P9-DWP-445

TODAY'S BEST

NONFICTION

TODAY'S BEST NONFICTION

SELECTED AND EDITED BY READER'S DIGEST

THE READER'S DIGEST ASSOCIATION, INC.
PLEASANTVILLE, NEW YORK

The condensations in this volume have been created by The Reader's Digest Association, Inc., by special arrangement with the publishers, authors, or other holders of copyrights. Letters, documents, court testimony, etc. may have been edited for space.

The original editions of the books in this volume are published and copyrighted as follows:

Reporting Live, published at $26.00 by Simon & Schuster
© 1999 by Lesley R. Stahl

A Song for Mary: An Irish-American Memory, published at $23.00 by Warner Books, Inc.
© 1999 by Dennis Smith

Show Me a Hero: A Tale of Murder, Suicide, Race, and Redemption, published at $25.00 by Little, Brown and Company,
© 1999 by Lisa Belkin

Daughter of China: A True Story of Love and Betrayal, published at $24.95 by John Wiley & Sons, Inc.
© 1999 by Meihong Xu and Larry Engelmann

FIRST EDITION, Volume 54

ISSN 0893-9373

Printed in the United States of America

CONTENTS

LESLEY STAHL

REPORTING

LIVE

Nixon's lawyer was briefing Republican leaders. When he emerged, I followed him outside, where cameras were waiting. A reporter I didn't recognize tried to elbow me out of the way. There was a code among the reporters: We were as civil to each other as possible. I thought, Who is this galoot violating the rules? I dealt with it by chopping *my* elbow into *his* gut. It was as powerful a wallop as I could muster, delivered with a ferocious grimace. I know this because NBC ran it on the *Nightly News.* My mother called me, horrified. Bill Small, our bureau chief, loved it. I was one of the boys.

—*Reporting Live*

Part One

NIXON AND WATERGATE

I WAS born on my thirtieth birthday. Everything up till then was prenatal. By 30, I knew two things for sure. One was that I wanted to be a journalist, which would mean, in the environment of the early 1970s, surmounting my femaleness and my blondness.

I was right about the profession. From my first story, journalism has been a drug. I love it, every aspect, just as I knew I would. But it turned out I wasn't as much of a natural as I thought I'd be. I had to plug away. There are two kinds of reporters. There are those like the late Charles Kuralt, who wrote so well he could spin a good story out of one or two bits of information. And there's the other kind, door kickers like me. My reports have to have lots of hard facts.

The other thing I knew for sure was that I wanted to be like my father—not in his success at business, but in his character. He was patient, always respectful, gentle. I figured that in this matter too there'd be a lot of overcoming to be done.

By 1972, I was on the path toward goal one. I was an on-air reporter at Channel 5 in Boston.

I'D BEEN in Boston for two years, enough time to finish decorating my apartment and enough time to get snarled up in a going-nowhere romance. My boyfriend, Amos, was a sleek Cary Grant type. There was a time when his handsome face would live in my eyes all day long, even at work. My mother, Dolly, didn't appreciate him and—what a surprise—she wouldn't let me forget why. The why was that Amos had another girlfriend. She knew about me and I about her, yet we both clung to him for nearly two years. "He's agonized about this," I told Dolly. "Oh, sure," she said.

It was early April 1972. The Equal Employment Opportunity Act had just been passed, and the Federal Communications Commission had recently included women in its affirmative-action program for television broadcasting. In other words, the television networks were scouring the country for women and blacks with any news experience at all.

I applied to all three networks, sending them each an audition tape of my five best stories on Channel 5. I included a Thanksgiving feature about a group of hardy Bostonians living the way the Pilgrims had in the nonelectric, nonheated seventeenth century. They had ground up some wheat to make bread the old-fashioned way and offered me a piece. I took a bite, made a face, and almost heaved it up on-camera. That story attracted Bill Small, CBS's bureau chief in Washington, where I would have thought there was little need for a comedienne. But he invited me for an audition.

Small, at 45, was a gentle bulldog, known for his firm control of his bureau. He was a large man with a cherubic face and a voice so soft you had to lean in to hear him. After a brief chat he handed me two fat rolls of wire copy and said, "Here, read these. Then let's see if you can write up a few radio pieces."

I worked hard on those radio scripts because CBS had the premier news department and I wanted to work there. The anchorman, Walter Cronkite—"Uncle Walter"—was number one in the ratings, and his team, his horsemen, were inspired by the legacy of Edward R. Murrow, who, in creating television journalism, had insisted on the highest standards of reporting.

Without grading my radio reports, Small sent me off, saying, "We'll be in touch." I was back in my apartment in Boston a few days later when the phone rang. Amos was there trying to distract me, so I said, "Shut up! It's Small."

"Excuse me," said Small, the inaudible. He had heard me say "Shut up." It was a movie. I was living a movie. "How soon can you get here?" That's how he started the conversation.

"Well, I have to pack up my apartment here, find a place to live in Washington, which I know nothing about. I think I could do it in, say, two weeks."

"If you can't start tomorrow," he said, "forget it." Small's reputation was that he was tough. But with all his gruffness he had won the affection of the reporters in the bureau (as he would mine) because he simply would not tolerate attempts by the administration in power to chill him or his reporters. He stood up for his people, defending them from attacks either from outside the company or from his superiors at CBS, who were called, in those days, "those assholes in New York."

I said good-bye to Boston, to Amos (and the girlfriend), and started at CBS News in Washington the next day. My mother was ecstatic.

It was springtime. And my career was about to begin.

THIS was a time of prosperity and accomplishment for the CBS Washington Bureau. We had 21 reporters and correspondents (today there are nine), more than the other networks in numbers and quality. William Paley, who had founded and then controlled CBS, came close to pampering his News Division. We were his spoiled children, so money was rarely a factor in decision making. Experts were hired, boats rented, planes chartered. Physically, however, the Washington Bureau was a slum. The newsroom looked like a boneyard for old newspapers and coffee cups with floating cigarette butts.

I felt like Alice with everything oversized. On the left was a row of booths where editors were slumped over Moviola machines, cutting strands of film by hand with razor blades and splicing them together with narrow strips of Scotch tape. Along the back wall I gawked at a row of offices with no doors. The occupants were always on view, onstage. And what occupants! There, in one row, was the reason CBS News was known as the crown jewel. On the far right was Dan Rather, 40, then covering the Nixon White House. He was fearless, and I wanted to be just like him. Next came Dan Schorr, 55, CBS's famous investigative reporter, known for breaking stories and creating controversy about himself. To his left was the State Department correspondent, Marvin Kalb, 41, a foreign policy expert with a special interest in the Soviet Union. Next was Roger Mudd, 44, the best writer in the bureau, who covered Capitol Hill with a delicious sauciness. He was a giant of a man with hands the size of shovels. Last was the office of George Herman, 52, a refined man who moderated *Face the Nation,* the Sunday interview program, and managed to float above the feuding that entangled all the others in that upscale neighborhood.

In the middle of the newsroom was "the desk." Actually, it was an island of desks where Bill Galbraith, the assignment editor, ruled over a litter of assistants and radio editors with an authoritarianism expressed, incongruously, in a disturbing whine. It was made clear to me almost immediately that this "heart of the newsroom" had little use for the women and minorities raked in by affirmative action. I was introduced to the two other "affirmative-action babies" in what became known as the class of '72. Connie Chung, 25, loved to tell self-deprecating jokes about being Chinese, about how Bill Small had hired her because, she'd say, "I do his shirts with extra starch!" The other in our threesome was Bernie Shaw, 31, a handsome black man with a mild let's-be-friends manner.

In the beginning we had to scrounge every day for a place to sit. Not that we expected to have our own open-faced offices. But the space we got was, well, inconvenient. We were each given a desk in a narrow corridor in the back. I don't recall that there were any chairs, which was just as well, because if we had sat at the desks, our knees would have hit our chins. They were second graders' desks, useful only as a reminder of our status there.

After several weeks of doing radio, my first TV report on *The CBS Evening News* with Walter Cronkite was about a hijacking at Dulles Airport. It was brief, a minute long, and voiced over, meaning you never saw me on-camera. But as was the custom for such debuts, everyone in the newsroom gave me a standing ovation. It was the best day of my life.

A few weeks later I reported on a promising new cancer treatment, and I appeared in my first network on-camera stand-up. I was so proud. I couldn't wait to hear from my cheerleader-critic mother, but she didn't call. This was curious, since she called at every turn, even when she heard me on radio.

When I called home, my dad, Lou, had that she's-mad-at-you voice. What had I done this time? Dolly grabbed the phone. "Forty million Americans saw you tonight. One of them is my future son-in-law, but he's never going to call you for a date," she said, "because you wore your glasses."

I managed to finish my third story for the *Evening News* early enough to hang around the newsroom, making friends and getting to know the other reporters. I was chatting with another correspondent when one of the television producers hollered out, "Stahl! Where is she? Stahl!" I could tell I had done something very wrong. When he found me, he was livid. "You smiled. You smiled in the stand-up. Thank God there's still time for you to redo it. Kid, never, ever, ever smile. Ever." I was to be purged of all signs of humanity; the only display of personality allowed was a grimace. Women had to be trained especially hard to come across as authoritative.

As I worked on projecting a commanding presence, Dolly was waging a guerrilla war against my glasses. "Don't you think there's a reason Walter doesn't wear *his* glasses on television?" she would argue. "Don't you think Barbara Walters—she's so smart—has looked into this? *She* doesn't wear glasses on television."

My mother and I were fighting two different wars. She told me often enough that "good-looking people do better in life, and you'd better not forget it." She was always harping on me about my hair: "You need to go into New York and get Kenneth to style it. That's where Jackie Kennedy goes." About my clothes: "Where on earth did you pick up that little number? Get rid of it." It wasn't that I disagreed with my mother. It was just that her formula for success—being beautiful—had the effect of making people think I was brainless.

I knew my colleagues saw me as a lightweight, unqualified to join the champs of TV news. I had to find ways to convey my seriousness, to send out signals that I was resolute and earnest, not what the wrapping said I was. So I wore my glasses and worked around the clock.

I also promised myself I would never blame my setbacks on sexism. If thoughts like "It's just because I'm a woman" crept into my head, I sat on them. I told myself, "Lesley, work harder. If you're good, they'll have to use you." And I assumed that Bill Small hadn't hired me because he wanted me to fail. If you were one of "Small's people" (Dan Rather, Marvin Kalb, and Bob Schieffer), you were under a special cloak of protection, and he promoted you. I had to become part of that club.

I wondered if I ever would. One day Small came by and read over my shoulder in the newsroom: "Congress, resting on its collective elbow . . ." Making sure everyone saw, he ripped the paper out of the typewriter, crumpled it, and made a perfect hook shot into the wastebasket. "C'mon," he sniffed. Twelve thousand capillaries exploded in my stomach. *He's going to fire me. I can't write. He knows it. I want to die.*

I felt that way constantly in those days. One reason was that my very presence seemed to inspire resentment among several of the camera crews. They acted as though we new hires had cut in line, hadn't paid our dues. How do I know they resented our being there? Because they wanted me to know. I can still hear one cameraman as he argued into his walkie-talkie, "Do I *have* to work with her?" making sure I overheard. Of course, they did have to work with me and I with them.

An urge to weep became a recurring problem. If I got it in the office, I would hold it in until I could get to the ladies' room, where I'd duck into a stall and sob noiselessly. But out on a story there was no hiding place. Often, in the crew cars, I'd be locked up with these tormentors for hours, staring into their looks of contempt. The bullyragging was toughening me up.

I found an apartment in the Watergate complex, moved all my stuff from Boston, and didn't miss a day of work. Amos came to visit, though less and less often, but that was all right because I worked all the time. I was determined to show everybody I could do this—the crews; Bill Small, who had given me this opportunity; and David Brinkley. When I had worked at NBC News in the late 1960s, I'd asked his advice about a producer's job in London. Brinkley had told me I was not going to make it in journalism. "You're a pretty blonde," he'd said. "You should stay in New York and have fun." I decided I'd show him.

JUNE 1972. Most of the reporters in our bureau were on the road, covering the presidential campaign. Thus I was sent out to cover the arrest of some men who had broken into one of the buildings in the Watergate complex. That CBS let me, the newest hire, hold on to Watergate as an assignment was a measure of how unimportant the story seemed: just "a third-rate burglary," in the words of Nixon's press secretary, Ron Ziegler.

I was the only television reporter covering the early court appearances. When the five Watergate burglars asked the judge for a bail reduction, I got my first scoop. Unlike my competitors, I was able to identify them. That time the cameraman listened when I said, "Roll! That's them!" And so CBS was the only network to get pictures of the burglars. I was a hero at the bureau.

The judge asked one of the men, James McCord, what he did for a living. "Security consultant," he said. "Who have you worked for?" the judge asked. "The CIA." McCord said it so softly, I had to ask the people around me, "What did he say? Not the CIA?"

With each surprise I would race to a phone in the hallway and call the CBS Radio desk to offer a piece, often breathlessly: "These guys are from Cuba" or "They were carrying around phony passports!" While I was sensing an earthquake of a story, the editors in the bureau tended to rely more on *The New York Times* than on the new kid. So while I recorded piece after piece over the phone, I learned years later that they had rarely been used on the air.

Within a few weeks the case moved up to the federal court, where the only other press people were from the Washington *Star* and the Washington *Post.* I had a rule against flirting in the office, but technically this wasn't the office, so when the preppy-looking guy introduced himself—"Hi, I'm Bob Woodward with the *Post*"—I made sure he knew I wanted to be friends. He called me for a date later that day. And so I began to forget about Amos.

It was clear why so many sources confided in Bob Woodward. He had a way of making you feel you could trust him. He was also driven. I was like that too. We were at the same place in our careers: little-known rookies with no track records.

Everyone I knew in Washington was obsessed with his or her work, but Bob's tenacity bordered on clinical compulsion, which was why he was such a good reporter. He never left any doubt about his list of priorities: I came after Watergate, Carl Bernstein, and the entire staff at the Washington *Post,* including the pressmen.

It seemed odd that such opposite characters as Bob and Carl could form a partnership—until you got to know them. Together they were the complete journalist. Bob was the persistent, kick-the-door-down type who would make the hundredth phone call and pursue without letup. Carl, more of a loosey-goosey creative person, was an elegant writer. They were the real Oscar and Felix.

Once, when I called Bob, Carl got on the phone and barked at me, "The only reason you go out with Bob is because you're trying to get him to share his sources." Was I wrong to be insulted? The truth was that Bob told me next to nothing. I didn't even know there was a Deep Throat, though I was aware he was interviewing some guy in a garage, as well as White House secretaries, late at night. Several times when I thought the Watergate story was dying, he'd encourage me to stick with it. "You must hang on to this," he would say. "Trust me."

Late in the summer of 1972 "Woodstein," as the *Post* team was known, began writing stories about secret "hush money" flowing from the Nixon campaign to the burglars. But Watergate was not registering with the public. Newspapers around the country were reluctant to follow the lead of two young reporters who rarely revealed their sources, and it was a story without pictures. In television if it wasn't visual, we couldn't cover it. So between then and late October the White House managed to contain the story.

But that changed right before the election. Walter Cronkite decided to put together a Watergate primer, and I was called in to help. Relying heavily on Woodstein's reporting, our producer, Stanhope Gould, wrote a script and designed a package of graphics to explain as clearly as possible what we knew about the scandal. Cronkite was the narrator. The piece ran for 14 minutes, well over half the broadcast. That by itself would be a signal that CBS News considered Watergate momentous and pressing. Cronkite put his personal prestige behind it.

The first time I met Walter Cronkite, I was surprised at how young he looked in person. Television put 20 years on him. I liked him right away, but then most people did. Convivial and unpretentious, he is of that rare breed who wears the cloak of fame comfortably. He was our leader in the true sense. If he as much as breathed that we in the bureau had been second-best on a story, we'd pour ashes on our heads for a week. And in the unusual case when he took a stand on an issue, it had enormous influence. Now Cronkite was taking a stand on Watergate.

His 14-minute story ran on Friday, October 27, 11 days before the election. There was great excitement in the bureau. We all knew that allotting so much time to reporting the charges of wrongdoing would incite the wrath of the Nixon White House and campaign. A large group gathered in the newsroom to watch. When the Watergate piece ran, we all applauded because it was powerful and brave, and I was filled with pride. Cronkite and Gould set to work immediately on part two, a 14-minute follow-up about the Nixon campaign's money laundering. What we didn't know was that over the weekend White House aide Charles Colson called CBS chairman Bill Paley at home. (Colson was famous for his comment that he would drive a truck over his grandmother for Richard Nixon.) Colson accused CBS News not only of irresponsibility but of being in the pocket of Nixon's Democratic opponent, George McGovern.

I had swallowed the CBS promise that there was an unbreachable wall between management and the News Division, that reporters were insulated from corporate pressure. The wall, if it had ever existed, crumbled like old newspapers. On Monday, Paley all but ordered the president of CBS News, Richard Salant, to kill part two.

Putting his job on the line, Salant refused, though he did instruct the *Evening News* to trim down the time. Some say he stood up to Paley and preserved a hard-hitting Watergate report, but Stanhope Gould felt that Salant had caved in to corporate pressure, and was furious. He stomped around accusing our bosses of cowardice and timidity, but the deadline pressure impinged and he was forced to cut part two nearly in half. Even in that truncated form, it was two to three times longer than most pieces.

This report implicated the White House chief of staff, H. R. Haldeman, and former Attorney General John Mitchell, chairman of Nixon's reelection campaign. The final stroke was Cronkite's conclusion that White House denials about Watergate were not convincing. Yet eight days later Nixon won the election by a landslide. When the economy is healthy, as it was in 1972, the public is reluctant to change leaders, even in the midst of a scandal.

IN EARLY 1973 Bob and I decided to go to New York for a weekend. I assumed we were there to take a break from Watergate, go to the art galleries, take in Greenwich Village. But Bob wanted to work. He insisted we try to find John Mitchell's wife, Martha, who had taken to calling reporters late at night with on-the-record gibes at Nixon. When we couldn't find her, Bob wanted to sit in the hotel and read.

When the weekend was over, so were we. I had made it through without one display of emotion. My self-discipline at work was leaching into my personal life.

As the Watergate story got bigger, CBS made Dan Schorr the primary Watergate correspondent. I became his backup, his slave. And I was eager to learn from the master. My job was to gather up information and feed it all to Dan for his reports on television. We covered the first trial of the Watergate burglars together.

I was a regular. I lived at the court, chasing after suspects as they came in to plea-bargain or staking out the grand jury. I often sat on the floor outside the prosecutor's office with my main competitor, ABC's hyperkinetic Sam Donaldson, long-lost brother of Mr. Spock on *Star Trek*. He was fun to be with and so competitive that he put my drive into warp speed. From time to time the judge, "Maximum John" J. Sirica, would invite small groups of us in for a chat. "I can't tell you fellas and gals anything about the case," he would say. Then he'd tell us stories about his boxing career and his friend Jack Dempsey. He had a fondness for the press that was unusual for a conservative Republican.

As the trial progressed, Sirica grew increasingly impatient with the prosecutor, Earl Silbert, who one day pointed to defendant G. Gordon Liddy, general counsel on Nixon's reelection committee, and declared, "He's the mastermind." Liddy was the only one of the seven men on trial who talked to the press. During the breaks he would lean over the bar in the front of the courtroom and boast about his exploits. Once, he told us that he liked to hold his hand in a candle flame, just for fun.

Sirica wasn't buying Silbert's theory about Liddy. "He kept needling the prosecutor," I reported. "What about the higher-ups?" Sirica would ask Silbert. "Aren't you going to ask about the higher-ups?" I questioned the propriety of a judge second-guessing a prosecutor like that in open court, but Sirica went even further. To the chagrin of the defense team and the prosecutor, to the amazement of the press, the judge began cross-examining. "Isn't it true that you have been under great pressure to plead guilty?" he asked one of the burglars, Bernard Barker. "I want to know where the money comes from. There were hundred-dollar bills floating around like coupons." It was incredible.

When the defendant replied that he had gotten the money "in the mail in a blank envelope," Sirica shot back, "I'm sorry, I don't believe you." When the defense lawyers protested the judge's intrusions, he responded, "I don't think we should sit up here like nincompoops. The function of a trial is to search for the truth."

With each judicial intervention I would bound out of the courtroom, race down the corridor—not so easy in my spike heels—then down three flights of stairs to the pressroom, where a microphone with an open line to CBS had been installed for the trial. On rare occasions the news was dramatic enough for a bulletin: "This is a CBS News instant report," I'd pant. "I'm Lesley Stahl, reporting from the U.S. District Court in Washington, where Judge Sirica has just accused one of the Watergate defendants of lying." Because I had just run a sprint, I sounded as if I were in distress. I was reprimanded. When I complained to a friend that I was at a gender disadvantage, she said, "Well then, wear sneakers." Which was bitchy, since I loved my high heels and she knew it.

Five of the Watergate defendants pleaded guilty; James McCord and G. Gordon Liddy were convicted of conspiracy, burglary, and illegal wiretapping. Sirica postponed the sentencing for three months to squeeze them into breaking their silence. He signaled that he'd be lenient if they "spoke freely." It worked. On March 23, 1973, the day of sentencing, Sirica read a letter in court from defendant James McCord revealing that indeed there had been higher-ups and that perjury had been committed at the trial. Dan Schorr was out of town, so I got to tell the country that the lid was about to blow off the Watergate cover-up.

RIGHT around that time I met Senator Bob Dole, then chairman of the Republican Party. Recently divorced, he too lived in the Watergate complex. One night when we were both in the lobby picking up our mail, he asked me out.

I found him funny, attractive, and marvelous company, even though, as he admitted, he never read books—"only newspapers and the *Congressional Record*." But who needs book smarts when you have an acerbic tongue? He had an amiable way of forgetting I was a reporter, jabbing slyly at his fellow pols.

At dinner he would ask me to cut his meat; he couldn't, because his right arm had been injured beyond use during World War II. He told me that before the war he had assumed that he'd be able to ride out his life on his good looks, but then in Italy he had been hit by machine-gun fire. "Everything, everything was shattered," he said. "I had never studied much in high school. Without my looks and my body I felt there was nothing I could do." He said he had had to build a whole new person. This was a man who had suffered and overcome, and while I was sure there was bitterness there, he showed me none of it.

While we swapped stories about ourselves, we also discussed the topic that was consuming Washington: Had Nixon known ahead of time about the Watergate break-in and/or the cover-up? Dole told me he wanted to ask Nixon face to face, but he was having trouble getting in to see him. "Haldeman and [John D.] Ehrlichman [Nixon's close aides] have built a wall around the President." He was perplexed: "I'm chairman of the Republican National Committee, and they're keeping me away. They've decided to cut me out."

"How do you know it isn't Nixon himself?" I asked.

" 'Cause I know."

"Oh, come on," I said, "it has to be Nixon, who for one reason or another doesn't want to confront you. They're only following his orders. How could you possibly think they run him?"

If Haldeman and Ehrlichman were controlling Bob Dole's access, then they were the ones who were running the Watergate cover-up. I could see him fighting the inevitable conclusion that Nixon was involved.

THE stakeout is an opportunity for reporters to relinquish their dignity by loitering around someone's office or house waiting to ask a question the target wants to avoid. Once "Woodstein" had guided the Watergate story into the Nixon White House, it was hard to reach anyone close to the President, so CBS decided to intercept the principals at their homes before they left for work in the morning. I was one of the instruments through which CBS practiced this degrading form of journalism, chosen because I was too new to say no. I became a stakeout queen.

There was a time in 1973 when I, at the home of one or another of the Watergate suspects every morning, caught many of them in their pajamas as they opened their doors to pick up the Washington *Post.* It was dirty work, especially when wives came running after you in their bathrobes, hollering, "Get off my lawn!"

One morning the desk called to send me to the home of

Supreme Court Justice William O. Douglas. "What has *he* done?" I asked.

"We want pictures of him jogging for a profile," said the deskman.

"But it's hailing out," I said, "and he's seventy-five years old."

"If you knew more about this town, kid," the assignment editor said condescendingly, "you'd realize that Douglas is a great outdoorsman, and if he doesn't jog per se, he'll be out there walking his dog. So get there . . . before the sun comes up."

The crew was just delighted to be sitting in front of Douglas's house at 5:30 a.m. They blamed me.

There was no sign of activity around the Douglas house till 9:30, when Justice Harry A. Blackmun pulled up in a limousine—they were carpooling—that went right up the driveway. Douglas made a shaky trip across the icy pavement. The crew and I waited at the base of the driveway. The Justice lowered the electric window.

"Good morning, sir. We're here to get pictures of you jogging," I said.

"Are you crazy?" asked Douglas. "I'm seventy-five, and it's hailing!"

Failure never discouraged the assignment editors, and every now and then a stakeout paid off. I got an interview with Jeb Magruder the morning he was fingered by Woodward and Bernstein as a central Watergate player. Even if an official refused to talk, I often got pictures—manna in my world.

I usually drove back to the bureau with the crew unless my pictures or interviews were "hot" and it was possible I could get them onto the *Morning News*. Then the assignment editor would send a courier to pick me up. The couriers—CBS had a stable of them—were good-ole-boy motorcycle cowboys. If we were on deadline, I, in a dress, would sit sidesaddle on a Harley-Davidson hog and worry about my hair.

THE Senate hearings on Watergate got under way on May 17. I was progressing, cultivating sources, breaking a few stories. I was still tethered to Dan Schorr, but even as his number two, I was glad to be covering the biggest story in the world.

The Senate Caucus Room has towering 50-foot Corinthian columns, mahogany-and-pink-marble walls, a coffered ceiling, and pendulous chandeliers. It says, This is where important business takes place. It was *the* place to be. People fought to get a VIP seat for a day. To me it was home.

A Senate source on the Republican side passed a big story my way. I transmitted it to Schorr for his *Evening News* piece, as I was expected to, and he reported it on the air that night. When I went back to the office, I was surprised that no one said, "Great get, Stahl." I had begun to bridle at my role as Schorr's factotum. I had assumed he would be my mentor, but unfortunately, he acted as though I were a threat. But as long as my bosses knew when I had brought home the bacon, it was tolerable. So that night I said something: "Hey, what about my story?" I was told that Schorr had gotten that one on his own. That was too much to take. Instead of tears, out came temper. Before I could control it, there it was, a loud growl: "I will *never* give him a story again."

Schorr responded by telling me I was finished at CBS.

That was a Friday. All weekend I worried that my career was over. On Monday I went to see Small: "You must hear my side of this. I hope you haven't formed any opinions about me not being a team player without hearing me out." Small was inscrutable. All he said was, "You need a haircut." (Dolly was instructing me to keep my hair long.) "But Mr. Small, I have my version of what happened."

"I was beginning to think you would never stand up to that s.o.b.," he said. "I was beginning to think I was wrong about you. Now that you've shown me a little spine, I think you're ready to go out and report on your own."

From that day on I was the official *Morning News* correspondent covering the Senate hearings, and if I could come up with my own story, I would get on the *Evening News.*

Every day I read every word written about Watergate in sources ranging from the Washington *Post* to *Women's Wear Daily* to *Time* and *Newsweek* to the AP and UPI wires. Part of the daily ritual among the reporters in the hearing room was complimenting one another's work. Great embarrassment came with not knowing about the most obscure scoop in the smallest publication.

Every reporter there wanted to provide a piece of the puzzle and make a mark on what was clearly historic. So the competition was intense. But we became friends too. The hearing room became a village, one I loved. Someone would write a poem or a joke about a witness, and as in high school it would be passed from one table to the next and then up to the Senators. Reporters consulted one another constantly; we hung out together and had parties. I threw several myself, once sending out subpoenas as invitations. In this sense we were similar to a press corps on a presidential campaign. But here we were covering the *un*-making of a President.

I came to know all the Senators on the Watergate Committee. Chairman Sam Ervin became the second Watergate hero, after the unlikely John Sirica. Like the judge, Ervin, at 76, had lived long enough to have perspective. With his wispy white hair Ervin charmed with his wit and coyness, as when he'd protest in a slow southern cadence, "I'm just a simple country lawyer." This was a simple country lawyer from Harvard Law School who wowed everyone with his mixture of country homilies and off-the-top-of-his-head quotations from the Bible and Shakespeare.

The vice-chairman, Republican Howard Baker, could have been his son. Another southerner, Baker was so good-looking that *Women's Wear Daily* added him to its "stud list" alongside Robert Redford. His repeated question about the President became a mantra: "What did he know and when did he know it?"

You can't imagine the electricity in that room, day after day, as we careened from a sense of doom for the presidency to a feeling of outrage at the corruption. And there was a constant punctuation of raucous hilarity as one witness after the next came out with code names and expressions you couldn't believe were bandied about the White House. Not telling the truth was "modified limited hangout," John Mitchell was the "big enchilada," there were "black bag jobs," and documents were "deep-sixed." Secret operations had names such as Gemstone and Sandwedge; campaign dirty tricks were called Sedan Chair.

Three nights a week CBS did a 30-minute sum-up of the hearings. Bill Small asked if I thought I was ready to join some of the senior correspondents in a round-table discussion on the shows. I lied and said I was ready. But my two male partners (not always the same) argued so much with each other, I rarely got a word in. Night after night I'd be introduced, but except for a few scattered bleats from me, I was drowned out. Finally the bosses explained that telegrams and phone calls were pouring in complaining that the men were being rude to the girl. The bosses said, "If she doesn't talk tonight, no more round table."

That night our moderator in New York, John Hart, asked a mischievous opening question about "the gossip" about John Ehrlichman. I said to myself, Why should I, the woman, answer a question about gossip? Let the men do that. But naturally the men, Dan Rather and Dan Schorr, waited for my response until the silence became excruciating. Finally Schorr said, "Well, if you want to start with 'gossip,' I'd better turn this over to the woman."

I wanted to punch him. Instead, I gibbered incomprehensibly, not parsing, not tracking. When I wound down, Schorr made my humiliation complete. "Well, let's fill in a couple of facts here," he said, "before we go off on our wild gossip."

Mercifully the show ended. I raced upstairs and called home. "Daddy," I said, "they threw me the ball, and I dropped it. Help me write a letter of resignation."

Being a dad, he said, "Don't be ridiculous. You were, in a word, magnificent. Smarter than those two. What thoughts! What ideas you had! And you looked good too."

"Dad, if you can't be honest with me—because I know how dreadful I was—put Mother on the phone."

There was a pause. "Mother can't talk right now," he said. "She's too upset."

Eventually my mother called me and did her magic, bucking me up and sending me back into battle.

After each subsequent round-table show I would call home for my parents' affirmation. I needed their assurances that I hadn't been as garbled as I feared. Because I didn't have an office, I would make these almost nightly calls from the newsroom, so I was often overheard. While I was seen as toughening up in some ways, this unwinding with my parents exposed my self-doubts.

THE star of the hearings was to be John Dean, Nixon's counsel, but the committee agreed to postpone his appearance one week because Soviet leader Leonid Brezhnev was in town for a summit meeting with Nixon. That week I went to Dean's house in Alexandria, Virginia, early every morning, hoping to get a picture or get off a question. Sam Donaldson was usually there too. By then Sam had taken to calling Nixon "the felon," which he would bellow out at every opportunity. But he didn't get a chance to bellow at Dean, who stayed hidden inside.

Sam and I were bumping into each other constantly. He was ABC's chief staker-outer. We both got word one day that the newly named special prosecutor, Archibald Cox, was at a meeting in one of the Senate office buildings where camera crews were not allowed to shoot except in designated areas. Abiding by the rules, I went searching for Cox without my crew. The daring Donaldson said to himself, What a silly rule. As Cox appeared, so did Sam—with crew. "What's this?" I asked. "A camera?" As I hurled myself in front of the ABC camera lens, one of Sam's colleagues put his two arms under my armpits, picked me up, and removed me from the area. Sam got an interview with Cox. I did not.

A certain, shall we say, rambunctiousness was becoming my trademark. One afternoon I drove to Dean's house and knocked on his door. "Who's there?" It was his voice! I got down on my hands and knees, opened the mail slot in his door, and begged him for a quote. He got on his hands and knees too and peeked at me through the slit. And what was my big coup? All he told me was that he'd gotten a haircut and planned to wear his glasses when he testified. A soul mate! He wanted to convey a sense of soberness.

Dean, 33, testified for a full week near the end of June. The whole country watched as he plunged his sword deep into the President. He testified that Nixon—at the heart of the Watergate cover-up—had discussed paying the burglars hush money, and he revealed the existence of the President's "enemies list." I wrote a script for the *Evening News* about 20 people that Nixon had targeted with, among other things, IRS audits. Dan Schorr was on the list and loved it. To be on Nixon's list of political and journalistic enemies became a badge of honor.

It was the dead of summer, and the writer Aaron Latham was sent by *New York Magazine* to the hearings for the first time, meaning he had to compete with those of us who'd been sitting there since May. After a full day he concluded that his notebook had not one scrap of an original observation. He panicked. A friend of his told him, "If you want sidebar material, call Lesley Stahl." It was true that I had notebooks full of unused gossip and funny asides that were too frothy for CBS. When Aaron called and offered to buy me dinner, I said he could pick me up in the CBS newsroom.

In walked six feet four and a half inches of well-formed, well-proportioned, well-put-together Texas gorgeous with a bashful smile of straight teeth. And he wore a natty brown corduroy jacket with leather elbow patches and cowboy boots. If his reddish brown beard hadn't been scraggly, I would have found him too perfect. What also took the edge off the dazzle of his looks was his modesty and shyness. He was fetching beyond words.

He took me to a pizza joint. I had so many Watergate stories, I chattered nonstop. He filled up two notebooks.

I then invited him up to my apartment to see the Watergate subpoena I had sent out as a party invitation. He was positive that I was his, that he was going to score. But I handed him the subpoena and said good night. Finding himself unexpectedly *outside* my apartment, he was—how can I put this?—enraptured.

His boss at *New York Magazine* liked Aaron's article so much, he asked him to return to Washington every two weeks to write a Watergate column. So Aaron wooed me. We had dinner every other week and became good friends.

I COVERED Ehrlichman's and Haldeman's testimonies before the Senate committee. Ehrlichman, 48, in his half-glasses, was pugnacious; Haldeman, 46, in his crew cut, was mild-mannered. Even though they had both been forced out of their jobs at the White House, they denied everything and protected the President.

The most startling of all the testimony came on July 16. Senator Ervin announced a surprise witness, Alexander Butterfield, who supervised internal security at the White House. On the stand for a mere 30 minutes he revealed an Oval Office taping system. After the initial shock of his testimony the hearing room exploded with chatter as we all came to realize that there might be evidence on tape that would either clear the President or nail him. As it turned out, what brought the President down in the Watergate bugging scandal was that Richard Nixon had bugged himself!

Most days I'd make dozens of calls, asking hundreds of questions. I wanted to make sure that if someone got the urge to leak, I'd be there to catch the drip. Often I'd make a call just to get help on what questions to ask. If I couldn't get through to one of the principals or their lawyers, I'd ask for a secretary or junior assistant, hoping he or she would be flattered and eager to show off. If I picked up any information at all from one conversation, I would drop it into my next call to sound as if I knew more than I did. Or I'd throw out wild propositions just to test reactions. "I hear Dean is asking for no jail time," I once told a lawyer.

"That'll never happen."

Next call: "I heard Dean's talking about less than a year in jail."

"You're not far off."

By fall of 1973 Nixon's approval rating plunged to an arctic 27 percent. At a news conference in late November in southern California he declared, "I am not a crook," and tried to blame the press, calling the TV news coverage of him "outrageous, vicious, distorted." When my CBS colleague Bob Pierpoint asked what specifically about the coverage made him angry, Nixon said he wasn't angry. "You see, one can only be angry with those he respects."

Nixon finally agreed to turn over nine tapes, which had been subpoenaed in July, to Judge Sirica for a ruling on claims of executive privilege. I was back in Sirica's courtroom for a hearing on the matter when the White House revealed the existence of an

18-minute gap on one of the tapes. The White House said that the President's personal secretary, Rose Mary Woods, had accidentally erased the 18 minutes by pressing the RECORD button on the tape machine when she meant to push the STOP button. Sirica hauled the woman into court, where she tried to explain how she could have made the mistake. It was hard not to laugh as she demonstrated a stretch and a swivel, a twist to answer the phone, and a press of the wrong button, all at the same time.

In February 1974 the House of Representatives approved an investigation by the House Judiciary Committee into the possibility of impeaching the President. I'd wake up every morning wondering, How can he take the pressure? How is Mrs. Nixon holding up? On the night of February 14 the desk ordered me to "move, move now" to Trader Vic's on K Street, four blocks from the White House. It was Pat Nixon's birthday, and the President was taking her out to their favorite restaurant. The maître d' had called CBS.

Nixon had bunkered himself inside the White House—he had not held a news conference for four months—and his disappearance from public view was feeding rumors that he was degenerating into madness. This would be the first chance in weeks for any newsperson to see him.

There was only one other reporter there, the indomitable Helen Thomas of UPI. Of all the reporters on the White House beat, Helen had the biggest heart and asked the toughest questions. She and I joined forces. The maître d' gave us a table with a view of the President, Mrs. Nixon, and their friend Bebe Rebozo. We ordered spareribs and drinks that came with paper umbrellas. We wrote down what they ate and congratulated ourselves on our scoop.

Thomas and I had a plan: When the Nixons emerged, we'd be right outside in a perfect position to get off a few questions. But when we opened the door to leave, we were met by a swarm of reporters. The Nixons were right behind us, so Helen and I were run over and pushed to the back of the pack, out of hearing range. So much for our scoop. But we were not so hapless after all. Mrs. Nixon was also jostled to the back. It was a raw night, and there she stood, shivering in her brown cloth coat, looking frail, her eyes sad. The other reporters surrounded Mr. Nixon and shouted out one accusing Watergate question after the next.

Mrs. Nixon turned to Helen and me and said, "Isn't he wonderful? Just look at him. Can you imagine with all his troubles, all the pressure he's under, he took the time to take me out." Her eyes teared up. All I could think was, Look what he's put you through; this is the least he could do. I was once told by a Nixon adviser that at the many dinners he had attended at the White House, he had never once seen Nixon address his wife or even look at her.

I NEEDED a vacation, so when Aaron Latham asked me to go to Bermuda with him, it sounded like a good idea. By then he had become my best friend. When I was sad or happy or lonely or when I'd heard a good one, he was the one I called. We began to plan.

When my dad asked me, "Who's this Erin you're going to Bermuda with? Is she a new friend?" I told him about Aaron.

"But have you slept with him?"

"Dad!"

"I'm serious."

"If you must know, I haven't."

"Well then," he said, "you're not going."

"Excuse me? I'm not going?"

"No. Because it's inevitable that you'll get down there, have some bad experience with him, and call me. Well, sister, I'm not coming to pick you up in far-off places."

If my mother had said that, I'd have been on the next plane to Bermuda. But this was Lou, my dad. So I thought over what he said and decided he was right. You don't go to a romantic island with a "friend." I went instead to a tennis camp, alone.

My first night there Aaron, who'd stayed in Washington, called and said I was nuts to have left town. Every night there were Watergate parties where reporters dissected the Nixon transcripts. They were punctuated with "expletive deleted," which added to a sense that Nixon's Oval Office conversations were sordid and that the office itself was full of malice. Aaron said, "The whole town's alive with excitement. You have to come back—now."

It was early May. I flew home, took one look at Aaron, and realized I adored him and never wanted to be without him again. He was the smartest man I ever knew and the wisest, the best read, the funniest; and he was as good to me as my dad was to my mother. We hugged our first hug. He moved in that night.

Washington was swallowed up by the Nixon tapes. I went to a dinner party where a group of us, including Ethel Kennedy, sat in a circle and read the transcripts aloud. Though Nixon had obviously cleansed them, his dark side showed through in the passages where he and his inner circle cussed and plotted wicked wrongdoings like a bunch of gangsters. The impression was so damning, a Niagara of calls for his resignation drowned out whatever support was left him even within his own party.

Through May and June the House Judiciary Committee proceeded with its impeachment investigation. Then on July 24 the Supreme Court voted to uphold the special prosecutor's subpoena for 64 more tapes. The impeachment debate started in prime time that very night. I sat in the press section in the Impeachment Committee hearing room, moved by the speeches and impressed especially with the poetry of Congresswoman Barbara Jordan of Texas. She said that she, as a black, was determined to uphold the Constitution, which she *had* felt left out of. "But through the process of amendment, interpretation, and court decision, I have finally been included in 'We, the people.' "

As the proceedings moved forward, the seriousness of the process took hold. After six days of agonized debate the committee voted, several Republicans crossing over to answer "Aye" in a solemn roll call to recommend impeachment of the President for obstructing justice, for abusing his presidential powers, and for contempt of Congress. When it was over, Barbara Jordan left the room in tears.

On August 5, I could feel tension on Capitol Hill, but I couldn't find out what was going on. I went from office to office, learning of secret powwows but gathering little hard information. Together with Sam Donaldson I hopped onto the subway under the House office buildings; we both knew something big was happening.

We met up with a group of reporters staking out minority leader

John Rhodes's office. Dan Thomassen of Scripps-Howard rushed over to tell us about a statement Nixon had just released at the White House. No wonder there were so many secret meetings all over the Hill. Nixon was making public a transcript of a meeting six days after the Watergate break-in during which he had instructed Haldeman to have the CIA say falsely that the break-in had been one of their secret operations. The tape was the "smoking gun" evidence of Nixon's early involvement in the cover-up.

Nixon's lawyer, James St. Clair, was briefing the Republican leaders. When he emerged, I followed him outside, where cameras were waiting. I got a poke in the ribs as a reporter I didn't recognize tried to elbow me out of the way. It was one thing when the "primitives" (what the newspapermen called the cameramen) shoved me aside; they had to get a clear shot. But there was a code among the reporters: We were as civil to each other as possible. I didn't take it as a compliment that this stranger treated me as just another guy. What I thought was, Who is this galoot violating the rules? I dealt with it by chopping *my* elbow into *his* gut. It was as powerful a wallop as I could muster, delivered with a ferocious grimace. I know this because NBC captured it on film and ran it on the John Chancellor *Nightly News*. Dolly called me, horrified. Bill Small loved it. I was one of the boys.

As the day wore on, it became clear that if Nixon didn't resign, the House would impeach him by a wide margin. "He won't get ten votes," I was told by a head counter.

On August 8, for the second time in my CBS career, I was assigned to cover the Wholesale Price Index. Now, on the day I was sure Richard Nixon would resign, I was at the godforsaken Labor Department. This is how correspondents become paranoid.

Meanwhile, Aaron was at the White House. I called him on a mobile phone so he could tell me about the great drama in the pressroom, which had been sealed off. "They've locked us in!" Aaron said. "Everyone's running around yelling, 'Coup, coup!' We can't leave." Only later did we learn that it was because Nixon had wanted to walk around the Rose Garden one last time.

I listened to the resignation speech on radio. Nixon started by acknowledging, "I no longer have a strong enough political base in the Congress" to continue. In an unsatisfying phrase he said, "I regret deeply any injuries that may have been done." That was it. No "I'm to blame," no "Forgive me" or "I'm sorry." He accepted zero responsibility. There was no honor in his speech.

The next day, Nixon's last as President, he made his farewell address on television. Mrs. Nixon and their daughters, Tricia and Julie, stood with him, glassy-eyed but composed. What it must have taken to hold themselves together there in the glare—these three women who had been dragged into his disgrace. Nixon's speech was compelling because you kept thinking he was going to break down or go berserk. The most revealing part came at the end: "Never be petty; always remember, others may hate you, but those who hate you don't win unless you hate them, and then you destroy yourself." Did he understand himself that well?

Nixon boarded Marine One, the presidential helicopter, on the South Lawn of the White House, turned back, waved, and was gone. And so was Watergate.

Watergate changed journalism forever. It introduced an era of reporting through anonymous sources. It ushered in a swarm-around-'em mentality where reporters and cameramen hounded people. From Watergate on, nearly every government utterance would be subject to skeptical scrutiny. Thereafter, Presidents would view the press as a squad in a perpetual adversarial crouch, always ready to pounce.

There had never been a news story quite like it, and because the press had been so prominent, it glamorized journalism as a profession, turning some reporters into celebrities. Lost in all the myth-making was the fact that the courts and Congress had played the crucial role, not the press. Sirica and Ervin were the heroes, but as a friend once said to me, "Robert Redford didn't play either of them in the movies."

At CBS News our real contribution was in turning Watergate into a national story. This was a time when more than 40 million citizens were watching the same event, interpreted the same way night after night. That was the number of people who watched the

Cronkite news. Television had surpassed newspapers, magazines, and radio as the major source of news in the country. You could feel our growing strength.

WHENEVER I talk about the women's movement, I have more than a twinge of guilt because it did so much for me while I, a reporter, sat on the sidelines neither marching nor protesting. Here I was in the mid-1970s doing exactly what the feminists of the time were railing against: I was adapting myself to someone else's standards, to whatever the men who hired me wanted me to be. I wore curlers to bed and sprayed my hair so much I even called myself "helmet head." And I worked as hard as I could to project an image of malelike authority. Only when it came to my clothes was I true to myself. I have a taste for bright colors, frills, eyelets, and flounces. No one said a word to me about camera clothes, so I just wore what I liked, the most feminine outfits and highest heels I could find.

At the same time, feminists were burning the "tools of oppression"—curlers, *Cosmopolitans*, eyelash curlers, and girdles—much as Vietnam War protestors had burned their draft cards. Curlers. Was I oppressed?

I was ambivalent about covering the women's movement, as were most of the women reporters I knew. This was an issue we wanted to report on, yet one we were afraid would typecast us.

Barbara Walters told me that when she had coanchored the *Today* show in the 1970s, she'd had to fight to do serious stories and interviews: "I got letters from women saying, 'Hang in there. What you're doing is good for all of us.' " She said, "I did it for me, but I think it helped them too." I also told myself that succeeding at becoming a woman of authority on television would in itself help other women. By telegraphing an image of a woman with some power and heft, I rationalized I could help the cause.

I WANTED to be a political reporter. In 1974, I became one when CBS sent me to cover the congressional campaigns in the West. I put together a report on the Senate race in Colorado, in which

Gary Hart was the Democrat. One day he asked if I'd like to ride with him and his wife, Lee, to the next event. I sat in the back seat of what we'd call today a subcompact while Gary shut his wife up every time she tried to join in the conversation. "You don't know what you're talking about," he snipped. "Why don't you just be quiet?" And "Hush." And of course, "Shut up." I wanted to tell *him* to shut up; I wanted to reach out and touch Lee, but all I did was ask my questions and pretend to ignore his angry belittling of her. To me one of the lessons of Watergate was that the press hadn't done enough reporting on personal character. As I sat in that back seat, I wished I had film of Gary Hart browbeating his wife.

After covering the western campaigns, I went to New York, where I was going to be one of the desk anchors on election night. As the first CBS woman to do this, I felt a lot of pressure and I confided in CBS News president Richard Salant that I was scared. He told me that was silly and took me on a tour of the election-night set to prove it. The carpenters were still working on a large drum with seats marked off for each of the anchors.

"It's quite cozy," said Salant. "All of you are in a friendly circle. Nothing to make you nervous." We walked around the drum. "This is where Walter sits." He pointed to a desk with the name CRONKITE on it. "And here's Dan's seat." It said RATHER. Mike's place said WALLACE and Roger's said MUDD. "And here's yours," said Salant. It said FEMALE. He blushed.

I studied hard for election night, cataloguing interesting facts about all the candidates, gathering solid intelligence about why X or Y won or lost his race. When Walter and Betsy Cronkite invited Aaron and me to dinner, I was suspicious. "He's going to ask me to give him all my good information, and I'm going to have to," I told Aaron. "He wants to suck me dry of all my research."

I was dead wrong. Walter and Betsy lived in a brownstone on the East Side of Manhattan. Two other couples were already there. "No shoptalk, Lesley," Walter said. "Tonight, just fun." Up to then I had known "Uncle Walter" the way the audience knew him, as the epitome of rectitude. He was like the preacher in town, the man everyone looked up to for his integrity. What I saw that night was the other side: the worldly, hilarious, even ribald Uncle Walter.

He was sitting on an ottoman in the middle of his den telling stories about the war, courting Betsy, living in Europe. He played all the roles in the stories, imitating women, Germans, Frenchmen, and people we knew. And his jokes were earthy. Betsy was puckish and as sophisticated and full of fun as Walter. My favorite Betsy Cronkite line was, "I could never have an affair; I couldn't hold my stomach in that long!"

I think Walter invited us to lighten me up. Around midnight he announced he was about to tell a party-ending joke, one so raunchy that he was right—it cleared the room. Aaron and I had a wonderful time. I have loved Walter ever since.

Finally Tuesday night came. I wore a bright red dress with double-strand, opera-length pearls that jangled against the microphone and drove the director crazy. I was given my own hairdresser, who jumped up after each of my reports to recomb. When he'd finish, I'd call home, right there on the set: "Mum! How'd I do?" I'm still teased about that to this day.

The outcome of the 1974 election was breathtaking. The Republicans were sacked and pillaged as the voters punished them for Watergate and double-digit inflation.

I was convinced that my appearance on the show had propelled me into instant fame, certain that just walking down the street would become a race against the paparazzi.

The day after the election I put on a scarf to hide my hair and a pair of sunglasses. Aaron and I went for a walk down Fifth Avenue. He was slouching, worried that my new public stature would alter the equation of our well-balanced relationship. We walked from Bergdorf Goodman at 58th Street down to 56th. Not one person noticed me. I took off the shades. Still no one. By the time I got to St. Patrick's Cathedral, my scarf was off and I was staring at passersby, all but begging them to recognize me. We walked all the way to 42nd Street. Aaron wasn't slouching anymore.

I went back to Washington to be a general assignment correspondent. Gerald Ford was President. It was a boring time. We all missed the Trick.

IN THE FALL OF 1975, I WAS covering my first presidential campaign and had been assigned to Henry "Scoop" Jackson. But by early June 1976 Jimmy Carter was the only Democratic candidate left standing.

In the 1960s and 1970s the way to judge who was up and who was down in network news was to watch the national political conventions. Floor correspondents, those lucky few assigned to roam the convention delegations, were the A team, the first string, and I was disappointed when I wasn't chosen to be one in 1976. Instead, four of us junior reporters were each assigned to stand in for one of the starters when he got tired or had to relieve himself. Ed Bradley was paired with Rather, Dick Threlkeld with Mudd, Betty Ann Bowser with Wallace, and I with Mort Dean.

The Democrats held their convention in July at Madison Square Garden in New York City. The problem for the Carter forces was building some interest in the event, since the Georgian with the soft, soothing manner had the nomination sewn up. There was no suspense.

Each day, in the late afternoon, CBS held strategy meetings. We tried to agree on themes we could develop during the all-night broadcast, what issues to explore. At one of the meetings Rather was proposing an idea when, to everyone's discomfort, Roger Mudd started repeating what Dan was saying word for word, the way a child does in that irritating echo game. Rather shrugged it off and went on with his proposal, but Mudd escalated his taunt into outright heckling. I stopped breathing. So did everyone else in the room. Mudd had let his competition with Rather for anchorman—which of the two would succeed Cronkite—grow into a serious feud that made us all uncomfortable. Finally Mort Dean asked Roger to calm down so we could finish our business. I wondered what would have been said if a woman had acted like that.

For me to go out onto the floor Mort Dean, who had covered the space shots for CBS, had to come off. That first night, as Mort left to start our coverage, he said, "Lesley, remember those urine tubes the astronauts had? I'm wearing one of them. I won't have to come off the floor to go to the bathroom for a week!"

But the floor producer, Don Hewitt, whose regular job was producing *60 Minutes,* made sure there was a rotation, so about an hour and a half into the broadcast, around 9:30 p.m., he buzzed me: "Get ready, kid. Your turn is coming up." I suited up. I had to wear a big, bulky headband that was both a radio receiver and a transmission unit. A cup fit over my left ear so I could hear the CBS program and get directions from Hewitt. Connected to the headband was a mini-microphone that arced across my right cheek so I could broadcast from the floor. All of this posed an engineering puzzle because I did not want my hair flattened down. I looped clumps of hair over the headband, building a little teased house around it. Deep down I must have thought I *was* my hair. As I dressed for the floor, I thought of knights preparing for a joust. My squire, a CBS engineer, strapped a thick, heavy belt around my waist with pockets for the batteries and transmitter. It felt as unwieldy as armor. And he handed me my lance—a thin, wandlike microphone.

I forgot how hulky I looked the minute I walked onto the floor at Madison Square Garden, which was packed with more than 3000 delegates from 50 states. As I wandered, I kept searching for ways to get on the air.

Finally I was sent to find the youngest of the Carter women, eight-year-old Amy, the candidate's daughter. "Amy, Amy? Hi. I'm Lesley Stahl from CBS. Can you tell us what your impressions are of this convention? Do you think it's exciting?"

"Yes."

"Do you have any advice for the young people of America who are watching tonight?"

"No."

"Do you think that when you grow up that you'd like to run for President someday yourself?"

"No."

"Definitely not?"

"No."

"Okay. Thank you very much. Walter."

Now, that's a tough day at the office. Several months later, after the election, when Rosalynn Carter took Amy to her new school in Washington, I overheard Amy ask her mother, "Now that we won, do I have to be nice to the press anymore?"

On Thursday, the final night, I was out on the floor standing in a crush when the lights went out for a campaign-produced film on Jimmy Carter. When the lights came up, Carter was not at the podium, as everyone expected, but walking across the floor. TV screens were filled with one visual message: Here comes a man of the people, a Washington outsider—just what the country wanted after Watergate.

That night Carter seemed to have everything we would soon be complaining he lacked: the gift of inspiring, the ability to bring us together. He exuded leadership and strength. Was that a mantle he borrowed for the night like Cinderella's ball gown? A few days later a poll showed Carter 30 points ahead of Gerald Ford.

By Election Day, Carter's 30-point lead over Ford had melted like soap in a hot shower. There have been election nights when the networks knew who won as early as 4:00 in the afternoon from our exit polling, but in 1976 we had no clue when we went on the air at 7:00 p.m.

Finally, at 3:50 a.m., Walter said that Jimmy Carter would be the third Baptist, the seventh farmer or rancher, and the eleventh man whose mother had lived to see him elected President of the United States.

Aaron wrote an article for *New York Magazine* saying that each President comes to office having been shaped by a formative historical experience. For Dwight Eisenhower and John Kennedy it had been World War II, which had taught them to expect to win and made them optimists; Lyndon Johnson's had been the Alamo, where the Texans had been massacred. That's probably why he had turned the White House into a fortress surrounded by enemies. Aaron quoted James Schlesinger—Nixon's CIA director, Ford's Secretary of Defense, and Carter's soon-to-be Secretary of Energy—as saying that Jimmy Carter's formative experience had been the Civil War. And so he would expect to lose and also to be good at it.

Part Two

JIMMY AND ROSALYNN CARTER

I WAS in love with my boyfriend and with our life. We'd been living together in Washington for about a year and a half, though Aaron kept his apartment in New York. With a Texan you expect ten-gallon gasconade and swagger, but he was more like my New England father and brother, reserved and laconic. One reason Aaron became such a successful reporter was that he can ask a question, then wait patiently for an answer—however long it takes.

I had friends who warned me that Aaron and I came from worlds too far apart to ever be compatible: he from a small farming town, population 1500, in *The Last Picture Show* part of Texas; I from an upscale suburb in Massachusetts. But we never thought we were that unalike. He was the only man I ever met who called his parents as often as I called mine.

Aaron wanted children; I didn't. I was so happy with him, I was afraid this would drive him off, but I didn't think I'd be a good mother. Besides, Dolly had been telling me for years, "Never have children; they'll ruin your life." Thanks, Mum. She pounded into me the idea that a career was the real route to happiness. I bought into her prescription for my life wholeheartedly. But I was coming up on my thirty-fifth birthday. At the time it was firmly established that 35 was the end of the childbearing years. But then, right before my birthday, I got a three-page letter from Dolly.

"Dear Only Daughter," she began. "I've made so many mistakes." She laid out an argument free of sentimentality on why I should have a baby—right away. Never once was the word "grandmother" mentioned. Her first point was that we are all animals. "What do you think we were put here for anyway if not to procreate?" The second point came from a study she had read. "People (men and women) with children go much farther in their careers," she explained. "Do you realize that if you never have a child, you always see yourself as a child. Only a parent can take charge." Finally, she argued, women without children are "unfulfilled and feel cheated. I know I've been on your back a long while not to have children. Intuitively I knew I was right, but now I don't want my kid to have regrets."

She went on to say that Aaron would be a wonderful father and that I would not have to give up my career. "Don't wait until I'm too old to help you. Please. M."

How much of my life my mother controlled was unclear to me. I knew I had the career she had encouraged. And I looked the way she wanted me to—probably because she had bought my clothes until I was 30. On the rare occasion when she saw me in something I had picked out myself, she'd treat me as if I'd besmirched the family name. When she was angry at me, I'd get so distraught I could barely breathe, at 35. I thought all mother-daughter relationships were like ours and was fascinated but disbelieving when my friends told me that ours was, well, unusual.

I had always felt I wouldn't be a good mother. I was too single-minded about my career, too absorbed with my independence (I never saw being under my mother's spell as a form of dependence), and too impatient. Of course, I said those things at a time when my mother was instructing me not to have children.

What happened next is open to argument. Aaron swears I asked him, "If I did get pregnant, would you marry me?" I have no recollection of this, and if pressed, I will swear I never said it. And yet it appears that within a few days, *poof!* A little angel was on the way. Whatever magic brought this on, I didn't realize my condition, because it was impossible. I had taken every precaution.

Two months later, when I fainted in Senator Ted Kennedy's office, I didn't know why. As I say, it was impossible.

I went to the doctor. I was in my office around 3:00 when he called to say, "It's positive." I was so surprised, I ran to my sanctuary, the ladies' room, and locked myself in a stall. How could this have happened? Was it that I had deep down wanted Aaron's baby? Or did I simply do whatever Dolly told me to?

Aaron was ecstatic. And after the initial shock, so was I.

Two weeks later I was writing a story on how Medicare patients in New York City and Beverly Hills pay more for gallbladder and cataract operations than do the elderly in rural Nebraska or Findlay, Ohio. When I finished, I did the forbidden and slipped away at 4:30 in the afternoon. The rule was that correspondents with stories in the broadcast didn't leave before the show aired. I told my producer that I had to do something very important and asked her not to tell anyone I was gone.

Wearing an old blue dress and a new pair of shoes, I borrowed a necklace from a friend and sneaked out to elope. Aaron and I met in Judge David Bazelon's chambers and got married at five. The only ones there were my brother, Jeff; his wife, Paula, who was our photographer; Aaron's college friend Tom Plate, who was our best man; and my friend Mickey Bazelon, the judge's wife. We finished early enough for me to get back to CBS before the show went on the air at 6:30. My producer later told me she'd thought I had gone across town to ABC for an interview about jumping networks.

It turned out that eloping was a mistake. When I called to tell my parents, instead of feeling triumphant as I thought she would, Dolly went silent with anger because I hadn't invited her. I had hurt my mother, which was certainly not my intention. She refused to talk to me till the baby was born.

Two days after our wedding I flew to New York to meet up with Aaron, who had returned earlier. I had been teasing him that there was something unnatural when a wife has never seen her husband's face: He still had the scruffy reddish beard he'd had the day we'd met. When I got to his apartment, I walked right past him. Who was that man? He was wearing Aaron's corduroy jacket. I ran back. He'd shaved. I burst into tears. Poor Aaron. He was only giving me the wedding present he thought I wanted. He never shaved again.

The last thing Aaron needed was a crank for a wife. Only a few weeks before, Rupert Murdoch had managed to wrest control of *New York Magazine* in a hostile takeover. Aaron and most of the other writers and editors walked out, but this act of principle left Aaron with a pregnant wife and no job. Thus started his career as a freelancer. He was feeling insecure, but under pressure he became more prolific and made more money than ever.

Maintaining an atmosphere of sublime tranquillity for my child became my first priority. Everyone in the office seemed to conspire with me; they were all so solicitous of the pregnant lady, especially the cameramen. I was a novelty—one of the first women at CBS News to try anything so revolutionary. I was certainly the first pregnant on-air reporter.

I kept working as my body began protruding in every direction. I felt like one of those pink elephants in *Fantasia*—a big hulk daringly bobbing around on a pair of incongruously dainty toe shoes. I can still hear my click-clacking heels in the halls of Congress as my bulging body ran in a swaying motion after an escaping Senator. I worked right up to August 13, when my water broke.

When we got to George Washington Hospital, I thought I was in labor and that I was handling myself with remarkable fortitude, given my nonexistent tolerance for pain. But after 18 hours I was informed that it was time to induce.

I had interviewed several obstetricians, settling on the one who said he'd give me painkillers the earliest. So I called him on his pledge and got an epidural almost immediately. But then the doctor handed the stethoscope to Aaron—this was peculiar—and asked, "Do you think the baby's heart is skipping beats?" Just then I went into shock. I was raced into the operating room for an emergency cesarean, leaving Aaron behind. "We can name her Taylor," he said as I was wheeled off. Taylor was my choice, Tara his.

Taylor was born pink and perfectly shaped. Everyone agreed that she looked just like Aaron, even Dolly, who, having forgiven me the minute I went into labor, had rushed to Washington.

For the week we were in the hospital, Aaron and I would stare at Taylor for ten, 15 minutes, saying nothing. We were like swooning lovers. She barely cried, and we thought we had the sweetest baby ever born. Then we took her home, and we noticed a change. It was hard to miss. Our daughter cried. She cried all the time. Our little angel had colic. Some of the pressure was relieved when the pediatrician recommended drugs. After a few weeks we relented and began giving Taylor drops to stop the paroxysms of pain.

Soon I was back at work. I've often been asked how I did it, how I worked full-time with a baby. Simply, I had enough money to pay for a reliable nanny. Yet even with that, like all mothers who work, I lived with a constant, insidious guilt. This perpetual gnawing became so ingrained, I didn't realize it wasn't a natural part of me until Taylor went off to college 18 years later.

I took a ridiculously short maternity leave, just three weeks, and never dreamed of asking for any slack. I was so afraid CBS would treat me differently, give me less challenging assignments, that I felt I had to prove I was just as available as ever.

After a few weeks I was asked if I wanted to coanchor the *Morning News.* Not only did I think I could handle the job, I realized the schedule would get me home in the afternoons to be with Taylor. I also wanted to work with Hughes Rudd, a wonderful, unusual television personality from Waco, Texas, with a gravelly voice and sardonic wit. He called to tell me how enthusiastic he was about our teaming up, making me feel he'd been waiting to work with me his whole life. Taylor was six weeks old.

The first show on October 3, 1977, was straightforward. Hughes led off reading an item about skyjackers in Syria; then I followed with a story about President Carter raising taxes on imported oil. Back and forth we went—he in New York, I in Washington—for an hour, from 7:00 to 8:00 a.m.

Five days after I started, Hughes was told he was being taken off the show. We were both stunned. He joked cavalierly, but he admitted to me that he was hurt. He said "they" had told him that he was overpowering Lesley Stahl and that he was too gruff for the morning. I don't know one person who agreed with that.

Hughes's replacement was Richard Threlkeld, good-looking and one of the best writers among the younger correspondents. Our publicity photo made us look as though we were starring in a sitcom: a happy couple, Mr. and Mrs. Jones.

I wasn't doing a great job as anchor. I often stumbled over words. "President Kimmy Jarter . . ." When I'd try to correct myself, I would do it awkwardly. I had jumped into the unknown of live broadcasting, never imagining that the rip cords wouldn't work. I had built a reputation as a sedulous, grind-it-out-on-the-ground reporter. As I was so often told, I'd earned my spurs. I had been chosen because of that, not because I registered high on the warm-quotient meter. That became obvious.

My greatest enemy was the TelePrompTer. Eventually a genius invented a machine that reflects words right across the eye of the camera, making it possible to read and look directly out at the same time. But in 1977 the prompter consisted of a roll of paper that scrolled several inches above the eye of the camera. If you were an expert like Walter Cronkite, you figured out a way to read and give the appearance of making eye contact with the audience. I, on the other hand, had an annoying habit of darting my eyes back and forth between the copy and the camera.

Even harder than that was smiling. First the bosses make you incapacitate every smile muscle in your face. Then they make you an anchorman and complain that you're not warm enough: Smile more. But I just couldn't get the hang of looking into the glass-eyed camera-monster and giving it a sincere grin. After a few weeks Dolly came up with the name of a television teacher, Dorothy Sarnoff, and sent me to New York for a smile lesson. Dorothy set up a video camera, got me laughing and smiling into it, then taught me how to reproduce my own smile on call, like Pavlov's dog.

Only one producer came in early with me, and his job was to organize the taped pieces. I was left by myself to write my copy, which I rarely finished before I had to go to makeup. So I struggled nearly every morning to finish writing the show in the commercial breaks. It was hard to admit I was having trouble. But the job was daunting, I was sinking, and I finally asked for help.

Four months after I started, the cavalry arrived in the shape of Terry Martin, a radio producer sent to Washington to be "Lesley's person." Terry—sharp and quick, shrewd and gruff—was an answered prayer. He came in at 3:30 a.m. with me, and we'd sit there together reading the Washington *Post* and the wires. Terry and I would decide which items I should write up and tell.

Along with writing and reading items on the *Morning News,* I did some long pieces: a tour of the new National Gallery of Art with the architect I. M. Pei, a report on disposable diapers, and a farewell tribute to Eric Sevareid when he retired. Nixon once explained why Sevareid was the one newsman he would never attack: "We were scared to," he said. "He looked and dressed exactly like God."

In my interview I asked Sevareid, "What do you hope television news will look like in the future?"

"I think we have to find a way to make room for the word as well as the picture, because there are a lot of things you can't do with a camera. You can't take a picture of an idea."

WITH Terry Martin on the scene I was able to slip into a routine. I never acclimated to getting up at 2:30 in the morning, though there was a compensation: I could get home in the early afternoon and play with Taylor. Her colic cleared up right on schedule at three months, and she became the world's easiest, cheeriest baby. At seven months she would light up when I got home, so that if I had any worries at the office, they would fade away the minute I opened the door and saw her beaming face.

Aaron worked at home, which made a big difference in my life. He had an office that was off-limits to everyone else in the apartment, yet I knew that if something happened with Taylor, he was right there. He would emerge from his office around five, as though he were coming home from a day downtown. We'd have dinner together early, and then I'd go to bed. Most of my countrymen went to sleep with Johnny Carson; I went to sleep with Walter Cronkite.

IT WASN'T long before our coverage of President Jimmy Carter on the *Morning News* reflected the country's verdict—he was failing as President. He had won the campaign by attacking Washington insiders and by use of populist symbols (as when he carried his own bags), but once he was in office, both backfired on him. He started off by "de-pomping" the presidency, cutting back on limousines, silencing the Marine Corps band at his official functions, and wearing an unassuming, common-man beige cardigan on national television.

These little pantomimes were meant to announce his message: I am not Richard Nixon. It was well received at first, but soon the one-of-us image transposed into a he-lacks-presidential-stature image. Some of the blame had to go to the inexperienced staff of young southerners he brought to the White House, especially his 33-year-old chief political adviser, Hamilton Jordan. In March 1978 *Esquire* published "Hamilton Jordan: A Slob in the White House," written by Aaron. As he was researching the article, Aaron would amuse me with the stories he was hearing. Ham had lived in his green Corvair when he went to the University of Georgia. Ham was such a slob that he would throw his dirty clothes and half-eaten burgers into one big pile in the back seat until he got mice. Aaron's piece guaranteed he would never again get an interview at the Carter White House.

Carter recovered some public confidence at the end of 1978, when he pulled off his greatest foreign policy achievement—the Camp David Accords—which led to peace between Egypt and Israel. The accords grew out of a grueling 13-day meeting at Camp David with Anwar Sadat of Egypt, Menachem Begin of Israel, and President Carter. When it was over on September 19, I interviewed Prime Minister Begin on the *Morning News*. Right before we got our cue, he pinched my cheek and said, "*Shayne mayd'l*"—Yiddish for "Pretty girl." I squirmed as I wondered what Roger Mudd would have done if some Prime Minister squeezed his cheek.

In addition to calling on Israel to return the Sinai to Egypt, the accords created something called Palestinian autonomy. "What's the difference between autonomy and sovereignty?" I asked Begin.

"Ha-ha! Well, you have to look into the encyclopedia, my friend." Begin beamed. "The difference is very simple. Sovereignty means a state, a government with a parliament, et cetera, and with all the attributes of independence. Not so autonomy."

When I asked what it was like being sequestered for so long at Camp David, he said it had become tedious. "I said to Professor [Zbigniew] Brzezinski [Carter's national security adviser], 'This is a concentration camp deluxe.' He told me that 'you have got experience. Perhaps you started already to dig a tunnel.' There came a moment when we all felt we must bring it to an end."

The Camp David Accords succeeded because Jimmy Carter midwifed them, massaging and cajoling. It brought his presidency back to life.

I HAD become addicted to the stress of holding down a full-time job and taking care of a year-old baby. When we went on vacation, I couldn't unwind and, in fact, began inventing stressful situations to simulate the atmosphere at work. I'd contrive phony deadlines, such as going shopping 15 minutes before I'd have to meet a friend or starting dinner 30 minutes before the guests were due. *The New York Times* ran an article explaining that people who live under constant deadlines secrete a mildly addictive chemical related to adrenaline that we actually crave whenever we relax, and it said there was nothing unhealthy about benign activities that help pump out the chemical. From then on I accepted my hyperactivity and Aaron agreed to stop with the irritating "Why don't you relax?"

He had written an article for *Esquire* called "The Ballad of the Urban Cowboy" about oil workers in Houston and their favorite hangout, Gilley's, a ten-gallon Texas honky-tonk with a huge dance floor and a bucking mechanical bull. We were in Nantucket for two weeks "relaxing" when half of Hollywood began calling. Twenty different producers and studios wanted to make a movie of "Urban Cowboy," and they were all wooing my husband. Eventually there was an auction, and the story was sold to Paramount.

More exciting, Taylor began to walk.

ON DECEMBER 1, 1978, CBS announced that Dick Threlkeld and I were being replaced by our White House correspondent, Bob Schieffer. I wasn't sorry I wouldn't be getting up in the middle of the night anymore, but I didn't think I had fully mastered the job.

Threlkeld and I anchored the *Morning News* as lame ducks for five weeks, worried about our next assignments. I was imagining the worst when, one afternoon, our new CBS News president, Bill Leonard, called me at home and made a proposal: "How would you like to be the next White House correspondent?" I accepted instantly, without thinking. I didn't ask about the travel, the days and nights away from home. I only asked, "Are you serious?" To me the White House was the pinnacle. When I hung up, I turned to Taylor, who was playing with her stuffed animals and my lipstick. I read her some pop-up books and began to shake with fear.

I called Aaron at Paramount Studios. He was writing the screenplay for *Urban Cowboy.* "We'll work it out," he said. "Don't worry."

I called Dolly. "I don't know if I can do it. I'm scared."

My cheerleader said, "You can do it, and Dad and I will take Taylor whenever you want."

AARON and I were at a black-tie Christmas party with a mix of congressional leaders, White House officials, and reporters, all engaged in the typical Washington shoptalk.

"I start at the White House in February," I told Jody Powell, the President's 35-year-old press secretary.

"Everything will work out," he drawled, "if y'all just trust me completely."

A few days later Bob Woodward called to warn me that "the Big Three at the White House" were not pleased that I was coming over there and that there had been "some attempt to get CBS to change its mind about the assignment."

"Who are the Big Three?" I asked. They were Ham Jordan, Jody Powell, and the President himself.

Bob said, "They think you're a hatchet man from your Watergate reporting, but more important, they hold Aaron's *Esquire* piece about Ham against you."

"Come on," I said, "that's absurd."

"No, it's the truth, and if I were you, I'd spend my first two months doing nothing but straight substantive reporting."

Finally I went to get my credentials as a permanent member of the White House press corps. After having my picture taken for a laminated pass, a badge I would wear around my neck at all times, I spent the day with Bob Schieffer, the outgoing CBS White House correspondent, to get the feel of the place. He told me how demanding the job was. "You're totally out of control of your life."

Bob and I, my old Watergate stakeout partner Sam Donaldson, UPI's Helen Thomas, and many other White House regulars stood outside in the biting cold, huddled around what was called "the stakeout position," an area where reporters and cameramen were allowed to lollygag as we waited for people who were meeting with the President. As we waited, the fellas asked Judy Woodruff, the NBC White House correspondent, and me to stand back to back to see who was taller. It was a weigh-in for what the men saw as the inevitable catfight between the two network ladies.

The pressroom was really two rooms. One was a small theater for the briefings; the other, an area with booths for the wire services and TV networks and two rows of cubbyholes, where the major newspapers and magazines had phones and desks that their reporters could use for a few hours a day. Those of us who worked for the wires and networks used our booths as full-time offices.

We were a short walk from the Oval Office in our own little precinct within the White House, encased in the tomblike CBS booth, which was painted a cheerful shade of khaki and so incommodious that every time we turned the doorknob, as Woody Allen had said of his first apartment, we rearranged the furniture. It was four feet wide, with a long table for three correspondents and a radio technician. In the back there was a small soundproof room for recording our TV tracks and radio spots. Four of us spent eight to ten claustrophobic hours a day in there.

Our next-door neighbor, Sam Donaldson, had invented a new way to cover the leader of the free world: shouting. Sam had a bong of a voice with a built-in echo, much like Big Ben. When he bonged at the President, the walls quivered and the President more often than not responded, providing all of us with that thing most precious to television correspondents—a sound bite.

Sam told me, "Jody [Powell] is the *only* source in the White

House." I wasn't sure if he was being a pal or trying to throw me off the scent. But Sam had a nifty little scoop that night: Carter had invited Richard Nixon to the White House to meet Chinese leader Deng Xiaoping.

I went back to the White House the next day as an observer at Powell's daily briefing. It seemed to me that Powell spent more time attacking the reporters than answering questions. He often answered a question by saying, "That's simplistic," or "What a dumb question." There was nothing defensive about this cat.

The White House correspondent I wanted to emulate was Dan Rather, crisp and tough. I wanted to stand up to bullying and ferret out dishonesty. When Dan had left the White House in 1974, he had gone to *CBS Reports* as anchor, then, in 1975, to *60 Minutes*. When I called him for advice about covering the White House, he suggested lunch, so I flew to New York and met him at Alfredo's, a favorite CBS hangout. He spoke to me the way he delivered his on-air pieces: in bullets. These are the notes I took.

> #1. Hours to reach sources: 7:30–9:30 am, 7:30–11 pm.
>
> #2. Work the Hill and the Pentagon. People in the agencies are more likely to talk to a WH correspondent than the reporter on their beat . . . less traceable.
>
> #3. Be the cutting edge. Tell when what the WH is spoonfeeding you is nonsense. Write scripts about what they *do* say and what they *don't* say. When you don't buy the line they're selling, convey that to the public.
>
> #4. Said he'd picked up rumblings at CBS that my writing is not very strong. The vultures [my word] are already saying I'm slow and won't meet the deadlines.

I thanked Dan. We had been friends in Washington; I considered him an ally.

I STARTED getting calls warning me that Jody Powell and Hamilton Jordan would probably take reprisals against me because of Aaron's piece. A *Time* reporter told me that "a whole slew of Ham loyalists will never deal with you, never return your calls."

I spent several days at the White House as an observer, trying many times to get together with Jody, but he avoided me. I went home in a state of apprehension, sure I would never catch on to the intricacies of covering the White House. And I ached about not having enough time with Taylor. She usually fell asleep at 7:30. On a normal night I'd just be walking in the door.

I finally got in to see Powell. I'd been warned by the other women covering the White House that he had trouble dealing with us. Until the mid-1970s the White House press corps had been a white man's brotherhood. I was the ninth woman in that first wave to cover the President's side of the White House for mainstream magazines and networks. Most of us were in our thirties, the same age as the Carter aides. Actually, I was three years older than Jody.

Powell sat behind that famous press secretary's desk, crescent-shaped so reporters could crowd around in a semicircle. He drank iced tea, snorted nose spray, and smoked incessantly, smashing out his butts in a large, overflowing ashtray. I liked him—his open, doughy face, his fidgeting, his machine-gun wit, and the seriousness with which he took his duties. I wanted him to like me, but he made it clear that the rumors I'd heard were true.

I asked if I'd have any trouble at the White House, said I'd heard I would, and wanted to find out why and clear the air.

Jody stared at me for a while; then stuttering, as he often did, he said, "Look, Lesley, er—uh—we know you're against us." He accused me of being unfair to the President on the *Morning News*. "You seem to delight in zinging him."

I was dumbfounded. I was not antagonistic to Jimmy Carter. Like most everyone I knew, I thought he was not the most effective President we'd ever had, but on the other hand, I respected his diligence and his integrity. Either Jody was trying to chill me, or he really did see me as an enemy.

I said I hoped he would be fair with me. He said he would.

As I thought about it that night, I decided that part of my problem was that I wasn't southern. When the President or his Georgia inner circle was criticized as incompetent (Hamilton Jordan was widely known as Hannibal Jerkin), they'd circle the wagons and blame it on "southern-hating northerners," which to them included the media.

In these early weeks I was overwhelmed by the number of issues I had to be up on and was often lost in the briefings. I felt swamped. The White House was more than just another stakeout.

I found that the deadline pressures meant there was no time for polite discourse about my scripts. I never heard, "Gee, we love it, especially the way you said that thing about Carter's slumping entrance." I never heard, "Lesley, we have a little problem with time in the broadcast tonight, so we'd really appreciate it if you could find ten seconds to cut." It was just, "Cut ten seconds. *Do it.*"

I had to get up early to read three papers from front to back, clipping and underlining obsessively, and to wash my hair and spray it into a cap of cement so I wouldn't have to think about it again all day. During the day I phoned smart people constantly and checked the wires. I lived in perpetual vigilance.

Night after night I got on the air with pieces that didn't have as much information as Sam's and Judy Woodruff's. They seemed to have sources I could never find, insiders who provided them with insights and trenchant quotes. Each day I made more and more phone calls—sometimes as many as 30. But still I wasn't getting as close to officials in the loop as my competitors were.

This all came to a head when Israeli Prime Minister Begin came to Washington in early March to discuss the collapsing Camp David Accords. On the last day of his visit, around lunchtime, NBC went on the air with a bulletin: "NBC News has learned"—the dreaded words—"that President Carter has decided to go himself to the Middle East." He was going to both Jerusalem and Cairo to try to save the accords. This was a huge story. My phone rang. "Lesley!" the producer was yelling. "Can we go with it too?"

I said I'd get it confirmed and get right back to him. Jody Powell wouldn't take my call. I couldn't reach a single high-level person. Five minutes went by, and ABC was on the air. AP's bells began ringing . . . and UPI's . . . and still I couldn't get anyone to help me. I finally told my office to go on the air and say, "The Associated Press is reporting that . . ."

Humiliation and ruin. I was sure CBS would yank me out of the White House. At least the story broke in the middle of the day. I was able to come back with a strong script for the *Evening News,* but the feeling of defeat was hard to shake.

I would later come to realize that Jody's harsh treatment of me was becoming a badge of honor—at least within the halls of CBS. As long as he made it clear I was *persona non grata* at the White House, my job was secure because my bosses lived by the commandment that no government official could interfere with the network's internal decisions, especially who covered what.

The next morning Sam pulled me aside. There was something he wanted me to know. "Day after day," he said, "Jody Powell has Judy Woodruff and me up to his office for a private one-on-two background briefing. He's deliberately cutting you out."

How stupid I'd been. Of course! Jody, the only source.

"I'm telling you," said Sam, "because one day he'll get mad at me and have you and Judy in and cut *me* out. If he were leaking great scoops to me alone, I'd never say a word. But this ganging up on one of us is wrong." You don't get menschier than that.

"I know what you're doing, Jody," I said when I finally got a private appointment with him. "I know about your daily sessions with Sam and Judy." I thought he would try to deny it, but he just stared. "It doesn't make any sense," I said. "CBS reaches more people than either of the other two networks. All you're doing is depriving my audience of the message you're trying to put out. You're only spiting yourself. And besides, you told me you'd treat me fairly."

"You're right."

He said he would stop singling me out. And he did. As far as I know, Jody was evenhanded from that day on. That doesn't mean he did me any special favors. He didn't. Never. Not once.

THE year 1979 was the peak of network news power. Something like 120 million viewers tuned in to the three networks every night. We were so predominant that our deadline at 6:30 eastern standard time became the deadline of the entire federal government. The daily rhythm at the White House was synchronized with our rhythm.

CBS, with Walter Cronkite number one for 12 unbroken years, was at the crest of power. Cronkite was so much an institution (in Sweden a news anchor was called a "cronkiter") that he began not only influencing policy but making it. *The New York Times* called it "Cronkite Diplomacy" when Egypt's Anwar Sadat told Walter in a TV interview that he was willing to meet with Israel's Menachem Begin without any preconditions. Within hours Cronkite had Begin on the air, inviting Sadat to Jerusalem.

Carter left for Cairo on March 7 at 6:30 p.m., so the takeoff would lead the *Evening News* live. I was one of the pool reporters on Air Force One, which sounded like a treat. All the events on foreign trips were covered by assigned "pools," small groups of reporters who went to events on a rotating system and wrote up reports for all their colleagues who were left behind. I should have known better the minute Sam told me I would *love* it. As always, there were four pool reporters. We sat cramped around a table for the entire 13 hours. We never saw Carter during the flight.

Unlike most presidential trips abroad, this one had been put together too quickly for the usual meticulous scripting. There was no prepackaged final communiqué and therefore no guarantee of a smiling final photo and handshake. Carter was taking a huge risk.

After a full day of pool assignments, the real work began. We went to private briefings at our hotel with "senior government officials" where the progress of the talks was explained as long as we agreed not to reveal the identities of the briefers. These sessions were usually held one hour before our "feed time," 1:30 a.m. local time, when our reports were sent to New York by satellite. The networks each fed three or four pieces a night in rotation through one outlet in one small sliver of time. Just as you unwound from the deadline pressure, you were desperate for sleep, but what you did was shower and get ready for your first pool of the morning. Before long both we in the press and the staffers we dealt with were fatigued, irritable, and short-tempered.

On the third day we flew to Jerusalem, where Carter's motorcade from the airport was pelted with eggs. When Carter pleaded with the Israeli parliament, the Knesset, to "seize this precious opportunity" for peace, he got a cool reception. When Begin spoke, he was heckled.

That was the day we were supposed to leave for home. But the departure time kept slipping, and we couldn't find out why until, finally, at 10:00 p.m. Jody Powell announced that we would spend one more night, even though, he admitted, "I see very little possibility that these issues are going to be resolved."

It was close to midnight when Jody Powell's secretary, Carolyn Shields, invited me to Jody's hotel room: "He wants to see you." I found this very peculiar. His room? The invitation was a pleasant change, but there was no way I was going to allow anything untoward to happen. As I made my way along the corridors of the King David Hotel, I rehearsed ways of letting him down gently.

Carolyn answered the door. Jody had a grand suite. When I turned a corner and entered the living room, I had to laugh at my vanity. There were Sam and Judy! This was one of Powell's background sessions to make sure we got the story right.

He told us that Secretary of State Cyrus Vance and Israeli Foreign Minister Moshe Dayan were holding a late-night meeting to see if the peace plan could be salvaged, but he was pretty glum: "To say [the peace mission] is hanging by a thread is putting too optimistic an interpretation [on things]." He did add, "You never know."

We dashed off to give the story. We at CBS were pretty strong that night about the collapse of the talks. Walter led the show: "All indications now are that President Carter's high-stakes gamble in the Middle East has failed."

After our broadcast I was approached by an Israeli official who told me that the Americans were painting a far too gloomy picture in an effort to apply pressure on Begin to make concessions. "It's psychological warfare," he accused.

Yeah, but it worked. The next morning the American briefers told us the peace process was back on track. As Carter and the rest of the White House press corps went back to Cairo to consummate the agreement, I stayed behind to report that the Israelis were furious at the U.S. briefers, who had "deliberately overplayed the gloom and doom" and "distorted the facts."

Several reporters were steaming at Jody, believing he had deliberately deceived us. But rather than apologize for leading us in the wrong direction, Powell attacked CBS for our "arrogant" coverage.

No wonder Jody was put out with us. Jimmy Carter had pulled off a miracle. Through stubbornness and persistence, he engineered the first peace agreement between Israel and an Arab state by investing his personal capital in it. Carter deserved at least one news cycle of undiluted praise. There's no explaining it, but news organizations were soon focusing on how many billions of dollars the peace process would cost the U.S. taxpayer. Once again Carter got very little reward for his historic and personal accomplishment and virtually no bounce in the polls.

Sadat and Begin came to Washington to sign the peace treaty in late March. The signing took place on the North Lawn of the White House because a giant tent covered the South Lawn, which was usually used for such ceremonies. That night 1340 guests attended a sit-down state dinner in the tent. Just about every reporter who had been on the Middle East trip was invited except . . . guess who?

Well, that was all right. I told myself I didn't really care. I was embarked on a journey into self-control. It was something I had decided was absolutely necessary—both for this job and for Taylor, who was now two. Whenever I walked in the door, she would hurl herself into my arms. There was never love like that. And yet I had chewed her little head off one day when I had come home and found huge red and green crayon marks all over the walls. Aaron came out to see who Taylor had murdered. He told me coolly, "Either change or pretend to change, I don't care which." When I told Aaron he was right, as usual, and that I felt bad, he hugged me and calmed me. He seemed to love me in spite of it all.

I worked on mastering my temper and deadening that reflex of tearing up whenever I got particularly angry. Little did I realize that I would do such a good job of containing my emotions that one day I would have trouble finding them.

CARTER was one of the most accessible Presidents. He held 59 full-fledged news conferences, many more brief ones, and countless interviews. His aides will tell you today that this was a mistake, that he was overexposed and it hurt his image. While I generally disagree, there was an undisciplined air about his approachability. A photo opportunity in, say, the Oval Office was bedlam. We'd wait outside until the doors opened, at which time we'd all rush in together, jostling for position—cameras, microphones, reporters—as if someone were giving away free tickets to the Super Bowl.

It was even worse when the President traveled. The problem was that Carter was so prone to answer questions thrown at him on the spot that it was risky to leave his side. So we all swarmed in and formed a writhing cocoon around him. He was accessible and we appreciated that, but on television it looked like mayhem and added to a sense that no one was in control.

On foreign trips there was more restraint. In June 1979 we went to Vienna for the President's first and only summit with Soviet leader Leonid Brezhnev, a meeting Carter had been seeking ever since taking office. Jody Powell wisecracked, "The Reds and the Rednecks were going to square off!" Actually, they were going to sign the SALT II arms control treaty.

The leaders met first in an anteroom of Vienna's gilded Hofburg. President Carter arrived on time, but Brezhnev didn't. As Carter cooled his heels, we in the international press gallery just stared in silence. POTUS—President of the United States—spent a long five minutes wilting. Brezhnev finally arrived, shuffling, halting, and unsteady. That his health was failing was obvious, and yet he held his substantial body proudly erect and towered over Carter, who was, by then, so ill at ease that he seemed to shrink before our eyes.

Embarrassing television pictures are like a time-release poison, since they are played over and over, and in repetition can come to be defining. One such picture was shot as the summit in Vienna was ending. After the two leaders signed the SALT II treaty, Carter, on an apparent impulse, drew the enfeebled Brezhnev to him in an emotional embrace, and then to everyone's astonishment—gasps rose in the gallery—he kissed the Bolshevik on the left cheek.

As happened repeatedly with Carter, he was unable to profit from the successful summit. The buss on the cheek fed the notion that he was shrinking. Constriction was becoming an affair of state. President Jimmy Carter was dwindling in size, partly from his vigorous jogging, mainly from an impression that he was overwhelmed by his job. Reporters took to calling him the Little Peanut; cartoonists drew him as a little kid in a big chair, then eventually as nothing more than a row of protruding teeth.

Then OPEC, the Arab oil cartel, announced another price hike, increasing oil prices tenfold over 1973. There could not have been worse news for Jimmy Carter. In July he canceled his planned television speech on the energy crisis and disappeared to Camp David.

For several days the only people who saw him were his wife and a few close aides. It was an intuition, but I felt that Carter was collapsing from the frightening realization that he was failing. After a week of near solitude he invited a select group of aides up to see him, a decision that wrought resentment among staff members who were not invited. This produced agreeable repercussions for me as those left behind began returning my calls and giving me quotes—unattributable, of course—such as "A bunker mentality has set in up at Camp David." My 20 calls a day were paying off at last.

As Carter flagged, Rosalynn became his anchor. There were those who took to calling her the "deputy President." On the margins of memos Carter would often scribble, "Ros. What think?" or "Have you shared this with Rosalynn? She needs to know this too." When asked about her influence at Camp David, she answered disingenuously, "I don't know that I had any. I sat in on the meetings, I listened with him and then we—uh—then he made the decisions."

When Carter finally descended from the mountain, he went right on national television. I listened to his July 15 speech in the CBS studio. The beginning was an extended self-criticism, Carter quoting one of his visitors at Camp David as saying, "Mr. President, you're not leading this nation." After his *mea culpa* he went on to give a thoughtful analysis of the state of the nation, describing a "crisis of spirit" in the country.

The initial reaction was positive. "An extraordinary speech," said the usually skeptical Roger Mudd. "A very strong one, very upbeat."

I thought that the analysis of a gloomy national mood was right on the money. And instead of looking defeated, the President had managed to convey an air of confidence the public hadn't seen in him for months. His performance had been as important as the speech's content. Carter jumped 11 points in the national polls.

The Deacon—his Secret Service code name—embarked on "a revivalist crusade," as I called it on the air, starting in Kansas City and Detroit. Things were going exceedingly well. Then, two days after the speech, he blew it.

On July 17 the White House announced that the President had asked for the resignations of his entire 12-member Cabinet. It was called a slaughter, a purge. The dollar plunged, and Europeans, with their parliamentary systems, assumed that the Carter government had fallen.

By now there was a detachment of officials and aides eager to spread disparaging stories about the President, and who better to leak to than me, the Georgia crowd's bête noire. I began to break stories and to hear inside accounts of the President's meanness. I was told about his brusqueness, his cold glance of disapproval, his judgmental aloofness. Carter, it was said, was like Lucy in the *Peanuts* comic strip, who said, "I love Mankind; it's people I can't stand."

In the end, the resignations of half the Cabinet Secretaries were accepted. And in late July 1979, I began trying to find out who the new appointees would be.

Judy Woodruff found out who the Education Secretary, a new post in the Cabinet, would be. Each evening Sam, Judy, and I stood near each other on the White House lawn to record our stand-ups in sequence. That night, as I waited my turn, I overheard her. She saw me there; we even chatted. When I finished my report, I raced inside, made one phone call, and got her scoop confirmed by one of my new sources immediately—even before our broadcast started. What I should have done was sit with the information until Judy's piece aired. It was, after all, her story. But I called CBS, and Roger Mudd was able to lead our show with the name of Shirley Hufstedler, actually beating Judy's report by a few seconds. She was livid. Soon everyone was mad at me for "stealing" her story.

I was surprised at the reaction. I told myself, "You didn't eavesdrop; you weren't being sneaky about it. Judy knew you were listening and never said, 'Please step away.' " I worried about losing Judy's friendship, but still my reaction was to tough it out and say I had done nothing wrong. And I believed that, until I asked my colleague Bob Pierpoint, whose judgment I had come to rely on. I knew Bob was a man of integrity and decency. So when he told me that what I had done was like cheating on an exam, I was stricken low. I never "overheard" anyone again, and if I did, I forgot what I heard. Fortunately, Judy and I are still friends.

IN AUGUST, Taylor and I went to visit Aaron in Houston to watch the filming of *Urban Cowboy*. I had never understood why Aaron hated CBS functions or coming with me to parties connected with my job. Now in Houston I got it. The cast and crew had their little inside jokes. Aaron and Debra Winger would make eye contact and break up laughing. Or Aaron and Jim Bridges, the director, would sink into shoptalk minutiae about the next day's shoot, leaving me with recovered memories of the wallflower I had been in seventh-grade dancing school.

In other words, Aaron and I had a huge fight. I returned home early and got ready for a trip down the Mississippi with the President on the *Delta Queen* to gather support for his new energy conservation measures. We went 660 miles down the river from St. Paul to St. Louis. The boat was scheduled to make four stops, but Carter got it to stop 47 times, driving the press crazy with his "Hi, I love you" at every dinky little lock along the route.

He also drove the 15 other passengers crazy from day one with his jogger's thumping 22 laps around the decks at 6:30 in the morning. I wrote that in my script one night, but I also showed the large crowds along the banks. The White House was so pleased at the reception and the coverage that Powell joshed, "From now on we're only going to campaign on navigable rivers."

AARON and I made up. I figured out that I was jealous of the movie. I thought he was smitten with Debra Winger and that the Hollywood gestalt had turned his head. He confessed that he had fallen in love with the movie business, that he wanted to make screenwriting his career, but he also made it clear that Taylor and I were home base.

I did my best to avoid going to Plains but was rarely successful. "Town" in Plains, Georgia, population 680, was one row of stores, many owned by the Carters themselves. The largest industry after peanuts seemed to be worms. I got the impression that the Carters owned half of everything, including the land and the worms. Plains mirrored a lot about the White House, which, it seemed, Carter had tried to mold into something familiar and manageable, an insular community with a closed circle of small-town boys.

On Sunday, September 2, 1979, the Carters went to Sunday school at Maranatha Baptist, the eleven-o'clock service at Plains Baptist, and lunch at Plains Methodist. I had never been to a Baptist Sunday school, and there I was, the pool reporter, when the President taught the class of a dozen adults. He chose a short passage from Exodus about laws for protecting the male Hebrew slave—*Thou shalt not raise a false report*—which he analyzed for nearly 30 minutes. At the end he walked right up to me, pierced me with those cold blues, and said, "I hope you got something out of that."

ON NOVEMBER 4, 1979, nearly 3000 Iranian "students" stormed the U.S. embassy in Tehran and took 66 Americans hostage. They held 52 of them for 444 days.

The embassy takeover was precipitated by Carter's decision to allow the deposed Shah of Iran to come to the United States for medical treatment of his lymphatic cancer. The Iranians threatened to kill the hostages or put them on trial as spies if the United States did not return the Shah to Iran at once. Carter refused.

Over the next several weeks the networks fed the American people a diet of Iranian demonstrators chanting anti-American slogans and burning effigies of Jimmy Carter. Critics charged that our coverage intensified the crisis and prolonged the hostages' captivity. But in the beginning the White House encouraged our approach. And President Carter's ratings went up. The ordeal was unifying the country behind the President. The more the Iranians attacked

Carter and called him the Great Satan, the more his stature grew.

What Carter didn't grasp was that his strategy of keeping the story on the front page would increase the value of the hostages to their captors. But in the short run Carter was gaining from the publicity, and so were we. More people than ever, over five million more, were watching network news. The country was riveted.

On December 4 Carter made a brief announcement at the White House that he would seek reelection. He had pledged not to leave the White House until the hostages were free, so I began signing off, "Lesley Stahl, CBS News, with the Carter campaign at the White House." The President was able to run effectively that way, beating Ted Kennedy in the Iowa caucuses in January 1980 and the New Hampshire primary in February. But then, with inflation roaring and a sense of paralysis over the hostage situation, his weakness issue revived and his poll numbers drooped.

When Carter finally succumbed to the pressure for action, it was a catastrophe. On April 25 we learned that a secret operation to rescue the hostages had ended in disaster at a desert staging area 200 miles from Tehran. Several of the helicopters failed because of a desert dust storm; then, in retreat, one of the helicopters crashed into a C-130 transport plane, leaving eight crewmen dead amid a tangle of fiery debris. The incident came to symbolize a country that was no longer master of its destiny, and Carter had become the personification of the country's loss of control.

I TOOK a few days off and flew to Los Angeles with Taylor to see Aaron. He was working on the final cut of *Urban Cowboy.* Our relationship had plunged back into unhappy phone conversations in which we accused each other of selfishness and indifference. But there I was, hoping for a rapprochement. Instead, we had a blowout on the second day. "It isn't that I don't love you; I don't *like* you," I said in a quiet rage. Aaron retorted, "Well, I don't like you either." It hurt more than I'd expected.

"I'm leaving here, and I'm leaving you," I said. I called the airlines for a reservation, called a cab, and, with Taylor under my left arm, began hurling clothes into my suitcase with my right.

"You can leave as far as I'm concerned," Aaron said in his soft voice. "I won't miss you. But I know that in two years you'll be in a similar room, packing in a similar way, walking out on the next guy, and then, two years after that, on the next one, and one day you'll look back and say, 'What do I have to show for the last ten years?' "

I kept throwing my clothes and Taylor's into the suitcase in one big jumble. "But," Aaron went on, "you could stay and work this out with me. And in ten years you'll look back and say, 'I preserved this family.' And that will be the thing you will be the most proud of, no matter what else you do with your life."

I stopped cold, frozen by the clarity of what he said. There aren't many times in your life you hear a truth so piercing. There was no attack, just a simple assessment of my future.

When the cab came, he sent it away. We talked. We cried. And we agreed to try. Now it's 19 years later, and it is the thing I am most proud of.

IN 1980 CARTER'S team had welcomed the prospect of running against Ronald Reagan, whom they saw as a right-wing extremist the American people would never accept. Carter warned that it was too risky to leave the serious business of leadership in the hands of a cowboy actor. Confrontation in the nuclear age, he said, "is not just another shoot-out at the O.K. Corral."

Rather than bring up his own performance in office, Carter took to pouncing on Reagan's gaffes and emphasizing his intellectual shortcomings. Reagan gave Carter plenty of ammunition, expressing doubts about evolution and blaming trees, not cars, for smog.

Several of Carter's aides had urged him not to debate Reagan. His negative strategy of scaring the public about Reagan had seemed to show some promise. The week before the October 28 debate in Cleveland, CBS News polls had them in a statistical dead heat. If Reagan could convince the public that he wasn't the sort of person to start a war, all would be lost. But that's pretty much what Reagan did with his low-key, reassuring tone of voice. Not only did he defuse the warmonger issue by asserting that military force should be used only as a "last resort," but whenever Carter came after him, he replied with a mocking sigh, "There you go again!" He made the President seem whiny.

The Reaganites had worried about an "October surprise," a last-minute breakthrough in Carter's negotiations with Iran. Just before the election there was a glimmer of hope, and Carter raced back to the White House for one final attempt. But there was no deal when we went on the air on November 4, election night. By 11:00 in the East it was clear that Reagan was swamping Carter.

Jimmy Carter simply lacked the temperament for strong presidential leadership. He demonstrated that fine moral character—virtuous uprightness, godliness, marital fidelity—is not necessarily the prescription for effective governance. And his presidency poses the question: Can a President of the United States who hates politics succeed? The answer is no. Because of his aversion to the necessary protoplasm of governing, Carter was unable to sell many of his ideas even at a time when his party controlled both houses of Congress. He simply wouldn't do what was necessary to marshal support for the policies he had so diligently devised.

And then, when he did succeed, he couldn't seem to translate his victories into support. He got no credit for saving the hostages' lives. That was only one of his many unappreciated accomplishments. Carter started the smart-bomb program by launching the cruise missile and the Stealth bomber technologies; he put Pershing missiles in Europe to intimidate the Soviets; he took on the pro-Israel lobby—gutsy for a Democrat—by selling AWACS and F-15 fighters to Egypt and Saudi Arabia. And he pre-positioned the U.S. military in the Persian Gulf because he saw that any Middle East peace would have to be secured by the United States. In other words, he gave Ronald Reagan the leverage to bring the Soviets to their knees and George Bush the ability to fight Iraq in the Gulf war. But while he was President, Carter rarely got the credit he deserved.

Reagan won by a landslide, 51 to 41 percent. I recall James Schlesinger's prediction that Carter would expect to lose and then be magnificent in defeat. Which probably explains why he became such an inspiring ex-President.

Part Three

RONALD AND NANCY REAGAN

RUMBLAGE should be a word. Rumblage: vicious gossip reported to the target of the rumor, as in "I thought you should know what everyone's saying about you." In my case it was that my bosses were about to pluck me out of the White House and replace me with Bill Plante, who had covered the Reagan campaign. There was no doubt that he'd have better sources in the new Reagan administration.

The rumblage seeped through me like mad cow disease. My gut churned; my teeth ground. "I know they want me out of there," I told Aaron.

"Why don't you just ask them?"

I was afraid. When I asked Presidents tough questions, I wore the protective shield of CBS News; before my own bosses I'd be naked. But not knowing was worse. So in December I flew to CBS headquarters in New York and asked pitifully, "Can I keep my job?"

"Of course, of course," said Bud Benjamin, the number two man at CBS News, smiling and oh so puzzled by the question. They were happy with my work, and yes, everyone wanted me to stay on at the White House as chief correspondent. What a dark monster, the imagination. I was a cripple gone to Lourdes, instantly cured.

Within a few days I was assigned to cover the Reagan transition. It was clear early on that Reagan had innate potential for strong leadership. If Carter's take on the world was micro, every day for Reagan was a scene in an epic movie on the big screen. At six feet one inch and 185 pounds, he even loomed large. But mainly it was his sweeping view, as he'd displayed in the campaign. If Carter's perspective was farmer's plot, Reagan's was CinemaScope.

In early January, Reagan announced that his press secretary would be James Brady. I liked him; we all liked him. When someone leaked a story that Nancy Reagan had objected to Brady's appointment because he wasn't good-looking enough, the press corps grew to love him.

"I'm getting to be an irate husband at some of the things I'm reading [about Nancy]," said Reagan with a smile. It was my first Reagan news conference—my first close-up look—and all I could think was, "He's irresistible." My view of him over the last year had been from inside the Carter White House, where Reagan had been demonized a hundred different ways every day. I was surprised at how simply likable he was.

Now he was making sweet little jokes—"Nancy thinks he's absolutely handsome"—defusing the Brady dustup. But as affable as Reagan was, he couldn't defuse all of Nancy's time bombs. She simply drew fire. Her adoring gaze seemed phony, and her Rodeo Drive tastes rankled. I had learned about the Reagans' affinity for the Hollywood value system during the transition by following them to parties. One night I staked them out at a Beverly Hills mansion where young valets parked Rolls-Royces and Bentleys on the lawn. If you had sold all the jewelry that walked in the front door, you could've fed Cleveland for a year.

I was enjoying the change, getting to know the Reagan players, when I was summoned to New York. Bud Benjamin told me he had decided after all that Bill Plante and I would share the White House beat. Share? If he had slapped me, I would not have felt such pain. "What made you change your mind?" I asked.

"There was no change of mind."

"But you told me I had the job, the job of chief correspondent, the same job I have now." I could not control my agitation.

"No, I didn't."

I left the office in an aching fog, bumping into one of my old White House producers. He confided that indeed, after they had told me I had the job, they had asked Bill Plante to be my number two. He had refused, and that's when the sharing idea had come up. If they'd said, "Lesley, we changed our minds," I would have gotten over it. But to tell me I hadn't heard what I'd heard was unbearable; it felt like a double cross. I got angry and stayed that way for a long time. In fact, I entered what I now call the angry years. A decade of rage. As unhappy as I was with my new arrangement, I got along with Bill Plante, a fastidious man with a sonorous voice. Bill and I decided to "share" by rotating every other week. When it was his turn to do the *Evening News* pieces, I did *Morning News*. And vice versa. It worked, though I stayed angry at my bosses.

I WAS back at the White House for Jimmy Carter's last full day as President, which began at 4:56 a.m. He came into the Briefing Room at that predawn hour to say, "We have now reached an agreement with Iran which will result, I believe, in the freedom of our American hostages." But between 5:00 a.m. and 5:00 p.m., as during so many days before, nothing happened. I said on the air that night that White House officials believed "the Iranians want to deprive 'The Great Satan' of his final wish."

CBS went on the air the next morning at 9:00 to cover Inauguration Day. At noon Ronald Reagan, 69, became the oldest man to take the oath of office as President of the United States. The cameras got a shot of Carter on the podium with his eyes closed.

Two hours later Walter Cronkite reported that the planes carrying the 52 American hostages had cleared Iranian airspace; in his luncheon toast at 2:16 the new President announced, "The hostages are free!"

Carter's intimates are convinced that the Reagan camp had worked behind the scenes to delay the release of the hostages until Reagan was sworn in. This was never proved.

Later that afternoon Reagan visited Tip O'Neill's office, where the Speaker of the House showed him the desk that had been used by Grover Cleveland. The new President noted that he had portrayed him in a movie. O'Neill reminded him that he'd played Grover Cleveland Alexander, the baseball player, not Grover Cleveland the President.

The White House would be run by a troika: James Baker as chief of staff, a corporate lawyer–type conservative; Edwin Meese, representing the right wing; and pragmatist Michael Deaver, a public relations man. They liked to call the setup a board of directors, but it was more like a raging windstorm. Reagan's first-term White House would be a swirl of conflicting ambitions circling an eye that too often gave only sketchy guidance and paid little attention. The Reagan White House was more riven with palace intrigue and machinations than anything else I'd ever seen.

What emerged from this trifurcated organization was something close to a Hollywood studio with a movie star at the heart, supported by an agent-lawyer, an accountant-manager, and a publicity director. Most movie stars don't read their contracts and don't see to their own finances; many don't even decide which films to accept or reject. On-screen there's someone who tells them where to stand, what to say, and when to say it. There was even a head of the studio, a Michael Eisner type, who *really* ran the place: Nancy.

REAGAN held his first formal presidential news conference on January 29. Before it started, Jim Brady told the assembled reporters that he expected us to conduct ourselves with decorum and dignity and wait to be called upon. This would be a far cry from the way we had shouted and whooped at Jimmy Carter. My colleagues were sure it would never work. Ted Knapp of Scripps-Howard said, "I think this is the first true test of the Reagan presidency: not whether he can stand up to the Russians, but whether he can get control of the animals at the press conference."

Well, he did. It started with Reagan, tall and trim, doing his John Wayne walk down a long, red-carpeted hallway into the East Room. What a picture! It said, This is a President.

He made some news. Setting a confrontational tone for U.S. relations with the Soviets, the new President said, "They reserve unto themselves the right to commit any crime, to lie, to cheat, in order to attain [their one-world government]." Such throw-down-the-gauntlet rhetoric hadn't been heard from an American President in years, and it wouldn't be popular.

But generally, Reagan ducked the hard questions, explaining at least five times that he hadn't finished studying whichever issue was being asked about. And when he pointed to Judy Woodruff and then me, he called us both "young lady." It wasn't, we learned, that he didn't know our names. He simply couldn't tell us apart.

We should have known things would be different when Reagan got his Secret Service code name. Carter's had been Deacon; Reagan's was Rawhide. Reagan seemed to love the little "household" chores and amenities Carter had found so odious: for instance, picture taking with Congressmen and their important constituents. His many acts of courtesy would make it difficult to cross him. He was Rawhide, with a core of natural sweetness.

AROUND that time our radio tech, Lil Zimmerman, grew sullen. She was having her bathroom at home retiled, and right in the middle of the job her contractor put the project on hold. The White House had called. Nancy Reagan wanted her bathroom retiled, and Lil's job would just have to wait.

When the tile man returned to Lil's a few weeks later, he told her a fascinating story. One day while he was caulking away, Mrs. Reagan was getting ready to host a luncheon to promote volunteerism. Her co-host, Barbara Bush, showed up and horrified the First Lady. The tile man reported that Nancy, aghast, had exclaimed, "You're wearing red!" That was *Nancy's* color. The tile man reported that Nancy sent Barbara home to change: "And never wear red again as long as I live in this house."

When Lil finished the story, I saw visions of a nifty little scoop, but first I had to get the encounter confirmed, something I knew Nancy Reagan would never do. So I called Mrs. Bush's office, but her press secretary stiffed me with a firm "No comment." I had no choice but to sit on the story for years; in fact, I never reported it, though I believe it to be true.

On February 5 Jim Brady escorted Sam Donaldson, Judy

Woodruff, and me to the library in the lower level of the White House. We were to get a three-on-one interview with the President, but no cameras were to be allowed. It was 4:00 in the afternoon, leaving us just enough time to put together a one-dimensional story about what the President said. No leeway for reactions. Brady told us we'd have no more than 40 minutes.

With that, in walked Rawhide. My first impression: more wrinkled and frail than I'd realized. He stood straight and tall, but up close he didn't seem sturdy. The word "vulnerable" came to mind. Within a minute that voice, warm as cashmere, was apologizing to Judy and me for calling us "young ladies."

We asked about the budget, but Reagan talked in circles, curlicues, and mazes. Trying to pin him down on the inconsistencies of Reaganomics was like sawing into fog. We did not get a single quote that made sense.

REAGAN had made lowering taxes the main focus of his campaign. When candidate George Bush had called the plan "voodoo economics," Reagan and his supply-side sidekicks had argued that there would be such a burst of savings and business activity from the tax-cut stimulus, the government would be rolling in revenues, and major cuts in government programs would be unnecessary.

It came as something of a surprise, then, when the President began talking of massive reductions in social programs. Specific details of the budget cuts were not made public, so I worked the phones, calling as many Congressmen as I could. Bingo! A Republican from the Midwest got on the phone himself and told me he had a book of Reagan's proposed budget cuts. "It's confidential," he said.

"Could I come see it?" I asked.

"Sure. I don't see why not."

So I went to his office on the Hill and met with him privately. Then he and I together made a Xerox copy of the entire book.

My producer quickly managed to build a package of graphics to go with my script: that the biggest budget bites would come out of subsidies for the poor, such as food stamps, child nutrition, job training, and unemployment benefits—190 programs in all, including Medicaid. I also reported that even Social Security was on the chopping block. This was a healthy scoop and the first real sign that tax cuts would involve some serious pain.

Reagan became the mean stepfather of the government he'd been elected to oversee but that he held in contempt. He named anti-environmentalists to run the environmental programs and foes of civil rights to run those programs. It was cynical, as was the supply-side program, which had as a subsidiary goal the starving of Lyndon Johnson's Great Society programs into malnutrition by calling for nearly $50 billion in budget cuts. They were supposed to offset the more than $50 billion in tax cuts and a three-year, 27 percent rise in military spending—an increase so huge that experts questioned whether the Pentagon could spend it all.

The Democrats and many columnists swung wildly at the plan. Reagan ignored the criticisms and flew to Santa Barbara for the first of many vacations at his ranch (he would spend 345 days of his presidency there) in the Santa Ynez Mountains. His mornings would include horseback riding and chopping wood. Rawhide.

THE problems with the Reagan presidency were forgotten on March 30, 1981. He addressed the building and construction trade unions of the AFL-CIO at the Hilton Hotel in Washington. After he left, I stayed behind for a few minutes, wandered outside, and found a scene of choking fear: a man lying facedown, a narrow river of blood trickling from his head. What happened? I asked. "The President was shot at."

"The man?"

"That's Jim Brady."

Shaken, I ran inside, called the assignment desk, and blurted out what I'd seen and heard. "We know," said Bill Galbraith. Our cameraman had rolled even as shots rang out. John Hinckley, the would-be assassin, had been standing in the press area.

As I headed back to the White House, Dan Rather went on the air. For the first time in years the country would have to get through a national trauma without Walter Cronkite, who had retired on March 6. "President Reagan, according to the White House, is unscathed," said Dan. "The President—I repeat for emphasis—was not hit."

A good 20 minutes after Dan and the other network anchors reported that the bullets had missed the President, Lyn Nofziger, Reagan's political counselor, announced that indeed the President had been hit—in the left side of his chest. "But he's all right."

Poor Dan. He was at the mercy of wire copy and rumors. "Well, this is a change," he said. "What you have had in the last minute, in the last few seconds, is a change. The President was struck or at least grazed. We don't know the extent of it."

This was rough, spontaneous television, covering a crisis while the White House was trying to play down any sense of real danger to the President's life. The press and therefore the public were kept in the dark. We learned later that when Reagan had first arrived at the hospital, he had gone down on one knee and said, "I can't breathe." But everything we were told for the next several days was intended to minimize the gravity of the President's condition.

I was back at the White House in time for a four-o'clock briefing by Brady's deputy, Larry Speakes, thrust so suddenly into the role of press secretary. He had been a press aide in the Nixon and Ford administrations but had had no relationship at all with Reagan.

"Larry, is the President in surgery?" I asked.

"I can't say, Lesley."

"We have confirmed reports," I told him. "So have other networks, so have the wires. Can't you help us?"

"As soon as we can confirm it, we will and—"

"Larry," I interrupted, "Reagan's brother, Neil, has been told that the President is in surgery right now, that he's already had blood transfusions. Is your information going to be that far behind what we're getting from other sources?"

"No. We will do our very best to keep it up."

About an hour later we began hearing about the President's quips and one-liners. We were told that when he had first seen Nancy at the hospital, he had said, "Honey, I just forgot to duck." He was quoted as joking with the doctors in the operating room, "Please tell me you're Republicans!" These were meant to reassure the country that he was all right. By contrast, doctors sounded dire about Jim Brady's brain injury. There was extensive damage of the right hemisphere of the brain, though there was some hope: He was responding to commands.

In a briefing the next morning doctors gave us more one-liners: " 'If I got this much attention in Hollywood, I'd never have left.' " The jokes became the heart and soul of the information we got, along with assurances that the President was perfectly able to make decisions.

The idea that all was well with this 70-year-old man who had just been shot in the left side of the chest was not believable, at least not to me. I did a story that night strongly suggesting that the White House was orchestrating a cover-up. What we didn't know was that the head of the studio had taken over. Nancy was in charge of all decisions, including one to hide from the public just how close the President had come to dying.

Years later the President's daughter Maureen told me that when she arrived at the hospital a few days after the shooting, she found Nancy, her stepmother (whom Maureen had once called the Dragon Lady), all alone in the room adjacent to the President's, huddled in the corner of a couch listening to the nurses pound on Reagan's chest to get the phlegm up. "She looked so vulnerable and afraid. He was so much sicker than anyone realized," Maureen said, "and so I sat there with Nancy, and we listened together, and I forgave her for all those years."

All doubts about Reagan's fitness vanished when he left the hospital, waving and shining his handsome smile. It was 12 days after the shooting. "What are you going to do when you get back to the White House?" one of my colleagues shouted. "Sit down!" said Reagan. His wit and the grace with which he handled what could easily have been a crisis were comforting, his courage admired. His poll numbers sprang up by 11 points, and he emerged with a new dimension of heroism and specialness.

REAGAN's budget plans were drawing more and more criticism, especially his proposal to cut Social Security benefits for early retirees. I was hearing from my sources within the White House itself that the plan was flawed. On May 28, I did a story about how the deficit was creeping up $8 billion higher than projected. When asked, "How much longer can you blame the Carter administration for the increasing deficit?" Speakes said, "A while longer."

It began to bother me that a man as ill informed as Ronald Reagan was setting the economic course for the country against the advice of so many of his own people. That was true of his foreign policy as well. My concerns were heightened at his third news conference on June 16. Asked about the Israelis' recent attack on an Iraqi nuclear reactor in which they had used U.S.-made jets, Reagan replied, "I can't answer that." On Israel's refusal to sign the Nuclear Nonproliferation Treaty? "I haven't given very much thought to that particular question there." Earlier in the week he had bumped into his own housing secretary at a reception for big-city mayors and said, "How are you, Mr. Mayor? How are things in your city?" There were quiet little suspicions among the reporters that Reagan, the course setter, was sinking into senility.

Newsweek ran a devastating article in its September 7 issue entitled "A Disengaged Presidency." It reported "displays of inattention and ignorance," of Reagan's reliance on "cue cards" when he dealt with Congressmen and foreign leaders, and of his repeated inability to answer questions about issues. "He is easily bored, alternately joking and yawning through subjects that don't interest him. All he wants to do is tell stories about his movie days." The White House tried to discredit the piece. Jim Baker attributed the remarks to a few "dissatisfied staffers." But it rang true to me.

IN LATE 1981, I was 39½ years old. It had not been a particularly good year. I was feeling the stress of the job—the incessant competition, the need to know something about every issue under the sun every day—all this and raise a child and maintain a marriage. I kept thinking I'd lost my freedom. The only upside was that for the first time in years I didn't have to diet. My metabolism was running so fast, I ate anything I wanted and still lost weight. Losing weight, though, did not appeal to the camera; I began to look drawn, and Dolly told me so—often: "You're haggard. You may have to do something about it."

"Like what?"

"A face-lift."

"But I'm *only* thirty-nine!"

Meantime, CBS News had a new president: Van Gordon Sauter came over from CBS Sports. My only previous contact with him had been when he had sent me a message that I shouldn't wear my fur coat on television. I had ignored the advice. Right after his new job as my boss was announced, I went out and bought a lavender down coat that I wore for the next six years.

Sauter looked like a cross between Hemingway and the Schweppes man with his conscientiously groomed beard with flying buttresses. He was a man of considerable bulk who wore bow ties and, legend had it, had trafficked in eccentricity when he ran the CBS affiliate in Los Angeles, where he lived on a houseboat and walked around the office with a parrot on his shoulder. Now, in his new office in New York to discuss contract negotiations, I found a man with boundless enthusiasm and great charm, which he directed at me.

Swigging on a can of Tab, he asked what I wanted from CBS. I complained that every other White House correspondent had gotten to anchor a weekend newscast. He proposed a solution not uncommon to sports figures: "What if we write a window into your contract? We'll write that if you don't have your own show within a year and a half, then you can exercise an option to leave or renegotiate with us." I accepted.

Sauter was introducing a new sensibility to the News Division, preferring the magazine style with "breathing," which meant more picture and feature stories. In 1981 Dan Rather's ratings had fallen off the cliff. Sauter was trying to make Dan friendlier by having him smile more and soften his tone. None of it worked. But then one night Dan wore a V-necked sweater—and presto, he warmed up. So did the ratings. By the spring of 1982 Rather regained the lead and held on to it for 212 weeks. But I worried about the program's new direction.

June 28, for example. Around 4:00 p.m. the *Evening News*'s producers met in New York to decide on the lead. Their choices were some exclusive combat footage of the war between Argentina and Great Britain over control of the Falkland Islands, Reagan's meeting with Israeli Prime Minister Begin on a day when the Israelis bombed Palestinian strongholds in Beirut, and the birth of Prince Charles and Princess Diana's first child, Prince William. In Cronkite's time it would certainly have been the Falklands or the Israelis. On the night of June 28 you could hear the snap, a loud unhinging in the Washington Bureau when Dan Rather led off with the baby.

By late 1982 the Washington Bureau was suffering from post-traumatic stress syndrome. A report from the State Department about U.S. attitudes toward the Israeli bombing of Lebanon would be dropped to make room for a "flock 'n' roll" story about some singing sheep. Sauter was changing the very definition of what was network news; we felt he was downgrading us to some second-rate tabloid. We had thought of ourselves as chroniclers of daily events, television's counterpart of *The New York Times*. But if any of us complained, we were clumped into the category of "yesterday's men."

I wasn't opposed to all the changes, but then the producers in New York began fiddling with my scripts "to improve my writing." I suspected what they were really up to was cleansing my copy of any hint of criticism of the President. One of the producers told me that Sauter thought my coverage was "knee-jerk" critical on Reaganomics. I argued, "This isn't bias. My sources are White House officials." But I was told, "They think you're zinging the President."

When the Carter White House had said that, my bosses had encouraged me to be "tougher." These bosses were guiding me away from the kind of coverage I'd been trained to produce.

Sauter was trying to steer the whole ship onto a friendlier course to mesh with the new sweatered Dan. The nice approach was working for Rather—why not for all of us? Sauter wanted a feel-good broadcast; it's the ratings, stupid.

AARON'S movie, *Urban Cowboy*, with John Travolta and Debra Winger, opened, and I threw a party for my husband. Judge John

Sirica came, as did Zbigniew Brzezinski in a ten-gallon hat. These were great times. The movie was a megahit. Country-western bars sprang up everywhere, some with their own mechanical bulls; Levi Strauss was reborn. We saw a convergence of politics and popular culture. Aaron and I debated whether the craving for our old, romantic cowboy roots had made way for the election of Ronald Reagan or whether Rawhide had created the craving. He tended to be a politician who stood still with his immutable beliefs, waiting for everyone else to catch up with him or drift back to him.

Aaron was hot in Hollywood—and happy. Except that we were still living in Washington. He lost all interest in writing about government and politics. "This is such a one-industry small town," he would say. We both knew that if it were not for Taylor and me, he'd have moved away. His career heart was in Hollywood.

THE nature of the President's mind was a source of endless discussion and speculation in the press corps. Just as I would decide that he was vacant and mindless, someone like Deputy Chief of Staff Richard Darman would assure me, "He's far more intelligent and involved than you guys in the press realize." There was always the caveat "when he cares." But I kept hearing about Reagan doodling his way through national security briefings and sleeping through budget meetings, and meanwhile, the gaffes and errors continued to trill off his tongue.

Years after Reagan left office, I filed a request at the Reagan Library for one of his speeches and had to rethink my assumptions about Reagan's level of involvement in his presidency. His handwritten revisions are all over every page of the draft that was submitted by speechwriter Tony Dolan. On page 1 Reagan crossed out six lines and wrote the phrase "I believe in intercessionary prayer" in the margins along with a quote from Abraham Lincoln. He wrote out in longhand whole new pages 4 and 5 about illegitimacy and abortion, and on page 9 he scrawled in, "Unless and until it can be proven that the unborn child is not a living entity, then its right to life, liberty and the pursuit of happiness must be protected." Generally, he improved the speech, making it more colloquial, livelier. He was good at this.

I had been told that he rewrote many of his speeches, but I had such a fixed notion of him as a floater over the events of his presidency that I was startled when I actually saw the hard evidence. I called a friend who had worked for Reagan, and my friend said, "If you could get a pen or pencil in his hand, he'd engage. He seemed to think more sharply when he wrote out his thoughts." Speeches became far more central in Reagan's presidency than in most. They became an occasion for decision making, since the staff knew the speeches were one of the few things Reagan would concentrate on.

Reagan's ideology grew directly out of what he saw as injustices during his career in Hollywood—and these resentments were embedded in his brain like the deep roots of a 500-year-old tree. His anti-Sovietism had been born when he was president of the Screen Actors Guild. It was then, he told Larry Barrett of *Time,* that he had discovered the Communists' "brutality," "cold-bloodedness," and "lack of morality." A diatribe in Orlando, Florida, was as much a reaction to Stalin's invasion of Hollywood in the 1950s as it was to Brezhnev's aggressive policies in the 1980s.

It was the same with Reagan's other lodestar, cutting taxes. In the early part of his career he was outraged by his 91 percent tax rate—so outraged that he became a lifelong bulldog on the subject, dragging the rest of us along with him.

THE window clause in my contract was on my mind. It said I would anchor my own weekend newscast within 18 months. With the deadline just eight weeks away, I poked my head into Van Sauter's New York office one day and said offhandedly, "By the way, those eighteen months are up in May."

"Glad you're here." He got up from his desk and moved around to greet me. "Come in." He seemed so happy to see me. "Sit down." He guided me to a couch, sat down beside me, and engaged me in a discussion of issues and movies and sports.

"I hope you remember about the weekend show," I said at last.

I was pretty softened up and off guard as he replied, shaking his head, "Lesley, Lesley, we're not going to give you a weekend show. We never were."

"What? But—but—" I sputtered, "I have it in writing."

"Oh, I know. I wrote that down so you wouldn't leave."

My mouth opened, but only sighs came out. I had no idea what to say. Sauter got up and went to the door. "I'm locking this," he said. "I'm not letting you out of here until we find something else that will make you happy enough not to leave CBS." I was paralyzed—not by his cunning, but by my own naïveté. What an idiot.

"What about *Face the Nation?*" he asked.

"No way. That's George Herman's show, and besides, I'm not interested."

He told me that he wanted to revamp the Sunday morning broadcast, "bring it into the 1980s," that George was closing in on 65 and would be replaced anyway. "What if we designed a new Sunday show for you? Give it a new name, new format, new look."

I balked, but the more he talked of "creating something new," my starch went limp. He had seduced me with his enthusiasm, his willingness to experiment. And to be honest, I surrendered to the flattery of it all. I was more excited than I'd been in years. I agreed to take on the Sunday show without thinking through how I was going to handle what was essentially a second job.

TAYLOR would call me every afternoon unless I had arranged a play date for her. When I was growing up in Swampscott, Massachusetts, I'd ride my bike home from school, change into pants (Dolly dressed me up for school), and go outside and play. But Tay lived in a high-rise apartment in the middle of a city. No way could she, at age five, run outside and play without the supervision of an adult. How was she going to learn to be independent? I worried about it constantly and tried to give her as much freedom as I could.

Taylor was the easiest child. She was never sick, and she was always happy. As she got older, I wondered how I, of all people, had been so blessed. I didn't think I was a great mother, though Taylor knew I loved her and that she could always find me.

My colleagues used to tease me that Taylor was the only child on earth. If she called me, I'd get on the phone right away. I'd hang up on sources, put officials on hold, talk to her on deadline: "Hi, angel. What happened at school today?" "Nothing." Every day, the same conversation. And if she didn't call me, I'd call her.

More than anything I was her social secretary. I prayed my bosses wouldn't find out how much time I spent organizing her social life. Carmen, the nanny, didn't drive, so there were the pick-ups and the drop-offs—who had to be where at what time to retrieve her from whose house and who was coming over to ours.

When I got home at night, she'd act out what she'd seen on *Sesame Street.* She adored it. We gulped our laughs like Ernie and wondered what Mr. Snuffleupagus ate for dinner. I told a magazine that year, "Since I've had this child, there is no such thing as depression. I walk in the door, and there is that smiling face. You can just see how sweet human beings are when they start out."

The interviewer asked how I balanced it all. "I think I'm exactly like any other woman with a five-year-old," I said. "Whether you work or not, Monday, Tuesday, Wednesday you think: 'Gosh, I'm terrific. I can handle anything.' Thursday and Friday you can't handle anything at all. Saturday and Sunday, you coast."

I BEGAN planning for the new *Face the Nation.* The ideas my producer Joan Barone and I came up with were approved by Sauter, but they were also leaked to Walter Cronkite, then a member of the CBS board of directors and an outspoken critic of Sauter's approach to the news. Cronkite took one of our proposals—on the contraceptive sponge—to the board and passed it around as an example of how Sauter intended to remold *Face the Nation.* Walter was quoted as telling the board, "He's ruining CBS News on every front."

Face the Nation dated back to 1954. Its premier broadcast with Senator Joseph McCarthy aired on the eve of the Senate debate that resulted in his censure. It was not a tradition to be trifled with, and now Sauter had to assure his bosses at corporate headquarters that *Face* would remain the venerable, hard-news broadcast it had always been. He called me and said, "Let's start off with

Left: my parents, Dolly and Lou. Below: my father playing airplane with my daughter, Taylor, in 1977. Dolly, who stopped talking to me when Aaron and I eloped, forgave me the minute I went into labor.

Right: at three, Taylor was the most adorable little girl alive, with the bluest eyes and the sunniest disposition. Aaron was the father of all fathers.

Above: shortly after Reagan moved into the White House, Sam, Judy, and I were invited to a private meeting with the President.
Below: interviewing Hosni Mubarak at his ornate palace in Cairo.

Right: calling Mommy from the set on election night. Below: the Bushes appear on *Face the Nation* during the second Bush-Reagan administration.

Below: I brought Aaron and Taylor to meet with President Reagan on my last day as White House correspondent. When we first got there, Reagan looked frail and didn't seem to know who I was. But as soon as Aaron mentioned Hollywood, the glaze in Reagan's eyes cleared and the color came to his cheeks.

Above: with Charles Kuralt during our brief experience co-hosting a series of nightly Persian Gulf specials. Below: my beautiful family, all grown up. Aaron was right—it's the thing I'm most proud of.

some traditional shows. Once we persuade everyone we're serious, then we can start experimenting."

Even after weeks of preparation our first show sneaked up on us. We decided to make Lebanon our issue. The old *Face* had been built around a single interview. We were going to have multiple guests discussing a single topic. President Reagan had sent U.S. Marines into Lebanon as peacekeepers, and we had booked the Lebanese President, Amin Gemayel, as our big, look-at-us headliner to discuss the civil war and the U.S. Marines caught in the middle. But at 5:30 Thursday evening he canceled on us. It was three days before our debut. I went numb and stayed that way until the Monday after the show. Actually, I managed to be numb and panicky at the same time. Joan got on the phones and somehow persuaded the marine commandant, P. X. Kelley, to be our leadoff guest. Gemayel showed up on *This Week with David Brinkley.*

Sunday morning I got two dozen yellow roses with a card from my sweetheart that said, "Break a leg and all their hearts. Love, Aaron." If you were watching CBS at 10:30, September 18, 1983, then you saw me—eyes in a semi-pop, neck veins in a full pop—and you heard me say, "Lebanon is at war. This time a unit of a U.S. Marine brigade is caught in the cross fire." I was so nervous, my usual alto approached Tiny Tim range. "Four U.S. Marines have died in Lebanon, and Americans are asking why." P. X. Kelley, tall and ruddy-faced with ramrod posture, made one ask if looking the part was a criterion for the job of commandant. Speaking of parts: mine, as hostess, was to relax the guest. But on this day it was P.X. who reached over, patted my hand reassuringly, and said, "You'll do great." With that, I got a cue that meant "Go!"

"Are you personally concerned that we are getting into a situation that is so tangled we will not be able to get out gracefully?"

"That's something," he replied, "the administration and the government far above my pay grade is going to have to answer."

Kelley continued to duck and circumvent, but I was so grateful he'd shown up, I didn't push. I would have to get over the idea that I was a "hostess" in the homey sense. If I didn't toughen up, this was going to be a Sunday morning tea party.

The show was reviewed the next day as if I had opened on Broadway. Most of the articles dwelled on my limp style and failure to ask tough questions.

From then on I worked at a maniacal pace: Monday through Friday at the White House, Saturday at *Face.* We were determined that no one would ever again say I didn't pursue or follow up. We would try to guess what the newsmaker might say to various questions, then fashion comebacks. I never went on the air without a thorough blueprint. The trick, though, was not to stick with it, but to use it as a backup system that would leave me free to listen and point out when a question was ducked. Many officials actually took lessons in how to avoid answering tough questions. I can't count the times administration officials told me flat out that their goal in coming on *Face* was to escape without making one parenthetical phrase of news.

Face's most daunting challenge wasn't the interviewing, it was the booking. Not only did we have to convince top officials to be grilled at the height of a crisis, but we had to compete with two other Sunday shows for the same officials. Actually, we had to beg for guests, and beg we did.

My being at the White House was an advantage; I often did the begging and bargaining in person. I was able to book Jim Baker for our show called "Will Ronald Reagan Run Again?" It came as no surprise that Baker said, "In my personal opinion, he is going to run." I mentioned a possible opponent, Senator John Glenn. We had gotten a clip from the new movie *The Right Stuff* about Glenn the astronaut, which we ran in the middle of the Baker interview. "So what do you think of celluloid heroes?" I asked. "How worried are you that this movie is going to turn John Glenn into a big national hero, if not a myth in the country."

"Well . . ." He seemed caught off-balance. I thought, These guys are always so prepared, they know just what we're going to ask. But this time I had surprised the great Jim Baker. "I can't— For one thing, I can't believe that the voters are going to base their voting decision on a movie."

"You don't think Hollywood can create a President?" One of my all-time favorite questions.

For the next Sunday, October 23, we lined up Defense Secretary Caspar Weinberger to talk about the escalating violence in Lebanon, along with the Syrian ambassador, Rafic Jouejati. My phone rang at about 3:00 a.m. A truck bomb had exploded at the U.S. Marine barracks in Beirut, and more than 70 Americans were reported dead. The number would reach 241.

Joan and I went into the bureau very early, relieved that we had lined up the perfect guests. But our little bubble did the proverbial pop when I finally got through to David Gergen, director of communications at the White House. "We're awfully sorry," he said, "but Cap's in a national security meeting in the Situation Room, which we think will go on for several hours." I was discovering that live Sunday morning television was the twin brother of terrorism.

"But David, don't you think the American people are going to want some word from the administration?" I implored him to lean on Weinberger. "Let us set up a camera crew in the White House. All Cap would have to do is leave the meeting for ten minutes max. We'd carry him by microwave. Please ask him."

Gergen called back with word that Weinberger was considering my proposal. "We'll send our crew right over." It was after nine o'clock, 90 minutes to air. It would take the cameraman at least an hour to set up.

As I worked on my questions, Joan positioned herself at the front door to greet our other guest and escort him into the makeup room. Wire-service reports out of Beirut were laying the blame for the bombing on Syria, so we thought even if Weinberger stiffs us, at least we'll have the Syrian ambassador, who, to our great relief, finally showed up. When he arrived, he told Joan, "Oh, miss, I cannot stay. I only came by to apologize in person that I must not appear on your broadcast. This is not a good time. Please forgive." But as he bowed and begged Joan's pardon, she was gently guiding him back into makeup. He continued to protest, but somehow the self-effacing Joan eased him into the makeup chair, all the while sympathizing, understanding.

Meanwhile, I was sitting alone in the studio, staring into the camera, still not certain whether Weinberger would show up.

David Gergen was with our crew in the Roosevelt Room, telling us that he "hoped" Cap could get away. "No guarantees."

Minutes before the red light went on, Secretary Weinberger eased into a chair in the Roosevelt Room. I almost wept. I asked about a U.S. military retaliation, pointing out that the President had recently said he would "not stand idly by and have our marines brutalized."

"That is part of the agenda this morning," said Weinberger. "[We're] trying our best to find out exactly who was responsible." He said that the "circumstantial evidence" pointed to Iran. Was Syria also involved? He said that the investigation was just beginning but again fingered Iran.

During the commercial the Syrian ambassador was ushered into the studio. "Ambassador Jouejati," I asked, "did your government have anything to do with this tragic bombing this morning?"

He put his hands together in the prayer position and arced forward in a slow bow so low that he almost touched my knees with his forehead. This was done in silence. Finally, on the upswing, he made a long speech of condolence: "The marines are our brothers, and we regret that very very very deeply."

I eventually got to reask my is-Syria-involved question, which provoked a bout of petulance: "You have been asking Mr. Weinberger once and again, Is Syria responsible? . . . Syria is not interested in partitioning Lebanon."

After the show we congratulated ourselves. We had talked the Secretary of Defense into an extraordinary middle-of-a-meeting appearance; Joan had persuaded a reluctant Syrian ambassador to participate. And we had pulled it off all by ourselves.

AFTER a while, when it wasn't my turn at the White House, I began taking Mondays and Tuesdays off. I would pick up Taylor at school, run errands, and sleep. There's no question that I had taken on too much. But I never once considered shedding either of my jobs: the White House or *Face*. I would just have to adjust, manage my time, figure it out. Meanwhile, I lost 15 pounds.

We ironed out a few more kinks on *Face*, but still, every week was a booking agony. Soon I was developing a reputation for toughness as an interviewer. My attitude was that public officials are obliged to explain and justify their policies, decisions, and actions. So I was proud of being tenacious; I liked being called tough. But I was also called impolite, and that I didn't like. I told one critic, "The pressure of the clock is why so many interviewers get the reputation for being discourteous. The time is being eaten up [by the interviewees' filibustering] and you're still stuck on question two. It's a constant balancing act between moving it along and not being rude."

TAYLOR swears she never resented my being at the office as much as I was. She has told me she even considers it auspicious. I'm not sure that's a compliment. "If you didn't work, you'd be miserable, and we'd all be miserable," she said. I'm grateful that she feels that way. But more, I'm grateful that Aaron filled the vacuum, though I must say he was the most permissive parent ever.

Taylor wanted a chicken. All I could think of was the visit my father, Lou, had taken us on when I was a kid to his cousin's chicken farm in Sharon, Massachusetts. I can still smell the place and see all those pecking monsters. "Our apartment is too small," I explained to Taylor. Thus began a test of wills.

When I was off to work, she went straight to Aaron, who never could say no to her. "Dad, can we get a chicken?" Of course, said he.

So while I was scuffling over the White House's refusal to supply *Face* with a high-ranking guest for Sunday, I was negotiating with my six-year-old about a chicken. We agreed to launch an investigation, which mercifully culminated in a compromise: a parrot, a kelly-green male parrot we named Paley, after Bill.

THE first sign that Reagan's reelection campaign had started in earnest was the President's sudden slam of the gears into reverse on Soviet policy. In a major foreign affairs speech he once again turned the issue into a little movie about an Ivan and Anya and a Jim and Sally who meet and discover all the things they have in common: "Ambitions and hobbies and what they wanted for their children and problems of making ends meet." On a dime the Evil Empire was transformed into a Peoria of folks like us. Nancy Reagan, the grand impresario, had decided that her husband should go down in history for making peace with the Russians.

The President formally announced that he was running again on January 29, 1984. The date, we would later learn, was chosen in accordance with Nancy's astrological consultant.

Nancy Reagan was always a force to be reckoned with. She wanted the public to think she was a Tammy Wynette kind of gal, an un-Rosalynn First Lady who kept her nose out of issues. But Nancy Reagan's nose was deep into everything. Over the years I have grown to appreciate her, even admire her, but back then I had little sympathy for the Imperial One.

As someone pointed out to me: First she picked the chief of staff; then she made him obedient. Late one Friday afternoon I was meeting with Jim Baker in his office. At 5:20 we both heard Marine One, the President's helicopter, land on the South Lawn. Baker looked at his watch and went pale. "What time do you have?" he asked. It was 5:20, all right. "Oh, my God." It was the one and only time I ever saw him flustered. He jumped up. "Just wait here. I'll be right back."

"What's wrong? Is there an emergency?"

"I think I may have missed the helicopter." He looked frazzled. "The President's leaving for Camp David any minute. Maybe I can still make it." With that, he bolted out the door and ran through the Rose Garden, trying to catch the President. I was sure he had a grave matter he had to discuss; maybe a political scandal was brewing, maybe a message had come from the Soviets.

A few minutes later Baker was back, all smiles. "Phew," he said. "I made it!"

"Well, tell me, what was so urgent?" I had my notebook open to a fresh page, a new pen in hand that wouldn't run out.

"Oh, I didn't have anything special to tell them," said Baker, his composure restored. "I just wanted them to see me standing there as they left for the weekend."

I was floored: the steady chief of staff intimidated by the mild-mannered Ronald Reagan? But then I told the Baker helicopter story to someone in the higher reaches of the White House, and he just laughed. "It wasn't Reagan Jim was afraid of." He chortled.

"It was Nancy! Reagan wouldn't have noticed whether Jim was there or not. But Nancy—she expected things to be done just so."

Nancy and Ronnie were a salt-and-pepper set. He was as sweet as Brie, she was sharp cheddar; he was as unpretentious as Chianti, she was Dom Pérignon; he bore no grudges, she never forgot; he was the browser who liked window-shopping, Nancy was the buyer. And what Nancy was buying in 1984 was détente with the Soviets. According to a White House official, "She thought this was the only thing between Ronnie and the Nobel Peace Prize. It would cap his career, and she really pushed it with him."

THERE was a lot of criticism after the 1984 campaign that the media hadn't covered the issues, that we had concentrated our coverage on style rather than substance. That was in large measure true, but it was true because Reagan ran a feel-good campaign.

Every effort was made to ensure a constant flow of content-free, positive visual images. If Reagan's team managed to eclipse the competition, all the better. Which is what was happening in early June. Just as Gary Hart won the California primary and Mondale won New Jersey, Reagan went on a triumphal tour of Europe. As I said on the *Evening News:* "When it comes to political one-upmanship, Ronald Reagan is a master. Upstage the winner of the California primary? Piece of cake: Have lunch at Buckingham Palace with the Queen of England, meet with Britain's Prime Minister Thatcher, and pay tribute to the thousands who died on the beaches of Normandy."

While the President was in France, Michael Deaver produced his masterpiece: Reagan's commemoration of the fortieth anniversary of D-day from high atop the cliffs at Normandy—a filmmaker's Valhalla. Reagan gave one of his finest speeches, crafted by his new speechwriter, Peggy Noonan.

On the site of the Normandy invasion Reagan won the almost awed attention of the country when he read, " 'These are the boys of Pointe-du-Hoc,' " referring to the veterans sitting before him. " 'These are the men who took the cliffs. These are the champions who helped free a continent.' " The "boys," now in their sixties, wept.

I loved my job. I know I've said that before, but there were times like this when I stopped to live in the moment and say to myself, "Wow, kiddo, you are there. You are a witness, you lucky son of a gun. Just be still, slow the engine, and make sure you remember."

I MIGHT have even teared up a little at Normandy, but that was unusual. I had tried so hard to kill off my crying spasms, my internal quakes when things got hairy, that by now I had pretty much succeeded. When critics scraped me over, I simply flexed my well-developed I-don't-care muscle. I was being called a tough cookie, and through careful training, I was actually becoming one. And not always a pretty one.

Joan Barthel of *TV Guide* ran a picture of a sneering me in the June 30, 1984, issue with the line "Her questions range from sharp to stinging." But it was Barthel's description of me as "difficult" that was the real stinger. Quoting me on the *Face* set one Sunday morning, she wrote, "She asked: 'Do I have enough rouge on?' A technician relayed the word that came through his headphones from the control room: 'They think so, Lesley.'

" 'Not on this monitor, I don't. And there's a shadow under my left eye.' " She portrayed me as one demanding monster. I cringed when I saw the mirror and suffered for days, hating myself and resolving to ease up, to remember the job was fun. Just when I thought I was inured to criticism and attacks, one would come along that would throw me off my pins.

REAGANITES were worried about the gender gap, which was brought on by the budget cuts and issues such as the arms race, the environment, and abortion. That's why Nancy was begging her husband to skirt those subjects.

On their side the Democrats wanted to exploit the gap, but would Mondale go so far as to pick a woman as a running mate? Mondale's team concluded that he couldn't beat Reagan unless he did something dramatic and unorthodox. So, defying advisers, he chose Geraldine Ferraro, 48. She was a three-term Congresswoman from Queens, someone even more liberal than he was.

I watched his televised announcement at the Minnesota statehouse on July 12 and must admit that like most women I knew, I was filled with a sense of pride. Mondale, never a sparkler on TV, said, "This is an exciting choice. . . . Let me say that again. This is an exciting choice."

The next day at her first news conference, Ferraro attacked Reagan's character: "The President walks around calling himself a good Christian. I don't for one minute believe it, because the policies are so terribly unfair." She never made a dent.

By early October, Mondale was lagging so far behind in the polls that whatever chance he had left was riding on two debates. I was there for the first one in Louisville, Kentucky, which was a stunning role reversal. There was Mondale, confidently in control, while the Great Communicator kept losing his train of thought, groping for words. "The system is still where it was with regard to the . . . uh . . . the . . . uh." The synapses finally connected: "progressivity." Reagan's closing soliloquy made little sense. He summed up, admitting, "I'm all confused now." Both the press and the public saw clearly that Mondale had won.

The next morning op-ed columns were filled with speculation about Reagan's fitness for office. The White House's greatest and perhaps only fear—the age issue—was rearing up.

The Democrats did what they could to keep the age issue alive. But in the second debate in Kansas City, Reagan did better, delivering a slay-the-dragon line. Looking over at the 56-year-old Mondale, he said, "I will not make age an issue in this campaign. I am not going to exploit for political purposes my opponent's youth and inexperience." With that, Reagan smote the age issue. It just went away.

A few weeks later Ronald Reagan won the election in a landslide of historic proportions. He got 59 percent of the vote, carrying 49 states—all but Mondale's home state of Minnesota and Washington, D.C. Even the gender gap shrank. Reagan got 55 percent of the women's vote, as opposed to 64 percent of men's.

The election was about rewarding a President when the economy is sturdy, but even more it was about personality—a personality made for television. Like a besotted woman, the entire country ran off with the dashing cowboy, even if he was 73. It was romance.

Part Four

NANCY AND RONNIE

RIGHT after the election we asked the President when his next news conference would be. "Look," he said with a mischievous smile, "I won. I don't have to subject myself."

I was back in my cell at the White House, feeling like the little man on *The Ed Sullivan Show* who ran back and forth twirling wobbly glass plates on top of long poles. My wobblers were the White House, *Face the Nation,* Aaron and Taylor. I wasn't unhappy; there wasn't time. And besides, I was beginning to master the beat. This would be my seventh year in that place, and I was finally clicking into my pace and my voice.

The real reason I was able to keep those glass plates in the air was Aaron's devotion to Taylor. Aaron says it started at childbirth. Because I had a cesarean, he was the first one to diaper and feed Taylor in the hospital. And it didn't hurt that she looked exactly like him. Whatever the reason, I had never seen anything like it. He was working out of an office in our apartment but never got annoyed when she interrupted his work. He would go with her to the park whenever she asked and would take her and five or six friends to hockey games at the Capital Center or to Chuck E. Cheese. And he always volunteered for field trips with her class at Sidwell Friends School. Starting in third grade, he went on all the camping trips, and he videotaped every game and play she was ever in. After a while Tay signed him up without asking. It was a given that her dad would come along. She knew that he never said no.

"Did you ever resent that I wasn't home more with Taylor?" I asked my husband recently. "Did you think, 'She's not doing her share'?"

"Never. I mean it," he said. "I guess a pattern was set that first day in the hospital that I was the primary caregiver. It sounds pretty Pollyannaish, but I liked it." Can you believe I gave this dear man only one child? It hurts just to write this down. He should have had a battalion.

JIM Baker was a trim 54, with graying temples and patrician good looks. I have a soft spot for plodders, and that he was: a diligent and disciplined man who studied hard, plotted his moves, and prepared almost as much as I did. And he had a sense of fun about him, a twinkle. I liked him very much.

Now, after nearly four years as chief of staff, Baker was aching for a change. He'd been bruised by Nancy's open disapproval of him, and he resented that the Reagans treated him as little more than "staff." When Treasury Secretary Donald Regan heard that Baker was itching to leave, he proposed that they swap jobs. Regan, 66, a bull of a man, had come to Washington after making multimillions running Merrill Lynch in New York. He was bored after four years at the slow-moving Treasury and looked at the chief of staff's job as more powerful and center stage.

But it was inconceivable that Reagan would ever let Baker go. After all, he had engineered the most successful presidential term in more than 20 years. Not only did Reagan get his major goals enacted (tax cuts, military budget increases), he had won a second term resoundingly, in no small measure due to Baker's stewardship. Yet Reagan signed on to the swap without a flicker of hesitation. I was told that Baker was crushed that the President had agreed to his leaving so blithely. But if Baker was hurt, Don Regan was surprised that Reagan hadn't asked a single question. What the future chief of staff didn't realize was that the deal had been greased. Mike Deaver, the go-between, had finally won Nancy Reagan's approval. I've been told she resisted the change but was persuaded "with a degree of anger." Don Regan didn't know that Mrs. Reagan's okay was a prerequisite. He didn't get her—or grasp her influence. This was his first mistake. His second was not appreciating how submissive Reagan could be.

It is fair to say that the day Reagan agreed to the Baker-Regan switch was the day his White House lost its magic. The first-term team of Jim Baker, Richard Darman, Michael Deaver, and David Gergen understood what this President could and could not do. They knew Reagan had a great store of common sense, but they also knew he was ill informed. Issues had to be explained to him simply, often with pictures or videos. The President rarely asked questions.

Don Regan knew none of this. And there was no one left to explain it to him. Deaver left in 1985, saying he could no longer live on $100,000 a year. Ed Meese was about to become the Attorney General, and Baker was taking Darman, with his knack for damage control, to Treasury. Now the only one who understood how Ronnie functioned or how to protect him was Nancy.

Meanwhile, the Middle East was sapping Reagan of his Irish luck with one act of terrorism after the next: bombings followed by hijackings followed by kidnappings. On the third Sunday in March I reported on *Face* that Terry Anderson, chief Middle East correspondent of the Associated Press, had been taken hostage in Beirut.

Three months later, on June 14, 1985, TWA flight 847 to Rome was hijacked by Lebanese Shiites, who showed they meant business by killing a U.S. Navy diver and dumping his body onto the tarmac. The gunmen said they would not release their 39 hostages until Israel released more than 700 Shiite prisoners.

The networks would again be accused of "providing a platform for terrorism" when we interviewed the families of the hostages. But in this case, we had not pursued the families; they had come after us. Almost immediately they began issuing statements, offering themselves for debates and interviews. They figured out that if they humanized and personalized the hostages—turned them into sons and fathers—it was less likely they would be abandoned and sacrificed to the war on terrorism.

The criticism about our putting hostage families on TV was heated but not nearly as intense as when we put the hostages themselves on. ABC got the first scoop on June 19, when correspondent Charles Glass came up with an exclusive interview with the TWA pilot aboard the plane. Smiling rigidly, Captain Testrake said the crew was being treated fine. He was speaking from the window of the cockpit with a gun held to his head. Far from treating this questioning at gunpoint with indignation, as we should have, we at CBS were crestfallen that we'd been beaten.

The hijacking story was increasing the ratings of all the news shows, which encouraged us to maintain the intensity of the coverage. And as with Jimmy Carter in the beginning of his hostage crisis, the country rallied behind the President.

But with Carter's experience as a guide, Reagan made sure the hostages did not linger in captivity. On the seventeenth day, a Sunday, they were set free while *Face* was on the air. "The American hostages are on their way to freedom," I reported. "They're traveling in a convoy to Damascus before flying off to Frankfurt." My guest, Vice President Bush, joined us via satellite from Paris, "taking an oath" that there had been no "deal" to win the release.

The administration continued to deny publicly that any deals had been made, but it was later learned that the Reagan team had leaned on the Israelis, who, after the Americans were safely home, released the 700 Shiite prisoners in stages.

The major critic of the network coverage was journalist Fred Friendly—champion of the First Amendment. He said he had been disgusted by the networks' "unseemly . . . haphazard frenzy of competition." He even accused us of "probably advancing the cause of terrorism."

A few years later Friendly illustrated his point in a PBS seminar on terrorism in which a group of jurists, government officials, and journalists—I among them—were put into a hypothetical hijacking predicament and called on to make instant decisions under pressure. We sat around a U-shaped table as the moderator, Arthur Miller of Harvard Law School, laid out the crisis: the hijacking of an airliner much like TWA 847. Among those around the table were CIA director William Casey, playing himself; Sir Kenneth Newman, head of Scotland Yard; and Peter Jennings, the anchorman. I was there as the reporter on the scene.

At a critical moment Miller turned to me: "Miss Stahl, the plane is on the tarmac, and you have been invited onboard for some exclusive interviews. Do you go?"

"Yes." I don't hesitate.

At which point Miller says that the terrorist leader orders me to keep the camera rolling while he executes one of the Americans onboard "as an example."

The glow on my face goes out like a match in wind. I'm on that plane, and my heart is beating, and I have to decide *now* what to say to this murderer in whose hands I have so carelessly placed myself. I pause, and pause some more trying to find a way out. Finally, I say I will tell the cameraman to stop rolling. Maybe that will discourage the killing.

With that, Miller springs at me, building the tension in the room and true terror in my heart. If I don't keep the camera going and tape the hostage execution, he will shoot my cameraman.

I can hardly breathe. I am in the throes of real fear, with all the bodily manifestations of a panic attack. Peter Jennings tries to help, but Miller quiets him. I am on the hot seat, holding the fate of two men. I can't choose, I cannot, but Miller just waits until finally I say, "I'm sitting here thinking I don't want to be a reporter anymore when this is over if these are the kinds of choices we have to make."

JANUARY 28, 1986. On the day of Reagan's State of the Union address the anchormen were invited to a series of briefings at the White House, which were to culminate with a Q-and-A session over lunch with the President. Peter Jennings, Tom Brokaw, and CNN's Bernie Shaw were there, but for some reason Dan Rather couldn't make it, so I went in his place.

We were sitting around the oblong table in the Roosevelt Room waiting for the President. Don Regan sat at one end, Pat Buchanan at the other. As Vice Admiral John Poindexter, the new national security adviser, began his presentation, an aide brought in a note for Regan. He read it, looked up, and interrupted: "I'm very sorry to have to tell you, the space shuttle *Challenger* has blown up."

Peter, Tom, and Bernie dashed off, sending in reporters from their White House teams. Regan had a big-screen TV wheeled in so we could watch the excruciating reruns of the deadly tufts of smoke divide into two separate arcs in the sky. We watched over and over as we waited to see if the President was going to go ahead with his speech.

At 1:00 Reagan poked his head in. Ever gracious, he'd come to apologize for not joining us as scheduled. "I'd looked forward to coming in here and having a little session with you and some briefing, but in view of the tragedy that has befallen us, I don't think we'll do that."

He hesitated, which gave us an opening. "Mr. President," I asked, "can you give us your comments on the tragedy so that we can tell the American people your thoughts?"

"Well, what can you say?" He moved into the room. Without his cue cards he spoke movingly. "It's a horrible thing that all of us have witnessed and actually seen it take place. And I just can't rid myself of the thought of the sacrifice and the families that have been watching this also." It was Reagan who had pushed the idea of having citizens aboard the space shuttle. Christa McAuliffe, a teacher, had been aboard with the six astronauts. One of my colleagues asked the President if he was having second thoughts.

"Well, they're all citizens," he said sadly. "And I don't think anyone's ever been on there that isn't a volunteer. I know I've heard many times—reasons why they or someone like them should not be included in flights of this kind. So, no, that is the last frontier and the most important frontier."

He said he was determined to go ahead with his speech that night. "You can't stop governing the nation because of a tragedy of this kind." I was seeing a fiber I had not expected.

Finally Reagan was asked to say something to the children. Because of the first teacher in space, classrooms all across the country were watching the liftoff on television. "We've always known that there are pioneers that give their lives out there on the frontier," he said. "And now this has happened. It probably is more of a shock to all of us because of the fact that we see it happen now and, thanks to the media, not just hearing about it as if something that happened miles away. . . . Life does go on, and you don't back up and quit some worthwhile endeavor because of tragedy."

As I took notes, racing to keep up with him, I thought of how many times Reagan had faced challenges and had come through. We made fun of him and I myself thought he was slipping mentally, but not that day. That day he was magnificent.

By *Evening News* time Reagan had changed his mind about delivering his State of the Union speech, which was supposed to be upbeat. Instead, he led the nation in communal mourning. To the families he said, "Your loved ones were daring and brave, and they had that special grace, that special spirit, that says, 'Give me a challenge and I'll meet it with joy.' " A President who doesn't understand the power of words simply can't lead.

A week later Reagan turned 75. "Seventy-five," he said, "is only twenty-four Celsius!"

THE movie *Perfect,* based on Aaron's *Rolling Stone* article about the health-club dating scene, opened, and I gave Aaron a screening party. The stars—John Travolta, Jamie Lee Curtis, and Marilu Henner—came, as did my parents, Dolly and Lou, and half the White House. It was a great celebration at a health club in the suburbs. I danced with John. Bethesda Fever.

Columbia Pictures spent that first weekend doing exit polls, which, according to the experts, showed that Travolta, the man who had personified the 1970s, was marooned in the 1980s. Based on the surveys, the studio decided to kill its expensive promotion campaign. The TV spots were pulled, newspaper ads scrubbed. When the movie was not the big hit everyone had expected, Aaron slumped into a depression.

My husband turned into a man with dark days and nights. He would pull himself together for Taylor, but otherwise he receded into a state of semi-reclusiveness. I went out alone, or if I managed to drag him to a party, he often walked out, leaving me stranded. I knew how sad he was, and I often blamed myself. Had I caused this? Was my success making his life worse? But he didn't want to talk about his problems, and I didn't want to add to them by insisting.

In 1986, I began negotiating with Sauter for a new assignment. I thought if I could cover something other than Geneva summits and the gross national product, I could loosen up. Show some humanity. And besides, I wasn't enjoying Reagan II.

After fretting and hashing it out with Aaron, I called Sauter: "Van, I've hit the wall at the White House. It's been seven years, and while I thought I'd never get bored, my time has come. You have to get me out of here."

We finally agreed that I would be the national affairs correspondent, a roving reporter for the *Evening News*. I looked forward to taking a few days to research a subject, sleeping on a script overnight, mulling, pondering, weighing. I had become a quick-sketch artist. Now I would try to be a painter.

"I would like to acknowledge the end of an era." On July 31 Larry Speakes, in the Briefing Room, announced my imminent departure from the White House. "Lesley works the telephones probably better than anybody I've ever seen," he said. "She's tough but fair."

Sam Donaldson started wisecracking.

"You be quiet," I said. "I like this."

And then it was my last day. As was the custom for a departing correspondent, I was to get a farewell audience with the President. Aaron and Taylor were invited to join me.

We were expecting a little good-bye present from the President in the way of a story. A hole was reserved for me in the *Evening News* lineup. But on the way to the Oval Office, Larry took my arm and guided me to a corner in the hallway: "Look, no questions. No questions at all, about anything. Those are the ground rules. And I swear, if you even try, I'll shoot you on the spot."

If Aaron and Taylor had not been there, I would have told him to go shove it. "Okay, okay," I said.

With Larry leading the way Aaron, Taylor, and I entered the Oval Office. Standing in front of a Remington sculpture of a rearing horse, the President looked stiff and waxy. My anger subsided. I had a story.

Reagan was as shriveled as a kumquat. He was so frail, his skin so paper-thin, I could almost see the sunlight through the back of his withered neck. His bony hands were dotted with age spots, one bleeding into another. His eyes were coated. Larry introduced us, but he had to shout. Had Reagan turned off his hearing aid?

"Mr. President!" he bellowed. "This is Lesley Stahl." He said it slowly. "Of CBS, and her husband, Aaron Latham."

Reagan didn't seem to know who I was. He gave me a distant look with those milky eyes and shook my hand weakly. Oh, my, he's gonzo, I thought. I have to go out on the lawn tonight and tell my countrymen that the President of the United States is a doddering space cadet. My heart began to hammer with the import. As the White House photographer snapped pictures of us—because this was a photo op—I was aware of the delicacy with which I would have to write my script. But I was quite sure of my diagnosis.

Larry was shouting again, instructing the President to hand us some souvenirs. Cuff links, a White House tie tack. I felt the necessity to fill the silence. "This is my daughter, Mr. President," I said. "Taylor. She's eight." He barely responded but for a little head tilt.

Click. Click. More pictures. A flash. "When I covered Jimmy Carter," I said, "Taylor used to tell everyone that the President worked for her mommy. But from the day you moved in here, she began saying, 'My mommy works for the President.' " I wasn't above a little massaging. Was he so out of it that he couldn't appreciate a sweet story that reflected well on him? Guess so. His pupils didn't even dilate. Nothing. No reaction.

"You know, sir, I've covered the White House more years than you've been here. After I'm out a few weeks, I'll write you and tell you if there's life after this place." Again, only a modest acknowledgment that I was there.

This was painful. How had he deteriorated so quickly? I had seen him just the week before. There were more photos. And then Larry was shouting, "Sir, Lesley's husband, Aaron, writes for Hollywood. He's a screenwriter out there. Wrote pictures for John Travolta."

As Reagan turned his head to find Aaron, the glaze in his eyes cleared, the freckles on his hands faded, the skin on the back of his neck tightened, and color came to his cheeks. Clark Kent. "Aaron, who did you work with?" he asked, jaunty and alive.

He pulled Aaron away from me and walked him over to the yellow couches to discuss a movie idea he had in which he would star, not as himself, not as the President.

I was clearly cut out of this and too astonished to move. "Sir, it's time for them to leave," said Larry. We'd been allotted ten minutes, but the President brushed him off. He wanted to talk Hollywood. Five minutes later Larry became insistent. As the President shook my hand to say good-bye, he said, "Lesley, you don't have to write me. I was governor of California for eight years, so I already know what it'll be like when I leave here." He was beaming, as engaged as he'd been disengaged ten minutes before. "The first night Nancy and I were back in our own home," he said, "we were invited to a big, fancy party. Well, we got all dressed up, went out, got in the back seat of our car, and waited!" We all roared. I could see that Aaron, who had been railing for years at this man and his policies, was a puddle. Reagan had cast a spell. My husband was enchanted.

Somehow Larry managed to ease us out of the Oval Office, but Reagan called out, "Taylor, Taylor!" He was heading toward us down the hallway. When he caught up, he said, "Taylor, I can't let you leave without telling you the truth." She was looking up at a tall, robust figure. "Taylor, I worked for your mother too."

AT THE White House stories had fallen into my lap; now, as national affairs correspondent, I not only had to forage for an idea, I had to make sure I wasn't stepping into anyone else's precinct. The worst of it, though, was that I was losing my visibility. If, by chance, I ever forgot that I had not been on the air for a week, I would get a comforting call from Dolly: "Where the hell have you been? You're disappearing."

I'm afraid I wasn't suffering my loss of visibility in silence. Everyone, it seems, knew I was unhappy. At the White House I had averaged three stories a week. My second report as national affairs correspondent ran two weeks after the first. I had *Face,* though, where I was still able to cover the lead stories.

While I was unhappy about the pace of my new assignment, there was an upside. The daily panics were gone, and I had more time for Taylor, a fourth grader now. She was tall, with beautiful hair almost long enough for her to sit on, and she was still perpetually sunny. This was a year in school with more and more homework for her—and for us. When her teacher assigned a major report on something of local interest, she told Aaron and me, "I'm going to do it on Maryland shellfish."

"Are you kidding?" said Aaron. "Shellfish? That's boring. Why not the Washington Redskins?" Poor Tay. She argued for crabs, but Aaron was insistent, so she caved. But then when it came time to write the thing, he went out of town. That left me. On football. I suggested she become a reporter and interview people about the team. So she called Shirley Povich, the Washington *Post*'s renowned sportswriter (he lived in our building) and Jack Kent Cooke, owner of the Redskins. It was a triumph, if I do say so. She not only got an A, but she became a devoted and knowledgeable fan.

Someone asked me how we disciplined Taylor. It struck me that we never did. She was never bad enough. Then I remembered that the only time I had ever been punished was when I fought with my brother. Tay had no one to fight with. That year we asked her if she wanted a brother or sister. She was adamant: no.

EVERY President in my adult lifetime who won a second term ended up being involved in a whopper of a scandal. Reagan's giving arms to Iran was so explosive, it in effect ended his presidency prematurely.

Right before the election the Lebanese magazine *Al-Shiraa* broke the story that former National Security Adviser Robert McFarlane (accompanied by marine lieutenant colonel Oliver North of the NSC staff) had flown to Tehran that May with a planeload of weapons, a Bible inscribed by President Reagan, and a cake decorated with a brass key "to open U.S.-Iran relations" and negotiate the release of seven U.S. hostages held by Shiite terrorists in

Lebanon. But Reagan himself had signed a law banning arms sales to terrorist nations such as Iran.

I did the first of many *Face the Nation* shows on the scandal on November 9, 1986, when Democratic Senator Patrick Leahy, vice-chairman of the Intelligence Committee, clarified the issue: "Colonel Oliver North and others were running their own CIA, State Department, Defense Department out of the White House without anybody looking over their shoulder."

Republican Senator Orrin Hatch, also a member of the committee, responded, "It was an attempt to bolster the moderates [in Iran]."

The President broke his silence on November 13 in a televised speech in which he dug a hole for himself by admitting that he had sent "defensive weapons" to Iran, but so few they "could easily fit into a single cargo plane. . . . We did not—repeat—did not trade weapons or anything else for hostages nor will we." So the swap had not been a swap.

As the White House tried to explain, Don Regan wounded himself by telling *The New York Times,* "Some of us are like a shovel brigade that follows a parade down Main Street cleaning up." Nancy Reagan seethed at this shot at her Ronnie.

The White House needed some credibility, so they all but forced a reluctant George Shultz to appear on *Face.* It was a miscalculation, since it was well known that the Secretary of State had opposed the Iran initiative. Naturally, I asked him why, and found myself in the midst of what Washington *Post* critic Tom Shales would call "the bombshell appearance." When the interview was over, Shultz would have half the Republican Party and most of the White House furious at him, including the Vice President and the President's protector in chief, the First Lady.

"We need to, of course, respond [to terrorism]," said Shultz, "and among our responses is our denial of arms shipments to Iran. That policy remains our policy. It is in effect, and there it is."

Holy moly, I thought, what does that mean? We sent arms, but we have a policy not to send arms? Was he slapping the wrist of the President on national TV?

"I don't want to badger you," I said, "but you are not answering my question."

"Well, no, you can badger me."

"Okay, good."

"The basic truth is that we continue to have a very firm arms embargo, and we continue to—"

This was like looking at modern art. I said, "You try to tell us that a swap wasn't a swap; you are trying to tell us that we have a policy of not sending arms when we have sent arms directly. . . . How can you look at the American people and tell them that?"

As Shultz went on in his circuitous way, it became clear that he was not going to fall on his sword for the President. He left the unmistakable impression that he did not approve of Reagan's actions. This was the Secretary of State in open defiance, a public embarrassment.

We had budgeted Shultz for two segments of seven minutes each. I had been getting "cut" signals from the floor manager, but I thought we were on a roll and decided there was nothing wrong with an eight- or even nine-minute segment followed by a shorter one. "Did you ever consider resigning over this?"

"Oh, I talked to the President. I serve at his pleasure. And anything that I have to say on that subject, I'd just say to him."

Shultz seemed to get bolder as time went on, at one point remarking, "It isn't the right thing for governments to trade arms or anything else for hostages just because it encourages taking more."

Now the cuer was gesticulating wildly, and the producer was in my ear begging, "Lesley, cut. We have to break."

"Will there be any more arms shipments to Iran either directly by the United States or through any third parties?" I pressed on.

"Under the circumstances of Iran's war with Iraq, its pursuit of terrorism, its association with those holding our hostages, I would certainly say, *as far as I'm concerned,* no."

The producer screeched at me, "Wrap this up! Now!" I thought, So it'll be an 11-minute segment followed by three minutes. What's the big deal? Shultz and I were locked in a special place, the two of us tense as cats, aware we were doing something big and maybe dangerous: he going public as Secretary of State with his lack of confidence in the President; I getting the interview of my career. I had one more question I had to ask: "Do you have the authority to speak for the entire administration?"

His eyes were braced on mine. With a strange, hard-to-read smile (was it the expression one wears as one jumps off a cliff?), he said firmly, "No." He had decided that no matter what, he was not going to lie.

"On that note," I said as calmly as I could, "we'll take a short break. We'll be back after this message."

Both of us were drained. "I think we have another five minutes," I said. "What should we discuss when we come back?"

"Anything you want."

The producer was back in my ear: "Come back? Are you kidding? We have run completely out of time."

We usually allowed wire-service photographers into the studio after the show to take pictures of the guest, but Shultz asked if I would mind if he slipped out. "I never should have come on," he said. He thought he would surely be fired. He looked pale, and I felt bad. Had I pushed too hard? I told his aide, "I hope he's okay."

Late that afternoon I got a call at home from Kay Graham, chairman and CEO of the Washington *Post.* "George and I played tennis today," she said. "Lesley, he has no hard feelings toward you. None at all. He wanted me to tell you that."

With the interview as the lead story in almost every newspaper the next morning, Larry Speakes issued the very statement Shultz had been demanding: There would be no more arms deals with Iran, and the Secretary *did* speak for the administration on this issue.

AS NATIONAL affairs correspondent, I was now doing the off-lead scandal story. I said that Reagan's foreign policy was "marked by confusion and inconsistency." I spoke of "a sense that [Reagan] is making policy for emotional reasons" and used critical sound bites such as "The emperor has no clothes."

At the same time, the emperor became a figure of fun. Robin Williams played Reagan at a news conference on *Saturday Night*

Live. His staff was prompting him through his hearing aid, but due to some radio interference, he tells the press corps the latest traffic report. Ridicule is the scourge of politics.

Things got worse. As I noted on *Face,* that "small cargo plane" of "defensive" weapons "turns out to have contained two thousand TOW antitank missiles and two hundred and thirty-five Hawk antiaircraft missiles." This was a significant *offensive* capability.

Then there was another first: The President delivered the bad news himself. On November 25 Reagan appeared uncharacteristically bleak in the Briefing Room and dropped the second shoe, revealing that Iran had been overcharged for the weapons and the profits diverted to the contras. National Security Adviser John Poindexter resigned; NSC staffer Oliver North was fired; Attorney General Meese investigated. "The President knew nothing about it," Meese later announced. This is when, it is believed, the cover-up began in earnest.

While the Reagans were on their December vacation in California, Don Regan explained, "I was never briefed thoroughly on all of this. Does the bank president know whether a teller in the bank is fiddling around with the books? No." Someone was quoted in the Washington *Post* anonymously: "Big take-charge Marine ducks the minute the flak comes in." This is when Nancy Reagan began urging Reagan to fire the chief of staff. She became so persistent that the mild-mannered Rawhide snapped and told her, "Get off my g--damn back!" So she resorted to a stealthier tactic: leaking. And she sent an emissary to George Bush to ask him to encourage Regan to resign. The Vice President said no. According to some of her allies, Nancy never forgave him.

The President was careening between two contrary positions on Iran-contra: claiming ignorance and defending his actions. He told *Time* that Oliver North was "a national hero" and dismissed the furor as "a Beltway bloodletting." When a Gallup poll registered the largest one-month decline in popularity ever recorded for a President (from 67 percent to 46 percent), Reagan appointed a commission under former Senator John Tower to investigate.

The government was paralyzed. On top of the Tower Commission the Senate set up a select committee headed by Senator Daniel Inouye of Hawaii to look into the Iran arms deal; the House chose Congressman Lee Hamilton of Indiana to head a similar committee; under the Ethics in Government Act, passed after Watergate, a special panel of three federal judges appointed an independent counsel, Lawrence Walsh, to investigate the scandal; the Justice Department was already investigating the Attorney General; everyone you can think of was calling on the chief of staff to resign; and CIA director William Casey was in the hospital with a brain tumor.

I was leaked an important story by a member of Congress, someone I trusted completely. When I went on the air on January 15 with what he told me, I touched off a thermonuclear reaction.

Here's what I said: CIA director William Casey was emerging as "a key actor" in the diversion of money to the contras. I quoted a congressional source as saying that Oliver North's computer tapes showed that there had been many meetings and phone calls between North and Casey during the period under investigation. In his congressional testimony Casey had denied having any knowledge of the diversion before early October.

Within an hour the wires were dinging with bulletins. The CIA, which, as a matter of policy, never comments on news stories, was blasting us, denouncing the report as "totally untrue" and a "disgrace to journalism."

I called my source and asked if I had gotten anything wrong. He reassured me that what I had said was accurate. I told him that given the severity of the CIA response, I would have to reveal his identity to my boss. He understood. CBS decided to stand by the story.

The Tower Commission Report was a thunderbolt. Issued on February 26, 1987, it said, in effect, that while there was no evidence the President had known of the diversion of funds to the contras, he was, well, doddering. He'd forget meetings he'd attended and key decisions he'd made. Moreover, it concluded that his team of advisers had lied constantly to Congress and the public.

The President first told the Tower panel that he had approved the arms sales to Iran in advance; then he changed that and said he had not. Finally, he wrote a letter to the board saying, "I don't remember—period." The President admitted he could not remember if he authorized shipping arms to Iran and then could not remember if he remembered. My piece that night asked the question: Can the President recover? And pretty much concluded no.

The Tower panel placed much of the blame for "the chaos" in the White House on the chief of staff. And so, finally, the President agreed to replace Don Regan, who learned about that from a TV report. Regan was so incensed, he "blew a gasket," as an eyewitness reported, and stormed out of the White House for good. Mrs. Reagan was said to be ecstatic.

In our special that night Bob Schieffer made the observation that Don Regan thought he could run the White House like a business: "Put in a chain of command, tell people what to do, and if they didn't do it, fire 'em." He compared Regan to Jimmy Carter, who had thought he could manage the government "like a hardware store, by keeping a close eye on the books, always reading the fine print." Schieffer said both men had found out that politics can't be run like a store. For one thing, no business ever had a roomful of reporters watching every move. "But Regan committed the ultimate business sin," said Bob. "He got crosswise of the boss's wife."

THE implications of the Tower Commission's conclusions were devastating. If Reagan couldn't remember making such a momentous decision, you had to wonder, What could he remember?

The President's first response to the Tower Commission was a 13-minute speech on March 4, in which he acknowledged that the Iran-contra affair had been "a mistake," though he was careful not to say he was the one who had made it.

He penciled in a few changes in speechwriter Landon Parvin's draft. Parvin had written, "I've paid a price for this silence in terms of your trust and confidence, but I have simply believed that the truth should not be rushed."

Reagan crossed out the end of the sentence and scribbled in,

"Since November I've told you all I know about this." He crossed that out and started again: "In November I told you everything I knew about this situation. Since then I've waited as have you to learn the complete story." That too was crossed out. His final attempt: "I have had to wait, as you have, for the complete story."

Someone else was editing as well. This person changed Parvin's line—"I approved it, I just don't remember when"—to "I did approve it; I can't say specifically when." The change is less significant than who made it. I am hardly a penmanship expert, but I do have a few samples of Nancy Reagan's handwriting.

THE Iran-contra hearings were a soap opera with a handsome hero named Ollie, whose medals gleamed from his marine uniform. On the stand Oliver North said that he had never carried out a single act without first seeking approval from his superiors. "I was not a loose cannon on the gun deck of state." But in his testimony he shot off one explosion after the next. He told of five memos he had written for the President's approval of the arms sales to Iran and the diversion of profits to the contras. "I assumed the President was aware . . . and had approved it."

Of particular interest to me, he revealed that CIA director Casey had been at the heart of it all. On July 8 and 9, in my off-lead story, I recounted North's testimony that "Director Casey had specific and detailed knowledge [of Iran-contra], because I briefed him frequently in detail." He also testified, as I reported, that Casey was the one who had authorized the diversion of funds to the contras.

Over the next five days North boasted that he had shredded documents in the presence of Justice Department officials, that he had lied to Congress and prepared false and misleading documents. He didn't duck, didn't equivocate, didn't apologize.

The chairman and vice-chairman of the Iran Contra Committee, Senators Daniel Inouye of Hawaii and Warren Rudman of New Hampshire, were our guests on *Face* that Sunday, July 12. At that time Senator Inouye said, "The most depressing thing I've heard all week long was that if the cause is right, you may do anything: cheat, lie, manipulate, mislead."

The hearings were heading toward the next pivotal witness, John Poindexter. Inouye said, "There's an important document in which [Poindexter] says, 'I briefed the President, the President agrees on the use of these residuals . . . for other purposes.' " It sounded like a smoking gun, so I asked Inouye if I'd heard right. He leaned over to Rudman for backup: "You saw it. . . . We all saw it."

Face made headlines all over the country. But at the hearings Poindexter claimed that he alone had authorized the diversion of funds to the contras, that he had kept the President in the dark in order to "provide some future deniability. . . . The buck stops here with me."

It was in this atmosphere that British Prime Minister Margaret Thatcher came to Washington. The British press wrote that Thatcher was coming to bolster the President, buck him up, and help improve his image. To our delight she accepted our invitation to *Face* on the condition we tape the interview on Saturday at a location convenient to the airport. We found a large, ornate room in the Capitol, but one with no separate enclosure for a makeup table. When she arrived, I apologized, "Hope you don't mind that we had to set the table up right here in the middle of the room."

Mind? She loved it. Her entourage of male advisers, most of them strikingly handsome, elbowed in to get closer as she primped at the mirror. Her features were far more delicate than I'd realized from television. She wore a well-made soft gray couture suit with a stark white, V-necked collar. The assembly at the mirror was like a levee in the boudoir, with the Prime Minister fussing over her lipstick and hair and laughing coquettishly with her boys.

Had power become an aphrodisiac for *her* too, the one we called the "stern nurse"? She flirts with Reagan, I thought. Of course! And probably with Gorbachev. Who would have thought that the flinty Margaret Thatcher, with that silly handbag and gruff manner on television, had found the key to blending her power with her female sexuality?

But I put those thoughts away because I had already planned my own stern-nurse interview. I started by mentioning a report that on the day McFarlane and North were in Tehran with a planeload of weapons to trade for hostages, the Reagan administration had been assuring her government that no such deal was in the works. "What about trust?" I asked Thatcher.

She disliked the question. Her eyes daggered mine as she refused to answer: "I won't comment; it would be discourteous of me. You may go on asking the same question in a hundred different ways and you will still get the same answer."

I stuck with my game plan and asked again. And then I looked apologetic—this pains me to ask—but I ask, "Are you saddened by what's happened?"

Thatcher was poised, confident. "No. I think you are taking far too downbeat a view." She perched on the edge of her chair, leaned in, and began scolding me: "Cheer up! America's a strong country with a great President, a great people, and a great future."

I smiled. "Lighten up—is that what you're telling us?"

"Cheer up! Be more upbeat." There was no return smile.

I called her a "cheerleader" and repeated that the United States' credibility had been damaged. The nanny in her emerged with a two-minute lecture that, not to beat around the bush, demolished me by seeming to question my love of country. "Why are you doing your level best to put the worst foot forward? Why?" she asked. "America is a great country. . . . I beg of you, you should have as much faith in America as I have."

I was down on the mat, bloodied, but labored on, asking whether the President was depressed.

"He's fine. He's fine. . . . Aren't you pleased?"

I said I was and thanked her.

"Delighted."

I didn't think Thatcher was really angry at me. I felt that she saw this as a game, one she knew she was winning. But later that day the press officer at the British embassy called to say I had gotten that wrong. Mrs. Thatcher was livid to the point that his job was on the line for setting up such an unpleasant session.

But then the mail started—stacks and bundlesful, all of it like this. From Virginia: "Your carping criticisms wrapped in gloom and doom . . . does [*sic*] not serve the national interest." From Washington, D.C.: "We applauded when Mrs. Thatcher chopped you into bits."

A Mailgram from Ellicott City, Maryland, called me "a perverse and bigoted mental midget." Another from Los Angeles called me "lizard-lips." And my favorite, from San Francisco, "On that Thatcher segment: I loved you both. What a life."

It seems that Mrs. Thatcher got her own bagsful of mail, and her letters were mostly positive. In fact, she got so much mail complimenting her performance that she changed her mind about the interview. I wrote her a thank-you note (as I did most of my guests) and got back, handwritten: "Please don't worry about the number of critical letters. In politics we get far more than that! And like you, we just carry on. Every good wish." That from the Prime Minister who had chewed me up, stomped on me, and left me in tatters.

And then the Iran-contra hearings were over. The public, so eager to make allowances for the President, clung to Poindexter's testimony of "deniability" and lost interest.

But Reagan would never be the same. His great assets, his integrity and invincibility—his hero quality—were diminished.

TV Guide gave me a Christmas present, declaring that I was the "toughest" of the Sunday morning interviewers. Roderick Townley, asked to study the Sunday shows for bias, had concluded that I was not promoting a political agenda: "Essentially, she'll shoot anything that moves, on the left or on the right. . . . [She's] first and foremost, a watchdog . . . with perhaps a streak of pit bull somewhere in her ancestry." I wanted to frame it.

May 1988. Reagan was on his way to Moscow for his fourth meeting with Gorbachev. Some of the aides on Air Force One were concerned. Reagan seemed more unprepared and remote than ever. But as happened frequently, just when they were certain he had something like Alzheimer's, Reagan pulled himself together. In Moscow he made more than two dozen appearances, including speeches and negotiations, and—as far as I can determine—faltered only twice, though they were doozies. First he fell asleep during Gorbachev's toast at a state dinner in the Kremlin.

Then the exhausted President met with the Foreign Minister of Japan, who was also in Moscow. Each time Reagan's eyelids closed, according to an eyewitness, George Shultz said loudly, "Who would like coffee?" Within minutes a waiter arrived with Valvoline-strength java for the President, who would rebound to wakefulness, but only momentarily. After a second round of coffee Reagan was drooping again. So Shultz looked at his watch and told the Japanese Foreign Minister, "Oh, my, we have to catch a plane!" Catch Air Force One? But it worked. Everyone got up, then watched in horror as Reagan shook hands and said, "Well, Mr. Foreign Minister, it sure has been a pleasure"—to the interpreter.

By now the campaign was well under way, and polls showed George Bush 16 points behind Michael Dukakis. There was a sense of inevitability about Dukakis, a consensus that Bush—with Iran-contra and his "wimp" image—couldn't win. His team calculated that a public endorsement from Reagan would help, and they began planning a big gala where Reagan would pass the baton. George and Barbara thought their loyalty had earned this, but Nancy kept finding ways to keep it from happening.

Finally Reagan promised to do the deed. Endorsement Night! The balloons were there, the flags, the crowd. But Bush was all but cellophane. It had to be the most halfhearted endorsement of all time. Reagan spoke mostly about himself, then ended with a short, perfunctory "next President of the United States" remark, mispronouncing Bush's name, rhyming it with blush.

I took particular notice that Barbara Bush was wearing red that night. There the four of them stood at the head table holding hands, arms raised in the air: Barbara, then George, Ronnie, and Nancy, also in red. The only one not smiling was the First Lady. To my knowledge this was the first Barbara-in-red sighting in seven years. She wore the color from then on.

LEE Atwater, Bush's campaign manager, was a wreck. Nothing was working. George Bush, with an overall negative rating of 40 percent, was in hopeless shape with women. Of even more concern, the Reagan Democrats were shifting to Dukakis. Atwater was in search of one of the so-called wedge issues he was famous for—gun control, crime, school prayer, racial quotas—that would recapture those northern white Democrats.

In late May the campaign videotaped a focus group in suburban Paramus, New Jersey, and Lee leaked the tape to me for a report.

> ATWATER: We had two groups of 20 Democrats who supported Reagan in 1984 and were supporting Dukakis in '88.

On the tape you heard the moderator tell the group about Dukakis's prisoner furlough program in Massachusetts, where a first-degree murderer, Willie Horton, a black man out on leave from prison, had raped a white woman in Maryland and stabbed her fiancé.

> WOMAN IN GROUP: He favors a policy of giving weekend furloughs to convicted felons for good behavior?
>
> MAN: No, that'd be bad. That'd be awful. I'd like to know why he would—
>
> ATWATER: After that, between 40 and 60 percent of these people changed over to Bush.

Lee had found his issue: "If I can make Willie Horton a household name, we win the election." Republican candidates had been keeping their coalitions alive by playing the race card ever since the 1960s. But I was convinced that George Bush would never do this. I thought he would refuse on principle. I was wrong.

A MID-AUGUST CBS News/*New York Times* poll on the eve of the Republican Convention at the Superdome in New Orleans showed Dukakis ahead by 17 points. I set up shop in CBS's trailer city, where I stayed put, since I didn't want to find out what that humidity would do to my hair.

My guest on the preconvention *Face* was George W. Bush, the Vice President's eldest son, who was playing a central role in the campaign. "Can you name an issue that your father has cared consistently about," I asked, "that he fought for in the Reagan administration, that he would continue as President to stand up for?"

"Peace through strength," he answered.

"But that's a slogan," I said. What did George Bush stand for? Even for his son, it was hard to say.

I asked who would be his father's running mate. "Lesley, I don't know. I bombarded Big Boy with all my suggestions."

"Big Boy?"

"Well, Dad, of course." He smiled.

I asked if Dan Quayle would be the one. He said I shouldn't forget Kemp, Dole, or Governor of California George Deukmejian. This was a chance for candidate Bush to make every known Republican think he was being considered.

I'd been picking up the name Dan Quayle on the convention floor and offered him an interview. I asked the inevitable, "Why do you want to be Vice President?"

"The only way I'd want to be Vice President," he said nervously, "is if George Bush wants me to be Vice President, because it's so doggone important that he be elected the next President of the United States. If he thinks I can help him, so be it." This was a chance for Quayle to make a good impression. Bush's campaign team watched with disdain.

"They say you would help with the gender gap," I said.

"Well, there's no doubt about that," said Quayle. "In the end, the polls and everything show that I have done very well. I do not have the so-called gender gap. Hopefully we'll be able to carry that over to the rest of the country. Who knows?"

I spent the next day in a CBS trailer with Diane Sawyer, both of us trying to crack the who's-the-veep secret. Yet even though we called everyone we'd ever known, we were beaten. NBC broke the news that Bush was choosing the young Senator from Indiana.

I watched Bush's announcement on television in the trailer with several other CBS reporters as Quayle leaped onto the podium in a fit of hyperactivity that made you want to shout, "Get that boy some Ritalin!" He bounced around, flapped his arms, and crawled up Bush's back.

"Believe me," said the future running mate, "we will win because America cannot afford to lose!" He grabbed Bush's shoulder, startling the man, and went on. "Let's go get 'em!" Bush had a look of "What have I done?"

That night Dan Rather opened our convention with the news of the Quayle choice, saying, "A thunderbolt has hit the Superdome, and the lightning has yet to subside." Then he tossed it right to me. Behind me the Indiana delegates were cheering as I looked straight into the camera, trying to ignore them. "Why did Bush choose him? First off, Dan Quayle is conservative, someone to activate the right. Second, he's a proven vote-getter with women. We don't know if that's because of his good looks, but it is a move to deal with the gender gap. Third, he's 41, so it's an appeal to young voters. Lastly, he's a midwesterner, and they're hoping he will appeal to farmers and blue-collar workers. But in our survey, Dan, we found only two delegates in this entire convention hall who listed Quayle as their first choice for Vice President."

Later in the evening I found Bush's son Neil. "I understand there was a family meeting a week ago to make a decision about the Vice President," I said. "How many voted for Quayle?"

"One person," he answered. Those were Quayle's odds: 12–1.

By the third day of the convention Quayle was mired in reports that despite his enthusiastic support for the Vietnam War, he had avoided the draft by joining the National Guard. He made matters worse by explaining, "I did not know in 1969 that I would be in this room today, I'll confess." It began to seem that every time Quayle opened his mouth he made things worse. I reported that while some of the delegates were discussing dumping him, campaign operatives were arguing that it would be too damaging to Bush, since this had been his first presidential decision.

Peggy Noonan proved she was the best speechwriter in the country. Bush's acceptance speech was a knockout: "Read my lips! No new taxes!" It was one of many memorable lines. Bush drew a graceful self-deprecating self-portrait: "[I] hold my charisma in check." The best line: "I may sometimes be a little awkward. . . . I am a quiet man. But I hear the quiet people others don't."

Bush also differentiated himself from Reagan: "We need a new harmony among the races. . . . I want a kinder, gentler nation." This did not stop him from bringing up Willie Horton.

IT IS often the case in campaigns that one side gets all the breaks, and then suddenly the tide turns, as if Poseidon were directing the flow. For whatever reason, the gods had turned against Dukakis. He couldn't do anything right.

Dukakis had become complacent, gravely miscalculating the potency of Bush's message: that the Duke was a man who let murderers out of jail and wouldn't let little kids say the Pledge of Allegiance. (Dukakis had vetoed a bill in Massachusetts that would have required teachers to lead the pledge in classrooms.) Bush had achieved the usual convention "bounce" in the polls; then, with his message and Dukakis's failure to fight back, Bush kept on rising.

To illustrate that he wasn't "squishy soft" on defense, the Duke put on a large green helmet, climbed into the turret, and drove around in an M-1 battle tank for the cameras. That Sunday in Jack Kent Cooke's box at the Redskins game, Jim Baker, Bush's new campaign manager, couldn't contain his joy, telling Aaron that Dukakis in the tank was a gift from heaven: "He looks just like Snoopy!" The Bush campaign quickly produced ads making the Duke look like an idiot in that tank, while Bush himself issued the helpful hint: "If the tank doesn't fit, he shouldn't wear it."

BUSH'S revolving-door, or turnstile, TV spot graphically criticizing Dukakis's prisoner furlough program was becoming a cause célèbre. A CBS News/*New York Times* poll showed that it had the biggest impact of any ad in the campaign, effective because it was symbolic of the larger case Bush was trying to make about Dukakis: that he was a capital-L Liberal. But the ad had racial overtones, and as I reported, it was inaccurate.

I grilled Jim Baker about the ad on *Face* ten days before the election. "While the announcer says Dukakis let first-degree murderers out," I said, "the screen says '268 escaped,' clearly suggesting that 268 first-degree murderers escaped. In truth, only four *murderers* escaped. Two hundred and sixty-eight is the number of all prisoners. Why have you not corrected that?"

"It is off the air," said Baker, "but I don't admit it's incorrect."

"You don't admit that saying 268 escaped while the announcers say 'murderers' is misleading?"

"I do not admit that this is misleading."

"I'll tell you something," I said. "As a television reporter, if I say something and put some words up on the screen that conflict, that's inaccurate."

"Well, we make our judgments with respect to that," he said coldly, "and you can make yours. . . . We think it's very appropriate because it speaks to values and judgment."

Baker left the studio angry.

IN THE final days of the campaign both candidates went on exhausting cross-country trips with the same strategy: attack, attack, attack. Bush kept Quayle off the air and out of his ads. One Democrat told me, "If Bush wins, it's because Willie Horton is better known to the American people than Dan Quayle."

The consensus among the Democrats was summed up by Bob Slagle, chairman of the Texas Democratic Party: "Dukakis made a mistake in trying to fight by Marquis of Queensberry rules when the other guy kept hitting below the belt for ten straight rounds."

But Bush had done far more than just beat Dukakis in the attack department; he bested him in every aspect of the television game. The Bush people had figured out that to get "free media"—that is, exposure on the *Evening News*—they had to master the nine-second sound bite. They worked at sharpening and polishing the candidate's lines, donating a pithy zinger we couldn't resist: "Dukakis favors furloughs for murderers." *Bam!* And it was only three seconds.

Forget the issues. It was all slogans. It wasn't until the Dukakis people finally caught on that their candidate began to pull up in the race: "We're on your side." "He's riding on easy street, we want to improve life on Main Street." They had finally gotten the Bush-is-elitist message into short bursts—but too late.

We knew the Bush campaign was staging its events as commercials that we ran for free. We discussed simply not airing the "message of the day." But our election producer, Brian Healy, said that we did have a responsibility to tell people what the candidates were saying, even if it was mush. If it was inaccurate or distorted, we had to say it was, but to stop reporting what they were saying would have been tantamount to censorship.

On Election Day we called it for Bush at 9:17 p.m. Bush beat Dukakis by 54 to 46 percent. Voter turnout was just 50 percent, the lowest in more than 60 years.

WAS this the end of the Reagan era? Or would the Bush administration be a continuation, the third Reagan term? It was *the* question during the transition.

One thing was for sure: These were two very different animals, Bush and Reagan. I began to reflect, as everyone did, on the Gipper. What an enigmatic force. He had managed to change the agenda, alter the American conversation—what we wanted, what we thought our goals were. He demonstrated that government could work (even as he bashed it and sought to dismantle it). What confounded me and many other Reagan watchers was that he did what he did as a man prone to delusion. He continually presented a false self. Steven Weisman of *The New York Times* said, "He wasn't a cowboy, he wasn't a war hero, he wasn't a family man. Reagan was a mysterious combination of fakery and authenticity."

Reagan had three main accomplishments. One was as a truly gifted negotiator. He took pride in this, and with justification. He stood down the unions, and he stood down the Soviets.

The second was the unleashing of a new force of entrepreneurship in the country. But it is not clear that Reagan and his deregulation policies were as responsible for this as the mugging American corporations received in the 1970s, which spurred them to retool and downsize in the 1980s—a painful process we at the TV networks were hardly immune to.

With all the positive economic news Reagan did not lift our standard of living. During his time in office there was a shocking increase in female poverty: 13 million women living in poverty, the majority of them white and the sole supporters of their children.

The third was that Reagan lifted our spirits, no small attainment for a leader, even if he did so by painting a mythic picture of 1980s America as shining and triumphant. In the real America, despite his "family values" rhetoric, there was more greed, more sex and violence in our movies and on TV, more AIDS, more divorce, and an increase in the number of single-parent families.

You cannot look back on the Reagan years and not wonder if the President had Alzheimer's even then. We will never know for sure. There are those who were close to him who like to say, "Oh, he was always like that, even when he was governor of California: unprepared, bored in briefings, ignorant of the substance of the issues." But others who were also close say that there was a marked difference, especially in the last two years. They talk about his little vacations from the scene when he would be there, yet not be there. They were concerned, and yet Reagan always seemed to recover. I had seen it in the Oval Office with Aaron and Taylor that day in 1986.

Whatever was going on—Alzheimer's or something else—Reagan held on to his good common sense and was able to "break through" when he really had to. I'm convinced that Nancy Reagan suspected something and many on the staff did as well, and they chose to protect him and keep silent. The President's doctor, Burton Lee, was quoted in *USA Today* on November 29, 1996, as saying that late in his second term, "it was noticeable that there was something wrong there, but we figured it was just the natural aging process. Nancy was going to protect him and she did. She kept him further and further out of the flow."

When Reagan had a competent and steady staff, things ran smoothly, if not always brilliantly. And a great deal of the credit for that goes to Nancy Reagan, who, I suspect, did far more than we'll ever know to hold him, the White House, and by extension the country together. We'll never know exactly what Mrs. Reagan did, because she has chosen, as always, to protect her husband's image, which I think she will to the end. But I am quite certain we owe her considerable thanks.

Part Five

GEORGE AND BARBARA BUSH

IT WAS a coup getting an interview with the Vice President–elect. Dan Quayle had been under wraps since the election, recovering from the mauling he had endured during the campaign. He liked to blame alternately his handlers and the reporters, none of whom had made him say that the Holocaust had been "an obscene period in our nation's history" or "the real question for 1988 is whether we're going to go forward to tomorrow or past to the— to the back!"

My producers, Janet Leissner and Brian Healy, and I mapped out a line of questioning: I would concentrate on foreign policy, but I would ask about his lack of experience and what appeared to be Bush's eagerness to pretend his running mate didn't exist.

Quayle comported himself well in the interview. There was no blaze of genius, but he was botch-free. Sitting there knee to knee with him, I saw no trace of the trademark stare of terror that had so often betrayed him during the campaign. His press secretary didn't hide his relief. If the veep-to-be could get through a televised interview without a single mulligan, all would be well. I'm not going to lie about it: We on our side were bereft. How could we tell the *Evening News* that Quayle had been so disciplined that there was not a shred of news, not a single flub?

Back at the bureau, as I wrote a script, Janet screened the videotape, and pretty soon I heard laughter from her edit room: "Lesley, this is great stuff! What do you mean you got nothing?"

There it was, filling the screen: the very stare I had not seen in person, the Quayle freeze of fear. Somehow the camera had reached behind his mask, yanked out his insecurities, and magnified them. His lack of confidence was so evident on the TV screen that it changed the sense of what he was saying.

The camera has an emotional life of its own. It adored Ronald Reagan and John F. Kennedy. It shuddered at Bob Dole and Dan Quayle. Quayle's real enemy was the camera lens.

DAVID Burke, the new head of CBS News, summoned me to New York. "It's no secret you've been unhappy as national affairs correspondent," he told me starchily. That was hardly something I could deny. I'd been unhappy with my ill-defined role for some time. And yet when he said, "We'd like you to go back to the White House," I saw all the possibilities of misery and defeat.

Burke said he wanted to showcase me and would be my patron saint. Soon my reluctance gave way to a stronger sense of salvation. I had not found the formula to life without a news beat. By Inauguration Day I was back on my old beat at the White House. I had studied more than I had for final exams in college. Bush's record, Barbara's background, the new Cabinet, the five kids, the ten grandkids. I was out on the lawn in my Klondike coat and boots.

It was Monday, January 23, 1989, the nanny's day off, so I had to get Tay ready for school, including pulling her hair back into a ponytail, which produced a meet-the-day domestic donnybrook—just what I needed on my first official day back at the White House.

I had butterflies. Bush beat me in on the first day. As I said in my piece, "Reagan moseyed in at nine fifteen; Bush got in at seven twenty. By eight twenty he'd had breakfast with Quayle, a CIA briefing, a meeting with his top aides, and he'd sworn in his White House staff. He's wearing us out." And he was just getting started.

When Bush held a 45-minute news conference, he remembered our names, unlike Reagan. He answered two-part questions without having to use five- by nine-inch index cards. Instead of lopin' along with the tumblin' tumbleweed like Reagan, this man sprang and darted and flitted and arced across the television screen. No inner calm here! But somehow it made him likable, if not lovable.

If Jimmy Carter's frame of reference was the small town and Ronald Reagan's the big screen, George Bush's was comradeship. This President saw the world not in terms of issues or even values, but in terms of personal relationships. What counted was loyalty, keeping your word. No windmill tilting for the President, though he did have a political signpost that read DON'T RILE UP THE RIGHT.

During his first weeks in office Bush was sending conflicting signals: a strong antiabortion statement one day, announcement of a centrist Cabinet the next. His new national security adviser, Brent Scowcroft, was a protégé of Henry Kissinger's, a signal that Bush was siding with the pragmatists over the ideologues.

If Bush's actions were unclear at first, I chalked it up to the loss of identity any Vice President would experience after eight years of "cooperating." I believed he intended to undo the excesses of Reaganology, even though he had been there at the Crusade and had brought back many fellow Crusaders to help him unravel what they had wrought. More than half his Cabinet members were recycled from the Reagan years. One analyst said, "There are more retreads here than in Akron, Ohio!" But most were pragmatists.

One who wasn't a retread was John Tower, nominated for Secretary of Defense, a mistake that would consume Bush's first 40 days in office. Sharp-tongued and prickly, Tower was not well liked by his former colleagues on the Senate Armed Services Committee, where he had served for 19 years.

In fact, Tower had built up such ill will that few in Washington came to his defense when stories of his drinking, womanizing, and coziness with defense contractors began to surface.

I was at my White House post on February 7, working the phones, concentrating on the Hill, a nest of Tower's enemies. I found a press secretary who told me in a conspiratorial whisper, "I hear Sam Nunn [chairman of the Senate Armed Services Committee] is, as we speak, at the White House in a secret meeting with the President."

"Why's he here?" I asked.

"To tell Bush he's against the Tower nomination. If Nunn votes against the guy, he's probably dead. And Lesley, you didn't hear any of this from this office." A story!

I reached a source in Nunn's office who refused to confirm the story but danced around enough to convince me it was true. I called the office and told my producer, "I think we've got a big one for tonight." I started writing a script and then decided to wander nonchalantly up to press secretary Marlin Fitzwater's office. But I was waylaid when a colleague came running after me: "Your daughter's on the phone."

Taylor, in sixth grade now, wanted to throw a party. "You know how you're going to have my room painted? Can I have my friends over to paint it some wild color before the real painters come?"

"We'll discuss this tonight." This was curious—my mother's voice coming out of my mouth.

I went back to my script and was interrupted again when Dolly called, just to chat. I eased my mother off the phone, and Taylor called again. "I'm on deadline, honey," I told her, straining to sound patient.

"But Mom, if you say yes, then I can start inviting kids. Mom, I want to have boys too."

"Boys? How many?"

"Six, eight, whatever you say. Please say yes. Please."

"Well, how much of a mess are you going to make?"

"We'll clean it all up."

I looked at my watch. It was late, and I hadn't yet reached anyone from the White House. "I surrender. You can have your party."

I finished the script, recorded the middle section, and—Taylor. "Can it be from one in the afternoon to ten at night?"

"Yes." Anything you want.

Then on my way to Marlin's again, in the corridor outside the Cabinet Room, I bumped into John Sununu. Who better to ask than the chief of staff? "Governor, I'm told Senator Nunn was here today informing the President he's now against the Tower nomination."

"Not true. Where do you get these stories, Lesley?" He was playful.

"Are you denying that Nunn was here?" I was in my don't-be-cute-with-me mode. "You're telling me he did not warn the President that he's opposed and that Bush should consider withdrawing Tower's name?"

"It's not what happened. You got a bum steer."

I raced back to the booth and called my original source: "Sununu says it's not true."

"Well, I'm telling you it is true. Nunn told Bush he'll vote no on Tower and urged Bush to dump the guy. Call Sam yourself."

Taylor called again. My rule about always taking her calls no matter what was facing a mighty test. But I have this theory that working mothers are afraid of their kids. I took the call and found myself talking to her best friend, Lauren.

"I'm the only one brave enough to ask," Lauren said. "You know Tay's painting party? Can boys sleep over too?"

"No!"

Lauren passed the phone to another friend, Zoe, who begged.

"No. No means no means no!"

I put in a call to Sam Nunn's office. "I'll get the Senator to call you back," his press secretary said. It was 6:20; I had to get out to the lawn. The cameraman set up a phone outside, so I got in position and waited with a nervous pounding for Nunn to call me back. With just two minutes to air, the phone rang: "This is Sam Nunn."

"Thank God," I said.

"Lesley, Sununu was not exactly telling you the truth." And he gave me the story himself.

On March 9 the Senate voted against Tower, 53–47. Bush quickly nominated Dick Cheney, longtime Congressman from Wyoming and former White House chief of staff for President Ford. He sailed through Congress, where he was respected and liked.

A few weeks later Taylor had the painting party. She and her friends threw buckets of color against the walls till the shade was a putrid deep khaki. The kids all had dark green-brown linings along their fingernails, and everyone's hair was coated with an ugly glop. And they were all bellowing at top volume. What could possibly be more fun . . . more uninhibited and disgusting? But all I could think was, What will their mothers say if it doesn't come out? "Everyone," I drill-sergeanted, "into the showers."

The paint washed off. And boys slept over.

IN THE fall of 1989 Aaron started coaching Taylor's basketball team, part of the Montgomery County girls' league. He had never coached before, so he studied videotapes and talked to his dad, Clyde, almost every night, sketching out plays on yellow legal pads that his father had taught his players when he'd coached Texas high school basketball in the 1940s, 1950s, and 1960s.

In addition to Taylor, there was Makay Woods, the fastest, and Kyra Taylor-Grossman, a gifted athlete with an impala's spring and a Magic Johnson dribble. The tallest was Theresa Ann, who played with the same doggedness as her father, the former New York Knicks star Senator Bill Bradley. But the soul of the team was Jillian Cutler, who had cerebral palsy. Here was a child who, after 11 operations, ran up and down the court, albeit in a stiff, jerky gallop. I sat next to her father at the first game and saw him weep.

Bill Bradley came to every game and never intruded except the one time the referee didn't show and Bill, much to Theresa's embarrassment, was called upon to substitute.

Aaron never missed a practice or a game, no matter how blue, how down, how despairing he was. Despite all the information on television and in magazines about the telltale signs of clinical depression, I didn't recognize them in my own husband. He was in the grip of the disease, but I was either too busy, too self-absorbed, or too irritated with him to put it all together. But you could go down the list of symptoms for depression and check off one after the next for Aaron. He was sleeping away most days, locking himself in the den. How many times I called from the White House booth and he wouldn't answer the phone. A cold fear would take me: Is he all right? Is he— Is he alive?

"Aaron, please see a doctor. You need a shrink."

"I don't need one. I'm fine." He was dead set against psychiatry. I felt helpless, afraid, and at the same time furious at him.

I commuted back and forth between "This misery of his is all my fault; I'm suffocating him" and "How can he do this to me?"

I HAD volunteered in mid-March to give a group of Sidwell students a tour of the White House pressroom. To my surprise one of Fitzwater's assistants in the press office took us out to the South Lawn to watch the President leave for a speech across town. Before I knew it, POTUS was heading our way. "Hey, guys." That's the way this POTUS talked. "I used to jog on your track over at Sidwell." He was loose and lanky. "So what are you doin' here?"

"We're studying broadcast news!"

"Well, you've found the right person to explain that with Lesley." I grinned. "I wish I could stay and chat some more with you guys, but I'm late for my speech." And he was gone. Like an extraterrestrial landing and takeoff. We rubbed our eyes: Had that really happened? I explained to the kids: "No one ever gets to see the President like that. Not even me." How could I explain how hard it was not to like George Bush? The public felt the same way. Bush had a 70 percent approval rating.

I did a piece on Bush's first 100 days, asking, Why is he so popular? John Sununu explained it this way: "It's because he's the guy next door. If they had a problem, he's the kind of next-door neighbor they would go to to try and get it solved."

Bush's friendliness, his over-the-fence regular guyness was, indeed, what the White House was selling. And the fact that he was nothing like Ronald Reagan. Television had been Reagan's best friend. Bush treated it like an unwelcome relative—except when it came to televised news conferences, where Bush showed off his un-Reaganesque ability to get through them without making mistakes. He met more often with the press in his first 100 days than Reagan had in his last two years.

If Bush clutched, his anchor was nearby. Barbara Bush was strong. I once told one of their friends the story about Nancy Reagan's tile man and the red dress. "I'll bet George told Barbara to just swallow it," I said.

"Oh, no," said the friend. "Barbara's tough. Much tougher

than George. He hasn't told her to swallow it or do anything else in twenty years!"

I was pleased to be one of eight reporters whom Barbara Bush invited to lunch at the end of April. No cameras were allowed, but it was on the record. Mrs. Bush wore a white dress with black polka dots and puffy sleeves. Very stylish. She looked beautiful.

We were up on the second floor of the living quarters in a charming private dining room that Jackie Kennedy had decorated with wallpaper depicting Revolutionary War battles and bluish green curtains draped back with a flowing valance and fringed tassels. Over artichokes stuffed with salmon mousse, Mrs. Bush revealed that George often called her from the Oval Office just to say hi. She could see into the Oval Office from the Truman Balcony, where she would occasionally poke out to wave to him.

As Mrs. Bush described their early morning strolls together around the South Lawn, a glow came over her and a girlish grin crept up. One of the reporters, a young woman, asked exactly what I was thinking: "Mrs. Bush, are you finding that the White House is a romantic place?"

The mood broke. Barbara flashed her eyes. "That's a dumb question. If you'd been in Washington for the last eight years, you'd know that George and I have always been close." This was the side of the First Lady the public never saw. The young reporter was humiliated.

I jumped in to spell my colleague. "I kind of like that question," I said, smiling to take the edge off.

"You would," snapped the First Lady.

"At night, in bed, the pillow talk?" brave Jim Mickleshevsky of NBC asked. "Do you discuss abortion?" Barbara Bush had let it be known that she tilted pro-choice.

"None of your business." She glowered at Jim.

She was most impressive when she talked about parenting. Working moms shouldn't come home "too tired," she said. I felt a pang. "People are going to have to reevaluate their lives a little and put their children first."

Then Mrs. Bush took us on a tour of the living quarters. In eight years of covering that place I had never had such a day. She walked us through Reagan's old workout room, now transformed into a grandchild's bedroom. We got a history lesson in the Lincoln Bedroom, where Abe had signed the Emancipation Proclamation. Teddy Roosevelt's huge hand-carved bed makes the room seem like a chapel. President Bush set up his own office right there, as FDR had done. George's toy soldiers decorated the mantelpiece, and in the corner was a big toy chest for the grandchildren.

A FEW weeks later I was with the President in Kennebunkport, where we got pictures of Mrs. Bush lambasting him because the Secret Service had torn up her garden to build a helipad. I was in Maine getting ready for a "chat" with Dan Rather on *48 Hours,* which he was anchoring from Beijing. Dan was the only anchorman who went to China to cover Mikhail Gorbachev's state visit. While Rather was there, the students went on a hunger strike in Tiananmen Square to protest the lack of freedoms, and workers began to join them. The government reacted by imposing martial law, and Rather was the right man in the right place.

My producer had picked a pretty spot outside, near the ocean, and when Dan came to me, I said the White House was relieved it was Gorbachev and not Bush who had been in China when the student protests started. "How could the leader of the Free World not have endorsed the cries for liberty?" I asked rhetorically. "How could he *not* have walked among the hunger strikers? Yet it would have been an excruciating decision for George Bush, Deng's [Xiaoping's] old friend."

Bush wasn't saying a word about the student protest or the government's order to fire on the protesters in Tiananmen Square if they didn't leave. What the White House did say was, "Things are in a state of flux; we're waiting to see what happens." That Sunday I interviewed Democratic Senator Christopher Dodd on *Face:* "How deeply we are moved as Americans when we watch a model, a six-foot replica of the Statue of Liberty," he said. "I would like to think the President might be able to express views that only a President can, expressing the feelings of the American public that would reach those students in China . . . that we really care and what you're doing is something we profoundly agree with."

But Bush would not.

After months of criticism over his reticence in foreign policy, George Bush surprised the world. At the end of May he went to a NATO meeting in Brussels and proposed a major reduction in U.S. and Soviet conventional force levels in Europe. Until then it was Gorbachev who'd been enchanting European public opinion with a series of disarmament offers. Now the headlines were announcing, BUSH UNIFIES NATO. There was a swagger in the Bush camp.

Standing in a little square in Bonn with a yellow post office behind us, Dan Rather asked me if Bush's new position was a flip-flop. "Up to now George Bush has seemed to be fighting the end of the cold war," I said. "What he did in this initiative was acknowledge that those days are over. The era of dismantling is upon us. He went beyond just recognizing that. He told the Europeans he wanted to lead in this new era, and that's just what they wanted to hear from him."

Many of the CBS people on the trip, including Dan, were strung out. They had not had a rest since China, but we all plunged on. The next day the press pool choppered to Mainz, West Germany, in a marine CH-46 helicopter, many of us dozing along the sides on canvas benches with military-style seat belts and earplugs. The door was open, admitting a cold, hard wind.

In Mainz, Bush challenged Gorbachev to tear down the Berlin Wall. "That wall stands as a monument to the failure of communism. It must come down—now. . . . Let Europe be whole and free." In my script that night I called George Bush "the conqueror."

WE WERE no sooner home in early June 1989 than the Chinese army began its assault on the prodemocracy student protesters in Tiananmen Square. CBS News owned this story. Because Rather had been there, we had swarms of reporters and producers in place. This allowed us to run new footage on *Face* of China's People's Liberation Army opening fire on the people in the square, shooting with automatic rifles, beating, and crushing hundreds of students and others who had been peacefully demonstrating.

Our guest was Senator Jesse Helms of North Carolina, who spoke for the right wing, which so intimidated Bush: "Lesley, we need to stand with these young people who are trying to achieve freedom."

"The Bush administration says they don't want to undermine seventeen years of diplomacy just because of one weekend," I said.

"This is the trouble: Make a deal, get along. You just can't make a deal with a communist government anywhere in the world. Every time we've tried it, we've been taken to the cleaners—and so has freedom."

For the next several days we at the White House watched the horror of Tiananmen on television. But wherever there was a TV on in an official's office, it was tuned not to CBS, ABC, or NBC but to CNN. This was when I realized that I was no longer top dog, as I had been through the Carter and Reagan years, when the clocks, as I used to say, were set to Cronkite and then Rather time. Now we had the round-the-clock CNN vigil. When I wanted to speak to an official, I found myself in line after the CNN correspondents. If Bush wanted to send a message, he wanted it to resonate globally. This was disconcerting for those of us with only a national reach. My power as a network correspondent at the White House was wasting away.

I LEFT for vacation with my contract negotiations with CBS up in the air. We were going on safari. I bought hiking boots, rain gear, and batting gloves. Aaron had decided to write a book about African safaris. He wanted to see specific things: a cheetah, a bull elephant charge, and especially a kill. So we set out each day with a mission.

I had decided by August 1989, in my forty-eighth year, that I had already had the best day of my life. Even with the little annoyances of my job, I was on an even keel. There were no more deep despairs, but no rapturous highs either. This was okay. I was not the least bit unhappy. Maybe a little wistful, concerned about a degree of numbness, but I thought this was what "middle age" was all about.

Then we went to Rwanda to see the mountain gorillas, Dian Fossey's gorillas in the mist. This was why I had bought the hiking boots and batting gloves. Our guide said he hoped we were in shape for a grueling climb up the mountain.

Off we went—Aaron, Taylor, and I. Not off, but up. I was assigned a Sherpa just for me, which I thought was silly. What did I need my own Sherpa for? As it turned out, I needed him to keep me from quitting. We started our climb through a bamboo forest. The sun came through in sharp spikes. When we broke into a clearing, climbing more steeply, there were nettles everywhere. That's why the gloves. By now my Sherpa was carrying my backpack and my camera. Taylor was at the front of the line, moving jauntily along as we tracked the gorillas. Aaron and I were at the back, huffing.

Soon we were in a thicket of underbrush so impenetrable that the guides had to cut holes with a machete for us to crawl through. Imagine, on our hands and knees slithering through mud or squeezing through nettles. I couldn't believe I was doing what I was doing. We'd been at it for two hours when I announced I would not take another step. I was finished. My Sherpa got behind me and gently but firmly kept moving me along. A young Rwandan in our group was climbing just ahead of me, barefoot, with a refrigerator balanced on his head.

After two and a half hours we were walking on a mattress of bamboo, then climbing straight up at a 45-degree angle. My Sherpa was either pulling me up or cupping his hands on my buns and hoisting me. He simply would not let me stop. And believe me, I was insisting. I, who never exercised, was beyond exhaustion, near tears when we were hushed by the guides.

And there they were: two baby gorillas frolicking like any four-year-olds. We snapped and stared. We were right there, in their lives, in the middle of their open-air house. And then the silver-back, the patriarch, seemed to welcome us, as three females kept grooming him. The guides called him Ndume, which they told us meant "powerful" in Swahili. We were told to bow, to keep our heads lower than his, as in *The King and I.* I was crouched down, staring up into his eyes, and he was staring right back.

We spent one hour in their world, watching them tumble and wrestle, nurse their babies, swing in the trees, forage for food, and just commune in small groups. We spent time amid them, so close that a female reached out to touch me.

My exhaustion was gone. Everything was gone except a total body-and-mind exhilaration, a joy so strong and complete I wanted to laugh and cry and sing and fly. It came partly from the almost religious experience of being among those magnificent creatures who were so hospitable and gentle with us. It came also from my beating the elements. I had somehow endured.

What I decided that day with the gorillas was that the best day of your life may not have happened yet. No matter what you think.

NOVEMBER 9, 1989. The Berlin Wall began coming down. At Gorbachev's urging, the East German government opened the border for free travel, and a flood poured through into West Berlin. The President decided to speak about this on-camera, so an Oval Office "tight pool" was organized. It was my turn to be the lone broadcaster. Bush was at his desk, a map of Germany spread out before him. Jim Baker sat to his left, Brent Scowcroft and John Sununu to his right. This would be the President's first comment on the coming down of the odious wall, communism's most sinister symbol, the very wall he and Reagan had nudged Gorbachev to destroy. But Bush, with what looked like a frown, sat there so limply, he actually listed in his chair. And his voice, instead of expressing the excitement of the moment, whined. We poolers were standing in a knot, the still photographers clicking and weaving around us. "You don't seem very elated," I said.

"I'm very pleased," Bush answered in a gray tone. "I'm not an emotional guy."

"Well, how elated are you?" I asked.

"I'm very pleased, and I've been very pleased with a lot of other developments, and as I've told you, I think the United States' part of this, which is not related to this development today particularly, is being handled in a proper fashion."

Bush was missing a characteristic essential for a President, an emotional ignition key. He couldn't seem to light up to these surges of human freedom, to ring out with appropriate poetry in times of crisis or exaltation. He was trying to send Gorbachev a message that the President of the United States was not going to gloat over his defeat, but what about a message to the American people? What about expressing *our* communal joy? I thought Bush's assuring the Soviets was the right approach, but surely there was a way to satisfy the soul without threatening Gorbachev. Reagan would have found it.

By Sunday the Berliners were dismantling the wall and West German Chancellor Helmut Kohl was already saying, "One nation; we belong together." But, as I pointed out on *Face,* the prospect of a united Germany was sending panic waves through the Western world. Margaret Thatcher was especially alarmed. She flew to Washington two weeks later, on November 24, and went to Camp David to persuade Bush to help her put the brakes on German reunification. She arrived in a helicopter that whipped up a huge snowdrift, which floated in the air until it fell on my head. Wet ice. On my *hair.* I was there to see Maggie and George get into a golf cart and drive off. Yet Thatcher was never as successful at manipulating Bush as she had been with Reagan.

Bush finally decided to offer Gorbachev a public endorsement by meeting him at an impromptu summit in Malta in early December. The central issue was to be Eastern Europe.

For CBS the summit in Malta was an opportunity to recover ratings ground we had lost. So we showed up in force with more than 100 reporters, producers, and technicians. Despite budget cuts, we spent a fortune on this one story—more than $1 million. We brought "flyaway" portable satellite dishes and microwave "hops" to transmit the signals from the Russian cruiser *Slava* and the U.S.S. *Belknap* anchored in Marsaxlokk Bay. Bush wanted a summit at sea. This was no easy technological feat: We had to relay signals from the ships, up to a church bell tower, and across the island to our newsroom at the Excelsior Hotel in Valletta.

I did my first report, a bulletin, live from the newsroom, standing next to Rather in front of an open window. The wind was wild, a storm so strenuous—winds up to 60 miles an hour—you had to wonder how Bush and Company slept out on the U.S.S. *Belknap,* how they were going to survive the inevitable seasickness. Having the summit on naval ships was Bush's way of keeping the press away.

We had brought along our high-powered camera with the extender lens, so the next day we got extraordinary pictures of Bush's launch trying to get back from the *Slava* to the *Belknap* after the morning session. The storm was now producing waves of 12 feet. Bush's small launch was swamped and pitching about. "They can't dock!" our producer boomed out. "Great pictures." You could see POTUS drenched by the hurling waves, Secret Service agents holding him. You had to wonder about the President's judgment.

We taped the *Evening News* in front of the open window. I was "chatting" with Dan about how the storm had forced Bush to cancel the afternoon session and the dinner; how he was stuck out on the *Belknap,* a hostage. As I talked, a blast of wind lifted my hair—I had to reach up and hold on. Said Dan, "Make no mistake, this wind would drive Sinbad the Sailor or Lord Nelson to cover."

I called home as the wind howled like Heathcliff on the moors. Taylor said she'd had one of her best days ever. Skating, movies, three boys were over. And I'd missed it.

We flew directly to Brussels for a NATO meeting. At a news conference Maureen Santini of the Associated Press showed she had real guts. "Weren't you hotdogging when you were out on the launch submerged by the waves and spray?"

"Hotdogging?" said Bush. "No!" He laughed. "Well, you know, these charismatic, macho, visionary guys, they'll do anything." I found that so disarmingly funny, I threw my head back and laughed so hard, I slid out of my chair onto the floor. Oh, God. At NATO. Embarrassing. I picked myself up and prayed no one had seen me.

THE peace dividend—would we ever get one?—was heating up as an issue. On February 4, I suggested to Defense Secretary Richard Cheney on *Face,* "If you cut out the B-2 Stealth bomber, everyone could get health benefits; if you cancel the Trident-2 submarine missiles, public education could be saved."

"The reason we are here today where we can talk about the collapse of communism . . . in part has been the success of our strategic deterrent for over forty years."

"But communism has collapsed."

"It has not yet collapsed," Cheney contradicted me. "There are still three hundred and eighty thousand Soviet troops in East Germany."

President Bush went on a cross-country campaign to fight the move for massive defense cuts, dragging the press corps around until we begged for mercy. After the lazy days of Ronald Reagan this felt like a death march. We started with a 6:00 a.m. takeoff from Andrews Air Force Base and found ourselves in a war by mid-morning California time. We raced up a hill in Humvees and, like Pierre in *War and Peace,* watched from a hill as the army staged a simulated battle in the Mojave Desert. Gorbachev was chairing a meeting in Moscow right then about ending the Communist Party's monopoly of power, and here was Bush battling to build strategic weapons to fight the Soviets.

The next day Bush took us to the Lawrence Livermore National Laboratory in northern California to promote Reagan's SDI (Strategic Defense Initiative). I sat in a mound of grease on the press helicopter, then stood in a shower of mud splatter from Bush's chopper. "He's here on the warpath," I wrote, "while Gorbachev is promoting democracy." I called it his "we're-not-ready-to-let-down-our-guard message."

From Livermore we went to the Strategic Air Command, where the President got into the cockpit of a B-1 bomber. He spoke to SAC troops by radio: "For you missile crews," he said, "the pointy end is up." The Bush White House was catching on.

There were no breathers in early 1990, as one momentous event bumped up against the next. I was in the Oval Office pool when President Bush admitted he had been caught by surprise when Gorbachev suddenly reversed himself and accepted a plan to speed German reunification. "Changes are goin' on so fast there that it's hard to keep up with them all," he said. Gorbachev had even gone so far as to stop fighting the idea of a united Germany in NATO.

"We're dealing with historic change," said the President. "I'm beginning to be very elated about this and—" Looking right at me, he smiled. I smiled back. He pointed at me. I pointed back. Everyone laughed. "Seriously," he said, "it's . . . it's very very fast." Later Fitzwater told me that Bush often asked his aides after news conferences, "Do you think Lesley thought I was elated enough?" It was a running joke: "Will Lesley say I was emotional enough?"

This would be one of his great achievements, German reunification, and it was bold. Mitterrand and Thatcher opposed it. But Bush kept pushing. Richard Holbrooke, who would later serve as U.S. ambassador to Germany, told me, "This was Bush's brilliant move. The wall came down; all Eastern Europe was in an uproar. Then Bush backed unification, and the transition was peaceful. There was stability, after all."

AARON, so bright after our Africa trip, was back in the dark corners of depression. I was troubled that I wasn't doing more to help him, but if I tried, he would just shut down. He simply would not see a doctor. When I pushed too much, he made me feel I was punishing him. He drove me to work one day, and I lectured my heart out: "You have to get out of the house. Exercise. Call people." He acted as though I was cutting his skin with a sharp razor.

But no matter how much he was suffering, he still managed to coach Tay's basketball team. That year they won the championship.

I was going to New York to substitute-anchor the *Evening News*. When I kissed Aaron good-bye, he had a pink, soupy look in his eyes. I called him before the broadcast, but there was no answer and I got a pang of panic. I had begun to fear he might take his own life.

Earlier in the day I had shared a cab with Mike Wallace. "How's Aaron?" he asked.

"He's depressed," I said, not really thinking about Mike's well-publicized bout with the disease.

"What's he doing about it?" he asked.

"He won't see a doctor."

"Well, make him," he demanded.

"I can't. He's a grown man. He's adamant," I said.

Mike grabbed me by the shoulders and began shaking me. "Listen, you," he said sternly, emotionally, piercing my eyes with his gaze, "you find a way. Whatever it takes, you get him to a doctor.

You must not let this man suffer another minute. Do you understand? Not another minute. Find a way." My eyes burned with tears. Why hadn't I come to this on my own?

Aaron has an expression: "So suddenly, there's God." Well, that's what happened. There was God, the very next day. I was back in the White House booth, looking for the producer assigned to work with me. "He's gone to his psychiatrist for his depression pills," I was told. What? What do you mean?

With everything that had been written about depression, I still had not fully realized that Aaron could be helped with a pill. I look back at my ignorance, my neglect, and want to weep. "I need your help," I told the producer when he got back. Within a half hour I was on the phone with his doctor. "Would you see my husband as an emergency patient?" I burst into tears. She said she would. Now I had to do what Mike Wallace said: find a way to get Aaron there.

That night I told him, "You have a physiological problem, a chemical imbalance. Please try this. Please." I thought I would have to claw and scrape and beg. But my sweet suffering husband looked out through his foggy eyes and said yes, he'd go. So suddenly, there was God.

Or so I thought. The doctor said his symptoms were those of "classic depression" and put him on medication that, I learned, takes several weeks to kick in. One night during that time, Aaron was in such despair he stayed out all night in the rain. I was so scared, I sat up in a frenzy. Should I call the police? The hospitals?

When he came home at 6:00 a.m., shivering and soaked, I called his doctor. "My husband's in crisis," I cried. She assured me he would get better in time.

Soon after, Aaron—who had been on an antidepressant for a month—was out. I noticed an unopened letter from his editor. He had submitted his book on Africa nearly a month before. What if she didn't like it? I was so worried, I called her. The book needs a lot of work, she said.

When Aaron got in, he read the letter and went quietly to the den. As he told me later, "I went off to be alone and let the darkness take me, the inevitable plunge into the pit. But something extraordinary happened. I hit a floor. It was physical; something solid was preventing my submersion into the misery. I could *feel* it. At first, I was sure this floor would give way. But it didn't. So I got up and joined you and Taylor." The next day he sat at his computer and rewrote his book in one long gush.

I'm not sure what triggered Aaron's depression, but once it took hold, I am sure it changed his chemistry to such an extent that he was incapable of pulling himself up out of that pit. The pills saved his life—I don't say that lightly. They saved mine too.

IN MID-MAY I ran into Mike Wallace again. This time he asked if I would be interested in joining *60 Minutes.*

"I'm bowled over," I said.

"Don't say a word to anyone," urged Mike. "Just wait. We're going to work on it. Be patient." I thought, This'll never happen.

AUGUST 2, 1990. I woke to the news that Iraq had invaded Kuwait. The cold war had just ended, and the very first thing we did was go to war.

Bush's first public comments were tentative. When asked if the United States would intervene, he hesitated: "I'm not contemplating such action." And then he flew off to Aspen, Colorado, to meet with Margaret Thatcher.

Bush made a desultory statement about Iraq, emitting traces of his old wimpy self. Her Ironness, on the other hand, belted out a ringing condemnation of Iraqi leader Saddam Hussein. But belying his cautious public posture, Bush, who had always insisted that economic sanctions didn't work, decided to organize an economic embargo. In an early morning meeting the President had overridden his foreign policy team, whose advice was, in so many words: Too bad about Kuwait, but it's just a gas station. It was President Bush who had asked the right question: "What happens if we do nothing?" And the answer soon became clear. Iraq would go after Saudi Arabia next, and more than half the world's oil supplies would come under Saddam's control.

It was widely said that Saddam had invaded after taking George

Bush's measure by observing his appeasement of China during Tiananmen and concluding that this American President would not resist an Iraqi move on Kuwait. But Iraq was threatening a vital U.S. interest, the oil supply.

When Bush returned from Aspen, I was on the White House lawn to hear his ultimatum: "This will not stand, this aggression against Kuwait." It sounded like a threat of military action.

One of his inner circle called to tell me that Bush was employing his "Rolodex diplomacy"—getting on the phone with foreign leaders. He planned and implemented a painstaking process of coalition building. "He's cajoling, persuading, changing the world. And he's so calm," the source said. Less than a week after the invasion the President announced that the United States was sending troops to Saudi Arabia. In all the years I covered the White House, I cannot recall having so much admiration for a President.

THE last thing this White House wanted was Bush appearing to be held hostage by Iraq. They had Jimmy Carter's example to learn from. So the President went on vacation to Kennebunkport. If he could go on his holiday, I could go on mine.

We had rented a lovely little cottage on Nantucket that we filled up with our friends. One day as we were going off to the beach for a picnic, the phone rang. It was Eric Ober, the new CBS News president. "How would you like to take on *Nightline?*" he bubbled. He said he had a plan: "We go on the air at eleven thirty every night with Persian Gulf specials, and then we never relinquish the slot. The network has given me the green light to try it—with Charles Kuralt and Lesley Stahl." My role would be hard-hitting interviews in Washington, while Charles would do well-written packages out of New York. I said yes right away.

"We start tonight," said Eric, "if Dan, who's in Baghdad, gets an interview with Saddam." We were to launch the show with Dan Rather's exclusive. Ober asked me to call him in one hour. If they needed me, they would send in a charter and fly me to Washington.

I had one more day in the sun. Rather got his interview on August 29, and I dashed home.

When the interview came to pass, Dan asked tough questions about Saddam's stockpile of poison gas and the American hostages he denied he was holding. Kuwait, Saddam said, was part of Iraq, a "province."

We led our first show with Rather's interview, followed by my interview with Rather, who described the Iraqi leader. "He's tough . . . with tattoos on his arm representing his manhood. . . . He thinks he's the one who has Bush backed into a corner." Responding to my question, Dan related how Saddam's bodyguards had separated him from his crew and taken him off alone to do the interview, using an Iraqi cameraman. It must have been frightening.

After the show there was a postmortem with the producers, who thought there had been too little communication between Kuralt and me. Charles and I had agreed that we hated forced chitchat between anchors. So there hadn't been any chat at all. But I was so dazzled to be working with Kuralt, grateful to be given the chance to grow, that I had that everything's-right-with-the-world feeling you get once every ten or 12 years.

Any fool should have known that a cold shower was on its way. It arrived the next morning, when our executive producer, Lane Venardos, asked who my guest would be that night. Only then did it dawn on me that I would have to come up with guests to interview *every* night—not to mention for *Face* on Sundays.

After a day of rushed phone calling, we finally landed the Iraqi ambassador to Washington, Mohammed al-Mashat. Saddam was holding hundreds of Americans and other Westerners hostage, planting them at strategic locations the United States might bomb. After trying to elicit information about the condition of the hostages, I threw off any pretense of impartiality: "Is there any wonder . . . the American people see this as an act of unbelievable inhumanity and view your leader, Saddam, as a monster?"

"Well, I'm sorry to say," the ambassador responded, "we feel it is most inhumane what you have done to us by denying us food and denying our children milk. This is the most inhumane." He was referring to the U.S. economic sanctions.

The ambassador and I went back and forth like that until the six minutes were up, when he stormed off swearing he'd never do our show again.

Don Hewitt of *60 Minutes* called: "You jumped right off the screen. You're the next Mike Wallace."

"You're just looking for an old fart to come aboard." I laughed.

"You can't be an old fart at *60 Minutes* till you're seventy-two," he said.

When the war was over, I would be going back to the White House, where I was in the tumble cycle coming back round and round: the yearly budget, the summits with the Soviets, the hot-house competition, the sucking up to my sources after a swipe at the President. *60 Minutes* was the answer, of course, but I told myself not to get my hopes up.

CHARLES Kuralt was the best writer and best reader in TV news. But with all his informality and warmth on the air, most people confronted a wall when they tried to get close to him. Our being in different cities made it hard to develop a rapport. When I saw him in New York, I asked what he wanted me to call him on the air. I'd been saying "Charles," but it felt stiff and formal. He said he didn't care. "Are you sure? Is Charlie okay?" Yes. He smiled. Really? "Yes, some people even call me Chuck." So I called him Charlie, and the producer phoned after the show and said, "Call him Charles. That's what he prefers, but he'd never tell you that."

I confided in Diane Sawyer that I was having trouble establishing a chemistry with Kuralt. She had been his partner on the *Morning News* for a year and a half. "It's his rhythm," she explained. "It's so stylized and idiosyncratic, no one can mesh with it." She said she had also called him Charlie on the air and gotten a note from their executive producer. "On the whole, Charles is better."

Ober had persuaded the network to approve our specials as a regular nightly show, at least until the end of the year. Aaron proposed that we call it *Taps,* but we settled on *America Tonight.*

From our first broadcast in late August, the eleven-thirty news specials had been exclusively about the Gulf war. On October 1 *America Tonight* debuted as a whole new show with a wider portfolio. But no one had thought through what we were about. Our only mandate was "Be different from *Nightline.*"

It was no surprise, then, that our debut was a clutter, a little of this and a little of that. I moderated a debate on the Gulf war between defense expert Richard Perle, who advocated a let's-attack-now policy, and former Secretary of the Navy James Webb, whose position was "Why so fast?" You knew as the clock ticked toward midnight on that first show that the wind was not with us. And the critics were not kind.

The good thing about daily journalism is that you get another chance every day, and we did better on Tuesday. We booked the House G.O.P. whip, Newt Gingrich, who was fast becoming George Bush's antagonist. Newt was leading the fight against Bush's budget agreement.

We also booked Carol Cox, a feisty redheaded budget expert, a real match for Newt on the subject of taxes. The debate crackled—so much so that Lane Venardos, the executive producer, let it run an extra 30 seconds. Everything ran smoothly. Charles did a nifty piece on the Humvee as the new military jeep. "Great show!" boomed Lane in my ear. I bounded into the control room on a high. Everyone was elated.

Gradually the show improved, and we settled into a rhythm. We were finding our voice, and New York began to treat us country mice in Washington more like partners than underlings.

AFTER the election Bush announced a massive buildup of U.S. troops in Saudi Arabia to 430,000. With those numbers an attack on Iraq could be launched by January 15, the deadline set by the United Nations for Saddam to withdraw from Kuwait.

It was as if George Bush had been preparing his whole life for this crisis. One of his advisers remarked that all the jobs he had held were coming together. He had been CIA director, so he knew which department to call for the best intelligence; he'd been U.N. ambassador, so he was receptive to the notion of using that body. It was because of the many personal relationships Bush had so carefully nourished over the years that he was able to persuade 26 nations to send troops to join his coalition. Reagan had been the cowboy hero who liked to ride alone; Bush liked to do things in concert, so, as it was said, he rounded up a posse.

Producer Janet Leissner came up with an idea for *America Tonight.* "Let's go home with a Senator and televise a town meeting with him on Iraq." We chose Democrat Bob Kerrey of Nebraska, who had lost a leg in Vietnam and was now opposing Bush's war.

Lane Venardos, several producers, Charles, and I were in Omaha the afternoon of the event, November 29, going over the format, when the phone rang. Kerrey was pulling out. He was objecting to our having invited Hal Daub, a former Republican Congressman from that area. Either we cancel out Daub, we were told, or we lose Kerrey. It was three hours to air.

We lost Kerrey. Charles and I, up on a stage, took turns asking questions, but mostly we let the assembled citizens debate the war. Some agreed with Bush: "What about the country's honor? Our credibility?" Others had kids over there: "They've sent fifty-five thousand body bags over to bring our children home in." A priest said, "That royal family [in Kuwait] isn't worth one drop of our blood, but we have to support our troops." A businessman called for patience, but a mother said her son, a marine, was a hostage, "a guest" in Baghdad. She did not want to give up her son, but *he* thought the principle, standing up to naked aggression, was worth dying for.

They were raw and honest, and they all cared deeply. What you learned was that the country was divided. Bush had not yet done the work of bully-pulpit convincing that he needed to.

When the hour was up, the audience gathered around us. It was too soon to end—there was so much more to say—so we stayed there on the stage and kept up our discussion. This show made us a team. Charles gave me a rose. I decided I liked him a lot. Not because of any personal relationship; we still had none. But I had come to respect his toughness, his doing what he wanted to do on his own terms. Mostly I liked him because he was grounded in principle and integrity.

On the flight home we sat together. I read three newspapers, underlining stories about the Persian Gulf, the White House, the budget, the President's poll numbers. Charles flipped through the Lifestyle sections and did the crossword puzzle.

The buildup in the gulf was a preoccupying story on *America Tonight.* I interviewed Crown Prince Hassan of Jordan, a longtime U.S. ally now tilting toward Iraq. Prince Hassan used the interview to plead with President Bush to give a little on the Palestinian issue "so the Arabs can feel the U.S. is not irrationally pro-Israel." I asked Israeli Deputy Foreign Minister Benjamin Netanyahu about Saddam's threat that if Iraq were attacked, its first act of retaliation would be to bomb Tel Aviv. Netanyahu said that Israel would not stage a preemptive strike: "We will have to be dragged in."

One of the President's shrewdest moves in this build-up period was downplaying the American hostages. He never talked about them, never made demands about their safety, mindful of the trap Jimmy Carter had fallen into by allowing *his* hostages to consume his presidency. Bush's tactic paid off. The hostages were of so little value that Saddam released them in December.

One of my guests, retired *New York Times* columnist James Reston, was critical of Bush's handling of the Persian Gulf buildup. He charged that the President was "continually issuing ultimatums that he can't live up to."

Reston had covered ten Presidents. Who was the smartest? Carter. "Jimmy Carter was very smart and not a very good President, so that intelligence is not necessarily the test." The worst? Reagan. "The worst but the nicest. The most delightful fraud we've ever had." The best? Ike. "He knew it was so much easier to get into wars than to get out of them."

I remarked about those Presidents who, in spite of their success, hadn't felt they'd "arrived" and sat in the White House still trying "to prove something to themselves and to the world."

"All these guys are beyond journalism," said Reston. "They're all psychological novels. How do you explain a guy like Nixon? He lived a life of pretense; tried to be a tough guy when he wasn't tough, tried to be vulgar when he wasn't really vulgar. The real Nixon was better than the phony Nixon, you see?"

"Is Bush trying to be what he isn't?"

"Bush is essentially a New England gentleman, but he's trying to overcome it."

ERIC Ober called in early December—*America Tonight* had been on the air for four months—and announced our cancellation after the end of the year. I was either relieved or disappointed, I didn't know which. "But if there's war," he said, "we're back with war specials every night at eleven thirty with Charles and Lesley."

Charles sent us all invitations to a party "To celebrate a failure." And we kept going.

By January 15 *America Tonight* was still on the air. The U.N. deadline for Saddam to withdraw from Kuwait was less than 13 hours away. Eric Ober announced, "Our cancellation has been revoked indefinitely."

The next morning there were rumbles at the bureau that this would be the day we would go to war, which would mean we'd go into round-the-clock coverage. We stayed on alert all day. Then, as Dan Rather was suggesting on the *Evening News* that an attack was imminent, the wires started pinging with a bulletin: "Flashes over Baghdad." Just then our CBS phone line to our reporter in Baghdad went dead. Someone hollered, "Switch to CNN." CNN was reporting tracers in the skies over Baghdad. You could hear the U.S. bombs going off. The President had launched an air war over Iraq.

I put on my boots and raced over to the White House in a heavy snowstorm. Fitzwater was briefing: Bush had learned of the attack he had approved from CNN and ABC.

Bush went on-air from the Oval Office at 9:00 p.m. It was a short, to-the-point speech, the most watched broadcast ever up to that point—65 million households tuned in. I went on right after: "He said he had 'no choice.' He said, 'We will not fail. We will knock out Saddam's nuclear potential, chemical facilities, his entire military arsenal.' "

We were now on the air nonstop. But with no phone connection to Baghdad, we were being badly beaten by CNN, which alone was able to keep its line open. CNN's live reports from inside an enemy capital were extraordinary. John Holliman: "Whoa! Holy cow! That was a large airburst that we saw." Bernie Shaw: "This feels like we're in the center of hell." Peter Arnett: "We're crouched behind a window in here. . . . The antiaircraft is erupting again."

DAY two. Colin Powell, chairman of the Joint Chiefs of Staff, and Defense Secretary Cheney briefed together. The air campaign was a success. There had been 1000 sorties, with no aerial resistance to the initial air attack, equivalent to an atomic bomb in payload (18,000 tons). And there were no reports of any U.S. casualties. The stock market soared.

I was back at the White House, where all the TV sets were tuned to CNN. There was still no Iraqi resistance, only sporadic and ineffective surface-to-air firings. I was watching the news from the booth when, at 7:05 p.m., CBS correspondent Tom Fenton, on a phone line from Israel, came on with terrifying news: Alarms and sirens were going off in Tel Aviv. There had been hits. Iraqi Scud missiles were pelting Israel. This was disaster. Now Israel would strike back.

I ran to Marlin Fitzwater's office. He had turned off his TVs and had his hat and coat on. "We're reporting Scuds hitting Tel Aviv!" I sputtered. Marlin slouched and slowly put his briefcase down. "Can you find out anything?" I implored.

Marlin called the Situation Room. "I have some reporters with me. What do you know?" When he hung up, he said, "They say they saw the TV report. They're checking." Other reporters began streaming back and joined us, camping out around Marlin's office.

Tel Aviv had been hit. In Israel newsmen were on-camera speaking through gas masks. Around 10:00 p.m. an exhausted Marlin Fitzwater posted a sheet of paper confirming that Iraq had sent missiles into Israel and Saudi Arabia. By then we had been on the air with pictures of the hits in Tel Aviv, which again was how the White House was getting much of its own information. Buildings had been demolished. By some miracle there had been only a handful of injuries.

I went on the air after midnight to describe the extraordinary, if not desperate, phone calling by Bush's foreign policy advisers to make sure the anti-Iraq alliance held together. I commented on the exceptional act of restraint on Israel's part in *not* retaliating.

DAY three. Everyone was worn out, including the President, who looked drawn at a *Morning News* conference. "Are we trying to kill Saddam?" I asked. "No one is being targeted," said Bush.

Throughout the day there were terrifying reports of more Scud attacks on Israel. Piercing sirens would go off, but then there would be all clears.

I left the White House at 9:00 p.m. and went to the bureau to get ready for *America Tonight.* This was to have been our last night; instead, it was another war show. We were all dead, but we had to move quickly because I had an interview with Israel's Netanyahu at precisely 10:40. Satellite bookings were very tight, with four nets vying for time. But then the sirens went off in Israel again, and everyone there was ordered into sealed rooms with gas masks on. It was a false alarm, but it meant that Netanyahu was late. By the time he arrived, we had just four minutes, but he was eloquent in describing the courage of his people in not striking back.

Iraq kicked out the foreign press on day four. A convoy of 110 foreigners drove to Amman, Jordan, praying the whole way. Everyone left but CNN.

U.S. planes were flying as many as 2000 missions a day against Iraq. At a Pentagon briefing Lieutenant General Thomas Kelly said, "We control the skies." Never before had the generals held daily televised briefings during a war. The briefings were aired live on CNN and at least in part on the networks. This had its downside, since the public was horrified to see how rude and irreverent we in the press could be. What business did some pip-squeak reporter have probing and pestering a four-star general during a war?

Often, the only way to pluck out information is to ask a lot of questions that may seem like nit-picking or sound uninformed (which they often are) or argumentative (which they also are). But this is what we do. As my CBS colleague Bill Plante said, "The public watched us make the sausage, and they didn't like it."

General Norman Schwarzkopf was the quarterback of the war. He had the build of a lineman and the presence of George Patton—perfect for television. He came on *Face* by satellite from U.S. headquarters in Dhahran with all the trappings of his military power: epaulets, bars, stars, stripes, and khaki everywhere. "We have cut Saddam's command and communications networks," he said. "In other words, Saddam is no longer communicating with his troops." I asked a *Saturday Night Live* question: "What does that mean?" He explained very patiently, "A lot of them aren't getting orders."

I took a break: Sunday afternoon at home, sitting on the bed, staring out. Aaron was watching the football play-offs, which were interrupted several times by bulletins: "Scud attacks on Dhahran and on Riyadh proper. You could see the streaks in the sky."

This was breathtakingly new: a war fought in real time on television. Vietnam had been reported after the fact on film that had to be flown to New York and developed. The Gulf war was bombs going off and the wail of air-raid sirens filling us with terror in our living rooms.

DAY six. CBS reporter Bob Simon was missing. He had taken a four-wheel-drive vehicle and, with his cameraman, sound man, and producer, had headed for the Iraqi border. By the time *America Tonight* went on the air, he was at least eight hours late.

Two days went by. No one heard from Simon or the others. I thought about them all the time. CBS morale could not have been lower. When the Saudis found the van with the keys, $6000, and TV equipment inside, we got desperately nervous.

By early February the planning and pre-positioning for the ground war into Iraq were grinding on. Tanks were moving forward from the Saudi desert. One of our reporters there said that the line of tanks was so long, you couldn't see from one end to the other. The thing the U.S. troops feared the most, he said, was that the Iraqis would use gas, as they had in their war against Iran. Bob Simon and the crew were still missing. It wasn't until two weeks later that Peter Arnett of CNN would report that Bob and his team were alive in a Baghdad prison.

Don Hewitt asked me to meet him for lunch in New York. He wasted no time on preliminaries: "I hear you're difficult." I braced for a lecture. "Show me someone who isn't difficult," he said, "and I'll show you someone with no talent. I want you for *60 Minutes*." After all those months of my being too afraid to want it too much, here it was plunked down unceremoniously before me.

So I said, "Oh, Don, I'm ecstatic!" Right? That's what anyone in my shoes should have said. But my first words were, "Can I keep living in Washington?" My very first reaction. I'd been churning over the idea of moving Taylor to New York.

"No. You have to move to New York." Then Hewitt said, "Well, maybe. I don't know." Clearly I had flummoxed him. He had been led to believe I was salivating for the job.

When I reached Aaron and told him about the offer and the possibility of staying in Washington, he went wild. "It's my turn," he said. "I hate Washington, always have, and you know that."

"But Taylor," I said.

"The perfect time to move Taylor is in ninth grade."

"Well, if we move, you have to tell Tay it's *your* idea. If she thinks it's because of me, she'll never forgive me. But she'll accept it if it's you who wants to move." He agreed and begged me to call Hewitt before he got second thoughts.

I phoned Don. "Doing this from Washington won't work," I said. "I spoke to Aaron, and yes, we'll move to New York." Now I was jabbering with enthusiasm.

"Oh, great!" said Don. Then the cold shower: "Now I have to bring this to my war council, to Mike, Morley, Ed, and Steve."

"Huh?" Not a firm offer?

"But you have Mike and me," said Don. "Don't take this as an audition or anything, but maybe you should do some pieces to show us what they look like."

The following night I took Aaron and Taylor out to dinner. I told Taylor, "*60 Minutes* might want me."

"We're not moving," she shot out. "We're not!"

I assured her that nothing was definite, there was no clear offer, and there was no point worrying until there was.

When Aaron went to the men's room, Tay asked, "What did you get Dad for tomorrow?"

"What's tomorrow?" I asked. Then I told her I'd owe her forever if she never told Aaron I'd *almost* forgotten our wedding anniversary. Married 14 years.

ON FEBRUARY 22, 1991, after five weeks of aerial bombardment, Bush issued an ultimatum: Saddam, you have until noon tomorrow to leave Kuwait. Otherwise the ground war will commence.

The next day, Saturday, Aaron and I watched the ground war begin on television. There were amazing logistical feats: fuel trucks, mobile hospitals, food caravans speeding through the desert, keeping up with the 100,000 troops dashing across Saudi Arabia and into southern Iraq. One of the pilots flying cover said it had looked like ants eating their way through a giant sandwich.

The ground war against Iraqi troops was brilliantly executed with lightning attacks that threw the enemy, already "attrited" (one of the Pentagon's many sanitized euphemisms), into chaos. The truth was, the dreaded Iraqi army was not any good. From the opening shot of the ground war its soldiers fled. It was a rout; the air force didn't even go up for a fight.

Bush had managed the war with a sureness of touch that impressed even those who had initially opposed our going in. All the way through he kept up his tireless phone calling: to keep the Israelis from retaliating, the Soviets from rescuing Saddam, the Iranians from sponsoring terrorism, the Germans and French in line, and the Syrians on board.

There were strategic reasons why Bush stopped the war before Saddam was deposed, including a desire to maintain a balance of power in the region by keeping neighboring Iran in check. That required a relatively strong Iraq. Without Saddam, Iraq might well have imploded into civil war. The moderate Arab allies told Bush that the disintegration of Iraq would be the worst possible outcome. Not pursuing the war to Baghdad would come to be seen as a mistake, but on the night of February 27 there was jubilation at the victorious cease-fire.

When the war ended, Bush's popularity rating soared to 88 percent. The last time a President had scored that high was Harry Truman at the end of World War II. Like most Americans, I thought Bush had led the effort with sophistication and patience, even wisdom. He had turned the conflict from an American-Iraqi contest into one between the civilized world and a madman. It was a diplomatic and military tour de force. But within a short time his image of resoluteness faded. As Bush turned back to domestic affairs, he reverted, as *Time* put it, to his old pattern of "deliberate drift." He was hurt too by the economy, which was in a recession.

A key to George Bush, I thought, was the son-of-the-great-man syndrome, the son who can never compete with or live up to the force or heft of the father. Bush had actually fled his father, the great Senator of principle, and went to Texas to make it on his own. But then when he went into politics, he did it by yoking onto powerful patrons, taking on the coloration of these new father figures. And so he flipped from a Goldwater conservative to a moderate Nixonian, from a critic of Reaganomics to one of its ardent defenders. When he finally hooked up with Reagan, he allowed himself to fade into Reagan's shadow. Perhaps that's what sons of great men do: find themselves another man of force and heft, latch on, and, as destiny would have it, suffer in the comparison.

President Bush, the Warrior King, gave a speech of triumph to a joint session of Congress and got 22 standing ovations. The pundits were saying he was invincible. But with the economy in recession, his popularity soon receded. By the 1992 election his job approval rating was down to 37 percent.

EARLY March. A Saturday morning. Bob Simon, producer Peter Bluff, and the crew were released after being held in an Iraqi prison for two and a half months. I heard Bob's news conference on the radio at 7:00 a.m., apologizing to his family for putting them through the pain. When I opened my *New York Times,* I read, "According to Don Hewitt, he has two candidates to replace Meredith Vieira on *60 Minutes:* Lesley Stahl and Bob Simon." I went shopping.

Bob and the crew went to London, where a doctor examined

them and said they were in good health. Bob told CBS he wanted to go home to Tel Aviv right away and write a book.

That's when Don called me from London: "This is going to happen; you're coming to *60 Minutes*." Was it me by default?

"I have to do something that I'm so afraid is going to make you angry," said Don. "You're going to be really upset with me. I hate to say this. We're getting along so well."

"What? You can say anything," I said. "What?"

"Don't be mad, okay?"

"What, already?"

"I hate your hair. You have to change it. It's too stiff. Too Nancy Reagan."

If I'd been younger, I would have chafed at the insult—how dare he! But I wasn't offended. It was settled. New hair.

I flew to New York. At *60 Minutes* everyone greeted me warmly. Mike Wallace was there, which was surprising, since he had had a pacemaker put in over the weekend. I got a big welcome hug, gingerly executed since he was in some discomfort. Ed Bradley hugged me too. They made me feel I was in the family.

It was definitely time to tell Taylor. We were on our way to Vail for her spring vacation, waiting in the airport lounge. "It's going to happen," I said. "You'll love New York," said Aaron. "I promise." She cried and sobbed and heaved. I myself had lived in that zone my entire fourteenth year, but this was unusual for Tay. Was I ruining her? Aaron and I kept exchanging looks of helplessness. I signaled, "Do something." He signaled back, "What?" As agreed, Aaron insisted it was his idea, his desire to leave Washington: "I've always hated it here."

Taylor fell asleep instantly on the plane. When she woke up, she offered me a deal: "I'll move to New York if I don't have to take piano lessons anymore." Taylor had been begging me to stop piano lessons for years.

"Deal," I said. She never cried about it again.

OUR last *America Tonight* broadcast was a call-in show from New York with General Thomas Kelly, the Pentagon briefer, in Washington; CBS correspondent Bert Quint in Kuwait; Mideast expert Fouad Ajami with us in New York; and Bob Simon in Tel Aviv—his first TV appearance since his news conference.

"It's finally time to play taps for *America Tonight,*" I said in my farewell. "A show that was born because of the Gulf war."

As the credits rolled, everyone came up on the podium and hugged Charles and me.

It was much harder to say good-bye to *Face* after eight years and 300 appearances. With everything I had done, those shows were my proudest work. I didn't "make news" every week, but I did get my teeth into a subject, explore it for 30 minutes, and try to achieve some depth. And the excitement of live TV is a kick. It was heady and hard, and I loved it.

"I'm going to miss this good old chair," I said in my good-bye broadcast. After thanking all the wonderful men and women I had worked with—the producers, the editors, and the crew—each by name, I said, "So long, and I'll see you on *60 Minutes.*"

SO WHAT had I learned in 20 years in Washington? I learned that it's not only "the economy, stupid." It's also television, stupid. Television had become the center not only of campaigning and governing but also of diplomacy and decision making. I also learned to have enormous faith in our system. Democracy works. It even intrudes on the way the media functions. I came to see that the press is far more reactive than influential, far more reflective of public opinion than most people realize. Jimmy Carter wasn't unpopular because the media battered him; we battered him because he was unpopular. We had license. And Reagan got an easier press because the public loved him.

As I packed up to leave Washington, I thought sadly of my ride on the decline of network news. Much of the erosion had been brought about by technological change, but deregulation had been the other factor. Deregulation was one of the few policies Jimmy Carter initiated that Ronald Reagan adopted and carried forward. In fact, he turned it into part of his free-market religion. In the old days the Federal Communications Commission used to mandate that those of us who used the free airwaves broadcast a set amount of public-service programming. To win "brownie points," in Don Hewitt's words, we put on hour-long documentaries and lots of other hard-boiled news shows.

When *60 Minutes* came along, it showed that news could make money. Now, as Hewitt says, "You cannot do news on television *unless* you make money."

Deregulation brought us more stations, and technology brought us cable and even more stations, more competition. When there was a strong FCC and only three networks, we were encouraged to be the front page of *The New York Times.* Today, in the 300-channel universe, we compete with tractor pulling on ESPN, game shows on the independent channels, and *I Love Lucy* reruns on cable. To compete, we eventually succumbed to wet-fingering like the politicians, relying on polls so we could give the public what they wanted.

Enter the blurring of hard news and tabloid news, where the concentration is on personalities. By the early 1990s we were covering O. J. Simpson and Princess Di as if they were Charles de Gaulle and Mao Tse-tung. The same pressures began intruding on political reporting, except there we called it "character" journalism.

With the falloff in audience, we also began to introduce more conflict into our reports. Actually, the drift toward hostility journalism developed out of the best of intentions. When we realized that the new technology allowed us to squeeze three or four sound bites into one piece, we began to look for "opposing views" to flesh out our reports. We thought of it as good journalism, but it had the unintended effect of exacerbating a public discourse of disputatiousness. Our bosses began asking for a "stable of arguers" in the hope that the audience would like the dueling. Soon we were searching for the most polarized views so we could get a real battle going.

Even with all these changes, and while other broadcasts have softened up their content, *The CBS Evening News* is still a place where you find solid, old-fashioned journalism. Dan Rather is first and above all a hard-news reporter who has managed to preserve his edge and the highest of standards.

And I was going to another grand institution of the old values.

60 Minutes, with its unshakable ratings, had not felt the pressure to melt into an electronic grocery-store tabloid. *60 Minutes* kept its lust for hard-edged investigations and jabbing interviews. Don Hewitt had invented the television magazine in 1968 and simply refused to change his tell-me-a-story format.

I would get questions about being the "only" female at *60 Minutes.* But nearly 40 percent of the producers—11 out of 29—were women (today it's 36 percent: 9 out of 25), and both Hewitt and I said publicly that we thought the next correspondent hired would be a woman. And in fact, the next was Christiane Amanpour of CNN.

Don said he was afraid I was too Washington. "We're a repertory company," he told me at lunch. "Mike, Morley, each one of you has to play all the parts. One week you're Hamlet, the next Ophelia, the next Iago. I want you all to do it all." So one week I would profile Paul Newman at 70, the next investigate Medicare fraud, the next interview Yasir Arafat. Can you imagine after all those years of being straitjacketed into presidential issues what it was like to go out and cover any story I was interested in? It was a holiday. On my first day at *60 Minutes* someone turned to me in the elevator and asked, "Going up to Paradise?"

Working with the very best in my business, I was floating. More than that, I was getting younger. Well, you'd get younger too if you worked with guys that old! Morley used to say, "We've reached the point where if we do a story on Medicare, it's a conflict of interest!" Joking aside, there simply is not a better job or a better shop in all of television news—possibly in all of journalism.

I started at *60 Minutes* on April 2, 1991. I smiled all that day—so much my face hurt—and I haven't stopped yet, eight years later.

So suddenly, there was God.

A Song for Mary

AN IRISH-AMERICAN MEMORY

Dennis Smith

I have a high, clear, choirboy's voice, and I sing away. I try to make every word count.

"She was lovely and fair
As the rose in the summer,
But t'was not her beauty alone that won me.
Oh, no, t'was the truth in her eyes ever dawning
That made me love Mary
The Rose of Tralee."

They all clap and cheer when I am done.

"That Dennis," Aunt Helen says. "I wonder who his Rose of Tralee is."

"It's my mother's song," I say. "She's the Rose of Tralee."

Everyone laughs, and my mother says, "Blarney." But she's beaming.

—*A Song for Mary*

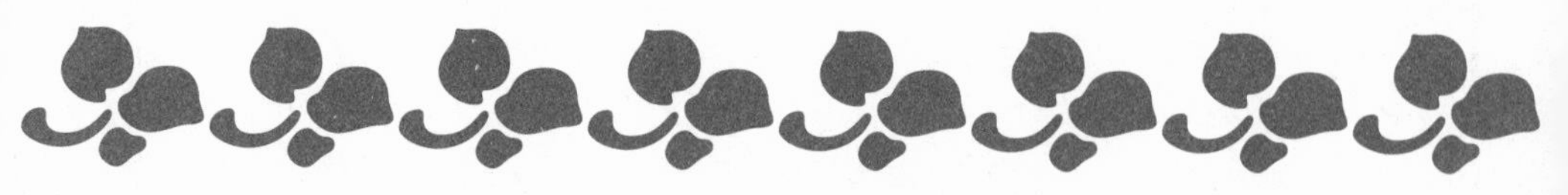

Prologue

SITTING with my brother in the first pew of Queen of Angels Church, I can hear the beeping horns and speeding cars and trucks on Queens Boulevard, and I wish it were quieter. I look around the church and into the faces of my five children and my brother's four, searching for some sign of grief. Do they miss her? I keep asking myself.

Do they know anything about her?

There are no flags or draperies on her casket, no brass or silver ornaments. Just a small bouquet of mixed flowers sitting on top, about where her folded hands would be. The casket looks strong and modest, words that apply to her like colors on a drab canvas.

These sons and daughters and nieces and nephews of mine have had privileged upbringings, and little has been missed for the wanting. But they are the grandchildren of a tough New York life. I study them now as the priest goes through the Mass, all of them young adults, each with a life of his or her own, each with a unique set of problems and confrontations, needs, and desires. Sure, they loved her, but I wonder if any of them have found time in their busy and complicated lives to touch themselves with her life, to be anointed with a memory that might protect them or help them or make them more complete.

Why didn't I think of it beforehand? There will never be another opportunity like this. I could have written something; the priest could have introduced an oration. But she wouldn't have approved of that kind of singling out, even at the funeral. No, keep it modest, she would advise. Remember that railroad tracks are plain and ordinary, but they'll get you where you're going.

Still, I want them to remember this moment, for it should be a monument moment.

The priest is at the Communion, and I go to the altar.

"I want to say something," I whisper.

The priest is shocked out of the usual.

"Who are you?" he asks.

The children are lined up behind to receive.

"Their father," I say, gesturing toward them.

I stand to the side until the Communion is finished, but the priest goes past me as if I am invisible. He busies himself at the altar, paying me no mind, but I stand my ground. I'll have my say in or out of his agenda.

Finally he looks up to the small group and says, "A family member wants to say something."

I look at the small casket enveloping what has become no more than ninety pounds of skin and bones. There is not a cough or a sneeze or a shuffle in the church. The traffic sounds have momentarily disappeared, and it is perfectly quiet.

"Just one thing," I say, "that I want to ask you to think about as we're all gathered here trying to commemorate a life. The true epitaph is not the message epitomizing a person that is etched into a headstone, but the memory that resides in the swelling of the heart. Each of you might have hundreds of memories, but you have to make sure you find the right one, the one that speeds the blood. Sometimes you have to search long and deep within yourself to find that particular memory, and when you find it, you'll know, for this is the epitaph that will stand your test of time. So I ask you to remember Mary like this, and like anything in your life that is worthwhile, there is no time like now to start."

One

I AM seven years old, and I know the difference between right and wrong.

It's been my job for more than a month to take the erasers out to the schoolyard at ten minutes to three each day and clap them against the brick wall so they'll be nice and clean for Sister Maureen in the morning. But today, when we were standing for our afternoon prayers, Peter Shalleski knuckled me in the back of the head. We were in the middle of the Hail Holy Queen. It's too bad that Sister Maureen didn't see that. She only saw that I took Shalleski's ear right after "O Clement O Loving O Sweet Virgin Mary" and twisted it so that it nearly came off. I should have bopped him right there in front of everyone, in the middle of the Hail Holy Queen, but I know he is tougher than anyone in the class, and I know as sure as Charlie McCarthy has a wooden head that Shalleski is going to get even with me later for the twisted ear.

I don't care.

My head is hurting from where he knuckled me, but I know it is going to hurt even more, as Sister is about to give me a whack with the pointer. I wish I had corduroy pants instead of these thin gabardines. Here I am, standing on the bare wood-slat floor, eyes closed, biting my teeth together as hard as they will go, my hands flat against the chalky blackboard, leaning over for all the class to see, as the thin pointer goes *shwitt* across my shiny pants.

The sting goes through my body. I want to scream out, but I can't. None of the boys ever screams out, even if Sister gives three whacks, which is the most she gives. The girls never get it, and even if they did, it wouldn't hurt so much, because there is so much material in their blue uniform dresses. I can feel my face becoming red as I turn and try to straighten up.

"Sit in the back of the class until three o'clock," Sister said.

"But what about the erasers?"

"Never mind the erasers. There'll be no more erasers for you."

It is the first job I ever had, the first time I am doing something the others do not do, something different. She gave me the job because my marks led the class on the vocabulary tests, and to lose it now makes me want to cry.

But I know you can't cry in front of a whole class of boys and girls. It would be like screaming out when Sister whacked you with the pointer. They would start to call you Phil the Faucet or Blubber Baby or some stupid thing, and take out their snotty handkerchiefs every time you passed them in the hallway.

"Shalleski hit me first, Sister, and I don't see why I should get punished because of what Shalleski did."

"Don't raise your voice to me, young man," Sister scolds. Mommy is always saying this, too, calling me young man in a voice that means being a young man is not so good and that it gets you in trouble. Maybe Mommy and Sister are related, long-lost cousins or something. Sister waits a few seconds. "If Shalleski jumped off the Brooklyn Bridge, would you?"

"So?"

"So next time don't hit back. Turn the other cheek. Think about what Jesus said in the Sermon on the Mount and pray for anyone who you think is mean."

I am not so sure about this turn-the-other-cheek thing, because I know Shalleski, and just as I am praying for him, you know what Shalleski will do? Shalleski will clout the other cheek, too.

I THINK about telling my mother all the way up the four flights of stairs at 337 East 56th Street. I count the gum blotches on the twelve marble steps of each flight to keep from crying. No one ever told me about how to keep from crying, but I figured out that if you just thought about something else, concentrated on it, the tears wouldn't come. Thirty-one gum blobs, each a square inch or so, mopped over a couple of hundred times so that the edge of the gum looks like it's blended into the marble.

There is an O'DWYER FOR MAYOR sticker on the windowpane at the fourth-floor landing, and I begin to peel it off. I want to wait for another while before I see my mother, to relax a little. I always tell her everything, and I want to get it right about Sister Maureen. I can feel my eyes begin to get tight, and I stretch them wide open.

One of the apartment doors opens, and Mr. Gentile comes out to walk his dog. He raises his hand toward me, and I flinch.

"Leave that sticker alone before I give you one."

I feel embarrassed to let him make me flinch like that. I want to curse at him, but I know that I will meet him again in the hall. So I run the length of the long dark corridor back to apartment 26.

"Damn kid," he says as he pulls the dog down the stairs.

"MR. GENTILE cursed at me."

"Don't pay any attention to him."

Mommy pours a bit of Karo syrup onto a piece of white bread and places it in front of me. The table has a piece of red linoleum across the top, and the linoleum is cracked and splitting apart. The wood below is rotting out.

"Why shouldn't I pay attention to him?" I pick at the linoleum.

"He's just one of those guineas who don't know nothing," Mommy says as she slaps my hand away from the linoleum.

"Sister Maureen must be a guinea, then."

"Why do you say that? What happened?"

Mommy can always tell when something is not quite right.

I again feel a tug of the skin around my eyes, and so I begin to make the dreaded face as I tell Mommy the story, pulling my chin down and stretching my eyes up. It feels good. It gets rid of the tug.

"Stop making faces."

I do it again because I can't help it, and my mother reaches for the strap. I freeze because I know I can't run. The three rooms are each not more than eight feet long, and the kitchen is about five. Not much space to run.

"Mommy, no."

The strap comes across my shoulder, stinging. But I don't flinch. Flinching from Mommy is like running. It gets you nowhere.

The strap is a piece of belt a little more than a foot long. It has a slit at the end to fit over the back rung of the kitchen chair.

The faces are hard to control, and so I put all my energy into the story about Shalleski, but before I can get through it, I begin to feel the tears building up in my eyes and my nose begins to run. I am not supposed to cry about such things, but I put my head on the table and let my shoulders heave up and down.

"It is so unfair of her to take the erasers away from me."

"She was right to punish you," Mommy answers. "Stop the crying, alligator tears. Sister Maureen was right."

"She wasn't."

"Don't correct me. You have no control. You have to learn to control yourself, or you'll never get out of trouble."

I love the way Mommy always finds a way to the back end of a situation. If there is something on her mind and she does not know how to speak it head-on, she goes around it. And so she begins to tell a story that I suppose is about Sister Maureen.

"When you were a baby—this was just before your father went to the hospital—you were sitting in your stroller. Your father was holding Billy in his arms. You leaned forward, and the stroller tipped over, and as you fell, you put your little arm out to block your fall. Well, the handle hit your little thumb, and your little thumbnail just popped off your finger."

I want to tell her that, since I was just a baby, my arm and my thumb and my thumbnail would have had to be little.

"Oh, how you howled, even after we bandaged it all up. You must have howled for three days. I felt so bad because I guess I just wasn't paying attention, but it does show how you have to watch out for yourself in this world and don't ever rely on someone taking care of you. So if you lost the eraser job, there is not much you can do but find some other way that might bring you joy and satisfaction. You have to take care of yourself, Dennis."

She is a pretty woman, Mommy is. I know because the guys on the street sometimes whistle to tease her. The sun is bouncing off the window box where we keep the milk in winter. Her teeth sparkle as she speaks, and she wraps her arms around me. She is always wrapping her arms around me and kissing me on the head.

"I just let my eye wander for a moment, and there you were on the ground. Your own mother let you down. And now you have to find something to replace the erasers."

"Are there any bottles?"

"Look under the tub. I think you'll find some."

The bathtub is in the kitchen, next to the sink, and is topped by a shiny metal cover. The three Rheingold beer bottles are in shadow, and I can barely see them. They are worth six cents, but they are also pretty risky. I know I can't just pick them up, so I put my hand in carefully and shake one, hoping that if there are any roaches there, they will scurry away. I take the bottles out by the neck, one by one, and roll them over and over on the floor.

Mommy told me that the builders put the roaches in the walls because they had a grudge against the Irish and the Italians. There are fifty roaches in the walls for every one you see, and sometimes when I am lying on the top bunk at night, I think that the walls are shaking with all the roaches running around behind the plaster. I can never get used to roaches. Some nights I just can't go to sleep thinking about the shaking walls.

Taking back the empties before my brother, Billy, gets them is always a special treat. It could take a half hour at Abbie's candy store on First Avenue to spend six cents, because it isn't easy to decide between the candy corn, the dots on the sheet, the banana marshmallows—all two-for-a-penny treats. The bottles are a chance in a lifetime opportunity, and they come two or three times a week. They are like an allowance. Anyway, the only kind of allowance I have.

But the bottles do not come without the risk. I turn them upside down over the sink, then shove them into a paper bag.

At Rossi's grocery, I wait in line until Mrs. O'Bannon gets her roast pork sandwich—the hero I dream about, oozing with mayonnaise sprayed with salt and pepper and topped with lettuce leaves. The roast pork is the most expensive one you can get at Rossi's, except for the roast beef. We hardly ever get sandwiches, and when we do, it's just salami or cheese, but I had the roast pork hero once when Mr. Dempsey from the delicatessen on First Avenue gave me a half dollar for sweeping up, and Mommy said I could keep all of it.

The nickel and the penny chime together in my hand as I leave Rossi's and walk down the First Avenue hill in the shadow of St. John the Evangelist Church. My church. The traffic light changes, and I have to wait. I look at the church and decide to pay my uncle Tommy a visit. A navigator, he went down with six others in a B-29. In a fog. In Bayonne, New Jersey, searching for an airport on their return from Germany. He had been on forty missions in the war, and so St. John's put a plaque up for him in the back of the church.

Forty missions in Germany and lost in Bayonne. My uncle Pat says it is like winning the Kentucky Derby and then getting killed by your horse in the stall.

I genuflect at the back end of the center aisle. The church is huge and beautiful, with paintings on the ceiling and great big columns going down either side. I walk up to the shrine of the Immaculate Conception at the small altar to the right and kneel before it. I always do this because the Virgin, her hands spread far apart, smiles at me in return for any request. She lived for requests and applications, Mommy says.

I know that I have to say a prayer, and so I begin the Hail Mary. "Hail Mary, full of grace! The Lord is with thee, blessed art thou amongst women, and blessed is the fruit of thy wound, Jesus."

I always think about this wound of Jesus and what wound it is and what kind of fruit they are talking about. I suppose it is the bloody gaping hole in his side where the soldiers put in a big spear, and I am thinking that the fruit might be bananas and oranges because I don't think they grow apples in Bethlehem, which is the neighborhood Jesus comes from.

Today I ask her to make my father better, and she says she will and smiles at me. She doesn't actually talk, but gives me a message. I always close my eyes and think that I am swimming in the bottom of a deep well, and, looking up, I see just a small circle of light, and there in the light is the Blessed Virgin.

Now it is time for the deal. What am I going to do in return? Last time, I promised to wash the kitchen floor for Mommy, and so now I promise to wear a clean shirt whenever I can remember. The Virgin seems to think that is a square deal, and so she smiles.

I return to the back of the church, which is really the front, and pass the plaques of all the St. John's men who were in the wars. Uncle Tommy has his own plaque, a small one.

I never knew him, my uncle Tommy, never even saw a picture of him, but whenever I look at his plaque, I invent his face and I put words in his mouth, just like I do with my father. Sometimes I put my father and Uncle Tommy together in a room, and they always argue about what ball game they want to take me to, for I think my father likes DiMaggio and Yankee Stadium and Uncle Tommy likes Pee Wee Reese and Ebbets Field.

And so I talk for a few minutes to my dead uncle, kiss my fingers, and touch the cold bronze of his name. Just next to him is the heavy wrought-iron poor box, and I separate the penny from the nickel. For a second I hold the penny up like an offering and bless myself with the sign of the cross. I do not want to give the penny up, but my mother says that if you forget the poor of the world, the world will someday forget you, so there is no choice.

That is two rolls of caps, the poor-box sacrifice, but I still have the nickel for Abbie's candy store, and a nickel will go a long way.

"C'MON already," Abbie is saying, "there are things to do instead of waiting for you to make up your mind. What's your name?"

"Moniker," I say. I might be seven, but I know it means a different name. My uncle Tracy always says that his name is Tracy, but his moniker is Your Lord Worship Tracy.

"Monica is a girl's name. What's your name?"

Abbie is always rushing you, and he always asks your name so that if he catches you stealing, he can tell the cops. A lot of the guys in the neighborhood steal every time they go in.

"Just an old Jew," the guys say, "that gots lots of dough. He'll never miss a little candy."

I guess everybody thinks that stealing candy from Abbie is like stealing a million dollars from the Rockefellers. So it's probably a venial sin, and you'll get a few Hail Marys in confession. But if you steal a nickel from an old woman, you are sure to go to hell.

Mommy says that if you steal from somebody one day, the next day you'll lie to somebody else, and your life will be worth nothing, because nobody loves a liar. If you're a liar, you'll never have a true friend, and what's the point of living if you don't have true friends?

I have red wagon wheels in one pocket and licorice in the other and a bagful of Good & Plenty. It is like a miracle what a few beer bottles will do.

Kips Bay Boys Club is just around the corner, and I am going there to have a game of Ping-Pong and maybe pool. Near the corner I see Peter Shalleski and his brother Harry, who is my brother Billy's age. I know that I should put my Good & Plenty in a pocket as soon as I see Shalleski, but he is on me, punching, before I can take another step. The bag goes out of my hand, and the pink and white candy spills all over First Avenue. I am so mad that Shalleski does this. I want to fight back, but Shalleski has me by my shirt collar, screaming about his twisted ear and how I got him into trouble with Sister Maureen.

What is the matter with me? I am frozen with something. I'm getting smashed, and I can't help thinking that Shalleski shouldn't be doing this. Why does Shalleski have to punch and knuckle people all the time? He is yelling with every punch. "Take that, you son of a bitch," he is saying.

Stop, stop, stop, I am thinking as I press my arms into my face.

Finally Shalleski stops, I guess because I'm not fighting back.

No one says anything, not another word. The two brothers just walk away, and I look at my candy all over the ground.

Is there any of it that isn't too dirty to pick up? No, I am thinking. It's now dirty like the devil's ashes. Both my ears hurt, and I feel the blood at my nose. I put my fingers to the top of my lip and throw my head back as I walk down 52nd Street.

Archie is standing at the top of the stairs at Kips. He is always there if he isn't playing dodgeball in the lower gym.

"Where's your club card?" Archie asks.

"Come on, Archie," I say, "you know me."

"Doesn't matter. You have to have the card."

I have the black "midgets' card," the youngest age group. Midgets can just go to the lower gym to play schoolyard games, but the intermediates, like Billy, can use their gray card to play full-court basketball on the third floor.

I know that Billy will be in the upper gym. He's always playing basketball or baseball, or reading. Mommy goes to the library every week to get the books, and Billy always reads them.

I have lived with Billy all my lifetime, and when you live with someone, you don't think a lot about them. They are just there, like the kitchen sink. But recently I've been thinking that Billy has been pretty good with me, making sure I learn things that he has found out, like how to play rummy and Ping-Pong.

I run to the gym and see Billy taking a foul shot. "What are you doing after the game?" I call to him.

"I don't know," he yells back. "Going home?"

"Could you take a little bit of time with me?"

"What do you want? Ping-Pong?"

"To learn how to fight."

Billy looks at me like I am asking him for twenty dollars. He stops shooting the ball and comes over to me.

"You don't learn how to fight. You just do it."

"No," I answer, "I gotta learn, 'cause I fell outta the stroller and lost my thumbnail, and I have to beat the brains outta Peter Shalleski. I have to plan it."

"What?" my brother says, a little confused. "Meet me in the weight room after the game."

The weight room is below the swimming pool and has a punching bag hanging from the ceiling. There is a pair of black punching bag gloves on the floor, three sizes too big, but I put them on.

As I begin to punch away, I remember the rules of dancing the nuns taught us in the church basement. Keep your head up straight, your chin out. Keep your knees buckled just a bit. Bring your shoulders back. Control the change of your weight from one foot to the other. Maybe a good fight is like a good dance, I think.

I am now bouncing around, jabbing at the punching bag, making it swing with each jab. I weave, and bob up and down. Hit the bag, hit the bag, hit Shalleski the Ratski.

Billy comes into the room and watches me some.

"You're doing pretty good," he says. "You want to box?"

"No," I say, taking one last hard punch, pleased that I beat the bag to a pulp. "Let's go home."

Billy puts his arm around my shoulder as we walk up Second Avenue, past Moe's Diner, past the newsstand. He's only nine, but he knows how to do everything. He's the basketball champ, the baseball champ, and he's never in fights, because nobody wants to tangle with somebody that moves as fast as Billy. And he is always good with lessons, no matter if it's history or boxing. "Just don't take any crap from people," he is saying. "Shalleski may give you some lumps every time, but he'll begin to respect you."

"I don't want his respect," I say. "I just want him to stop bothering me and maybe kick the crap outta him."

We turn at 56th Street, and when we pass the Hotel Sutton, we cross to the other side of the street. It is only at the stoop that my brother takes his arm from around my shoulder. He takes a good look at me, and gives me a small smack at the back of my head and laughs. I guess he sees the dried blood at the end of my nose.

A few women are sitting there, newspapers under them to protect their skirts. One is drinking out of a cardboard container of beer, which she got at Billy's Bar and Grill on the corner. If there is any blood showing on me, I don't want them to see it, and so I whiz by.

My mother sees the blood before I get a chance to wash it off. She is dishing out the tripe. It is like the inside of a dead sponge, and she puts it beside a few carrots and peas. I hate the tripe. It smells like the inside of my shoe.

"What's with the bloody nose?" Mommy asks.

"Dodgeball at Kips," I say, sitting down.

I know I am risking all my future friends by lying, but she will strap me for sure if she finds out I was fighting in the street.

"Go wash your face."

I go to the sink in the middle of the kitchen and wash.

"Don't they have people there to make sure you don't get hurt?"

"Archie was there."

"Archie is always there," my brother pipes in.

"What does Archie do?"

"He hits you with the dodgeball," I answer.

"He just plays the game," Billy says. "Archie is the greatest."

The tripe is making me sick. "I can't eat this, Mommy," I say. Billy kicks me under the table.

"Eat it and shut up," Mommy says. "You need the vitamins of this, so I don't want to hear another word."

I have to think of something to take my mind off this tripe.

"Tell me about Daddy in the hospital."

"Daddy is fine," Mommy says. "I saw him last week when you went to Aunt Kitty's to play with your cousins."

"You didn't tell me. Why can't I go?"

"I told you a million times that they don't let kids in."

"Tell me again about the accident," I say. "How did he fall off of the truck?"

"He just fell, is all."

"So why are his legs so bad?"

"Because he can't move them. Just eat your dinner."

"So why can't he use crutches or something?"

"They don't want him to," Mommy says. "And you are going to be in trouble, young man, if you don't put your fork in."

I notice Billy cutting the tripe into teeny pieces and mashing it into his peas before he puts it into his mouth. He doesn't say anything. He never says anything when we talk about Daddy.

"Mommy," I say, "if we didn't put the nickel into the sacrifice box on Sunday, would we buy different food?"

This makes her mad. She reaches for the strap behind her.

"I don't want to hear another word."

I am getting sick from the smell of the tripe, and I feel the tugging at the corner of my eyes. So I stretch my eyes upward and my chin down, and before I know it the strap has gone across my neck.

"Stop the faces and put the fork in."

The sting at the side of the neck feels like it is glowing, like the saints glow in the picture books. I want to curse, and I want to cry, but to keep my mind off everything, I begin to cut the tripe into bitsy pieces and mash it into the peas and the carrots. I make little balls, and I chew as quickly as I can.

It works. If I hold my breath long enough.

Billy even knows how to eat tripe without getting into trouble.

"Run the water for a bath," Mommy says.

I look at Billy, who is putting his plate in the sink. He disappears into the bedroom.

"I can't get the tub top off," I say.

"You did it before, so just run the water."

I don't want to take the tub top off, because I know there will be the roaches there, standing upside down under the tub top. Sometimes there are ten or twenty of them, and I am afraid that one of them will get on my arm or, worse, into my shirt.

I pretend to try to take the top off. "It's too heavy, Mommy."

"For goodness' sake. Billy, get in here."

When my brother comes in, I go into the bedroom. I sit on the windowsill, waiting for the water to get high. The room is just large enough for the bunk beds and a dresser. Suddenly I hear a great thump, like somebody threw an elephant from the roof. And then I hear a great scream coming from the apartment next door, and so I run into the kitchen.

"It's the guineas again," Mommy says.

I look out the window into the courtyard, and I see Mrs. Giambetta next door at her window, screaming her head off. My mother looks over my shoulder and pulls me away. But just before she does, I can see Crazy Mario sprawled and splattered across the concrete five stories below. Crazy Mario is Mrs. Giambetta's son.

"I want to see," Billy says.

"There's nothing to see," Mommy says. "Go take a bath."

"Crazy Mario jumped outta the window," I say to Billy.

"Shut up, and take a bath, both of you."

Mommy turns away from us. It looks like she is looking for the strap, but I can see her shoulders going up and down. She goes into her room, and she tries to shut the door, but it can't shut because there is no closet in the room and all the clothes are hung on the back of the door and on the doorknob.

I go in and see her on the bed. She is thin, and the bed is so much bigger than she is. Her face is pressed against a pink spread, and she is crying. I never knew she cared about Crazy Mario.

"I'm sorry, Mommy," I say to her.

She turns to me and catches her breath. Her eyes are so pretty, and it makes me sad to see them so red and swollen.

"Oh," she says, trying to smile, "it doesn't have anything to do with you. Tenement tears, you know? It's just that everything is so hard for everybody . . . especially mothers. . . . Poor Mrs. Giambetta." She gets up and sits on the side of the bed. "I just wish we could move out of midtown, maybe to Queens or back to Brooklyn." She smiles, and gets up and pats my fanny. "If I could only get off this welfare, we could get a better place. Someday."

I never think much about being on the welfare, because Mommy told us to never tell anyone about it. I know she doesn't like it, though. She keeps saying if only me and Billy were older, she could get a real job instead of cleaning all these Sutton Place apartments and then hiding the money from the welfare.

"Poor Mario is dead, huh?" I ask.

"I guess so," Mommy says. "I never knew him, except I saw him sitting on the stoop like he was hypnotized."

That's why they call him Crazy Mario. He just sat around staring at the cracks in the sidewalk. He made no response if you talked to him, even if you said "Excuse me" when you passed him in the hall. He was old enough to be in college, but now he is dead, plopped like a pancake in my backyard, and I hope he is in heaven because in heaven your eyes are opened and you see everything, and Mario could have his voice back, and he could say hello to everybody.

Two

ST. JOHN'S schoolyard is filled with running and shouting children, the girls all in blue jumpers and white blouses, the boys in white shirts and blue ties. Billy and I get there just as the principal rings the big brass handbell. Everyone walks quietly to his or her class line and gets lined up like boxes on a drugstore shelf.

Sister Stella looks old to me, older than Mommy, and her face is always in shadows and just barely sticks out from her bonnet. On the first day of class she wrote on the blackboard, "Be happy and you will learn." She is the only nun I ever heard of who talks about being happy. Petey Poscullo says she probably takes opium.

But she told us that her favorite saint is Saint John Bosco, who was a teacher like her and who said that the teacher has to love the students or else nothing happens. So she is always talking about love and being happy.

There are twenty-one of us in the classroom, and I am sitting in the front row, doing my penmanship lesson, practicing the capital letters Sister Stella has written on the board. It is the Palmer Method, and it works out pretty good if you remember to use the Sunday cane at the front of the H, K, M, N, U, V, W, Y, and Z.

"More than a third of the alphabet," Sister Stella told us, "depends on the straightness of the Sunday cane."

I think I am doing them all right, but Sister Stella is now behind me and hits my knuckles with a ruler. It doesn't hurt. Sister Stella wouldn't hurt anyone, because it would interfere with them being happy, and if you are not happy, you can't learn.

"Your Sunday canes," Sister says, "are wiggly."

I work on my Sunday canes, especially the starting lines on the M's and N's, making them perfect half-moons at the top and lines straight as a fire pole at the bottom. I do this, and I am happy in my learning, the way Sister wants us to be.

MOMMY is punishing me because I was ten minutes late for dinner yesterday, and so I cannot go to Kips this afternoon. Instead, I have to sit around Mrs. Grayson's apartment on Sutton Place while Mommy works the vacuum and washes Mrs. Grayson's clothes.

She puts on a housecoat over her skirt and sweater. As she buttons it up, she tells me to sit in a kitchen chair and read.

"I don't have a book," I say.

Mommy takes a book from her bag and hands it to me. It is a library book, *Hans Brinker.*

You can always tell a library book because the corners are usually popping out with frayed cardboard. I don't think I have ever seen a new book. I take this book and begin to read, and soon I am rooting for this Hans guy to win the skating race. All the time, I am watching Mommy out of the corner of my eye. She keeps running from room to room, whistling and carrying things. She is mopping and dusting and lifting photographs from the piano.

In the kitchen Mommy puts the washboard in the sink and runs the water. There is a mound of clothes on the floor. She is sweating and looks tired from so much running from room to room.

"Can I help you, Mommy?" I say, dropping the book on the table. "Could I wash those things for you?"

"Go read your book," she says. "Boys don't do people's wash. They read books if they know what's good for them."

I am always reading books, anyway, and so I don't know why she won't let me help her. Mommy scrubs up and down the washboard, and her eyes are closed.

It is too bad that Daddy isn't better. It's too bad that he doesn't have the good legs, so that he can go to work and Mommy could go to one of the parks down by the river, like the other women on 56th Street. And Mommy could sit there and read magazines, and knit, and talk about the Italian kids who wear pegged pants and get away with murder by their parents and the way everything at Rossi's store is so expensive. And Daddy could come home at night, and we could talk about the Dodgers being in Cuba for spring training and how come the Dodgers couldn't just practice underneath the 59th Street Bridge the way we do at the Police Athletic League games.

"Mommy," I ask, "could you buy me a new book someday?"

"You mean, *would* I buy you a new book. There are so many books in the library you should read first. After you read all of the library books, we can think about a new book. Okay?"

"Okay, Mommy."

"Now." She is standing with her hands on her hips looking around. "The kitchen floor once over, and we can go home."

"Mommy? I think I read all the books in the library already."

"You're full of soup, Dennis. You haven't read all the books."

"How many more do I have to go?"

Mommy's hands are still on her hips. She looks like a model in a magazine because she is thin and curvy. She's smiling, and her long brown hair swings back on her shoulders.

"Do you know our building?"

"Yes. Three thirty-seven East Fifty-sixth Street."

"Six stories high, made of bricks, right? How many bricks?"

"Maybe a hundred?"

Mommy laughs out loud. "No, Dennis. Thousands and thousands. And if you think of each brick representing maybe fifty books in the library, do you know how many books you've read?"

"How many?"

"Maybe two bricks' worth," she says. "So think about how exciting it is to have all that fun still before you."

"Yeah, and who is going to carry all those bricks home from the library, huh?"

She bends over in her laughter, a high giggle kind of laugh.

I don't even like to carry groceries up the four flights of stairs, never mind all these bricks she is talking about.

Mommy stops laughing and gets on her hands and knees. She looks around and begins to crawl across the floor, pulling a big bucket of steaming water next to her. She has a rag in one hand and a brush in the other, the brush going back and forth like an out-of-control clock. Every once in a while she stops and wipes the sweat off her forehead with the rag.

Suddenly, watching Mommy, my mind goes weird, like it is on fire inside my head. I don't know another kid whose mother does this anywhere except in their own houses, and I am getting awfully sad awfully quick. And mad. Why is my mother the only mother who gets down on her hands and knees for all these people? This is not our house; this is not our floor she is cleaning. Why couldn't Mommy be Mrs. Grayson, instead of the other way around?

And then maybe I could have a new book, and we could sit and read it together, even for just a day.

IT IS Tuesday afternoon. I'm at altar boy practice, holding a tall candlestick high up as if I'm offering it up to God.

It's not so easy to do this when you're only eight. It is made of gold, and it's heavy, and I am afraid of dropping it. I know that there are people in the church making visits, and Father O'Rourke is behind me giving us instructions. I should be paying attention, but there are big holes in my shoes. I had cardboard in them, but it rained and the cardboard went like soggy liverwurst. I forgot to put in new cardboard, and there are holes in my socks, too, and I can picture the threads falling out of the holes and all the people in the church laughing, and I pray to God to make Father O'Rourke get it over with. I don't even have the Latin memorized yet, and here he is giving us the instruction to serve at High Mass.

"Okay," Father says, "we are at the Consecration now, and the priest has the Host high in the air, so you're on, Delaney."

Richard Delaney is in charge of the bells, brass bells that look like three round upside-down bowls, and he hammers each bell, so that it sounds like NBC on the radio. It makes me think of sold American, look sharp, feel sharp, be sharp, the Shadow knows, Henry, Henry Aldrich, coming, mother, and I am thinking of these things to get my mind off the holes in my shoes and to forget how my arms are hurting from holding this thing so high. And then my eyes tighten, and I make the faces.

Father Hamilton comes on the altar, and the first thing you notice about him is his white socks. The boys in school can't wear white socks unless we have a note from home saying we have foot scurvy or the creeping crud or something. I wonder if Father has athlete's foot. He is a lot younger than Father O'Rourke, but he is completely bald and has skin the color of Chinese apples—a sort of red and brown mixed together.

"Okay," he says to the group, "I am going to teach you how to pronounce the Latin of the Suscipiat."

Father Hamilton recites the Suscipiat slowly. It is the hardest prayer to memorize, and we all listen carefully because Latin doesn't always sound the same way it looks on a page.

"There are two words here," he says, "that you have to practice, and if you don't get them right, you will never get on the bus for Coney Island."

Father knows that will get our attention because the only real reason we become altar boys is to get that extra day off from school and go on that trip every May.

"The words are *sacrificium* and *totiusque,* okay, and you will repeat them now as I say. *Sa-cra-fee-see-umm,* okay."

Someone is heard to say, *"Sa-cra-fish-ium,"* and Father makes us say the word ten times before we can get on to *totiusque.*

"*Toe-tea-us-quay,* okay," Father continues.

Someone says, *"Toe-ta-as-quay,"* and when we do that word twenty times, Father Hamilton looks over and sees I have put my hands, cassock and all, into my back pockets.

"Stand up straight, Smith," Father barks, "and put your hands at your side."

I jump, and then I get angry that he singled me out this way, embarrassing me. You would think that I was walking off with the tabernacle itself, the way he yelled. I feel like telling Father Ford, who is the nicest priest I know and the boss next to Monsignor O'Connor. He would tell Father Hamilton to let a kid put his hands in his back pockets if that's where he wants them.

Finally it is over, and Father O'Rourke says we can go home. The next time, he says, we will get to the *mea culpa,* and we should read in our missals about the Offertory.

I love being in this church. The lighting is always perfect, little candles throwing these big shadows that change whenever anyone walks around. I am always studying these gigantic paintings on the ceilings, and the ones on the walls with the gold around the halos that flashes like it is part of a huge neon sign. I mean, you can talk to God anywhere, but it is better here somehow.

Father Hamilton is just being a pain, I am thinking as I walk up First Avenue. I am the youngest in the altar boy class. Even though I'm only in third grade, I got high marks in vocabulary, so they made an exception. Usually, you have to be nine.

But school has been a lot of trouble to me recently, and I don't know why. I haven't been memorizing hardly anything, like the dates for the discoverers I have to know for the tests and the rivers in Brazil. You have to know these things to be promoted from third grade, but I just don't care. It's not that I want to do anything different, either. I just feel that school is as important to me right now as swimming in the East River in the wintertime.

I have tried to study my lessons every night, but after ten minutes I begin to get fidgety, and so I quit and listen to the radio. Sister Stella yells at me every day for not doing my homework, and then she puts her arms around me like she is sorry. Mommy knows that my grades aren't as good as they used to be. She thinks Sister doesn't pay much attention to me. But I keep telling her Sister Stella loves all the students because of Saint John Bosco.

MOMMY has made me put on a tie, and Billy, too. We don't have a real suit to wear, either of us, but we have on our best clothes, each in a white shirt, tie, school pants, and a plaid lumberman's jacket. I am wearing my old Klein's-on-the-Square shoes, but Mommy keeps talking about going to Thom McAn's to get new ones. I hope it is soon because the holes are getting to be silver-dollar holes, and I have to change the cardboard every night.

Mike Shurtliff did not pay Mommy for washing and ironing his shirts for a long time, because he is in show business and hasn't had a job. But he is our next-door neighbor, and Mommy told him he could pay her when he got the money. And today was the big day, the big payoff, because Mike gave her twice as much money as he owed her. He got a good job on Broadway with a play about the death of a salesman. Mommy said we should celebrate Mr. Shurtliff's good works, and so she is taking us out to dinner.

I am nine years old, but this is the first time I have ever gone to a restaurant. Well, I've been to Riker's for a Coke and to Nedick's for a hot dog and a couple of times to Emiliano's for pizza pie.

It is cold, and Mommy and Billy walk so fast that I have to run to keep up with them. We race to Third Avenue and then up to 58th Street. Mommy points, and I can see the big sign surrounded by lights. It says JOE'S ORIGINAL RESTAURANT.

Mommy holds the door for us, and I see as we go inside that the floor is made of marble and there are many small tables covered with white cloth, every one with a little vase of flowers. A man in a short black jacket and a bow tie asks Mommy what she wants.

"A table," Mommy says, "a table for three."

She is smiling, and I am glad to see her so happy.

"Do you have a reservation?" The man does not smile back.

"We don't even have a telephone," I whisper to Billy.

"I don't know," Mommy says, looking down at us.

I shrug my shoulders, and Billy looks dumb. He hardly ever looks dumb, but that's how he looks as he puts his hands out, palms up.

"I guess we don't have a reservation," Mommy says, "but we've been planning this for some time. A lifetime."

She smiles at Billy and then at the man.

He takes us to a table in the very back end of the restaurant, near two big double doors. Mommy stops in her tracks.

"Do you have another table, maybe where it's quieter?"

"This is what we have, lady," the man says.

"What about those?" Mommy asks, pointing at some empty tables.

"They are reserved," the man says.

"What for?" Billy asks.

"For people," the man says. "This is all. You can have it or not."

"Sure," Mommy says as she sits. I think Billy is going to argue with the man, but Mommy grabs his hand, and she never stops smiling. She is so happy to be here. As happy as I am.

Another man comes over and asks what we want.

Mommy picks up a menu from the table and reads it a minute. "Oh," Mommy says. She looks surprised.

"Well," the waiter says, tapping his foot.

"Could you give us a minute?" she says. She is still smiling as she watches the man leave, putting a pencil behind his ear.

"Boys," she says, "I was here once, but they have changed the menu since. It costs more than I thought, so we'll have a light touch, huh? I will have a salad to begin."

"Look," Billy says, "a shrimp cocktail. What's that?"

"It's too expensive is what it is," Mommy says.

"How about pork chops?" Billy asks.

"Too much."

"Probably," I say, "they give the tripe away for free here."

Mommy laughs at this.

"What's a Salisbury steak?" Billy asks.

"It's good for you," Mommy says.

"That means we can afford it, I guess," Billy says.

"It means it is very good for you," Mommy answers. "They put onions and a gravy over a steak that is chopped up."

"Chopped up how?" Billy asks. "Like a hamburger?"

"Better than a hamburger. You'll like it."

I can see that Mommy is pushing the Salisbury steak, and I am thinking I'll be glad to get it with the flowers and the linen napkins.

The man comes back, and Mommy asks him for a couple of the Salisbury steaks, a salad, and something called a knockwurst. All the names in this restaurant are strange and new. There is something on the menu called escargot, which Mommy said is a snail in a shell, and I can't think of anything that is more disgusting. I'm glad Mommy didn't tell us that escargot is good for us.

The Salisbury steak comes, and it's a big football of a hamburger, covered with gravy and surrounded by mashed potatoes. Mixed together it's the best hamburger I ever had, and if my fork could lift it, I would eat the bottom of the plate with a little more gravy. The man comes back after some other guy takes our plates away, and he asks what we will have for dessert.

Mommy gives him one of her smiles. "Could you come back in another minute?"

The waiter leaves, and Mommy turns to us, saying, "I have a great idea. Why not pick up some of the good and expensive Bryer's ice cream on the way home, from the French place on Second Avenue? They pack it by hand there."

"Okay," Billy says.

"Better than anything," I say.

Expensive or not, it would be nice to get something that is better than anything, anyway.

Mommy is holding the ice cream as we are walking home. Billy is holding her one arm, and I am holding on to the other as we walk into the wind.

"The ice cream," Mommy says, "will never melt in this weather."

I feel proud of my family as we walk together like this, just coming home from a restaurant, as good as anyone else in the neighborhood, as good as the Scarry family, who go out to eat once a week because the father is a bartender and gets a lot of big tips from the drunks on First Avenue. I know we shouldn't envy anyone and we shouldn't want anyone to envy us, but I can't help feeling good and special that we have been to Joe's Original Restaurant tonight.

THERE is always a line outside of Kips Bay Boys Club on Saturdays. Sometimes it goes down 52nd Street and around Second Avenue. Two boys come out; two boys go in. Everyone wants to be inside, and not just because everyone else is in there. The place is hopping with things to do. Boys are playing pool or Ping-Pong, swimming in the downstairs pool, making wooden lamps or pottery bowls in the shops, or they are in the main gym or the small gym on the roof or the lower gym in the basement. Midget mayhem, Archie calls the lower gym, but I don't know what mayhem is.

I am just a couple of boys from the entrance, and Archie sees me. He's got this way of whistling and then putting his hand in front of his face and pointing at you. He then curls his finger and yells out, "Hey, son." That means he wants you to stop something. Or sometimes, like now, it means he wants to see you.

Archie brings me to his office, a small cubicle with a desk, and then he leaves, saying, "I'll be right back."

I've never been in this office before, and I am wondering, What is the story here? Archie Mangini is the second banana at Kips Bay Boys Club, but he is the one you see every day. Mr. McNiven is the club boss, but he is always out trying to get money from people on Sutton Place.

I look around and read the brass plates on the trophies Archie has on his desk and on top of the filing cabinets—swimming trophies, basketball trophies, one for debating. I don't know how old he is, but he is out of college, someone told me. Maybe he's twenty-five, maybe a little more. I've heard guys say they wished Archie was their father because he's fun.

I would rather have my own father, though. I think about this for a minute as I sit down in a hard wooden armchair.

I know so little about my father. I wonder if he ever got any trophies. I saw a photograph of him in Mommy's drawer where he is standing in an empty lot, wearing a baseball glove. Maybe he got a baseball trophy. Who knows?

It's funny the amount of things I don't know about him, like would he want to go to the nine-o'clock Mass with Mommy? Or would he go to the twelve fifteen, like so many of the fathers I know, like Mr. Walsh and Mr. Scarry? And I wonder if he would wear a suit, like Mr. Walsh. I wonder if my father uses hair tonic in his hair. And would he make us eat tripe and beef liver, or would he buy us a dog so we could feed it the bad stuff under the table? Jeez, there are so many things to know, and I don't know any of it.

Archie comes into the office and closes the door behind him. He throws a pile of folders down on his desk.

"You know what these are?" he asks, holding up a folder.

"How should I know?" I answer. I have no idea what Archie wants me in his office for.

Archie looks at me for a minute. I am ten years old, and I guess he thinks I am being a snotty wise guy.

"These are reports I have to send to the city youth agency about certain kids who have gotten in a lot of trouble."

"So?" Why do I want to know this? I ask myself.

"So, Dennis," he says, "the reason kids get into trouble is that they begin to not care about things—their family, school, homework. Then you find out they don't even care about their future."

I know that if he is calling me Dennis and not calling me son, he means business here. Somebody from school must have talked to him. Maybe even my mother.

"So?" I ask, looking down.

"So," Archie says, "I met Father O'Rourke on the street yesterday, and he told me that you were having a hard time at school."

"I am not," I say. I don't like people talking behind my back, even if it is true. "Father O'Rourke has a big mouth, anyway."

"He didn't say you were in trouble or anything, but only that your brother gets such good grades in everything and you are not doing so good. Are you?"

"What does Billy's marks have to do with me?"

"I guess everybody expects more of you. You're in the fifth grade, and you should be doing things the right way by now. Is it too much to ask that you pay better attention to your schoolwork?"

I don't know why I should have to do as good as my brother in anything. He gets all the good marks, and he is great at all the sports, and what has that done for anybody? My mother is still over there every day on her hands and knees going from one end of Sutton Place to the other, nobody caring about her. Nobody cares if she has a decent day in her life, and she does everything right.

"You can do better, Dennis," Archie says. "And you know it."

All the statues in Archie's office are shining with the light that is shooting in from 52nd Street. Billy has a couple of trophies, but all I ever got is a silver medal for coming in second when I swam the breaststroke at the all-city swim meet.

"I don't give a s---, Archie," I say, still looking down.

"Watch your language, pal. Don't be like that with me."

"I just want people to mind their own business," I say.

"Business, son, can be all of life, caring about everything. That's the way it is at Kips Bay. If you're a part of this boys club, we're going to care about you."

"But," I say, getting up from my chair, "there's nothing wrong with me, and anyway, I don't care who cares."

I know I don't have to talk about it to Archie or to anyone if I don't want. It's a free country. I go to the door, thinking I don't need Archie and I don't need Kips Bay.

I turn the doorknob and pull, but nothing happens. I yank with all my might, and it is like the door is riveted shut. I look at Archie.

He is smiling.

"I can't get out," I say to him.

Archie gets up and walks to the door. He grabs the doorknob and kicks the bottom of the door. It opens like a garden gate.

"There's a certain way of doing everything, Dennis," he says, winking at me. "Running away from me is just not the right way."

He puts a hand on my shoulder and leads me back to the chair.

"We just want to give you a boost up," he says.

All right, I am thinking. I'll have to sit now and tell Archie that I'll do better in school. It won't take long.

I AM kicking a can all the way home, thinking that with every kick I am telling everybody to leave me alone. School is not the greatest place in the world, anyway, and if I wanted a trophy, I would practice my breaststroke. If I wanted good grades, I'd spend more time with my homework.

I give the can one last, mighty kick, and I can see the small crowd of women in front of my building. My mother never sits around with them, on the stoop or anywhere. And she never tells anybody anything. She doesn't want us to tell anybody anything, either. What they don't know won't hurt them, she always says.

Inside the apartment, my mother is sitting at the kitchen table, going over the little notebook where she writes down all the money she spends. She has a pencil in her hand. There are just three things she has to have money for all the time. She has to pay the bill at Rossi's grocery store, or we won't be able to get milk and bread. She has to pay the man that comes from the landlord every month. Also there is Mr. Karp, the insurance man; he comes every week to get twenty-five cents from us and from almost everybody in the building and in all the buildings on the block. My mother says she has to pay the insurance because if she dies without insurance, they will just throw her in the river, and the tide will take her to Africa or somewhere she doesn't want to go.

"If the tide would take me to Ireland," I remember her telling the insurance man one day, "I wouldn't have the insurance at all, but I'd put my bathing suit on and hope to die."

My mother has never been to Ireland, but her mother and father were born there and told her that it was more beautiful than heaven. I believe it. Everyone is always saying how beautiful Ireland is, and I wonder why they left it at all.

Now she stops writing in her book and stares off for a minute.

"Dennis," she says, "I think you should get a job. Every little bit we can put together would help. Now that you are ten, you are getting old enough to have a real job. Working, you know, is the second key to heaven."

"What's the first key?" I ask.

She laughs, saying, "Obeying your mother."

"I had a job, Mom," I say, "but you told me to quit it."

I had worked for two Saturdays at the drugstore on 49th Street and First Avenue. It was a delivery job, and the doctor there paid me ten cents a delivery. The only thing was that, after dusting every bottle on every shelf and washing the floor and cleaning the glass cases with the perfume, there were only two deliveries all day, and the doctor gave me twenty cents.

After the next week, when there was only one delivery and I did the floors and the cases and the bottles, my mother went down to the drugstore and showed the doctor the ten cents and told him he should be ashamed of himself. I was very embarrassed, but my mother told him that she wouldn't let me go to his drugstore again, even if I was dying with the consumption and he was giving away cough syrup. She left the dime on the counter and held my hand as we walked out of the store.

"You have to be careful about people," my mother said as we walked up First Avenue, "because you'll meet some who are never sorry for their sins."

I wish I could find a good job because every time someone talks about somebody being rich, they say he has a good job. I don't know where you get these good jobs, but I am going to ask Billy to help me.

IT IS Saturday morning, and I am playing off-the-point with Bobby Walsh down by the tennis courts on 55th Street. I am wearing a brand-new pair of dungarees my mother just bought me, and I'm feeling like I could win at anything today. Usually I get Billy's old dungarees, but these were a surprise and fit just right.

We are playing games of eleven, and I'm a little tired. I started the paper delivery job this morning, and I had to get up at five thirty to carry all those *New York Times* and *Daily News* through the hallways of Sutton Place.

I should have some money soon, because Billy got me the job. It's not a good job, but it will help. I am getting twenty cents an hour delivering the papers for Fat Walter, who runs the candy store on 57th Street and First Avenue. It takes about an hour and fifteen minutes to take the papers up the service elevators and through the hallways, but they only pay for an hour. "If you go fast," Fat Walter says, "you can do it in an hour."

Next week I'll have my own thirty cents to spend. I told my mother that I will give the rest to her.

SISTER Urban is looking over the class with that funny look she has every time she wants to lash out at someone. Raymond Rabbitscabbage, whose real name is Rasakavitch, farted, just a little noise. But it gives me an idea, and I put my hand in my shirt, cup it under my arm, and squeeze down. I am good at this, and it makes a terrific fart noise. Petey Poscullo laughs out loud, pointing at me, and Sister Urban is flying down the aisle.

"It wasn't me, Sister," I cry out, "I swear."

But that doesn't stop her. She grabs me. She pulls me by the arm, and I can see her hand go way back before she swings it around and slaps me hard across the face as she pulls me from the seat. I am stunned that she does this, and I yell.

"S---," I say, "I didn't do nothing that bad."

She pushes me to the back of the room and has me standing with my nose one inch from the brown wall. She puts her mouth next to my ear and yells at me.

"If you ever curse in this room again," she screams, "I will have you thrown out of this school as fast as you can blink."

Here, with my nose against the wall, I listen to the class start talking again about one of the saints. I wonder how come God lets a nun cream a kid like this in front of everyone.

My face is burning, and I try to rub it a little. But Sister Urban sees me and calls out from the front of the room. "You just put your hands at your side," she says, "or I'll tie them behind your back."

Whenever I go to church, I always ask God to help make everything better for everyone. I know that I'm ten years old, and it's 1950, and I have a job, and I'm supposed to act older and not care about God or church. But I love talking to God because I know He cares about me. Just like my mother does. But I worry that He has too many people talking to Him at the same time, and doesn't have time to get to me.

MY MOTHER holds my face in her hands.

"Look at this," she says. "What happened?"

There is no mirror in our bathroom, so my mother pulls me in front of the mirror above the kitchen sink.

"Just look," she says, pointing.

I can see Sister Urban's handprint in red across the side of my face. Now I guess I have to tell her what happened. And so I sit down in a kitchen chair and tell her about Rabbitscabbage and Petey Poscullo and how Sister Urban ran down the aisle.

"You just made a crack underneath your arm?"

"That's all I did, and Petey . . ."

"It is kid stuff," she whispers, "just kid stuff. Put your jacket on."

Now I am in the dark corridor of the second floor of St. John the Evangelist school, hoping against hope that Sister Urban is not to be found, but there she is, sitting at her desk reading papers.

"You wait here," my mother says.

I don't think I have ever seen her this mad.

The door is wide open, and I listen to what my mother has to say.

"I just want to tell you," she says, "that my son has a red mark across his face the exact size of your hand, and I don't give a fiddler's anything what he has done, you are never to touch him again, and you can come to see me and I will do all the punishing, but if you ever put your hand on my child again, I swear on all that is holy and good that I will come across the street to this school, and I will find you, and before everybody I will tear the hood off your head and put a match to it."

Sister Urban is as stunned as I was when she whacked me, and in less than a second my mother has me by the hand, and we are walking out of the school, across the street, and back up the stoop on 56th Street.

"She is going to hate me, Mom," I say as we walk up the gum-stained marble steps of the hallway.

"She'll do no such thing," my mother says. "She'll respect you."

I guess my mother is right. I know she wouldn't do anything to get me in trouble. But I'm glad about one thing, anyway: that there were no kids in the class when my mother got there.

Three

MY MOTHER has been seeing this guy named Tommy Quigley. Billy says that Quigley is a queer name and not a name to make you like someone. But she goes out with this Quigley sometimes, too much if you ask me. Quigley comes over and has dinner with us at the kitchen table. My mother makes fish sticks or something good like that when he comes.

"He is just a friend," she said one day when Billy asked her why he comes around.

I think of Daddy every time I see this Quigley guy, but Billy says that I shouldn't worry about it, that she has to have friends. She only has Aunt Kitty and Aunt Helen to make her laugh.

"Don't tell anyone he comes here," she told me and Billy.

She always wants to keep everything a secret. I guess she feels bad that this guy comes here when she already has a husband up in the hospital. I don't even know how she met him, and she wouldn't tell me, anyway. She never talks much about herself, except when she tells us how hard it was for her mother and father when they came here from Ireland. One day, though, I got her talking and she told me about growing up beside a firehouse in Brooklyn and that she loved the firemen, who would send her to the store for sandwiches when she was a little girl because they couldn't leave the firehouse, and then they always gave her a big tip. That's as much as I know about the way she grew up.

Billy told me he thinks her big secrets come from her being poor when she was little, that she didn't want to think about it anymore. I don't know what it's like to be poor like that, but I remember her saying that you are only poor if you miss a meal when you want one.

My mother went out with Quigley tonight. She said she'd be home at nine thirty, but she came back at eight. Billy was listening to the radio in the living room, and I was on a kitchen chair reading about Heidi. I don't know why my mother gets me these books. I'm in the sixth grade now and should be reading mystery stories.

She didn't say anything much when she came in. She just put her robe on and read a magazine, the way she does most nights.

Later, in the middle of the night, I hear an explosion.

Bang.

It is frightening, and I jump up out of my sleep, and I can see Billy is out of bed completely, in his underwear.

"What is it?" I ask.

"Somebody has kicked the door," Billy says.

I feel my stomach turning. Where is my mother?

Bang. The crash comes again.

I can feel my body shake. My mother is now up. She turns on the kitchen light.

Bang, pow.

Another loud kick, and this time I can see that the wood at the bottom of the door is caving in. I jump down from the bed, and Billy and I are standing here, shivering in our underwear, staring at our mother, wondering what she will do.

My mother reaches for the key to Mike Shurtliff's apartment, the one across the hall. Besides doing his shirts, she now cleans for him, and she hands me the key.

"I am going to open the door," she whispers, "and he will rush in, maybe. I don't know."

"Who is it, Mom?" Billy asks. His hand is on her arm, and it looks so small there even though he is thirteen.

"It's Quigley," my mother says, still whispering. "Dennis, you have to go across the hall. The lock is easy. Just turn it and push.

There is a phone in Mike's living room. Call the operator. Tell her to send the police. Can you do that?"

Oh, God, I never had to do anything so important as this.

"What about Billy?" I ask. "I want Billy to come with me."

"I need Billy here," she says, pushing me to the door.

"Can I get dressed?" I ask.

"No," she says. "There isn't time."

Bang. Pow. Bang.

This time the door is cracked open. I can see Quigley's shoe.

"Go away!" my mother screams at the top of her lungs. "Go away, Tommy. The police are coming."

There is another kick, and his foot comes all the way through the door. He kicks more, and his foot gets higher and higher.

My mother pushes me to where she wants me to stand, and she puts Billy behind her. She gives me a wild sort of look, and her eyes seem like they are on fire. She then opens the door in one sudden jerk, and Quigley grabs her, and I don't know if I should try to stop him, to hit him with something. I am eleven, and I should be able to beat this Quigley up.

"Go, Dennis!" my mother screams. "Fast."

I push past them and run to the door across the hall. But my hand is shaking too much. Christ, I am thinking, help my hand put this key in the lock. Finally it falls into the lock hole.

I go into the living room, but I can't find the light. Oh, God, turn on the light for me. I go back into the kitchen and feel around for the string that I know is hanging from the ceiling, but I cannot find it, and my body is shaking much worse now. At last I pull the string, and the light shines right on the telephone, and I dial zero and tell the operator to send the police because someone is killing my mother. She asks me for the address three times.

"You just stay here on the phone," the operator says, "until I make a connection."

"What connection?" I say. "I have to go."

"Stay on the phone!" She is yelling at me. My mother is being killed, and this operator is yelling at me.

A man comes on the phone now, a policeman, I guess.

"What is the address?" he asks.

"I already told the operator," I say. "Three thirty-seven East Fifty-sixth Street."

"What is the matter?" he is now asking.

"What is the matter? My mother is being killed by Quigley. He's killing her! Don't you understand?"

I want to hang up the phone, but the policeman keeps asking why all this is happening, and I tell him that I was sleeping, and how should I know why any of this is happening?

I am still on the telephone when I hear the police. They are right outside. They are running down the hall; then I can hear them wrestling with Quigley.

I drop the phone and run. Quigley is cursing, and the policemen are punching him as they drag him. All the neighbors have opened their doors, and I know that my mother will be mortified.

Where is she? I wonder. I begin to panic. I don't care about the neighbors and if they see me running through the hallway in my underwear. I just want to see my mother.

MY MOTHER is holding me in her arms. I am eleven years old, and my mother is holding me in her arms like I was two. She is sitting on a kitchen chair, and she is just staring at the hole in the kitchen door, and she is rocking. Billy is standing next to her, with his hand on her shoulder.

"I just have you guys," my mother says, wiping a tear off on the shoulder of my undershirt. "I just have you guys to help me."

THE summer breeze is whipping my face, and it seems like we are going a hundred miles an hour. Billy has gone on a sleep-away trip with Kips Bay Boys Club to play a basketball game at some other boys club in Connecticut. His junior varsity basketball team has won the finals in New York City, and now they are playing other states for the championship. Billy is beginning to collect more trophies than Archie has in his whole office.

My mother has a new friend. His name is Artie, and I am sitting in the back of his brand-new 1952 Chevrolet. It is a hot day, and all the windows are open. This is the first new car I have ever been in, and we are going along some highway, just taking a drive, and I put my head out of the window. The force of the breeze is like being on some ride in Coney Island, like flying through the air.

Suddenly I hear the sound of a siren, and I turn to see a policeman riding beside us on a motorcycle.

"Damn," Artie says.

The policeman tells Artie to stop, and we go up on the sidewalk of the highway. It is just like I have seen in the movies, and I watch closely as the policeman slowly gets off his motorcycle and slowly takes his gloves off and slowly walks over to Artie. It is like he practiced it a hundred times.

The policeman leans over into the window.

"You know how dangerous that is?" he asks.

"What is that, Officer?" Artie says. "I don't think I was speeding or anything."

"The boy," the officer says.

"You mean Dennis?" my mother says.

Artie turns to look at me. I can feel myself shrinking up.

"What did you do?" he says in a voice like he is yelling.

"I didn't do anything," I say.

They are all staring at me, and I don't know what I've done.

"He had his head out the window," the policeman says.

"You had your head out the window?" Artie repeats.

"You should get an act together," I say.

"Don't be smart, young man," my mother says.

The policeman warns Artie to control the passengers in his car.

"I'm sorry, Officer," Artie says.

"I'm sorry, Artie," my mother says.

"I'm sorry, Mom," I say, though I don't think I've done anything so bad. But I know it will make her feel better. People always feel better when you say you're sorry, and instead of saying hello to people, sometimes I think we should just say I'm sorry when we meet them.

There is a silence in the car as we drive forward.

"It's very dangerous to put your head out of the window," Artie says after a while. "Twelve years old, you should know better."

There is more silence. I know that Artie wants to say more, but he is waiting for my mother to say something. He has known her for just a short time. I know he doesn't want to make her upset.

But my mother doesn't say anything.

I wish it were my father driving the car instead of Artie. Sometimes I feel so alone when I think about my father. I see other boys at church or going to the subway with their fathers, and I wish I could do what they do.

I can't talk to anyone about it. Even Billy. Sometimes I wonder what Billy thinks about it, about our father, but I know that if I ever say anything, I will just get him pissed off that I brought it up. I'm just the youngest in the family, and everybody expects me to keep my mouth shut, I think. There is just this forget-all-about-it attitude that covers our lives like wallpaper.

But here is Mom with this Artie guy, and I don't know what to think about him. He is not such a bad guy, and at least he doesn't get drunk like Quigley did, but he has no right to yell at me, not for anything.

He's an Italian, and my mother never really talked so nice about the Italians on the block. She used to call them the guineas, but I haven't heard her say that since she met Artie.

Sometimes I think she should marry somebody like Artie; then she wouldn't have to work so hard cleaning apartments. She wouldn't have to hide the money she earns from the welfare, either.

I know, though, she could never get married again, because we are Catholic, and being a Catholic means that you only get married once. Maybe if she were born a Protestant or a Jew, she would have a better deal, but she says that it's bad luck to wish that you were someone else. Maybe things will change for her someday. Maybe things will get better enough so that she can get up from her hands and knees on Sutton Place.

Damn. I love my mother so much, and I can't understand why God doesn't change things for her.

SOMETIMES on Sundays all the aunts and the uncles come over. They get together to sing or to talk politics. *Diddley-do and the gen-*

eral's through is what Uncle Bob sings, because he doesn't like Ike. It is always a day for Irish songs and the chances of the Democrats and some salami and bologna sandwiches and lots of pretzels.

Billy and I look forward to these days because the cousins are good stickball players, and we get a game going on 56th Street. There are about ten of them. They come from Brooklyn and Queens, the cousins, and coming into the city is a hotshot thing for them. City guys, they think, are somehow tougher.

Billy and my cousin Bobby are fourteen and always after the girls. Sometimes they go down to the river with the girls to watch the Pepsi-Cola sign blink on and off. The 51st Street park down by the river is always dark, because there are so many trees there, and they sit there with whatever girls they can get to go with them, and they try to feel them up.

I am only twelve, but I wish I was thirteen, because the girls don't mind walking down by the river with a teenager.

There is not much room in the kitchen, and the four kitchen chairs and the one from Mommy's room seemed squeezed. The women, along with Mom's cousin Tim, sit in the chairs, and the rest stand around, leaning on the stove or the icebox. Uncle Andy is sitting on the top of the bathtub, next to the sink.

Uncle Bob pulls me aside and asks me how I am doing in school. I know I hate school, but I don't want to say this to anyone. It is like being on welfare, and you have to keep it a secret.

"Okay," I answer him, "I guess."

"That's the boy," Uncle Bob says. "Always do good in school. You could get to be a bishop and kiss all them nuns."

Uncle Bob is a bartender and makes fun of everything. He slips me a dollar bill, new and crunchy. It is not my birthday or my confirmation day or anything, and I feel funny about it.

"Thank you," I say.

I take the dollar to our little room and put it in my top drawer. Later on I can give it to my mother.

It is getting late, and the keg of beer that Uncle Andy plopped in the sink is almost empty, but Mom says she has some bottles of Ballantine in the icebox. They are all singing "At a Cottage Door" for the millionth time, and I know it by heart now, and "God Bless You and Keep You, Mother Macree" and "Let Erin Remember."

I always sing "The Rose of Tralee" whenever anyone asks me. The first verse, anyway, and the chorus, because I never learned the second. It is my song, my party song, and everyone always has to do a party song.

"C'mon, Dennis," Aunt Kitty says, "give us a song."

"Yeah," my cousin Eileen says, "belt it out, will ya?"

It doesn't take much encouragement to get me in the middle of the kitchen. My left hand is on the keg of beer, my right on the kitchen table, which is filled from one end to the other with glasses and bowls of potato chips. The aunts and uncles all around, and the cousins, and my brother, Billy, too. All standing in this kitchen where you wouldn't think more than three people could stand.

I have a high, clear, choirboy's voice, and I sing away at "The Rose of Tralee" the way I sing away at the "Gloria" or the Kyrie at the eleven-o'clock High Mass. When I get to the chorus, which I know my mother loves, I try to make every word count.

"She was lovely and fair
As the rose in the summer,
But t'was not her beauty alone that won me.
Oh, no, t'was the truth in her eyes ever dawning
That made me love Mary
The Rose of Tralee."

It is my favorite because it always makes me wonder how someone can know when they see the truth in someone's eyes. Most people I know have eyes that make you want to hide, stern eyes, like the nuns. I guess my mother's eyes have the truth in them, especially when they shine with a tear or two. Maybe that is why she cries when sad things happen or when she gets fed up with something, these tenement tears that she says are not really important, but that just come with the territory.

They all clap and cheer when I am done, and Uncle Bob tries to give me a cigar, but I laugh it off as Aunt Kitty gives me a kiss. It all makes me feel good.

"That Dennis," Aunt Helen says. "I wonder who his Rose of Tralee is."

She grabs me and begins to give me a kiss. I try to be friendly, but I think I'm too old to be getting kissed by everyone. I look at my mother, and she's got her hands together as if she's praying.

"It's my mother's song," I say. "She's the Rose of Tralee."

Everyone laughs, and my mother says, "Blarney." But she's beaming. It's like I just gave her a Christmas present.

Everyone sings in the family. Uncle Bill sings "Phil the Fluter's Ball," and everyone tries to sing along as he slaps his knee and stamps his foot. Mom sings "Paddy McGinty's Goat," because it is the one song her own mother taught her as a kid. I like listening to her voice. She only sings when she is with the family like this. She never sings around the house.

When Uncle Andy sings "Danny Boy," Aunt Kitty complains.

"It is such a sad song," she says, "leaving flowers on the grave and all. Let's just sing about the good times."

"Are there good times really?" Mom says. "Sometimes I think there's just different times, maybe a little good, maybe a little not so good."

"Oh, come on, Mary," Aunt Helen says, "there's lots of good times. We are all here, and that's something."

"Well," Mom replies, "good or bad, you still have to get through the day."

"Yeah, sure," Aunt Helen says, "and the Queen of England has to get through the day, too. But I bet we are having a better time."

Four

I AM standing in the courtyard, yelling up between the corridor of the high walls. "Hey, Mom," I am yelling, trying hard to avoid looking at the spot where I remember Crazy Mario Giambetta sprawled out like a pancake. The courtyard is dirty, garbage piled up in the corners, some old newspapers blowing around in the breeze. The supers don't do such a good job in the backyards on 56th Street.

"Hey, Mom!"

Looking up, I try to see between sheets, pillowcases, and underwear that are in lines from window to window, and from window to the line pole in the middle of the alleyway.

"Hey, Mom!"

Where is she? I wonder. I want to see *The Greatest Show on Earth* with all the guys from 56th Street. And the girls. Marilyn Rolleri is going, and there is no one in the seventh grade as pretty as Marilyn Rolleri.

Finally, between the army of flying sheets, I see the fourth-floor window open, and my mother is sticking her head out.

"Yes," she says. "Stop yelling."

"Mom," I say in a slightly lowered yell, "can I have a quarter to go see *The Greatest Show on Earth?*"

"No, not today." The window closes, and she disappears.

I feel very sad suddenly because I can see in my mind all the guys walking down to the Loew's Lexington, cracking jokes under the Third Avenue El, trying to sneak up past the lobby goldfish pool to the balcony, where you have to be more than sixteen, or going off to the side of the loge and grabbing a smoke.

And I can see one of the guys putting his arm around Marilyn Rolleri's chair, then bringing his arm down until he feels her arm, then maybe over more until she slaps him. But maybe she won't slap him, and I very much want to be the boy she doesn't slap.

"Hey, Mom!" The window opens again.

"Mom," I say, "please?"

"No."

"Mom, please. Why can't I go when everyone else is going?"

"Come up here," she says, and closes the window again.

"Hey, Mom!" I see her head once more. "C'mon, Mom, I just want you to wrap a quarter in a piece of newspaper and throw it down to me."

"No," she says, "and you come up here right this minute. Don't answer me again."

I can see the window slamming down. I don't want to climb the stairs, but I know now that she is mad, and she'll only be madder if I don't go up. I know, too, that she is going to say no again.

In my living room, I am sitting on the hard spring that is popping up almost through the cushion of the couch. Mom sits in the small chair across from me. There is just room for the couch and the small chair and the radio.

"I wish you wouldn't do that," my mother says.

"Do what, Mom?" I am in for it, because she always begins complaining when she says "I wish."

"Yell up in the yard," she says, "so that all the neighbors on Fifty-sixth Street will know that I am a woman that does not have a quarter to give her own son when he wants to go to the movies. You have to learn better manners than that."

Here we go again with the better manners, I am thinking. My mother is always saying that I should get better manners, and my brother, Billy, too. It's like an excuse to not talk about something.

My mother is looking at me now in a kind of hard way. Not in an angry way, but still, I can tell she is unhappy.

"It is not right," she says, "that I don't have the quarter to give you to go with your friends, but I don't. Can't you see that I would give it to you if I had it in my bag or saved up somewhere? But there are no quarters, Dennis, not even any of your money from the newspapers, or Billy's, and you shouldn't make me say that out the window to the whole world. Can't you understand that?"

Well, I do understand. But I also want to go see *The Greatest Show on Earth* and try to get my arm around Marilyn Rolleri. I can't say it, though. I couldn't say that to her.

MY AUNT Kitty lives down on the ground floor of our building, and she always has her door open. She is my father's sister, the one that always has a bottle of beer in her hand.

Aunt Kitty has a high whining voice, and I can hear it as I jump the last five steps of the stairs. So I walk down the hall to her apartment and find her sitting at her kitchen table with my uncle Tracy, who is married to my father's sister Josie. There are two quarts of Ballantine beer on the table. I begin to think about the empties, but I know that I won't ask, because my mother would be pretty mad if I asked Aunt Kitty for anything.

"How's the little rug rat?" my uncle says to me.

This is what my uncle Tracy calls everyone under fifteen, so that he doesn't have to remember anyone's name. He's got eight kids, and he calls them Doodlebug, the Wheel, Sore Thumb, Kit Kat, Hole in the Head, Granite Head, Betty Boop, and Tarzan. They have real names like Tommy, Joey, Elizabeth, and so on, but I think he has forgotten the originals.

"Great, Uncle Tracy," I answer. "What are you doing?"

He's got a puddle of beer in front of him, and he is soaking a dollar bill in it. On the other side of the table he is soaking a twenty.

"I'm going to show Aunt Kitty," he says, "how to make eighteen dollars seventy cents, and two beers, out of absolutely nothin'."

I sit next to my aunt. She is talking at the top of her lungs, and so I pretend to lean on my elbow and hold a hand over my ear to soften the cackle of her voice. It is only ten thirty in the morning, and they are both red-eyed.

"See, Kitty," Uncle Tracy says, "just take the corner of the bill like this and keep picking at it, slowly. See? A bill is nothing but two pieces of printed paper stuck together."

The twenty-dollar bill is now in halves, and he lays them out carefully in the puddle of beer, pressing out every wrinkle. He does the same with the one-dollar bill. He is like a surgeon doing an operation, and when he has the four parts laid out before him, he puts the back part of the dollar on the front part of the twenty, and the front part of the dollar on the back part of the twenty so that it appears he has two twenties.

"You see," he says as he presses them smooth, "you have to do this in a bar that has just a little light, 'cause the bartenders never turn the bill over. And so you lay the twenty down, dollar side down, for one fifteen-cent beer, and he shoves it in the cash register and gives you nineteen eighty-five change. And then you go to the next bar and do the same thing."

Uncle Tracy always does things that are like magic. He works at the Brooklyn Navy Yard, and since he has so many kids, he never has enough money for drinks after work. So he has all these tricks that he bets on at the bar. He can make an eight-toothpick square into an eight-toothpick rectangle by moving just two toothpicks.

"Uncle Tracy can do anything," Aunt Kitty says, wiping up the beer on the table.

Uncle Tracy is the only relative I know who has a car. And he has a great car, too, a '38 Buick, a huge boat with a floor shift.

"Hey, Uncle Tracy," I say, "can you teach me how to drive?"

"Are you kiddin'?" he says. "The cops will throw away the cell key 'less I get sober. Don'tcha know anybody else?"

"I know lots," I say, "but they don't have cars."

Aunt Kitty pours another beer for Uncle Tracy.

"Hey, rug rat," he says, "here." I am twelve years old, and my uncle throws me his car keys. "Find someone to teach ya. The car's in front, but don't use too much gas, will ya?"

Aunt Kitty laughs. "Uncle Tracy is a riot," she says in a very loud voice, and I hope my mother isn't passing in the hall. My mother would give back these keys faster than a camera could take a picture.

On the stoop, I see Davy Weld coming up the block. I think he is sixteen, and maybe he has one of those junior licenses I heard about. I know he's got a piece of a sister named Tuesday, and I heard she's an actress on television. We don't have a television.

"Hey, Davy," I call out to him, "you have a license?"

"Yeah, sure," he says, "I have a license from California."

"You want to teach me how to drive?" I ask.

"Sure," he says, grinning. "I only drive Cadillacs."

"I got a '38 Buick, floor shift with an on-the-floor starter."

"No bull?" Davy says, his eyes now open pretty wide.

Fifteen minutes later we are driving down the East River Drive. The speed limit is thirty, but Davy is going seventy, and I'm beginning to worry that the cops might be around.

"Do you have any cigarettes?" I ask him. I don't smoke yet, but I am thinking that this might get him to slow the car up.

Davy hands me a cigarette from his shirt pocket and pulls over on 14th Street to strike a match.

"Maybe later," I say, putting the cigarette in my pocket, "but, for now, could you teach me something?"

Davy lights one and then drives into a deserted street by a large Con Edison plant. He tells me to get behind the wheel.

"You can drive home," he says. "I don't want the risk anymore."

"What risk?" I ask.

"Getting caught," he says, "without a license."

I think about this as I go around the car to get behind the wheel.

"I thought," I say to him, "you had a license from California."

"Naw," he says. "I have a sister lives out there, but I'm not sixteen yet." He offers me another cigarette. "It looks cool if you are smoking behind the wheel. It will make you look older."

But, I am thinking, I'm still only twelve, and I can't even see over the steering wheel. So how cool can I look?

I put the cigarette between my lips and both hands on the steering wheel. This is as close to king of the mountain that I've ever been. I turn the wheel back and forth.

Davy lights a match for me. He is already smoking heavily on his cigarette and flicking it like crazy. But I think of my mother. She has a way of finding out everything. She will smell smoke in my clothes or in my nostrils. And then she will take me to Father O'Rourke, who will throw me out of the altar boys and make me take a don't-upset-your-mother pledge or something. Or worse, he'll give me to Father Hamilton to face my punishment, and I'll have to say three months' worth of prayers.

I hand the cigarette back to Davy.

"Not today. I don't want to smoke and drive at the same time."

"Okay," Davy says. "So step on the clutch and put the gearshift way up into first."

I look down, and I can see that there is about three inches between the clutch and the end of my foot, even with my toes stretched out. I am already on the edge of the seat.

It is impossible to drive this way, and so I get out of the car. Davy gets back in the driver's seat.

"So teach me how to drive, anyway," I say. "Just show me."

Davy goes through the motions, and I ask him to do a couple of things twice. I think I know it all by the time he parks the car back on First Avenue and 56th Street, and I can't wait until I get another three inches on my leg.

Uncle Tracy really is a riot, I am thinking as I begin down the hall to my aunt Kitty's to return the keys.

Aunt Kitty has the door open, and I can hear her jabbering a mile away. They are sitting in her living room.

"It's rotten what they do to him," Aunt Kitty says. "They are always beating him up and taking his smokes."

Who is she talking about? I am wondering as I lay the keys down on the kitchen table. I stand by the door and wait.

"He tried to run away once," she goes on, "during the time they were giving him the shock treatment, and they beat him up good. They said he fell in the shower. What a mess he was."

"Holy s---," Uncle Tracy says. "Where is this place?"

"Someplace called Greenland State Hospital."

I know that Greenland State is the insane asylum. The nuthouse. I've heard guys in the street sometimes say that other guys should be sent away to Greenland State.

"He'll never get better," Aunt Kitty says. "I feel sorry for poor Mary and the burden she has with those two sons."

What burden? Is this my mother she is talking about?

"And the welfare," she says. "What a mess. At least I have the pension. But she's lucky she got that apartment upstairs."

My mind is now racing. Is there somebody upstairs who is on the welfare and has two kids and is named Mary and who isn't my mother?

I am running up the stairs now, two by two, and I feel the tears running down the sides of my face. I'm twelve years old, and I shouldn't be crying, but I want to yell at her, to tell her how mad I am that she has told me all these years about my father having the bad legs and that the hospital won't let me and Billy in because we are too young, that something fell off the truck at Railway Express and landed right on top of him and on top of his legs, and all these years I have pictured him being squished underneath some great package and his face tormented by the pain, and I always thought he was getting well and he would come home and take me to the ball game at Yankee Stadium.

But it is all a lie. Why didn't she tell me?

The O'DWYER FOR MAYOR sticker is still on the fourth floor window, and I stop there to catch my breath, stretching my eyes as wide as they will go, thinking of the words I will say to her.

I know every time I think of something that I won't say that. I can't. I can't yell at my mother. I can't make her sad. I am already a burden, Aunt Kitty said. And Billy, too.

And it is my fault. How could I believe that he was in a hospital with bad legs? All these years, no one said anything. Maybe Billy wanted to believe it, too, that his father is in the hospital with bad legs, or bad something, but not because he was flipped, not because he was walking around with wide eyes and a blank, scary stare or beating himself against a wall or lying in a corner of a padded cell with a straitjacket on.

I am twelve years old. I should have known.

My mother should have told me. Why doesn't she trust me?

Five

FINALLY I am thirteen and old enough to go to the teenage canteen at Kips Bay Boys Club, but my mother is acting like I am still twelve or something.

"I'm in the eighth grade," I am saying, "and I don't know why I can't stay out until midnight. Everyone else stays out."

I am sitting at the kitchen table. My mother is at the sink cleaning those pork chops that she boils with sauerkraut and potatoes.

"C'mon, Mom," I say, "just until eleven thirty, then."

"You have a lot of nerve," my mother says, "to expect to go gallivanting around with the report card you brought home. When you start getting marks like your brother, Billy, I will think about giving you any special privileges, but for now you'll be here at ten o'clock if you know what's good for you. Otherwise you can stay home and brood about it."

This is exactly the trouble with trying to make sense with my mother. She's always saying if I know what's good for me, but when I tell her what's good for me, she never pays attention. It is only her definition of good that we get to talk about.

Billy is up in the Bronx at school, Cardinal Hayes, and he is probably still at basketball practice. Even on a Friday. He made the varsity team, and he is only in his second year. Billy is good at everything, and when he graduated from St. John's, most of the parents got pretty mad because he won so many of the medals.

Just recently Billy won the Boy of the Year at Kips Bay, and they gave him a scholarship to a place called Exeter up in New Hampshire, a boarding school. Mom went up to Cardinal Hayes to talk to the principal, Monsignor Fleming, and he told her that Exeter was a Protestant place and it would not be good for Billy's soul, so he is not going. He's got a scholarship at Cardinal Hayes, anyway, because of the fact that we are on welfare and Billy plays basketball.

I wonder about Billy's soul, and then I wonder, What is a Protestant and why is it so bad to be one? I only know that being a Catholic is better. We have to do things, like love God, do good, avoid evil. Protestants don't even have to go to church on Sunday if they have something else to do. If we don't go to church on Sunday, we go right to hell when we die.

We never miss Mass in our house, and even if we did miss once in a while, I don't think Billy would be available to be a Protestant, no matter how many teachers at Exeter tried to get him to be one. Anyway, Billy's too tough, and it would take four or five guys to hold him down if they wanted to make a Protestant out of him.

I wish my mother would treat me like a teenager.

"I don't want to stay home," I say.

"Then be home at ten," my mother says, now scrubbing out a big pot, "and do your homework the way your brother always does his homework before he goes to sleep."

She is always telling me that I should get better grades, and I guess she doesn't have any choice except to use Billy as an example. Sister Alphonsus always does that, and Archie down at Kips does it, too. Everybody thinks Billy is doing great in everything, and it's easy for them to say I'm not doing so great.

I wish I could tell my mother how much I think school is a waste of time. That I would rather be out working somewhere and having a quarter in my pocket to go to the movies or get a hamburger at Riker's if I want one. But she would just argue with me.

Everyone at school is always yelling at you, making you feel like you did something wrong by getting up in the morning. My mother doesn't realize that there is so much yelling at St. John's. The nuns yell at you for running in the playground during recess; the principal yells at you if you're late to lineup. And everyone yells about getting better marks.

Sister Alphonsus doesn't let the smallest thing pass without yelling, and almost everyone stays after school every day for something or other. Yesterday I had to stay because I got out of the line at lunchtime to tie my shoe. I feel like I am in some prison movie when I am in school, where everyone is against you and your only job there is to find a way to escape.

I AM sitting on the floor now in the auditorium-size game room of Kips Bay. The room is pretty dark, and there are spotlights shining down on the dance floor in the middle of the room.

I am in my powder-blue sports jacket, and I am talking with Walsh and Scarry, drinking the small bottles of Coke they gave us for free. Archie is at the door, checking the club cards.

Some slow music starts, and there is a rush of boys going across the dance floor for the girls.

"I'm going to ask Marilyn Rolleri to dance," I say, getting up.

"Good luck," Walsh says.

"Those Italian girls," Scarry says, laughing, "like the sausage."

"Yeah, yeah," I say as I walk away and toward Marilyn.

She looks at Gilda Galli as she gets up to dance with me, saying, "Mind my place."

I walk to the middle of the dance floor and turn to see if she followed me. She is there, her hands flat against a tight black skirt, which wraps her down to her ankles. It is so tight I can see the outlines of her thighs.

I don't know what to say to her and just grab her around the waist and pull her close to me. The nuns say that you should leave room for the Holy Ghost when you dance, but I don't think there is enough room between us for one of Uncle Tracy's toothpicks.

Her hair is falling behind her, halfway down her back, in long black curls. We are dancing, but we are hardly moving at all. I put my face against hers. My lips slide softly over her cheek.

I could ask her any number of things, like "How are your ballet lessons?" or "How do you get along with your parents?" But I wonder how many opportunities like this I am going to get. Just get it over with, I say to myself.

I slide my lips up to her ear. "Could I take you home tonight?"

She knows I like her, but she doesn't seem impressed.

"I have to go," she says, "with Barbara Cavazzine and Gilda Galli to Emiliano's for a pizza after the dance."

I picture myself, just for a moment, saying "I can't go. I have to be home before ten, or my mother will kill me."

I would never say that to Marilyn. She would think I'm a stupid shmo, a kid. Oh, Marilyn.

Johnnie Ray begins to sing "The Little White Cloud That Cried," and I feel myself up against her thigh. She is pushing into me. Oh, God. There are a hundred kids around us, some doing the fox-trot, some doing the fish, but we are grinding. I feel like I won the grand prize in some happiness contest, and I'm hoping that Archie doesn't see us. You're not supposed to do the fish, and you're especially not supposed to do the grind.

"As I went walking down by the river," Johnnie Ray is singing, and I am thinking that I would like to take Marilyn down by the river, to sit with her on a 51st Street park bench, to put my hand all over her tight skirt, to watch the Pepsi-Cola sign blink on and off across the river, to move my hand softly, quietly, into her blouse.

"Why don't you come to Emiliano's for a pizza with us?" she asks in a whisper.

"I can't," I say, " 'cause I have something to do."

"What do you have to do?"

Her breath is going all over my neck and the side of my face, and her legs are like hot wax against me.

"Just something to do," I say. "That's all. Some other time."

My mother, if you think about it, has ruined my whole night, just because of my report card. And I don't care what anybody says, it isn't fair to get punished like this. I could get good grades like Billy if I wanted, don't they know that?

It just doesn't matter to me, the famous report card, is all.

I guess my mother thinks that somewhere between ten and eleven o'clock that, because of a bad report card, I am going to murder someone or that someone is going to murder me. So I have to leave everyone and be home at ten. It's not right.

No one has to go home at ten o'clock. And everyone but me is going to Emiliano's for pizza.

So now I am alone on Second Avenue. Everyone else is behind me, walking slower, taking his or her time. I suddenly want to run, and I sprint forward. It's not that I am late. I am running like mad because I want the wind against my face, and if I didn't have to be home at ten, I think I could run all the way to the Bronx.

I AM lying here under the bunk bed, thinking. It's dark. All I can see above me is the metal of a bedspring and squares of swollen mattress protruding down.

Yesterday, Friday, was a two-time-terrible day.

Diane Gillespie threw up in the girls' clothes closet, and Sister Alphonsus sent me down to the basement to find the school custodian. On the way up I met Marilyn Rolleri in the stairway. I thought she was a gift from heaven when I saw her there, kneeling down to pick up a pencil case she had dropped. I knelt down and put my fingers around the case just as she was picking it up. Her large brown Italian eyes were looking me up and down.

Oh, Marilyn, I was thinking, what am I going to do? You are here in the quiet of the staircase, you with a smile of perfect teeth and a backside molded by an artist.

We were both standing then, our fingers wrapped around her

pencil case, and her smile was coming closer to me. No, I was moving closer to her. I don't know what got into me. I closed my eyes a little and leaned in so close. I thought her breath smelled like what love should smell like, soft and airy and warm. I let go of the case and put my arms around her, and we leaned back onto the wired glass of the staircase wall, and we kissed.

I breathed in her life's breath and let the wetness of her lips enter my mind so that it will never be forgotten.

Not a single word was said between us. She gave me that one long kiss, and trotted up the stairs so fast she was already sitting when I opened the door to class.

I waited for her in the schoolyard when we broke for lunch. She was with Barbara Cavazzine, and I asked if we could talk.

They both stopped, and Marilyn came toward me.

"I know," she whispered, "that you want to ask me to go out with you, but I am going to go steady with Raymond Connors."

"Right."

That was all I could get out. "Right."

But it wasn't right, not after having her lips pressed against mine for, what, a minute at least. One glorious, historic minute. It was like she had given me a hundred dollars and then took it away. And now I have this love in my heart for her, but there is no her.

I wanted to shout, but I remembered what my mother said about being polite all the time. If you are polite in the good times, you will also be polite in the bad times, when it matters the most.

Raymond Connors, who had enough red hair and enough teeth for triplets. I like Raymond Connors, but he doesn't even know how to do the lindy. Why would Marilyn go steady with him when she could, well, get anyone she wanted?

All afternoon I could hardly pay attention to Sister Alphonsus. We were going over the grammar part of the state regents examination, and I was getting all the right answers. At least when I did them, for I was doing one and skipping one, and every time I skipped one, I thought about Marilyn.

Sister Alphonsus kept looking at my answer sheet and shaking her head, and at the end of the day she asked me to stay.

"You're hopeless, Dennis," she said, "and I don't think we will be able to let you graduate unless things are changed around here. I want to see your mother."

"What for?" I asked. I suddenly got very nervous.

"Your report card was not good," she said, "and you are falling behind in everything."

"I do my homework," I said.

"You have not done a complete homework since the term started, Dennis," she said, "and do not argue with me. Bring your mother in fifteen minutes before the start of school on Monday morning, no ifs, ands, or buts. Good afternoon."

Good afternoon, b.s., I was thinking. I was exploding inside. I am so tired of all of it, everyone telling me what I should be doing, nobody doing anything to help me, Marilyn Rolleri making out with Raymond Connors, my father walking around in circles in some upstate hospital, Archie telling me I could be great, but he never says what I could be great at, and my mother crying, sighing, yelling, and pleading with me almost every day to spend more time with my homework. It is just too much to put up with.

"Good afternoon, Sister," I said quietly, being polite.

But something inside me was running, running into some dark forest where you can't see two inches in front of you. I felt myself walking slowly away from Sister Alphonsus, but my feet were going fifty miles an hour, and the next thing I knew, I had changed my clothes and I was in my mother's room and I was searching through the drawers of her dresser, looking for the welfare money she keeps hidden away. I looked in every drawer. I needed some money, but I didn't know why. I only knew that I had to keep running, that I couldn't stay and talk to my mother and tell her that Sister Alphonsus wants to tell her that I am not going to graduate, because I only did some of the grammar questions when I wasn't thinking about Marilyn kissing Raymond Connors with teeth enough for three people.

I needed a cigarette. I started smoking just after I learned how to drive with Davy Weld, but I have never smoked a cigarette in my house. I grabbed the carton of Old Golds that my mother had in her bottom drawer and shook out a pack. I know that she knows how many packs are left, the way mothers just know these things, so I can't take the whole pack. But I can get a cigarette out without her knowing, the way Uncle Tracy would do it, and I carefully opened the bottom end of the cellophane and then the bottom of the pack. I pulled out one cigarette from the exact center, ran to the kitchen for the glue bottle, glued the paper and then the cellophane back together again, and put the pack back into the carton.

In the living room, I lit the cigarette and leaned far back into the couch. I knew that my mother was cleaning some apartment down on Sutton Place, and so I just relaxed. I sat there feeling for a minute that I owned the building, that I owned my life.

But only for a minute.

What was I going to do? I couldn't tell my mother that I was going to get kicked out of school. I just couldn't.

Run away, I thought. Run away. Anywhere.

If I could run away, everything would turn out okay. Something good might happen somewhere, and I wouldn't have to explain about why I am not doing what they all expect me to do.

Outside, I knew something lucky would happen, and the first person I met on Second Avenue was Henry Castle. I know him from baseball games under the Queensboro Bridge, and Henry promised that he would stick by me all the way. I think he liked the excitement of somebody running away. It was a little unlucky that he didn't have any allowance left, so a bus or train was out of the question. At least I didn't have to think of where I could take a bus or a train. I don't even know what stop to get off at when I visit my cousins in Brooklyn.

We went to the 54th Street Gym because Henry wanted to work out to get in shape for the Golden Gloves. We hit the bag a little and ran a zillion times on the running track that goes around the ceiling of the gym, and then we were hungry.

I sat on a radiator in the hallway while Henry went in to have dinner at his house. He put a fish stick in a paper napkin and brought it out to me, and we went down 53rd Street and watched the older guys play craps.

I think Henry felt that I would just go home at eleven o'clock, but I stuck to him like roof tar. After all, who said he would stick by me? I couldn't be alone at a time like this, and he knew it. So we went back to his house and crept up the creaking stairs.

Henry has three sisters, and so I tiptoed into the bedroom, where there were two sets of bunk beds. Henry made me get on the floor and pull myself under the bed. His sisters were already sleeping.

I lay there in the dark and wondered what my life was coming to. Everything was all confused. I only knew that if I didn't run away, everyone would be sad and angry. No one was going to forgive me, anyway. I was wrong in everybody's eyes, and I just said to myself that I wasn't going to think about it anymore.

So I said my night prayers and made all the blessing requests like nothing had ever happened. I blessed my mother and asked that my father gets okay again and that Uncle Tommy forgets about the airplane crash and is happy.

AND now I am here. Still under the bed. I am just opening my eyes. It is a new day, and I am hoping it will be better than yesterday. I raise up a little and bump my head on the bedspring.

Now I am hearing voices, and I remember where I am. Is my mother here? Where is my mother? Probably sitting in the police station. She is going to give me blue murder, and now that I've been out all night, I can never go home.

I listen for a minute or so. The whole Castle family seems to be sitting around the kitchen table.

Henry comes in, and he lies on the floor next to me.

"My father," he whispers, "will pull my eyes out of my head if he finds out you're here. It's like harboring a criminal."

"You want me to jump out the window?" I ask.

"That would work," Henry says in a whispering laugh. "But that gives me an idea."

"Yeah, so?" I ask.

"We'll have seven seconds, maybe less, so you gotta run like hell. You got it?" His eyes are sparkling like he invented something.

"Got it," I say. I don't have a clue about what is going on.

I have my shoes in my hands now, lying under the bed and waiting for something to happen. I hear Henry opening the front window of the apartment.

"Holy God!" he screams. "Look at this!"

I can hear his family running to the front window, and everyone is crying, "What, what, what?"

I am now bolting like a racehorse to the front door, and I hear Henry say, "It's not even raining today."

It is not yet noon, and Bobby Walsh and I are playing pool in the intermediate game room at Kips Bay. Bill Egan is the instructor for the room and a great Ping-Pong player. He's swinging the paddle near the three big windows that look out onto 52nd Street.

Walsh is taking a shot when I look up and see my brother Billy. He has rage in his eyes, and I have never seen him like this.

"There you are," he says, "you freakin' punk."

He is coming after me. I am in the corner, behind the pool table, and I sprint the other way. He is coming fast, as if he can't wait to get to me. There is nobody as fast as Billy. I go back to the corner. He fakes to one side, and I fake to the other.

"You tried," he says, snarling at me, "to steal Mommy's money."

"I did not," I say, knowing I am saying an outright lie.

"You're nothing but a punk," he says. "You know that."

He fakes again. My heart is pounding. I know that he is going to beat me good when he catches me.

"Lookit," I say, "just leave me alone. I didn't steal anything."

Walsh drops his pool cue on the table and slips past Billy in a flash. Bill Egan is looking our way. Billy picks up Walsh's cue stick, and I know now that I can't get past, but I have to do something. And so I fake one way and then run the opposite way at full speed. Billy swings the pool stick, and it is a blur coming at me.

It is like there has been an explosion, and I fall to the floor.

It feels like the stick is stuck in my arm, that the bone has broken and wrapped around it. The pain is shooting through every part of me. The room gets dark for a moment, and I can't see anything.

Bill Egan is now on his knee, my face cupped in his hands.

"Dennis," he is saying, "look at me. Say your name."

"Dennis," I say.

"What's my name?" he asks.

"Bill."

Billy is standing behind Egan as he lifts my arm, bending it, and squeezing it and pulling on it. It hurts like the skin has been burned away, but I don't say anything. I don't want to give my brother the satisfaction that he has nearly killed me.

"It's okay," Egan says. "No break, anyway."

"It's okay?" Billy's voice seems nervous.

"It will leave a bruise big as a house, though. What the hell is going on? Think your brother is a baseball or something?"

"I just wanted to stop him," Billy says. "It's a family matter."

That's all you have to say in the neighborhood. Just mention the word "family," and the mouths shut like clams.

We are outside the club now, and I am sitting on a car fender on 52nd Street.

"I have to take you home," my brother says.

"Yeah?" I say. "Well, I don't want to go."

"Mommy is worried," he says. "She was up all night."

"I don't want to go through it with her," I say. "Sister Alphonsus wants to see her. They are going to kick me out of school."

"They are not going to kick you out of school," he says.

"Sister said it, that I won't graduate."

Billy is quiet for a while. Finally he grabs me by the neck, but gently, and pulls me off the car.

"Let's walk a little," he says, " 'cause I want to tell you what I read at school yesterday. It's a poem by Robert Frost, and in it he says that home is the place that, when you go there, they always have to let you in. Get it?"

"So?" I say, because I really don't get it.

"So," Billy says, "you have to feel that there is something between you and Mommy that will let you tell her all about Sister Alphonsus and let her at the same time believe in you so that she'll go to Sister Alphonsus and work it out."

"What about running away?" I ask.

"Work it out with Mommy and take your punishment."
"What kind of punishment?"
"You can handle it," he says.
"And why are you saying 'Mommy' like a kid?"
"I don't know," he says. "She's feeling so bad, it just seems right. Mom, Mommy, what difference does it make?"
Billy puts his arm around my shoulder. We walk a couple of blocks like this, without saying anything more.
Then, as we're passing 55th Street, I look into his eyes. I never saw his eyes so blue. I smile at him, saying, "So they hafta let you in when you go home, huh?"
"Yeah," he says, "they have to."

Six

I AM in the library now at Kips Bay Boys Club, a long and narrow room with polished wooden walls. It is like being in an apartment on Sutton Place, because it has a rich smell and the furniture is all made of wood and is shining.

Betty Fallon is the librarian, and I have been sitting with her almost every night for the last few months, trying to read more, like I promised my mother I would do. She has been giving me a different book every week, like *The Last of the Mohicans* and *The Prairie.* I read them sitting at a spindly table, and we talk a lot whenever I'm there. I feel I can really talk to Betty. She is always laughing and putting her hand on my arm. She gave me a book called *The Corsican Brothers,* and the book made me feel sad because of how close these brothers were. I wish I had someone who I was close to.

I guess I feel close to Billy, no matter what happened with the pool stick. But he is so much older than me, two years.

"You know, Betty," I say, "I don't have anybody to be close to like in *The Corsican Brothers.*"

"You have your friends," Betty says. She is sitting behind her desk at the front of the room, up on a step, like an altar.

"You can't tell guys things that are bothering you 'cause they'll call you a faggot."

Betty smiles. "Now, what kind of things are bothering you?"

"Lots of things, I guess." I say this looking away for a moment. "I am always thinking about things in my life."

"Like what?" Betty smiles at me, and I smile back at her.

I begin to think about the talk my mother had with Sister Alphonsus, and how I had to promise that I would work harder to do all my homework and to study for tests. But no matter how things are going, if they are good or bad, I still am not crazy about school. And there's something else lately. I've been thinking a lot about my father, that I don't know what is going on with him and what kind of place he's in and if people are still being mean to him, tying him up or beating him. The thoughts about him just come up without expecting them. I could be washing my toes in the kitchen bathtub, and I could suddenly wonder if my father washed his toes, too, or if someone was washing them for him. It bothers me all the time.

"Betty," I say, "can I tell you something you can't tell anyone ever?"

"Sure you can," she answers.

"I mean, it is like confession, where you can't say anything even if I murdered someone."

"Did you murder someone?" she asks, pretending to be surprised.

"No," I say. "I want to tell you about my father."

Betty leans over and cups her chin in her hands.

"My father," I say, "is in a place where they beat him up and give him shock treatments—you know, they put wires into his brain and all that." I am trying to be as casual as I can be, like I am talking about the color of my brother's basketball uniform.

"Your father is in a mental institution?" she asks.

I am staring at Betty. It is so hard to speak, and I think she knows this. She waits until I can put the words together.

"My mother always said," I continue, "that my father was in the hospital because he fell from a truck when he worked for the Railway Express and he can't walk, but I heard my aunt Kitty talking about him being in this asylum."

"Oh, Dennis," Betty says, reaching out to hold my hand, "that's too bad he is sick like that, but you know it is just another sickness, like having the mumps."

"Yes," I say, pulling my hand back a little, "I guess I know all that, but my mother doesn't know that I heard Aunt Kitty, and she keeps talking about him being in the hospital because of his legs and all."

I feel like crying now, so I look around for something to take my mind off my mother and the way she lied to me.

"What are you doing?" Betty asks.

"I am counting the books because . . ."

"Because?"

"Oh," I say, a little embarrassed. "I—I don't know. I just count things if I think I might start to bawl."

"Oh, Dennis," she says, "why do you want to cry?"

"Because my mother didn't tell me the truth."

"But can't you see that she wants to protect you?"

"Yes," I say. "But—but—why should she lie to me? Why couldn't she just trust me?"

"Did she tell Billy any different?" Betty asks.

"I don't know," I say, shrugging my shoulders. "I think I'm mad at Billy, anyway, because he hit me with a pool stick."

"Your brother didn't hit you with a pool stick."

I roll up my sleeve and show Betty the bruise that is still on my arm, the one that I don't think will ever go away.

"Well," Betty says, "brothers fight sometimes."

"I suppose," I answer. "But I don't know if she told Billy, and I don't want to ask him."

Betty gets up from her chair and puts her arms around me. I try to move away, but as I feel her pressing me into her, I just relax there until she holds me out by the shoulders.

"Maybe," she says, "you should ask. You have these questions in your mind, and they have nowhere to go unless you let them out of your mouth, and there is no one better than your mother to ask about them."

She gives me another little hug and takes a book from her desk. It is called *Tom Sawyer.* She hands it to me.

"You'll like it," she says. "I promise. Take it home for a week."

I run out of the library and jump down the black marble stairs in twos. It is a surprise to me that Kips Bay has all these men in the pool, the gym, the shops, the game room, and, besides all that, a woman like Betty who can help you out if you are in a jam with homework or have trouble with a drunken father or something.

I wouldn't mind so much if I had a drunken father, though. At least he'd be home.

I THROW *Tom Sawyer* on the kitchen table. I can see my mother's legs in the living room. She is sitting on the couch, reading a magazine. She has been pretty mad at me since I ran away, and I wonder how she'll act with me now.

I sit next to her. She kisses me but doesn't say anything. She is staring at me, and I wonder if she smells the cigarette smoke of the one cigarette I had before I went to Kips. A long time passes.

"How are you?" she says finally.

I lean in next to her, and I inhale the smell of Clorox coming from her white blouse. Anything white in my house smells of bleach, because my mother is such a stickler about getting things clean. It is a hard smell, but it is such a clean smell that it is relaxing. And I do need to relax as I figure out a way to ask her about my father.

"Okay," I answer.

"I've been reading this interesting story about the pope," she says. "Let me read it to you."

My mother loves to read to us. When we were kids, she used to read the Letters to the Editor column to us every day. She is reading now about how the pope was the first pope ever to come to America, when he was a monsignor or something, and her voice is light and singsong. I love to hear her read.

Now, though, I am trying to figure out a way to get her to stop reading. I want to say something before Billy gets home.

"Mom," I begin with a hesitation, "could I make you a cup of tea?"

She puts the magazine down beside her. "You should say excuse me," she says. I knew she would say that.

"I'm sorry," I say. "Excuse me, your most worshipful lady."

She laughs now and pats my leg.

"No thanks, Dennis. I could never sleep if I had tea now."

I shift some on the couch. "Could I ask you something?"

"Sure," she answers.

"Did you ever have a conversation with Daddy about me? I mean, doesn't he want to see me? Does he ever ask about me?"

"Of course he does, honey," she says. "But they don't let kids in the hospital there. I told you a hundred times."

I was hoping she wouldn't say that again, even now when I'm thirteen, and I can't just let her say it again and leave it alone.

"I know, Mom," I say, shaking my head, "but you never told me he was in a mental place."

I can feel all the muscles in her body get tight, and she picks the magazine up again and begins to flip through it. She doesn't look at me but keeps flipping the pages. Two minutes must pass.

Finally she stops. "Who told you that?" she demands.

"I heard it," I say.

"Where did you hear it?"

"I heard Aunt Kitty talking to Uncle Tracy, that's all. And I told Betty about it down at the Kips library, and she said I should just talk to you about it."

My mother turns on the couch and faces me.

"You told Betty about your father being in an insane asylum?"

"I told her you told me he hurt his legs."

I can almost feel how upset she is, because the couch seems to be shaking.

"Dennis," she says, her voice getting louder now, "you must never tell anyone these things about your father or us being on welfare. Or anything in our lives. This is our secret. It's our lives. People are always trying to butt in." She points her finger at me. "Nobody should know our business. Do you understand, Dennis?"

She makes this ugly face when she is mad at me, like she is disgusted with something, like there is some dead fish around or something that smells wicked. I am so sorry that she is angry with me, and I feel ashamed, and I don't know why. I get up from the couch, grab *Tom Sawyer* from the kitchen, and go into my room to read.

Why are we so different? Different from everyone I know. Why do we have to have all these secrets that separate everyone, including us here in apartment 26? Why should I have to feel so apart from my mother?

I am in the upper bunk reading as my brother comes home. He doesn't say anything and quickly gets into the bottom bunk. I am wondering if I should ask him what he knows about Daddy and about the mental asylum. But what if he doesn't know? Will I make him sick with worrying about it?

"Turn the light out, will you?" Billy says.

I can't read, anyway, and so I turn the light out. But I know I'm not going to get any sleep, not when I have all these questions. Like Betty said, they will have nowhere to go unless I let them out of my mouth.

"Billy," I say, "what do you know about our father?"

There. I've said it. I can't do anything about it now.

"He's in a mental institution," Billy says, and I can hear him pulling the sheet up over his head.

"How come you never told me?" I ask.

"There's never any reason to talk about it, Dennis," he says. "And a long time ago Uncle Andy told me that I shouldn't talk to anyone about it, so I didn't."

"Uncle Andy told you that? How old were you?"

"I don't know, eight, maybe nine."

"You knew all this time and never said anything?"

"We never talk about it, Dennis."

I am climbing down from the top bunk now.

"Dammit," I say, over and over as I walk to my mother's bedroom. I pull the light cord, and she jumps up.

"Could you get up?" I ask.

"What's the matter?" she asks, sitting up in the bed.

"I just want to know one thing, Mom," I say, standing there in my pajamas. "Why didn't you tell me a long time ago? Why didn't you think I was old enough to know about my own father?"

I can see her shoulders going into a slump. She suddenly looks so tired, and she begins to whisper, "Oh, Dennis, Dennis, Dennis."

"Well?" I ask, folding my arms.

My mother looks away for a second, and she says, "What do you want to know? What do you want me to tell you?"

"Is he okay? Is he hurt? Is he getting beat up?" I ask these questions like they are bouncing off the sides of a pinball machine.

My mother smiles. "He is not in that awful Greenland Hospital anymore but up in Poughkeepsie State, and the people are very nice to him. Believe me, I have seen them being nice many times."

"All right, good, Mom," I say. "I'm sorry to wake you up."

"You didn't wake me up, Dennis," she says.

"Good, Mom," I say, "because I wouldn't want to disturb you."

I go to our room and climb back to the top bunk. I pull the sheet up and adjust my eyes to the dark. Billy doesn't say anything at all, and I leave him to his own thoughts.

Anyway, at least I'm not alone in all of this anymore.

BILLY is a junior counselor at Kips Bay Summer Camp this year, and so I'm home alone. It is a hot night, and I have a wet rag around my neck, and I'm trying to sleep on the floor. Anything to cool off. My mother is asleep and probably dreaming about how mad at me she is, because she found the tiniest pieces of tobacco in my shirt pocket.

She treats me like I'm in the third grade. And she never would have found it if she didn't have to iron my polo shirts all the time. I'm the only guy on the street who has ironed polo shirts.

Now the sweat's coming out of my neck like Niagara Falls. All I can do is toss and turn on the hard floor, and so I decide to sleep out on the fire escape. I grab a blanket and go out the front door, then down the hall and climb out the window.

I am in my short cotton underpants, barefoot and bare-chested, and I throw the old army blanket across the rusty iron strips of the fire escape. I lie down. There is not much room, and I'm curled up like a puppy in a corner. Still sweating like mad, I say a prayer to Saint Jude, the patron of hopeless causes, to send a breeze my way. I'm maybe as uncomfortable as I have ever felt in my life. I'm

Above left: my mother and father in 1940. Above right: my favorite picture of Mary—gloves and determination. Left: Mary and me in Central Park—we walked on Sundays after church.

Right: Christmas, with a hole in Billy's shoe. Below left: me working the ranch in Nevada. Below right: my first week at Engine Company 82—and the beginning of a new life.

not sure of what is bothering me: the spaces between the iron slats, or thinking that I could be up at Kips Camp if we could afford it, or maybe just that my mother hasn't mentioned our father since we had that talk in her bedroom.

I don't know why she avoids it. She could tell me what happened to him, how he got that way, why they won't let me in to see him. There is still this big empty hole in our lives.

And then, there is Barbara Cavazzine, who I now like more than Marilyn Rolleri. I asked her to go to the movies with me.

She said no.

She didn't say "No thanks" or "My mother won't let me" or "I like you but I like some other guy more." She just said, "No," and that was that. I guess I will have to ask her again.

I DON'T know how long I have been sleeping, but I awake suddenly because I feel the whole fire escape shaking. I smell smoke as I open my eyes. There is a giant in front of me, with big boots folded over below the knees, and he is picking me up as other firemen run up the stairs behind him.

"Hey, kid," the fireman says.

"Let me down," I say, thinking, I'm not a kid, for Chrissakes.

A cloud of smoke sweeps down over us, and I begin to choke uncontrollably. I look up and see the flames coming from the apartment window above us, Mr. Sorenson's apartment. My eyes are hurting like someone put mud in them.

"Sure thing, kid," the fireman says, putting me down. "Let's get you off this fire escape, anyway. You'd be in a lot of trouble when they break the windows upstairs."

He has me by the hand as we go to the hallway window.

"The firemen," he says, "have to break the windows, you know."

He grabs a huge axe that he had put down, climbs in first, and helps me into the hallway. The fire is above, but I can still smell the smoke in the hall.

"Hey, kid," the fireman says as we walk into the hallway, him in his huge boots and me in my bare feet, "what do you think of that DiMaggio? Is he a hero, or what?"

Mr. Sorenson's apartment, and maybe even Mr. Sorenson himself, is burning up, and he's asking about Joltin' Joe DiMaggio.

"Nobody better," I say.

I love this fireman. I wonder what you have to do to be a fireman.

There is a lot of noise in the hallway as the firemen drag up the hose. My mother sticks her head out the apartment door.

"Just stay in your house," the fireman says to her, "and you'll be okay."

He messes my hair and runs back to the fire escape, and in a second he is gone out the window. It must seem to my mother that I came out of thin air. She puts her arm around me and squeezes hard as the door shuts.

"It's Mr. Sorenson's, upstairs," I say. "There's a lot of smoke."

"Ohh," my mother says.

I look at her hazel eyes, and they show that she is afraid. Her eyes are like street signs to me, because you always know where she is when you look at them, and now I can see fear.

"It's okay, Mom," I say to her. "The fireman said so. He said that we'll be okay and that DiMaggio is a hero."

I am back on the floor in the living room, the wet rag again around my neck, and in the new quiet of the dark I am thinking about that fireman. It must be something to be a fireman.

I wonder if he has children, maybe a boy or a couple of boys, that he takes to Yankee Stadium to see DiMaggio.

Seven

It is now fall. I am fourteen years old and in public school.

There was a big ruckus about going to a public school. Everybody knows that kids go to Catholic high schools when they graduate St. John's. Even Sister Alphonsus, who was going to fail me in everything, told me that I would be better off going to a minor-league Catholic school.

And my mother, too. She went on and on about how good Billy

is doing at Cardinal Hayes, but my mother doesn't realize the difference between us, which is simple. Billy *likes* school.

I begged her.

Another Catholic school would kill me. It's like being a duck-stepping Nazi storm trooper to be in Catholic school. Everything is all precision and discipline, and you can never talk without being first asked a question.

All my friends who go to public school tell me that no teacher ever gives you a bad time and you can either do your homework or not, no sweat off their back. Public school is like heaven, where nobody bothers you.

And so now I'm in a school where I never go.

The School of Aviation Trades (SAT) is on East 63rd Street. I get up in the morning, and I go to Jimmy's candy store on 62nd Street, where the jukebox is always playing and the guys wear leather jackets and have key rings hanging from their belts.

At least I don't have to wear a white shirt and blue tie anymore. I have this black windbreaker with my name printed on the front pocket. I know my mother would never be able to afford to buy me a leather jacket, but those jackets are so cool.

I did go to class a few times, but the homeroom teacher kept changing, and no one ever took attendance. There is no point in going to school if no one takes the attendance, because you'll never be missed, and no one will think that you are in Jimmy's candy store, where you can use the fifteen cents your mother gives you each day to buy singles, Lucky Strikes or Camels.

My mother thought I was doing great in my new school, because each day I would tell her about these swell guys I knew and how smart they were, and I would mix in a few names of books to make everything sound A-OK. She would ask about parent-teacher day, and I told her they sent reports at the end of the term.

I could always tell her that the reports got lost in the mail.

Today most of the guys went over to play pool, but I don't have the money for even a game of eight ball, so I am sitting in the rear of the candy store, watching Antone and a guy named Bullboy as they are dancing to the new Frankie Lymon and the Teenagers tune, "Why Do Fools Fall in Love?" They have imaginary partners, and they are twirling them out and in, and it looks pretty funny.

Antone comes over to me when the music stops. He's a couple of years older than I am.

"Hey, Smitty," he says, "give me a butt, huh?"

I have only two cigarettes left, and it isn't even noon yet. If I give him one, I'll be stuck for the rest of the day.

"C'mon, will ya," he says, holding his hand out.

His black leather jacket is open, and all the zipper chains are swinging back and forth. He has on a white shirt, and the collar is open and standing high in the back. His hair is in a million curls and falls down into a point just above his nose. The sides are greased down with Vaseline.

"C'mon, give me a bitchin' bastard cigarette."

The guys I grew up with don't talk like these guys do. Up here at SAT there is a never-ending contest to see how many curses you can get into a sentence. I take out one cigarette.

Antone doesn't say thank you, but this doesn't bother me too much. He'll never meet my mother, anyway.

Some other guys come in, and Antone and Bullboy leave. The candy store is just a place to smoke and to waste time. No one has put any money in the jukebox, and so I think about going around to the schoolyard to see if anyone is playing stickball.

I walk down 63rd Street, and I suddenly hear my name.

"Dennis," I hear.

I am stunned to hear my mother's voice.

"Hey, Mom," I say, trying to be nonchalant. It is always good to be nonchalant because it is cool not to be rattled by things.

"Give us a kiss," she says. She is carrying a big paper bag.

I kiss her on the cheek, hoping none of the guys are around to see me. I know I have to think fast, before she asks me any questions.

"I just came from shop class," I say. "Now I'm going around to history and social studies."

I know I am lying.

"Where is shop class?"

Her eyes now are like pinpoints, like she is a detective studying some clue.

"On Sixty-fourth Street." The school is divided between both streets.

She thinks for a minute and shrugs her shoulders.

"I have a surprise for you," she says, smiling as she changes from a detective back to my mother. I can tell she is happy for some reason. My mother is not happy so much, and I always feel good if I see her smiling. She opens the bag. "Just take a look at this."

She pulls out a green wool jacket and holds it up, here in the middle of the street. Across the back, in big white letters, it has the name of the school: AVIATION. It is brand-new.

My mother just began working for the New York Telephone Company, after all those years on welfare. I know she doesn't make much money as an operator in training.

Oh, man, I think. I feel so bad that she went and did this, spending all this money. Maybe I could have gotten a cheap leather jacket with all the zippers, and here she has gotten me this jacket from the school where I never go.

She is gleaming at me. She is so proud that she has given me this jacket.

I should smile, I think, and I do as I take my windbreaker off. Even if I don't like it. I can see in her eyes that she has a little happiness, and I wish I could add to it by loving the jacket. But I can't.

I put it on. It fits just right. I put the collar up so that I feel a little like a guy who's cool and with it.

"It looks great," she says. "It is just the thing now that you are in high school and everything is going so good for you."

She stands back a little and folds her hands one into the other the way she does when she is studying something. Her smile goes from one end of her face to the other.

I am feeling worse now, because I wonder if the guys around the jukebox will think the jacket is for faggots. But my mother has taken the windbreaker, and I have no choice but to wear this one.

"Thank you, Mom," I say, giving her a kiss on the cheek. "I have to go, or I'll be late."

I AM ON MY WAY TO KIPS BAY Boys Club. It is early afternoon, and it has just stopped raining. The street is crowded with people because the sun has finally broken through the winter. I go toward Second, past Ling's, the laundry down in the cellar, past Jasper's candy store where everybody plays the horses, past the empty lots and the corner vegetable stand. The old cobblestones on Second Avenue are shining with wetness, and everything in the neighborhood looks clean, like it has all been buffed with a rag.

I turn down Second because I'm meeting Walsh and Scarry and Jurgensen down at Kips. Pretty soon I won't have much time to play ball. I've been going after this job at the East River Florist, and they just told me yesterday that I can work Friday afternoons and all day Saturday. It's not a bad deal, either, thirty cents an hour.

I've been giving all my newspaper money to my mother, but I'm going to get to keep half of the florist money I earn, after I pay her back for a pair of Thom McAn shoes she bought me.

I see this guy I know, Frankie, on the corner of 54th Street.

I've known him for a long time, since when we were kids and we all had bikes. We used to ride through Central Park, a gang of us from different streets. Frankie is a quiet kid, but as tough as Rocky Marciano. Nobody mistakes his being quiet for a guy who can be pushed around. Now he is just standing here on the corner.

"Hey," I say to him.

"Hey, Dennis," he says, "where you going?"

"Kips."

"I never go there," he says.

"How come?"

"I dunno," he says. "Faggy stuff, waiting in line to play Ping-Pong. Got any smokes?"

"No," I say. "I'm gonna buy one-for-a-penny from Abbie. Want to walk me there?"

"I can't," he says. "I'm waiting for a guy."

"What guy?" I ask.

"You ever smoke pot?" he asks.

"No," I answer. This is something we never thought about in our crowd on 56th Street.

"This guy," he says, "is supposed to come with some pot. You wanna stick around, I'll give you some tokes."

"What's a toke?" I never even heard this word up at SAT.

"A drag," he says. "You know, a puff."

"You ever smoke it before?" I ask.

"Yeah, sure," he says. "Everybody in my school smokes it."

Frankie goes to the Machine and Metal Trades High School on 96th Street, and I am thinking if they are smoking pot and working those big machines, they will all end up like Captain Hook.

"I heard it makes you dizzy," I say.

"No, man," Frankie says. "High is not dizzy. High is like dreaming a great dream where all the colors are like on fire. Stick around, Dennis, 'cause here he is now."

I do not recognize the guy who comes to us. Everyone says, "Hey," and the boy gives Frankie a small brown paper bag. Frankie gives him two dollars.

"It's that easy?" I say. "Just stand on the corner?"

"Naw. You hafta set it up. He goes to my school."

"You like your school?"

"No," he says. "I never go. I just hang around there, you know? C'mon, we'll take a walk down by the river and smoke."

"No," I say. "I gotta go play basketball. Maybe Saturday night."

"Yeah, sure," he answers, "maybe Saturday."

I give him a small punch on the arm to say good-bye. He is such a friendly guy, but very different from my other friends, very mysterious. I could hang around with him and probably have a great time getting to know what makes him tick.

At Kips, I change into the club shorts and run out onto the basketball court in my undershirt. Scarry and Walsh and Jurgensen are there, doing layups, jump shots, sets from around the rim.

"About time," Scarry says. I guess they've been waiting.

Scarry is semi-kneeling as he throws a set shot. It is a basket, but I knew it would be. Scarry is playing ball for LaSalle Academy, and he is the team's star. Walsh is more like me. He just wants to take shots from the outside and look like he has some style.

Jurgensen is stockier than all of us. He moves over the court like a farm tractor plowing a field of rocks, but he puts his heart into everything. He would be a good ballplayer if he were lighter and if he didn't drink so much beer. Anytime we go down to 51st Street park to drink beer, Jurgensen always has his own package. Sometimes I'll drink two cans of Rheingold, and Scarry might drink one, but Jurgensen gets two quarts and gulps until he becomes legless.

Walsh and I play Scarry and Jurgensen, and we are at it for over an hour. But Scarry quits suddenly.

"I gotta go," he says. "I have homework."

"C'mon," I say, "we could do another half hour."

"I have homework, too," Jurgensen says. "If I don't get it done, they're gonna throw me outta school."

"It would take three Irish Christian Brothers," I say, "to lift you in order to throw you out."

Jurgensen just raises his middle finger as they leave the court.

And so Walsh and I are left alone to play horse. I take three games straight because Walsh can't do the around-the-back layup that I have perfected. I can tell he is getting bored. He has a defeated look on his face.

"Let's quit," he says finally. "I have to go do homework."

"You're such a queer, Walsh," I say, "like Scarry and Jurgensen. Where is all that homework going to get you, anyway?"

Walsh laughs. "It will get me through the night without my father beating my head against the wall with my algebra book."

ARCHIE grabs me as I am pushing open the big doors to the stairs out to 52nd Street.

"Hey, son," he says, "give me a minute."

Archie has a new office. There are photographs of kids all over the walls. He pulls his chair from the desk and sits next to me.

"So," he says, "you're up at Aviation Trades, huh?" Archie isn't one to beat around the bush, and I can tell what he is up to.

"Yeah," I answer, "right."

"And," he says, "you're going to school every day?"

"Right." I do go every day, so I'm not really lying. I just don't go to any of the classes.

"Tell me about it," he says. "Do you like it?"

Archie wants to suck me into something here, but I don't know what. He must have heard something, maybe from Billy. Billy has been asking me a lot of questions about school lately.

"Sometimes I do. Sometimes I don't."

"Is there a particular subject or teacher you like?"

I don't want to outright lie to Archie, but I don't even know any teacher's name, except for Mr. Donahue in shop.

"I like Mr. Donahue," I say.

"Mr. Donahue," Archie says. "Good. Why do you like him?"

"I guess he's a good teacher. He pays attention, anyway."

"Are you paying attention to what you're doing?"

This is the setup now. "What do you mean?" I ask.

"I mean," Archie says, leaning back in his chair, "you are telling me that everything is sweet and dandy, but that's not what I heard."

"Billy," I say. "Billy said something to you, right?"

"You know, son," Archie says, "we are not talking about another person here. There is just one name I am interested in. Dennis. I want you to know that people are interested in you."

I slouch in my chair, feeling that this is like a punishment just sitting here. People are interested in me? That's a big deal, right?

"Sit up, son," Archie says, "will you? Be proud of yourself. You may be a smart, talented kid, but I think you are in danger of wasting your life away like an unwatered vine."

I don't say anything, though he waits to see if I do.

"Who," he says as he gets out of his chair, "who are the people we respect around here? Think about this, because you know the answer. It's the guys who jump up and say, 'Let's do it,' and 'Let's do it right and have a darn good time doing it.' Look around the neighborhood, son, and think about who you want to be like, because I'll tell you this: If you don't start thinking about who you are and what you can do, you might be on the road to playing rummy with guys like Eddie Dunne up at Sing Sing."

Archie comes over and gives me a soft punch on the shoulder.

"We all like you, son," he says, "but you should know that wasting your life is as bad as taking food out of a starving person's mouth."

Eight

MR. DONAHUE is in my living room as I walk in the door. My mother's on the couch, crying, and Mr. Donahue has a sad look on his face. I know what he's doing in my apartment, and I hate him immediately for being here. For making my mother cry.

"Sit down," my mother says. She has a handkerchief to her eyes. I can see the anger in her eyes, or maybe it's sadness, I can't tell. Her voice is scratchy.

"What's going on?" I ask as I sit on a kitchen chair we brought in when the easy chair got a hole in the cushion and we threw it out. I am in my green Aviation jacket, and I wiggle out of it.

"The worst thing about this," my mother says, "is that you lied to me. You lied to me every day for months about going to school."

I know I can't give an excuse, not with Mr. Donahue here.

"Why do you do these things, Dennis?" she cries, her nose sniffling. "Billy never gives me a moment's problem, and you never give me a moment's rest. Why, why? When you are so smart? All the nuns at St. John's always told me how smart you are and how you never meet your abilities and how much everybody likes you. And you wanted to go to public school, and we let you go where you wanted, and now this?"

My mother is beginning to sob, and then she screams, *"Why?"*

I don't know what to say.

She is sitting there in her green housecoat, the one she wears when she is ironing, thin and pretty, the tears shining as they run down her cheeks, and I wish I could hug her and tell her that there is nothing really wrong. Tell her that school is just not what I want to do. I want to be out in the world. I just want my own life, and not have a life that has to be reported to every Tom, Dick, and Harry.

No one is saying anything. We all just look at each other and listen to my mother sobbing.

I guess these are those tenement tears she talks about, bad times that just come natural sometimes. Everyone knows that things could be better for all of us if we all lived on Sutton Place. The Walshes, the Scarrys, the Jurgensens, everybody. But I would still play hooky from school, because school is just not for me. You have no control over your life there. Look at my father, cooped up; he has no control over his life. We just get ordered around from minute to minute.

"We are going to have to give him a JAB card," Mr. Donahue says, finally breaking the ice.

"What does that mean?" I ask.

"It means," Mr. Donahue says, "that you are fourteen years old and have to go to the Juvenile Aid Bureau regularly until you are sixteen. You can quit school at sixteen, but until then the Juvenile Aid Bureau will be responsible for your going to school."

I know I can't wait until I am sixteen.

FRANKIE is waiting for me in Riker's on 53rd Street. I just got paid three dollars for three hours on Friday and seven hours on Saturday at the florist. I'll give my mother half, but I am still flush, and I order a hamburger on an English.

"You want something?" I ask him.

"No," Frankie says. "You shouldn't have too much in your stomach if we are going to toke on some smoke."

"I was on a boat once," I say. "Everyone got sick but me, 'cause I got an iron stomach."

After my hamburger we walk down to 48th Street, where another Dennis, this one named Buckley, set up a club room in the cellar of his building. Buckley is funny-looking, with a big wide mouth and a nose that almost comes over his lips. And he's got a lot of pimples, like he has a disease. But his clothes are sharp, and his shoes look like they come from Flagg Brothers.

"Where did you get such cool vines?" I ask him. I am just trying to make conversation as I sit in a heavy brown sofa with a hundred cigarette burns in it.

Frankie has taken a bag from his jacket, and he opens it. He also opens a package of paper, folds a piece, and places it between his fingers. He pours some pot out of the bag onto the paper carefully.

"The fags," Buckley says.

"What's that mean?" I ask.

"I would never let them near me," Frankie says.

"It's easy money," Buckley says. "I never let them go on top of me or anything."

I am getting nervous as I watch Frankie put the cigarette in his mouth and wet it so that it is closed all around the edges. It is all pretty sloppy. I am beginning to wonder what the hell I'm doing with these guys.

I don't like Buckley's talk. I have heard about guys who hang around Third Avenue by Clark's Bar until some man offers them money to let them get kissed and worse in an alleyway. It is pretty sick, if you ask me, pretty sick and weird.

Guys like Scarry and Walsh would never even know about this kind of stuff, making it with fags and smoking pot. I wish it were just Frankie and me here alone, so that I could swear him to secrecy like a blood brother or something. I don't want anyone to know that I am here with these guys doing this.

More secrets. Everything's a secret in my life.

I don't know this guy Buckley, and he gives me the creeps. I wish we could just get it all over with.

Frankie lights the cigarette and takes a deep puff, holding it in. He passes it to Buckley, who does the same and then hands it to me. I take a little drag. I hold my breath, the smoke inside of me, and I don't feel anything. Good. I hand it over to Frankie.

"If I could get a job, I wouldn't let the fags near me," Buckley says, "but nobody wants to hire me."

I am thinking that I don't believe him. Everyone I know who wants a job can find one in my neighborhood.

"I don't need a job," Frankie says, "because I just help my old man, and he gives me a buck ten an hour. Pretty good, huh?"

"A buck ten an hour," I repeat.

Frankie takes another long drag and hands it off to Buckley. Some guys are so lucky, I am thinking. I can't even keep my newspaper money. Even now with my mother working and off the welfare, she still says that I have to give her the newspaper money, because it's not much, three dollars, sometimes four.

The cigarette is again between my thumb and forefinger. This time I take a deep puff, and I hold it in until I choke. I give it to Frankie, and then it hits me. Everything begins to spin, and the spinning is so out of control that I don't think I can sit up straight on the sofa, and I am suddenly scared and trembling, thinking that something awful is about to happen, that maybe the door will fly open and a thousand cops will rush in and beat us, and they will tell Billy, and Billy will tell my mother, and my stomach can't take the spinning anymore, and the hamburger on an English is now pushing up through my throat and pouring through my mouth, and Buckley is cursing like crazy, pulling me out of his clubhouse and into the dark, smelly cellar, where I roll over into a knot and pray to God that the spinning will stop.

MONSIGNOR Ford looks over his desk at me. My mother and I are in the rectory of St. John's on 55th Street. There is a musty smell here, as if no one has opened a window in thirty years. The carpet is thick, softer than a paintbrush.

We are all sitting on big leather chairs. Father Ford was just made a monsignor, and I know he is doing my mother a favor by taking the time to meet with us.

He shifts a few papers, things my mother had given him.

"Do you think you want to try again?" he asks.

He used to be my favorite priest, but we don't see him so much anymore. He has a little stripe of red at the bottom of his collar and on the wrists of his cassock, a stripe like a military man.

"Yes," I answer, "I guess so."

"Your record shows," he says, lifting a paper, "that you haven't been at school more than twelve days in two terms. Not much different from saying you've never been at school at all, for I doubt in those twelve memorable days they ever once had your attention."

"I don't know," I say. "I don't think they cared about me being there or not."

"Mr. Donahue cared," my mother says.

She smiles, and I know that she does not want to get into an argument with me, especially in front of Monsignor Ford.

I guess she was very surprised that the High School of Aviation Trades sent her a letter saying that I should find another high school to go to. I was surprised, too, because nobody gets kicked out of a public school. That's what I thought. But here we are with Monsignor Ford, trying to find a high school to go to.

"You have caused your mother nothing but grief," Monsignor says, "and now we are going to give you a final chance to get yourself together, to fly the straight and narrow."

"Yes, Monsignor," I answer in the kind of Catholic school way that got me through nine years of St. John's.

"Can you play basketball?"

"Yes, Monsignor."

"That's something," he says, smiling. "They like basketball players up there at Hayes."

"Cardinal Hayes?" I ask, my eyes opening in recognition.

"That is where Billy is," my mother says.

"Good," Monsignor Ford says. "All the more reason for them to take a chance on Dennis."

I am suddenly excited.

It would be great to hang around with my brother. He's still two years older than me, but the age difference does not matter so much in high school, and maybe I can hang around with him and those guys from the Bronx who are his friends. These guys are the stars, the jocksters, the guys who get the girls, the big shots. I could be a part of them.

Maybe.

I STILL have the East River Florist. Since I have been playing so much hooky, Mr. Schmidt has given me work three days a week. He is paying me forty cents an hour now, plus tip money. Not many tips, though, because the maids answer the doors on Sutton Place and the River House, and if the people leave any money, you can bet the maids pocket it. I don't blame them, either, because they probably need more of everything in their lives.

Like my mother. She could use a new everything, especially a new ironing board. Hers is covered with old sheets and stitched at the bottom, and the sheets are always getting creased, and my mother is always saying Hail Marys to keep from cursing as she irons.

I don't think we have anything new in the house, except for the Bible and the Formica table in the kitchen with the four puffy chairs that she bought in a deal that took two years to pay off.

I have been saving my money, though, and I have thirty dollars tucked under my bed. I saw a ring in Bloomingdale's, a little gold one with a blue stone. It is fourteen karats, and I just need ten dollars more to get it. My mother used to wear a wedding ring, a plain gold one, but I haven't seen it in a long time. I don't know if she lost it or sold it. A new ring would look nice on her hand, and as soon as I have the forty dollars, I am going to get it for her.

I wonder if she would like a ring more than a new ironing board.

I WALK up the hill to Kips Bay Camp, in Valhalla, New York, a big canvas bag over my shoulder. The country air smells like a package of Chinese laundry, clean and soft. The dirt road under my feet makes me think I am in another country, like Ireland, but Valhalla is just ten miles above the city. Still, it's greener than Central Park.

Billy got me the job of kitchen boy for the summer. He's a counselor, and he told me that next year, if I did okay at Hayes, I could become a counselor, too.

The kitchen boys' cabin is at the end of a long row of eight cabins and two double cabins. I throw my duffel on a bed, and I lie down to rest from the hike up the hill from the train station. I am still huffing and puffing, but I light a cigarette, anyway.

A guy named Spango comes in with his suitcase tied together with a wash line. I know him from 55th Street. He has dark skin and a gold tooth. He has brought a record player that plays the new 45 rpm records, and he has a collection of rock and roll.

It is great having Spango and having Frankie Lymon, the Platters, the Four Tops, all of them, always available on the 45s. I can tell there is never going to be a dull moment this summer.

The time passes quickly at camp. Some days I have to work in the mess hall, cleaning tables or washing the floors, and on other days I work in the kitchen. I practice my set-and-jump shot every day, and read as much as I can. Billy gave me the complete works of Sherlock Holmes and Shakespeare. I like Sherlock Holmes better, because he always knows what he is doing, but the Shakespeare characters seem never to. My brother also gave me a paper edition of the *Confessions of Saint Augustine* after he read it, and I carry it around in my back pocket, half thinking that Archie will be impressed and half thinking I might read it.

Now the summer is half over. Two days ago I was scheduled to work in the kitchen, but when I woke up, I had a stomachache and heaved all over the place. It was a bug of some kind. Spango knew I was going to be late for work if I didn't get a move on. It was his day off, and I guess he felt sorry for me.

"You stay here, Dennis," Spango said, "and I'll work today."

He didn't say that he would change days off with me or that I owed him something. He just said that he would do the job for me. I'll never forget him, that he did that for me.

He died last night.

The whole camp is in shock. He and a guy named Charlie Spaskey went to town to have a soda. When they were coming home, they hitched a ride at the bottom of the hill coming up from town.

The driver was drunk, went eighty miles an hour, and slammed into a tree. They say Spaskey will live, but his brain is damaged.

All my life I have been thinking about how rough it is for my father to be cooped up in a hospital, and now I am thinking about Spango, dead at fifteen years old. I am fifteen years old, and I can't imagine hitting a tree and having everything go black, every breath crushed out of you, and not even having a chance to get life started.

That accident makes me think that I have a lot of years before me, and I shouldn't be wasting any of my time. I want to make something of myself. I could be something important, too, something that will make people think, Holy God, Dennis did that?

I remember that I said three Hail Marys as soon as I heard about the accident. What else is there to do but pray for a guy, to hope that God won't be too hard on him?

After the funeral and visiting Charlie in the hospital, I practiced my basketball, set shots and layups, all summer long. I was feeling good, so good, about going to high school, about becoming more like my brother. I wanted to try to be a better student, and I wanted to work to be a sports star. I've always known I can do it, and everybody tells me I can do it. Archie and Betty down at Kips, Monsignor Ford, my mother, all of them telling me that I can recognize my famous abilities if I just pay attention.

I HAVE been at Hayes for more than a month now, and I want to pay attention, too.

Or, at least, I wanted to.

It is Sunday, a crisp fall day, and I am at the French bakery on 54th Street. I went to the eleven-o'clock Mass.

I used to wait until the priest said, *"Ite, Missa est"* (Go, the Mass is ended), but lately I have been standing in the back and slipping out after the Communion. Father O'Rourke says it is insulting to God to come late or to leave early and that if you insult God, you'll insult your mother and father and your friends, too, and what kind of a person goes around insulting everyone like that? But I think God has a lot more important things to think about.

I come here every Sunday to buy three seeded rolls. Sunday would not be Sunday if I didn't get the rolls for my mother and Billy and me to have with our Sunday egg.

My month at Cardinal Hayes has not been a great one, and I don't think Monsignor Ford will be happy with me. I tried, but I just can't get my heart into it.

I made the freshman basketball team, and I went to practice for the first couple of weeks, but the boys are much better than I am. No matter how much I practice, I am not going to be a starter. My brother plays like a poet, and I think it's a gift that God gives you. I guess I have a little gift, but when it comes to basketball, it's like God gave Billy a pair of shoes and I got the shoelaces.

A pretty French girl puts the rolls in a bag. On the way home I see Father O'Rourke still standing on the corner of 55th Street talking to some parishioners. It is not very cold, but there is a woman who has a fur coat on that comes down to her ankles, and I suppose she's from Sutton Place.

"A real howdy-do," my mother would say.

My mother has one coat, a red one that comes to her knees. She has had it ever since I can remember. I guess she won't get a chance to have nice things. My father will never come out of that hospital.

It makes me sad to think that Mom never has anyone to go out with. I don't know what happened to Artie. He just disappeared. She is always alone. Even when she is doing just ordinary things, like walking at night around the corner to 57th Street to get the *News* and the *Mirror.*

Father O'Rourke is now waving good-bye to the fancy woman and gives me a wave, too, as I pass by. I wonder if he will go into the rectory now and tell Monsignor Ford that he saw me on First Avenue and that I did not look like I was doing too well at Cardinal Hayes High School. I am feeling that I might as well hang a sign across my chest saying, "I have not been so good for high school, and high school has not been so good for me."

I want to pay attention, but maybe not to what people want me to pay attention to. If I could just study what I want to study, instead of math and science and religion. If I could just read stories by Hemingway and F. Scott Fitzgerald and O. Henry, or if someone would just pay me thirty dollars a week to go to school. But I'm not doing anything that I like, and I don't know why I should stay with it.

I walk slowly up the stairs to my house. As I open the door, my mother and my brother are by the stove, and they raise their heads to look at me. Billy had gone to the midnight Mass after his game last night, and my mother went to the nine o'clock this morning. She has her old pink robe tied tightly around her thin waist. Her hair is combed in long waves coming over her shoulders, and she is wearing a shimmering red lipstick. The bright morning light makes her look like she is Rita Hayworth. She smiles a little when she sees me. I can always see how much she cares about me when she smiles like this. She has a spatula in her hand, turning an egg.

I kiss her cheek and punch my brother on the arm.

"You guys beat the Mount?" I ask.

"Sixty-four, fifty-nine."

"Did you go to church?" my mother asks.

"Yeah," I say.

"What was the Gospel about?"

"I don't know. It was about religion."

"Did you really go to Mass, or didn't you?"

"I was there," I say. I don't like her checking up on me this way. After a long pause I add, "It was about the angel Gabriel coming to visit Mary."

"Okay," my mother says, satisfied. "So you were there."

I am thinking that I want to change the subject. "How many points you score?" I ask Billy.

"Eight," he says. He's reading *The New York Times* that I brought home last night.

VIRGINIA Sabella came around last night, and we walked to the 51st Street park. She was wearing one of those black felt skirts that spread out like a tent and a black sweater. We were looking across Welfare Island at the blinking Pepsi sign, and I was kissing her.

"Do you still like me?" I asked her as I rubbed my hand up and down her back.

She didn't answer, and I kissed her again.

"Well," I asked, "do you?"

"Yes," she said, "I still like you."

I brought my hand across her stomach, constantly worried that she'd tell me to stop, but I found the courage inside and I slid my hand up over the outside of her sweater in one fast movement, until suddenly my hand was fully over her breast, and for one small moment I thought I was approaching heaven.

She grabbed my hand suddenly and brought it into her other hand. "But," she said, "I like somebody else, too."

This word "like." You never know what it means.

Virginia is such a terrific girl, and I wanted so much to say, "Let's just go together, Virginia, and the guys can talk about Virginia and Dennis the way they talk about Gail and Joey, or Maureen and Vinny, or Margaret and Dante."

"Who do you like?" I asked.

"Well, if you keep it a secret, it's Bobby Seelaw."

"But he's going out with someone."

"My cousin Maryanne," she said. "But Maryanne really likes Raymond Connors."

Oh, dammit, I thought, Raymond Connors again.

I didn't say much after that, but I began to wonder where Marilyn Rolleri was recently. I haven't seen her hanging around.

"EIGHT points," I say to Billy, still sitting at the kitchen table. "I would have done better."

"In your sleep," he says.

Flipping through the newspaper, I think about the angel Gabriel from the Gospel and how misnamed Brother Gabriel from school is. I saw him take a kid and push him against an open window and punch him over and over again until the kid was almost on his way three stories down.

Being in Brother Gabriel's class is like being in a torture chamber. I don't know *a* to *b* about algebra, and so I usually get a whack across the back of the head when I am standing in front of the blackboard without a clue as to what is the next step after taking the chalk in my hand.

I know that there is something wrong with a situation where the person in control has hatred for everyone. And I know, too, that this is something I don't have to put up with, that I can fight back.

I am quitting school. It's in my mind now, solidly.

Nine

FRANKIE has entered his father's candy store. I am in the back, playing the pinball machine. It is Saturday morning.

I haven't been going much to Kips lately, because I began to hang around with the guys in the candy store on 55th Street: Frankie, Nicky, Mikey. We just hang together, like a club, every day and night. I like the way we're all friends. It's different from the way Scarry and Walsh and Jurgensen are friends. Here on 55th Street all the guys have quit school, and everyone is trying to figure out what he's doing and trying to get work here and there.

When I got to the florist this morning, Mr. Schmidt asked me if I could come back at one, because there was a wedding or something. And so I am here to kill a couple of hours.

"Hey," Frankie says as he sees me, "how come you're not at work?"

"I don't have to be there until one or so."

I guess I could have gone to Kips to play Ping-Pong or pool. But I am feeling that I belong here, that the guys on 55th Street care more about each other than they do about themselves.

"Hey, great," Frankie says. "How'd you like to come up to 120th and score some horse with us? We'll be back way before noon."

Horse? I wonder what that is. But if it is on 120th Street, that is Harlem, and it must have something to do with getting high.

"I don't have any carfare," I say. "How are you getting there?"

I am thinking that going to Harlem is something I am not so hot about doing. Harlem is dangerous, and going there is like walking the wood on the third rail, like testing the saints and the angels. Guys carry knives up there and are pretty easy about using them.

"First Avenue bus," Frankie says. "I'll give you the carfare."

One o'clock is more than three hours away. I guess testing the saints and the angels is as good a way to pass the time as any.

"As long as you pay the bus both ways," I say to him. I can tell he just wants company.

"Great," he says. "We'll go pick up Mikey around the corner."

WE ARE walking across 120th Street toward Second Avenue. It is a strange feeling being here. Everyone sitting on the stoops, walking along the street, driving cars, managing the shops, looking out the windows, is colored. We are the only whites.

"Are we all right here?" I ask.

"They know we must be here on business," Mikey answers. "They ain't gonna mess up somebody's deal without knowing whose deal they's messing up, you know?"

"They know," Frankie adds, "that we just want some smack."

"How do they know?" I ask. It's like walking into the lion's den because the lion's eyes are closed.

"They just know," Frankie says. "What else they gonna think, that you're the insurance man?"

Suddenly Mikey turns up a stoop and slips into a building. We follow him. The hall is dark. There are no lightbulbs in the fixtures. There is garbage in the hall, paper and crunched cigarettes. The smell of piss and stale booze fills my nose to the brink.

If my super kept our halls like this, the neighbors would beat him up. I am beginning to wish I stayed with the pinball machine in the back of the candy store.

One flight up Mikey knocks lightly on a door. All of a sudden a short colored man is pulling us into his kitchen. The kitchen has a bare wooden table in it, with one chair. There is a pot on the stove and a box of breakfast cereal on the table. Nothing else. We go to the next room, where a woman is sitting on another kitchen chair, and she seems to be sleeping. Three wooden milk boxes, some newspapers, and a *Hollywood Confidential* are also in the room.

"My man," the colored guy says. He is slapping Frankie's hand. "What's the word?"

"Thunderbird," Frankie says.

"What's the price?" the guy continues.

"Sixty twice."

"Where do you cop?"

"At the neighborhood shop."

The room has two windows, which are covered with a blanket. The old linoleum has holes. It hasn't been washed, I am thinking, since it was brought into the building.

The man goes into the kitchen and takes a shoe box from inside the stove. I can see roaches scurrying around inside the open oven.

"How many?" he asks as he opens the box. There are a great many small packages wrapped up in white paper and tape.

"Just one," Mikey says.

He takes one and hands it to Mikey. It looks to me that Mikey has done this a hundred times.

What if the cops come? I am thinking. What would happen to me? This is not like playing hooky. Drugs is serious business, and some judge could send me to jail for years.

What am I here for? I don't even want any drugs.

"Can I taste?" Frankie asks.

"Hell no," the guy says. "You can't taste. How you expect to come to Harlem to buy some horse and taste it first, 'cause that don't sound like you think I am your friend. And I am your friend. You know that."

Frankie just nods and gives three dollars to the colored man.

In the street again, I am glad to breathe in a chestful of air that is lighter and cleaner than that dank tenement smell. It is all done. We have scored a hit.

And, strangely, I feel like I won something. I've never done anything like this before. But I did it. Something scary.

I like this feeling I have, this strength, knowing that I have done something that Scarry, Walsh, Jurgensen, any of those guys, have never done. Scoring horse in Harlem.

Even if all it proves is I did it.

I WONDER how long it will be before everyone finds out.

I've been putting on a shirt and tie when I get up every morning to do the papers, and Billy and my mother think that I go straight to school. But, instead, I go to the greasy spoon Greek diner on 53rd Street, where I read the *Daily News* and drink coffee until the florist shop opens.

I've been reading a lot about the polio epidemic that has all these kids locked up in iron lungs. Every time I read the newspaper, I take a little time out to explain to God that it's the biggest fear in my life to be trapped like that, to be locked in a tube or a room, and that's why I do all this shuffling from the papers to the florist, all this lying to my family about going to school.

I like the florist. I like the forty cents an hour. I like being on my own, controlling my own life. I wish I could get around the lies. My mother thinks I'm working only on Saturdays. I wish I could tell her the truth.

I TOLD Mr. Schmidt that I had something special to do this afternoon, and he let me go early, and I am now coming back from Bloomingdale's, where I finally bought the ring with the blue stone for my mother. I guess I could wait for her birthday to give it to her, or even Mother's Day, but I want to give it to her now. This is the day I finally put the forty bucks together. It's like something to celebrate, this forty bucks.

I pick up my three-ring binder from where I hide it under the stairs. My mother's working the four-to-twelve, and I catch her as she is putting on some lipstick before the kitchen mirror. I throw my binder on the top bunk in my room, and I come out to the kitchen, the little blue box deep in my pocket and burning a fast hole.

"How you doing, honey?" she asks.

I give her a kiss on the cheek. She seems surprised.

"I'm okay, I guess, but I have this pain in my leg."

She turns quickly to look at me.

"What pain, where?" she asks.

"Up here," I say, patting the upper part of my thigh. "It's like there is something pressing into my leg, like a sharp corner of something. Holy cow, what's this?"

I'm patting my leg like crazy, and she has no idea of what's going on. Finally I pull the ring box out of my pocket, saying, "Look, Mom, a little box with all these sharp edges."

I give the box to her, a dark blue box with a gold stripe around the sides, and I watch as she holds it to her breast.

"What's this?" she asks.

"Just something I think you need. And it's brand-new."

She sits on a kitchen chair as she pulls the ring out.

"And expensive," I add. She always thinks things are better if they're expensive.

"Oh, Dennis," she says, "you're something else. This is . . ." She can't finish the sentence right away, and she waits.

"You drive us all to the brink of despair," she says finally, "and then you do something like this."

I don't say anything, and I am happy to see how she likes the ring as she slips it over her finger. It fits perfectly.

"How could you afford this?" I knew she would ask.

"I just saved," I answer, "a little here, a little there."

"You know, Dennis," she says, holding the ring out in the light, "to do this shows something that's in your soul."

I don't want her to make such a splash about it. I don't want the ring to do anything except give her something to be happy about, something out of the blue that will make her smile.

"Oh, c'mon," I say, "I just wanted to give you something."

"Yes," she says, "you have given me something. And I hope you never lose it."

"The ring?" I ask.

"No." She laughs. "Not the ring. C'mere now and give us a kiss."

I laugh, too, saying, "I already gave you a kiss, Mom. I gotta go to meet the guys on Fifty-fourth Street."

I'm not meeting the guys on 54th Street at all.

I'm meeting the guys on 55th Street, but I don't want to tell her that. I don't want her to know.

IT IS now two weeks later, and the three of us are sitting around in the basement of number Two Sutton Place South, on 57th Street. I come to this building a lot with the flowers, and I know the lay of the basement delivery area. So does Mikey, because his father is a janitor here. We are in the boiler room, down a deep stairwell.

We came here straight from making a score on 120th Street.

It is hot, steamy. The walls are dark and shining with the sweat of the moisture. There is a water bug on the ceiling, a large one that seems frozen by the sound of our voices.

Frankie takes a set of works from under his shirt. There is a small metal cap from a medicine bottle, and he puts it between the prongs of a bobby pin, which acts as a handle. It is like a miniature cooking pot. There is a weird sense going through me as I watch this. It is like being at a High Mass, where the priests do things you don't quite understand. Mikey wraps thread around the tip of a large eyedropper and jams a needle on it. Frankie has the junk, and he opens the package and creases an edge of the paper to pour out the white powder.

"Careful, man," Mikey says.

"I know what I'm doing, man," Frankie says.

"Easy, guys," I say. This is the first time I have said anything since we got off the Second Avenue bus. The last time I was with them, we just scored the horse, but today I'm going to try it.

Frankie pours the powder in and goes to the water faucet on the side of the boiler. He puts a little water into the cap and mixes the powder. It looks like white mud, but when he puts a match to the bottom of the cap, all of it begins to boil, and the white substance disappears. It now looks like plain water.

"Perfect cook, man," Mikey says. "Perfect cook."

"Okay, Dennis," Frankie says, "you're up."

Until this moment I was thinking that I could still be along for the ride, but now, in a split second, I am a real part of all this. I have heard so much about how taking drugs just once will make you a drug addict for life, and drug addicts are the slime and the sewer scum in any neighborhood.

"C'mon," he says.

I never think about Frankie being a drug addict, but I guess he is. He's far from being a dreg, though. He's a good friend. I can tell the difference between a good guy and a dreg.

"C'mon, Dennis," Frankie says again.

Maybe there's still time to back out, I think. As exciting as this is, there's no reason for me to do this, except to try it.

"Naw," I say.

I don't know what to expect. So there's nothing wrong with being worried about it. Yet still, there is something that makes me wonder what is it all about, what it feels like.

"C'mon, Dennis," Mikey butts in, "you don't have to take it mainline. You could skin-pop."

"Is it habit-forming?" I ask. I don't know why I asked, because I know the answer.

Mikey laughs. "Yeah, man," he says. "But that's what's great about it. You're always looking forward, man."

"You can't get a habit," Frankie says, "if you just skin-pop. Don't listen to this guy. You can only get a habit if you mainline. Like this, see?"

Frankie has filled the eyedropper and wrapped his arm with a belt, holding one end between his teeth. He is smacking his veins with two fingers, getting a vein to rise. And then he jabs the needle into a vein until he finds the hole he is looking for. Then he spits the belt out, just as he is squeezing the bubble top.

I watch the solution disappear into his body, and I watch his lips change in a second from being pursed and all business and serious to a round smile.

I don't know what to think as I watch him close his eyes for a long minute. He tries to talk, but I can see it is hard for him to open his mouth. Finally he is able to say something.

"Just skin-pop, Dennis," he says. "It is okay, man. I wouldn't screw you up. You know that."

I do know that. Frankie wouldn't do anything to hurt me.

"All right, man," I say. "Just one time."

Frankie has his eyes closed again, and so Mikey takes the needle out of Frankie's hands and refills it. He leans over and pinches the skin on my upper arm, around my muscle.

"Watch, man," he says. "It's like darts."

I feel the steel going into my arm, and I flinch. But he is holding me firmly. And then he lets go of my skin as he squeezes the bulb.

I begin to watch Mikey load up for himself and tie the belt around his arm, and then, suddenly, out of the blue, it feels like someone has coated my eyelids with lead. They are so heavy. I am thinking, okay, I am not spinning, but my hands, my head, my fingers, all feel like they are nailed down. I try to open my eyes, but I cannot. I think about that water bug I saw, and I begin to worry about it. I know that it is going to let go of the ceiling and fall through the wet air and land in my hair, and I try to open my eyes to see where it is, but I can't, and I am sweating with the fear, and I can't move my hands to smack it off.

But then, just as suddenly I forget about the bug. I don't care about anything except raising my hand. But my hand is made of concrete, and it is welded on my lap, and I can't raise it, but I don't care. And time begins to pass. I can't think of time. There is no time. There is just now, and the now seems to be endless, with no beginning and no end, like God himself.

I don't know where we are, but all of a sudden we are moving. I sense these moving shadows along the cellar walls, and then there is sunlight, and we're in the park on 57th Street. I sit on a bench, and it seems like days go by as I sit there, the green strips of wood gently wrapping around me, my body like a tub of granite floating miraculously over the trees and then down into the East River, like a concrete coffin floating on top of the water. I am so afraid. I don't know why I have done this. And what makes me most afraid is that I don't know what to do when I'm afraid.

I just want to float in this blackness, thinking that if I had one wish in the world, I would wish that my brother and my mother knew to come get me.

I HAVE been trying not to think about all the letters from Cardinal Hayes High School that I have been ripping up.

I guess they will send someone down to 56th Street sometime soon, but it won't get me anywhere by worrying about it. I worked a long day today at the florist, and I have a few extra dollars in my pocket besides what I spent on a case of beer.

It is a hot night, one of those Indian summer nights just before Halloween, and I have been drinking beer down by the river. I was going to meet the guys on 55th Street, but I met Terry and Jackie Morgan just as I came out of my building. They're always a lot of laughs, and we've been arguing for more than an hour about why the Yankees lost to the Dodgers in the World Series.

Terry just left us. He went to have dinner with some girl he met in a hallway when he was delivering papers down on Sutton Place. Her parents were taking him to the Russian Cafe. Except for Joe's Original Restaurant and Emiliano's pizza place, I still have never been to a restaurant for a meal.

"How do you get a rich girlfriend like that?" I ask, holding a can of Rheingold beer.

"Just walk the streets around Sutton Place," Jackie says. "They are desperate over there, 'cause they don't have guys like us."

"How come you don't have one?" I ask.

"Because I have Annie," Jackie says. "That's why."

"Who's Annie?"

"Give me some beer," he says. "Can you keep a secret—a secret like if you tell anyone at all, I will personally cut your personals from your person?"

"I can keep anything," I say, "even a girlfriend if I could find one. A secret's easy. So who's this Annie?"

"Annie Dunne."

"Annie Dunne, with the husband in Sing Sing Annie Dunne?"

"That's the one," he says. "I went to bed with her three times."

"Jackie," I say, trying to remember the things I heard about the Dunne family, "isn't the husband in jail for murder?"

"No," he replies, "I think for beating somebody up. But he's in jail for another ten years or something."

"Jackie," I say, swigging the beer, "ever hear of jailbreaks?"

"This ain't the movies," Jackie says, laughing.

"But Jackie," I say, "even in the movies they don't all get killed in the jailbreak. Some of them go on to become priests, and some others come back to kill the guy that was banging his wife."

"Come on," Jackie says, "let's go pay her a visit."

"It's almost midnight," I say.

"C'mon, don't be such a punk," he says. "It's something to do. Your mother waiting for you or something?"

"Don't be a pain," I say. "My mother went out to her sister's house in Queens."

"So you don't have to go home. C'mon."

We hit 56th Street and walk to 333, the building next to mine. Jackie has his finger to his lips as we creep down the alleyway.

"Shh," he utters in a kind of whisper. "If we wake up old Mrs. Dunne, that will be the end of it." Old Mrs. Dunne is Annie's mother-in-law, and she is the super of the building.

Underneath my windbreaker I can feel my polo shirt sticking to my back. I guess it's sweat made from the heat, but maybe also because I am a little afraid. Jackie is three years older than I am, and I don't know him the way I know Walsh or Scarry or even guys like Frankie and Mikey.

Now we're in the backyard, and Jackie wants to climb up the drainpipe to the second floor.

"Up the drainpipe," I say. "Why can't we go in the front door?"

"I been thinking about what you said about the jailbreak," Jackie whispers, "and I gotta make sure nobody sees us."

Jackie shinnies up the drainpipe to the window above us and shoves the kitchen window open. I am right behind him. He climbs in and pulls me in after him. I feel a strange sensation inside my body. It's not that I am afraid, but I just know that we are doing something that is very wicked.

Jackie takes his clothes off right there in the middle of the kitchen, and he is as naked as the day the doctor smacked him on the ass.

"You go sleep on the couch," he whispers, pointing to the living room.

I don't like that he is telling me what to do. I thought I would get to see Annie in her nightgown or something, but I didn't expect to climb up a drainpipe all this way to go sleep on a couch.

In a moment, though, Jackie is gone, his clothes spread around on the kitchen floor, left there like he was a leprechaun.

Suddenly I hear a long scream, a woman's scream, and in a whirl Jackie is going through the kitchen. He's searching madly for his clothes, picking them up, and running.

I am standing here, feeling my stomach turn over and over.

"Get going!" he yells to me.

I race after him through the back bedroom window, the one that leads out to the fire escape. Still naked, Jackie runs up the fire escape stairs. I find him in the darkness of a corner of the roof, doubled over, out of breath, and laughing madly. He begins to hop frantically on one leg as he puts the other through his pants.

"Holy God," he is saying over and over. "I climbed into the bed.

I saw her lying there, and she turned around, and she yelled like hell, and she scared the crap outta me, and it wasn't even Annie Dunne, Dennis, it was old Mrs. Dunne herself, there in the bed."

"Fat Mrs. Dunne?" I say. "What's she doing there?"

"Annie must've gone away, who knows, up to Sing Sing maybe."

"With a file in her girdle," I say. "That guy is gonna escape."

Jackie laughs a big one and pushes me.

I raise my finger to my lips. Jackie is making too much noise.

"The cops are sure to come," I say, whispering.

"Who cares?" Jackie says. "I'm going home anyways. Just be quiet in your hallway."

Our buildings are all in a row, mine and Annie Dunne's and the Morgans'. I watch Jackie as he crosses over two roofs and goes down the stairs in his building, and I cross just one roof in the other direction and go down the stairs in mine, thinking that this has been a crazy thing to do. Why do I do these things? Why am I living outside of the normal?

I run quickly down the dark narrow hall to my apartment and search for the key under the ripped hall linoleum. I quickly shove the key in the door and swing it open. And then I am flabbergasted. My mother is standing right there before me.

"Where have you been?" she asks.

I am completely surprised. She told me she probably wouldn't be home, and I promised her that I would be in by eleven thirty. She is in her pink bathrobe, her arms folded in front of her.

"I thought," I answer, "that you were staying at Aunt Kitty's."

"Well, young man," she says, "I came home because I want to know where you are spending your time when you go out at night. It is almost one o'clock in the morning. Who were you with?"

I know she doesn't like the Morgan family, because the mother and father come out on the street drunk once in a while. My mother thinks that if you have to be drunk, you should not share it with everyone on 56th Street.

"Walsh and Scarry and those guys," I say in a low voice.

"Did you say Walsh and Scarry," she says, "and those guys? Huh? Listen, Dennis, tell me who you were with."

"I was with them," I say, lying. "We went to a movie."

"Where did you get the money to go to a movie?"

"Scarry treated us all." It's another lie.

My mother looks very angry. "I don't believe you," she says. "Scarry and Walsh would not be out at one in the morning."

"I was so with them," I say in one last try to get out of it.

"You weren't," she says. "And I'll say this to you. Tell me who your friends are, and I'll tell you what you are."

"Can I go to bed now?" I say more than ask.

"Yes," she says with a biting, bitter voice and that terrible disgusted look on her face.

I turn into our room, and she is following me. I just wish she would shut up and leave me alone. I don't take my clothes off, but jump up fast into the top bunk and turn my body to the wall. But she is right behind me and gives me a good shove.

"And don't think," I hear her say as my body goes flat against the wall, "that I don't smell the beer along with the cigarettes."

A FEW weeks pass, and my mother doesn't say much more than hello to me.

It is now Sunday morning. Early. My brother has just come back from a midnight-to-eight shift throwing the mail sacks for the New York Central Railroad, and he is sitting in the bathtub in the kitchen. I don't say anything to him as I go to brush my teeth.

I didn't get up to do the papers this morning. Last night I hung out with Frankie and Mikey, and, besides the junk, I took a few tokes on some pot. My head aches, and I wonder, since it feels like the size of a watermelon, if I will ever get completely awake again. I am also wondering, as I grab the toothbrush, if Billy can see the marks in my arm where I have been skin-popping. I should have worn a long-sleeved shirt when I got out of bed.

My mother is in her room. Thank God. I don't want to talk to anyone, especially my mother.

I'm not going to go to Mass today. I don't feel good. It's okay to miss Mass if you're sick.

I'm still worrying about my arm in a short-sleeved shirt, and I go into our room and throw myself into an old flannel shirt. I pour corn flakes into a chipped green bowl and look for the sugar. I can't find it. I look all around, but I don't see it.

"Where's the sugar?" I ask.

"Don't talk to me," Billy says.

I really don't like it that he is talking to me this way.

I open the refrigerator door. I see the can, and I pour two tablespoons over the cornflakes.

"Don't give me the bug up in your ass," I answer Billy.

Billy points a finger at me. "Just watch your mouth, Dennis," he says, "or I'll take your teeth out of it."

"Yeah, yeah," I say. I put my head down close to the cereal bowl so that I don't have to look at him. We don't argue so much, but sometimes he just thinks he has to play the father around here.

"You know," he says, "you're not going to get away with everything."

"Yeah, yeah," I say again. I don't know what he is talking about.

"I played basketball up at Mount St. Vincent's yesterday," he says. "And I met Father Jabo."

Father Jablonski, the dean of discipline at Cardinal Hayes.

"Yeah?"

"He told me you haven't been up at school for more than a month, and so I told Mom."

"S---," I say. "Why'd you do that?"

" 'Cause she should know how you're screwing up."

"Yeah, yeah, friggin' squealer."

Billy raises his voice now. "I told you to watch your mouth."

"I need a mirror to watch my mouth, and why can't you just mind your own business?"

"Because you are a little wise guy, you and the punk brizzers you hang around with."

My mother now comes running out of her bedroom.

"Just stop it, you two," she says. "Stop arguing. Arguing doesn't settle anything," she says.

She boils the water for her tea. I can tell she is upset, because she is pursing her lips and shaking the kettle to help the water boil faster. Billy doesn't say anything. I just chew my cornflakes.

She pours her tea and slams the cup on the white Formica, and the tea spills over.

"So what time did you come home last night?" she asks.

"You mean me?" I ask, looking up. And then she lays into me.

"You are such a fast-mouth," she says. "You know I don't mean your brother, who has been out since midnight working to bring a few extra dollars into the house, and you nowhere to be found."

I suddenly think that I not only do not know what time I came home, but I don't even know where I was, for I only remember the heaviness of my eyes, and the nodding, and the sitting in the cellar of the candy store on 55th Street, and the nodding, and the walking to Riker's on 53rd Street, and the bite of a hamburger from someone I don't remember, and then an endless stream of nodding, and I don't know where and I don't know what time.

"So," she says, louder, "what time did you come home?"

I don't want to be forced to lie again.

"I don't know what time, Mom, so just leave off, will ya?"

She pours milk into her tea, and a half teaspoon of sugar. "Where were you that you don't know what time you came home?"

"I was just out."

"What were you doing?"

"Nothing, and just leave me alone, huh?"

"And what went on at the florist's shop yesterday?"

"Nothing."

"Nothing went on?" she asks. "What did you do there?"

I am thinking that it is just going to get worse for me here, and we haven't gotten to playing hooky yet. And so I don't answer.

"Answer me," she demands. "You say nothing went on?"

"No," I answer. "Nothing went on."

"You're absolutely right nothing went on," she says. "Because you never went there to begin with. Mr. Schmidt came here looking for you because you left him high and dry, and you tell me nothing happened? So you are turning into a liar, too?"

"I didn't lie," I say. "Why can't you just let me alone?"

"Who were you with?"

I am now feeling the skin all over my face begin to tighten, as if a corner was being twisted like a rubber band, and I want to make one of those terrible stretching faces that will make her madder than anything. I just want to get out of the apartment before everything explodes. My head is filled with grease and rocks, and I can feel my heart pumping like a tommy gun. I close my eyes.

"Where were you?"

"Mom," I yell, "c'mon, huh? I am so f------ tired of everyone being on me, you and Billy—"

I don't have time to finish my sentence, because Billy is out of the tub in a flash and coming for me.

I know I shouldn't have cursed. And I know, too, that I have to run. But where can you run in a four-room apartment?

My mother's room? Maybe I can lock him out.

And so I run as fast as I can, but my mother has so many clothes on the door that I can't close it, and Billy has pushed the door open and is punching like a Golden Gloves contender, and I begin to fall on the bed, and Billy, all naked and soapy, is on top of me, and I feel my head sinking down into the mattress with each punch.

And now my mother is screaming.

"Stop it!" she is screaming. "Stop it! Don't ruin this family."

And I wonder if she is talking to me or Billy.

She is trying to pull Billy away, but he is so wet and slippery that she keeps losing her grip, and Billy punches me twice more, and then suddenly he stops and walks away, naked like an Indian hunter, and my mother is just standing there, tears streaming down her face, her hands clutched together.

I don't do anything. I wish I could say something that would make her stop crying. Maybe if I said I was sorry, but I don't know what to be sorry about. Playing hooky? Staying out late? C'mon, I am fifteen years old, for Chrissakes.

It is my life, and those guys are my friends, and what else do I have but my life and my friends?

Ten

IT DIDN'T take much to quit Cardinal Hayes. My mother had to go up to the Grand Concourse with me, and we sat in Monsignor Fleming's office.

"When will you be sixteen?" Monsignor asked.

"A few months," I answered.

"You won't have much of a future," the monsignor said. "An education is the safest thing to put between us and despair."

"Monsignor Ford is getting me a job when I turn sixteen," I said. "At Catholic Charities."

"That's something," Monsignor Fleming says. "It's good you have a friend in Monsignor Ford."

And that's all there was to it to quit high school—no fanfare, no trouble, no pledge in the rectory office. I just left Cardinal Hayes for the last time, and that was that.

Now I am one of two office boys at the Catholic Charities building on 22nd Street. It takes hardly any effort to sort and deliver the mail up and down six floors, and I am getting seventy-five cents an hour. Thirty bucks a week. I give my mother fifteen, and I can buy whatever kind of shoes I want from now on.

I'm still working on Saturdays at the florist. Working two jobs and being on my own is what I want. I am controlling my life, and if you don't count my mother, Mr. Schmidt at the florist, and my boss, Mr. Lacy, at Catholic Charities, and maybe Monsignor Ford, I don't have anybody to answer to. I can do as I want.

I AM standing in the back of the church now. I've been missing Mass a lot lately, and I am making a stop-in. No matter what is going on in my life, I always try to make room for church.

"Just stop in once in a while between Sundays," I remember Sister Stella saying, "and that's the quickest way to heaven."

I don't have anything to especially pray for, and so I am sitting in a back pew, sort of basking in the soft evening light and the wild mix of colors coming down from the saints and the angels on the ceiling. It is like basking in the sun at Coney Island, when you don't think about hardly anything, but just let the warmth sink in.

Suddenly someone comes into my pew and sits next to me. It's Father O'Rourke, and he gives me a big pat on the back.

"We miss you at the altar boys, Dennis," he says.

"Just getting old, Father," I say, "growing up."

"Level to level, huh?"

"Right. Grammar to high school, and high school to working."

"I heard you are now down with Monsignor Ford. How is it?"

"It's okay," I answer. "Okay."

"Why'd you quit school?"

"I failed everything," I say. "And instead of going into my third year, I would have to do my first year all over again. I'd be old enough to vote by the time I graduate."

Father O'Rourke laughs.

"I know what you mean. Most days I'm trying to catch up with what I was supposed to do yesterday, but could I give you some advice?"

"Sure, Father."

"Keep reading books. No matter what's going on in your life, always care about what you are putting inside your mind. It's what's up here"—he is now pointing at my head—"that will let you grow, level to level."

"I WOULD start with Hemingway," Billy says. It's a Sunday afternoon, and we are shooting baskets up at the 61st Street park.

"I already read some Hemingway," I say.

"I'm reading all of Hemingway, all of Faulkner, and all of Sinclair Lewis. You read all these books, and you'll know something of how America got to be like it is."

Billy is in Hunter College now. Hunter is a free city college, but you have to pass a pretty hard test to get in there.

He got a scholarship to Oberlin College in Ohio, but first he had to get a hundred bucks to cover the book and lab fees. My mother didn't have the money, and so he didn't go. I wonder, though, if it was because she just didn't want him so far away. It was a disappointment to Billy, but he never complained about it. But lately I notice something about Billy that I never saw before. He's been spending a lot of time down at Jasper's Bar on Second Avenue, and sometimes he doesn't come home until it closes at three a.m.

"LAST night was a close call," I say to Frankie, leaning into the velvet crunch of the back seat.

He is driving his father's car, and we are going out to Rockaway Beach. His father has gone on an all-day moving job and won't be home until late tonight. I don't think he knows that Frankie took the car. Frankie doesn't have a driver's license.

"That Bobby Sutton is something, huh?" Frankie says.

"I didn't know he had a zip gun," I say. "I was wondering why we went all the way almost to Queens on the Fifty-ninth Street Bridge, and then he takes this gun out of his pocket and shoots it off into the sky. I'm glad there were no airplanes flying over."

"Yeah," Frankie says, swerving in and out of the traffic. "And the Keegan brothers should be happy they weren't on Sixty-fifth Street, either, or else Sutton would have let them have it."

The Keegan brothers are boxers, Golden Gloves champs, and nobody to fool around with. But their sister Eleanor had a problem at the Kips Bay dance with someone from 55th Street, and she blew her stack. Her brothers came down to the candy store the next day and said everyone on 55th Street was a punk unless we came up to 65th Street to fight it out. Frankie said we couldn't let them get away with putting us on notice like that and called Bobby Sutton to come in from Queens. Sutton completely dominated the Machine and Metal Trades High School when Frankie went there, the toughest guy in a tough turf.

After testing the zip gun, twenty of us marched up First Avenue to 65th Street, two abreast. I liked being lined up with all the guys, like going into a war or something, all of us being a part of something big, something that people would respect.

When we turned the corner there, we saw four guys standing on a stoop, and Sutton went right up to them and started punching. I never saw anything like it. These guys were just minding their own business, and this madman began punching at all four of them.

I had no beef with these guys from 65th Street, but here we were, in their territory, with Sutton punching everyone he could see. I wanted to tell him to stop it, that we had defended ourselves, and maybe now we could all go home.

But then the cops came running up First Avenue.

"Chickie!" somebody yells. "Chickie, the cops!"

I ran like I was in a race in the stadium up on Randall's Island, first down to York and, thinking that everyone would probably run back downtown, I made a left and zoomed up to 72nd Street. I could walk then, across to Lexington, down to 56th Street, and then slowly, like nothing happened, around to 55th Street.

"IT'S amazing no one got caught," Nicky the Greek says. Nicky just started hanging around with us, and I've been seeing a lot of him since I quit the job at Catholic Charities.

It was a boring job, just going from floor to floor dropping the mail at people's desks. Also, Mr. Lacy began to yell at me for being late or not fast enough or any little thing, and so I told him to get someone else to take his b.s.

"Some cop got close," Nicky says, "but he never got up to me."

"What are we going to do, anyway?" I ask.

"Go to McGuire's Bar on 108th Street," Frankie says. "Maybe watch a little basketball in the beach court there, maybe have a couple beers, maybe shoot up."

"Maybe get some Irish girls to sit on our laps," Nicky says.

"I don't want to shoot up," I say.

"You can skin-pop," Frankie says.

"I think I'll drink beer," I say, " 'cause I got a few bucks."

My brother is in the fenced-in basketball court alongside the beach near McGuire's Bar. There is a fast game going on, and I sit along the sidelines, watching, until he comes over at a time-out.

"What are you doing?" he asks.

"Looking for some broads, maybe. How you doin'?"

"I got such a hangover," he says. "I'm going to have to play fifty games to clear it all out of my system."

"Where were you?"

"Jasper's," he says, "and I was completely ossified, drinking beer out of my shoe. Jasper threw me out and told me that the only reason he wasn't locking me in the refrigerator was because neighborhood kids get two tries."

"I wouldn't go back for a while, Billy," I say.

"Right," Billy says, "I'm banning myself."

At least Billy goes to his jobs, and he never misses college. He's getting things done. But I don't know when to stop, to ban myself from anything. I want to try to change, and that's why I told Frankie today that I don't want any horse. I don't want to be a dope addict. I just have to tell them I don't want it. I have to think about this dope stuff the way Billy thinks about Jasper's Bar. At least, Billy is smart enough to ban himself.

I AM sitting in the back of the car now as Frankie and Nicky are shooting up. I am looking out the back window to make sure the police are not driving by. It is a hot day. I had about five beers in McGuire's, and there were no Irish girls, not that I wouldn't take a girl from Istanbul if I could get one.

Frankie and Nicky are nodding, and I am beginning to sweat. I can't wait for the car to get going again.

"Hey," Frankie says, "Dennis, man . . . man. You got anything to eat, like a Yankee Doodle, man?"

"No, Frankie, I don't."

"Man, we gotta go to Fifty-fifth Street to get Yankee Doodles."

Frankie starts the car, and I half know that he cannot drive while he's nodding. But I also half don't care.

It's hot, and I'm a little woozy. I should have gone to work at the florist today, but I asked Mr. Schmidt if I could take the day off. I don't like delivering flowers anymore, either, and I would quit if it wasn't for my mother.

"If you quit," my mother said, "it would be the last straw and I will kick you out of the house."

She would kick me out of the house, even though home is the place that when you go there they always have to let you in.

But poetry isn't always right. It is hard to get back in the house when you have been kicked out. I know, because Mikey Fallon and Dennis Buckley have been kicked out of their houses, and they live from park to park and cellar to cellar. And they are not the kind of guys that Archie said we respect, the guys we look up to.

I always thought I would be one of those guys, the guys people respected, but it wasn't working out that way.

On Queens Boulevard at 78th Street we stop for a red light. A car behind doesn't stop in time and bumps us.

"Hey, man," Frankie says, "my old man's car. Any dents, and he'll know we took it."

I look out the back window. There are six guys in the car behind us, maybe in their late twenties. As the light changes and we go forward, I see the license plate. "From New Jersey," I say.

"Not even America," Frankie says.

"Six guys," I say.

"If they're from New Jersey," Nicky says, "you count in halves."

"So, man." Frankie laughs. "There's only three of them."

At 74th Street we again stop for a red light, and the same car comes behind us and bumps us again, this time a little harder.

"Oh, man," Frankie says, "they ain't gonna do that again, man, no way." He opens the door and grabs a monkey wrench from under the seat as he gets out of the car. "I'll break their windows."

I find myself climbing out of the car behind Nicky. The six men from New Jersey are all out of their car, and each one seems bigger than we are. Why did they bump us? What did they want? Maybe Frankie cut them off or something. I don't know.

But now here I am in the middle of Queens Boulevard, punching some guy who has me around the neck and is dragging me to the street, kicking me as he pulls. It is like I entered some weird ride out in Coney Island where you never know what to expect, and this time you have to fight as hard as you can without knowing why.

And so I am lying on the ground, horns blaring in the middle of traffic, with some guy's hair clenched in my fist, and I won't let go, and he is screaming as he punches me, and I am punching him, and another guy comes and starts trying to kick me between my legs, and I am covering myself and punching and holding and pulling. I feel my skin breaking apart and the blood running down my chin.

And in the middle of all of this I look over and I see Frankie on the ground, and he is hitting some poor fellow again and again over the head with the monkey wrench, and their clothes are full of blood, and there is blood everywhere on the street, and I can hear the sirens in the distance.

NOW I am in this strange place, a place dark in the corners, the bare lightbulb in the hall casting dim stripes shooting over the bare mattress and the black-stained stainless steel bowl, and I am thinking of my mother, remembering that Mrs. Fox upstairs will have to tell her that there is a phone call for her from Queens, and I can see my mother walking through the dark hall and up the stairs, with each step worrying about who is dead and who is injured and where were her two sons?

Oh, Mom, I think, I am sorry I am making you go through this.

And so many thoughts follow this one, because you know that you are powerless to change your life all by yourself. You need help because, after everything is said and done, all the prayers uttered, the Sorrowful Mysteries finished, and you're alive and in trouble like this, you know that it is all your fault. That you got here on your own, but you can't get out without somebody who cares about you.

THE Queens County Court building looks like a schoolhouse, red and gray stone, with two dozen steps to the front door.

I see Marty Trainor on the steps, his arm around my mother's shoulders. For the first time in my life she looks frail to me, huddled there in a yellow-flowered dress beneath Marty's arm.

I have no clue as to what is going on, except that I know I am in trouble and that Marty Trainor is the guy everyone in the neighborhood calls when there is trouble. I haven't seen Frankie or Nicky since I got up from the ground on Queens Boulevard.

My mother doesn't say anything, and I can hardly look her in the eyes, those keen hazel eyes now reddened at the corners.

"Your mother and I have talked this over," Marty says, "and I think I can get you off, but you'll have to give us your word that you are willing to change your life."

Marty Trainor is an old Kips Bay Boys Club guy, and he knows that giving your word means something here.

"What kind of trouble," I say in a shaking voice, "is this?"

"Pretty serious," Marty says, pulling me away from my mother's earshot. "Felonious assault is pretty serious. The guy you were fighting with has twenty-six stitches."

"Not the guy I was fighting with," I say, thinking that the worst thing with the guy I fought is that he could be bald.

"It doesn't matter who," Marty says. "The fact is someone has all those stitches from a fight on a public street, and the judge won't care about who actually did what."

"The guy hit me first, Marty."

I have always believed that if someone hit you first, it was not only fair to hit him back, but almost a personal responsibility.

"Look, we have to go in. Your mother is a wreck. This is going to cost her three hundred and fifty dollars for getting me out here, but I am not going to take the money from her. I want it from you."

"Yeah, sure," I say, "but I don't have that kind of money."

"You'll pay me ten a week until it's paid, understand?"

"Yeah, sure."

"And this is what you are going to do."

"What's that?" My voice is not so shaky now, and I am thinking that Marty Trainor is a smart man and a good lawyer.

"You have never been in this kind of trouble before," he says, "and the judge will like that. But what he will really like is when we tell him that you are going to be seventeen years old in just three weeks, that it has been your lifelong ambition to join the United States Air Force, and that you will be on your way to a boot camp in a month, far from your friends and the neighborhood that made it possible for you to end up here in a courtroom for criminals before your weeping mother."

I don't know what to say to Marty, but I am thinking that I don't have much to say about any of it, anyway. I guess he talked this over with my mother, so I just shrug my shoulder in agreement. I look over at my mother, hoping that she will smile, but she has a rock-hard look on her face.

IT IS still early morning, and we are again at the top of the court's steps. Marty Trainor has just gone, and my mother and I are standing quietly, waiting for the right words to come.

Here she is, prim and proper in her yellow-flowered dress, but haggard, looking beaten from a sleepless night and from being forced to stand behind her son before a judge who only wants to know if her son would join the air force, and if her son would join the air force, he would dismiss the charges so that her son could still be a cop or a fireman or a postal clerk or anything you could be if you aren't convicted of some crime. And so I know there is only one thing to say to my mother.

"I'm sorry, Mom," I say to her. "I am."

She smiles for the first time and begins to walk down the steps.

"You know," she says, "you're going to have to pay Marty Trainor. It's a lot of money."

"I'll pay him back, Mom," I say. "I promise, every last penny."

"I'll remember," she says. "And for you, remember that the road to going backwards is made out of unkept promises."

On the subway, the train rollicking at sixty miles an hour, my mother puts down her *Daily News* and holds my hand.

I shift a little on the airy, cane-covered train seat. She sees that she has taken a reluctant hand, and she squeezes my fingers.

"I know you'll look handsome in a uniform," she says. "What do those air force uniforms look like, anyway?"

"I don't know," I say. "I never saw one."

"You never saw one? Then, why are you joining the air force instead of the marines or the navy?"

"I don't know," I say. "I thought you and Marty agreed about it."

"Oh, goodness," she says, laughing. "I guess when I told him that it was a great hope of mine that you would finish the Aviation

High School, he just thought the air force was the thing for you."

"Yeah," I say, laughing, too, "I guess so. What difference does it make, anyway? I'll be okay."

She laughs a little more, quietly to herself, and lets the train rock her back and forth. She sighs.

"You know, there isn't much time before you'll be away in the service. We have a lot to do."

"Yeah," I say. "Like what?"

"Well," she says, "you are leaving New York, and I don't know how long it will be before you come back. So I think it's time. . . . I think you should come with me up to see your father."

There is a great silence now as the train screeches to a stop at the Grand Central Station stop on 42nd Street.

God, I am saying to myself, dodging in and out of the crowd as I walk up the subway stairs to Lexington Avenue. I haven't thought about going to see my father in a long time.

Eleven

THE Poughkeepsie State Hospital is a large, brown brick fenced-in building that reminds me of all those poorhouses and asylums that the English and the Irish writers describe in their stories, except that it is not so dark and wet.

We are now walking through the main corridor, and I am looking for the reception desk.

"There is no one ever on the first floor," my mother says. "We have to take the elevator to three."

I am trying to act calm, cool, and collected. It's not easy being in an insane asylum for the first time, but it's even harder to see your father for the first time you can remember.

There is a small corridor before us when we get off the elevator, and on either side there is a door with wired glass.

I can see a nurse reading a newspaper through the door on the left, but my mother pulls me to the right. Inside I see about twenty beds, most with men sleeping in yellow pajamas. Some are sitting on the floor, some walking around in circles, bumping into each other. I wonder who my father is and watch to see how many men turn as my mother raps her keys on the glass. Hardly anyone turns.

"He was here last time I was up," she says.

She raps harder, and the nurse unlocks the door to our left.

"We are looking for John Smith," my mother says.

"I think he's on four," the nurse says. "Try four."

There is the same configuration on the fourth floor, but this time the nurse is on our right. She unlocks the door, and we cross the hall, and she unlocks the other door.

Like on the third floor, there are twenty or so beds, and my mother and I cruise around the room, looking for my father, but I don't know who I am looking for.

A man comes quickly up to us, almost on a run. His yellow pajamas are two sizes too big for him. Suddenly he grabs my arm.

"Give me my money," he says. His eyes are wide and seem directly connected to mine. I don't think this is my father.

"I don't have your money," I say, trying to be calm.

"Tell him," my mother says, "the nurse has his money."

"The nurse has your money," I say.

"The nurse has my money?" he asks, like I told him his horse came in in the sixth race.

"Yes," I say, "the nurse."

The man turns and walks away.

My mother smiles. "They respect the nurses," she says.

There is a post in the middle of the room, and my mother begins to walk around it. But she stops and gently lifts a finger. "There he is."

I see my father for the first time, lying there in a bed behind the post. He looks much older than his forty-five years. He is thin, but his stomach is large. He looks so different from how I remember him in the two photographs I have seen. In one he is in an empty lot in Brooklyn, holding a baseball glove, looking like a kid, trim and fast, trying out for maybe the Railway Express team, center field, casually leaning to the left, knowing he'll make the cut.

In the other he's in a big velvet chair, my mother on his lap, her legs, long and shapely, kicking out from a summer dress, him, good-looking in a white shirt and tie, his face a grin from ear to ear. Both photographs flash happiness like a neon sign, and I look closely now at my father for the smallest sign that he is happy.

But there is no expression on his face.

"Hello, John," my mother says.

"Hello, hello," he says quickly. His voice quivers a little.

"It's Mary, John," my mother says. "Mary."

"Hello, hello," he says again. "Give me a cigarette."

"They used to be able to smoke," my mother whispers to me, "but there was a fire somewhere."

"Do you remember me, John?" she asks.

"Hello, hello," he says, this time adding, "Mary."

"This is Dennis, John," she says, pulling me forward.

"Dennis," he repeats.

"How are you, John?" she asks.

He is staring across the room at nothing in particular.

"Give me a cigarette," he says.

"How have you been?" she asks again. "Are you eating anything but dessert, John?"

There is a stain on the front of his yellow pajamas, still wet, and I am guessing it is from his lunch. My mother takes a handkerchief from her pocketbook and wipes at it. He pushes her away.

"Who's this?" he asks, gesturing toward me.

"This is Dennis, John," my mother answers. "Your son."

"Give me a cigarette," he says.

"Do you remember Dennis, John? Dennis and Billy?"

"Hello, hello," he says.

The hair at the side of his head is sticking out, and my mother pushes it back with her hand.

"You are looking pretty good, John," she says. "I bet all the nurses are after you, huh?"

"Give me a cigarette," he says in the same crispy voice.

"John," my mother says, her hand on my shoulder, "do you remember Dennis? Dennis is now a man, see?"

"Hello, hello," he says.

My mother goes around the bed, fluffing things up, taking the wrinkles out of the sheets. I notice that she doesn't kiss him. He has been away more than sixteen years, and I wonder how many years it is since she kissed him last.

"Okay, John," she says in the middle of a sigh, "you're looking pretty good, and so I guess we can go."

My mother pats his hand. My father doesn't say anything.

I have my hands in my pockets, and I think I should at least reach over and shake his hand. I grab a cigarette out of the pack in my pants pocket as I pull my hand out.

I take his hand as my mother begins to walk away.

"Good-bye, Dad," I say, something I've never before said.

"Give me a cigarette," he says.

I lean over next to his ear, and I whisper.

"I dropped one," I say, "on the sheet."

I am thinking as I walk into the main entry hall with my mother that these places are not dangerous. Things are just quirky here.

Ever since I heard Aunt Kitty jabbering away that day more than five years ago, I have been reading everything I came across about mental disease. I realize that there is a special kind of sadness that comes with the territory in these places. People get locked away and forgotten, and that is a desperate thing.

Maybe it is easier on the family to make up stories. It was hard for my mother to talk about my father. It's easier to have a secret than to explain to people, especially the children, that he is locked up and forgotten because no one else knows what to do.

It's a very personal thing.

WE ARE now speeding back toward the city on the New York Central Albany Special. My mother is quiet.

I'm quiet, too, sad from seeing my father like that. But I'm glad I was there, finally. At least, I saw him. In all those years when I wanted to see him, I couldn't. Then after I found out where he really was, I didn't much care to see him at all.

I used to dream as a kid in St. John's that one day a classroom door would open, and there would be my father on a pair of wooden crutches, and the whole class would cheer as I ran to him. But his being in an asylum was a letdown to me, an embarrassment.

All my life, I guess, I've been wishing that things would get better for us, for Billy and me, that my mother would be happier.

And that my father would get better.

But I can see now that my father will never get better, and that is a hard and a bitter thing to know for sure. Before, when I thought about it, I thought it could get better for him if I prayed enough. God has kept him alive, anyway. I'll just thank Him for that.

My mother pats my leg and breaks the silence.

"I'm glad," she says, "that you came with me."

"I'm glad, too, Mom," I answer. "Even though it was pretty strange, like looking at someone in a movie or something."

"He loved being around you and Billy. His memory is completely shot now. Those shock treatments, you know. But he used to always ask about you." My mother has a soft, resigned look on her face. "He would remember you and forget me, because the wires for his short-term memory were completely cut somehow."

"How did that happen, Mom?" I ask. "How did you find out?"

"Nobody knows, really. They call it catatonic. I had no idea anything was wrong," she says, looking down at her hands. "Everything was so normal. We were living in Sterling Place in Brooklyn. You had just been born, and Billy was two."

She stops now and looks at me, smiling.

"I remember," she continues, "we were out for a walk. I had you and Billy stuffed in that carriage like socks in a sock drawer, and when I got home, I rang the bell for your father to come down to help me, and I rang and rang.

"It was his day off, and I was hopping mad that he never came down, and so I asked some man on the street, a passerby, to help me up the two flights. I opened the door, and I saw your father's legs in the living room as I thanked the man for helping.

"I guess it was a funny scene," she says, "because I saw him sitting in the big, blue velvet chair, and I began right away to complain about him not coming down to help."

As she is talking, I can see tears in the corners of her eyes, but she is laughing as she talks. "And then I started to raise my voice a little," she goes on, "because he wasn't answering. 'Well, say something,' I said, 'and don't sit there like a wrapped package.'

"Then I went in and saw him sitting there, his hands grabbing the chair as if he was falling off a cliff, and his eyes staring out like he saw a ghost. Oh, Dennis, I was so frightened."

"What happened?" I ask.

"I have never seen a person like that, just completely frozen, unable to speak or utter a sound. 'What's the matter, John?' I kept asking over and over. But he couldn't move even his mouth. And so I went to a neighbor and asked him to run to the bar where your uncle Bob worked. Uncle Bob came, and then the doctors and the ambulance. He was a completely different person forever after that, never knowing where he was or what was wrong."

"God, Mom," I say, "that was pretty hard on you, huh?"

She takes the handkerchief from her pocketbook and dabs at her eyes.

"Well, I would say it was harder on your father."

Her voice is cracked and small, and she breaks into a laugh.

"Yeah," I say quietly. My throat is dry; it feels as if a two-by-four is going through it when I swallow.

"So," she says calmly, "it was just the three of us after that"—she pauses—"just me and you two little guys."

"Well," I say, trying to make her feel good, "you did okay."

"Did I, Dennis?" she asks.

I'm not sure she wants me to answer, but I answer, anyway.

"I mean," I say, "Billy is in college, and I am going into the air force. This all came from you."

There are just a few people, maybe a dozen, on the train. I have been coughing because my mouth is still dry. My mother gets up and walks to the end of the car, where she fills a paper cup with water from the spigot. Everybody watches her as she moves past them. She takes a sip and brings the cup to me.

"This will make you feel better," she says.

She sits again and puts her pocketbook on her lap. There are so many things I would like to ask her: about how she grew up next to a firehouse in Brooklyn, about graduating from high school, about what boyfriends she might have had, about how she and her brother and two sisters lived in a two-bedroom apartment, about how she met my father, about her wedding day. But she has settled back and closed her eyes and seems to be keeping some inner rhythm in tune with the clacking of the wheels against the tracks.

I think she is sleeping, but she begins to whisper.

"Dennis," she says, "would you do me a favor?"

"Sure, Mom," I answer, "anything."

"Would you sing me," she asks, " 'The Rose of Tralee'?"

God, I'm thinking, I don't want to be singing on a train in front of the whole world. Maybe if I just don't answer her, she'll fall asleep and forget all about asking me to sing in the middle of a crowd, even if it is just a dozen.

" 'The Rose of Tralee,' " she whispers.

She must be thinking about all those Sunday afternoons sitting around a keg of beer on 56th Street.

It's funny how people are and what makes them happy.

I am thinking that the only time I saw her being really happy was when I sang that song for her, and then again on that night she took us to Joe's Original Restaurant. And it seemed she was pretty happy when I gave her that ring. Three times is not many in a life.

I felt so close to her those times, like she knew her life was safe with me and she trusted me completely.

I never gave her much reason to trust me after that.

But she brought me with her today. She told my father I was a man now. She trusted me to be there with her.

And so here I am, seventeen years old and about to leave home for God knows how close to forever, and I take a deep breath to sing this song for my mother.

I strain my voice to be above the clacking of the train, and I know that the whole train is looking at me. But I look over at my mother as I sing the first verse.

"The pale moon was rising
Above the green mountains
The sun was declining
Beneath the green sea
As I strayed with my love
O'er the pure crystal fountain
That stood in the beautiful
Vale of Tralee."

Her eyes are still closed, and I believe she is happy behind the smile on her face. She seems, for the moment anyway, to have forgotten all those tenement tears I caused her over the years, and her smile makes me sing louder as I enter the refrain.

I don't care what the people on this train are thinking.

Twelve

IT IS now three years since I rode that train to New York with my mother, and the air force came and went.

And I am talking to a horse.

The time has sped by so quickly, and I still haven't made anything of myself. In fact, I think I've gone backward a little. I'll be twenty soon, and as sure as I can feel the Nevada wind against my face, I know I have to make a change somewhere.

It's a clear day, and before me I can see forever over generations of mountain peaks. And I am talking to this horse.

It's not just any horse. It's my horse, and it's funny how life can shift you onto roads where you never expected to be.

"Easy, Patches," I am whispering as I pull back on the reins.

I bought Patches about a year ago, and I've been working as a cowboy whenever I get the chance. Patches isn't as easy to handle as a well-trained cow pony, but I have come to love this impatient horse, every brown and white patch that runs through his coat.

I'm now working as a per diem ranch hand, riding through the open range in these northern Nevada hills about twelve miles from the town of Gerlach. There is no feeling I know like what I am now feeling on this high, shale-covered mountain. I can't see anyone before or behind for twenty miles.

I see thirty or so cows and calves grazing on a flat about a mile distant. Patches and I will amble pretty easylike in that direction, because I don't want to scare them off. It's hard enough to rope them when they are corralled, and here they have half a state to roam.

I have an old and torn straw hat pulled down low to protect my Irish skin. It's desert-hot up here close to the sun, and I was sure to pack a couple of long-sleeved shirts for the week, along with a change of underwear and a toothbrush.

We drove as far as we could in the truck, an old government-surplus weapons carrier, the kind ranchers up here buy for the hills. Dave is the boss, and there are four of us who have packed into the hills for a week. Even with a four-wheel-drive vehicle, though, we could drive just so far, and then we had to ride into the hills for about three hours before we found the high corral, made about twenty years ago of sticks and rope, where we could put the horses.

I don't know how much Dave will be paying us, but I guess it'll be ten dollars a day or so, which isn't so bad if you're spending most of the time lazing in a saddle. There is not much to do but think, and until we get to those animals, I have a lot to think about.

The air force made me a radar operator at the Fallon Naval Air Station, sixty miles east of Reno, and I liked the job well enough. But the hours were not great, and I had to work the midnight shift one week a month. Our country's distant early warning system never sleeps, and I dutifully watched through the nights for enemy planes from Quemoy and Matsu and other communist hotbeds.

It was monotonous work, but you are not given many choices in the military. You fall into an empty slot when you graduate basic training, and that is that, and my empty slot was in this desert aircraft control and warning squad.

Who knows how things would've turned out if I fell into a Boston, a Los Angeles, or an Italy slot, or if the bus from Las Vegas had not been exactly on time?

I had been to an Indian powwow in Carson City. Paiute Indians from all over the state came to dance and trade, a colorful event with more energy than a prison riot. Dancing, singing, and those constant tom-toms always in the air. It was hard leaving, but I knew I had to be back at the base in Fallon at midnight. The nine-thirty bus from Las Vegas would have done it for me.

There is no excuse that I got to the depot five minutes late. It doesn't matter that I was told that this was the only day in decades that the bus was on time. I was more than an hour late for the midnight shift at the radar operations building, and here is where the bad luck comes in. This was the same night that orders came in for me to transfer to the U.S. base in Bermuda.

I had not been home in two years, because I could not afford the transportation. This transfer would not only have taken me into one of the world's greatest playgrounds, it would have paid my way to New York. The captain on duty that night redlined the transfer and submitted a request for company discipline, an Article 15.

That was a year ago, and up until then I was a pretty good airman. But now, sitting here on top of Patches, I am thinking that I have failed again.

I have no skills, I'm almost twenty years old, and I'm living from hand to mouth with a dollar here and a dollar there, bucking bales of hay or milking cows, living with friends a week here and a week there.

The only thing I have working for me is that I still have a lot of freedom to make choices for myself. But what's the point if there are no choices lined up?

If only the bus had been a little late. If only there had been another captain on duty. If only my transfer order had come in the day before. All these ifs turned my life around from being an ordinary live-by-the-rules airman to being a guy from the streets of New York who would go back to living by his own rule, the rule that says I am always right and everyone else is always wrong.

So have as good a time as you possibly can, and the hell with everything else.

And I did have a good time. It seemed there was a party every

Saturday night in the town of Fallon, with wild cowboys and great-looking women. I still had never had a steady girlfriend, but there was always someone to dance with, and hug when the moon was up. Maybe it is the times, and maybe it is Nevada women, but I can never seem to get past the hugging part out here.

Having sex, like getting transferred, is something that other guys seem to do. There have been times when I thought the stars in the sky would rattle with sex, and the moon would fall climaxing into the desert, but it never quite happened, and I find myself in the morning with a lingering disappointment and a memory that doesn't explain why.

The hugging part isn't bad, though, and I keep hoping.

PATCHES begins to shift in his steps as we get closer to the calves. He knows he will run as soon as we get them riled.

"Whoa," I say, and I pat his neck, which calms him a little. But not much. Horses are too excitable to calm completely. I think that is why I like Patches so much. He won't just settle into anything I want him to do. I have to work at it.

This thought makes me think of my mother, because I wouldn't own Patches if she didn't come through a year ago.

"How much do you need?" she asked, and I could imagine her looking for a place to sit down as she carried the big black phone around the living room, the phone the telephone company gave her as an employee benefit.

"It's a lot of money, Mom, but I really need it."

"What do you need it for?"

"I want to buy a horse."

There was a long pause.

"Dennis," she said, "people from Fifty-sixth Street don't buy horses. They buy tickets to the circus if they want to see a horse."

"C'mon, Mom, I can pay you back, honest."

"How much?"

"Two hundred for the horse."

"What?"

"And another fifty for the saddle. I need the saddle, Mom."

"The Indians never use a saddle. Don't you go to the movies?"

"Well," I answered, trying to contain my joy, because I know she would never joke unless she was willing. "The Irish from Fifty-sixth Street always use saddles. I read it in a book."

I heard her begin to cough as she laughed.

"Are you okay, Mom?" I know she smokes too much, and she is near fifty and never gets any exercise.

"I'm okay. I just came up the stairs, and I need to rest a little. So did you pay Marty off?"

"Completely, Mom. I sent the last ten dollars a few months ago."

I miss my mother and brother and being part of a family, and lately I have been thinking about going home. If I stay here, I will just, well, get by. Since I passed all the General Educational Development tests, maybe I can get into a college and learn something that might give me a leg up on things.

Sure, I've been reading tons, like my brother said, and Father O'Rourke, too. All the works of Sinclair Lewis, J. P. Marquand, Eugene O'Neill, James T. Farrell, Hemingway, and Fitzgerald, and anyone whose style of writing appeals to me. But that and fifteen cents will get me on the subway, something my mother used to say.

I came pretty close to serious, lifelong trouble when I was hanging around with the guys on 55th Street. But I also know I have been drinking too much beer out here, and I am beginning to feel about beer what I feel about drugs. It comes with trouble, and trouble comes with it.

There are only three streets in Fallon, and one of them is filled with casinos, where, like the bars, you have to be twenty-one to get in. Because it is a navy town, there are SPs, who are like MPs, on shore patrol at all hours, and they think all airmen have it too easy and are easy prey in an idle night's work.

I got picked up twice by the same SPs, was put into the back of the patrol wagon and taken to my barracks. Each time, they said I was drinking alcohol as a minor and was drunk. And they filed a complaint with my commander.

The commander confined me to the barracks for a week each time. But the third time was like they were picking on me, and I wasn't going to let these SPs pick me up again without giving them a hard time.

They said I punched them, but I didn't. I just twisted myself out of their grip, one on each side of me, by flailing my arms. They couldn't hold me, and they pushed me to the ground and sat on me until the patrol wagon came.

Resisting an order by a shore patrol was punishable by another Article 15 discipline, and the commander sent me to Hamilton Air Force Base for an evaluation. The officers there gave me an honorable discharge. It was like they were saying, "No hard feelings, but we have eight hundred thousand other guys who can do your job."

And so here I am without any more excuses.

No more ifs. It was me who didn't make the bus. It was me who became a slacker after my transfer was redlined. It was me who drank all that beer, who resisted the SPs. If I have a black and a bleak future, the fault is all mine.

But there is a difference between admitting your fault and trying to rectify it. If I go back to New York, at least I will have my mother and Monsignor Ford and Archie and people who have been "interested" in me, to use Archie's word. I don't know how many second chances a man can get in this world, but I know I have to ask God for one more.

Thirteen

MY MOTHER was right. There are no good times in a person's life, just different times. Or maybe all time is just a series of little difficulties and challenges wedged between big ones, and if you're lucky, you are able to squeeze in as much happiness as is possible. The key is to know when you are happy, and I have recently come to think that I know when I am happy.

It is hard to put into words, but I can feel my soul dancing.

This is my first week working as a mechanic's helper in the pipefitting shop of the New York Central Railroad. I just received my first paycheck, ninety-four dollars for forty hours' work, which, when you consider I was making a hundred and eighty dollars a month in the air force, you can understand why my soul was dancing.

I have no great interest in being money hungry or in the accumulation of things, but I don't know of any other way to make a judgment about how I'm doing. I'll be able to pay my mother back for Patches in just a couple of months, and everything seems to be going great.

My mother is still working for Ma Bell and still doing the ironing for neighbors.

Billy left Hunter College, but he started up again at New York University. He's working full-time at Kips Bay as the gym instructor, but I have the best-paying job in the family.

"The Irish are getting up in the world," my mother said at breakfast this morning, folding over the pages of the *News.*

"You bet," I said.

My mother laughed. "I'm talking about Senator Kennedy," she said. "He's running for President."

"If he can get me on the police department or the fire department," I said, "I'll vote for him."

There is enough money in the family now to buy all the clothes we need and go to a movie whenever we want. There is a chicken in every pot, so to speak.

Billy told me recently that New York University is trying out a special program for people like me who have no high school, but who have a GED certificate from the military. I'm going down to Washington Square tomorrow to see about it.

I AM now in the street, watching Donald Doran fold the moving blankets. He is sweating heavily, and I am feeling guilty that I am so cool and collected. All the furniture is in and up.

It was the only day Billy could organize the move, and I had a final examination at New York University. I felt I was letting my brother down, but he understood. If you fail a course, the loss will put you in the hole for almost a hundred and fifty bucks. You could get a moving company to move a palace for that kind of money.

But a neighborhood moving job like this one costs just a case of beer and a half-dozen heroes from Rossi's. All you have to do is round up the guys on their downtime.

We have moved two blocks away, to 54th Street off Second Avenue. It is still up three flights. I was hoping my mother would find something on a lower floor, but she told me it was a good deal, a classy apartment, rent-controlled 'til death do you part.

My mother is under the sink as I enter the apartment for the first time. She is scrubbing away as Billy and the others are moving the furniture around to make everything fit. It's another railroad apartment and a little smaller than 56th Street. I am wandering around, looking to see what happened to the bunk beds, so at least I will have somewhere to throw my books.

"Not a roach in the place," my mother says, popping out from under the sink, "and if you look out the back window, you will see a tree, green leaves and all."

Sure enough, there is a tall backyard tree, full and waving slightly in a breeze. My mother smiles from ear to ear. She is drying her hands with the bottom of her apron.

"How," she asks, "did you do on the test?"

"A hundred."

"You got a hundred?"

"No." I laugh. "That's how many questions there were."

"C'mon," she says, "how did you do?"

"Mom, it was all Greek to me, but I knew about the wine-dark sea and poor Mrs. Oedipus, so I guess I got a B."

"Oh, I am so proud of you," my mother says. "But I'd be prouder if there was an A."

"I guess," Billy says, "it's okay to get out of a moving job for a B."

THESE are salad days for me, even though I got caught in the layoff by the railroad and have to drive a cab, when I can get one in the shape-up, or work as a chauffeur for the limousine company. I am not making a decent salary by a long shot, but I am reading everything in and about literature I can get my hands on and sensing that I am changing with every page I read.

It is now a September morning, and I have read that the city of New York is accepting filings to take the police and the fire department examinations. I am in the middle of breakfast, and I have an early morning class, but the news sparks an enthusiasm inside me that I have hardly known. I am going to the department of personnel first thing today. I dress fast, and then I do something I haven't been doing much lately. I grab my mother around her slender shoulders and give her a kiss on the cheek.

"Mom," I say, "the Irish are really going to get up in the world this time."

She gives me a welt on the rear end as I head out the door and says, "Good luck to you now, Dennis."

FOUR years later I am twenty-five years old, and it is 1966. The war in Vietnam is beginning to boil over, Black Power is taking over civil rights, Muhammad Ali is beating everyone, and Bobby Hull has scored fifty-four goals for the Rangers.

My mother's good-luck wish seems to have worked, because I got the fire department job.

This is the job that has saved my life.

I could go on from here and make a million dollars, but that wouldn't mean half as much as having gotten through all the trouble of my young years and still being able to take the oath of office for the New York City Fire Department.

I am now crossing the wide, dirt-strewn, cobblestoned surface of Intervale Avenue. I look up at the front entrance of Engine Company 82, at the high, red-painted doors. The red is so vibrant it makes me think that a flashbulb has gone off.

The corner of Intervale Avenue and 169th Street is filled with action. There is loud Latin music blowing out of a loudspeaker in front of a bodega. I can hear a couple of bongo drums coming from another block. There is garbage at the curbs, and the buildings are stained with roughly painted initials. It is everything you expect to find in a neighborhood the newspapers refer to as a ghetto.

This is my first day here, and I am scheduled to work the night tour, from six in the evening to nine in the morning, fifteen hours straight. I am not a "Johnny" firefighter anymore, but neither am I a seasoned vet. I've only been in a few fires these last three years, but up here in the South Bronx it's a different fire-fighting story and miles from the quiet firehouse in Queens where I have been working the last few years. Here the firehouse is like an island surrounded by a sea of fire. Engine Company 82 responds to forty alarms a day.

I am feeling good, real good, because this is my firehouse now. Engine Company 82 is on the top of the list of the busiest fire companies in New York, and I asked a friend of mine to get me transferred here. I have no idea of what to expect. I was only told that if there is anything easy in this company, it has been hidden away for years.

I remember the day I became a firefighter as clearly as any President remembers the day he was elected. I passed a firehouse on the way to the subway that day, the one on 51st Street, ecstatic that I would soon be a part of the whining sirens and clanging bells. I felt reverence when I was presented the three-inch silver Maltese cross, which is the firefighter's badge.

My wife, Pat, was there, and my mother, too; one prouder than the other that I had made it through the mental and the physical tests and the character investigation.

I was now in a job that was a fulfillment of a goal, a job that I loved. There is so much good about it, particularly the way it makes me feel good about myself. Maybe that comes with putting yourself on the line for other people.

This job will not make any of us rich, but I can't help thinking, after three years of fire fighting and four years of college, and with a fabulous wife, two kids, and a healthy mother, it would be hard to be much richer than this.

If I could go off to war or perform surgical miracles or nurse the dying or teach in a paint-worn classroom in the South Bronx, I would have a job that would let me look in the mirror and say that the people need me. I think that's true for a fireman, too. And when the alarm gets pulled, I'll do my best.

I know I didn't have much success as a kid in school, and I

didn't make such a good job of it in the air force, either. But I was given another second chance, and a great chance it was. It got me into college. It got me married to a wonderful woman. And it got me here to the front doors of the busiest fire company in the world, just where I want to be.

And the funny thing is, I don't know where that another second chance came from if it didn't come from God.

I remember that firefighter who came when I was sleeping on the fire escape so many years ago. They carried Mr. Sorenson out, and he just spent a day or two in the hospital after being knocked cold by the smoke. The firefighters seem to come when you need them. Even when you think no one can help you, the firefighter is going to do something that helps.

I guess I've always wanted to be like that fireman. "Hey, kid," he said, "how about that DiMaggio?" What a great way that is to keep a youngster from being frightened.

I think being a fireman made all the difference to Pat, too. No smart girl would marry someone with no future, without the ability to provide. And now I am becoming a man with definable abilities.

My famous abilities. All my life people have been telling me that I have to recognize my abilities, and now I'm beginning to waltz in the cloak of those abilities.

I met Pat the year before I went on the fire department. Walsh and Scarry and I were in East Durham, a resort village upstate they call the Irish Alps. Pat was with friends, and we danced a hundred dances in some Irish ginmill a hundred miles away from the city and had the best time. We did the Stack of Barley and the Siege of Ennis, and then we did the New York Savoy, and since I didn't know anyone with a car, we walked what seemed a hundred miles under the moonlight to where she was staying.

We dated steadily after that, the first steady girlfriend I ever had, and it went straight down the road called serious. So serious that we just had our second son, Dennis, who will probably wrestle his brother, Brendan, for a good seat at the table for the next decade.

My wife is from Queens, the daughter of a roofer, like my grandfather, but her family is from county Kilkenny and mine from county Cork. Meeting Pat was also part of the good luck my mother wished me, like a good-luck prediction of a seventh son of a seventh son.

We are building our future together, and little by little we are doing more than getting by. We even bought a new car, a Volkswagen Bug, and we go to a play off-Broadway once in a while. I have the good city job, and I have the twenty-year pension that goes with it.

My brother, Billy, has become a schoolteacher in Harlem, 127th Street and Lenox Avenue. He's read more books than anyone I know and hasn't disappointed anyone in meeting the potential of his intellect. Things could've been a lot easier for him, but he's not the complaining type. He didn't go to Exeter, and he didn't go to Oberlin, and he never had a year in college when he didn't work two jobs. But if you asked him, he'd tell you that he got a good deal and the deal paid off.

I can hardly ask a question about literature, philosophy, history, art, or music that he doesn't know the answer. And he cares about everything. He leaves the humanitarian talk to the civic theorists and do-gooders and commits himself to the education of children.

Billy was offered an assignment in a softer school out in Queens or in midtown Manhattan, but he wanted to go where he would be challenged by the toughest kids in New York.

I know my life was hanging for too many years by a very thin thread, like the sword of Damocles, threatening to crash into and destroy the thin structure of my future. But I know that I am not living so precariously now, the dangers of fire fighting notwithstanding. My feet have become planted into the concrete of New York, and I have a newfound stability I trust.

You can tell how much someone cares about his future by how much he cares about his present. In the same way my mother used to smile at me, that smile of regard and confidence, I am now smiling at myself and giving myself a wink in the mirror once in a while.

I am doing what I want to do, and I realize how lucky I am that I can do this. I have changed, and I am changing. What is the point of talking about literature or history or religion if we don't believe we should get a little better in all things as we go through our years? Our lives, like our morality, our sense of fairness, and the quality of our love, should improve measurably from decade to decade, and I am thinking that if I don't sense this about myself, I am missing out on the real excitement of it all.

So here I am, looking up at the towering, yellow-bricked building of Engine Company 82.

And I'm hoping I have whatever I need to fight the fires that I know will be before me. I guess that is mostly courage, which is not a personality trait you can train for at a training school.

Courage is like character, something you build up in small degrees from the day you are born.

There are dozens of things I might think of, but I'm now seeing my mother's face, in her apartment, probably reading the paper and having a cup of tea, and I wish she were here, even for a moment, as a smile slides across my lips and as the blood begins to gush through my veins, to see how happy I am.

Suddenly, as I am thinking these things, the huge red doors of Engine Company 82 and Ladder Company 31 fly open, and the trucks come out like drag racers, big and powerful, careening around the corner, speeding up 169th Street, air horns and sirens blaring all the way. All around, the bongos are beating out their quick rhythms, the crowds are snapping their fingers and feet to the music or rushing about from one side of a litter-strewn street to another. I watch the trucks until they disappear from view, off to some unknown emergency in our country's most forgotten, falling-apart, crime-ridden neighborhood. It is like the doors have been opened to a new world, one I have not seen before.

God.

This is going to be exciting.

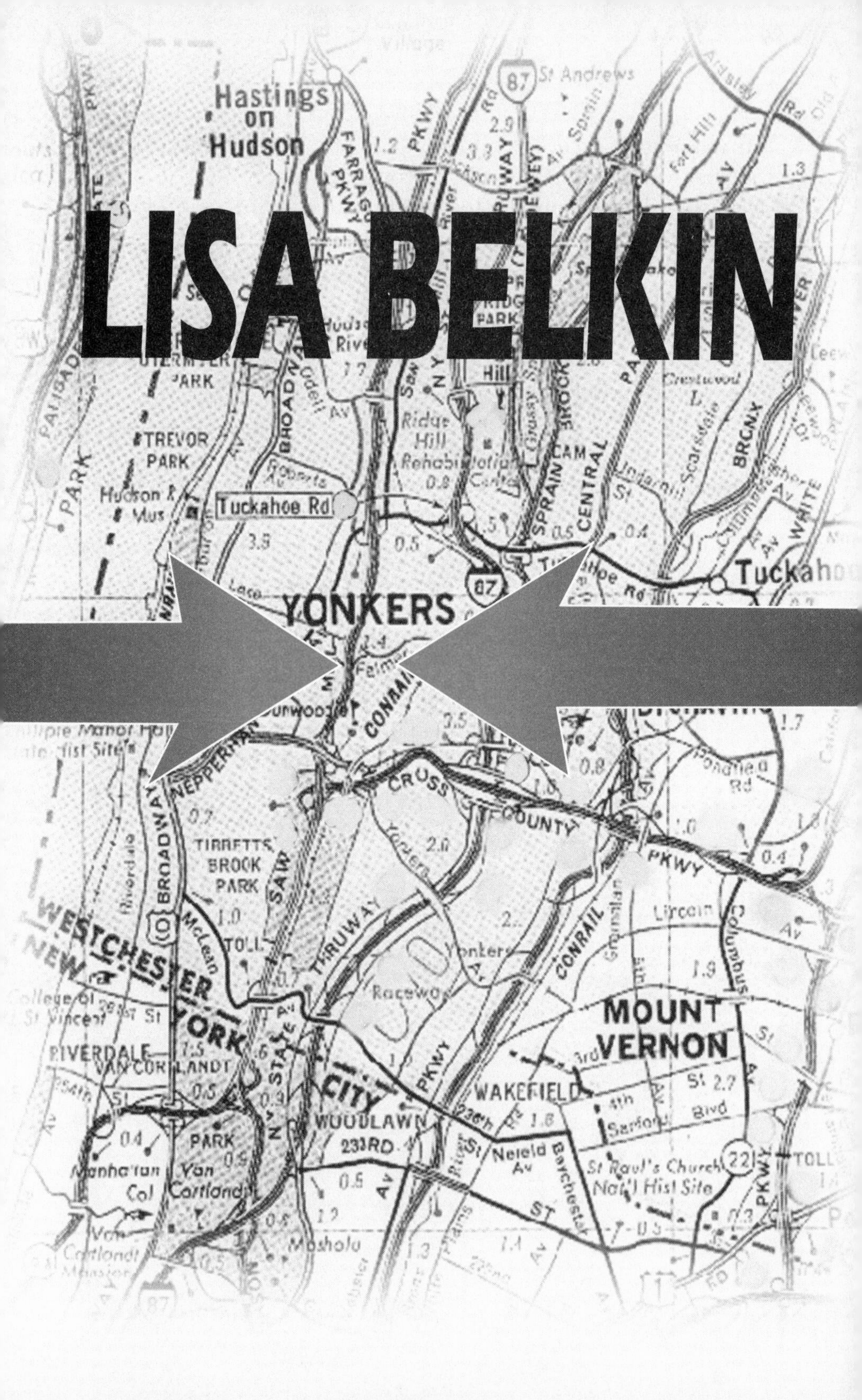
LISA BELKIN
Hastings
on
Hudson
Tuckahoe Rd
YONKERS
TREVOR
PARK
TIBBETTS
BROOK
PARK
WESTCHESTER
NEW YORK
CITY
MOUNT
VERNON
WAKEFIELD
WOODLAWN
RIVERDALE
St Paul's Church
Nat'l Hist Site
Tuckaho
CROSS
COUNTY
PKWY
THRUWAY
CONRAIL
BROADWAY
SPRAIN
CENTRAL

Show me a Hero

As mayor, Nick knew he shouldn't allow the protesters to feel they were disrupting city business, but there was no way to hide the fact that they were. There had been bomb scares and death threats. And there were bullets. Three white envelopes that were left in the men's washroom at City Hall each bore the hand-lettered name of a different council member. Each had a single .22-caliber bullet inside.

Nick was determined to mask the effects on his life. Tonight he collected his poker face, took a long, unsteady breath, and walked through the door into the packed council chamber.

As soon as the mayor appeared, Mary Dorman leaped to her feet with the rest of the crowd, joining in the catcalls and the boos.

—Show Me a Hero

"Show me a hero, and I will write you a tragedy. . . ."

—F. Scott Fitzgerald

PROLOGUE, 1992

The Pipe Bomb

THE pipe bomb was small as pipe bombs go, but the explosion could be heard from several blocks away—a sharp bang as rows of factory-fresh ceramic tiles shattered into a pile of razor-edged rubble. Neighbors who were drifting off to sleep sat upright, awake. Family members who were preparing for bed looked at each other, first with questions, then with certainty that they had the answer. "I guess somebody is trying to blow up the new housing," one man joked to his wife. But it wasn't a joke. That's exactly what someone was trying to do.

Everyone heard the bang, but only one person called the police. The dispatcher decided it was an electrical transformer problem, so there were no sirens, no searches in the night. The next morning, crews of workmen arrived at the sprawling site, which had once been the overgrown ball fields of an abandoned school and now held the nearly finished shells of forty-eight cream- and lemon-colored townhouses. Seeing the damage, they, too, called the police, who quickly rimmed the area in yellow-and-black tape.

Soon the FBI was there, and the federal marshal's office. The Bureau of Alcohol, Tobacco and Firearms. The director of the Yonkers Municipal Housing Authority. Assorted politicians who came to say "I told you so." They stood in the dirt outside apartment 120, relieved to see the townhouse was still standing.

The pipe bomb had been placed on the outer windowsill of a ground-floor bathroom. The window was blown out, the newly laid tiles on the floors and walls were shattered, and a mirrored door of the medicine cabinet was knocked from its hinges. Parts of the bomb were found a hundred feet away.

The crowd grew, as it always does in Yonkers. Some onlookers were nearby homeowners who had heard the explosion the night before. Others were just curious, drawn by the emergency lights. They hadn't wanted these buildings from the start—hadn't wanted to be part of this court-concocted experiment in social history. A few were, not so secretly, glad about the bomb. Maybe it would do what their years of protests couldn't and cause the housing literally to crumble.

Eventually the work crews took a break for lunch, but everyone else stayed for most of the day. The authorities searching. The politicians talking. And the neighbors standing and staring.

PART ONE: THE EXPLOSION 1988–1991

1988

The Youngest Mayor in America

NICHOLAS Wasicsko had always wanted to be mayor of Yonkers. Growing up in a two-family house on the west side—the wrong side—of the Saw Mill River Parkway, he was not one of those who set his sights on escape to the east. Instead he looked even farther west, to the beaux arts spires of City Hall. Bright, brash, and confident, Nick let other kids have dreams. Nick had plans.

Both he and his younger brother, Michael, stopped growing at about five feet six, but that did not keep them from spending afternoons of their teenage years on the basketball courts of a nearby schoolyard. During one game Nick mentioned that he would run the city one day. For months after that his nickname was "the Mayor."

Nick sensed early on that he had a knack that made things go his way. At age ten he talked the other paperboys in his neighborhood into letting him take over their routes; then he hired younger boys to actually deliver the papers. By the age of thirteen he had his own checking account, but because he was underage, it had to be co-signed by his mother, who was a teacher's aide, and his father, a factory worker.

He paid for four years at Manhattan College by working at a Carvel plant near the Hudson River. He saved for New York University Law School by working as a Westchester County police officer. Pictures of him in uniform, he reasoned, could help his political career.

That career began in force in 1985, when he won a seat on the Yonkers City Council using the slogan "Don't get mad, get a new councilman." He was twenty-six years old, with a baby face that he tried to mature with a slash of black mustache. He had not yet finished law school when elected, and he was still living with his mother.

He didn't do much as a councilman—mostly watched, listened, learned, and planned. Then, two years later, five days after he passed the New York State bar exam, he announced he was not seeking reelection to the City Council. He was running for mayor instead.

It was not, on the face of it, a rational decision. For one thing, the mayor of Yonkers was a largely symbolic position in 1987, a bully pulpit with no real administrative power. It was the city manager who drew up the budget and signed the checks. The mayor was technically just the first among equals on the City Council. He had one vote like everyone else, but he got to hold the gavel.

At $35,914 a year, it was considered a part-time job, usually sought by successful businessmen looking for a prestigious cap to their careers. Nick's opponent, Angelo Martinelli, was just such a man—a millionaire publisher who had held the mayor's office twelve of the previous fourteen years.

First Nick tried to portray the race as a referendum on youth versus age, but fifty-nine-year-old Martinelli, though twice as old as Nick Wasicsko, was hardly ancient, and the attempt fell flat. Then he tried to paint Martinelli as explosive and confrontational, but in Yonkers those qualities are not necessarily seen as negatives, so that didn't work either. Nick was a candidate in need of an issue.

Summer came, and Nick had raised $5170 in contributions. Martinelli had raised $67,388. The Wasicsko campaign organization consisted of Nick, his brother Michael, and Jim Surdoval, a young political consultant.

Meanwhile, everyone at City Hall thought Nick's political career was soon to be over, so they kept their distance, and he often felt as if no one in the building spoke to him at all. The only person who was consistently friendly was one of the secretaries, Nay Noe, a young Ecuadoran woman. At the age of twenty Nay was one of the few people at City Hall younger than Nick. She had little interest in politics but wound up with her very political job because Harry Oxman, the vice mayor of the council, asked Father Duffell of St. Peter's Church to find him a bilingual secretary, and the priest thought of Nay.

She started her job as secretary to the council just after Nick started his mayoral campaign, and at first she saw his isolation as arrogance. Over time, she came to feel sorry for him. She started to think of him as "the Lone Ranger sitting there all alone in the back." Maybe, she decided, politics interested her after all.

One evening Nay walked into Nick's office and said, "My parents have a house on Pier Street. Do you want to put a campaign sign on my house?" He sent Michael over with the sign a few days later. On her next trip into his office she was bolder, and she asked, "Do you need help on your campaign?" They spent part of the evening in front of the ShopRite on Riverdale Avenue, where Nay watched Nick shake strangers' hands. She was charmed by his enthusiasm as he bounded up to shoppers, sometimes carrying their groceries to their cars if it meant they would take a few minutes to listen to his ideas. Soon it was Michael, Nick, Jim, and Nay.

The quartet worked hard, covering every part of the city. Nick even insisted on going into the projects. Nay came along sometimes to translate to residents who spoke Spanish. More often Nick went there alone. His only company was his own determination—and the .38-caliber revolver he always wore strapped to his ankle, a habit left over from his days as a cop.

But it was not hard work that turned the campaign around in the middle of the summer. It was Judge Leonard B. Sand, who was running out of patience.

FEDERAL court case 80 CIV 6761, *The United States of America and the Yonkers Branch of the National Association for the Advancement of Colored People, et al.*, against *The Yonkers Board of Education, the City of Yonkers, and the Yonkers Community Development Agency* was filed back in 1980, when Nick Wasicsko was still in college. Though it would soon shatter his life and redefine his city, he paid little attention to the case at the time. Neither did most of the people in power in Yonkers. They were certain that this problem could be quietly made to go away. Back then it was seen merely as "yet another" school desegregation case, albeit with a twist. It charged that race determined location and quality of education in Yonkers and went on to argue that the Yonkers schools were segregated because Yonkers housing was segregated. Black and Hispanic children went to the same few schools because black and Hispanic families were forced to live in the same few neighborhoods, and any judicial order to change the schools would also have to change the neighborhoods.

The lottery that distributes cases at the federal district court in Manhattan handed this one off to Judge Leonard B. Sand, whose expertise had been in tax law before President Jimmy Carter appointed him to the bench in 1978. A reserved, elfin man with silver hair and bushy, wizardly brows, Sand could not have been more of a contrast with the raucous city whose future was now his to shape. Sand was a member by marriage of the powerful Sulzberger family, who owned *The New York Times*. He was a wealthy man in his own right, too, an early partner in a prosperous law firm. When not presiding over court business, he could be found padding around his office in worn leather slippers, talking jurisprudence with his clerks the way others talk the stock market or sports.

Sand heard the Yonkers case himself, without a jury, at the request of both sides. The trial took up most of 1983 and 1984. There were 93 days of testimony from 84 witnesses, 140 depositions, thousands of exhibits. By the end it was clear that the city's schools were segregated: 23 of the city's 34 public schools were over 80 percent minority or 80 percent white. And there was also little question that its housing was segregated. The southwest quadrant, which contained 97.7 percent of the city's public housing, also contained 80.7 percent of the city's minority population.

Sand's job, however, was not to decide if Yonkers was segregated, but to decide why it was segregated, why this city of twenty-one square miles and 188,000 people came to have nearly all its minority citizens living within one square mile. Why the Saw Mill River Parkway, the road that divided east from west, became a barrier of sorts—white and working class to the east of it; black, brown, and poor to the west. If it was happenstance, then there was no wrong to be righted. But if it was intentional, then Yonkers could be forced to make dramatic, difficult, history-making amends.

Sand decided that it was not happenstance. Yonkers looked the way it did, he ruled, because its politicians, acting on behalf of its very vocal east side voters, wanted it that way. He said so in a 657-page decision, filed with the court in November 1985. It was a chronicle of what Sand saw as a forty-year pattern. Housing sites were proposed for the white east side; outraged residents responded by packing the City Council meetings—sometimes a thousand people at a time; council members ordered a search for other possible sites; the housing was eventually placed on the mostly minority southwest side.

"It is," Judge Sand wrote, "highly unlikely that a pattern of subsidized housing which so perfectly preserved the overwhelmingly white character of East Yonkers came about for reasons unrelated to race." That said, he ordered Yonkers to move some of its poor, minority residents from the poor, minority side of town into public housing, to be built just for them, on the white, middle-class side of town.

Nick Wasicsko was a brand-new member of the City Council back when Sand first issued that order. The council voted to appeal Sand's decision to a higher court. Nick voted for the appeal. Martinelli voted against. For a long time the problem was considered solved—it would somehow disappear into the court system. There were spurts of outrage ("we never discriminated against anyone") and defensiveness ("why is the judge picking on us for decisions made forty years ago?") but almost no self-reflection. From where the council members and the voters sat, Sand's decision had nothing to do with *their* Yonkers.

That is because the judge's monumental opinion was missing one thing: The central fact of Yonkers is that it only *looks* like one city. It *acts* like thirty-eight separate cities, or at best a loose confederation of neighborhoods, each singular, organized, and proud. Dunwoodie, Seminary Heights, Wakefield Park, Kimball—home to secretaries, bus drivers, teachers, policemen. Lawrence Park West, Sunnyside Park, Beech Hill—where some houses are mansions and deer sightings are not uncommon. Runyon Heights—the only middle-class black neighborhood in town. Fleetwood—filled with co-ops and young professionals. Locust Hill—a longtime Hungarian neighborhood. Bryn Mawr, Woodstock Park—mostly Scottish and Irish. Park Hill—Italian. The Hollows—Slovak, Russian, Polish, and Hungarian.

Sand recognized this, but he did not understand it, not the way the people of Yonkers did. He saw such cliquishness as the way people lived until they learned how to live better. Born in 1928, Sand spent the first sixteen years of his life in the Bronx. His neighborhood was working-class and Jewish. Over by Fordham Road nearly everyone was Catholic. To the east was a section called Brooke Avenue, and the Irish kids who lived there were called the Brookies. When he graduated from high school, he went on to the New York University School of Commerce, which at the time was essentially a trade school, and he came out with a degree in accounting. "I really wanted to go to Columbia," he says, a place that represented to him the lyrical world of literature rather than the practical world of balance sheets. But it was also a time of quotas and anti-Semitism, so he did not even bother to apply. That his life turned out just fine—Harvard Law School followed N.Y.U.—does not dull the what-ifs.

Sand ordered Yonkers to do better: To open its neighborhoods, its enclaves, its safe ethnic pockets. To let outsiders enter and to give them a turn at transforming their lives. It was the logical, rational, right thing to do.

The citizens of Yonkers, however, didn't see it that way. The separateness that Sand saw as a limitation, they saw as a strength. They viewed their barriers and boundaries less as a way of excluding others than as a way of defining themselves. They did not need lectures on discrimination, they said. Being Italian or Irish or Polish meant a childhood filled with stories of grandparents who could not find jobs or homes or respect because of their accents or their names. Neither did they need lessons from the Bronx. Many of them had also lived there, more recently than Sand, and then fled to Yonkers as their neighborhoods decayed. This was about their pride in overcoming the barriers this country places before all newcomers and about the lives they had built—modest, perhaps, but theirs. Mostly it was about their fear that someone was trying to take it all away.

By 1987, when Nick decided to run for mayor, Yonkers was no closer to building the new housing than they had been two years earlier. Trying to be patient, the judge allowed the city to decide the specifics of the plan: how many new units, where and by what date they would be built. But after numerous deadlines came and went, Sand permitted the Justice Department and the NAACP to work out the details instead. On their say-so he ordered Yonkers to build two hundred units of low-income public housing and eight hundred units of moderate-income subsidized housing on the east side. Still trying to be patient, he asked the city to submit a list of construction sites. More deadlines were ignored. Yonkers had come to assume that stalling would work forever.

But just before Nick launched his campaign, Sand decided to shake up that assumption. He ruled that since city leaders were having such trouble finding appropriate housing sites, they should hire a consultant to do the choosing. The City Council conducted a nationwide search. Hours before Sand's Valentine's Day deadline and much to the judge's surprise, the requisite consultant was actually chosen.

"They hired me," Oscar Newman would say, years later, of his

$160-an-hour contract, "with the expectation that I would fail."

If that is what they expected, they were surprised. Newman's book, *Defensible Space,* is about using architecture to influence human patterns of behavior, and Yonkers was a chance for him to further test his theories on a very large, very public scale. A man of immense vision, immense presence, and immense ego, Oscar Newman soon became one of Sand's closest advisers.

By spring the judge had accepted Newman's philosophy as his own. The large housing projects being planned for the east side were doomed by their very design, Newman argued, and would be a disaster both for the public-housing residents and the surrounding community. The future of public housing, he believed, was a "scattered site" model—small clusters of private units, with no shared space such as hallways, that would blend into the community. At first this change of plan pleased the members of the council, though not necessarily because they agreed with the underlying theory. Besides, it would take more time to find numerous sites (Newman's plan called for eight) than it would to find one or two, giving the city more time to drag its heels.

Newman, however, found the sites after just a few days. Spending the city's money, he hired a helicopter and pilot and flew low over Yonkers, making maps of vacant areas of land. He identified twenty-six possible parcels, about forty acres altogether. The City Council then hired a team of lawyers who discovered legal loopholes that would prevent most of the sites from being used. Newman went back to his maps and compiled a list of additional sites. The lawyers tried to reject those sites, too.

By July, Newman was no longer reporting to the City Council but was working directly for the judge. With Newman at his side Sand's language turned tougher. It was at Newman's suggestion, for instance, that Sand placed a moratorium on four private commercial development projects. If there was such a shortage of buildable land in the city, Sand scolded, what's all this talk about building a retail mall? An executive park? The city would first meet its federal obligations, thank you very much. And for good measure, Sand, who had threatened Yonkers with contempt fines before, repeated that threat with greater specificity. The fines would begin at $100 and double every day. At that rate the city's entire $337 million annual budget would be wiped out in twenty-two days.

IN THE escalating debate over the housing, Nick Wasicsko had found his issue. His slogan in this campaign was a variation of the one that had worked before: "Don't get mad, get a new mayor." Jim Surdoval had the slogan printed on several hundred lawn signs, and to his astonishment they were snapped up by east siders. When the printed signs were gone, people started making their own. Nick was more than just a candidate. He was becoming a cause.

As a result, he began to spend more time campaigning on the east side, reminding voters that Martinelli believed the housing was "inevitable." Nick believed the city—the voters—deserved a "second opinion." He knew he was leaving anti-housing voters with the impression that he would continue their fight to the death, but the fact was, he didn't know what he would do. He thought he would be a good mayor. He would worry about the rest later.

On November 3, 1987, Nick Wasicsko defeated Angelo Martinelli by a vote of 22,083 to 20,617. "I never thought I'd lose for one minute," he lied to reporters after the votes were counted.

Late on election night Martinelli drove over to concede the race in person. Shaking Nick's hand, he said, "The voters have lifted a tremendous burden off my shoulders and placed it on yours."

Nick knew why he won, and he didn't care, just as he didn't care that he had $20,000 in law school debt and a new job that would pay him less than that after taxes. All that mattered to him was that at age twenty-eight he was the youngest mayor in the country. He was "the Mayor" now, on and off the basketball court. In a few years maybe he could change that title to congressman. In the distance he could see the governor's mansion and the White House.

THE first thing Nick did as mayor-elect was to ask Nay Noe out to lunch. They were like two giddy kids as they stepped into Louie's restaurant in south Yonkers, running a gauntlet of well-wishers.

When their waitress had come and gone, Nick looked across the table at Nay and thanked her. "I appreciate your support, everything you've done," he said. His fingers fiddled with his mustache as they so often did when he was nervous. "Come work for me," he blurted suddenly. "You're the only one I can trust."

A week later she accepted the job. She understood enough about the ways of City Hall to know that she owed an explanation to Harry Oxman, the man who had hired her in the first place. When she offered one, Oxman accused her of chasing after Nick to advance her own career. "That's not it," she answered. "I helped him because I felt bad for him. I thought he was going to lose."

Nick put Nay in charge of "the fun stuff," including planning the inauguration and the party afterward. Nick wanted to do something different, something that symbolized youth and energy, so instead of planning a traditional gala in a catering hall, he rented a large boat equipped for dinner and dancing. Every day he gleefully read the updated list of people who had paid $150 apiece to attend his bash. His City Hall office was neither quiet nor lonely. He practically strutted from one task to the next: hiring a new city manager, sending out press releases declaring a "fresh start" full of "fresh ideas," schmoozing with the other members of the council, allying himself with a coalition of Democrats, Republicans, and Conservatives who were opposed to the housing.

A PHONE call came on December 28 that would change everything. It was Nay who tracked Nick down and put the lawyers through. It was four days before Nick was to be sworn in as mayor, and the United States Court of Appeals for the Second Circuit had ruled on Yonkers's fate. This was the appeal Nick had staked his campaign on, the appeal that was supposed to persuade the higher court that Judge Sand had overstepped his bounds and that the housing should not be built.

Instead the 163-page opinion from the three-judge panel unanimously rejected the city's arguments. Sand's order, it said, was "well within the bounds of discretion."

Other members of the council reacted to the news quickly and defiantly. "We will take it to the Supreme Court," said Nick's fellow

Democrat Henry Spallone, the beefy former New York City cop who was always ready for a good verbal brawl, whose political views were described by the local paper as "medieval."

The councilmen waited for Nick to join them in their outrage, but the young mayor-elect was unexpectedly quiet. "It is too early to tell whether the city will appeal," was all he would say.

It was probably good he kept his early reactions to himself, because they were those of a petulant child. "I can't believe the timing," he complained to Nay. "It will put a damper on everything. I don't even get a chance to have some fun." Quickly, however, he went from feeling cheated to feeling overwhelmed. He was twenty-eight years old. He had never been responsible for his own rent or telephone bill, and now he was responsible for this.

Briefly, he thought he should join the shouting. That would be the political thing to do. Take it to the Supreme Court, he reasoned. He was elected to appeal. So why not go all the way?

But since the day after his election the expensive lawyers working for the city had been warning him that the Second Circuit Court would reject the initial appeal, and they were right. Now they were telling him that there were no constitutional grounds for an appeal to the Supreme Court. He suspected they were right about that, too. An appeal would be expensive, and the city had already spent millions fighting the case. An appeal would also risk Sand's further wrath. The judge would see it as a desperate stalling tactic and would impose the threatened fines. Vowing to appeal would make Nick popular for the moment, but would it risk the ruination of the city he had just been elected to lead?

Few men have ever had to grow up so quickly. In his inaugural address five days later Nick made his answers clear. Yonkers, he said, would comply with the integration order because "the law is the law" and compliance was the only way to avoid crippling fines. He thought it unfair to punish the homeowners of today for discriminatory decisions made by political leaders decades ago, but unfair or not, it was within the judge's power.

The phone calls started as soon as he finished his speech. They were venomous and violent. Nay took one message after another but drew the line at transcribing the obscenities. "Tell the mayor to go to hell." "We should have known better than to trust that child." "Tell the mayor he's a traitor." "Tell the mayor to resign." "Tell the mayor we'll impeach him."

He read all the messages, responded to none of them, and wondered if he had done the right thing. As the pink stack of while-you-were-out slips grew higher, he cheered up. All his life he had been able to talk people into seeing things his way. He had to believe he could bring them around now.

A City Like No Other

CITIES have ways about them, eccentricities and quirks as distinctive and basic as those of the people who live in them. And no place feels quite like Yonkers, rough-hewn and jagged, a working-class bridge between the towers of Manhattan to the south and the pampered hills of the rest of Westchester County to the north.

Its history began with a tribe of Native Americans who "sold" the land to a Dutch nobleman, Adriaen Van der Donck, in 1646. His title was Jonge Heer, or Lord. Eventually Jonge Heer's holdings became known as *Yonkeers.*

The city grew with the railroads. The first trains followed the paths of the waterways, and because Yonkers was trisected by the Hudson, Saw Mill, and Bronx rivers (the latter two are now reduced to mere trickles), it had twenty train stations during the late 1800s. By the turn of the century it was the industrial center of Westchester County, with 129 factories counted in 1912. The Waring Hat Company, the largest in the United States, turned out 18,000 hats every day. The Otis Elevator Company employed 7000 people, or one out of every three workers in the city. Another third worked at the Alexander Smith Carpet Mills, the largest in the world, with 56 acres of floor space. Even Nicholas II, Russia's last czar, had a carpet made in Yonkers.

Waves of immigrants manned those factories and left their imprints—English, Scottish, Polish, Slavic, Ukrainian, Italian. Each started at the bottom, in the mills, the smelting rooms, and the refineries, then made the climb up, onto the assembly lines and into the managers' offices. As they moved up, they also moved out, heading east of town, where, spurred by the age of the automobile, farmland was being transformed into neighborhoods.

When they reached the open spaces east of the Saw Mill River, the groups kept to themselves, forming enclaves that felt less like America and more like whichever country used to be home. The electoral ward system was born of that deliberate separateness. The Yonkers City Council was made up of twelve members who worked more like a confederation than a union. There was an unofficial rule back then that each councilman had final say over proposals for his electoral ward. It was de facto veto power. If the councilman from the ward said no, no other member of the council would vote to place a housing project in his territory.

Some blacks made it across the Saw Mill into the one black middle-class neighborhood in Yonkers. Called Runyon Heights, its existence is an example not of how blacks were welcomed on the east side, but of how they were not.

During the building boom of the 1920s a developer made a bad purchase—land too rocky and hilly for ranch-style houses with big, flat yards. To salvage his investment, he announced that he would turn the land into a Jewish cemetery, a plan that enraged the owners of surrounding parcels. Some people later said that the developer, angered by attempts to stop him, took his revenge by selling the land to blacks; others said that he gave the objectors a choice, and it was the neighbors who decided "it was better to live next to live Negroes than dead Jews."

Mainly, minorities stayed on the west side, making their homes in the places that earlier generations of newcomers had eagerly left. They lived near where they worked, in tenements behind the factories and mills. The east side became ever more middle-class and white. The west side became ever more minority and poor.

Yonkers, of course, was not the only place in the country with slums and with a growing gap between blacks and whites. Periodically the federal government would talk about improving the nation's slums, but nothing was done until the Great Depression, when public housing was born. Helping the poor was just a side effect of that program; its real goal was providing construction jobs and rebuilding the economy. After World War II public housing was expanded, this time as a way to house returning veterans.

The boom in housing provided the city of Yonkers with a dilemma. The city badly wanted—needed—the money made available for the growing public-housing infrastructure, but it did not really want the public housing. Funds were applied for and granted, but any neighborhood the planning board chose for the housing would convulse with protests and a councilman's no vote.

For more than forty years, therefore, one huge public-housing complex after another was built on the west side, the only part of town that offered no resistance. Mulford Gardens, with 550 apartments, opened in October 1940. Cottage Place Gardens, with 256 apartments, opened in 1948. The William A. Schlobohm Houses, 415 apartments in eight buildings, opened in 1953. Calgano Homes, better known as School Street, had 278 units completed in 1964.

By 1988 not one of the city's subsidized-housing projects for families was located in any of the overwhelmingly white neighborhoods of the east or northeast. In all, the southwest contained 97.7 percent of the city's subsidized housing.

Eventually, when Congress ruled that public funds could not be spent in a way that would create a housing ghetto, the City Council voted to sacrifice the funds. No public housing for families was built in Yonkers after 1964, because that was when the Department of Housing and Urban Development (HUD) started paying attention to where all such housing was located.

Yonkers, to be sure, is not the only city to cluster its public housing. Others did the same thing, and the year that the Justice Department began its investigation of Yonkers, it also looked at Chicago; Lima, Ohio; Marshall, Texas; Charleston, South Carolina; and Rochester, New York. All were potential targets for the first of what was expected to be a series of groundbreaking lawsuits linking school segregation with housing. Any one of those cities could have been chosen as the test case, but only Yonkers was, less because of what it did than how it did it.

"What got them in deep problems was they couldn't keep their mouths shut," Oscar Newman says. Other cities apologized for their past. Some built a handful of low-income units in middle-class neighborhoods. Once that was done, the Justice Department went away. Yonkers, however, came out swinging. City officials said that low-income housing was purposefully placed in the poorest corner of Yonkers because that's where it *belonged.*

So it was Yonkers, not Rochester or Chicago, that was successfully sued for discrimination in federal court. And it was Nicholas Wasicsko, who always wanted to be mayor of Yonkers, who inherited the legacy of that lawsuit and who came to learn more than he really wanted to know about his city and about himself.

FOR a few weeks at the beginning of 1988 it looked as if Nick might actually be able to do the impossible: to unite the council on a vote to implement a housing plan. With the help of the city's law firm and the new city manager, Neil DeLuca, Nick persuaded nearly everyone on the council that voting to comply with the order was the only way to maintain some control over the end result.

Two councilmen—Harry Oxman and Charles Cola—needed little persuading. Oxman, a courtly, quiet man, was the only member of the council who fully favored compliance, and Cola represented the district that included all the city's housing projects, so it was his political responsibility to vote yes.

Two other councilmen were never really subjects of Nick's full-court press. Hank Spallone had lived in the South Bronx and had seen how a neighborhood could change. He had been elected because he had vowed to go to jail, if need be, to stop the housing. Nick did not even try to change his mind. And Edward Fagan was such a puzzle that Nick didn't bother to make an effort. All the relationships on the council were based on business, not friendship, but Fagan, wiry and wary, gangly as a scarecrow, seemed to go out of his way to keep his private life out of the office.

By process of elimination, therefore, Nick directed most of his talking at his two remaining colleagues, Nicholas Longo and Peter Chema. Longo, with sixteen years on the council, was probably the shrewdest politician in Yonkers. Peter Chema, too, was a veteran of Yonkers politics. His father had won a council seat when Peter was a child. Peter earned a degree in civil engineering, then opened a tire business before running for council for the first time in 1979. At thirty-seven Chema was eight years younger than Longo and less certain of himself.

During his first weeks in office Nick tried to outpolitic these two longtime politicians. Many years earlier, he reminded them, Yonkers had accepted federal money to build public-housing units on the east side. The money was kept, but the housing was never built. So Judge Sand saw these two hundred low-income units as payback, and he would not be persuaded to compromise on that part of the plan. Wouldn't it be better, Nick asked, to have some say over where those inevitable units went?

On January 20, 1988, what began as a vote on a routine procedural matter became a showdown on the housing. To qualify for the $10 million renewal, Yonkers had to submit a housing assistance plan, which outlined the city's housing plans for the coming year. The city's plan included the statement that two hundred units of low-income housing would be built on the east side. If the council voted to approve the plan, Judge Sand said, he would see that as a pledge of cooperation. If not, he said, he would levy the fines that would start at $100 a day and double every day.

So at the last possible moment the council voted as the judge had ordered them to and as Nick had begged them to. The single no vote was from Spallone, who stormed out of the meeting. "I am not about to be intimidated by any judge," he shouted. "If it takes going to jail to prove to America that everyone should have constitutional rights, I'm saying to you, 'I am willing to go to jail.' "

Spallone's theatrics aside, Nick was pleased with the results. He must be "one helluva politician," he figured, to have been able to pull this one off. But Judge Sand was less pleased. Although he praised the council's vote, he asked for more. Stated intentions are fine, he said, but now he wanted specifics. He gave the council a week to develop and vote on a binding "consent decree"—a list of locations where the housing would be built.

The five who reluctantly voted yes held meetings toward that goal and pointedly did not invite Spallone. The list they compiled included seven sites. Six of the seven had been on Oscar Newman's original lists, but the seventh was a surprise. It was a serene slice of land that was part of the St. Joseph's Seminary.

The councilmen and their lawyers appeared in court the morning of January 26, 1988, and presented the list to Judge Sand. He praised the council again and stressed the importance of having the city make these decisions rather than the court. "A court can order bricks and mortar," he said. "Only the citizens of Yonkers can create an environment that is conducive to good relations."

He gave his blessing to the list and asked for one more thing. He wanted the city to give up plans to appeal the case to the Supreme Court. The vote scheduled that night to approve the list of sites would have no meaning, he said, if it were done with the hope that the High Court would eventually rule the consent decree null and void. Lawyers for the city agreed to waive their right to appeal.

BECAUSE the expected crowd would overwhelm City Hall, the council meeting that night was to be held in an east side high school gym. As Nick and the others arrived at Saunders High School, they could hear the roar of the crowd before they entered the building. Inside, it was pandemonium. Nine hundred people had passed through the metal detectors, and four registered handguns had been confiscated. Five dozen policemen lined the gymnasium walls. Henry Spallone was already at the microphone, whipping the crowd into a frenzy.

More than sixty people had signed up in advance for the public comment portion of the evening. For more than five hours they paraded to the microphone to scream, plead, and threaten.

"Put your jobs on the line tonight," yelled Rabbi Bernhard Rosenberg of the Midchester Jewish Center, his fists clenched. "Get some guts and stand up to it. Or put it in *your* neighborhood."

Eleven-year-old Judy Guldner, whose neighborhood would get sixty of the two hundred units, stood pale but composed behind a lectern with mikes from fifteen radio and television stations. "My parents worked hard for my house. I don't want people who have no morals, and take drugs, in my neighborhood."

Only one person spoke in favor of the plan—Laurie Recht, a thirty-four-year-old white secretary from south Yonkers. She stood four feet ten inches and could barely be seen over the crowd. She read her brief written statement. "Low-income housing in small groups does not necessarily increase crime," she said. "There are good and bad in all races. It is important to realize that no one group should be blamed for all social or societal problems." When she was finished, the jeers were so loud and frightening that she had to be escorted from the room by the police.

At 1:00 a.m., after the list of speakers was exhausted, it was the council's turn to speak. Nick kept it short. "Majority rules in America," he said, "but it cannot rule contrary to law."

Last on the list was Hank Spallone. "Nuts to the judge," he boomed. "This is a sellout of the worst kind."

With that, the crowd tried to rush the stage, hundreds of people pushing at once. Nick could see the tension in the officers' faces as they linked arms to hold the protesters back.

The clerk took the voice vote at 1:30 in the morning.

"Mr. Wasicsko?" Yes.

"Mr. Spallone?" No.

"Mr. Longo?" Yes.

"Mr. Oxman?" Yes.

"Mr. Chema?" Silence. "Mr. Chema?" Peter Chema made a fist, then turned his thumb down.

"Mr. Cola?" Yes.

"Mr. Fagan?" Yes.

The consent decree had passed 5–2. The battle was over.

The war had barely begun.

Mary Dorman Joins the Fight

MARY Dorman sat in the front row of the City Council chambers. A sinewy gray-haired woman with the sturdy, roughened hands of one who values hard work, Mary gazed slowly around the room, absorbing every detail. That she was even sitting in this room was because of her own transformation—from a quiet, bespectacled lady into a loud, determined warrior for a cause. Only four weeks earlier she had never been to a political meeting, and now she was warmly greeting dozens of people by name.

Mary had paid no attention to the housing fight until the near riot at the Saunders gym. Mary was not the joining type. Aside from her bowling league and her Sundays at St. John the Baptist, her world was her husband, Buddy, who was an engineer with AT&T; her grown daughter, Maureen; and her job as an assistant to her brother-in-law, who was a veterinarian.

Twenty years earlier, when she and Buddy first moved from the not yet dangerous Bronx to the comparatively open spaces of Yonkers, they had lived in an apartment over the animal clinic where she worked. Maureen, an adolescent back then, took the only bedroom, and Mary and Buddy slept in the living room on a pullout couch. They tried not to waste much time complaining about the lack of space. To their mind, sofa beds were simply where you slept while you worked for something else.

Whenever they talked of moving, Mary would say, "If I can't have a brick house on St. John's Avenue, I don't care if I never have a house." To her St. John's was one of the city's prettiest streets, a winding boulevard lined with neat, modest Georgians and Cape Cods, ending with St. John the Baptist Church.

Then, on a snowy day in 1978, she saw a sign at the local drugstore offering a one-story two-bedroom brick house on her perfect street. She and Buddy fell in love with it at first sight, but the $58,000 asking price was more than he was willing to pay. When Mary heard that another buyer had already bid the asking price, she went back to her suddenly cramped apartment, shattered. But within days the owner called. The other buyer had talked about tearing out the arch over the kitchen door. Would Mary and Buddy be willing to pay $53,000? The house became hers because she loved it as it was. She swore she would never let it change.

Now two of the seven sites on the consent decree list were within walking distance of that house, and Mary was drawn to the meetings. To Judge Sand the battle of Yonkers was about what was right. To Nick Wasicsko it was about what was realistic. To Mary Dorman it was about her home.

She fell in with a group called the Save Yonkers Federation, a coalition of thirty neighborhood associations. Her attraction to the group was its loyalty to Hank Spallone. There were a lot of politicians doing a lot of talking, she decided, and Spallone was the only one who seemed to make any sense.

Mary's days were soon shaped by Save Yonkers. She found herself attending meetings, sometimes nightly, where she listened to speeches to the converted by people who had been strangers before the fight but now described each other as good friends.

Her first meeting in hostile territory—at City Hall—came two weeks after the one at Saunders, on the second Tuesday in February. This was a regularly scheduled council session. She arrived at 5:00 p.m., one hour before the public comment portion of the evening. As she waited with her new compatriots in what would soon become her usual seat, someone handed her a small American flag, a symbol of the right to appeal to the Supreme Court. That had become the rallying cry in the weeks since the council forfeited that right by approving the consent decree. "Appeal. Appeal. Appeal!" they shouted.

Mary Dorman shouted along with them. She waved her flag; she booed; she screamed; she closed her eyes and joined the others in a tuneless hum to drown out any councilman other than Peter Chema or Hank Spallone, the two who had voted against the consent decree. When Nick Wasicsko tried to speak, someone hurled pink disposable diapers at him. "Go back home to your mother," Mary yelled, her anger white-hot and oddly cleansing. For fifty-four years she had been a polite woman, the type who said "Excuse me" when she bumped into furniture, so she was amazed at how easily she took to the rhythms of disobedience.

She was intimidated only for a moment that first night, when a group of protesters near the back of the room stood up on their chairs, linked arms, and looked defiantly at the thirty policemen and their leashed police dogs. Mary watched the cops approach lawbreakers who were also their neighbors. It was over in a moment, as several dozen protesters were escorted out of the building.

The mayor adjourned the meeting soon after that, leaving much of the agenda as unfinished business. When Mary got outside, there was a party of sorts going on, lit by the television cameras. Those who were ejected were being high-fived and hugged.

The next two weeks went quickly, filled with meetings, phone calls, plans. Now, on the fourth Tuesday of the month, Mary was back in her seat, holding her flag, waiting for the meeting to start. Waiting, most of all, to feel that liberating anger once again.

WHILE Mary was out front getting ready to chant, Nick was in his office getting ready to take it. He knew he shouldn't allow the protesters to feel they were disrupting city business, but there was no way to hide the fact that they were. There had been bomb scares and death threats to the five who had voted yes. And there were bullets. Three white envelopes that were left in the men's washroom at City Hall each bore the hand-lettered name of a different council member—Nicholas Longo, Charles Cola, Ed Fagan. Each had a single Winchester .22-caliber bullet inside.

Full-time police escorts were assigned to the five council members. When Nay visited Nick at home—they were a couple by then, but a deliberately low-profile one—she was frisked by armed guards before she was allowed to walk in the door.

If it was impossible to mask the effect of the protests on the government, Nick was determined to mask the effects on his life. At home he stood in front of a mirror and practiced keeping his face impassive, rehearsing a calm, steady tone of voice. Tonight he collected that poker face. Then he took a long, unsteady breath and walked through the door into the packed council chamber.

As soon as the mayor appeared, Mary leaped to her feet with the rest of the crowd, joining in the catcalls and the boos. When Nick put his hand in place to salute the flag, Mary waved her own miniature flag and chanted, "Appeal. Appeal. Appeal."

When it came time for the business at hand—a list of twenty resolutions, none of which had anything to do with public housing—

the noise from the spectators was so loud that the clerk had to walk up to each councilman in order to hear and record his vote.

The meeting was supposed to conclude with a ceremony honoring city firefighters and police officers for acts of bravery in the line of duty, but that too was drowned out by the crowd.

For a moment Nick lost his cool. "These men risked their lives for the city of Yonkers," he screamed into the microphone. The boos became even louder.

"Wasicsko, you're crazy. You're a sleaze," Mary yelled.

"Would the officers please eject this woman?" Nick thundered. Mary Dorman was escorted out of the building.

Mary had seen something in Nick's face that she thought was regret, and on a whim she called him the next morning. She expected to leave a message, but he answered the phone himself.

"I just called to tell you that you're wrong to support the housing," Mary said.

"The law is the law," he responded.

"Do you think Yonkers is guilty of racism?" Mary asked.

"I think Yonkers is getting a raw deal," he said, "but the judge ordered it, and the appeals court upheld it, and the law is the law."

"Why can't you say you think it's wrong? Let people know that, at least."

"That's not what a leader is supposed to do."

It was not the answer Mary was expecting. For a moment she was quiet. "You threw me out of the last meeting," she said finally.

Nick heard something in her voice that he thought was sympathy. "Which one were you?" he asked.

"I'm older, gray hair, glasses. I always sit on the right-hand side, first row."

"That's you?" he said. "I promise I'll never throw you out again."

Alma Febles Struggles Through the Night

THE eight red brick buildings of the Schlobohm housing project stand within sight of City Hall. Mary Dorman passed the eight-story structures on every trip to the council chambers, but she had never been inside. Fighting to keep "those people" out of her neighborhood became her all-consuming goal, yet she had never thought to detour one block north to see "those people" for herself.

Alma Febles, in turn, could see City Hall from her bedroom window in building 1 at Schlobohm. She paid as little attention to the protesters at City Hall as the protesters paid to her. She saw no connection between the goings-on at City Hall and the events of her own life, a life that was crashing down around her.

While lights were burning, while Mary was chanting, Alma Febles was crying. She had cried every night in the weeks since she'd come back from Santo Domingo, leaving her children behind. She'd barely eaten since she'd returned home, replacing food with two or three packs of cigarettes a day. She avoided sleep, too, because when she managed to fall asleep, she would dream: Frankie getting lost, Virgilio getting hit by a car, Leyda getting sick. She would wake up with a pain in her stomach. Then the tears would come again, and she would wander the empty apartment until dawn.

During the seven years she had lived there, Alma rarely called apartment 151 at Schlobohm home. She called it the apartment. That was because the two-bedroom flat, with its muddy green walls, was not home, not to Alma Cordero Reyes Febles, thirty-one years old and still sure there was a place for her to live that would bring her a feeling of peace. Alma was chasing the memories of her childhood in Santo Domingo, the capital of the Dominican Republic. Her mother owned their modest house back there. Alma, close to the youngest in a family of two brothers and six sisters, would wander the streets without worry, feeling safe in the invisible cocoon of neighborhood.

Although she loved life on the Caribbean island, her mother decided the children should have more, and slowly the family began to emigrate to the United States. Alma stayed in Santo Domingo while her mother worked to bring her and her siblings stateside one by one. Alma was eight when her mother left. She was fourteen when her mother sent for her to come to Yonkers.

Life in Yonkers was different from life in Santo Domingo. Alma knew no English, and although she was a serious student back home, she was miserable at the city's huge high school. She hated the winters. She hated sharing a two-bedroom apartment with her mother, three sisters, two brothers, and one cousin. Her goal in life was to find a place with a room all her own.

The pull of home brought her back to the island for frequent visits, and when she was sixteen, she met Virgilio Reyes there. They were married in Santo Domingo when she was nineteen. Virgilio junior was born two years later. Alma's new husband was drawn to the United States, so the young family moved to Yonkers in 1979. At first they lived on the top floor of a five-story walk-up. The $212 rent was the most they could afford with Virgilio's job at a local factory. The apartment was freezing all the time, and before she could bathe her baby, Alma had to turn on the kitchen stove and prop open the oven door.

Eventually Leyda was born, and Alma's marriage grew significantly worse. "That's when we started to hate each other," Alma says of Virgilio senior. Suspecting she would soon need to take care of herself, Alma started working toward a degree in special education at a local college. In 1981, when Leyda was a year old, Alma and her husband were divorced.

Alma took her children to Santo Domingo for Christmas that year. When she came back to Yonkers at New Year's, she found that a fire in the boiler had destroyed everything she owned. As a result of the fire, she moved into Schlobohm.

To enter her building, she had to walk through courtyards that seemed to radiate dread and despair. Everywhere the smell of trash mixed with the smell of disinfectant. Apartment 151, two bedrooms, no view, was supposed to be a short-term stopping place, but Alma was still living there three years later when she took another trip to Santo Domingo and met Jose M. Febles. They married within months; their son, Frankie, was born within a year; they were divorced by the time he was five months old. Now there were three children to feed, and Alma quit school and took a job selling office furniture at a Yonkers showroom.

For a few years she managed to keep Virgilio, Leyda, and Frankie sheltered from the world outside. They were not allowed to leave the apartment without their mother, and they rarely left it with her, because Alma feared that the small, ill-equipped playground in Schlobohm was really gang territory.

When Virgilio and then Leyda reached school age, Alma walked them each to the bus stop in the morning before she left for work. Frankie spent the day at cousin Miriam's apartment, and when the school day ended, Miriam would meet the older children at the bus stop and walk them to her house, too, carefully locking the doors. But no number of locks could shield them completely. By the time Virgilio was nine, Leyda eight, and Frankie four, their heads were filled with scenes that children are not supposed to see.

Leyda: "Once the elevator doors open and there was a drug deal happening inside, and they tried to pull me in, but they didn't."

Virgilio: "There's gunfire every weekend."

Realizing that her short-term solution was quickly swallowing her children's childhoods, Alma moved back to Santo Domingo in 1987. Once back on the island, she rented a peach-colored house on the street she grew up on. Although the house had three bedrooms, Alma still did not have a room all her own. She and Leyda shared one of the bedrooms, Virgilio and Frankie shared another, and the third was for the sleep-in baby-sitter. The woman would watch the children while Alma worked as a teacher's aide from seven in the morning until seven at night.

Virgilio and Leyda loved the freedom of the island and spent their days as Alma remembered spending hers. Because the children were safer, it took Alma a year to face the fact that she was not earning enough to afford the life she wanted to build. Her salary was less than 2000 pesos a month, worth about $300 at the time. Each month, with rent, the baby-sitter, and food, she spent slightly more money than she brought home. But American dollars went far in Santo Domingo in 1988, and she knew that if she went back to Schlobohm alone and began to work again in the furniture store, the $1200 she would earn each month would be enough to support her children back on the island.

On a February day in 1988, when tropical breezes were blowing in Santo Domingo and the temperature was below freezing in

Yonkers, Alma boarded a $550 American Airlines flight. She cried through the entire three-hour trip. She returned to the apartment she had fled a year earlier, which she had sublet to some cousins. She spent her days at work and her nights weeping. When her first monthly phone bill came, she disconnected the telephone in the apartment because she was wasting hundreds of dollars in nightly calls to the tiny peach house in Santo Domingo.

Removing the phone did not stop her from calling, however; it just made the calls more dangerous. She would sleep, then dream, then awaken in fear. More often than not she would race off to the pay phone on the rough streets near Schlobohm. It was the only reason she would ever dare to venture outside in the projects in the middle of the night.

The War

PENT-UP anger explodes. Unleashed anger expands and multiplies. Every day there was more anger in Yonkers—more protesters, more bullets in the mail, more Pampers and tiny American flags. As the weeks passed in 1988, as winter became spring, the web of anger widened. It moved beyond Yonkers, beyond control.

In February it went to Washington. At 7:30 one morning, five hundred protesters boarded ten rented buses and caravanned to the Capitol building, where they held signs that pleaded PRESIDENT REAGAN, HELP YONKERS, N.Y. Mary Dorman was part of that crowd. A small group of coalition leaders arranged a meeting with one of New York's U.S. Senators, Daniel Patrick Moynihan, and Mary tagged along. But Moynihan made it clear there was nothing he would do to help Yonkers fight Judge Sand.

By April the anger had ensnared the Catholic Church. Mary and her compatriots had come to blame the church for the consent decree because the agreement was made possible by the donation of land by the St. Joseph's Seminary. In the weeks that followed, parishioners throughout Yonkers defiantly kept their wallets closed when the collection plate was passed.

In June the anger reached the judge's front door. This time

there were two hundred protesters, and their purpose was to show Sand that they knew where he lived. Following a hand-drawn photocopied map, they drove north to Pound Ridge, an affluent pocket of Westchester, where most homes cannot be seen from the road. They stood in front of his fence for two hours, waving their fraying American flags and carrying placards that compared Sand, who is Jewish, to Adolf Hitler. They shouted "Integrate Pound Ridge" into bullhorns. On the trees and mailboxes along the narrow, curving road they taped signs saying LOW-INCOME HOUSING TO BE BUILT ON THIS PROPERTY, COURTESY OF JUDGE SAND.

As the circle of anger widened, the entire country began paying attention. Mail arrived on Nick's desk addressed "City Council, Yonkers" or "Yonkers, New York."

A letter writer from California described Sand's order as "nothing but garbage." A farmer from Missouri wrote that federal courts were leading the country "right down the drain." Judges like Sand were "just a bunch of dictators who won't be happy until they ruin our lives." From Tennessee: "Public housing is wrong and I would not permit it in my neighborhood without a fight."

Nick's days had become a spiral of less sleep and more vodka, and politically, he became the first to bend. If a symbolic appeal to the Supreme Court would calm the frenzy, then he would go to the Supreme Court. One night at the end of a particularly draining council meeting, when one hundred and forty people were on the speakers list and two hundred were outside chanting, he quietly announced that the city would ask Sand to restore the right to a Supreme Court appeal.

In a written statement to the judge Nick blamed himself for "sorely underestimating" residents' fears. "They are very frightened people who can see in the court's decrees a callous government destroying . . . the only real asset which [many of] these people have managed to acquire. If the furor is not dispelled, the hostility will scare away prospective public housing tenants and destroy chances of racial harmony—the goal of the case."

Sand turned down the request. "To allow [the appeal]," he wrote back, "would reward intransigence, reward threats of violence and reward conditions which lead, rather pitifully, the leaders of Yonkers to say 'Help us, court, we can't govern.' "

The City Council heard Sand's response, then decided to appeal to the Supreme Court anyway. They knew they risked contempt charges, and they knew the High Court probably wouldn't help them, but that did not stop them from filing the papers.

The next to blink was the Catholic Church, which threatened to withdraw the seminary site, saying they had been misled regarding the number of housing units planned for the site. Sand ordered Yonkers to condemn the property and seize it.

Nick, a lapsed Catholic but still a Catholic, was personally troubled by that fight. But he was much more troubled by the effect the standoff was having on Nicholas Longo, who had reluctantly voted in favor of the consent decree because it would theoretically give the City Council control, only to find they were being ordered to seize land from the church.

"As a Catholic," Longo said, "I in good conscience cannot proceed against the Catholic Church."

Nick suspected that Longo and the others were actually more interested in saving their council seats than in saving their souls. He believed that all the more completely when Sand offered to drop the seminary site from the plan if the city found a replacement. Instead of being relieved, Longo was outraged. "No more sites," he said. "That's it. Period. Sand is anti-Catholic, anti-Christian, and ought to be removed from the bench."

On June 13 the Supreme Court announced it would not even hear the Yonkers case. The next night the City Council voted a moratorium on the housing, officially refusing to cooperate with the judge. Sand immediately answered back, instructing the council to take a vote reaffirming support for the consent decree. As ordered, a vote was taken, and the tally was 5–2 *against* the housing.

The grenade was now in Sand's court.

MICHAEL Sussman, the lawyer for the NAACP, hoped this would be enough to push the judge to use the full force of his office and finally take control of the housing away from the City Council.

That is what other judges had done in other standoffs. In Boston, for example, U.S. district judge W. Arthur Garrity, Jr., took control of the city's schools in 1974 after finding that the city had segregated blacks in inferior schools within its system. He retained that control for eleven years, finally relinquishing it in 1985, when the city's first black school superintendent was hired.

Sand seriously considered the same route, but from the beginning of the case he had believed that the only way the housing plan would work was if it came *from* the city rather than being forced *on* the city. His intention was not to erect some buildings and declare victory, but to make those buildings into homes and make those homes part of a diverse but unified community.

In the end, Sand's decision was to fine Yonkers, not dismantle it. He was wagering that hefty fines would work. A student of judicial history, he knew that in every other case when sanctions were imposed for obstruction of a federal desegregation order, the showdown fizzled within hours after the fines took effect.

If the council did not vote to reaffirm the consent decree by August 1, Sand announced, he would impose personal fines of $500 a day against each recalcitrant councilman. In addition, the long-threatened fines would be imposed against the city, starting at $100 a day, then doubling every day. The money would be nonrefundable. It would take an act of Congress to recover even one dime.

On day 1 Yonkers would owe $100. Day 2, $200. After a week a daily fine of $6400, for a total of $12,700. By day 14 the daily fine would top $1 million for the first time—$1,638,400 to be exact. On day 22 the daily fine of $209,715,200 would bring the total fine paid to $419,430,300, more than the $355 million in the city's budget. By day 29 the total fine would be $53,687,091,100, which would be greater than the U.S. trade deficit with Japan. By the end of the month the total fine of $107 billion would be more than the gross national product of Finland.

Hours before the midnight deadline on August 1, 1988, the council met again. Driving to City Hall that night, Nick wondered why he was bothering to go at all. Hank Spallone, Peter Chema, and Nicholas Longo had been clear and public about their plans to vote no. Nick and Harry Oxman were planning to vote yes. Charles Cola had said that he was worried about the effect the threatened fines would have on the city's bond rating, but otherwise he had been firm in his opposition to the housing. Only the ever mysterious Ed Fagan had refused to say which way he would vote. That left the most optimistic projections at three votes in favor of compliance and four votes against.

Another death threat had come in the mail for Nick recently, scribbled on an invitation he had sent out for a political fundraiser that would double as his twenty-ninth birthday party. "This is your last birthday" had been scrawled across the card. A small-caliber bullet was in the envelope. It was hot outside now as he drove to City Hall thinking about that bullet. He was sweating in spite of the air conditioner. He wanted to go back home.

Before he saw the protesters, he heard them singing. There were hundreds of them, more than the steps or sidewalks could hold, kept in place by thirty police officers. Linking arms, they sang "We Shall Overcome," then "God Bless America."

Inside City Hall, only eighty people could fit in the council chamber, a relief after the riotous meeting of nine hundred at the Saunders High School auditorium. But here the protesters sat almost nose to nose with the councilmen, separated only by a six-foot barrier of klieg lights and television cameras. The air inside was stifling and became even more so when Nick was forced to close the windows to drown out the shouting from the street.

First came the speeches, familiar faces saying the same things they had said before. But this time there was a cockiness. This time they believed they would win.

When it came time to vote on the reaffirmation of the consent decree, Nick voted yes, as did Harry Oxman. Charles Cola, to Nick's amazement, voted with them. Henry Spallone and Nicholas Longo voted no. Peter Chema did the same. The vote was tied, three for and three against. The last to vote was Ed Fagan, who had remained a puzzle during the week before this meeting. The clerk called Fagan's name, and he paused dramatically. One second. Two seconds. More. Then he leaned his body toward the microphone, stared into the spotlight, and delivered an emphatic, "No."

The single word shot through the silence with the force of a starter's pistol. The crowd went wild, giving Fagan a standing ovation and dancing in the narrow aisles. Like a jolt of electricity, the news traveled out of the council chambers, down the stairs, and onto the street. The council had taken on the judge. The whoops of celebration could be heard even through the closed windows of City Hall. People screaming inside. People screaming outside. Soon it sounded to Nick as if all of Yonkers were screaming.

The Homeless Motel

DOREEN James* sat on the bed at the motel for the homeless, bouncing slowly against the surprisingly firm mattress. Doreen was a large, imposing, fleshy woman, made rounder by her recent pregnancy, and she held Jaron, her newborn, in her ample arms, snuggling him against her chest, trying to keep him from crying. Some young women, alone with an infant for the first time, would be frantic, but Doreen was not the frantic type. "You be quiet now," she said, patting the wailing baby with her dark brown hands.

As she bounced, she glared at the pot of water bubbling lazily on the hot plate across the room. Until the water boiled, then cooled, she could not mix the powered baby formula. And without the formula she could not quiet Jaron. Leaving her parents' home, with its fully equipped kitchen and two extra pairs of helping hands, had seemed like a good idea at the time, an overdue declaration of independence. But here in this state-funded motel room she was having second thoughts.

Doreen was born in Yonkers in 1965 and had spent her childhood in the projects on School Street. It was different there then, she remembered: "No drugs, no dogs, and they didn't have all that traffic." Her father and several other men took turns patrolling the hallways at night. Doreen was the fifth child in a family of four girls and two boys, and her memories of public housing were ones

---

**Not her real name.*

of safety and togetherness. Alma Febles wanted out of Schlobohm; Doreen James wanted in, or thought she did.

A life spent in and around public housing meant she knew how to navigate the rules, and she understood that there were two waiting lists—the regular one and the emergency one. The first route took years, so Doreen went to the Yonkers Department of Social Services and presented herself as an emergency case—a twenty-one-year-old new mother who was homeless. The caseworker immediately found a room for Doreen and Jaron in a motel for the homeless in the upper reaches of Westchester County, a temporary stopping place until an apartment became available.

What Doreen never mentioned to the caseworker was that there was an entire bedroom available for her at her parents' house, a room her parents said would be hers to call home whenever she wished. And she also failed to mention that her parents were leery of her entire plan. Pearl and Walter James had struggled to get their children out of the projects, and they could not understand why their youngest daughter was hell-bent on moving back in. Doreen had been ten years old when her father took a job maintaining a golf driving range in New Jersey, proudly moving his wife and children to Essex County, where they lived in a two-family house.

Still, despite their move, the James family did not cut off all contact with Yonkers. Sheila, the oldest of the children, was nearly twenty at the time, and she decided to stay behind. Doreen went back to see her often. After high school graduation Doreen attended school to learn to be a medical office assistant, but she discovered she had an unconquerable fear of needles, so she dropped out. Next she became a home health aide and enjoyed that until one of her patients died. For months after that she worked as a salesclerk.

During one of her visits to Sheila she met Joe Bailey. He was the brother of a mutual friend and a symbol of how the projects had changed. Joe sold drugs, cocaine mostly. Doreen didn't really mind his profession, because he rarely sampled his wares himself. "He's nice to me; he's a good listener," she would explain in her languid, laconic way. Then she would shrug her shoulders.

A year after the couple met, they decided to marry. They never set a date, but they did choose a solitaire diamond ring, which they put on layaway. Soon after that, when Doreen learned she was pregnant, Joe was thrilled. Doreen was less so. "This wasn't part of the dream," she tried to explain to Joe.

In her seventh month of pregnancy she went to the hospital clinic for her prenatal checkup. It was a crowded, uncomfortable room, and she hated her appointments there. She kept them only because Joe insisted. He had suffered from asthma for years, and his source of income aside, he was always preaching healthy living. When her name was finally called at the clinic that morning, however, it was not by a nurse, but by Joe's father, who made his way across the room, his face sagging. Joe was dead. Asthma. Doreen gripped the flimsy chair so tightly that the edges bent. She tried not to faint. As she sobbed in the arms of her fiancé's father, he patted her kindly and warned, "Don't you have this baby on me right now."

That same night she escaped back to New Jersey. "Mommy and Daddy to the rescue as always," she said. The jewelry store would not refund the money for her ring, so she exchanged it for a gold cross for her baby, a last gift from his father.

Jaron was born early in the summer of 1988. At first Doreen burrowed into the cocoon of home, the chance to be a child while she cared for her child. Then one night she dreamed that Jaron called his grandparents Mommy and Daddy. Despite her parents' objections, she applied for her own apartment.

The motel in Yorktown Heights was nicer than she had expected, but Doreen felt trapped in the rural town, nearly an hour north of Yonkers. She spent her days trying to feed her child with only a hot plate, and her nights worrying about noises from outside. Someone had told her "there was Klansmen in the woods," and after a few sleepless nights she left. She had to say she was homeless, she reasoned, but she didn't have to *live* like she was homeless. She could room with her parents in New Jersey until her name reached the top of the emergency waiting list.

The Glare of the Spotlight

As THE television cameras turned their attention to Yonkers, they magnified and electrified events. On August 1, 1988, the night that the city hurled itself into contempt, there were fifty reporters in the council chamber to watch the vote, including one from the Jerusalem *Post.* Yonkers was now international news.

The next morning, August 2, the council members were summoned to Judge Sand's chambers to have the fines officially imposed. The press was there, too. In the middle of the hearing Hank Spallone walked out. A U.S. marshal soon found the AWOL councilman in a nearby telephone booth, where he was chatting on the air, live, to a radio talk-show host.

From then on, there seemed to be reporters everywhere. Nick knew that every reporter who called him also called Hank. Their remarks would appear under a single headline. Their faces would be shown in the same video segment, one right after the other, point-counterpoint, a debate in front of the entire nation between two men who had more or less stopped speaking months ago.

The lawmakers were not the only ones caught in the seductive pull of the spotlight. For months, from the January meeting at Saunders until the August 1 showdown at City Hall, the protesters had been posing only for the council. Now they were posing for the cameras. During the second week of August, Hank Spallone took his Kodak Instamatic over to Schlobohm, where he took photos of peeling paint, overflowing trash bins, and broken windows, then glued the snapshots onto a huge piece of oaktag. Mary Dorman was on the national news that night, holding the collage in front of City Hall. Shortly after that, producers from the CBS program *48 Hours* came to town, and Mary Dorman was on in prime time, talking in her kitchen. She yelled at Phil Donahue one morning and Morton Downey, Jr., one afternoon.

Mary welcomed the cameras, sought them out, assuming that everyone believed as she believed, but each encounter left her a little stunned and bruised. The video lens can be a two-way mirror, and what Mary often saw reflected was what the world thought of *her.* The reporters used the word racism a lot. They compared this city to cities like Selma and Montgomery. Mary did not think of herself as racist. To her this fight was not about race at all, it was about *principles,* and she thought she could make the reporters see it her way.

One sweltering afternoon a writer for the Boston *Globe* sat with Mary in her kitchen for several hours, talking above the roar of an aging air conditioner. The woman ("a nice black girl," Mary said) asked a lot of questions about the east-west division between the races in Yonkers. Mary tried to explain that it isn't only white people who choose to live with others like themselves. When black people move across town, she said, "they also stick together."

In a front-page story the reporter wrote, "Mary Dorman is white and lives on a pleasant, tree-lined street on this city's east side. Her view on housing desegregation, voiced one day last week in the air-conditioned parlor of her modest brick home, is this: 'I don't think you should take people with one lifestyle and put them smack in the middle of a place with a different lifestyle. You have to expect them to resent us.' "

Another woman, the article continued, "is black and lives on a busy, treeless street on this city's west side. Her view on housing desegregation, voiced in a steamy hallway outside her apartment, is this: 'I think all people should be together and equal as one.' "

The Emergency Financial Control Board and the Supreme Court

NICK Wasicsko stood on the spectator side of the waist-high partition that on more usual days separates the City Council from the public. The room looked different to him from back there, more somber and imposing. He tried to seem at ease with the role of outsider.

It was Tuesday, August 9, day 8 of contempt. The city had paid $12,700 in fines (another $12,700 would be due by 4:30 that afternoon), and the councilmen had paid $3500 each. Later in the day, in the opening scene of what would become a multi-act legal drama, the U.S. Court of Appeals would put those fines on hold, pending an appeal.

There, at the seat graced by a sign that read NICHOLAS WASICSKO, MAYOR, sat a woman who was clearly not Nicholas Wasicsko. She was arranging her pads with the manner of someone comfortable being in charge. The other council seats were filled with other people whose names did not appear on the nameplates in front of them. They were there to take control of the city's finances.

This was not the first time Yonkers had flirted with bankruptcy. The city had careened within inches of disaster more than once and always managed to find a last-minute rescuer. During the winter of 1976 Yonkers was technically in financial default for one weekend because it had spent years simply rolling its deficit into the next year, until the debt reached $83 million. That time Governor Hugh Carey stepped in and bailed the city out. Then, in the spring of 1984, the Yonkers Board of Education announced it would close the schools in April instead of June because the City Council would not provide the funding needed to complete the school year. The schools remained open when Governor Mario M. Cuomo signed a financial bailout and the council agreed to enact a local tax surcharge.

The bailouts of 1976 and 1984 came with strings attached. The state legislature established an Emergency Financial Control Board for Yonkers, which was authorized to keep an eye on the city's finances and to step in, when necessary, to prevent another crisis. For years this board had been reviewing, advising, and overseeing all fiscal decisions. Now, on day 8, its members had come to Yonkers to wield the full force of their authority for the first time.

It was not the solution Nick had wanted. He and his interim city manager Neil DeLuca had asked Cuomo—begged Cuomo—to save Yonkers from itself. On the first day of the contempt crisis Neil asked Cuomo to remove defiant councilmen from office, "to save Yonkers from bankruptcy and further national embarrassment." The same day, Nick called the governor and asked him to come down to Yonkers himself to "talk some sense" into the rebellious four. Cuomo turned both men down.

Cuomo's problem was that this battle had lined up his two natural constituencies against each other. If he had said what some would have expected him to say—that racism, however it might be cloaked or sanitized, is still racism and is still evil—then he would also have been saying that workingmen and -women, most of them immigrants like his parents, could sweat and save only to have their labor be for nothing. And if he had said just the opposite, that good, honest hardworking people had a right to protect their dreams, he would also be saying that other good, honest hardworking people, who happened to be stuck in a cycle of discrimination and poverty, were not entitled to dreams of their own.

Given that choice, he said both. He stayed distant enough from Yonkers that he had that luxury, one Nick Wasicsko and Neil DeLuca didn't share. They didn't understand why one day Cuomo called Judge Sand and warned that the plan in its current form would hurt property values, and why the next day he warned the councilmen that "the rule of law" must prevail. What they did come to understand was that the governor was not going to bail them out. Instead Cuomo had sent Gail S. Shaffer, New York's secretary of state and the chairman of the Emergency Financial Control Board, a tough-as-nails woman who was used to playing hardball up in Albany. Everything about Gail Shaffer—from her blood-red manicure to her perfectly coifed brunette hair—showed she was in control. It was she who sat in Nick's chair, looking stern and ready for business.

A long table had been set up for the board members in the middle of the room on the inside of the horseshoe formed by the desks of the councilmen. But Gail Shaffer knew Yonkers, had come to know it during the years she had spent on the control board, and knew she had to send some strong messages from the start. What the city saw as quirky independence and Sand saw as discriminatory obstinacy, Gail Shaffer saw as simple immaturity. Politics in Yonkers resembled a preschool classroom, she thought, and when she prepared for her visits there, she would tell her staff, "I'm going to teach potty training 101." Her goal was to dissolve the control board, to push Yonkers to the point where it was mature enough to act like "a normal locale," one that could "take charge of its own destiny and make these decisions themselves."

By the time the meeting was over, the control board had taken away almost all financial authority from the city manager and the City Council. The city was still allowed to pay employee salaries, court judgments, and previously approved bills and bond payments, but nothing else. All other spending, every single item over $100, would have to be personally approved by Gail Shaffer.

"APPEAL, appeal, appeal," the protesters had shouted, and on August 17, 1988, more than two weeks into the crisis, dozens of lawyers had their chance to do exactly that. Attorneys for the city and the councilmen filled the courtroom of the U.S. Court of Appeals for the Second Circuit and explained why nothing about this situation was their clients' fault. They stood before the three-judge panel and pointed at the other guy. "He" started it, the city said of the councilmen. No, "he" started it, the councilmen said of the city.

Michael Skulnick, who represented the city of Yonkers, told the court that his client wanted to obey Judge Sand but was "powerless to comply with the order." Compliance required a majority vote of the council, he argued, and there was nothing the city could do to change the four council members' minds. To fine the city under those circumstances was like blaming a hostage for failing to flee.

Then Hank Spallone's lawyer stood up and argued that the city, not the councilmen, should be fined. "If the city has failed to act, then punish the city," he said.

The judges shook their heads. "*You're* telling us the city should do something, and the city is telling us *you* should do something," one judge said, clearly annoyed.

"Never before has a federal court commanded a city councilman or other state or local legislator how to vote on legislation," Spallone's lawyer argued. "What we have here is an attempt to erode the integrity of the legislative process."

Michael Sussman, speaking for the NAACP, responded that Sand was not really telling anyone how to vote. He was simply requiring affirmation that the city would implement something—

namely the consent decree—the councilmen had already voted for.

Throwing out his hands in frustration, one judge said, "I don't understand how anyone keeps their word in this group of people."

In the end, the circuit court upheld the fines against the councilmen but tinkered with the fines against the city. Saying that the formula Sand had used could reach "unreasonable proportions," the panel limited the fines to a maximum of $1 million a day, so the city would go bankrupt on day 79 rather than day 20.

Knowing that both sides would appeal their decision, the judges extended the stay on the fines until the Supreme Court had its chance to rule. The appeal to the Supreme Court was filed within hours, and the decision was issued at 11:55 p.m. on September 1. In that decision the Justices unanimously rejected the city's request to continue a delay on the fines. Although technically that was not a rejection of the city's point that the fines were unconstitutional, the practical effect was the same, because by the time the Court would finally hear the full arguments, sometime in the fall, the city would already be bankrupt.

The decision surprised Nick. He never believed that the fines would be found unconstitutional, but he had assumed that the Supreme Court would continue the stay until October, giving him a month of maneuvering room. And if the first part of the Supreme Court's decision surprised Nick, what the Justices said next left him nearly speechless. They lifted the fines from the councilmen. The councilmen were freed while the city kept on paying.

The decision also distressed Judge Sand. Judges commonly say (in public, at least) that they do not regard it as a personal slap when they are reversed on appeal. Just as commonly, no one believes them. Sand's irritation at the ruling of the Supreme Court stemmed only partly from ego, however. He was far more distressed because the Justices had removed the part of the sanctions that Sand felt was most likely to work. Faced with paying $500 a day every day, a councilman, he was certain, would change his vote.

Nicholas Longo had a different reaction altogether. The Court, which was theoretically above petty politics, had issued a decision that Longo recognized as a stroke of political brilliance. The way the Supreme Court set things up, the city continued to suffer, and the councilmen were the reasons why. Now they were more likely to look like stubborn roadblocks, watching the city swerve toward bankruptcy while their own checking accounts were safe.

Well, I'll be damned, Longo thought with fear and admiration. In his gut he suspected this was the beginning of the end.

Shutting Down the City

GAIL Shaffer spent a large part of every day saying no. No to new trash bags for the meals-on-wheels program, to postage stamps for the board of elections, to repairing potholes, upgrading fire hydrants, repainting the walls of traffic court. No to the department of parks, recreation and conservation, who wanted $325 to charter a bus to take forty senior citizens to the Platzl Brau Haus restaurant for lunch. Each no was met with howls of outrage. "This isn't saving any money; they're just nickel-and-diming us," grumbled the parks commissioner.

"Isn't there anyone in that city who understands the gravity of the situation?" Shaffer asked. Though each individual "no" would not make a dent in the city's looming problem, she knew, together they were far more than just nickels and dimes. Each rejection should have given the people of Yonkers a taste of what would be if fines swallowed the entire budget. But the indignant whining made her wonder whether that message was getting through. Yonkers was like a millionaire after the market had crashed, still hiring limousines because "they don't really cost *that* much more than cabs." The reality was that Yonkers couldn't even afford cabs.

Hoping to further make the point that Yonkers had entered another realm, the control board ordered nearly all city executives and administrators to turn in their city-owned cars, the ones stamped NY OFFICIAL on the license plates. Nick Wasicsko and Neil DeLuca, along with the police and fire commissioners, were among the few who were allowed to keep their cars. The six members of the council were not, and they did not take it well.

"What next?" Peter Chema asked. "Cut off our legs?"

The plumbing bureau lost its three cars, and shortly after 6:00 p.m. that day a water line burst at the Bowling Green Storage and Van Company, spewing one million gallons thirty feet into the air. It took inspectors two hours to get there.

As the cuts mounted, so did the fines. "What's $200,000?" asked the local paper on Labor Day morning, September 5, day 11 of the contempt crisis. On day 12, $192,000 would be hand-delivered to Judge Sand's office at the federal courthouse in Manhattan. Once it was delivered, the city would have paid the aggregate sum of $204,700, which led the *Herald Statesman* to do some math.

How much is $200,000? Enough for each resident of Yonkers to buy a $1.35 pack of cigarettes, a $1.21 gallon of gas, a 73-cent quart of milk. It would pay the salaries of ten employees at the department of public works animal shelter. It would cover the yearly operating costs of Nick Wasicsko's office, including his salary, Nay's salary, and the paychecks of his four other employees.

How much is $200,000? A lot of money. But within days, when the daily fine reached $1 million, the old level of $200,000 would be looked on with nostalgia. One million dollars a day was roughly $30 to $40 for every citizen of Yonkers. In two months, when the total reached $66 million, the city's entire cash supply would be gone. All that money, which could do so many other things, sent off in an unmarked envelope transported by anonymous courier.

And not one cent was refundable.

WHEN the Supreme Court upheld the fines, when the totals reached $200,000, the councilmen began to talk. Not to the cameras, but to each other, for the first time in a very long time.

On the afternoon of Labor Day they all but locked themselves in City Hall. They started their conversations in Neil DeLuca's second-floor conference room at about one o'clock, then broke into small groups. For the next few hours these clusters broke apart, came back together—a kind of cocktail party in hell.

At one point Longo and Chema retreated to the men's room with Wasicsko and Cola for some particularly intense conversation. Fagan loped in and was asked to leave.

"It felt like a bunch of high school kids," he said, pouting, as he retreated to the hallway. "Everybody standing around smoking and talking. The only thing missing was the graffiti and the guys singing a cappella doo-wop in the stalls to get the echo."

The four who had voted no were focused on what amendments might be made to the plan to induce them to change their minds. They talked of reducing the number of units, scattering them across a larger geographical area, or not building any housing but using money to upgrade housing that already exists.

The three who had voted yes focused on returning the talk to reality. The judge seemed in no mood to entertain any amendments to the plan, they warned, until after the council voted to reaffirm the consent decree. There was no possibility of negotiation until someone changed his vote. In the midafternoon Spallone and Fagan walked out, saying that unless Sand changed the plan, they would not change their minds.

Those who remained talked for several hours more, then sent out for pizza and gathered to watch Spallone and Fagan on the six-o'clock news. "The only thing Judge Sand gave away was ice in the wintertime," they saw Spallone say. "No deal."

At 8:30 the meetings finally ended, and the exhausted councilmen had their turn to face the media.

The sticking point, said Wasicsko, glancing over at his worn-out adversaries, "is that they want to show their constituents that they accomplished something with their defiance. I think the court is reluctant to give them that appearance of victory."

SENSING some momentum, the Emergency Financial Control Board added its own extra push. On Wednesday, September 7, when the fines reached $409,600, Gail Shaffer announced sweeping layoffs. On Saturday, when the fines would be $1 million a day, 447 people—a quarter of the municipal workforce—would lose their jobs. Shaffer's plan was to cut between 109 and 439 people per week until November 5. By then the only remaining city employees would be the police officers and firemen necessary for bare-bones protection. Dramatic, immediate layoffs, she hoped, would change the political equation for the "spineless" council and force them to change their vote faster.

"The city of Yonkers must confront reality in a very decisive way," she said. "The time for finger-pointing is over. The time for punting is over. We must save Yonkers from itself."

The results could be seen twenty-four hours later, on Thursday evening, September 8, at the next meeting of the City Council. At first it seemed like business as usual. The room was packed to overflowing, the police strained to keep order, the heat was oppressive, and tempers were short. But as Nick Wasicsko called the meeting to order and the members of the public approached the microphone to speak, he heard that something was different. Instead of yelling at the council, the people were yelling at each other.

"I'm tired of these idiots supposedly representing my interests," shouted Martha Darcy, a librarian whose job was scheduled to be cut, pointing toward the protesters.

"I have a wife and two kids. How am I going to feed them if I'm laid off?" asked Russell Deutchen, a motor equipment operator.

"Sixteen years with the city is going down the tubes," said Mary Rudasill, a single parent who worked in the office of human rights.

"I'm a taxpayer, too," said her boss. "Settle the mess."

There were people speaking against the housing, too, trying to rally the crowd to their view that the layoffs were a noble sacrifice some would have to make in the name of a greater cause.

Nick let them shout for a while, then acted to end the meeting. He was getting smarter. The judge had ordered the council to meet once a week until someone changed his vote. Nick asked, "Does any councilman desire to change his vote today?"

Receiving no answer, he ordered the meeting recessed. He left the room feeling somewhat hopeful. He had always known they were out there—the Darcys, the Deutchens, and the Rudasills. He had sat in these meetings and wondered where they were. This had been the best meeting he'd had in months.

ON FRIDAY, September 9, 1988, day 15, the fines reached $1 million, and the layoffs began. Black flags of mourning were hoisted at all three library buildings, which were ordered to close at noon.

At the Grinton I. Will Library, on the east side, a group of senior citizens refused to leave. They had been playing bingo in the ground-floor senior center there when the building officially closed, and they decided that if their councilmen could be defiant, they could, too. "If they want me out of here, they're going to have to carry me out like they did those kids in the '60s," one septuagenarian said.

The bingo game continued, and the winners joked that they would chip in and buy a cemetery plot for Judge Sand. As they played, laid-off workers interrupted to say good-bye and offer encouragement. One employee sent in sandwiches. "If the cops are going to take you away, I want you to have full bellies," he said.

The police did come, at 5:30 in the evening, and the residents started chanting, "Hell no, we won't go."

The leader of the group, sixty-six-year-old Harry Preis, shuffled up to the three officers, waving his cane. "What if we said we're not going?" he asked.

"Oh, we have tear gas we can bring in," said Lieutenant George Kovalik, tongue firmly in cheek. "Everybody who goes to jail today is getting cornflakes. Without milk."

"Will you please escort us out of here?" Preis asked.

Kovalik took his arm.

"Attaboy, Harry," people yelled.

The library was dark and empty by six o'clock.

WHILE the bingo players were chanting, the councilmen were talking. The million-dollar-a-day mark had brought on what Peter Chema called the chill of reality. It was time for Yonkers to choose its fate: desegregate its housing or dissolve its government.

They knew they could not talk at City Hall. There were too many eyes there and too many cameras. Paul Pickelle, one of the city's many lawyers, offered his Tudor-style home in nearby Scarsdale.

Michael Sussman, the lawyer for the NAACP, was the first to arrive, at 8:00 a.m. on Friday. He and Pickelle, adversaries for years, took off their jackets and shot some hoops in Pickelle's backyard. "I was going to offer to play you for the housing plan," Pickelle joked. "But then I saw how well you play."

Neil DeLuca arrived at 9:00 a.m., as did Michael Skulnick, the city's lawyer on the housing case, and lawyers for Nicholas Longo and Peter Chema. Over coffee and doughnuts in the Pickelles' kitchen they agreed to suggest the following to Judge Sand: that the 200 townhouses be reconfigured as 100 townhouses plus 100 units scattered throughout mixed-income developments.

After two hours of talking, the lawyers phoned Longo and Chema, who were at home waiting for word. That done, they broke for sandwiches. One thing they forgot to do was update Nick, who was holding the fort back at City Hall. When he found out about the off-site meeting, he was furious. He had called a council meeting for noon because the council had to vote to release the $819,200 needed to pay the contempt fines for that day, but DeLuca, Pickelle, Chema, and Longo were nowhere to be found.

Nick had been suffering from severe stomach pains all week. With no time for a checkup, he had called his doctor, who prescribed ulcer medication over the phone, but that made a small difference at best. Nick had had to keep excusing himself from the meeting so he could run to his office and double over in private agony.

"Four of the key players aren't here, and I don't know why," he fumed at Nay. Noon came and went. Nick swallowed more pain pills. Then he went back out and recessed the meeting.

At 2:30 Michael Sussman arrived to fill him in. Chema and Longo came soon after. The payment was authorized, and a check was sent to Foley Square. Nick again recessed the meeting, reserving the right to resume it again on a "two-hour call."

At 3:30 the lawyers gathered once again at the Pickelle house, bringing Chema and Longo with them. They all sat in the living room, which had been immaculate that morning but which by the afternoon was strewn with soda cans and snacks. By 4:20 the deal was done. The two councilmen had agreed to the reduction to one hundred townhouses that had been worked out earlier in the day. After months of stalemate it almost seemed easy.

They should have known that nothing in Yonkers is that simple. At 4:30 the lawyers held a telephone conference call with Judge Sand, who was in Pennsylvania at a judicial conference.

Michael Sussman began by telling the judge that the city and the NAACP had been negotiating in good faith. The proposed changes "might make it a better plan, more acceptable to the community."

Michael Skulnick spoke next and began to tell the judge the specifics of the compromise. Sand angrily cut him off. He had expected a phone call pledging compliance. Instead all he was hearing was a proposed list of changes. "The court will not entertain" any mention of changes, he said, "until the council votes to comply."

In light of the recent progress, Skulnick asked, might the judge consider suspending the fines?

Sand said no, he would not consider that.

Would the judge consider not sending the checks on to the U.S. Treasury? Would he consider putting them in escrow—where they might eventually be refunded—instead?

No, he would not consider that either.

Might the council be allowed to adopt a resolution of intent, promising to adopt the plan if the amendments were worked out?

No, Sand said.

The conference call was over seven minutes after it had begun. The judge's message was clear: Comply first. Negotiate later.

"The judge was in no mood to hear new plans," Pickelle told Longo and Chema, who were pacing in a nearby hallway while the lawyers made the conference call.

About twenty minutes later Sand's law clerk called back, saying the judge was willing to compromise a smidgen. The court would forgive Thursday's $819,000 fine, as well as Friday's $1 million fine, if the council voted to comply at a meeting that began before midnight on Friday night.

With seven hours left until midnight, all remaining energy in the Pickelle house was spent pressuring Chema and Longo to change their votes. Yes, the weary councilmen agreed, they wanted to end this, but they didn't want to break their word. Nick arrived at six o'clock and upped the stakes even further. Gail Shaffer, he said, had promised she would suspend the layoffs if the city complied before midnight that night.

Paul Pickelle's wife made beef stew for dinner. At 9:55 Nick realized he had five remaining minutes in which to give the required two-hour warning that there would be a council meeting, or he would miss the midnight deadline. At ten o'clock everyone left for City Hall, with no commitment from either Chema or Longo.

Nick went home for a quick shower and another dose of medication. Then he drove to City Hall and raced up the steps past a sea of workers who were about to lose their jobs.

Nick called the meeting to order at 11:57 p.m. At 11:58 p.m. he called for a recess so that the clerical staff could type up the resolution on which the councilmen would vote.

It was an arcane resolution, listing specific building incentives that would promote the construction of the eight hundred units of low- to moderate-income housing, but by voting these incentives into effect, the council agreed to move forward with the housing plan. It took more than an hour to type, copy, and circulate the resolution. Nick spent that time in his office, urging the police chief to keep the protesters quiet "so they don't spook Nicky Longo."

Longo and Chema spent most of that hour in Neil DeLuca's office, being spooked. Chema called his wife twice while he waited. During the first call he said he would change his vote. During the second call he said he "couldn't do it."

Just before the council was to reconvene, one of DeLuca's assistants came in and handed everyone a list of the six hundred and thirty workers who had received pink slips earlier in the day. Chema and Longo shook their heads as they scanned the names. "We're about to economically murder six hundred families," Longo said.

At 12:45 a.m. the councilmen returned to the chamber. Nick's gavel could barely be heard when he reopened the meeting.

As the council members took their seats, Mary Dorman found herself putting her hands over her eyes and staring through her fingers. She couldn't bear to watch, but she couldn't bear not to.

"Does any council member wish to change his vote?" Nick asked.

Longo gave a short speech. Until tonight, he said, the fines, the threats of bankruptcy, the layoffs, the cutbacks—all of those had been distant and abstract. Now they were terrifyingly real.

"These are people I've shared backyard barbecues with," he said, and Nick knew the fight was finally over.

Mary, defeated, let her hand slip, motionless, into her lap.

The historic vote came at 1:15 a.m. on Saturday, September 10, 1988. Nicholas Longo voted yes. Moments later Peter Chema did so, too. They would comply with the judge's order. The housing would be built.

1989
A House on a Hill

THE house at 175 Yonkers Avenue is hidden in plain sight. It sits on one of the west side's busiest streets, at the top of a hill, making it visible for miles. But the only way to reach that hill is via a steep private road, which is unmarked and easily missed.

Only because of a Realtor's arrow did Nick and Nay make their way up that driveway in the first place. At the time, they were not in the market for a house. They were in the middle of Nick's reelection campaign and were headed to the Cross County Shopping Center to shake some hands. Nick had come to hate those campaign stops on the east side. A few weeks earlier a passerby had actually spit at him. What he was looking for was not a house, but a detour. When he saw the OPEN HOUSE sign, he made a U-turn across four lanes of traffic and drove up the hill.

It was love at first sight. Nick and Nay were both instantly smitten by the huge unkempt building, with its withered green shingles and peeling green brick. They knew they couldn't afford it, and they had no idea how to begin repairing it. They also knew they had to buy it.

There was something that drew them to this house, something beyond privacy or space. One seventy-five Yonkers Avenue could be a grand house. They sensed there was a mayor's house beneath the hideous linoleum on the floors and the cracking acoustic tiles, maybe a home worthy of a Senator or a governor. Buying the hilltop estate would be a statement of faith that there was a future.

Nearly a year had passed since the night that Longo and Chema changed their minds. Nick had assumed—naïvely, he now realized—that once it was over, it would be *over.* Instead property owners near the sites filed suit to block the plan. A group of pro-compliance taxpayers sued the recalcitrant councilmen for $166 million, charging dereliction of duty. A local congressman introduced a bill to refund the fines that Sand had declared nonrefundable. Only one of the many suits and petitions met with any real results. The Supreme Court agreed to hear the appeal by the four councilmen who had incurred personal fines and who wanted their $3500 back.

In the middle of it all, just in case Nick had somehow missed the absurdity of his city, came word of Laurie Recht, the secretary whose short speech at Saunders had so enraged the crowd. After she made her lone plea in favor of the housing, Recht had become a local celebrity and been called a hero. She had filed twenty-four police reports in the nine months after she stood up to the crowd. Most were for threatening phone calls, but one described a bomb threat, another described a swastika painted outside her apartment, and a third detailed an attempt to run her car off the road.

Secretly, police put a tap on her telephone and installed a video camera outside her door. Soon after that, Recht reported receiving three threatening calls in one day, but no such calls were recorded. The video camera did catch a guilty party, however. Reviewing the tape, the police clearly saw a person looking around, then scrawling a threatening message. That person was Laurie Recht. How fitting, Nick thought, that the only other person who stuck out her neck for this cause was now being led away in handcuffs.

He never really decided to run for reelection. Instead he saw the decision as one of "hanging in or quitting." A first-term incumbent was expected to run again. Nick was too tired for a fight, but to do otherwise would give Hank Spallone, who was threatening a primary challenge, too much satisfaction.

Once it became clear that Nick was going to run, some of the old adrenaline came back. It was a different kind of energy from that which had propelled him through his first mayoral campaign, however. What the housing fight had shown him was that the rush of victory lasts only through election night. After that you have to stand for something. Nick had come into office with ambitions. While he was there, he developed beliefs.

The first thing he did was spend $15,000 on a poll, with the hope that it would prove there really was a silent majority who supported his stand on the housing. What he learned was that although the general electorate was split between Nick (29 percent) and Hank (33 percent), among the Democrats who would decide the primary, 40 percent supported Nick and only 28 percent supported Hank. The Wasicsko campaign leaked the results of their poll. Hank Spallone, rather than simply dropping out, as Nick expected he would, switched parties and became a Republican.

Nick officially launched his campaign in front of City Hall. A crowd of one hundred and fifty stood on the steps around him, holding brooms and chanting, "Clean sweep." He was proud of his speech, a portrait of a city at a crossroads: "Our road leads to Yonkers once again being a fine city," he said. "Their road leads to Yonkers once again being a city fined. Our road leads to electing a City Council of lawmakers. Their road leads to reelecting a City Council of lawbreakers."

He tried to ignore the fact that seven hundred people were in the crowd when Hank Spallone launched *his* campaign.

Nick was challenged for the Democratic nomination by Dominick Iannacone, a former councilman. Wasicsko defeated him with 70 percent of the vote, and the victory gave him confidence.

Slowly the endorsements came. He received high-profile union support as well as praise from big-name Democrats. Senator Moynihan called the race one of "national importance." Governor Cuomo called Nick "clearly the superior candidate."

As the campaign unfolded, Nick tried to concentrate on these satisfying parts and not be distracted by the creeping ugliness. He tried not to see the group of protesters from Save Yonkers who appeared at all his east side campaign events to catcall and jeer. His campaign was going well, and he was feeling confident—as long as he stayed away from the east side. Nay would find him lying on the couch, unshaven and ill-tempered, when he was scheduled to appear across town. "I don't want to go," he would say. If he did go, he would strap his .38 to his ankle. The weapon he had previously used to protect himself in the projects was now needed in the safest parts of his city.

That avoidance instinct was what led him to his fixer-upper house on the hill, where he placed a $210,000 bet, in the form of a bid to purchase, that everything would work out okay. It was money he and Nay did not have, so they borrowed the down payment from her parents. The house provided them a distraction through the rest of the summer—filling out mortgage forms, planning renovations. On good days they imagined it as a center of political power, on bad days as an escape, a retreat.

Increasingly the days were bad. A poll after Labor Day showed Nick losing to Hank by nearly ten points, with 18 percent undecided. Nick's campaign contributions were disappointing. Since he had little hope of reaching that undecided 18 percent on his own dime, he put his hopes in a televised debate.

The tone turned nasty early when Spallone noted that the Supreme Court had agreed to hear his appeal of the personal fines and hinted that this might help the city stop the housing.

Wasicsko blasted his opponent for giving the voters false hope. "The Supreme Court has ruled on all issues of liability and remedy. That is forever closed. Mr. Spallone's case involves thirty-five hundred dollars of his money, but the housing situation will not change."

In his closing remarks Nick talked about putting history, and the housing, "where it belongs, behind us."

Spallone closed with, "It's time you recognized that you failed as a leader. I think if they vote for you again, you'll be a disaster upon this city."

The debate seemed to have an effect. A new poll found the race to be a virtual dead heat. Eighteen percent were still undecided.

Nick went to bed the night before election day thinking he might be able to defy the odds one more time. He was wrong.

NEARLY 70 PERCENT OF YONKERS voted in the mayoral election of 1989, twelve thousand more people than two years earlier. Fifty-three percent voted for Hank Spallone, and 45 percent for Nick Wasicsko. A ward-by-ward map showed a city divided by the Saw Mill River Parkway. Nick beat Hank on the west side. Hank made an equal sweep of the east side. There were more voters on the east side, and a higher percentage of them came out to the polls.

Nick made his concession speech shortly after 11:00 p.m. "Do not despair," he told the crowd of two hundred and fifty. "I believe I was there when the city needed me. I have no regrets. I endured death threats and all sorts of abuse. I think in the long run history will prove me right." Still, the loss hurt. That is the risk of running on an idea, not just a strategy. When you lose, you lose a lot more.

The next morning Nick and Nay moved into the house on the hill. For her sake he tried to be cheerful, a man starting a new chapter with the woman he loved. But even his jokes were tinged with pain. At lunchtime the couple took a break on the sunporch, where the windows were milky with age. "It's a lot like Yonkers," he said, his mouth smiling but his eyes sad. "With a little bit of work it could be gorgeous."

Billie Rowan Meets John Santos

THROUGHOUT the eight buildings of Schlobohm and all public housing in Yonkers, people are living where they are not supposed to be. Officially, allowing someone who is not on your lease to live in your apartment is grounds for eviction. But it is a rule that is difficult to enforce and regularly ignored. Home is a fluid concept in Schlobohm. And that is how Billie Rowan* first came to meet John Mateo Santos, Jr., during the summer of 1989.

Billie was technically living with the rest of her family over in building 6, but she spent as much time away from there as she could. Nineteen-year-old Billie was a teenage whirlwind, partial to cornrows and glittery costume jewelry. For nine years, since she

---

**Not her real name.*

first moved to Schlobohm with her parents, brother, and two sisters, their three-bedroom apartment felt cramped and claustrophobic to Billie. Now she was fighting with her mother. Janet Rowan had not approved of Billie's decision to drop out of school four months earlier. She insisted that her daughter get a job, and Billie spent each weekday as a nurse's aide at a home for mentally retarded children, the same work her mother did.

Billie hated it. "I don't have the patience for this," she would yell at her mother, begging to be allowed to quit.

"This is the real world," her mother yelled back. "Live with it."

Billie spent most of her time in building 4 with her best friend, Meeka. John Santos spent a lot of time there, too. Meeka's boyfriend, known as Mambo, was among John's best friends, and although John was officially on the lease in his mother's apartment over in building 1, he spent almost every night in Meeka's spare bedroom.

It was there one hot Saturday night in July that John and Billie sat talking alone in the living room. John's baby face was smooth, his big brown eyes were sexy, but what attracted Billie first was his voice. It was a voice that was both innocent and dangerous, that blended Yonkers with Puerto Rico. John could convince her of anything with that voice. That first night he used it to tell her that he was nineteen, when in fact he was only seventeen. He also told her that no one called him John; nearly everyone called him Hot, short for Hot Stuff.

He went on to explain that his constant fights at school, ones that led to his expulsion, were not *really* his fault, because the "white guys always provoked me." And he also explained how the robberies he and his friends "sometimes did" weren't *really* robberies, because "if there's another group and we fight, then the ones that we end up beating—we take what they have." Not like "armed robbery or nothing," he said. More like the spoils of war.

He was the smallest but the toughest, he said, describing the day that he fought off a gang of seventy-five wild men in the schoolyard, all of whom "had bats, pitchforks, you name it." He became tough, he said, because his father "used to beat on me." Not until he was in his teens did he learn it was because he was not his father's son. His mother was only fifteen when he was born, he said, abandoned by the man who'd gotten her pregnant.

John's own son, Noel, was born on Christmas Day of the year John himself turned fifteen. The baby's mother wanted to get married. John had lied to *her* about his age, too. "Then I told her the truth," he said. "I said, 'Now that you know how old I am, don't you think I'm too young for all this stuff?' "

Even then Billie realized that a lot of what John was saying didn't quite ring true. A mob armed with pitchforks? Who has a pitchfork in Yonkers? And she also sensed that all his stories had the same central theme—nothing that happened to John was ever his fault. But Billie was mesmerized by his stories. Everything about his life was so much *more* than hers—more tortured, more intense, more exciting.

As the hours passed, John gradually moved from the sofa to the love seat and finally to a spot on the floor at the base of Billie's chair. He looked up at her and asked, "May I kiss you?"

Billie was impressed because most guys she knew were never gentleman enough to ask.

He tapped her lips with his. A deep tap. Then he did it again.

Billie decided she would be with him forever.

A Night Without Dreams

DOREEN James was also having a sleepless night at Schlobohm. It had been months since she had slept the way other people did—from bedtime until morning. Most nights she did not even bother to get into bed. She sat in the living room of her hard-won apartment in Schlobohm and stared sadly at the few furnishings that she had bought at garage sales near her parents' home.

All through the summer of 1988—during the months that began with Joe's death and stretched out after Jaron's birth—Doreen had been wrapped in a blue, weepy mood. When she finally moved to Schlobohm in November, she spent weeks sitting listlessly in her living room, as if waiting for the very walls to make her happy. Now, during the summer of 1989, the sadness lingered. The feeling came most often at night. As was her ritual, she cried for a while, then fumbled in the drawer by her bed, where she kept things away from her one-year-old's curious fingers.

She was proud that she hid her stash from Jaron. It meant she was not so utterly lost that she couldn't protect her son. She held fast to her other rules, too. She would not make a buy unless there were Pampers and baby food in the house. Only an addict, she told herself, spends the diaper money on drugs. And she would not start to smoke unless she was certain that Jaron was deeply asleep. Only a hopeless soul does crack in front of her children.

Slowly, almost drowsily, Doreen took the crack vial from her drawer. Tonight there would be just one, because five dollars was all she could scrounge. She had been borrowing from her sisters too frequently lately. She would die of shame if they did the math and told her parents. Despite Doreen's current address, Pearl and Walter James still thought of their daughter as a child of the suburbs, not the projects. They would never understand how she had got so lost and had wandered so far from where she belonged.

Lumbering over to the window, Doreen pulled the garage-sale curtains shut so that her parents, miles away in New Jersey, could not see. Then she poured the tiny amount of white powder into the bowl of her smoke-shop crack pipe and lit a match. She held the flame to the powder and inhaled, coughed, then inhaled again.

Soon everything would look crystal-clear, as if someone had washed the windows of her soul, lifted her out of herself to a place that was shiny and brightly lit. Five dollars brought only a few minutes there, and when they were over, she would be more depressed than before, but for those few minutes she could escape, leaving Schlobohm, with all its disappointment and confusion, behind.

Defensible Space

NICK thought little had been accomplished during his last year as mayor. In fact, a lot had been accomplished, although very little of it happened at City Hall. Across town, in the Municipal Housing

Authority, steady, quiet progress was being made toward complying with the court order. Now that the list of sites was complete (Judge Sand had replaced the seminary site), the bureaucrats, not the politicians, were in charge. Drawing up blueprints, soliciting developers, awarding the contract would all be done by Municipal Housing. And behind every detail of that work was Oscar Newman, the towering architect with the Amish-style beard who had infuriated the city with his helicopter search for housing sites.

To Newman the Yonkers desegregation fight had never been about desegregation at all. Thirty years earlier Newman, then an assistant professor of architecture at Washington University in St. Louis, was struck by the fact that the older townhouses of Carr Square Village remained safe and livable while the brand-new housing project across the street was ruined by vandalism and crime. There was no difference in their surrounding neighborhoods. The only real difference between the two housing projects was the type of structure—two-story row houses on one side, eleven-story apartment buildings on the other. What was the dynamic of those designs that meant the difference between success and failure?

After years spent walking through countless other housing complexes, Newman thought he'd found the answer. Crime, mischief, menacing behavior—they all require anonymity, the feeling that no one is watching and no one will interfere. In public-housing high-rises, he concluded, there is too much space that belongs to everyone and therefore to no one. Hallways, stairwells, large public areas where—without such luxuries as the doormen, elevator operators, or superintendents that more middle-class buildings have—all visual clues say that no one is in charge.

He'd had his first chance to test his theory of "defensible space" at Clason Point in the South Bronx in 1969. This housing project consisted of forty-six buildings, mostly row houses, with a total of four hundred apartments. The buildings were constructed of exposed cement and had been built to house munitions workers during World War II. Few apartments faced the street, but instead looked out on a grid of internal walkways.

Oscar resurfaced each building with a stuccolike substance that could be made to look like stonework or brick. The material came in a variety of styles and colors, and he let the tenants of each row house select the color. Out front he used stone curbing to turn the neglected communal lawn into semiprivate front yards. In back he did much the same to create a series of smaller backyards. The grid of walkways was transformed into a kind of promenade. Down the center he placed benches and decorative streetlamps, each only eight feet high and made of real, breakable glass.

The New York City Housing Authority had never installed such an accessible, breakable lighting fixture before, and they tried to talk Newman out of it, but he argued that the reliance on the shatterproof lights in housing projects was part of the reason that vandalism occurred in the first place. "The materials are vandal resistant—and ugly," he said. "People go out of their way to test the resistance capacities."

The housing authority at Clason Point had similar objections to nearly all the other changes that Newman proposed. Their stated reason was that his plans were too expensive, but Newman believed the real reason was far more complicated. It has always been understood that public housing must not be too nice, that it must not have frills like balconies or bay windows, the kinds of things that inspire envy or hostility in the taxpayers who paid for it.

It is this "stigma of ugliness," Newman argued, that was largely responsible for the crime rate in many housing projects. Making a project look as different as possible from its surroundings, he said, "marks it off as clearly as if by quarantine." Unfortunately, he explained, "this practice not only 'puts the poor in their place' but brings their vulnerability to the attention of others."

Newman is a forceful personality, and over time he persuaded the housing authority to try it his way. In the first year after he made his changes, crime in Clason Point dropped 54 percent. The percentage of residents who felt they had the right to question strangers increased from 27 percent to 50 percent. Tenants planted grass on the lawns that they now thought of as their own. They went on to plant flowers and bushes and to add small white picket fences. There had been a 30 percent vacancy rate in the project before the redesign. Soon there was a waiting list of several hundred families. The streetlamps were not vandalized.

Over the years since then, Newman had redesigned countless neighborhoods. But Yonkers was different. It was the first time he would have the luxury of starting from scratch.

In Yonkers the first thing Newman did was to persuade Judge Sand to make the buildings townhouses. When he entered the case in 1987, the plan was for two high-rise apartment buildings to be built on one site and a three-story walk-up on another. Those designs had the support of the NAACP, the Justice Department, and HUD. Newman explained that such large, anonymous structures would serve only to destabilize the surrounding neighborhood.

HUD was wary because what he was proposing would set a bad—read "expensive"—precedent. In the end, it was the judge who made the decision to adopt Newman's scattered-site approach, a decision that led to the endless search for buildable sites and eventually led to the contempt crisis. Although resigned to a scattered-site strategy, HUD continued to lobby for two-story walk-ups rather than townhouses.

Newman responded with long memos to Judge Sand. Walk-ups have communal entries, stairwells, and yards, he said. Each townhouse, as he envisioned them, would have its own front and rear yard. Each front door would be close to and visible from the street. Each backyard would be defined by a small fence, and small groups of yards would collectively be fenced off from the surrounding streets by a taller, six-foot fence. "The smaller the number of families that share an area," he said, "the greater is each family's identity with it and the greater its feeling of responsibility for maintaining and securing it."

Eventually HUD agreed. Newman's next challenge was to communicate the plan to prospective builders. The Yonkers Municipal Housing Authority typically bids out such work by issuing a request for proposal, with only the most basic guidelines given for the job, but ultimately HUD allowed Newman more detailed language than was common. He filled dozens of pages with descriptions of the "two-story townhouse units," each its "own entity" and each with "its own front and backyard." They were to be attractive ("brick veneer at the first story") and different from one another ("variation in window sizes, color, texture, etc."). The front yards should face the street. Rear yards should be individual but grouped together "to create a collective private zone."

In May 1989 a developer was hired. Deluxe Homes, Inc., was in Berwick, Pennsylvania, where the prefabricated units could be put together with minimal interference from Yonkers protesters. HUD would pay them $16.1 million to build the first 142 of the required 200 units of public housing. In December 1989, days before Nick left office, Deluxe's neat white-on-blue construction plans, showing details of everything down to the towel rings, were submitted to HUD. Nick was sent a copy of those plans, but the fine points of architectural blueprints were lost on him, so he never understood all that had been accomplished on his watch.

Newman, on the other hand, spent days scrutinizing every detail of the blueprints. Years of reading these drawings meant that he could see a three-dimensional neighborhood on the flat, tinted pages. Each home was slightly different from the one next to it, some with peaked roofs, some with bay windows.

Beautiful, Newman thought. It had better work.

Billie's News (I)

BILLIE Rowan and John Santos were in the middle of breaking up when Billie told him she was pregnant. They had been together for three months by then, and Billie had stopped working so she could be available whenever John wanted her. The routine of their lives was that it had no routine. When John was ready to see her, he would stand outside her mother's building and summon her with a whistle, his trademark whistle. This man, this gentlemen who had asked permission to kiss her, would never come to her door to get her. She would have to go to him. Then they would hang out—at Meeka's, on the sidewalks of Schlobohm, at the corner store. More often, though, he would hang out with his friends. He would be gone well past midnight, and Billie would wait for him, at Meeka's or at his mother's.

She believed that eventually she could wear him down, keep him at home. When his friends called, she wouldn't deliver the message, and when they came to the door, she would tell them he wasn't there. She turned up the music on the stereo to drown out their whistles from the street, but he left every night anyway.

Before long John felt trapped and confined by her efforts. She was nice. He liked her, maybe even loved her, but he didn't like the way it felt, this wanting to be with only one person. In early autumn he decided to end the relationship, and as was his way, he tried to make her leave him first so it wouldn't be his fault.

"I'm nothing but a bum," he said, his voice smooth and soft. "I'm not good enough for you. Why don't you just forget about me?"

In answer Billie spat her news at him. It was her way of hurting him back. It was also her gamble that she could keep him. "I'm pregnant. And I'm going to get rid of it." Then she stomped off.

John did something he'd never done before. He went after her. He followed Billie across Schlobohm into her mother's building. For the first time in three months he climbed the stairs and knocked.

"It's for you to decide," he told her, but if she wanted to have the baby, he'd "stick by it." He also warned her that she shouldn't expect him to change. "If this is what you're doing to get me away from the streets, don't you understand that's the only family I have?"

Billie heard him, or said she did, but there was another message in his visit. If a baby had the power to bring John to her door, then Billie decided she definitely should have that baby.

Little Frankie

ALMA Febles was pacing the American Airlines terminal at Kennedy Airport, looking out the window, though she knew the plane was not due for hours. She smoked her cigarettes at a rate far heavier than the four to five packs a day she had been using in recent months. As she struck the match to light her next, she made a deal with the heavens. "God help me," she said, "if Frankie gets off that plane, I will not smoke one more cigarette in my entire life."

About a year after Alma had moved her children down to Santo Domingo, her second husband—Frankie's father—moved back down there, too. The gossip that drifted north to Alma said he had made a lot of money back in the United States. Alma did not know where the money came from, and she didn't want to know. She did not hear much about him for several months, until one summer evening when she called the peach-colored house and was told that five-year-old Frankie wasn't there. A man who said he was the boy's father had come for him, so the maid let Frankie go. No, she didn't know when he was coming home.

For the first week Alma felt concern but not panic. Maybe he just wants to spend some time with his son, she told herself. She called the house every afternoon, swallowing hard when she learned Frankie was not home. By the beginning of the second week she had to check her rising anger. After ten days she told her maid, "You call his house and tell him Frankie's been there enough time. I want him back."

The next day the maid had a message for Alma from her ex-husband. "He said that Frankie's not coming back. He says if you want to discuss it with him, you should call him."

Close to hysteria, Alma dialed from work. She'd explain to her boss later. "Who gave you the authority?" she demanded of her ex.

"Frankie's my child," he said. "He's better off with me than with a maid who doesn't even know him. He's going to stay with me."

Her next words were low and angry. "I'm going to give you twenty-four hours to send him home. I haven't heard from you in a long time. You don't know the reasons Frankie's there and not here." She took a deep breath. "If I call tomorrow and Frankie's not home, I'm going to go there. I'm going to go over to your house, and I'm going to kill you and all of your family." She was speaking faster now, the volume and pitch rising. "The only person who is going to survive is Frankie, 'cause he's mine. I mean it."

Alma slammed down the phone. She was shaking uncontrollably and fighting the tears. She thought of how frightened Frankie must be, away from his brother and sister, with a father he didn't really know. He couldn't call them. He didn't know how to use a telephone. Then the thought struck her, clear and overwhelming. Frankie didn't belong in Santo Domingo. "He belongs at home," she said. "With me."

She found her boss, explained the phone call, and asked for a $400 loan. Then she called her ex-husband again. "I'm going to send him a ticket," she said. "You're going to put Frankie on a plane on Sunday. I want him to come home."

The next call was to a travel agent. The arrangements were made, and the only question was whether her ultimatum would work. She made one last phone call. "If you don't send Frankie," she said, "I'm not going to go there and kill you. I'm going to call the American embassy and press charges. Frankie's an American citizen. I'm going to put you in jail because you kidnapped him."

Now she smoked and prayed and hoped her threat had hit its mark. Frankie's plane was due to arrive at four o'clock. Alma was at Kennedy by two. When the hours finally passed and the passengers began to disembark, she knelt on the carpet in the gate area and began to pray. Her prayers became sobs as a stream of unfamiliar faces came off the Jetway. Then the parade of passengers stopped. The pilot came out, and the copilot, and there was still no sign of Frankie. Alma put her head to her knees, trying not to faint.

"Mama," someone said. "Mama."

She looked up, and there was Frankie, holding the hand of a stewardess.

Alma never smoked another cigarette again.

1990
Mayor Spallone

MARY Dorman felt a flash of personal triumph sitting in the audience at the Polish Community Center during Mayor Spallone's inauguration. The swearing-in ceremony was open to the public, but the section where Mary was seated was by invitation only. She carefully tucked the engraved card into her purse. It was a keeper.

Mary had worked hard so that Spallone might be mayor. Just as the housing fight was her first experience as a protester, Hank's run for office was her first experience as a campaigner. She distributed flyers, attended rallies, and became part of the group that followed Nick throughout the east side, rattling him at every stop.

This being Yonkers, it didn't take long before the euphoria over Hank's victory began to sour. The morning after the election he toned down his rhetoric. "We will abide by the decision of the Supreme Court," he said when asked about the pending court decision. "That is what law is about; that is what we are about."

Words like these, with their echo of earlier words from a previous mayor-elect, infuriated some of Spallone's core supporters, but not Mary. She still believed in him. She also knew a lot about the appeal. The case of *Henry G. Spallone* v. *United States of America and Yonkers Branch–National Association for the Advancement of Colored People*, she knew, raised the question of whether a legislator could be fined for not voting as a judge directed him to. The Constitution protected members of Congress from coercion and prosecution for their votes. Over the years, lower appeals courts had extended that right to include local legislators. But until *Spallone* v. *U.S.* the question had never made it to the Supreme Court.

When the Supreme Court decision came down eight days after the inauguration, it was welcome news. The Justices overturned the councilmen's contempt fines.

Mary read every word of the analysis in the newspaper. All the articles said that while the decision was a victory for the councilmen, it would have no effect on the housing order itself. Even Chief Justice William Rehnquist, who wrote the majority opinion, was careful to say, "The issue before us is relatively narrow. There can be no question about the liability of the city of Yonkers for racial discrimination."

Mary was reassured by the fact that Hank Spallone saw the decision as something to celebrate. He had ordered a case of pink champagne and a six-foot-long hero sandwich for an impromptu party at City Hall. "I don't think this is the end," he said, raising his champagne for a toast. "I think this is the beginning." And if Hank believed that, Mary Dorman believed it, too.

John Goes to Jail (I)

BILLIE was in her fourth month of pregnancy, dreaming of happily ever after, when John was arrested. She tied a new scarf around her head, buttoned one of his colorful shirts around her expanding middle, and went to see him in a foul-smelling visitors room at Rikers Island, where he explained that none of this was his fault.

It all started a few months earlier, he said. He went out one night with his good friend Stash. They found their way south to the Bronx, where "we was partying and we went to the clubs." At one club, he said, "Stash introduced me to another guy, who I really didn't know, but I trusted Stash. I trusted his judgment.

"Then we were coming back, and it starts to rain. I say, 'We can take the train,' but the other guys don't want to. These girls come by in a car, and Stash tells them to stop. So they did, and we started talking, and they said they could give us a lift."

Stash's no-name friend sat in front with two of the girls while Stash and John sat in back with two others. "We're all laughing. They ask for our names and telephone numbers, and I give them mine. Not my real name. Just Hot. But I give the real number."

Unbeknownst to him, he said, his friends did not do the same.

"A little bit later," John continued, "Stash's friend, he tries to rob one of the girls, and they're all screaming. I'm like 'What's going on here?' We all took off, and I thought that was the end of it. But I guess one of them went to the cops, and I'm the only one they could find. Now they're charging me with robbery two."

His excuses were so earnest, so detailed, that even he seemed to believe them. His voice was so confident, so smooth, that Billie chose to believe his story, too.

John plea-bargained for a one-year sentence, of which he would serve eight months. He told Billie that her visit to him in jail made him realize that they were meant to be a couple. "My friends turned on me, the cops scared me, and you believed me," he said.

Billie promised she would wait for him. John promised he would change.

Doreen's Father Finds Out

JARON James was an excited two-year-old, tugging his grandfather's hand as they walked along the glass-strewn path toward building 2 at Schlobohm. Doreen stayed several paces behind them, marveling, as she so often did, at the untainted joy that her son felt at even the simplest moments in his life.

Of all his favorite things, visits from his grandfather topped the list. Walter James visited Schlobohm as often as he could. He said he was coming just to see Jaron, but Doreen knew he was still taking care of her as well. He never lectured her on this life that she had chosen. He just brought his gifts and his hugs. As he headed home after each visit, he would say, "You know where to find us if you need us," or "Our door is always open."

Doreen followed Walter and Jaron through the front door of her building, then caught up with them as her father was lifting her son so he could push the button for the temperamental elevator. As he touched back down on the ground, something caught Jaron's eye, and he reached down to pick up a broken crack vial.

"No, Jaron, hot," Doreen yelled. He knew "hot" was something he should not touch. She grabbed the boy's forearm and shook it until the vial fell from his chubby hand, shattering at his feet. As it did, Doreen opened his palm and wiped his hand with the hem of her shirt, rubbing until the child began to cry. The elevator doors opened, and she guided Jaron inside. "I'm sorry. Mommy's sorry. Filthy junkies, leaving their crap where decent people try to live," she said as her father stepped in next to her.

Walter James said nothing as the car lurched upward. Then, as it reached the seventh floor, Doreen's floor, he said, "People talking about what other people are doing. And they're doing the same thing." He spoke quietly, almost a whisper, but his words had the force of an explosion.

There was no more mention of drugs that afternoon. Walter's embrace was stiff as he hugged his daughter good-bye. "You know where to find us if you need us," he said.

Doreen felt her parents' disappointment in that hug. After that the sadness that already swallowed her grew deeper, and she needed more drugs to make it go away. No one in her family would lend her money anymore. She borrowed from friends when she could, but mostly she "borrowed" from Jaron. One by one she broke her rules. Sometimes there was no milk in the house, and Jaron drank water. Sometimes she was not sure if she had remembered to feed him at all. He was not always asleep when she smoked. If he interrupted her, she shushed him, then sent him back to bed.

Every day became part of a rapidly descending spiral. When she was high, it did not feel as perfect as it had before. When she wasn't high, she was sick. One night she had smoked everything she had and still needed more. She ransacked her drawers, looking for money or a forgotten vial. As she searched, she thought of other ways she might pay for more drugs. She couldn't steal. She wasn't that desperate yet. She knew the dealers downstairs sometimes traded drugs for sex. Could she do that? Her body, already numb, was just something to escape from. Maybe she could.

Just then she came upon the tiny gold cross in Jaron's room, the one she had exchanged for the engagement ring she never wore. She held it up by its chain. What would it be worth? Ten vials? Fifteen vials? More? Then, with a life-changing snap, she let the necklace drop back into the drawer.

She had hit rock bottom. Crying and shaking, she went to the phone and called her parents. "I need help," she said. "I'm sick and tired of being sick and tired. Mommy, please help me."

Her parents drove over from New Jersey and brought their daughter home.

Alma Brings the Children Home

BY THE spring of 1990 Alma Febles realized it was time to bring her other two children back to Schlobohm. There was no single event that led to this decision, just the feeling that as the months continued to pass, Virgilio and Leyda seemed farther and farther away.

What troubled Alma most was her children's growing fear. Over time they became afraid of the peach house, certain that it was haunted by the ghost of an old man who died there one night while rocking in his rocking chair. She decided that if the children were going to be in danger and afraid of where they lived, then they might as well be in danger and afraid closer to her.

Leyda and Virgilio moved back to Yonkers in May 1990 after they finished their school semesters. Alma, exhausted from three years of worry and guilt, slept for the better part of three days. While she slept, the children made themselves hamburgers, which were an unaffordable luxury on the island, and took long, bubbly baths, because the peach house only had a shower. They elbowed each other for space in the small apartment, squabbling the way only siblings can. By the time Alma awoke, they were complaining that they wanted to go "back home."

But Alma knew what her children couldn't—there was no "back home." The hardest thing to accept was that she really didn't have a home. For a long time she had believed that when life became unbearable in Yonkers, she could always escape to the island of her childhood. But she had tried that and failed. Santo Domingo was not the answer to her problem. Did that mean there was no answer?

No Place for a Baby

JOHN Billie Santos III was just a few weeks old when Billie took him to Rikers Island. Her mother tried to talk her out of the visit, asking, "Why are you bringing a baby to that disgusting place?" But Billie couldn't wait to present her son to his father.

She took two buses to the subway, then took the subway to the Queens Plaza station. She waited in the cold for the bright orange bus to Rikers, then spilled the contents of her bag and pockets onto a table in the waiting room. Once the guards determined that she was not carrying contraband, she boarded a blue bus. That took her to the Correctional Institute for Men, one of ten separate jails on the island and the one where John was doing his time.

The entire trip took more than three hours, and by the time she found a seat in the communal visiting room, Billie was almost as cranky as her baby. Many minutes passed before John appeared, and she tried to examine her makeup in the glare from a barred window while giving herself a silent lecture to keep her feelings to herself. Their relationship during the months John had been in prison was far better than it had been when he was at home. They wrote letters almost daily, and with the baby, John said he now had a reason to "settle down, go back to school, go to college."

Finally John was escorted into the visiting room. He was dressed in his prison-issue work pants and work shirt. He had a scar on his cheek, a badge earned during a knife fight shortly after he arrived. The rules said she could not hug him, and she could not hand him anything—except their son.

John lifted Johnny from Billie's arms and gazed at him. Billie tried to concentrate on that gaze and ignore the other families, the screaming children, the guards, and the clock on the wall.

When their hour was over, Billie bundled up the baby and got back on the blue bus. She made her whole complicated trip in reverse, arriving at Schlobohm near dinnertime. The visit had been draining but not depressing. Eight months, she reasoned, was not a long time. John obviously loved his son, meaning he must love her, too. He would be home soon, and her life could take the shape she had planned.

Doreen's First Meeting

DOREEN kept her eyes on the door while waiting for the meeting to begin. She was here in this overly air-conditioned community room only because she had promised Sheila she would come.

During the months Doreen had spent back home in New Jersey, her sisters had reentered her life. Barbara, who was closest in age to Doreen, had taken the role of friend and confidante. Sheila, the oldest, was like a third parent. It took a long time before Walter and Pearl James could trust Doreen, and one of their first steps was allowing her to spend time back in Yonkers with Sheila. One of Sheila's plans for Doreen included this meeting of the Resident Empowerment Association Developing Yonkers, known as READY.

Sheila was one of the founders of READY. When the rest of the James family moved out of Yonkers years earlier, Sheila had been lucky enough to qualify for an apartment in the Dunbar Houses, the only public-housing project in Runyon Heights, the black middle-class neighborhood on the east side. One of her neighbors there was Sadie Young Jefferson, president of the Dunbar tenant council. A stern, dynamic woman who had raised seven children in Yonkers public housing, Sadie knew well that Dunbar was the best. She decided that residents of the other projects deserved housing as good as hers.

Sadie had been unimpressed and angered by the 1988 battle to bring public housing to the east side. Angry because "they say they're not prejudiced. Wrong. They're prejudiced." And unimpressed because she did not think that blacks should only consider their homes acceptable if they were near the homes of whites. The solution, she thought, was not to move people across town where they weren't wanted, but to give them power on their own side of town. "If we're going to live plantation-style," she said, "then we can run our *own* plantation."

During the previous year Sheila had traveled to Washington, D.C., with Sadie, to the library in the headquarters of HUD, and they emerged twelve hours later with suitcases full of information on tenants' rights. The National Center for Neighborhood Enterprises gave READY $5000, which it used to hire lawyers and incorporate itself. Then a philanthropic group provided $100,000 for office space and tenant training programs.

Doreen found herself in one of those offices attending one of those programs because she was trying to prove to her parents that she could be trustworthy and responsible. No one was more surprised than Doreen when she began to look forward to Sadie's teachings and to gain confidence in herself.

These sessions were rallies more than lessons. Sadie did not lecture at the front of the room, she chanted, and the event took on the character of a revival meeting.

"They say we are tenants," Sadie declared. "We are not tenants, we are *residents,* a *community.*"

"Amen, sister," someone said.

"Calling the projects 'projects,' " Sadie went on. "I recall projects being science projects. We are not a *project*."

"You say it, girl."

"Low income," she shouted, "does not mean low class!"

"Amen. Amen. Amen."

"They think that all the people in public housing want to do is lay around and smoke drugs," Sadie said. "I live in public housing. I'm nothing like they're describing. People in public housing are decent, educated, talented, everything that everybody else is. We just happen to make less money, so we need lower rent."

It was a most unusual kind of twelve-step program. Sitting in her uncomfortable folding chair meeting after meeting, Doreen wanted to be everything Sadie said she could be. Soon afterward she went to her parents and said she was ready to take control of her own life again. She wanted to move back into Schlobohm.

1988
Redux

SLOWLY, very slowly, a proud house was emerging from the whirlwind of renovation at 175 Yonkers Avenue.

When Nick and Nay first bought the house, they knew it needed "some work." After they moved in, they realized there wasn't a single part of the house that didn't need work. The cost of a professional contractor was out of the question, so most of the overhaul was done by Nick's brother, Michael, who was an electrician by trade and had spent a summer between high school and college working as a carpenter.

Nick and Nay spent their first weeks as homeowners living in their dining room while Michael knocked down a circa-1960s wall that had been erected down the center of the living room. When the living room was finished, Nick and Nay moved in there, and Michael moved on to the second floor, where he knocked down more walls, added insulation, put up Sheetrock, rewired the electrical system.

The third floor was next, and Michael and Nick turned it into an apartment for their mother. While pounding a sledgehammer through ancient plaster, Nick found a sepia-toned picture of the first owner of the house, along with a photo of the building back when it was part of a working farm. He spent hours in the local library poring over books of historic Yonkers houses, learning more of the erratic history of his city at the same time.

He was able to do these things because he really wasn't doing much of anything else. He was working part-time at John Jay College, teaching a course on the workings of local government. He also hosted a radio program on Tuesdays, called *Nick Wasicsko, Attorney at Law.* The only time he had spent in a courtroom recently was when he sat in the audience while the Supreme Court heard arguments in *Spallone* v. *United States.* And his real expertise was not how government worked, but how it *didn't* work.

Of course, government wasn't working particularly smoothly for those who succeeded Nick in office either. Hank Spallone was looking less like a street-smart operator and more like one of those hapless cartoon characters who throws trash cans and old chairs into the path of the oncoming monster but still the monster keeps coming. The new federal appeal Spallone had promised was filed; in fact, several of them were, but they barely slowed the beast, as the courts refused to hear them.

Within a year of his landslide election Spallone was openly feuding with the other council members, including those who were theoretically his allies. He was "incompetent," they said, "an embarrassment," "unable to work with anyone." He was also under attack from those who elected him. Save Yonkers took out a half-page ad in the *Herald Statesman* accusing him of "selling out."

Nick actually felt sorry for his longtime nemesis and bemusement at the fact that while he could not *get* the housing built when he was mayor, Spallone could not *keep* it from being built.

Ironically, Nick's only major victory during his punishing term in office was to change the governing structure of Yonkers. The frustration and paralysis caused by the system had led him to appoint a charter revision committee during his final year. The group proposed eliminating the city manager form of government and replacing it with a "strong mayor" system. The proposal was on the ballot in November 1989, and while Nick was defeated, his plan was approved. Spallone would be the last mayor to have a title but no clout. The new system would go into effect in January 1992. The city's first strong mayor would be elected in November 1991.

Hank Spallone clearly wanted to win that all-important election. In September 1990 he announced that he would run for reelection. If the early declaration was supposed to scare off challengers, it did not. Other Yonkers politicians began thinking that they, too, would like to be the first strong mayor. By the end of the year the list of rumored candidates was nearing a dozen, and the talk at the house on the hill started to be less about remodeling and more about politics. "I'm a mayor in exile," Nick would joke.

He did not make a definite decision. He was still too bruised. But he took pride in the fact that the strong mayor plan was developed on his watch, and he liked flirting with the idea of running again.

As the renovations progressed on their house, Nick and Nay each found a favorite spot to seek out when they needed solace. For Nick it was the living room in his mother's third-floor apartment. Every morning after Nay left for work, he would take his cup of coffee and his three newspapers up there. What he found most appealing about the room was the view. He could sit and sip his coffee and stare across town at the spires of City Hall.

Billie's News (II)

JOHN Santos was released from prison on September 11, 1990. He came home to Schlobohm and tried for a while to keep his promise to Billie. He worked two jobs—at a nearby grocery and at a men's clothing store.

Billie had moved out of her mother's apartment by then and into building 4. John's name was not on Billie's lease. Officially, he still lived with his mother in building 1, but that was just a technicality. He and Billie talked about making their living arrangement permanent, just as they talked about getting married, but they never got around to doing either of those things. Billie refused to marry John until they had the money to do it right.

So money was the reason there was no wedding, or maybe there was another reason, too. The adventure Billie thought she would find with John had not turned out to be so exciting after all. He went to jail, she waited for him, and now they had this infant who kept them up at night and inside during the day.

Whatever her frustrations, Billie had to admit that John was fiercely attached to little Johnny, willingly getting up to feed him in the middle of the night. John and Billie fought a lot. Often during those bouts Billie would storm out in anger. "Go ahead and leave," John would scream. "The baby stays here with me."

Between the fights they got along, and John soon decided that he wanted another baby. "Let's have a little girl," he cooed.

Billie had her doubts, but she agreed. John could be very persuasive. When she told him she was pregnant, he promised, not for the first time, to stop hanging out and using drugs.

Billie tried to feel happy but found herself crying instead. Near the end of her third month she told John, "One is enough. I didn't even want that one."

He was furious. "What are you? Crazy?" he screamed. His eyes became wild. It was the first time Billie was ever afraid of him.

"You're gonna have this baby," he said, "even if I'm going to have to lock you up in this closet and feed you under the door."

John never did lock Billie up. He did something even more effective. The following day she found him lying ill on the living-room floor, holding an empty bottle of Tylenol pills. "I need to go to the emergency room," he said, his speech slurred.

"You're faking," she said. "I'm going to my mother's. See you later."

When she did see him next, it was in the emergency room. "I'm sorry. I didn't think you took the pills," she said, sobbing.

He wiped away her tears. "I want you to have the baby," he said.

She promised she would.

Not until years later would he admit that he *had* been faking. He never actually swallowed any pills.

1991
Breaking Ground

THE phrase idle gossip does not apply in Yonkers. Gossip is not idle here; it is purposeful and serious, aggressive and active. For years gossip was enough to bring hundreds of people to City Hall. Now, in the spring of 1991, gossip sent many of those same people into their cars to cruise the Yonkers streets. Rumor was that ground would be broken at any moment on the new housing, though the developer, anticipating protests, was not saying exactly when. There would be no announcement and certainly no groundbreaking ceremony. The only way to know was to go out and look.

Mary never set out to check on the housing, but whenever she was in the car for another reason, she was likely to swing past one or more of the sites for a quick peek.

Nick's visits to the sites were more purposeful. He would take the wheel almost every night after dinner, and because he had agreed not to smoke his stogies in the house, he called the trips cigar runs. As rumors of the groundbreaking grew louder, the cigar runs were no longer aimless. He set out each night wondering if it would be *the* night.

For weeks there was nothing. Then, early on the morning of April 12, 1991, the construction began. With a grinding roar the housing announced its presence on Clark Street as workers ground the asphalt parking lot into dirt. Word spread with its usual speed, and soon a crowd of onlookers had gathered to watch.

"It's a dark day for Yonkers," Mayor Spallone said.

Two hundred demonstrators gathered at the site on Saturday, as they would every Saturday for the next few months. The marches did nothing to stop the construction. Deluxe Homes, Inc., was run by Don Meske, a man whose hobby was big-game hunting. The protests, he said, were an annoyance, not a threat. "When you're facing an elephant that weighs twelve thousand pounds," he said, "*then* you've got something to be scared of."

Mary did not join any of the weekly marches. They were organized by Save Yonkers, the group she had been part of until it turned its back on Hank Spallone. She did follow the marches from the sidelines, however, glimpsing the action as she drove past. Looking through her new lens, she did not see warriors committed to a cause. She saw foot soldiers flailing away at the air, not realizing that this was a fight they could not win.

Weeks passed, and concrete foundations emerged at four of the sites. While they were being poured, workers quietly removed the asbestos from inside school 4, one of the first sites on Oscar Newman's list for the new townhouses and the symbolic heart of the anti-housing fight. When that job was finished, a bulldozer began tearing the two-story brick building apart.

Again a crowd gathered, and again there was talk of continuing the fight. When Mary drove to the shell of the school, however, she didn't see anything left to fight for. When she drove on, it was with the mixture of regret and resignation. The fight was over. It had suffused her world, and now it was gone. Mary Dorman was no longer fighting the housing.

Doreen the Candidate

DOREEN James heard the swish of the envelope as it was slipped under her door. That is how messages from Municipal Housing are delivered at Schlobohm. In her two years there Doreen had never actually seen who distributed that mail.

This piece of paper was sent to inform all interested tenants that candidates were being sought for the tenant council. The group had been founded in 1971, when the idea of self-governance in public housing was very much in vogue. In Yonkers in 1991 the tenant council consisted of three representatives from each housing site who met once a month at the housing office on Central Avenue. Sadie Young Jefferson had told Doreen that on paper, the council had broad power, but in practice the council worked against the needs of the young, single African American and Hispanic women who were the overwhelming majority of public-housing residents. The problem, Doreen learned, was that there were more public-housing sites for senior citizens (seven) than there were for families (five). The size of the site did not affect the number of delegates to the council, so the senior citizens, most of whom were white, had a majority of 21 to 15.

READY could not change the number of delegates, but it could change the clout of those delegates by selecting and training candidates. Which is why Doreen carefully read, then reread the letter. For months Sadie had been telling her that she was "ready to fly," to become a leader in her chosen home.

That night Sheila came to visit. "You give me all that talk about being independent and being in charge," Sheila said, holding the self-nomination form out to her sister. "Here. Be in charge."

Doreen waited several days before signing her name. Even after she dropped the paper in the box at the Municipal Housing office, she was not certain that this was an election she wanted to win.

Reelection Redux

EVERY major turn in Nick Wasicsko's adult life had been linked in time with politics. Even his proposal to Nay carried political overtones. "You're the only one who's really stood by me," he said. Politics was everywhere in the spring of 1991 as the preparations for his wedding melded with preparations for his possible run for City Hall. He was certain that he wanted to marry Nay. He was less certain about whether he wanted to enter the race for mayor. To do so would mean a tough primary against Terrence M. Zaleski, a Democratic state assemblyman with much the same constituency as Nick but none of the historical baggage. If Nick lost the primary, would that seal his political fate? Would two losses complete the agonizing transformation from twenty-eight-year-old prodigy to thirty-two-year-old has-been?

In each of Nick's three other races—even the last, disastrous one—he was positive that running was what he should do. Polls, gossip, conventional wisdom, none of those had stopped him. Now they had him paralyzed. Then he learned that he was one of four finalists for the 1991 John F. Kennedy Profile in Courage

Award. A prestigious honor, one accompanied by a $25,000 check, it is given every year to a public official "noted for taking a principled stand on an issue in the face of political and public opposition." If he won the award, Nick decided, he would run for mayor.

Nick started to search for a campaign team. One of the first people he called was Jim Surdoval, who had launched his political consulting career as an adviser to Nick and was now an entrenched Yonkers "player." Nick assumed Jim would welcome his news.

"I'm sorry," Jim said. "I'm committed to Terry Zaleski." He told Nick that he and a group of other Democrats had actively recruited Terry Zaleski. "He's pro-compliance on housing, but he's not identified with it like you are. He doesn't have that negative."

"He's not identified with it," Nick snapped, "because he hid up in Albany in '88. He stayed as far away from the housing as he could."

"Right, so now he doesn't have that negative. It's the first strong mayor. We need the Democrat with the best shot."

Nick, dizzy with surprise, tried to find some way to bring his former adviser back around to his side. "It doesn't have to be a negative. I took a courageous stand, and I was a hero."

"Courage isn't the kind of word you use to describe yourself, Nick, even if we both know it's true. Don't try to make a comeback as mayor," Jim said, giving advice he knew would most help Zaleski. "They're not ready for you as mayor. Run for council instead."

Soon after his talk with Jim Surdoval, Nick learned that the Profile in Courage Award would be presented to someone else. His mind, his emotions, his life were all in chaos. The two subjects, the wedding and the mayoral race, became ever more enmeshed at 175 Yonkers Avenue. Nay admitted her relief that he would not win the award, because it would be presented during their honeymoon. What Nick heard was that she had not wanted him to win.

In the end, Nick decided to run for mayor anyway. He scheduled his announcement for May 8. As that day approached, however, he started receiving telephone calls from people he assumed would support him. They explained, as Jim Surdoval had, that Zaleski had a better chance because he was a "clean slate." The only thing they didn't say was something Nick already knew—that Surdoval had asked them to call.

At the last moment Nick abruptly changed his announcement to May 13, his thirty-third birthday, giving him another weekend to think. He asked Jim to set up a "face-to-face" with Terry Zaleski, and he spent much of that weekend at Zaleski's house, listening as Zaleski tried to talk him out of the race.

"You don't want this now," Zaleski said. "You're getting married. You don't need this." And there was mention of Nick being appointed deputy mayor once Zaleski was elected.

Nay had come too. Nick asked her along because he had come to rely on her sense of people. "He's a weasel," she said of Zaleski after they left. "Where was he while you were being crucified over the housing? He was up in Albany, and he didn't even pick up the phone once to tell you to hang in there."

But Nick rejected Nay's advice. He held his press conference as scheduled on May 13. He and Terry Zaleski stood side by side in the driveway of Nick's house as Nick announced that he would not run for mayor but would give his support to Zaleski instead. It was a political and personal sacrifice, Nick said, made for the good of the party. "The thing that matters is getting Spallone and the Republicans out of government."

Three days later Nick made another announcement. He would run for the City Council seat that had been held by Peter Chema, who would be giving it up to face Hank Spallone and Angelo Martinelli in the Republican primary.

Two days later, at noon, Nick Wasicsko married Nay Noe at the church where his own parents had wed. Nick had promised his bride this would not be a political event, but it was not a promise he could keep. An article in the *Herald Statesman* mentioned that the "wedding ceremony is open to the public." A Cablevision crew came to cover the event, a fact that made Nay more nervous than the idea of actually getting married. Neither Terry Zaleski nor Hank Spallone was invited, but Nay noticed them seated in the pews as she walked down the aisle. The reception was at a country club in the nearby village of New Rochelle.

Three days later the Wasicskos left for a two-week honeymoon in Spain and Morocco. While they were gone, the John F. Kennedy Library Foundation announced that Nicholas C. Wasicsko was one of three runners-up out of one thousand nominees for the Profile in Courage Award. The foundation said of Nick, "Although he came to the office of mayor with only two years' experience as an elected official, Wasicsko distinguished himself as a man of conscience under fire. He summoned the courage to uphold the rule of law and demonstrated extraordinary leadership for the people of his divided city."

Someone else had finally said it about him.

The Townhouses Appear

IN JULY the first of the townhouses arrived in Yonkers. It was driven to Clark Street on the back of a flatbed truck, and it had the eerie, disembodied look all prefabricated buildings have in transit.

Oscar Newman had never considered using anything but prefab units for what were, in so many ways, *his* townhouses. Not only were they less expensive but their creation was less public. Only the brick veneer would be laid at the site, meaning there would be less cause for protest and fewer targets for vandalism. The units were installed quickly. The one that arrived at Clark Street on July 9 was bolted onto its foundation that same day. After that, the completion rate was two or three a day.

Someone—mischievous kids, the FBI decided—painted NO NIGGER and KKK on one of the newly installed buildings and broke the windows of two others. Then the City Council tried its own form of vandalism, briefly threatening to withhold a sewer permit for the site. And HUD presented last-minute roadblocks, skirmishing with Newman over everything from the gauge of the tubing on the backyard fences to the location of the outdoor trash cans.

Newman lost the fight over the fences. He had envisioned wrought-iron, but HUD would not pay for even the faux version of wrought iron, so he was forced to settle for galvanized iron chain-link instead. He had more success with the trash cans. The agency wanted big Dumpsters shared by several families. Newman wanted each townhouse to have its own in-ground trash can. It would make tenants take responsibility for their garbage, he argued. In the end, Peter Smith, head of the Municipal Housing Authority, took Newman's side and cleared the way for the individual containers.

It was with a mix of pride and nerves that Newman took Judge Sand to visit the sites one dreary, chilly afternoon. While Sand said some complimentary things, mostly he was quiet. But when they walked into the backyards, he stared disapprovingly at the chain-link fencing. "They look like pigsties. Is the fencing really necessary?"

Newman explained how fencing, even the ugliest fencing, was better than none at all. Without the fencing, he continued, there would be "no sense of ownership, no feeling of responsibility."

Sand shook his head in answer. "I hope you know what you're doing," was all he said.

The Election of 1991

HENRY Spallone never made it onto the strong mayor ballot. Peter Chema won the Republican primary. Spallone tried to run as an independent, but Chema challenged his petitions. Fifteen hundred signatures were necessary to qualify for the independent line. A total of 2150 people had signed Spallone's petitions, but Chema proved that 675 of those were invalid, leaving Spallone 25 signatures short. Mary Dorman was in the courtroom when Spallone, the fight gone out of him, accepted the decision.

Outside the courthouse, Spallone vowed that this was the end of his *campaign,* not the end of his *career.* He would be back, he said. But hadn't he also promised that he would never permit low-income housing in Mary's neighborhood? When ground was broken on the townhouses, she had stopped believing in the fight, not the man. With this withdrawal from the race she could no longer believe in the man either.

Terry Zaleski received only 36 percent of the vote on election day, but that was enough to become the first strong mayor of Yonkers. "This has truly been a campaign for the future of the city of Yonkers," he said as he declared victory just after 11:00 p.m.

While Zaleski was celebrating, Nick Wasicsko was at home, stunned at the direction his own City Council race was taking. Because he had won the Democratic primary by 3 to 1 and because his was a heavily Democratic district, Nick had expected a fairly easy win in the general election. Instead the early results showed him losing to his opponent, Edward Magilton, a political first-timer. With 97 percent of the votes counted, Magilton led by forty votes. At midnight Nick obtained a court order to impound the voting machines for a recount. He went to bed at 2:30 in the morning wondering whether he should have conceded.

Morning brought the news that more of the votes had been counted, and Nick was thirty votes ahead. By the time he dressed and left the house, all the remaining districts had been counted, and he was trailing again—by two votes.

It was several days before the recount, and he spent that time becoming increasingly certain that his political career was over. He received some calls telling him to "hang in there," but there were not as many as he thought there should be, and more important, not one was from Terry Zaleski. "I sacrificed it all for that guy," he said. "He can't pick up the phone?" Eventually Zaleski did call. What Nick never knew was that Nay, frightened by her husband's growing depression, had demanded that Zaleski talk to Nick.

The recount was 3006 for Wasicsko and 2980 for Magilton. Nick was a City Council member again by a margin of 26 votes.

PART TWO: THE REBUILDING

1992

The Lottery

BY TWOS and threes, with fingers crossed and lucky charms palmed, hundreds of people stepped into the crowded School Street gym, scanning the endless rows of folding chairs in the slim chance of finding a seat. They had not expected that there would be a crowd, especially during a thunderstorm. But what was being offered in the gym on this night was a powerful draw, so the room was filled, and the crowd was still coming. While the children ran through the aisles, their parents were distracted by the battered metal-and-Plexiglas drum on the stage at the front of the gym. It was, literally, a bingo drum. Peter Smith, of the Municipal Housing Authority, had borrowed it from the Polish Community Center.

Standing on the stage feeding 220 names into the bingo drum, Smith was unnerved by all the eyes upon him and sobered by how fitting this contraption was to his task. It was a toy, and he was using it to play with people's lives. He knew that the people in this room, justifiably suspicious of anything they could not see, would have had no faith in a computer lottery. But still the symbolism of the bingo drum weighed heavy on him. Didn't it reflect the random nature of the housing case solution: 5000 residents of public housing in the city and, after all the years of turmoil, a first round of only 71 townhouses?

With a mixture of guilt and defiance Doreen James found an aisle seat. She peeled off her raincoat, helped Jaron out of his, shook the water off of each, and settled her little boy on her lap.

By the time she'd received the application for the townhouse lottery, Doreen had been a member of the Schlobohm tenant council for several months. She showed the letter saying she was eligible for the lottery to her sister Sheila, who argued that she should throw it away. "You need to stay here and finish what you started," Sheila said. "Nothing will ever happen if the best people leave." The townhouses, Sheila added, were a setup, a charade that was intended to fail. "They built them fast so they'll fall apart fast. Then they can point and say, 'Told you so. Those black folks can't take care of their things.' "

In the weeks since then, she and Sheila had carefully avoided all talk of the new housing. Instead Doreen replayed their last conversation continually in her head. Maybe the townhouses *were* destined to fail, but they were better than Schlobohm, where recently Doreen had walked into her building and learned that some kid had set a paint can on fire in the elevator, blowing the inside of the car apart.

By the time Alma Febles and her family arrived at the gym, the only vacant seats were in the back, and there were not enough of them for Alma, her sister Dulce, Alma's three children, and Dulce's two. Dulce's grown daughters took Frankie and Virgilio to stand near the rear wall, and Leyda sat between her mother and her aunt.

Alma was surprised that her sister had applied to be here tonight. This move was something parents do for their children, and Dulce's daughters were no longer children. They had made it into their teens, out of school, into jobs, out of danger. Not only that—Alma had learned English during her years at Schlobohm, while Dulce had not. Who would her sister talk to on the east side?

In the weeks since they sent in their applications, the two women talked about how they would decorate their apartments, the parties they would have there, the flowers they would plant in the backyards. They never talked about what would happen if only one was given the chance to move.

When the letter for the housing lottery arrived, Alma had recently started a new job, talking to Spanish-speaking clients over the phone at the personal-injury law firm of Fitzgerald & Fitzgerald. The lottery, coming on the heels of the new job, seemed like an omen to Alma. For the first time in years she began dreaming. She knew she shouldn't get the children's hopes up, and she tried to remind them often that there were so few townhouses and so many eligible people, but she was incapable of keeping her own expectations in check. One afternoon she arrived home carrying a large box. "What's that?" Leyda asked as Alma put the box down.

"New pots," Alma answered. "I bought them from a woman at work who sells through a catalogue. They cost one hundred and fifty dollars, but I can pay her thirteen dollars a week."

"We need new pots," Leyda said.

"These aren't for now. They're for the new apartment. They're too good for this place."

"Just like us?" Leyda asked. Alma didn't answer.

Billie Rowan arrived at the gym at the last minute, so she stood near the doorway, leaning her shoulder against the wall, not bothering to search for a seat. Her mother had agreed to keep the children for a few hours, and Billie was blissfully alone. It was an occasion so rare that it was worth celebrating, so Billie had taken the time to fix herself up, something else she had not done in months. Tonight she even took off the ratty kerchief that had covered her cornrows lately. She was almost certain no one could see the spots where stress had thinned her hair.

She was stressed because John was in prison again. He had pulled a knife on a couple whom he may or may not have been trying to rob, and he had been sentenced to eighteen months at the Cayuga Correctional Facility, which was a five-hour bus ride from Yonkers. He had been there when their daughter, Shanda May Santos, was born, and this time Billie did not rush her baby to a prison waiting room as she had done with Johnny. If John had cared so much about seeing his daughter, she thought, then he would have found a way to stay out of trouble.

She was angry at John, but she was not through with him. When he came home, she promised herself, they would have a real life. The children would behave. The house would be clean. She would learn to cook. He would get a job.

She tried to keep the thoughts positive, but pinpricks of reality kept intruding. In the three years that John and Billie had been together, the amount of time he had actually been home totaled less than six months. He had never spent her birthday with her. He barely knew his son, he did not know his daughter, and Billie did not have a single photograph of him not taken in prison.

In one of John's recent letters he had said it was fate that sent him to prison and fate would take care of him when he came out. Shortly after he'd sent that letter, Billie had filled out the application for the lottery. She was trusting those same fates to pick her name out of the bingo drum and hand her a new life, a new start.

WHEN Peter Smith walked to the microphone shortly before eight o'clock, the crowd became relatively silent. There were a few sneezes and more than a handful of fidgety children, but overall it was quiet enough to hear a bingo drum spin.

Smith wasted little time introducing himself before he picked the first folded paper out of the drum. "Number one, Delphina Paige." The owner of that name jumped up and did a little dance at her seat. Name after name was picked, and each was met by cheers or tears or a fist pumped in the air in a victory salute.

"Number nine, Doreen James." Doreen buried her face in her hands so Jaron would not see her cry.

"Number forty-three, Billie Rowan." Billie stood and grinned for about ten minutes, then gleefully ran home in the rain.

The noise level in the room rose, and Alma barely heard Smith call her sister's name. "Number seventy-one, Dulce Manzueta." Alma gave her sister what she hoped was a joyful smile.

Just then Smith stopped the drum from spinning. He held up his hands, asking for quiet. "The first seventy-one names have been chosen," he said. "There are only seventy-one apartments right now, and all those are now filled. We will keep picking names, but everyone else will be on the waiting list."

The crowd became more subdued. People who had their answer began to head for the door. Alma wanted to follow them.

"Number one sixty-seven," Peter finally said. "Alma Febles."

Leyda flung her arms around her mother's neck and sobbed. "They picked our name—they picked our name," she stammered through tears. Her mother simply stroked the little girl's back. She didn't have the heart to explain about the waiting list just then.

The Other Side of the Fence

MARY Dorman was sitting at the pockmarked wooden table in the conference room of the Grinton I. Will Library, taking notes on the legal pad in front of her. She would have killed for a cup of coffee, but although there was an automatic coffeemaker on the shelf near the door, it was always empty. There was a television and a VCR, too, but they were both unplugged. Mary suspected that Bob turned all these things off each evening so that there would be no distractions, nothing to do but listen to him talk.

Bob was Robert Mayhawk, who had entered her life with a phone call several weeks earlier.

"You don't know me," he said, "but you were recommended by someone for a project I am working on. About the housing."

Mayhawk explained that he ran the Housing Education Relocation Enterprise program, known as HERE, which had been hired by Municipal Housing to help move the new tenants into the townhouses. There would be orientation classes that everyone would be required to take before they could move in. Volunteers were needed to help with that orientation. Would Mary be interested?

She was very interested. In the months since she watched the first townhouses arrive, Mary often found herself thinking about the people who would occupy them. What would it be like, she wondered, to live where you are not wanted?

"How do you feel about the housing right now?" Mayhawk said.

"I think it's wrong," she answered. "But it's here. The people who are moving into it had nothing to do with what went on, and I feel bad for them."

"So you would like to be involved in our project."

"Yes," she said, "I would."

When Mayhawk called, Mary had assumed he was white and that the others in this program would be white. Who else to teach the new residents how to live on the white side of town? Instead Mayhawk was black, as was the rest of the team. There was one other white face in the room. Lucille Lantz had been the founder of an anti-housing group called the People's Union. Like Mary, she describes her fight as one of principle, not race. "It's about unfairness," she says in her deep, smoke-filled voice. "While I struggle to pay my rent to live in east Yonkers, others are allowed to live in the same neighborhood with better apartments paying lower rent."

A small, coiled woman, wound as tight as her auburn perm, Lucille was the type who was always protesting something. Before the housing, there was the school desegregation plan (she had been PTA president). Before that, a campaign for change in the rules about foster care (she and her husband, Paul, had been foster parents a dozen times over the years). Each fight made her more brassy, more savvy, more political.

Both Mary and Lucille had fought the housing, and both had

come to realize that their fight had been lost. But while Mary's disillusionment had been gradual and quiet, Lucille's had been very sudden and very public.

The night before the City Council voted to comply with Judge Sand, the executive committee of the People's Union had met at Lucille's apartment. The council would cave, they all agreed, and Lucille made what she thought was a practical suggestion. "It's time we woke up and smelled the coffee," she said. "We have to figure out a way to make the housing work."

Everyone in the room began to shout. Until that night Lucille had believed that people say things in anger they do not really mean. By the time the fracas in her dining room ended, she had come to believe that what people say in anger is what they really do mean but usually have the self-control to keep to themselves.

By the end of the night Lucille had submitted her resignation. The local paper ran a short article announcing her departure. She spent the day waiting for her phone to ring off the hook with calls begging "Come back; we need you," but no one called.

Until Bob Mayhawk. If Lucille could not beat the housing from the outside, she decided, she might as well keep her eye on things from the inside. It felt good to have a new cause. But she knew this wasn't her fight anymore. This time she was a visitor, an onlooker.

Mary Dorman's first conversations with Lucille Lantz were awkward. Although an outsider to the conference room would assume that the two women had much in common, Mary, at first, could see only their differences. One was a leader, the other a follower. One still thrived on confrontation; the other had lost her taste for it. But change is a process, not a destination, and the next part of the fight, the struggle to implement the housing, would bring a whole new set of transformations.

A Field Trip

A LINE was forming at the corner of Ashburton and Broadway, a short walk from Schlobohm, when Mary Dorman arrived. Seeing the crowd, she pulled a piece of paper from her pocket and quickly scanned the rows of names. There were obviously more people on the line than on the list. Municipal Housing had assigned each tenant a time—one group in the morning, one in the afternoon, two groups today and two tomorrow. But since this was the first group and everyone was so eager to see their futures, they had apparently decided to ignore the instructions.

The letter had also said "no children," but there were children everywhere. And it said only one member of each household could take the trip to see the townhouses, but no one seemed to have come alone. Billie Rowan brought her brother. Alma's sister Dulce brought her daughter Rita to translate the tour into Spanish.

The bus pulled up a few minutes later—a sleek luxury charter rather than the creaky yellow school bus Mary had been expecting. Mary had gotten her first official assignment from Bob Mayhawk a few days earlier. She had had to go door to door in the projects to survey those who would move into the new townhouses. She expected to feel fear, but instead she just felt white. For nearly sixty years she had thought of herself simply as a person—not a white person, just a person. Walking the hallways of Schlobohm, however, she started seeing herself as the tenants might see her. White. Middle-class. Irish Catholic. Proper. What more did they need to know? Had all this not been so new, she might have stepped back and seen that this was how it felt to be black in a white world. This constant awareness of living inside your own skin is what the tenants of the townhouses would feel every morning in a neighborhood where their face advertised their address.

As Mary made her way from one apartment to the next in Schlobohm, she became exquisitely aware of her words, her assumptions, the sound of her voice. Too often what she said turned out to be slightly wrong. "Everything is so clean," she gushed in the first few apartments. "You go from that dirty, dirty hallway, and then you're in this nice home. You keep it so clean."

She thought it was a nice thing to say until she said it one time too many. "Yep," one woman answered. "We try to clean the bathrooms once a week, whether they need it or not." The comment hit its target, and Mary felt stupid and small.

Afraid she would stumble again, Mary kept her mouth shut during the first part of the bus ride. Not until she saw her familiar neighborhood of Lincoln Park did she feel comfortable enough to take the microphone. "Right now we're passing St. John's," she said. "I go to church there.

"That's Morely's supermarket," Mary continued. "It's a good supermarket. The people there are very nice."

The bus turned the corner from Central Avenue onto Clark Street, the site of the first groundbreaking. The driver slowed but did not stop. The tenants pressed against the right-side window. It was the first time that most of them had seen the townhouses.

"They're gorgeous," one woman raved.

The buzz around the bus grew louder.

"That's public housing? Not like any public housing I've ever seen."

"I'm gonna plant me some flowers."

"Maybe my kids can have a swing."

"I would like to know why they won't let us get off the bus. Why aren't we allowed to walk around there?"

They would walk around soon but not yet, Mary explained, then directed the driver past the four other sites. First to Trenchard Street, built on the remains of school 4. Now twenty-eight townhouses stood in its place.

"See how convenient the public transportation is?" she said, pointing to a bus stop. "The number twenty bus goes right past here."

Next to Wrexham Road, another twenty-eight units surrounded by stately apartment houses. During the months of construction the site had been a favorite of graffiti vandals who were fond of several boulders too large to be removed. DEATH TO SAND was a favorite message. Or YONKERS FOREVER. But as the bus drove past, Mary saw no trace of the spray-painted anger.

"So close to the Cross County Shopping Center," Mary said. "Just a short bus ride away."

Onto Helena Avenue, just fourteen units on a street of single-family homes. A street almost exactly like Mary's. Finally, to Whitman, with forty-eight townhouses, the biggest of the sites and the one Mary liked the least. To her it seemed isolated, too much like the projects it was meant to replace.

"This is where we can get out and look inside."

Mary climbed down first, then waited at the bottom of the steps, helping the occasional toddler.

"Is this the place they bombed?" one young mother asked. "Which apartment was it?"

Not the ones they were visiting. Municipal Housing had unlocked two model apartments, both far away from the now repaired bombing site. For nearly half an hour the tenants peeked in every Formica cabinet in those apartments, nodding approvingly at the shiny linoleum, the two-door refrigerator, the gas range, the stainless steel sink, the oak staircase. They even used the bathrooms.

Billie Rowan paced the living room, gauging its size. All around her, others were complaining that the 12'9" by 12'6" space was too small, but Billie cheerfully announced that she didn't care. "I don't have nothing to fill up these rooms anyway," she said.

In the kitchen, Doreen James was opening and closing the back door. It felt flimsy in her large hand, just as Sheila warned it would be. And the window frames seemed cheap. She thought of pointing out the flaws to "the bouncy white lady" in charge of the trip, but she quickly squashed the impulse.

Outside, Rita and Dulce were pacing the fenced-in yards—four strides wide, ten strides long. Not nearly as big as they looked from the bus. As they walked back and forth, a white couple, who Rita assumed lived in one of the private homes nearby, came and watched them from the other side of the fence. "This is going to be a nightmare," the woman said to her companion. Rita did not translate for her mother.

Moving In

To Doreen's relief Jaron quickly fell asleep in his new room at Gaffney Place. The stalling and clinging she had expected never happened. He just put his head on the pillow, and that was that—a simple, trusting gesture that to Doreen seemed to say, "The bed is the same; Mommy is the same; the good-night kiss is the same."

Doreen wished she could find the same kind of comfort. Jaron's bed was one of the few familiar things in the apartment. In her determination to make a new start, she had left almost everything behind in Schlobohm—furniture, knickknacks, even some clothes. Let Municipal Housing figure out what to do with them.

As a result, the living room of her new townhouse was completely empty. Jaron had spent the day careering around it with joy—jumping, spinning, running in circles. Then he had dashed to the backyard and done the same thing there. His mother had felt safe and smug watching him, but now that he was asleep, the living room echoed with emptiness, the backyard was dark and threatening, and Doreen was having second thoughts. Someone had thrown a rock through the window of the maintenance man's car the day before yesterday. Sheila and the others at READY had wagged their tongues over that one. Was she right to have ignored them?

She had moved here to protect Jaron, but in this uncharted world she was uncertain about where to start. Protection in Schlobohm was physical: Don't stare at that screaming man; don't pick up that crack vial. In this new home, with lawns and trees and recycling bins, she felt she needed to protect him from words and thoughts, to somehow protect his feelings, his inner world.

Because old habits die hard, she started to map out a communal approach to the problem. Should she form a committee to explore a neighborhood watch patrol? Quickly she stopped. Worry about Doreen and Jaron, she thought. Protect yourself.

To that end she had already wedged two new twin beds into the tiny upstairs bedroom and made a home for her sister Barbara. If Municipal Housing found out, they would all be ordered to leave, but Doreen did not think twice about inviting Barbara to stay.

So her sister was here to make things safe. Then why was Doreen standing in the empty living room, afraid? She walked into the kitchen and spent a few minutes rummaging through the drawers until she found what she had only just realized she needed.

The steak knife felt reassuring in the palm of her hand. She had never once thought of sleeping with a knife under her mattress when she lived at Schlobohm.

Grasping the knife, she started up the stairs, stopped, and turned back through the kitchen and out the door to the yard, which was already scattered with Jaron's toys. Doreen spotted what she wanted—an aluminum baseball bat. With the knife in one hand and the bat in the other, she stepped back into her tiny house. She locked the door behind her. Once upstairs, she placed the knife under her mattress, the bat under her bed, and went to sleep.

"HAPPY birthday to me." Billie Rowan was humming to herself as she walked up and down the stairs of 115 Gaffney. This was the first place she had ever lived that had stairs, and she was fascinated with them. She was unpacking slowly, shaking one item at a time loose from its wrapping of newspaper.

How cheerful to move on your birthday, she thought, with boxes of surprises to unwrap. It didn't matter as much that her only gift for her twenty-second birthday was five dollars from her mother, tucked into a Hallmark card. Her own belongings would have to do, and she felt a childlike thrill when the newspaper fell away and revealed something that belonged in a bedroom or bathroom, because it meant another sprint up and down the stairs. Seven steps up. Pause. Turn. Six more steps and you were upstairs. Those thirteen steps made this a real house, not just another apartment. "You'll curse those stairs one day," her mother had warned her. But it had been a long time since she had listened to her mother.

By dinnertime her few boxes were more or less unpacked. She and the kids ate some farina (she would have to do some shopping soon) and sat on the bed in her bedroom, watching television.

A few minutes had passed when a noise that did not seem to come from the TV caught Billie's attention. She went down the stairs, slowly this time, with tension rather than joy, but found nothing wrong in the living room or kitchen. She opened the downstairs closet. Nothing. The back door. Nothing. The front door. Nothing. Everything was quiet.

She went back upstairs and settled herself on the bed, when

there was another noise, different from the last but equally unfamiliar. She went downstairs again, and again she found nothing. The problem, she thought, wasn't the noise; it was the quiet. She could not remember ever being anyplace this quiet. Then came another noise, another search. Finally she turned off the television and began to put a few of her belongings—toothbrushes, diapers for the kids, clean underwear—into a bag.

She would go to her mother's apartment in Schlobohm, she decided. After all, it was her birthday, and Shanda and little Johnny would be more comfortable there tonight. It would just be for one night. Except she had all those errands to run tomorrow for groceries and things, and the only stores she really knew were on the west side.

Maybe she would stay at her mother's tomorrow night, too.

Councilman Nick

IT WAS early in the morning when Nick first mixed the powder and water in a plastic bucket and carried it to the end of the long driveway. He and Michael pushed a long steel rod into the sloppy mixture. Then Nick, Michael, and Nay took turns holding it upright while the liquid languidly became solid.

As hours passed, Nay went back to the house, first for sandwiches, then magazines, then sunscreen. By midafternoon Nick tried to rig up a support for the pole, but it held only a few minutes.

All this effort was for a street sign that said WASICSKO LANE. It was green and white and looked like the real thing. But it wasn't. Michael had found a company that specialized in replicas, and he had given one to his brother and sister-in-law to help confused deliverymen find the hidden house. "Shouldn't have to wait until you're dead to have a street named after you," Michael had joked.

Nick had been touched and amused at the time, but now he was feeling hot, tired, and embarrassed. The end of his driveway was right next to a traffic light, and each time the cars stopped, drivers would stare and honk and wave. They must have thought he was an idiot standing there holding a pole.

Or maybe they thought the sign was real. When the townhouses were first going up, Nay said, "Wouldn't it be great if they named them after you?"

No, Nick had answered. "They start to name things after you when you're washed up or you're dead." If asked, he would graciously decline the honor, but no one ever asked.

He was painfully aware that no one had asked about a lot of things lately. Despite his expectations, he had not become part of Terry Zaleski's inner team. Neither had he been invited to the lottery, although other members of the council were there.

One day Nick and Nay had gone on a cigar run to the townhouses to greet the new residents. He knocked on doors, shook some hands, and was invited to tour a few half-finished apartments. All the tenants were polite, but they did not seem to know him, and they had no idea what he had done to get them there.

As dinnertime neared, the pole no longer tilted when left unattended. Nick brought out a shovel, dug a hole, rolled the bucket into it, and covered it with dirt.

In the waning sunlight he stood with Nay and stared at the sign. WASICSKO LANE. The pole was slightly crooked, and an overhanging branch obscured some of his name.

Sitting on the Lawn

FOR every cause there is a meeting. Mary Dorman's new orientation assignment was her own housing site, at which she would hold weekly meetings with her tenants. Mary's site was Clark Street, and she was holding her first meeting out on the lawn, in the narrow space between two clusters of townhouses. She had rung all twenty-eight doorbells, but she could not find one person who would agree to host this meeting at their home. At first she assumed that was because they didn't have any furniture or thought they would have to buy snacks, but now she believed it was something deeper. In the projects, apartments were places to escape to, not places where you threw open the doors and invited strangers inside.

So Mary gave up on finding a living room and settled for this newly planted patch of sod for her first meeting, grateful that it provided some shade against the June sun. Mary was the first to take a seat, hoping that she would not go home with grass stains on her khaki pants. When everyone was settled (only five people came), she tried to explain why the second meeting should be held inside.

"We can't keep coming out here," she said. "Winter's going to come. You're going to have to get together in each other's homes."

No one volunteered.

Then she tried a different argument. "You have to get to know each other," she said. "You're your own little community, and aren't going to be able to do anything if you don't know each other."

That seemed to work. Carolyn Dunclay, a single mother with a handicapped daughter, shyly raised her hand and said everyone was welcome to come to her apartment the following week.

Mary spent a moment enjoying that tiny victory, then asked if anyone was having any problems. The list, at first, was full of minor maintenance chores. Someone's stove didn't work. The water in one upstairs bathroom didn't turn on. "New-house problems," Mary called them, and promised to send them along to Peter Smith. Then the women started talking about "teaching the neighbors some manners." The neighbors, Mary learned, had made it a habit to sit on their front stoops and glare at the new residents, sending the tenants burrowing into their homes with the doors shut and the curtains drawn. In the projects they had kept their children inside for fear of guns and drugs. Did they move here only to lock the doors again against less tangible threats?

Mary didn't know what to tell them. Like a parent trying to advise a child on dealing with the playground bully, she told them everything she could think of and hoped some of it sounded useful. "You know what I think," she said. "I think you're probably a little nicer than they are across the street. You wouldn't sit in your house and stare at them. If I were you, I would just go about my business. If you see them or pass them, smile and say hello. If they don't say hello back, fine. But nobody can accuse you of not being polite."

That's what they were doing, they said. It wasn't really working. Not only that—there was the problem of the dogs. Every morning and every evening two neighbors marched their dogs across the newly planted lawns and let them do their business. The woman had three white poodles, the man a nasty-looking rottweiler.

Mary, herself the owner of a German shepherd–Labrador crossbreed, advised, "If you see them do it, you could ask them to please put their dogs on the street. If you don't see them, just pick it up with an old newspaper or something—that's what I do—because you don't want it there."

LUCILLE LANTZ'S site was Trenchard Street and Gaffney Place, now home to Billie Rowan and Doreen James. Like Mary, Lucille could not find anyone willing to host the first meeting. She sat outside with the tenants on the hot asphalt of the parking lot.

Lucille opened with a nervous joke. "I guess I should apologize for being white and Italian," she quipped, running her hands though her frizzy auburn curls. She was relieved when there was laughter.

"Is anyone having any problems?" she asked, turning her notebook to a clean page.

There were complaints—several pages of them—but they were not the "gimme gimme whining" kind that Lucille had expected. The problems these women spoke of really *were* problems.

"Kitchen," her notes said. "Grease splattered from stove leaves stains. Could Municipal Housing install backsplash tile?"

"Staircases," her notes continued. "Raw wood, no varnish, hard to clean. Could steps be refinished?"

Fair question, Lucille thought.

"Anything else?" she asked.

"The lawn mowers—" someone said, but before they could explain further, there came a scream from across the parking lot. Two Big Wheel tricycles had collided. Lucille stayed where she was, watching as Doreen James walked over and picked Jaron off the ground, then applied a kiss to each knee.

The gesture transfixed Lucille, not because it was extraordinary, but because it was not. She looked at the tenants: all women, all mothers, all representing what she had once feared the most. While others joined the housing fight to protect their property values, Lucille had joined in the name of morality. Public housing, she had thought, was filled with families that were not what families should be—single women with too many children, usually by different fathers, without even the decency to be embarrassed about their situation. Now Lucille felt seared by the knowledge that right and wrong were not as simple as they used to be.

Be careful what you hate, you might become it, the saying goes, and in 1990, two years after the protests ended, Lucille's youngest daughter had became pregnant. She was nineteen years old and still in college. The baby's father was someone who quickly disappeared from her life and whom Lucille would be happy to never see again.

Abortion was never really an option. The Lantz family did not believe in it. Shortly after the baby was born, Lucille and her husband, Paul, became their grandchild's legal guardians, turning their ordered lives upside down. Now there were Disney videotapes in Lucille's living room and magnetic letters on her refrigerator and stuffed animals just about everywhere.

Doreen settled Jaron in her lap. As she did, she caught Lucille's stare and tried to decide what to make of this woman who was alternately helpful and harsh.

"Where were we?" Lucille asked.

"Lawn mowers," said Doreen.

"I think I can help with that," Lucille said, explaining that she had persuaded the owner of Marden Hardware to give the new tenants discounts on hoses, sprinklers, mowers, and other lawn items. "Ask for Howard. He's very helpful."

Doreen clenched her teeth. The problem isn't buying the mowers, she thought. I work. Her current job as a bus monitor might not earn her a lot, but she certainly knew her way around a store. "We know where to find one," she said. "The problem is Municipal Housing—they don't give us anyplace to store them." Not only that, she added, there are no gates to the yards, "so after you mow the front lawn, you have to wheel the thing through the house to mow the back. I don't want to keep dragging a dirty mower through my house."

"Housing will lend you a mower," someone offered.

"Yes," Doreen said. "But you have to go all the way to Walt Whitman to get it, that's two buses, and you sure can't bring it back here by bus. And that still doesn't keep the thing out of my house."

"Who here has a car?" Lucille asked.

Two women raised their hands.

"How about this?" Lucille suggested. "If one person borrows the mower, they give as many people as possible a chance to mow their lawns. You help each other out." Not a perfect solution, she realized, but a start. Although there were nods of agreement from the women in the circle, Lucille saw little chance that any sharing would actually take place. Doreen James saw no chance at all.

John Comes Home

BILLIE had hoped everything would be perfect the day John came home from prison, and for a little while it almost was. She woke earlier than usual that morning. She straightened the few pieces of furniture in the apartment, wishing there was more of it. She had managed to buy a dining set, a secondhand bed for Johnny junior, and a new crib for Shanda. But there was only a bed and a television in her own bedroom—soon to be John's bedroom, too—and the living room held nothing but dreams.

When John finally arrived, she walked with him from room to room. Everything he saw left him wide-eyed with surprise.

"This is nice. This can't be true. They're playing with your mind," he said. "Tell me they're not messing with my mind."

"No, baby," Billie answered, thrilled that he was thrilled, because maybe now he would stay. "This is ours. This is home." That John wasn't on the lease and had no official right to live there was, to Billie's mind, just bureaucratic blather.

For the first few days everything was as Billie had hoped it would be. John was at home "twenty-four/seven" and helped take care of the house and kids. It was nothing like their life in Schlobohm—no gang to tempt John away, no summoning whistles from the street. As the days passed, however, Billie began to find John's evenings at home to be as trying as she had found his nights away.

"Why don't the children have a bedtime?" he asked near midnight one night, wanting to share passion, not parenting, with Billie and finding that Johnny and Shanda were wide-awake.

"They go to sleep when they want to," Billie answered. "If I put them to bed early, they won't go to sleep, so I let them tire themselves out."

"Why do they hang around here all day?" he asked late one afternoon when the children were still in their nightclothes in front of the television. "Why don't they play with the other kids?"

She had tried that, she said. Johnny would bring his remote-control car and Shanda would take her plastic truck, but it never seemed to work. The hitting would start, and the other mothers blamed Billie's children, so "now they play amongst themselves."

Billie did not blame John for thinking the children were undisciplined and out of control, because she thought the same thing. "My kids are crazy bad sometimes." They were born that way, she'd decided, and it didn't help that their father was never around to show them who was boss.

She said that during their first few fights, but then John would look sweetly into her eyes and explain that it was not his fault. He'd wanted to be with her, but the law had kept him away.

Billie found herself apologizing. "I'm sorry. It's not your fault."

They never had that fight again. Instead they held their battles on less dangerous ground: Why does he always leave his dirty clothes on the bathroom floor? Why does she always wear her pants so tight that she's "showing off the goods"?

John was not really bothered by Billie's nagging. He saw it as a sign that she loved him. Billie, in turn, did not dwell on the dissolution of her dream that everything about their new start would be perfect. The skirmishing was familiar. It was simply the way things were with the two of them.

Only the place where they lived had changed. They had not.

The Pretty House

ALMA FEBLES'S daughter Leyda was beautiful the morning she graduated from the sixth grade at school 29 in Yonkers. Her dress, made by her aunt, was a blue, floaty, satiny material. Pinned carefully to it was a single white carnation, her first corsage. Each girl in her class wore one—a gift from their teacher.

The ceremony was lovely. Afterward Alma, Leyda, Frankie, Virgilio, and the assembled crowd of aunts and cousins went to the Sizzler for lunch. The restaurant was crowded and the service so slow that Alma began to believe that the fates might rescue her and make the meal last long enough to preempt her afternoon plans.

But eventually the steaks were finished, the check paid, and the inevitable could not be put off any longer. It was time for Alma to take her children to the east side to see her sister's new townhouse.

Alma felt a few pangs of envy when she first walked in and saw the staircase, the kitchen, and the bedroom that was Dulce's alone. All these were smaller than she had imagined but somehow more beautiful. She must have used that word a dozen times during her visit. "It's so beautiful. Everything is so beautiful. So different."

The adults sat inside, some in the living room, where the plants were thriving in the sunny window, some in the kitchen around the new wood table. The children ran from room to room playing.

Every so often Dulce or one of her daughters would get up to refill a coffee cup or brush up some cookie crumbs or take a plate to the sink, and Alma would be jolted by the simple act of prideful ownership. Filling *their* coffee cups, cleaning off *their* table, placing *their* plate in *their* sink. Welcoming *their* guests to *their* home. Alma ached for her own purifying new start.

She thought of her closets back at Schlobohm, filled with countless kitchen items she had bought on hope and an installment plan. What had started with one box of pots had become a compulsion, a mania. By the time Dulce left Schlobohm, Alma could fit nothing more in her closets, and she began to stack her unopened purchases all around the apartment.

Alma was truly happy for her sister. She merely wanted the same thing for herself.

After a few hours at the townhouse Alma went to find her children to tell them it was time to go home.

"I don't want to go back to our house," Frankie said. "I want to stay here at the pretty house." Alma had to drag him out the door.

A Visit to Remember

THE doorbells were among the many things that chronically did not work in the townhouses. When pressed, they rang, but it was a muffled sound. Thomas Downer tried a few times with no result, then knocked loudly. Less than a minute later a woman's face appeared at the upstairs window. "Who's there?" she said.

"Thomas Downer. I'm here on a parole visit for John Santos."

The face disappeared, and Downer stood outside patiently while things were tended to within, knowing he would be admitted soon, not because he was welcome, but because they had no choice.

While he waited, he sized up the townhouses. Gruff and burly, Downer had been a parole officer for more than a decade, and he had rarely made a home visit to a place as nice as this. A few white-collar criminals, maybe, but not ordinary thieves like John Santos.

Technically, Downer knew, he had the right to haul John out of these townhouses and back to jail. Out less than three weeks, the man had already broken the rules. When John was first released, he listed his address as 132 Bruce Avenue, his mother's home. During his first meeting with John, Downer made it clear that "if you plan to move out of there, you ask me first."

But now Downer doubted that John had ever intended to live on Bruce Avenue. All evidence was that he was living here with Billie Rowan on Gaffney Place. This did not come as a surprise to the officer. He had learned to form quick impressions of his parolees, and his opinion of John Santos was that he was unnaturally agreeable. What a little weasel, Downer thought at the time. Experience had made Downer suspicious of people who "agree to everything you tell them." Usually, he'd learned, it's just a front.

Standing outside the door of John's new home, however, Downer knew he was not going to bust the man for breaking the rules. Even from the front stoop it was clear to him that this was a better neighborhood than the one he had already approved on the west side. What would be the point of muscling John for making a move that gave him a better chance?

John finally opened the door and asked Downer to come in. He introduced him to Billie, who was standing near the kitchen with one hand on each child's head, trying to hold them still.

Downer said hello, then asked if he could have a look around.

Upstairs, he was careful to note which of the two bedrooms belonged to Johnny junior and Shanda. (If I have to come there in the morning to take him, I don't want to terrify the children by kicking in the wrong door, he thought.) He looked through the bedroom closet, finding male clothes that appeared as if they would fit John. He opened drawers and in the bathroom paid close attention to the toiletries (two toothbrushes, shaving supplies). It was, he decided, "very apparent" that John Santos was in residence.

Back downstairs, Downer explained the rules to Billie: "I come by the house. I might come by early. I might come by late. I need to check that he lives here. That there are no drugs or alcohol. No illegal activity. Do you agree to allow me into your house?"

Billie nodded.

"Do you agree to have Mr. Santos staying with you?"

She nodded again. She could not imagine at the time how Downer's memory of that nod would one day shatter her new life.

Not long after that, Downer left. As he walked to his car, he found himself unusually optimistic. He still thought John Santos was a weasel, but luck can help even a weasel. By moving here, Downer thought, the weasel might have lucked into a future.

Dogs, Drains, and Decisions

MARY DORMAN'S second tenant meeting was held indoors, at Carolyn Dunclay's house, and it was a success. Carolyn provided soda and coffee and put out a plate of little sandwiches. Mary had stopped at the bakery and brought cookies. This meeting felt like a party.

Nine people filled the living room, and the first item of business was to pick a place for the next meeting. When Cynthia Napper, one of a handful of married women in the townhouses, volunteered right away, Mary resisted the urge to cheer.

Next they elected officers for the Clark Street tenant association: a president, vice president, and secretary. The problems raised at the second meeting were essentially the same as those raised at the first. The dogs were still using their lawns as toilets. The neighbors were still staring, stone-faced, from across the street.

The new secretary wrote all the comments down, and Mary promised to take them to Peter Smith the next morning. She said maybe Smith could have the police captain come over to talk to them about the dog problem. As for the staring, if Mary could figure out a way to stop people from talking and staring, she would use it in her own life.

LUCILLE Lantz's second meeting was not as successful. Once again she found herself sitting in the parking lot, although this time there were more tenants in attendance, and they had brought chairs.

She tried to hold an election, but when she asked for volunteers, no one wanted any of the positions. "You can't govern yourselves without officers," she said, looking around the circle. Her gaze stopped at the person she thought to be the most likely candidate.

"Don't look at me," Doreen said. "I don't want to govern anyone."

"You wouldn't be doing it alone," Lucille said. "There will be other officers, too."

Doreen looked around. "I don't see other officers," she said.

"I think you'd be good at this," Lucille said.

"I don't think I'm interested."

Once again the tenants recited their complaints. Lucille had heard it all before, but rather than being annoyed by the repetition, she was, for the first time, saddened.

Yes, these women had complained before, but apparently no one had listened, because nothing had changed.

A woman named Rose Campbell began to speak. Tiny and shy, Rose spent hours every day cleaning up around her townhouse, sweeping the sidewalks and picking up other people's trash. When she received a letter from Municipal Housing announcing that her mandatory house inspection would be held on Wednesday between 9:00 a.m. and noon, she took the morning off from work, without pay, and waited.

When the inspectors had not arrived by 2:00 p.m., she called the office and was told that inspections stop for the day at 2:00 p.m.

"But I have a letter that says today," she said.

Bring it down and show it to me, she was told.

"That means two buses, and I have two small children," she said.

Lucille went home that night troubled by everything—by Rose Campbell and the apathy and the complaints. Later that week she dialed Municipal Housing. Disguising her voice, she used the name of one of her tenants in place of her own and asked to be put through to someone who could help her. She spent a long time on hold before she was disconnected. She made several other tries and each time used a different name and described a different problem. She was transferred repeatedly and placed on hold endlessly. She left a few messages, but no one called her back. She did not get an answer to a single question.

LONG before Mary and Lucille expected it, Bob Mayhawk announced that their involvement with the housing was over.

"Just like that?" Mary asked.

"The job is done."

They would never get more of an answer from him than that.

The decision, whatever the reason, made sense to Lucille. "We had a role to play, and we played it," she said. Mary, however, announced that whatever Mayhawk said, she was not leaving. She would continue to visit the townhouses, to go to tenant meetings, to help if they asked her to. "I can't just drop them," she said.

Mary had started the HERE program as a follower and had

grown into a leader. She no longer needed Hank Spallone to tell her what to think or Bob Mayhawk to tell her what to do.

In response to a letter from the Clark Street tenants that Mary had suggested they write, Peter Smith asked a police captain to attend the weekly tenant meeting to see if something could be done about the dogs. Mary began knocking on doors that night, reminding people to come. By 7:00 p.m. the designated living room was full.

Mary began by explaining the problem to the captain. "People are walking their dogs on the lawn. They are letting the dogs go all over the lawns. One lady comes out with these three poodles and lets them go to the bathroom on this nice lady's lawn."

While she was talking, the woman she was talking about came out, the one with the poodles. Mary pointed her out to the captain, who sent his deputy to talk with her.

After what felt like a long time, the lieutenant came back and said only that he hoped "it wouldn't happen anymore."

Doreen Finds Her Voice

DOREEN James sat in the parking lot of Gaffney Place, her large frame balanced on a narrow kitchen chair, waiting for her meeting to begin. Circumstance had once again put her in charge. This time she was the president of this townhouse tenant association. There had never been an election, but Lucille had called and said that she would not be coming to meetings anymore, and since Doreen was the person with the most experience, Lucille thought it would make sense if she took over. Doreen was surprised at how excited she was about the title. She was also determined not to let that excitement show.

She had prepared for this meeting as carefully as she knew how. She made her own short list of problems, all chosen because she had ideas on how to fix them.

When the other women were seated, Doreen started with the easiest item on the list—a party. The few organized activities over on the west side were not available on this side of town. The children would come home and announce, "Mommy, we're going to Playland," because their friends back in Schlobohm had told them that Municipal Housing was having a trip. When their mothers called to inquire, however, they learned that the buses were only for those who lived on the west side. A party in the parking lot would not be a trip to Playland, Doreen knew, but she liked the idea of doing something exclusive to the townhouses.

"We could have a barbecue for our kids before they go back to school," she suggested to the group.

"That's a great idea," someone said. "Why don't everyone bring something?"

Someone asked how they would be sure that "everyone doesn't bring the same thing." After much discussion Doreen had the idea that a sign-up list might solve the problem.

The date was set for the Sunday of Labor Day weekend.

Item one had gone exactly as planned, so Doreen moved on to item two. "Let's talk about the Con Ed bills," she said.

A month after they moved in, the tenants had received their first utility bills in the mail, something most of them had never paid, because heat and electricity were included in the rent back in the projects. During the late 1980s, however, HUD had required that all new units must be equipped with their own thermostats. There was no mention of this added expense of the townhouses during orientation, however, and to the tenants the unexpected arrival of a Con Ed bill merely looked unfair.

"It's a double standard," one tenant said. "Why should we have to pay something that the people across town don't?"

Doreen had made some calls to Peter Smith, and she had some answers and some ideas. Municipal Housing could not simply assume responsibility for the tenants' utility bills, Peter told her. The new federal rules required that tenants themselves pay the bills. However, local housing departments could reduce the tenant's rent in order to offset the bills. The "allowance" for a two-bedroom townhouse would be $109, and for a three-bedroom townhouse it would be $129.

Doreen's listeners had not yet turned on their heat, and already their bills were between $70 and $80. The amounts Municipal Housing was offering would not cover the cost once winter came.

"Why do we have to pay any bill at all?" one woman asked.

"They pay most of it," Doreen said. "If you keep the bill down to $109 or something, then they pay the whole thing."

"How can we do that when there are gaps under the door?"

Doreen uncapped her pen. "How many other people have gaps under their doors?"

Nearly everyone raised their hands. Doreen suggested, "Maybe you should all call Peter Smith and tell him that. I think the more of us that call Peter Smith, maybe something will happen. Tell him you're cold and can't afford to pay for the heat. Tell him there'll be a lot of sick babies and people will start using kerosene heaters."

"Tell him we're freezing our asses off," one woman snapped.

"Be polite," Doreen warned.

The Beginning of the End

MEMORY is selective, and fame is addictive, a combination that allowed Nick Wasicsko to forget the burn of the spotlight and to remember only the adrenaline rush of being at the center of it all.

He had hoped to regain some of the glory, or at least some of that feeling of connectedness, by rejoining the City Council. But daily contact with Terry Zaleski made him feel like an outsider. As mayor, Zaleski seemed to see corruption everywhere, launching countless investigations. Nick was certain he was a target of one or another of those investigations. Vincenza Restiano, the City Council president, was certain that she, too, was being watched, and this unsettling suspicion soon became the basis of a most unusual friendship. Nick was a man who had few friends. Until Restiano, none of those friends were other politicians. But Vinni Restiano was not the usual type of Yonkers politician. Her position of City Council president was really Nick's old mayor post but with a different title. Soon Nick was spending more time in her office than in his own, strategizing, even role-playing the way she could run an upcoming council meeting.

Restiano had been a member of the City Council until 1987, the volatile year in which Nick was elected mayor, when she lost her seat to Nicholas Longo because she favored compliance and he did not. She once confided to Nick that she had been so despondent after her 1987 loss that she could understand how people could consider taking their own lives. The type attracted to politics, she knew, begins to confuse votes with love, and it pained her to go out in public in the days after she was defeated. "They didn't say, 'Vinni I love you, Vinni I love you,' " she said.

Over the months, Nick and Vinni talked about politics and about life and, more and more, about Terry Zaleski. The voters, Nick thought, would soon tire of Zaleski's "politics of investigation," and Nick planned to be in position when they did.

Partly out of crankiness and partly according to strategy, Nick began a very public skirmish with the mayor over the Yonkers Parking Authority. The Parking Authority brought in $2.5 million in revenue each year in parking fines and fees at the city's thirty garages. Nick's brother was a member of its board, a job Nick had given him before leaving the mayor's office. One of the first things Zaleski had done when he himself became mayor was ask Nick to ask Michael to help oust the man who ran the agency—John Zakian, who had been a supporter of Zaleski's opponent.

At the time that Zaleski made his request, Nay also worked at the Parking Authority, and her boss was John Zakian, putting her in a precarious position. Nick, still trying to show he was a team player, did as he was told and ousted Zakian. Now, nine months later, Nick was trying to show he was *not* a team player. Robert Jean, who had replaced Zakian, was an affable enough administrator, but this was politics, and Nick and Michael began lobbying other members of the board to remove Bob Jean. Citing irregularities in the wording of his contract, they argued that he should be voted out of his position and replaced with John Zakian.

By this time Nay, still at the Parking Authority, was happily working for Robert Jean. The first she knew of her husband's plan to oust another of her bosses was a newspaper article saying that Nick believed the agency was not being well run under Robert Jean's watch. It quoted Nick as saying that the reason he believed this was because Nay had been telling him so.

"You're trying to crucify me, aren't you?" Nay asked, knowing that she had never told him any such thing.

He promised her that her job was secure. "When John comes back," he said, "he'll be happy to have you work for him."

Mayor Zaleski, however, did not want John Zakian back. He realized this was part of a bigger plan, and he wanted to stop it immediately. He sent the message that Nick would face a tough primary to defend his council seat unless he stopped this shoving match over the Parking Authority. Trying to compromise, Zaleski said he would dismiss Robert Jean and launch a search for a replacement—anyone but John Zakian.

Certain that he had the votes he needed to get his way, Nick refused to talk about compromise. When the Wasicskos left for the Parking Authority board meeting, Nick was anticipating victory. Nay was worrying that her husband was losing his mind.

They watched nervously as Michael Wasicsko put forth a resolution containing a list of charges against Robert Jean. It called for his dismissal and the reinstatement of John Zakian.

Jean answered the charges in detail, blaming most of the alleged wrongdoing on Nay. She was too angry to speak. Michael tried to, but he did not get to say much.

In the end, the key vote, a man Nick was sure he had on his side, voted to keep the sitting administrator in office.

Two weeks later Robert Jean fired Nay Wasicsko.

The Wasicskos barely spoke for days.

"How could you play politics with our life?" Nay asked Nick.

He didn't promise to stop, just that next time he would win.

There was an opening for a deputy city clerk at City Hall, a job that essentially reported to Nick's friend Vinni Restiano. John Spencer, a Republican who was also at odds with Terry Zaleski, nominated Nay for the position. A few days of articles and editorials followed, saying the appointment was a nepotistic conflict of interest, since the city clerk worked for the City Council. "It is a conflict of interest, absolutely," Nay told Nick.

But in Yonkers that has never seemed to matter. Nick abstained from the vote. Vinni lobbied the council on his behalf. Nay soon had a new job, by a vote of 4–2.

Trick or Treat

WHEN Doreen James lived in Schlobohm, Halloween was not a problem. The first year she moved in, she taped smiling paper pumpkins and grinning cardboard witches to her door, but within days the decorations disappeared. She saw them later, stuck on someone else's door, laughing at her. After that, she did nothing for Halloween.

With her move across town Halloween became a tangle of decisions. What would she tell Jaron about trick-or-treating? If she took him door to door, should she venture beyond the townhouses?

And as president of the tenant association, Doreen didn't feel right simply letting this holiday go by. She called Municipal Housing and asked for help. The agency's budget, she learned, included a certain amount of money for holiday celebrations at each site. For Halloween, Gaffney Place was allowed $75. As president, the money was Doreen's to use, as long as she provided a receipt.

So the day before Halloween found Doreen at the Sam's Club warehouse in Elmsford, loading a cart with industrial-sized packages of M&Ms, Bit-O-Honeys, and Twizzlers. The total was $74.95, and Doreen carefully saved the receipt.

She and Jaron spent the night of October 30 stuffing the goodies into brown paper lunch bags. The next morning Doreen knocked on every door at the site. "You have one child, I give you two bags," she said. "You have two children, I give you four bags." The result was a reverse kind of trick-or-treating; instead of the children going to the candy, the candy came to them.

While Doreen was going door to door on Halloween morning, Mary was over at Clark Street visiting Pam Johnson, the tenant scheduled to hold the next meeting. She found Pam standing on a chair in the living room, taping cardboard ghosts to the ceiling. The couch was covered with paper napkins, plates, and cups.

"For the meeting?" Mary asked.

"For the party," Pam mumbled, holding a roll of Scotch tape between her teeth.

Climbing down, Pam explained that the party was a last-minute idea, a reaction—the only one she could think of—to a "problem" her younger daughter had had earlier in the week. Four-year-old Anita Johnson was "minding her business" with her own toys on her own lawn, Pam said, when a "little white girl" from across the street asked if Anita would like to come over.

Pam walked her daughter to the curb, helped her across the street, then returned to her stoop and watched as the two girls began to play. They seemed to be getting along just fine, Pam said, when a short while later Anita ran to the curb in tears, shrieking for her mother to take her home.

"The little white girl started calling her names and said she couldn't play with her, because she was black and dirty," Pam said. "She wasn't allowed to play with black kids. I told her that girl doesn't know what she's talking about.

"I was going to have them go trick-or-treating," Pam told Mary. Anita was going to be a ghost, and her eight-year-old sister, Valentina, was going to be a witch. "But I can't let them go out there now," she said. "I won't let them be rejected like that." So Pam organized a party. One neighbor bought the skeletons that decorated the walls and ceilings; another brought the balloons, the cake, the paper plates, the candy apples. Municipal Housing supplied the money for the hot dogs and the sodas.

"We invited everyone from the townhouses," Pam said. "I feel bad. I would have liked to invite some of the kids from across the street. I probably should. I know I should. Do unto others. Turn the other cheek. I can't."

Meeting the Poodle Lady

IT WAS not quite 8:00 a.m., and Anita Johnson was standing by the living-room window as she did nearly every morning, waiting for her mother to get Valentina ready for school. Anita felt more than ready to go to school herself, but she was only four, and her mother said she would have to wait until next year.

Lucky Valentina went off to school each morning and into realms Anita could only imagine. All those children to play with. The way Anita saw the world, the more playmates, the better. "Anita loves everyone," Pam Johnson liked to say of her sunny, outgoing daughter.

There were few children her age in the townhouses, and when she had tried to meet one of the white children across the street, the little girl had called her names and made her cry.

Standing by the window in the morning, Anita could see that little girl's house. She could also see the Poodle Lady. The lady walked around the corner, then down the block past Anita's house. Every morning she came. She had three dogs on leashes, two white and one a sandy color that looked almost pink. Anita was afraid of the dogs back where she used to live, but she thought she would probably like this kind of dog—all fluffy and bouncy. She wondered if the lady would let her pet them.

Anita knew her mother didn't like the Poodle Lady very much, but she was not sure why. Something about the dogs using the townhouse lawn as a bathroom. On this morning, as the woman and her trio of dogs came into view, Anita decided to ask her not to do that. Then she and the Poodle Lady could be friends. She opened the front door and practically skipped down the path.

"My name is Anita. Can I pet your dog?" she asked.

The woman nodded. "Pat their backs. They like that," she said.

Anita looked up. "Why do you talk like that?" she asked.

"I come from a country called Colombia," the woman answered.

Anita bent down toward the three dogs, reached out her hand, and patted the closest one hesitantly, behind its head, grinning her happiest grin. Then she pulled her hand back quickly and held it behind her back. The dogs were soft and silky, like she had imagined they would be. The Poodle Lady had started to walk away. As she walked, she called out her good-byes to Anita.

"Bye," Anita said, adding hopefully, "See you tomorrow." She couldn't wait to tell her mother that the Poodle Lady was her friend.

Christmas

THE afternoon before Christmas, Pam Johnson returned home after spending the day at her mother's apartment across town. She, Anita, and Valentina were still taking their coats off when a neighbor knocked on the door. "A lady was here looking for you and your girls," the neighbor said. "That lady with all the poodles."

Pam had often seen but had never met the Poodle Lady whom Anita was so fond of. Anita talked of the woman all the time, and Pam knew almost nothing about her. She did not know, for instance, that the Poodle Lady's name was Lillian Cadavid and that she had raised three children in her two-family house around the corner. Pam did not know that the poodles—named Martini, Brandy, and Alexander—were not really poodles at all, but were bichons frises, which cost between $800 and $1200 as puppies, or that each one was a gift for a different Christmas or birthday. And she certainly did not know that it was a source of amusement to Lillian that her bichons were "not too friendly with black dogs."

Lillian did not know Pam's name either. Fond as she was of Anita, she never asked the little girl her last name, although they met nearly every day. Lillian thought it best not to know. "So often the mother has a different last name than the child."

Lillian did not know Pam was one of the tenants who complained to the police about the "poodles" during the first summer in the townhouses. And Pam did not know that Lillian was unrepentant when the officer approached her the night of that meeting.

"I pay taxes. I don't see that anybody owns the street," she had said. "The people in these houses think I'm doing this because they're living there? They don't know that this is my routine. For a few days I thought, Where can I walk my dogs now, because the houses are there? Then I said, No, I'm gonna keep my route. And I did."

All Pam knew was that Lillian was kind to Anita and Valentina and had got Anita past her fear of dogs. She had got Pam past another fear, too. Knowing that one white neighbor could be friendly somehow made the other white neighbors seem less threatening.

All Lillian needed to know was that Anita was special. Seeing her stand on the curb waiting to pet the "poodles" made the morning dog walk fun. Lillian had feared the townhouses, even protested against them, but Anita made her think the new housing might not be too bad.

About an hour later Lillian stopped by again. This time Pam and her daughters were home, and Lillian gave them the small Christmas packages she had brought—bags filled with candies and hair ribbons—which were received with proper thank-yous.

Pam did not invite Lillian in. Lillian did not expect her to.

TWO days after Christmas, Virgilio, in a rare moment out of Alma's sight, was walking from Schlobohm to the store. He had instructions to pick up a few groceries for his mother, and he planned a detour for a slice of pizza for himself. He practically bounced as he walked, because of the virginal white Nikes on his feet, a Christmas present from his mother.

As he walked up the hill, he noticed some kids a few feet in front of him, older and unfamiliar. They were looking at each other, then at him. His steps slowed and lost their bounce.

"What size are your sneakers?" one of the boys asked.

"Why do you want to know?" Virgilio asked.

"Let's take the shoes," another of the boys said. "Take the mother-f---in' shoes."

"Ten and a half," Virgilio said, and he started to run, the sneakers thudding hard against the pavement.

The boys didn't follow. His Nikes were probably the wrong size.

"His feet are too big," Alma said with laughter bordering on hysteria when Virgilio arrived home out of breath and without any groceries. "They left him alone because of his big feet."

Later she scolded him. "If you weren't going anyplace special, you shouldn't have worn your new sneakers," she said. She needed to believe that the incident was caused by something he did.

"They're just sneakers," Virgilio said as he kicked the shoes off into the corner of his cramped, cluttered room.

1993
The Murder

THE screams began just before 8:30 a.m. at 28 Lamartine Terrace in southwest Yonkers, in a neighborhood tottering between fairly safe and somewhat frightening. "Help me. He's killing me. Help me. I'm dying," shrieked Helen Sarno, a seventy-year-old woman who lived on the seventh floor. "Help me! He's killing me!"

The couple downstairs pulled on their clothes, grabbed their baby, and ran up one flight to find the reason for the cries.

"Help me. I'm dying."

The man across the hall was about to walk his dog. He shooed the pet back into his apartment, yelled to his stepdaughter to call the police, and headed toward Miss Helen's door.

"Help me! He's killing me! Help me! I'm dying."

Another neighbor was shaving, and he raced out wearing only his undershorts, with a baseball bat in his hand.

Together they banged on the locked door and yelled, "Leave her alone" and "Open up." In time a male voice from inside said, "It's okay. It's her son. We're having an argument."

"Help me!" Miss Helen screamed again. Those were the last words from the apartment. Soon the cries turned to moans. Minutes later even the moaning stopped.

More time passed. Then suddenly the door burst open, and a man bolted into the hall. He was young and Hispanic, about twenty years old. He was wearing a jacket, green denim jeans, a red sweater, and Timberland boots, all covered with blood. There was a fuzzy white hat pulled over his head—an attempt at disguise perhaps? He quickly yanked the door shut behind him so it locked, keeping the neighbors from racing into the apartment.

He started to run around the men in the hallway, but there was not enough room, and his only option was to barrel through them. They tackled him. He tried to escape, so they pounded him with their fists and with the baseball bat. He crawled a few inches, lost the hat, and they tackled him again. Then he slithered out of his coat and out of their grasp and ran down the emergency stairwell.

As he left through the front door of the building, a police cruiser responding to a neighbor's call pulled up, and the officers saw a Hispanic man with no coat walking onto the sidewalk. A young woman leaned out a window on an upper floor, pointed, and yelled, "That's the guy. That is him. Stop him." The man dashed around the back of the building, and the officers followed. He was cornered, and after a struggle he was handcuffed.

"I was just trying to help the lady," he said as the officers placed him in the cruiser.

Another officer had gone upstairs and tried to open the locked front door. Then he climbed onto the fire escape of an adjacent apartment in order to try the kitchen window. That, too, was locked, but he could see through the curtains into a room awash in blood. He smashed the glass pane inward. Then he climbed onto the kitchen table and jumped down over a pool of blood, following two sets of bloody footprints through a small entryway and into the bedroom. It was there that he saw the elderly woman, Helen Sarno, slumped on the floor. She was dressed in a blood-saturated housecoat. There was a pocketbook open on her bed, containing a cafeteria club card from St. Joseph's Medical Center, a senior citizen discount card, some grocery coupons, and $13.60. In her lifeless hand she clutched a small change purse. Later detectives would find a single string of rosary beads inside.

The officer unlocked the door and let the paramedics in. There was nothing they could do. Helen Sarno had died from one of five separate puncture wounds from an ice pick found on the kitchen floor.

Detectives brought some of the neighbors out to look at the handcuffed suspect in the back seat of the police car. One at a time they said, "That's him." A short while later the prisoner was brought to the police station, where his bloody clothes were taken away as evidence and he was given a prison-issue jumpsuit. His fingerprints were taken, and he was questioned.

When he was asked his name, he answered, "John Mateo Santos." When asked his address, he said, "One fifteen Gaffney Place."

THE HEROICS OF HELEN SARNO'S neighbors were reported in the newspaper the next day, and John's address was soon the talk of the east side. John Santos. Now the abstract fears of the homeowners had a name. He stood for all the murderers and drug dealers that were, quite certainly, being imported from across town.

The outrage was aimed everywhere, at places that made sense and ones that did not. There were calls for a death sentence even though, at the time, New York State had no death penalty. There were demands that the townhouses be shut down.

Mary Dorman felt the full force of the outrage. Days after John's arrest there was a meeting of the Lincoln Park Taxpayers Association. Mary was pointedly not invited. "Mary lied to us," a former friend of hers shouted. For six months Mary had been assuring her neighbors that Municipal Housing was scrupulously policing the new sites and that anyone who caused trouble was swiftly removed. But news stories about John Santos included the fact that to date, not a single person had been told to leave the townhouses.

Billie Rowan, of course, felt the heat, too. Two weeks after John was arrested, she was faced with eviction from Gaffney Place. John was not on Billie's lease, but he told the arresting officers that he lived in her townhouse. Housing regulations require all *permanent* members of a household to be listed on a lease. But for too many women in the projects, permanence is a matter of definition. Was John a permanent part of Billie's life? Stopping in between stays in the penitentiary? Leaving for several nights at a time without telling her where he went? Why tell Municipal Housing that something is permanent when you aren't at all sure yourself?

But rules are rules. Peter Smith's department hired an investigator to track suspected cheaters. There was no shortage of tips, since people on the wait list for public housing in Yonkers—a list 1500 names and five years long—often snitch on people who are already occupants of the housing. Each year the housing authority holds about 180 informal hearings on charges other than nonpayment of rent. Of those, only 12 to 15 tenants are ever evicted.

One of those, Smith suspected, would be Billie Rowan. He had no choice but to begin proceedings against her.

On January 15 Smith signed a letter to Billie Rowan informing her that she was entitled to a hearing on the charges before a council of tenant representatives. She stood accused, the letter said, of violating "Paragraph No. 6 Clause B of the Resident Monthly Lease Agreement."

Smith knew he would not attend the hearing. Billie had two young children, and he expected that this case would break his heart. He would leave this to the agency's lawyers.

Doreen Raises Her Voice

"WHAT'S the matter with Municipal Housing?" Doreen James asked in outrage as she settled her wide self into Mary Dorman's compact car. "Punishing her for something that her guy did? She said he didn't live there. They should leave her alone. She's a fine person; she has two kids. She didn't cause the trouble. Why are they wasting their time bothering her?"

The meeting Mary and Doreen were going to was the first in a series of by-invitation-only meetings that Mayor Zaleski was holding to hear what neighborhood leaders had on their minds. The two women sat at an empty table near the back of the community room at the Scotti Community Center.

Up front were the mayor and his commissioners. Zaleski stood up and described the purpose of the gathering as "finding ways to make this city even better." He asked each of the commissioners to describe who they were and what they did. That done, the mayor stood up again and asked everyone in the room to introduce themselves.

Next the mayor opened the floor to a general discussion of ideas and concerns. First there was a lot of talk about graffiti. Then there was an even longer conversation about school crossing guards. As he was speaking, several members of Save Yonkers walked in and sat near the door. Mary knew these people and worried that they were there to "bring up the incident with the murder."

The murder did come up, but not because of anyone from Save Yonkers. Tired of hearing about graffiti and such, Doreen James raised her hand and said what she had come to say. As soon as she started speaking, the room became silent.

"I would like to talk about the comments of the two gentlemen on the City Council," she said, referring to a report she had seen on the news about calls for action in response to the murder. "The tenants who live in the new sites are very upset about what they are saying. We do not like their comments about screening people and checking on who we have as company and things like that. How would they like it if that type of thing were said about them? The tenants are decent people, and the tenant who may be evicted because of this is, too. That man Santos did not live at Gaffney Place. It shouldn't be assumed that he did just because he said so."

"She was magnificent," was how Mary would describe the speech to her husband, Buddy, later. "Eloquent."

When Doreen finished speaking, the police commissioner stood up to say yes, Doreen was correct, the man in question had just been released from prison, and it was likely he was not really living anywhere. The Second Precinct officers spoke, too, and said there were no unusual problems at any of the sites.

Then Doreen raised her hand again and asked if there were regular police patrols at the new housing sites, and the commissioner said yes, there were patrols all the time.

"I never see you unless there's a problem," Doreen said. Did the officers know that "at the park across from Trenchard the kids hang out and do graffiti and probably do drugs? Not the kids from the housing, because our kids aren't that old. It's the kids from the neighborhood."

The commissioner and the officers consulted among themselves, then said no, they had not known that, but would look into it.

The conversation moved on to other people and other topics, but the chief officer from the Second Precinct came to Doreen, handed her his card, and said, "If you have a problem, please call us. We're really interested in what goes on. It doesn't have to be trouble before you call us."

Then a man Mary knew from her protest days came over to talk to Doreen. He complimented her on her words and suggested she take pictures of the graffiti in her playground as evidence of the problem. Mary was dumbstruck. "This was one of the bigots," she said to Buddy later. "I have no idea how she won him over."

Billie's Hearing

BILLIE Rowan took the bus up Central Avenue on the morning of her eviction hearing. She had persuaded her mother to take care of Shanda for a few hours, but two children were more than the woman was willing to handle, so Johnny came along with Billie.

In the conference room, she was seated at one end of the table. Johnny had fallen asleep on her lap. It's like it's dinnertime, she thought, and they're all here to eat *me*. At the head of the table were two white men who looked like lawyers. Along the sides were five women, most of whom looked like her. They were the members of the tenants committee, the ones who would decide her future.

Billie was relieved that she already had some acquaintance with two of them. Sadie Young Jefferson had been Billie's boss when she worked as a trainee during a county employment program. Next to Sadie was Caliope James, Doreen's great-aunt. When John was arrested, Doreen had told Billie, "Call if you need anything."

The man who seemed to be the head lawyer opened the meeting by explaining that Billie was being evicted for violating her lease. He asked that Billie be sworn in—like in the movies, Billie thought—and she was told it was her turn to speak.

"They told me I would be getting evicted because John Santos was residing with me, which was not true," she said, holding Johnny tight with one hand and taking a folded sheet of paper from her pocket with the other. "He was released, and his place of residence was 132 Bruce Avenue. I have a paper here stating that."

She handed the letter to the lawyer, who unfolded it, read it, and did not look very impressed. For the first time Billie wondered if she should have brought her own lawyer, or at least a friend.

"This only indicates that as of August twelfth he indicated in his certificate of release to parole supervision that he would reside with his mother, Carolina Santos, at 132 Bruce Street," the lawyer said. "Do you intend to produce Carolina Santos as a witness?"

"Yes," Billie said. "She'll make it here." She said it with as much confidence as she could, since she had not even thought of asking Carolina to come.

Sadie started to speak. She sounded warmer toward Billie than the lawyer but not nearly as sympathetic as Billie had hoped. "Do you know that man they're talking about?" she asked.

"Yes," Billie said.

"How do you know him?"

"He's my boyfriend. He's the father of my two children."

Another tenant brought the questioning back to the letter Billie had introduced as her evidence. "Just because it states on that piece of paper that he said he was going to reside there doesn't mean anything," she said. "I could say I live in Washington, D.C."

"I understand," Billie said. "But I'm here now because he said he accidentally put my address, and they want to evict me for that."

Caliope James asked, "If he was living at 132 Bruce Avenue, why would he give your address?"

"Probably under shock or whatever," Billie said.

"Why," the lawyer asked, "would he give that address when he indicated to the parole board he was going to live at 132 Bruce Ave.?"

"Like I said, he was being arrested for murder."

Sadie broke in. "Has he ever stayed on your premises?" she asked.

"Well, no. He came to visit frequently. He was there constantly because of the kids and because of me."

"But he never lived there?"

"No, he never lived there."

"Did you tell anybody that Mr. Santos lived with you?" the lawyer asked. "Did you tell your caseworker?"

Billie thought of the glass-walled cubicle at the social services office, of her and John signing form after form, declaring him an "essential person" in her household, that they lived together, pooled their money together, prepared meals together. Of course she should have realized this lawyer would find out about that.

"Yes or no," the lawyer said. "Did you tell your caseworker?"

"No, I did not."

"Did you tell Mr. Santos's parole officer?"

"No."

"Are you, in fact, receiving an additional grant because Mr. Santos is allegedly living with you?"

"When he was home, I was receiving, yes, a grant for him."

"So you did report to the department of social services that he was living with you, did you not? You're under oath."

"Yes," Billie said softly. "Yes."

Sadie spoke next, any trace of sympathy gone. "Let me say this to you. These people here are residents of public housing. We know what we put on an application. It is not like we come out of the sky and don't know housing. We are familiar with their rules and regulations." In other words: We know he would not have been put on your grant unless he lived with you, and we know that you know that is against the rules.

From there the conversation became ever more hostile. Little Johnny felt hot against Billie's chest. She couldn't believe the sound of her pounding heart did not wake him.

"Since, I take it, he is incarcerated," Sadie asked, "has D.S.S. pulled that money out of your grant, or are you still getting it?"

"No," Billie answered, she had not stopped the money. "I've been going through emotional changes. I haven't gotten to them yet."

"In other words, you're still receiving money for him?"

"Yes."

"Is that legal?" asked the lawyer, clearly quite interested.

"No," Sadie said.

"No," Billie agreed. "I have to get in touch with them."

Sadie nodded curtly. "I have no more questions," she said.

The lawyer then brought in John's parole officer, Thomas Downer, who described how, at John's first meeting, "he informed me that he was moving in with Ms. Rowan at 115 Gaffney."

"Were you satisfied that he was living at 115 Gaffney?" the lawyer asked after Downer described his visits to the townhouse.

"Completely," the officer said.

"Did you tell Mr. Downer that he was living there?" the lawyer asked Billie.

"Yes," Billie said, giving up completely. "I told him that. Yes."

When all the witnesses had finished, the lawyer said, "I have no further witnesses. Ms. Rowan is free to make whatever statements she wants to the hearing panel."

Billie shrugged. "I have nothing to say."

The lawyer addressed the committee. "She's offered no concrete evidence to substantiate the fact that Mr. Santos was living with his mother. You have the uncontroverted evidence of these witnesses and the documentary evidence that substantially proves he was, in fact, living with her. I, therefore, would hope this panel would move for her eviction. You have thirty days to make your decision."

Out in the Street

BILLIE Rowan trudged through the snow to reach her mailbox one morning in March.

The first envelope she opened was her welfare check from social services, reduced to $479 a month now because the lawyer at Municipal Housing had sent a letter saying John was no longer entitled to his $84 allotment.

Next was a long, handwritten letter from John. Like the others he had sent from the county jail over the months, this letter was upbeat. "He's okay because his fingerprints is not on the ice pick," was how she described them. "They still want to hold him, though, being that he was there when it happened, so I don't know, maybe he'll be released soon."

The last letter was from Municipal Housing. Billie ripped it open, then waded through two pages of legalese. The information she was looking for was in the last paragraph: "After hearing all the testimony and reviewing the exhibits introduced into evidence, the Resident Hearing Committee . . . recommended for the eviction of Billie Rowan." She was told to be out by the end of the month.

She knew she could fight back if she wanted to. The odds were she would lose, but the fight could last a long time, and she would be allowed to stay in the townhouse until it was over. She just didn't have the stomach for that route. John would be home soon, she figured. Her plan was not to fight but to flee. Maybe to South Carolina, where she had distant family.

For several days Billie searched through the classifieds for a new apartment. There were very few places she could afford. John's sister, Yolanda, had agreed to share the new place with her, so they would need something large enough for the two women and their four children. A two-bedroom would do, if some of the children slept in the living room. They could afford about $600 a month. In Yonkers the average rent for even a one-bedroom was $682, more than they could afford.

Most of the ads hinted at a world that had nothing to do with Billie's life. Duplexes with gardens; two bedrooms with an on-site gym. All for more than $1200 a month.

A few ads, however, were clearly seeking her business and that of others receiving checks from the department of social services:

> YONKERS, DSS OK, Studio, 1,2,3 & 4 BR apts, $500 & up. IMMEDIATE.
>
> YONKERS 1,2 & 3 BR, A1 Condition, $500 & up.

She called the second of these numbers. A broker named Elias Rabady answered her call and told her he specialized in apartments on the southwest side of town on the "tree streets"—Elm, Maple, Chestnut, Poplar, Ash. Billie knew the area well. It was where people lived until they qualified for a shabby, noisy, depressing apartment in Schlobohm.

Billie and Yolanda were shown a four-room apartment at 63 Oak Street, a seedy red brick walk-up that even Mr. Rabady described as "a little crummy." The apartment was dark and cramped but reasonably clean. There was no refrigerator, but the heat seemed to work and was included in the rent, which was $650 a month. A one-month security deposit was required, as well as a broker's fee of 15 percent of the yearly rent, or $1170.

Billie and Yolanda said they would take it. Mr. Rabady filled out the shelter verification forms as required by social services to approve payment. He spelled Billie's name wrong on the application—instead of Rowan, he wrote Rowanne.

Billie dragged herself home, defeated. The children had not eaten dinner, but she didn't have the energy to fix a meal. When she lived in Schlobohm, she had always guessed that there was a better life. Now she *knew* that there was. It had been easier before, when she could only guess what she was missing.

The next morning, at the mailbox, Billie met Doreen James.

"You're going backward," Doreen lectured when Billie told her about the apartment. "Your man screwed you. It happens. Don't screw yourself double by not fighting back."

Billie did not move to Oak Street. She simply stayed where she was, past the March 31 deadline, in spite of the notice that arrived to inform her that Municipal Housing had asked the city court of Yonkers to enforce her eviction. A court hearing, the letter said, was scheduled for May 1. Two days before the hearing, Billie called Westchester/Putnam Legal Services. Papers were filed on her behalf, challenging the city court's jurisdiction over the case, and her future was put on indefinite hold while the Supreme Court of Westchester County considered that challenge.

She never contacted Mr. Rabady. She simply did not send him her money. A short while later he threw her file out.

Nick Runs One Last Time

Nick began the summer as he had begun so many other summers—deciding whether to run in the next election and, if so, for what office. A citywide redistricting plan was to take effect during the election of 1993, and Nick's house was in a heavily Hispanic district. A local activist named Fernando Fuentes had made it clear he would run for that seat, and Nick was not eager to challenge him.

The only other option, as he saw it, was to run for city judge, but when he approached the executive committee of the Democratic Party, the response was frosty. They were sorry, they said, but there was already a strong Democrat running for that position.

Nick approached Vinni Restiano for her endorsement, and he was stunned when he did not get it. Not knowing of his plans, she had already promised her support elsewhere.

What happened next would be the subject of much debate after the election. The way Nick described it, he was approached by Jim Surdoval, on behalf of Terry Zaleski, with a suggestion. There was an office perfect for Nick's experience and talents, Nick would remember being told by Surdoval. City Council president. If he challenged Vinni Restiano for that position, the mayor would support him.

The fact that Restiano was a friend and that Nay worked closely with her at City Hall did bother Nick, but he needed to run for office in 1993, and this seemed to be the only office available.

Telling Nay turned uglier than he had expected. When he came home, she was kneeling on the ground outside the house, pulling weeds in what she stubbornly insisted would one day be a garden.

"I'm going to primary Vinni," he said.

She jumped to her feet. "Stay the hell away from me," she said, pitching her spade and her gloves to the ground, then running toward the house. "I don't think I know you anymore."

When she reached the doorway, she turned and shouted, "You know what? I'm going to work for Vinni."

Nick knew the news would reach Restiano, and he was not surprised when the phone rang several hours later. Vinni was calling from her car, and Nick couldn't tell if they had a bad connection or if she had been crying. "So you made your decision," she said. "What a coward. You couldn't pick up the phone and tell me yourself? After all we were to each other, the friendship we had."

Nick noticed that she spoke of their friendship in the past tense.

"Don't think this is going to be easy," she warned.

Alma Searches for Home; Pam Finds It

ALMA Febles followed the news about Billie Rowan closely. She knew that one hundred and twenty-one more townhouses were scheduled to be built—eventually—but the furor over the murder, she feared, might mean that "eventually" would never come.

She paced and fretted; then tentatively, fearfully, she began to search for an apartment outside the projects. Unlike Billie, who looked at places she could afford and was unsettled by what her money could buy, Alma looked at places where she would actually want to live—three-bedroom apartments in safe neighborhoods.

A friend told her about an apartment for rent across the street from work. It had two bedrooms, but they were big, so she and Leyda could share. The building was clean and safe, with an intercom system and new carpeting in the lobby. The rent was $825.

With a recent raise Alma earned $360 a week at Fitzgerald & Fitzgerald. After deductions for health insurance and taxes, however, she took home $256 a week, or $1109 a month, meaning her rent at $532 a month was nearly half of her disposable income. So she certainly was not able to spend $300 extra dollars each month for a new apartment.

When school ended, she sent Frankie and Virgilio to Santo Domingo for most of the summer, where each one stayed with his own father. She worried constantly, particularly about Frankie, but she didn't see that she had any choice but to let him go. In early August she spent $300 she did not have to fly herself and Leyda to Florida, the cheapest summer destination she could find. They stayed with friends and they swam in the ocean, but the change of scene did not lift Alma's depression. When her sons arrived back home, they were tanned and rested. Frankie had spent all his days outside, he said, riding bikes, playing ball, and "doing stuff kids do."

It was during the brutal heat waves of summer that Pam Johnson loved her townhouse most. The thermometer would swear it was as hot here as on the west side, but it felt worlds cooler. The difference had nothing to do with air-conditioning, as unaffordable a luxury to her here as it had been before.

One August day when it was 100 degrees before lunch, Pam dragged her daughters' plastic pool onto the front lawn and filled it with water. As always happened, children materialized from the other townhouses, wearing bathing suits. And as also always happened, the neighbors across the street peered from their windows and their front stoops, not saying anything, just staring.

There was still hostility from those neighbors. The man in the brown house, for instance, who often yelled at the children, "Go home. I don't want you on this side of the street." But there were also signs of a possible thaw. There was the Poodle Lady, who had followed her Christmas presents with Easter baskets and then started to bring treats for no reason—headbands, coloring books, hair barrettes. And there was the man with the rottweiler, who had stopped letting his dog stand and growl behind the Plexiglas storm door, where it had petrified the children. One day Pam passed him while he was walking the dog, and he nodded hello. More recently, when a few children from the townhouses were playing a radio while standing on a corner, leading some homeowner to call the police, the man with the rottweiler came out to tell the officers that the music wasn't really too loud.

Watching the townhouse children play, Pam saw pure happiness. The splashing had been under way for about a half hour when Valentina went running into the house, then came racing back, her arms filled with plastic buckets. She and Anita filled them from the spigot out front and hurled arcs of water at their friends. Soon everyone was armed with buckets and cups, and everyone, children and adults, was soaked and gleeful.

The water fight went on for nearly an hour. Pam paused for a moment and glanced across the street. The neighbors were out on their sidewalks and stoops, dozens of them, standing and staring. But the looks on their faces were not what Pam expected. They were smiling. They were even laughing. They looked as if they wished they could join the ruckus.

This is *my* neighborhood, Pam found herself thinking. This is where *I* live. Then she doused Anita with a bucket of water.

A Death and a Decision

As summer ended, Doreen James's sister Barbara began having violent seizures, sometimes one every day. Minutes later, when she was conscious again, Doreen would try to persuade her to go to the hospital, but she always refused.

In early September, Barbara had terrible pains in her leg and felt too weak to walk. This time she agreed to go to the hospital, where Doreen learned that her sister's blood pressure was dangerously low and, more important, the circulation in her leg was nearly completely blocked. The leg would require surgery.

The operation was scheduled for early in the morning, and Doreen could not be there. Her mother had promised to call her when it was over. At lunchtime there was a knock on Doreen's door, and when she opened it, she found her mother standing on the threshold, frail and confused. "I have something to tell you," she said. "She didn't make it. She died during the surgery." Barbara James was thirty-four years old.

When Doreen came home from the funeral, she found a notice from Con Ed in her mailbox, warning that her power would be cut off because her bill was past due. She crumpled the letter into a ball and hurled it across the room. Then she sank to the floor and cried, tears of grief and frustration, tears for her sister but also for things she did not understand she'd lost until this moment.

"I don't want to live here anymore," she said. "This isn't home."

Doreen had left Schlobohm not because she was tired of fighting to make things better there, but because she was tired of fighting *alone*. She moved to the townhouses hoping things might be different, that her neighbors would stick together.

"But people don't stick together," she said. "They're doing the same thing they did on the other side of town. Their own thing."

During her last months Barbara had gently scolded Doreen, saying she was looking for something that didn't exist, adding that most white people ignore their neighbors, too. Maybe Barbara was right. Doreen alone could not transform this collection of townhouses into a neighborhood. This wasn't home. But she would not stop looking for someplace that was.

Several days later Doreen called Municipal Housing. Valerie Carroll, the tenant supervisor, came on the line. "I want to move out of here," Doreen said.

Valerie had never processed a request to leave the east side, she said. Hundreds of people were waiting for a chance to move in.

"You don't understand. I'm not asking to leave the east side. I want Dunbar Houses," Doreen said, speaking of the small enclave in Runyon Heights where Sheila lived, where Sadie lived, where Jaron would see black faces that lived in hous*es,* not hous*ing.* Maybe there she would feel like she belonged.

"There's a long list ahead of you," Valerie said.

Doreen said she was willing to wait.

Nick vs. Vinni

ONCE Nick launched his campaign against Vinni Restiano for City Council president, council meetings became ordeals for him. This was still Restiano's council, and his decision to try to change that did not sit well with most of the people who worked for or with her.

It had become an ugly campaign. The two former friends had nearly identical voting records, and that, coupled with Restiano's feelings of betrayal, left the candidates nothing to attack but each other. Restiano accused Nick of nepotism—putting Nay in a City Council job—even though Restiano herself had lobbied the council to make that happen. Nick accused Restiano of being more of a Republican than a Democrat, even though he had helped her craft many of her political positions.

Nay was caught in the cross fire. Each day a few more pieces of her job were taken from her and given to others in the office. Eventually the only job left her was handing out forms to couples needing marriage licenses. After spending each day launching other people's marriages, she would come home and widen the cracks in her own.

"I'm sick and tired of this whole ugly, disgusting mess," she would vent at Nick. "I paid for your politics when they fired me from the Parking Authority. Now I get to pay again? If you lose and she wins, that's it for me, for my job, for everything. Did you think about that?"

After the polls had closed the day of the primary, Nick and Nay went to Mannion's restaurant to wait for the returns. It was supposed to be a victory party, but it quickly became clear there was very little to celebrate. Three of the four candidates backed by

Terry Zaleski lost their races, including Nick, who trailed Restiano by 363 votes.

At ten o'clock Nick conceded the race. From the pay phone at Mannion's he called Restiano's home, where she was awaiting the returns with supporters. She was polite but icy, and Nick left the restaurant immediately after the call. Neither Nick nor Nay said one word as they drove back home.

A Hero

NAY was not fired the morning after the primary, a fact that provided the Wasicskos little peace of mind. The last time Nay had been fired, it made headlines, and the couple respected Vinni's political savvy enough to assume that she was waiting until her reelection was final before carrying through on her threat.

The kitchen renovation was well under way, and now the conversations on Wasicsko Lane were not about how to decorate it, but how to pay for it. They would find themselves awake at 4:00 a.m., worrying aloud in the dark.

"What are we going to do when you get fired?"

"Maybe we can ask my parents to help us out again."

"I've made a mess of everything, haven't I?"

Nick had started a job search cautious yet optimistic, as befits a politician. He believed he would get a job. A good job. What he wanted was simple—to stay in the Yonkers area in a position with visibility and prestige. He hoped eventually to run for mayor again, or maybe for city judge, with the governor's mansion still beckoning in the distance. He contacted Terry Zaleski, who directed him to Jim Surdoval.

He knew that politics was about never looking desperate, so he approached Jim with studied nonchalance. "So what's next for me?"

"There are no positions in the Zaleski administration for you at this time," Surdoval said.

Nick tried to maintain his team player poker face. "Make me commissioner of whatever," he said, thinking, Invent something. I have a home. I have a mortgage. I have bills to pay.

"It would look like a payoff for running against Vinni," Surdoval said. He paused and softened. "I'll work on something," he said before showing Nick the door.

At home, Nick scrawled his résumé in longhand for Nay to type. He had been a finalist for the Profile in Courage Award, he wrote of himself in the third person, "for his courageous stand against angry crowds and voters opposed to court ordered desegregation," and he "was elected the youngest mayor of any major US city in an upset election over a six-term Republican."

Then he wrote letters to accompany the résumé. He wrote to Henry Cisneros, President Clinton's Secretary of Housing and Urban Development, "I am enclosing my resume with the hope that a role for me may exist at HUD that will under your stewardship reinforce the message that quality desegregated housing is a national priority." And though the specifics were different, he wrote much the same message in his letter to Judge Sand, who was looking to appoint a federal master to oversee the final stage of the housing plan.

These letters and others were sent on September 20, 1993, less than a week after Nick lost the primary. By the second week in October, when he had received no response from anyone, he went back to Jim Surdoval. The mayor had passed Nick's name to Assemblyman Oliver Koppell, who was the nominee to be New York's attorney general, recommending Nick for a job as an assistant attorney general. Terry Zaleski had also recommended him to a number of New York City law firms.

Rather than being heartened by the help, Nick was frightened and depressed. He did not want a job as a lawyer. He had never actually practiced law and was petrified that he would fail. The depth of that fear became clear when his uncle asked Nick to draft his will. Nick spent an entire Saturday in the Barnes & Noble bookstore reading trade paperbacks on how to write a will, and he left with one hundred dollars' worth of merchandise. "I don't remember anything about this," he said to Nay. "I want to do it right."

He sent out more job letters, but where his earlier ones had been self-assured and eloquent, these clanked with a false bravado.

"I am writing with interest about the position of lawyer lobbyist," he said in response to an ad he found in the classified section of *The New York Times.* "As a former Mayor with high recognition among state officials, I believe I can be a strong asset to your organization."

He never received an answer.

A Tragedy

ON THE morning of Friday, October 29, 1993, Nick tried to get Nay to take the day off. He lay in bed at eight and watched her as she dressed for work. "Make it a three-day weekend," he said. "Go for a walk and look at the leaves."

"The leaves are all dead, and I don't have any vacation days left. Vinni wants me out. Let's not give her ammunition."

So Nick got out of bed, dressed quickly—green Dockers pants, white sneakers, and the green sweater Nay had given him to cheer him up the week before—and he drove Nay to work at City Hall. They talked of the things husbands and wives talk about when they catch a few minutes together during a hectic day. The kitchen cabinets had arrived and were lying in their cartons all over the kitchen floor. They had to shop for a refrigerator on Friday night. They had to meet the tile man at the house on Saturday morning.

On the way home, Nick picked up *The New York Times* and the *Herald Statesman,* which he read first, scanning it frantically for any news of the investigation into embezzlement at the city's Industrial Development Agency. As mayor, he had chaired the agency, and more recently he had been a member of its board, appointed by Terry Zaleski before their relationship went sour. Nick knew he had not done anything wrong while a member of the IDA board and that he was not among those being accused of wrongdoing, but lately he had been overwhelmed by a fear that in the uncontrollable arena of politics, innocence is no defense.

"They're making allegations, and they're ruining people's lives," he had said to Nay a few days earlier. "This is not funny. I hope when it's their turn, let's see how funny they think it is."

Nick's raw fear alarmed Nay. That night he told her he was being followed, but he did not say by whom. He spent hours at the library, searching through past newspaper stories, constructing a chronology he could use to make his case.

On the morning of October 29 there was no news of the investigation, and he spent a few hours making telephone calls, including one to his secretary. He asked her to reserve some tickets for him—two for a human rights dinner that same night and two for the Democratic city committee annual dinner to be held on Halloween. Shortly before 11:00 a.m. he changed out of his Dockers and into a suit and tie to do his councilman's duty at a ceremony to open a new county welfare office. The ceremony lasted no more than half an hour, and Nick returned home, changed back into his more comfortable clothes, and worked in the kitchen for a while with his brother Michael, unpacking the cabinets.

At one o'clock Nick drove to City Hall to pick up Nay for lunch. During their hour at the Broadway Diner he complained that he was tired of being followed, and because he was certain a tracking transmitter had been placed under both his cars, he planned to switch vehicles with Michael. Shortly before 2:00 he dropped Nay back at City Hall.

Early that afternoon Michael walked into the living room and saw his brother holding a gun, looking terrified. Nick raced out the door, saying only that he had to run an "errand."

Minutes later Nay paged him on his beeper. He called her back and told her he was at a pay phone a block from the house. He said he was going directly home to help Michael. Forty-five minutes later he drove up to the house, left the car engine running, ran up the stairs, then down them again. He took the cash out of his wallet but left the wallet behind. He took the keys to his Chevy Geo and his Ford Taurus off the key chain and left the key chain behind, too.

All afternoon Nay tried to page him because she was frightened at his stories of transmitters and tails, but he did not answer his beeper. At 4:30, when her work was done, she stood in her customary spot at the front door to City Hall and waited for Nick to pick her up. An hour later, when he still wasn't there, she called Michael and asked him to drive her home.

While Nay was waiting for Nick, he was sitting on a hill at the Oakland Cemetery, about two blocks from his house and a mile from City Hall. He was leaning against a tree, looking out over the cemetery where his father and grandfather were buried. Beyond their graves he could see the twin spires of St. Casimir's Church and the gables of City Hall.

It was closing time at the cemetery, and the caretaker, Fedor Feciasko, walked over and asked him to leave. Nick said he would and started walking down the hill toward his red Geo with the license plate that read WASICSKO. But when the caretaker came by again a few minutes later, Nick was back by the tree, staring down on Yonkers. The caretaker opted to give the former mayor a little more time. He waited until 5:15 to approach Nick again, and as before, Nick stood up and walked toward his car.

At 5:20 Feciasko made one last trip up the hill. He would tell one of the dozens of police officers who soon swarmed the scene, "He was lying over here. I saw the gun in his hand, and the blood."

Nick Wasicsko had shot himself once through the head with the .38 revolver he almost always carried. Nay could not believe he did not leave her a note, but none was ever found.

Within hours the stream of praise began.

Said Mayor Zaleski, "It's an extraordinary tragedy. All of the people of Yonkers send their heartfelt love and sympathy to the family. It's just a tragedy. A loss beyond words."

Vinni Restiano: "I feel like I've been in a car crash and the other driver died. Even though we've been political adversaries in this last primary, Nick Wasicsko was a friend, and I'm shocked and hurt for his family. Nick was a real intelligent individual and he had a life ahead of him. He must have really been hurting inside for him to have done this to himself. There was nobody smarter."

Hank Spallone: "Terrible. Tragedy. A real tragedy. We were on opposite sides of the political spectrum, but we were always very friendly. I'm just shocked. Such a fine man is gone."

Nicholas Longo: "He took the tough times with a lot of character and a lot of strength. The fellow who withstood what was taking place in 1988 was not the fellow who walked into the Oakland Cemetery tonight."

NICHOLAS Wasicsko had been baptized in St. Casimir's Church. He and Nay were married there, too. And on a gray and frigid election day morning St. Casimir's was where he was mourned. It was the first election day in almost a decade when his name did not appear on the Yonkers ballot.

More than a thousand people packed the church, filling the pews and spilling out into the entryway, where they stood, coats still on, tears flowing freely, through the hour-long farewell Mass.

From her pew in the middle of the crowd Mary Dorman was astonished to see Oscar Newman slip into a nearby row.

Nay sat in the front pew, stunned, numb, and in a haze of grief. From the time the police commissioner himself had arrived at her door and taken her to the cemetery to identify Nick's body, she had coped by refusing to think. Thinking was more than she could handle. It took all her energy merely to walk and talk.

Now, at the funeral, she was still willing herself not to think. It worked for most of the morning, but then near the end of the service the Reverend John Duffell took the pulpit to begin his eulogy.

It was Father Duffell who had found Nay her first job at City Hall. During her early years with Nick he would warn Nick to take care of Nay because "she's my favorite girl." From this same pulpit Duffell had married them.

Nick was "a man full of promise, a man full of suffering," Duffell said, and his death "makes us realize what's important: not the politics, but the human beings. If only all the things that were said about him these past few days could have been again and again said to him." But Duffell did not stop with soothing generalities. He spoke of the "McCarthyism of Yonkers" and described the city as a place filled with politics, hate, rumor, investigation, and fear. The kind of place where a man who had done the right thing, as Nick had done, could be destroyed because he was right.

Nay stopped feeling numb and began to feel angry. She was

angry at Yonkers and at the mourning politicians who surrounded her. As she followed her husband's casket out of St. Casimir's, she was angry at herself for being one of those politicians, playing by the rules Nick had taught her. As the four-block-long funeral procession snaked its way past City Hall, she was also angry at the screaming crowds who hounded her husband in 1988. So many of those people were watching now, she knew, as the motorcade passed by. People who had quieted their voices but never shed their hate, who made it clear with their votes that they could not forgive him.

Then, as Nick Wasicsko was buried on the same hill where he had died, Nay was angry mostly at her husband—for leaving her to rebuild her dreams from scratch because he could not bear to pick up the fractured pieces of his own.

1998: Epilogue

A DECADE has passed since the summer of contempt in Yonkers. It has been six years since the first tenants moved into the townhouses, and five since Nicholas Wasicsko's death.

For Alma Febles the townhouses have been everything that she had hoped, a gift made all the more precious because it took so long. On October 28, 1994, two years after the lottery, Alma and her children moved into their new home. She is past forty now and still does not have her elusive solitary bedroom. She says she doesn't mind. Virgilio has already left the townhouse; he joined the marines. In another blink of the eye Leyda will be gone, too; she plans to go to college and become a fashion designer.

It took far longer for the townhouses to bring contentment to Doreen James. Although her name remains on the waiting list for Dunbar, she is now less determined to make that move. She is still involved with READY and proud of the changes the group has helped bring to the west side, but even as she is seeing the clout of grassroots activism, Doreen is easing it out of her life. "Sadie says you can't solve other people's problems until you fix your own," she says. Part of her new life plan includes a full-time job at a chain hardware store on the east side, and night school, where she hopes to take the courses that will allow her to become a social worker in Schlobohm.

And Billie Rowan? She sees the townhouses as a cruel municipal tease, a trinket given to her briefly, then roughly snatched away. The five-week-long trial of John Mateo Santos was front-page news in Yonkers. He did not testify, but his legal aid lawyer argued that he had struck up a conversation with Helen Sarno at a local deli and she had invited him to her home for a cup of coffee. At first he declined, and they each went their own way. Then John changed his mind and returned to the elderly woman's apartment, only to find her covered with blood and near death.

Billie believed him. The jury did not. They found him guilty. Judge John R. LaCava gave him the maximum sentence of twenty-five years to life for what he described as a "cowardly, senseless, and inexcusable murder."

It would be several more years before another court decided Billie's own fate. In time she lost the last of her appeals and was evicted in October 1995, nearly three years after the murder. Shortly before she moved, she said, "I hope my kids remember this place so they can find a way back here." She fled Yonkers and left no forwarding address.

DESPITE fears that the ills of the west side would travel with the tenants, life is still relatively peaceful on the east side. There have been some problems that have brought the police to the townhouses—complaints of loud music, domestic squabbles, fights among the children. But in general, the police say, they are not called to the new housing sites more often than they are called to any other cluster of homes. Said Bob Olsen, Yonkers police chief during the years after the townhouses first opened, "The doomsday scenario never materialized."

The townhouses do what Oscar Newman had hoped they would do. They blend into the neighborhood. The tenants think of their homes as their own and care for them as well as they can. Lately there is talk of how they might eventually be able to buy the units.

There is still anger on the east side. A walk through the neighborhood, a knock on random doors finds that the anger is quieter than before, but it has not gone away.

"So far it's not so bad," says one homeowner, washing down his driveway with a hose. "But they're still on their best behavior. I feel like we were screwed over. I'm just too tired to fight about it."

A block away, another neighbor points to the FOR SALE BY OWNER sign on her front lawn. It has been there for several months, and she expects it will be there for several months more. "I'm not selling to get away from them," she says of the townhouses, "but it's because of them that I can't sell. Would *you* buy a house around here?"

It is, in fact, still difficult to sell a home in Yonkers—anywhere in Yonkers. But is that only because of the housing? Some argue that the real blame lies elsewhere. Yes, Yonkers has a black eye. But who threw the punch? Says John Spencer, the current mayor, "The damage that was done, the people of Yonkers did it to themselves."

NAY is still the deputy city clerk of Yonkers. On the wall of her City Hall office she has hung a framed newspaper from the summer of contempt and a poster Nick gave her called LOVE'S FIRST KISS. Since his suicide she has mended her emotional fences with Vinni Restiano, and each woman describes the other as a close friend. A scholarship fund has been established in Nick's memory, and an east side park has been named after him.

Unable to sell the unfinished house on the hill, Nay abandoned it to the bank. She now lives in a one-bedroom apartment. She took the WASICSKO LANE sign with her when she moved, but she left a pile of posters that said NICK WASICSKO FOR CITY COUNCIL PRESIDENT.

THE Department of Housing and Urban Development sees the townhouses of Yonkers as a success. Sprinkling low-income families throughout middle-class neighborhoods is now department policy. Across the United States—in Newark, Cincinnati, Boston, Chicago, and Houston—boxy brick towers, once filled with hundreds of public-housing units, are being declared failures and dynamited down to dust. From now on there will be only townhouses, like the ones built after all those years of protest in Yonkers.

"The lesson of Yonkers," says Oscar Newman, who retired to create giant totem-pole-like sculptures in upstate New York, "is that it is coming soon to a town near you."

Some of the lessons of Yonkers are practical: Spend resources on architects, not lawyers; accept the inevitable and move on. But other lessons are less tangible. To succeed where Yonkers failed means accepting that no neighborhood stays the same forever and that protecting our children might be better done by letting strangers in than by keeping them out.

Yonkers is what will happen—is happening—everywhere. In some places it will happen quietly; in others the shouting will be deafening. One by one each of those neighborhoods will learn what that means for a nation whose people preach diversity but are most comfortable when surrounded by others like themselves.

MARY Dorman is now a member of the city's civil service commission, with her name painted in gold on the door of her office at City Hall. One morning while out in her front yard she was stopped by the driver of a passing car who was looking to buy a house in Mary's neighborhood. Mary did know of one house, an attractive colonial with a big yard. She told the woman of it, then surprised herself by adding that the home was "across the street from the public housing." She knew it shouldn't matter. But she also knew that it does.

Alma Febles knows it, too. Shortly after she moved into her hard-won home, she worried aloud at a rumor that more of the same were to be built—on her new street. "They should build more, but I hope not right near here," she said with no hint of irony. "This is such a quiet, pretty block."

Meihong Xu
and
Larry Engelmann

Daughter

中國的女兒
OF CHINA
A True Story
of Love
and Betrayal

"I know you want to learn about China, and I'm trying to help you," I said. "But there is an invisible world here. I want you to be aware of it, because if you aren't, you can get into a lot of trouble."

"You've lost me," Larry said.

"Okay, let me make it very straight. When you write to your friends in America, please stop mentioning my name."

"How do you know what I write to my friends in America? Are you watching me?"

I could not answer his question directly. All I could tell him was that it was routine for agents of the government to read the mail of foreigners. "You have to remember that here in China, you don't have a private life," I cautioned him.

—*Daughter of China*

ONE

第一章

Red Aunt

THE room is small. It's like countless similar rooms I've seen in military barracks scattered across China. At some earlier time the room probably housed eight enlisted men. Tonight there are only four beds in the room, two of them pushed side by side against each of the longer walls. The narrow window has been nailed shut, and old copies of the *People's Liberation Army Daily* have been pasted over the glass.

Three female soldiers assigned to guard me perch close together on the bed nearest the door and occasionally whisper to each other. They never divert their gaze from me. Two armed soldiers are pacing back and forth in the hall outside.

Wearing only khaki trousers, a blouse, and sandals, I sit on the bed farthest from the door. I fold my arms tightly over my breasts in a futile effort to stay warm. I stare at the concrete floor and wait.

Before long, I know, there will be an insistent knock on the door. Surrounded by guards, I will be led from the room. I can see it happening. We pass into the darkness outside, transformed into mere silhouettes in a grim little parade. As if on signal, the guards stop. We are in an open space. The ground shines with a slick skin of ice; the sky is starless. Someone pushes me to a kneeling position. My arms are pulled back hard and tightly bound together behind me. I gaze at the ice and wait to hear the rustle of clothing when one of the soldiers raises his hand and holds his pistol a few inches from the back of my head. The others step away to avoid being soiled with my blood. Then there is complete stillness. I close my eyes tightly. I think of him one last time—my American. Will he hear my last unspoken words? Will he whisper my name when I fall? Will he remember me?

My military records will be purged. I will be erased from existence and become a nonperson. My family and friends will be told that I disappeared. They know what that means. They will not ask questions. When they mourn me, it will be secretly and in silence.

These are my expectations as I sit in this room with my three guards. I shuffle through a hundred memories of happier times, searching for something I can hold on to. I find again the face of the American. His eyes are so blue tonight. He smiles. I see his lips move, but I no longer hear his voice. I know I will never see him or hear him or hold him again. His face fades, and he is gone.

The sound of footsteps in the hall is the measured rhythm of death approaching. I know a few words might save my life. But I can never say these words. I cannot betray those I love. I am even unable to betray those I now know have betrayed me.

My thoughts come to rest on a familiar memory: Lishi—my village. I remember once more the story of the little girls lost in the fires. How many times have I heard the tale of their courage? Now I wonder if I have that same courage. I think of my aunt in Lishi. In my refusal to betray those I love, aren't I like her? On this night, without hope, condemned, do I feel at last what she felt? I sense pride and hope rising within me, filling me with strength. I am suddenly comforted. I am not afraid.

WE ARE simple people—peasants. Our birthright and destiny is hard work. We live by the cycle of the seasons. We know when to cultivate the earth, how to nourish it and renew it. In return, it gives us sustenance.

For sixteen centuries our village, Lishi, has survived in Jiangsu Province, near the shore of Lian Hu, south of the Yangtze River and west of the Grand Canal. The devastations of nature and man—floods, droughts, famines, plagues, earthquakes, wicked warlords, evil emperors, foreign devils, revolutionaries, and religious fanatics—have swept back and forth across our land, carrying away the handiwork of our labor. But we survive. We return to repair the damage and plant the grain once more. Life goes on. We have good fortune as well as bad, our elders constantly remind us. One follows the other, always, like the seasons, they say.

We believe it is important to remember and honor the courage of those who lived and died here before us. Their example inspires and instructs us. Memory is the sacred thread connecting us to our ancestors. There are a few memories, however, that are nearly unbearable. Such is the memory of December 1937.

It was a time of war. The villagers convinced themselves that the isolation of Lishi would deliver them from destruction. We were neither a fortress nor a great walled city, like Shanghai or neighboring Nanjing. We felt safe in our insignificance. Yet the Japanese Imperial Army—the short devils, as we called them—ignorant of our insignificance, passed through our village. They did not stay long—less than one hour, in fact. But we will remember and retell what they did there for a thousand years.

A road linking Shanghai to Nanjing cuts through fields south of the village. It was crowded with refugees and soldiers that December. The villagers of Lishi heard tales of the monstrousness of the Japanese soldiers who had long occupied distant parts of our country. Now they were on the move again, pushing all before them as they advanced on the Nationalist capital in Nanjing.

There were calls for the villagers to abandon everything and form a mass exodus. Yet there was also uncertainty about leaving the village. If there was no smoke from the cooking fires and if everyone hid, there was the possibility that the short devils would not stop.

As they prepared to go into hiding, they saw a lone Chinese soldier, lost and confused, stumbling through the fields. They attempted to question him, but he could not understand their dialect. With gestures and common Mandarin idioms they thought they succeeded in communicating with him. They were quite sure he said the Chinese armies were advancing and the short devils retreating!

It was possible, they said. If these Chinese armies were advancing, then there was no reason for the villagers to hide. A half-dozen elders hurried across a field and out to the main road to welcome the Chinese troops. They were followed by a boy who wanted to see the Chinese soldiers.

A few minutes later the boy returned alone, crying and out of breath. There was no Chinese army, he screamed. There were only the short devils, thousands and thousands of them. The elders were all dead. Now the short devils were spreading out across the fields and would be in the village within minutes.

It was too late to try to run away. One of the older women suggested a plan. Since the Japanese soldiers always looked first for the young girls, they were in the greatest danger, she said. They had to be hidden quickly. The villagers decided to conceal them in the stacks of rice straw around the village. Everyone else would hide in their homes until the danger passed.

All the young village girls—more than fifty—were quickly buried inside the haystacks. They were told not to move or make a sound and, most important, not to come out until their parents returned to uncover them. The villagers then scattered to their homes, blocked the doors, and huddled under their tables and beds.

Minutes later Japanese soldiers entered dwellings, turned over tables and pots, broke water jars. Many villagers had covered themselves with blankets. The soldiers ripped the covers away, jabbed the villagers with their rifles, then kicked them and spit on them. The villagers made no sound except for the chattering of their teeth.

A soldier found a small boy under a large wok inside one home. He carried him to the other soldiers and asked him questions. The boy understood nothing. The soldiers made hand motions and spoke in a soft soprano voice, like a young girl. The boy said nothing. Suddenly a soldier noticed rice straw in the boy's hair.

The soldiers laughed, as if they'd stumbled onto the obvious solution to a riddle. They walked to the nearest haystacks. A soldier affixed a bayonet to his rifle and prodded a haystack with it. He found nothing. He stepped to another and another, jabbing the bayonet in more forcefully each time. There was no sound, no movement, no resistance. But after jabbing a fourth haystack, he saw a vermilion smear along the entire length of the blade.

A soldier emerged from a house, carrying a can of kerosene. The other soldiers saw him and gave a shout of approval. He sprinkled kerosene on all of the haystacks and then struck matches and ignited the hay. The kerosene-fed fires blossomed quickly. There was still no sound or movement from the haystacks. After staring at the blazing mounds for several minutes, the soldiers moved on.

A short time later some of the bolder villagers peered outside. When they were sure it was safe, they shouted to the others that the short devils were gone. Then they saw the smoke and the glowing pyres. Some of the women screamed the names of their daughters and fell to the ground. Others raced to what remained of the haystacks and with pitchforks and shovels and bare hands pawed madly through them. But the round-faced little girls of Lishi were gone. None escaped.

The remains of the girls were gathered the next day and buried in a common grave. The bodies of the murdered elders were also recovered and buried near the girls. The past and future of the village seemed to have died on the same day.

When my mother was born in the spring of 1941, the burning of the girls in the haystacks was still a fresh wound. Her parents named her Yingdi. *Ying* means hero, and *di* indicated that they hoped she might soon be joined by a brother. A cousin born six months later was also a girl. She was named Lingdi, or Lead to a Brother. In the next years both families were blessed with sons.

Four years after the defeat of the Japanese the Communist armies liberated China from the Nationalists. When the liberators passed down the road near Lishi, Yingdi and Lingdi, dressed in their finest clothes, danced and sang with other village children and threw flowers at the soldiers. Later they joined the Young Pioneers. They became leaders in the Communist youth movement and, ultimately, members of the Communist Party.

In late 1959 the two girls, age eighteen, left the village, which was suffering from a severe and prolonged famine. They traveled thousands of kilometers to Shenyang, where they found work in a textile factory. Each month for three years they mailed home all but a small portion of their earnings. They ate only one meal each day—a breakfast consisting of thin rice soup. But the girls gladly made this sacrifice for their families.

They returned to the village in late 1962, and both married. Yingdi, my mother, married a young man from the village who was trained as a veterinarian. She worked in the fields on the collective farm. Lingdi, my aunt, married a man from Shanghai who had been a capitalist before liberation. He had been sent by the Communist Party to our village for reeducation through labor in the fields. His family, two generations earlier, had lived in Lishi. He was accustomed to a soft life in the city and was unhappy in our village.

I was born on December 6, 1963. My brother was born in 1965 and my sister in 1968. Lingdi and her husband had no children. Four years after they married, her husband announced that he wanted a divorce. He wanted to return to Shanghai and did not want to take his illiterate peasant wife with him.

To all outward appearances Lingdi was a perfect wife. She was a hard worker, a good cook, and a leader in community activities. Her only shortcoming was that she was childless. But that was not considered an acceptable reason for a divorce. Officials asked Lingdi's husband the reason for his petition. "My wife is not totally a woman," he said. "She is neither a woman or a man. She is both. And I can no longer share a bed with her."

The officials were stunned and scandalized by this revelation. Within days a pair of them called at Lingdi's home to notify her of her husband's petition. She understood little they told her. But she knew enough to be humiliated. When asked if what her husband said was true, she said nothing. The officials said she could visit a physician in Danyang—a female, they emphasized—for a physical examination. She had the right, of course, to refuse. But if she did, the officials could only assume that her husband's charge was true, and in that case the divorce would be granted.

Ashamed as well as frightened, Lingdi stayed in Lishi. Six weeks later her husband was granted his divorce. He departed immediately for Shanghai. We never heard of him again.

In the next years Lingdi's life was particularly dismal. Villagers whispered and joked about her. She was suddenly an outcast in the village where her family had lived for centuries. Yet she struggled to remain a perfect Party member. Invariably, she was the first to arrive at Party meetings and the last to leave.

As I grew older, I became aware that Lingdi paid lots of attention to me. She gave me gifts—new shoes and pencils, paper, ink, and brushes for school. I had never owned real leather shoes until Lingdi gave me a pair. My favorite gifts were always the children's storybooks she bought for me.

Shortly after the birth of my sister, Lingdi confessed to my mother that she was lonely and her personal life was empty. She wanted a child. "I would like you to give me Meihong to be my daughter," she said. She could provide for me better than my parents, and she needed someone to care for her in her old age.

My mother later discussed it with my father. He said he would never give away any of his children. My mother wept out of pity for Lingdi and reminded him of her kindness and constant loneliness. Finally he agreed that if Lingdi would take my younger sister, they might come to an agreement.

When Lingdi was offered my sister, she said no—she wanted only me. My father refused. So there was nothing more to talk about on the subject. Throughout the years, however, Lingdi treated me like her daughter, providing me with school supplies, books, and clothing. Many times she walked me to school and then, in the evening, home. I enjoyed her attention, and I responded to it.

During the Great Proletarian Cultural Revolution, which began in 1966, there was heightened political activity throughout China. People everywhere in the nation were swept up in fervent revolutionary rapture. At night there were torchlight parades and rallies and denunciations of revisionists, rightists, capitalist roaders, and landlords. Huge banners glorifying Chairman Mao and other leaders decorated the villages. On weekends the children were organized to scour the surrounding area in search of landlords plotting to overturn the revolution. It was an exciting time to be a child.

Then a troubling series of incidents began. Counterrevolutionary graffiti appeared in the villages. Some of it was simple: a picture of Chairman Mao or Comrade Jiang Qing, his wife, had an X across it. Several smaller posters appeared later, stating simply, DOWN WITH MAO. DOWN WITH JIANG QING. DOWN WITH THE PARTY. The source of these signs was a mystery. No one was above suspicion. Meetings were called at the school, and we were asked individually if we had written the counterrevolutionary slogans or knew who might have done this.

Then late one night we were awakened by someone pounding on the door of our home. A Party cadre had come to summon my mother to an emergency meeting at brigade headquarters. My mother was chief of the local brigade.

When she returned several hours later, she was very upset. I asked what had happened. She refused to tell me. She said only that there would be no school that day and in the morning there was to be a public rally. Everyone in the three villages of the brigade was required to attend.

At the rally, the local Party secretary came to the stage and announced that the criminal responsible for the anti–Chairman Mao graffiti had been identified. Then she shouted out triumphantly, "The class enemy is Xu Lingdi! Down with Xu Lingdi!"

There was a moment of silence and a loud gasp of astonishment from the crowd. But within moments everyone joined in the chant: "Down with Lingdi!"

The words, the loud hateful chanting, hit me like fists. I stood there stunned. I had never heard Lingdi say anything disparaging about the Party or Chairman Mao. On the contrary, she was the model Party member. My red aunt was an agent of the rightists? She had always been so kind and so generous. Maybe that was why, I thought. She had been attempting to recruit me into the ranks of the counterrevolutionaries all along.

The Party secretary said, "Xu Lingdi has admitted her crime. She has confessed, and she will be punished severely."

During the next days details of the arrest and confession spread through the village. When the first graffiti had appeared, the police pursued the most obvious suspects—a group identified as hooligans and troublemakers. These were young men who were seldom serious at rallies, flirted with the girls instead of paying attention to the speakers, were lax in their field work, and did poorly in school. A dozen hooligans were rounded up, held in jail, and interrogated over the course of a week. But none of them broke down and confessed, even when they were beaten.

The police decided to charge three of the hooligans, including Lingdi's brother, with writing the graffiti and to punish them as a warning to the other criminals. The police had no evidence against the young men, only their suspicions.

On the first day of the secret trial of the boys Lingdi appeared before the Party secretary and said she was the real criminal. She was told to return home and to stop being a nuisance by confessing to crimes she could not possibly have committed.

Lingdi persisted. She returned with newspapers from which the pictures of Chairman Mao had been cut out. She said that she had pasted the pictures up and x-ed them out.

When the Party secretary examined the newspapers, she asked how Lingdi, of all people, could do this? Lingdi only said that she was confessing because she felt that the young innocent men, including her brother, being tried for her crimes should be released. She said her mother's heart was broken by the mistreatment of her son. He was suffering for Lingdi's crimes. Lingdi was placed in a jail cell, and the trial of the young men was suspended.

Several weeks later another brigade rally was held. The Party secretary and other cadres pushed Lingdi onto the stage. She was wearing a tall dunce cap, and from her neck hung a placard with her name x-ed out and with a description of her crimes. Her hands were bound tightly behind her. The left side of her face was swollen and bruised, and her eye was completely shut. One after another the Party cadres stepped forward, denounced her, and then slapped her face. Each time they slapped her, the crowd cheered.

Then the sentence was read: Xu Lingdi was stripped of her Party membership and sentenced to ten years in prison. She was told she was lucky to escape the death penalty.

In school I wrote articles about Lingdi and read them aloud. I asserted that I hated her and that all students should hate her. I had copied the articles about other accused criminals from the Party newspaper and simply changed the names. That was accepted as scholarship for the young during the Cultural Revolution. But my mother asked me to stop writing denunciations of Lingdi. "Your aunt is guilty of no crime," she said. "None!"

I was nine years old and could not comprehend what I heard. Suddenly I suspected my mother was a covert counterrevolutionary, along with my formerly red aunt. It seemed obvious. They had been so close over the years.

I became more suspicious when I overheard conversations between my parents late at night, when they thought I was asleep. My mother said it was bored teenage troublemakers who were responsible for all the anti-Mao mischief. Lingdi's brother had tearfully told her this, she revealed, and had asked her what he should do. She told him to say nothing more about it, ever. Nothing could help Lingdi now. The Party secretary who had turned her in had become a local hero. To contradict Lingdi's tale would only make the Party secretary lose face. That would bring more problems.

Despite what I'd heard my mother say, I led my school in denouncing Lingdi. Not to do so would bring suspicion on myself, I thought. After one of my more colorful denunciations, however, a girl asked if we should not be suspicious of those who were related to this traitor. Might not these people try to avoid suspicion through their criticism of Lingdi? I ignored what she said, but I felt the other students looked at me differently after that.

Following the death of Mao and the fall of Jiang Qing and three of her cohorts—the Gang of Four—in the autumn of 1976, when I was twelve, thousands of political prisoners appealed to the government and were released. But Lingdi did not immediately appeal. She had been sent to a labor camp about fifty kilometers from our village and worked there for six years—until 1978—in a factory making gloves. I heard later that when they were about to set her free, she asked to be allowed to remain. If she returned home, it would be a shame for her elderly mother, her brother, and her cousins to have her nearby. But the state required that she go home.

When she came home, she was thin and pale. There were streaks of gray in her hair, and she stooped slightly when she walked. As she feared, there was little forgiveness for her in Lishi. She moved into a small dwelling beside the rice paddies. She visited her mother and cooked for her. My mother visited her often, late at night. They sat at a table in the dark and reminisced and drank tea. My aunt still liked me very much, but I kept my distance.

In 1981, I was one of twelve girls selected nationwide to attend the People's Liberation Army (PLA) Institute for International Relations in Nanjing. All of the village was proud of me and celebrated.

Late one evening there was a soft tapping on our door. It was Lingdi. She pressed a small red envelope into my hand and left as quietly as she had come. I opened the envelope. It contained three hundred yuan. A five-yuan gift was considered generous, given the fact that the average salary in the village was about twenty yuan per month. Lingdi's gift was incredible. My mother, however, insisted that I could not keep it. So we walked to my aunt's house to return the money. The two cousins whispered to each other as I stood beside my mother. My aunt didn't understand why I could not keep the money. It was her life's savings, she said. She had no use for it. She started to cry. "I have always cherished this little girl," she said. "She is like my daughter. I just want to contribute something to make her life easier. If you refuse me this, you are rejecting me, just like everyone else in this village. I will be deeply wounded."

I listened to her crying in the dark. My mother stood there, without responding, and I watched her hands gently caress Lingdi's hair. I saw the shimmer of tears on my mother's face, and then I heard her say, "All right. She can keep it."

Three years later I received a letter from my mother telling me that Lingdi was about to be married. Lingdi was over forty-three years old at the time. Her suitor was fifteen years older, a man who had been born and raised in our village, then moved to Shanghai, where he had become a successful manufacturer. He had four married daughters. His wife had died and left him alone. He wanted a wife from his home village, so he returned to Lishi.

Lingdi was told of the man, and she asked to be introduced to him. One afternoon he visited her. They talked all afternoon and into the evening. She prepared dinner, and the two sat outside her house talking most of the night. The next morning the man from Shanghai came to the village market alone, made purchases, and returned to Lingdi's house. They were not seen that day and that night. On the following day, again early in the morning, he walked to the market, bought a few items, and returned to Lingdi's home.

The next day he came to our house. He told my mother that he and Lingdi found they liked each other very much. (In the dialect of Lishi there is no word for love. In place of that, people use the words respect, like, and cherish.) He said, "We plan to marry next month, and we would like you to be the witness at our wedding."

My mother was surprised and delighted. "Good," was all she could say. "Good."

"Something else," he said. "About the divorce. You know the story."

"Yes," my mother admitted, and avoided looking into his eyes.

"Well, I want you to know that man was a lying bastard. And Lingdi has suffered for nearly twenty years because of it. Lingdi is a woman. All woman. More than that. She is a perfect woman."

I attended Lingdi's wedding. She was smiling and laughing like a girl again. She was happier than I had ever seen her before.

TWO 第二章 Winter

THE whisper of the guards slowly drew me from my warm memories back to the cold dreariness of the barracks room. I retraced in my mind the road that led me to this place. I saw now it had been clearly lined with warning signs. I was never blind to the warnings. But in thrall at that time to unguarded and innocent romantic optimism, I behaved as if I'd earned an exemption from the iron realities of the world in which I'd always lived. I was wrong.

On several occasions I had noticed a car with military license plates parked outside my dormitory at night, engine running, the occupants sitting stiffly inside. I began to receive disquieting telephone calls—the caller, upon hearing my voice, would hesitate, then hang up without saying a word. When I would return to my room after a brief walk, I would notice a pen or a book I'd placed in a certain way on the desk had been moved.

To an outsider any of these things might arouse suspicion. But there is no right to a private life in China, and we grow up with expectations of being under observation. Only a fine line separates the daily aggravations of being under general surveillance from those indicating one is under specific surveillance. But someone like me, trained as an intelligence officer, should always know the difference and take countermeasures.

I was changing at that time and wasn't thinking enough about the possible dire consequences of those changes. I was becoming increasingly optimistic about my future outside the PLA. I behaved like a child whose eyes had just opened and who was seeing the world for the first time.

I remember that looking at my reflection in the mirror one morning, I had the strange feeling that I truly was no longer Lieutenant Xu Meihong of the People's Liberation Army of China. That woman had become a stranger. I was just Xu Meihong, the naïve girl from the countryside who wanted desperately to live without restraints and to see all the wonders of the world. But my timing was all wrong. And in China, timing is often the difference between life and death.

My fate was sealed the moment I first saw the American walking so confidently with his long stride and his big grin down a hallway to his office. When we passed, he said hello, and just for a second we looked into each other's eyes.

Yet the roots of my trouble went back to my earliest days in the military academy, when my childish ideals began to fracture. The American merely had the misfortune to be pulled into the world of my disillusionment and longing. In his humor and compassion, his loyalty, fearlessness, and optimism, I saw a whole new world. In him and through him I found hope. For that we both paid a price.

IN THE summer of 1981, when I was seventeen, I became one of an elite group of twelve girls selected from throughout China to train and study in one of the most prestigious military intelligence schools in the country—the PLA Institute for International Relations in Nanjing. It was an experiment. China's relations with the United States were expanding. There was a greater need for intelligence officers proficient in English. Specially trained young women might have the capability of making contacts and gathering intelligence from Americans when male operatives could not. If the experiment looked promising, others were to follow in our path.

During our first day we were told that after graduation from the institute, some from our group would be assigned to China's foreign embassies. In that capacity they would serve in uniform. An elite few would be sent abroad to become "bottom-sinking fish." They would live as civilians and, like fish at the bottom of the sea, blend into the general population. Some would be called back within a few years, having made contacts and cultivated "friends" of China.

One or two, however, would be required to keep new identities all their lives, marrying, taking foreign citizenship, and starting families that would be useful in the next generation or even the one after that. These were "heroes without names," because their true undertaking could never be revealed even to their families and friends in China. This sacrifice—leaving our mother country and lives behind while still secretly embracing old loyalties—was, short of dying for the nation, the ultimate act of heroism.

After we were told of our probable future assignments, we were read lines from a poem by the American poet Robert Frost:

I shall be telling this with a sigh
Somewhere ages and ages hence:
Two roads diverged in a wood, and I—
I took the one less traveled by,
And that has made all the difference.

Those words, we were informed, described us. The twelve of us had taken the road less traveled, and it would make all the difference not only in our own lives but in the life and future of China. We were instructed to commit the poem to memory. We never learned anything about the author other than his name and nationality. We believed the poem was specifically about patriots like us. For years I thought Robert Frost was one of the greatest Communist poets who ever lived.

In our barracks we talked with great excitement about our journey together down the road less traveled and about the inevitable day when we would be separated from each other, a few to go underground and never to be seen again by the others. We were intoxicated by the realization that we were heroes in training. We were young and red, and we believed we could do anything.

Then something went wrong. It happened gradually, over the course of several years. We discovered that the longer we served in the PLA, the more our patriotic passion cooled. When we witnessed firsthand the sham machinations and corruption of the gods of our youth—the Communist Party and the PLA—our crisis of faith commenced.

Naturally, we sought to conceal such feelings from our superiors as well as from each other. The twelve of us marched and worked and studied and showered and slept side by side by side. We sang the old revolutionary songs and mouthed the requisite oaths of allegiance. We clung desperately to the faith of our youth when we felt it fading, and we feared that without it, we were nothing.

THE overseas assignments the twelve of us expected were not made following graduation. The world had changed, we were told, and further training was required. So in the summer of 1985 we twelve went our separate ways.

I was assigned to remain at the institute in Nanjing and became an aide to a brigadier general. In the spring of 1988 I married a former classmate. My new husband also served as an aide to a general—the president of the National Defense University in Beijing. Assignment to the NDU was often a stepping-stone to a higher position within the PLA. My husband and I lived nine hundred kilometers apart and saw each other twice a year, but we wrote every day. We counted ourselves lucky. Some classmates stationed in Tibet were unable to see their spouses for years at a time.

In the summer of 1988, I was selected to study for one year at the Center for Chinese and American Studies, a two-year-old educational joint venture of Nanjing University and The Johns Hopkins University. The center was located within its own walled compound adjacent to Nanjing University.

At the center Chinese and American students and faculty shared a large complex of classrooms, offices, assembly halls, and dormitory rooms, as well as a library and cafeteria. The Chinese students were customarily mid-career professionals chosen by their work units to study English and other academic subjects with a small group of distinguished visiting American instructors. American students at the center were almost all young graduate students, but also included a few military officers, who came to study Chinese language and history with Chinese instructors.

To the Chinese students at the center the facilities were luxurious. Each student room had a private telephone, a Western-style bathroom, and hot water part of each day. We were unaccustomed to such conveniences. But for the Americans, I learned, conditions in the center were considered spartan.

One month after I began my studies at the center, I received my stars and became a first lieutenant in the PLA. While I resided at the center, I reported back to my institute each weekend. I continued to carry out other regular duties. I also worked closely with my commanding general, helping plan his trips to Beijing and Shanghai and assisting him in the composition of his briefings, reports, and speeches.

At the center, for the first time in my life I came into close contact with American students and professors who spoke freely about politics and cultural values, who joked openly about their political leaders unafraid of retribution, who had great hopes and few fears for either the present or the future. The first time an American professor told a disparagingly humorous story about one of

Left: *Meihong at age seventeen, during the summer of 1981, before she joined the army.*
Middle: *January 1988, Meihong in her winter uniform at the Institute for International Relations.*
Bottom: *September 1988, Meihong newly arrived at the Center for Chinese and American Studies as a civilian student.*

America's founding fathers, we were stunned. After showing us a copy of a famous painting of George Washington crossing the Delaware River, he asked us why we thought General Washington stood up in the boat. The students spent several minutes guessing. When they finally asked for the "correct" answer, the professor told us, "Because he knew if he sat down, someone would hand him an oar." The students were dead silent. The professor said it was a joke. "Maybe it just doesn't translate well," he said.

Participating day after day in discussions with these Americans, reading and socializing with them, I felt something inside myself coming loose. I began to laugh at some of the absurdities of the world and lost my sense of awe of people in power. I felt I was finding my own identity. I began to think critically and independently. Like all Chinese students, I'd always mistaken memorization for education. I thought there was one truth and one way and one system that was best for all people. Now nothing was as simple as it once was.

During the last week of November in 1988 three of my colleagues at the center were summoned to our institute. They were called individually before the commanding general and asked detailed questions about the center. When they returned, one of them came to my room. The general had called her aside and told her to tell me to come to the institute immediately. He further directed that I come to his living quarters rather than to his office.

ONE of the general's passions was coffee. He'd acquired a taste for it during one of his visits with a Chinese military delegation to the United States. At official banquets, when he was offered tea, he would place his hand over his cup and ostentatiously order coffee—"Just like the Americans," he'd say—black and unsweetened. The junior officers envied his cosmopolitan conceit.

When I arrived at the general's living quarters, he and his wife had just finished dinner. He led me to his study, and we sat down to talk in two overstuffed chairs facing each other. The general was a rising star in the PLA, and I felt privileged to serve under him.

His wife brought him a steaming cup of coffee. I accepted the glass of hot tea she offered me. She closed the door behind her upon leaving the room. The general slowly sipped his coffee. Not a word was spoken for a minute or two. Then he asked several detailed questions—questions about the food at the center, about the food servers and the domestic workers. Several of them reported regularly to the National Security Police, he reminded me. I told him I was aware of that. He wanted to know about the American students and teachers. What did I think of them?

Then he turned to questions about me. What were my thoughts? Who did I think was unusual? Interesting? Funny? Friendly? Unfriendly? Suspicious? Then he cleared his throat and said, "Let me tell you a story, Meihong. A true story."

He spoke in a slow, steady cadence, as if he were testifying rather than carrying on a conversation. "There is a student, a very beautiful young woman, who was studying at the Shanghai Foreign Languages Institute. A professor there, an American teaching English, noticed her. They talked often after class. She gave him tours of Shanghai. They went for long walks together, always talking and laughing. People saw them and watched them. She visited his apartment. She trusted him completely. This professor said that he had fallen in love with her. She responded that she too was in love. He promised to bring her to America and to marry her. But as she prepared to leave with him, suddenly she disappeared. Just disappeared! And he quickly left China without her."

The general paused and waited for my reaction. I didn't know what to say. Finally, weakly, I asked, "What happened?"

"Oh, the National Security Police discovered, just in time, that this 'professor' worked for the Central Intelligence Agency. And the young woman of course was not just any young woman. Her father is a PLA general. She herself is not that important, but she has access through her father to certain information and influential people that might be of interest to others. But now she's gone. Even her father doesn't know her fate." The general concluded, "A true story. I thought you should know."

"Why?" I asked. "Do I know this woman?"

"No," he said. "But this sort of thing happens. Young women can be naïve. There is a moment of weakness and something feels like romance, and then suddenly it's too late."

"Why are you telling me this, General?" I asked.

He said nothing for a moment. Then he said, "I don't know what has happened to you. What is it, Meihong? What has gone wrong?"

"Nothing is wrong, General," I answered instantly. "What in the world could be wrong? Everything is fine."

"You told no one your background, did you? You've not spoken to anyone about intelligence matters, have you? You're sure?"

I could not tell the general the truth. There was no way to explain my life or my feelings or my dreams or my actions to him. So I lied. "I don't think so," I replied. I pretended to be going back over my recent activities in my mind. "No. I'm sure I haven't."

"Really?" he asked. Then he warned, "Be very careful, Meihong. Very careful. These are dangerous times."

I tried to lighten the tone of the conversation. "General," I said, "you are too nervous. Maybe you drink too much coffee. I've made no mistakes, and nothing is going to happen to me!"

He quickly changed the subject. We talked about the celebration of American Thanksgiving at the center. Everyone had a wonderful time, I told him. We also were preparing for traditional American Christmas and New Year's Eve festivities.

There was still time to catch the last bus to the center. The general offered to accompany me to the bus stop. On the way, he again expressed his concern. "I need you to promise me that you will never betray me."

"Never," I answered in a whisper. "I am incapable of that."

"Tell me right now that you love your country, that you love the army, that you will never ever betray either of them," he said.

"Never!" I assured him.

The following afternoon I called my friend and former classmate at the Ministry of State Security. His secretary said he was unavailable. I called his direct personal line three times, and there was no answer.

I locked my door and braced a chair against the handle. Then I went through my letters, notes, and photographs, tore them to pieces, and flushed them down the toilet. After that I took a short walk to get some fresh air. It was cold and overcast. Half a block from the center I saw a military vehicle parked at the curb, with headlights off but the motor running.

I returned to the center by a different route.

IT WAS past midnight, the start of the second day of December. A gentle mist of rain was falling. As the minutes passed, the air outside became tinseled with sleet that hissed as it ricocheted off the concrete in the courtyard three stories below me. I stood at the window in my room watching for something, unsure of what it might be. A sound? A sign? A friend?

The sleet slowly became a light rain once more, then faded to a mist, and soon even the mist was gone. What time was it? I looked for that first familiar hint of indigo and coral at the edge of the blackness along the horizon. When I saw it, I'd know that another day was about to take flight, and I could feel secure. But everything was dark.

I leaned forward and carefully rested my head against the icy glass of the window. What could have gone wrong? Someone must have betrayed me. Who? How? For what? I went over it all once more. The good soldier remembers every detail.

I slipped under the covers on my bed. I told myself to relax and stop worrying. Finally I fell asleep.

DURING my English-language class the next morning I was unable to concentrate. I told the instructor I didn't feel well and returned to my room to be alone. In the early afternoon I received a call from a friend from my home village who was studying at Nanjing University. She asked if she could visit me. I said I'd welcome her company. I told her the guard at the gate to the center could just ring my room when she arrived.

A short time later I was interrupted by a soft knock at my door. My heart raced. Was this it? When I asked who it was, I heard a familiar and welcome voice whisper, "Me."

I unlocked the door and let in the American. I sat on the bed, and he pulled the desk chair across the room and sat facing me. We looked at each other without speaking. Sometimes words are unnecessary. A peace settled in whenever we were together. In a short time we had shared many peaceful moments, many words, and many secrets.

"You're quiet today," he said at last. "What's wrong? I was told you walked out of your morning class."

I wasn't feeling well, I told him. I was uneasy. Something was wrong. I would have to account for some of my actions in the center. I was absolutely sure of it. So I was trying to prepare myself.

He noticed I was shaking. He reached out and took my hands in his and told me to stop worrying. "This has to be your imagination. You're probably overreacting to something."

I reached up and gently pulled his face next to mine so we could whisper into each other's ear. "I think my room may be bugged. They probably know everything we talked about."

"No. They couldn't. But even if they did, what's the problem? You've done nothing wrong," he said.

"Do you remember the list you made with the American professors after your first week here? The one we laughed at so much."

"Yes: 'One Hundred Things That Can Kill You in China.' "

"You remember what was on it?"

"Yes. Let me see. It began with the air. Then the water. Then the food. The electrical system. The heating system. The open sewers. Missing manhole covers near broken streetlights. Loaded buses with their lights and engines off, freewheeling down hills at night."

"You forgot something important. I should have told you to add it to your list."

"What is it?"

"Words kill you here too."

"Words," he repeated. He didn't go on, and I knew he was starting to appreciate my concern. "Words," he said again, and sighed. "Is there anything I can do?"

I thought, Can you turn back the clock three months? Can you grow wings and fly me out of here? Can you take me to Hong Kong or America? To some safe place? But I didn't say any of this.

"Yes, there is something I think you'll have to do," I said.

"I'll do anything to help you out of whatever trouble you're in."

"When you leave this room today, I don't think we'll see each other again."

"That's not going to happen!" he said, interrupting me.

"Oh, for once will you just listen? If I am not here tomorrow, I want you to promise that you won't ask about me and you won't try to find me. If you do, you will only cause more trouble for both of us. I want you to promise that you'll forget about me."

"That's not possible. You can't ask me that now."

"Just promise me. Someday you'll understand. If they come for me tonight or tomorrow night, you have to forget me. It is the only thing you can do to save yourself. Deny everything. Lie. Get rid of my notes to you. Tear up my pictures." I started to cry.

"You're not making sense, Meihong. This is crazy."

"No. This is China. These things happen all the time. You just don't understand China."

"Right after we met, you told me I understood China like no other American."

"Sometimes I'm wrong. You don't understand. I don't think you can. People with round-trip tickets and blue passports can leave whenever they want to. They can escape. I made some mistakes—bad mistakes. So you have to take my word for it now. I promise you, if you forget me, I will never forget you. It's the only way."

"It makes no sense."

"Promise me, I beg you. If you care for me, you'll promise."

After a long pause he responded, "Okay, I promise."

Neither of us spoke for several minutes. I was crying, and because our faces were touching and we were whispering into each other's ear, my tears ran down the side of his face.

He wiped them away with the back of his hand. Then he fumbled with his wrist, unlocking the clasp on a slim silver bracelet he wore. As he removed it, he whispered, "Now it's your turn. You promise me something." He carefully wrapped the bracelet around my left wrist and locked the clasp. "My daughters gave this to me before I came here. They asked me to remember them every time I looked at it. They said it would bring me good luck. It did. I found you. Now you keep it and let it bring you good luck. You need it more than I do now."

"I can't take this—it's from your daughters."

"Yes, you can. They'd want you to have it. But this is only a loan. I want you to give it back to me someday. After everything turns out all right, then you give it back to me! Promise me that?"

"You don't understand. I really don't think we'll be seeing each other again."

"I think you're wrong. This will all blow over. In a week we'll be laughing about it. But right now just promise me," he said.

"Okay," I replied. "I promise. Someday I'll return this to you." I didn't believe my own words, but that's what he needed to hear. "Tell me," I asked, "are all Americans like you? Are they all equally incapable of seeing reality?"

"I certainly hope so," he said, and flashed one of his silly smiles that always made me smile back.

One of the things I loved about this man was his ability to dismiss the darker possibilities of almost any situation. He expected good things to happen. He'd seen too many happy endings in American movies, and he'd started to believe them. In China we don't believe such nonsense. If something has a happy ending, we're surprised.

I covered his hand with my own and whispered, "You should go now. This won't look good if someone stops by."

"Okay. See you in the morning." He stood, stepped to the door, gave me a carefree wink, and mouthed the words, "Bye-bye." I mouthed the same words back. I held up my wrist with the bracelet and forced a smile. Then he stepped into the hall, quietly closed the door, and was gone.

I read the same page over and over again and finally gave up and dropped the book on the floor. I examined the bracelet, ran it back and forth through my fingers, and said a silent prayer. My prayer was interrupted by the loud ring of my telephone. It was the gatekeeper at the entrance to the center. "Miss Xu," he said, "you have someone here for you. Can you come down?"

My friend from Nanjing University, I thought. "I'll be right there," I told him.

I decided, since this would only take a moment, not to put on a jacket. I hurried down the stairs and across the lobby. Two American students stood talking near the door. One cautioned me good-naturedly, "Hey, Xu Meihong, it's freezing out there. You better put on a jacket, or you'll catch your death."

I laughed. "Thanks for the warning. But I'll be back in a minute."

Outside, I dashed to the front gate. My friend was nowhere in sight. Then I saw a military staff car parked at the curb only a few feet away. Dark curtains were pulled shut around the rear windows. A fellow officer from my institute stepped out—Major Song.

"Major?" I called to him. "What are you doing here?"

"I've come to bring you back to the institute," he said. "There is a meeting you need to attend. It's very important. Very important." He appeared both somber and uneasy.

"Okay," I assured him. "But I need a minute. I have a friend I'm supposed to meet here. I want to leave a message for her with the gatekeeper, and then let me get my coat."

"We don't have any time," he said, reaching out and lightly grasping my arm. "And there is a coat for you in the car."

I suddenly felt sick. I knew he was lying to me. I noticed his nervousness and felt a pang of pity for him. He was a personal friend as well as a fellow officer, and this was his official assignment—to get me into the car and to take me somewhere. Who better, after all, to help extricate someone calmly from a building than a friend? All of us in military intelligence had become practitioners of duplicity. It was standard operating procedure—the art of betrayal. Now, as I sensed the door of my trap closing, I felt sorry and ashamed for both of us.

Major Song quickly opened the back door to the car and motioned for me to get inside. I thought for a moment about breaking his grasp and running away, but it was too late for that. There was no place to run or hide. Not anymore.

Major Song got in and sat beside me, then locked his door and signaled to the driver to go. The car proceeded for only half a block before pulling to the curb. Two uniformed men trotted out from behind a wall. I recognized them—Colonel Meng Fan Yan, who was in charge of security at the institute, and his aide, a captain. The colonel got into the car beside the driver; the captain got in next to me. We sped off again.

I knew precisely what was happening because I'd been privy to "extractions" like this before. Someone under suspicion for a crime was seized, usually at night, without witnesses around. The Americans in the center had been correct—I'd gone outside without a jacket, and I'd caught my death.

Suddenly the nervousness and anxiety I'd felt growing inside me for days started to wane. There was no longer an unknown to be imagined and feared. What I felt instead was resignation and acceptance and a sudden clarity of vision.

We drove out into the countryside. I knew my captors would closely observe my behavior, remember every word I said, and relate it to others for their common enjoyment. Each would also write a detailed report. I didn't want them to report that I was afraid or that I cowered. If I was going to die tonight—and that was a possibility—then I would make no plea for mercy or compassion.

If I was asked to name a name to save myself, I would not do it. If I was asked to tell the truth to save myself, I would lie. If I was asked to lie to save myself, I would tell the truth. If I was condemned to death, I would go to that death with final sweet memories of life.

We pulled onto a road that led to a military base, surrounded by a high wall topped with tangled barbed wire. Four armed sentries stood at a post outside the gate. They snapped to attention when they saw our car approach. The colonel rolled down his window and handed one of the sentries a document. Then they pushed the gate open. We drove past a dozen darkened barracks before finally stopping at one that had lights on inside.

I was escorted into the building. Several guards holding rifles were waiting inside. They surrounded me as we walked down a long dimly lit hallway to the far end of the building. The colonel knocked on a door. It was opened, and I was led inside. The only furnishings were four bare military beds.

Three female soldiers waiting in the room snapped to attention. Surprise registered on their faces when they saw me. Two of the women I knew by name. The eldest, Li Xia, was a major in her mid-thirties. We'd worked together on various assignments. The youngest, Xiao Zhang, was an enlisted soldier who served as a switchboard operator at my institute.

The colonel pointed to the bed farthest from the door and told me to sit down. Then he summoned Li Xia out into the hall. I asked Xiao Zhang and the other guard, "Do either of you have an extra jacket I could wear? I'm freezing." They looked at each other, then shook their heads. They seemed terrified.

The colonel and Li Xia stepped back into the room. "This is where you will stay for now," Colonel Meng informed me. "Do not try to leave the room unaccompanied. If you do, it will make things much worse than they already are. Li Xia is in charge in this room. If you have anything to say, address her. The more you cooperate, the sooner everyone goes home."

"Am I under arrest?" I asked.

"You will know in due time."

"Wait," I protested. "If I am *not* under arrest, I have the right to move about, to leave this room or this post. I too am a PLA officer. Do I need to remind you of that, Colonel?"

The colonel studied me for a moment. "Right," he said. "You are in the army. You must obey your senior officers. Stay here. Do what I tell you. Get some rest. You have things to do." He was angry, and he made no effort to conceal it. "And if you don't mind, Xu Meihong," he barked, intentionally omitting my rank, "keep your mouth shut unless you are asked your opinion." He spun around, marched out, and closed the door behind him. Li Xia turned the bolt lock on the door with a key fastened to her belt.

The other women were dressed in trousers, blouses, sweaters, tunics, and gloves. Their long underwear showed at the cuffs of their pants and tunics. They could see I was trembling from the cold. Yet no one offered me a jacket or sweater. It was all right. I was from the countryside. I could suffer without protest. If this was going to be a test of wills, I wanted to win it.

I thought of the American. Had he destroyed my notes? At that moment was he looking for me to see if I was feeling better? Did he still believe that all of this would have a happy ending?

I felt the silver bracelet around my wrist and gently turned it back and forth between my fingers.

THREE

True Lies

I MADE up my mind to contest every allegation made against me. In defending myself, I could not rely on the truth. It could neither save me nor set me free. The Chinese Communist Party determines what is true and what is not in China. Party leaders may declare that they seek to discover truth from facts, but they really mean they will find facts that fit the predetermined Party truth. When necessary, facts are invented.

When someone is accused of a crime in China, he is assumed to be guilty until proven innocent. When the system is working as expected, an arrest is a prelude to a confession. Someone who initially refuses to confess is likely to be coerced. Acknowledging one's errors and naming one's accomplices are the recognized mandatory first steps on the road to rehabilitation.

I took a road less traveled by.

I SAT silently with my three guards for an hour before I became aware that my stomach was growling from hunger. I turned to Li Xia and called out, "Report!"—the formal equivalent of requesting permission to speak. "I'm hungry," I told her. "I would like something to eat."

The three women carried on a frantic whispered conversation. Finally Li Xia said, "Not yet."

About half an hour later there was a sharp knock on the door.

Li Xia unlocked and opened it. The colonel and his aides entered. I stood up slowly, saluted, and made a point of looking directly into the colonel's eyes. Without any preliminaries he began to read in a shrill, piercing voice from a document he held chest-high. "I am informing you, Lieutenant Xu Meihong, on behalf of the military headquarters of the People's Liberation Army in Beijing, that, first, you are charged with endangering state security and, second, you are ordered to cooperate fully with us or to suffer the consequences. You know what those consequences are, don't you?"

I didn't reply.

Suddenly he transformed himself from a stern accuser into an avuncular officer. "Do you have any comments, Xu Meihong?"

"There has been a mistake, Colonel," I told him. "You know I would never endanger state security. Someone has lied about me."

"Let's look for the truth. There is a chance that the charges against you are incorrect. That's unlikely, but sometimes mistakes happen. You can help us uncover the mistake and correct it." He flashed an almost reptilian smile. "I saw you when you first came to the institute. You are a good girl and a good soldier and a patriot."

His sentimental evocation of my background, his effusion of concern and of sympathy were, given the charges he'd just read against me, ironic, to say the least. But like most public officials in China, the colonel was completely devoid of a sense of irony.

"Think about what you have done, and later tonight you can tell me everything. Then tomorrow you may return to the center and to your studies."

He made a quick about-face and left the room, closely followed by his two aides. Li Xia accompanied the men and shut the door behind her. Less than an hour later she returned with several containers of food—four small bowls of rice with fried vegetables—and a large thermos of hot water. She had a military tunic and a thin cotton coverlet slung over her shoulder. Without saying a word, she dropped the tunic and coverlet on the bed next to me.

The others ate eagerly—they were as hungry as I was. I picked up the bowl of rice and ate some, but my appetite diminished as my stomach turned to knots from the colonel's words. I placed the bowl and chopsticks on the floor, poured myself a cup of hot water, and held it between my hands to warm them. The guards finished eating. After a while Xiao Zhang dozed off in a sitting position.

I precipitated a crisis when I turned to Li Xia and announced, "Report! I have to go to the toilet."

She jumped up and made a quick circuit of the room, looking for a chamber pot or a bucket. There was none. A crisis ensued. Xiao Zhang was shaken awake and told I had to pee. She looked at me as though this was a strange and exotic practice.

Li Xia left the room. Soon she returned with the colonel.

"You have to go to the toilet?" he asked me.

"Yes, badly," I confirmed.

He summoned his aides. Then our squad of seven soldiers—four women and three men—proceeded to a walled outside toilet a short distance from the building. All three women entered the enclosed area with me. I spied a line of holes in a long slab of concrete. I expected to be left alone at that point, but the guards remained next to me, and Li Xia impatiently ordered, "Pee!"

"Could I have some privacy?" I asked.

"Pee! We're freezing."

I did as she ordered.

Back in the room again, I buttoned my tunic to the neck and wrapped myself in the thin coverlet I'd been given. I leaned against the concrete wall and finally fell asleep.

BEFORE dawn there was a knock on the door. The major was allowed in by Li Xia. He escorted me to a room at the opposite end of the hall. The interrogation room was small and lit by a single overhead light fixture. A square table with four chairs was placed directly under it. Heavy curtains were drawn over the window. The colonel was seated when I entered the room. The other officers also sat at the table, and I was told to sit opposite the colonel. A tape recorder and a thick green folder stuffed with papers were on the table.

The colonel initiated the session. "Your name?"

"You know my name, Colonel. We're longtime associates. We're good friends. You reminded me of that last night."

He was thrown off guard for a second by my outburst of sarcasm. The atmosphere that he intended to create—the contrite prisoner and the capable interrogator—was shattered.

"This is an official proceeding," he shot back. "You must answer the questions. Now, your name is Xu Meihong. Is that right?"

I inhaled deeply to calm my nerves and then spoke softly as I exhaled. "Yes. I am Lieutenant Xu Meihong of the People's Liberation Army of the People's Republic of China."

"Where were you born, and what are your parents' names?"

"What does that have to do with anything?"

"Damn you!" he shouted, and slapped his hand on the table. "I ask the questions, not you. You had food last night. You drank hot water. You pissed in a toilet. That was all at my sufferance. I can stop the food. I can stop the water. You can piss in your pants from now on, for all I care. That is up to you. Can't you see I am trying to help you? Answer the questions as they are asked and spare yourself and your family unnecessary suffering."

He thought it important to remind me that those charged with crimes never suffer alone—for centuries in China, punishment was meted out at many levels of one's family and friends. Just as there is no private life, there is no private punishment either.

"I was born in Jiangsu Province," I responded. "In the village of Lishi, near the city of Danyang."

"Your date of birth?"

"December 6, 1963."

I fell into the monotonous staccato rhythm of the session, answering each question, waiting and watching for places where the colonel tried to set his traps, trying to avoid them. When he was finished with the vital statistics, he shifted his tone to something he must have believed sounded friendly. "Okay," he began. "Now I want you to tell me everything about your life in the Center for Chinese and American Studies. Begin."

"What could I possibly tell you about the center? You read the incoming and outgoing mail. The telephone lines are tapped. You have people on the housekeeping and administrative staff reporting to you. What can I add that you don't already know?"

"That's what I am about to find out," he said. "You tell me everything that happened there."

"Everything? All right. I came to the center in September 1988. I was assigned to room 213. I'm enrolled in three courses—two in American history and society and one in colloquial English." I droned on, providing him every imaginable banal detail of life in the center—classes, conversations, hot water, cold water, bad food, good food, parties, music, movies, speakers, library rules, leaking windows and walls, visiting delegations from the United States or Beijing. I tried to miss nothing, no matter how irrelevant.

Eventually the recorder clicked off. One of the officers removed the cassette and inserted a new one.

Suddenly the colonel stood, drummed his fingertips impatiently on the table, and barked, "Stop it! I think you know what I want to hear from you. Tell me. Now." He switched off the tape recorder. "We are here because you let yourself get into trouble. These dilatory tactics of yours won't work with me. Are your ears clean? Can you hear me, Xu Meihong?"

When he finished, we sat looking at each other for a long time, as if taking each other's measure. There wasn't a sound in the room. At last the colonel leaned forward and switched on the recorder again. "Tell me about the people at the center."

"Well, most of the people in the center are nice except one," I volunteered. "That person is the administrative assistant to the Chinese codirector. He snoops. I think he goes into the rooms of the Chinese students when they're in class. He has keys. He solicits sexual favors from the Chinese female students and staff."

"Go on," the colonel directed, not even bothering to ask the individual's name.

I went down the list of names of Chinese students and faculty members at the center. The colonel interrupted. "I am more interested in the Americans," he said. "Tell me about the instructors. Who teaches the courses you take?"

I named the language instructor. The colonel was unmoved. Then I provided other names and at last said the name he had been waiting for. I struggled to say it in an even and dispassionate way.

Before I could move on, the colonel withdrew a blank page from his folder and pushed it across the table to me, pulled a pen from his pocket, and asked, "Write his name down here, will you?"

I wrote the name of the American in both English and Chinese. Then I pushed the paper back to him.

The colonel studied it carefully and grinned. He showed it to the others. "Mr. Larry Engelmann. A German name."

"Originally, yes. The family was from Germany, three generations ago."

"You know that? Family history? How familiar are you with this man?" he asked.

"He's a friend."

"A friend? A *good* friend would you say?"

"A friend," I answered.

The colonel studied me closely for some indication that I was uncomfortable with this topic. I continued to look straight into his eyes, my heart pounding so hard, I feared they might hear it. I did not want to say that name again. Saying it seemed a violation of trust, a breach of something I considered sacred.

He asked, "How well do you know Professor Chu?"

"She's a friend too. She's a *good* friend. She teaches courses in politics and diplomacy. She is Chinese too, as you know. Hong Kong–born."

"Who else do you know at the center? The Americans."

"I know every American faculty member there. I know the American students too. Do you want to know about them?"

"No," he said in a voice indicating both boredom and exhaustion. "No, I don't." He clicked off the tape recorder, sat back, and pushed himself away from the table. "That was a good start. You talked a bit this morning, and it was helpful. I think we will make rapid progress." I had no idea what he meant. "You know transcripts of these sessions will be typed and you will be required to sign each page to verify they are true?"

"I understand," I assured him.

I was escorted back to my room.

I told Li Xia I'd like to wash myself. She and the other two women escorted me to a tiny washroom next to our room. It had a cold-water spigot over a cement sink. I rinsed my face and hands. Then I brushed my teeth with my finger, rinsed my mouth, and we returned to the room. The women talked in hushed tones and agreed that one of them would go to a nearby building to get food.

I was physically and emotionally drained, but my anxiety kept my adrenaline high. Replaying the interrogation session in my mind, I wondered what the colonel actually knew and what evidence he possessed. If the charge against me was breaching state security and if the colonel possessed what he considered to be proof of my crime, then I should have been executed within hours of my arrest. But I was still alive, and that led me to believe that the colonel did not have all the evidence he was seeking. He consequently needed a confession, which I was absolutely determined never to give him. And he was probably seeking co-conspirators. He might tell me I was charged with a capital crime in order to terrify me into trading names or information for my life. I decided I would never do that.

I contemplated the character of the colonel. He may have been an idealistic young recruit into the PLA, the same as I had been. But his reaction to the hypocrisy and corruption around him was to join it rather than correct it. He represented everything I loathed about the PLA and the Party.

If, as the great military philosopher Sun-tzu wrote, the first rules of warfare are to know your enemy and to know yourself, I had an enormous advantage. I knew the colonel. He had power over me for the moment. All he knew about me, however, was what he read in the folder he held, and that was no longer me.

I didn't know how much time I had. The questioning might continue for days and weeks. At the institute we'd studied China's wars and interrogation methods and practiced them on each other in order to learn how to question and how to avoid answering one's questioner; however, a prisoner could be made to confess to anything. Everyone has a breaking point far short of death. Prisoners only need to be convinced that death is imminent and that all that separates them from doom is confession and cooperation.

I prayed for timely help from my friends in the military. There were officers above me who now must be worried about my words. They might be in danger, so they must be working to find me, to free me before the danger spread to become a disaster. Either that, or they might work for my quick elimination. That too would bring them a certain security. But things as they were at the moment—in a standoff—could not continue for long.

THE next morning, December 4, I was escorted to the interrogation room again. As I sat down in the chair facing the colonel, I sensed a wave of self-doubt and vulnerability sweep over me. I wondered how long I might resist my interrogators.

The colonel switched on the tape recorder. "Did you eat?"

"Yes."

"Do you have anything to tell me now?"

"No."

There was a very long pause. Then suddenly, seething with anger, the colonel leaped to his feet and kicked his chair away from the table. He leaned across and put his face only inches from mine. "I don't think you heard me last night. I think you'd better clean your ears." Before I could reply or react, he slapped my face hard. There was a sharp crack, and my head snapped to the side. I tasted blood in my mouth, and my eyes teared. My ears were ringing. I turned back to face him again. I said nothing. I glared straight into his eyes with as much contempt as I could convey.

"Now can you hear me?" he bellowed. He raised his hand.

I kept my lips sealed tightly together so he could not see the blood in my mouth. I was tempted to spit it in his face, but I decided to resist the temptation. He had blundered. I felt a deep hatred for him bubbling up inside me. Hatred gave me strength.

The colonel slowly lowered his hand, turned, picked up his chair, and sat down again. His tantrum intrigued me. I guessed that he was working under a deadline to get the information his superiors required. If my friends and fellow officers were looking for me, he did not have unlimited time. The more time I wasted by leading him down meaningless paths, the better for me.

I listened to the colonel breathing heavily. "Take her back," he told his aides.

As we left the room, I turned and saw him start to rewind the tape in order to record over this session. He wanted no record of it.

EARLY the next morning, December 5, I was brought back to the interrogation room.

The colonel clicked on the recorder and began the session. "Do you recognize this man?" he asked, pushing a photograph of the American across the table. I'd seen the photo before—it was used on the ID issued to faculty members.

"Yes. That's Larry Engelmann," I replied.

"How well do you know him?"

"As well as I know any of the teachers at the center."

"Did you ever write letters to him? Notes?"

"No."

The colonel opened a folder. I could see some of my handwritten notes. "What are these, then?" he asked.

"I have no idea. Probably forgeries of my handwriting."

He laid the folder on the floor, next to his chair. "Did this foreigner—or should I say this *American*—ever write to you?"

"No."

"Are you absolutely sure? Think before you respond."

"I'm sure."

There was a long silence. "There is no need to lie. When you stop lying, we can leave. Nobody forged your name to those notes. They were taken from the apartment of the American."

"If you are sure, why do you need my confirmation?"

His demeanor softened again, and he spoke like a forgiving father to a daughter who had strayed. "We trusted you. Now we need your help. If you give us the truth, nothing will happen to you. I promise. You know that we have your best interests at heart. Please tell me more about this . . . *American*."

I thought I should give him something at this point and use up time. By providing some information and watching his response, I might determine what he knew. "I don't know him well. I just knew him for three months. We met the first time in September."

"Well, tell us what you do know about him."

"Okay. I believe he used to work in California. He is a history professor. He has written two books, and he is writing a third."

"And the book he is now writing—what is it about?"

"Vietnam."

"Vietnam? Interesting," the colonel observed. "Did you ever talk to him about Vietnam?"

"No."

"He writes letters to Vietnam, to the Ministry of Defense."

"I wouldn't know."

"Do you know about his family?

"Not much. He once spoke of his daughters in Chicago."

"What else does he do?"

"He helps Chinese students. When he found we had no textbooks in the library, he wrote to the American publisher. We all received free books thanks to him."

"Anything else?"

"Yes. He promised to take us to the Jinling Hotel for hamburgers and french fries. He said, I remember, that we could never understand America until we ate hamburgers and french fries."

"Hamburgers and french fries? How generous. Is he a millionaire in disguise?" The colonel and his two aides chuckled at this sarcastic suggestion.

"Maybe he's just . . . different."

The colonel and his aides burst into laughter when I said that word. "Yes," he said. "Now we're getting somewhere. He is different, as you say. Do you think he is just here to teach?"

"No. He also wants to learn about China."

My words elicited another round of laughter.

"Yes, yes, yes. I am sure he wants to learn about China. Did he ask you to help him?"

"Yes. He asks questions all the time of the Chinese students."

"But mostly he asks you, correct?"

"I don't know why he would ask me more than others."

"Perhaps because of your position. Did you ever consider that?"

"He has no idea what my position is."

The colonel riffled through another folder and removed a photograph of me in my military uniform that the American had taken. "Let me get this straight—he doesn't know what your position is?"

I stared at the photo. There was nothing I could say.

"Xu Meihong, of course he is *different.* His pose as a professor is his second occupation. He has been working for American intelligence for years. Teaching is just his cover."

"You are wrong. If there were an American agent in the center, it could be almost anyone but him. He doesn't speak Chinese. He can't get around Nanjing on his own because of language difficulties. He couldn't possibly be anything other than what he appears to be."

"Would it surprise you to learn he speaks Mandarin fluently?"

Now it was my turn to laugh. "Who told you that? He speaks no more than ten words of Mandarin and mispronounces those constantly."

"He was pretending. Didn't you ever think that?"

My crime was to befriend an American intelligence agent? If this was their only charge, then the colonel had to be depending on inept eyewitnesses, who were lying or stupid.

"Okay, let's not waste time today. First, we know that he works for the CIA. We know that he is here on an assignment, that he replaced someone who worked for American intelligence under the cover of being a teacher. He sought you out. And through you he met others. We think he is here to establish productive relationships and to . . . recruit! We believe he recruited you. But we also think he recruited people who are using you—other Chinese. That is why you are here.

"Think about it. You've known him for a short time. We have copies of his letters here. Did you know that he wrote to 'a friend' and invited him to China? He told the friend he'd found a good translator and guide—you. We believe this man is his supervisor. He has no children. The two people he writes to are co-workers."

The story was getting loonier by the minute. I was surprised at how convinced the colonel was of every word he said. I'd seen pictures of the daughters, their letters. I'd been in his room when he'd received a telephone call from one of them. Was that an act?

"We have evidence indicating you are involved with this man—how shall I say it?—intimately. Isn't that true?"

"If you know me, as you insist that you do, Colonel, then you know that is not true."

"But I do know that this *is* true. And your husband knows too."

I felt myself redden with indignation and embarrassment. I glimpsed for a moment another path they were sure to follow in this ominous fantasy.

"Your husband is currently an officer in the PLA, an aide to a general at the National Defense University in Beijing, correct?"

"Yes."

The colonel grinned. "And your husband has been in the United States. What a coincidence."

"What are you implying, Colonel?"

He clicked off the recorder. "You've been to the NDU before. You know what goes on. You know who the American is. You know how you met him. What do you think it means?" he asked.

When I refused to respond, he said, "Think about all we've talked about today, Xu Meihong. If you are honest, we can finish this business tomorrow. Cooperate, and you can leave."

THERE was no interrogation the next day. That evening, however, December 6, I heard a knock on the door. When Li Xia opened the door, there stood the colonel and his aides holding a large cake. They entered the room and shouted, "Happy Birthday, Meihong!"

I was dumbfounded. I was surrounded by six people singing "Happy Birthday" to me—the same six people I'd expected only days earlier to carry out my execution. They sang in English, then Chinese. They applauded, openly delighted at their success in surprising me.

The aides brought in a dozen containers of food. Tea was poured for everyone. The colonel toasted me and wished me a thousand years of life. Plates, chopsticks, and forks were distributed. The colonel lit the twenty-five candles on the cake and told me to make a wish before blowing them out. I did. But my wish didn't come true. When I opened my eyes, I was still in that cold room and the colonel was alive and standing beside me.

When we were almost finished eating the cake and the other food, the colonel announced, "Now, I have a special gift for you."

He handed me an unsealed envelope. I pulled out a letter and a card from my husband. On the card was a poem he'd composed for my birthday, telling me how he'd missed me and would always love me. In the brief letter he wrote, "Nothing has changed between us. I arrived in Nanjing to celebrate your birthday and was told you won't be available for a while. I hope you will cooperate with these people and help clarify the misunderstandings that have arisen. I know you have done nothing wrong. I won't leave Nanjing until I see you."

I was both touched and stung by the letter. At last I had contact with someone who cared for me and was waiting for me. His confidence in my innocence no doubt led him to encourage me to cooperate with my interrogators.

My determination buckled. For the first and last time I allowed my guards to see me cry openly. I placed the letter and poem back in the envelope and pressed it against my heart.

"We know that something unfortunate happened to you," the colonel said softly. "We were ordered to help you. Others in the military called for severe punishment, but your friends intervened. They said there must be some explanation." He added, "You are a twenty-five-year-old girl. When we were twenty-five, we too made mistakes. Everyone does. If you admit that you made a mistake and tell us what it was, everything will be all right."

Before the party ended, the colonel summoned me into the hallway. He spoke in a subdued and seemingly sincere voice. "I should not have struck you. I want to apologize now."

I knew, of course, that this too was another act. Everything he said—every word—was predictable. I said nothing, neither accepting nor rejecting his apology. I turned and went back into the room.

After the colonel and the other two men left, a few minutes later the three women tried to strike up a conversation with me. Wasn't my husband's letter lovely?

"Remember," Li Xia said, "he is still waiting for you. He was permitted three days of vacation. You're running out of time."

"Can you get me some clean underwear?" I asked her. "I've been here five days, and I'm still wearing the same underwear."

She was visibly shocked that I'd ignored her comments about my husband. Her sympathetic concern evaporated in a second. "No," she replied. "This will be over soon."

FOUR

First Love

THE interrogation resumed the next morning. The colonel pulled a fat new folder from his briefcase. "I have here three confessions," he said. "All signed. Two of them are true. But one is a lie."

He studied me closely as he spoke, waiting for my response when I realized what these documents were. "Do you remember these confessions?" he asked. "Do you recall your previous efforts to lie your way out of trouble? Your lies are part of your record, Xu Meihong. You wouldn't make that mistake of lying again, would you?"

THE colonel was correct. I had lied for love in the past.

When I entered the institute in 1981, all the new cadets went through an orientation session, during which we were warned of severe consequences of a relationship with a member of the opposite sex. The discovery of an amorous attachment would lead to expulsion from the institute and from the army. For three years the twelve young women of my class faithfully followed the rules. But things changed during our senior year. Some of my female classmates revealed that they had found boyfriends during the summer. They boasted that they wrote letters to them and mailed them off campus.

I fell in love for the first time in my life during my senior year. The object of my affection was a fellow cadet named Lin Cheng. He was handsome, tall and slim, the brightest student in his class, and a member of the Communist Party. He was expected to have a stellar future in the PLA.

Each morning the cadets jogged to the Yangtze River and back. I was usually the only woman to finish the entire distance. Lin Cheng led the men. I jogged close behind him, hoping he might hear my footsteps and turn around and say something.

At night in my quarters I whispered to Tao Hui, my closest girlfriend, about him.

"Maybe you should talk to him about your feelings," she suggested. "But be careful!"

I decided, in my romantic desperation, to send him a letter. I carefully composed several lines, telling him I had special feelings for him and that I wondered if he felt the same way about me. I carried it inside a book for several days. One evening I went to a classroom to study, and he was there alone. I didn't have the courage, however, to say hello. I dropped the letter on his desk and left.

The next evening I went to the same classroom. No one was there. I opened my assigned desk and took out my textbook. Inside it was an envelope.

Lin Cheng began by thanking me for my letter. He said he had wondered about my intentions, since he noticed me running behind him. "But we are not supposed to carry on a romantic relationship, not now. I really wish you would concentrate less on me and more on your work and on gaining Communist Party membership," he wrote. "We should be busy preparing for the future."

I read and reread the note, trying to find something hopeful in it. I wondered what he meant by the term "not now." I showed the note to Tao Hui. She advised me to forget him. "Do you know how many men would die to have a chance to speak to you privately?" she asked. There were two thousand male cadets and only twelve women. But I only cared for one man.

The next morning I ran behind Lin Cheng to the river and

back. He didn't acknowledge my presence. So in the afternoon I wrote to him again, saying I would wait for him forever.

The next day I received a reply. "We need to talk," he wrote.

That presented a challenge. To be safe, we'd have to meet far from campus. It took ten days and several more notes before we finally arranged a meeting.

We took separate buses to a park in Nanjing. We sat on a bench and talked nervously about the weather, our commanders, our classes, and our classmates. Finally, after several hours, we became bold enough to talk about our families and ourselves.

We talked into the evening, not noticing the passing hours, until the last bus to the institute had already gone. We had to walk back. We were supposed to be back in our barracks with lights out at ten p.m. We walked as fast as we could. When I had difficulty keeping up, Lin Cheng took my hand. It was the first time in my life I'd held hands with a man.

We did not arrive at the institute until two a.m. When we were close enough to see the lights of the sentry post, he turned and then, before saying a word, kissed me on the forehead.

If we tried to enter through the gate, he said, we'd be detained and held for questioning. But he'd heard that several nights earlier some cadets had sneaked in through a gap in the wire on the wall. We walked along the wall until he spotted the place. Lin Cheng helped me climb up first. I crawled through the gap and jumped down on the other side. He followed.

Before we parted, he kissed me again and squeezed my hand. Then we ran in opposite directions to our barracks. Tao Hui was waiting for me. "You have to be much more careful," she advised. "You have to cool down your heart." But I was in no mood to cool down. I was thinking only of the next time I'd see my love.

Lin Cheng and I continued to meet outside the institute whenever we felt it was safe. One afternoon we met in Nanjing. I wanted to buy some books, so we walked to an open-front bookstore. We were standing together, paging through some new books, when I saw an officer from our institute staring at us.

Early the next morning a guard appeared at my barracks and

summoned me to a meeting with my political commissar. Without any preliminary questions he asked me what I had been doing in Nanjing in the company of a male cadet. I told him I had no idea what he was talking about.

He warned me that I'd made a second mistake. First I had been with a male cadet off campus, and then I lied about it. "You are in serious trouble," he said. So I told him that I ran into Lin Cheng in the bookstore by accident.

He asked me to write down what happened and sign it. Then he dismissed me.

I needed to tell Lin Cheng what I'd done. But I couldn't find him. Other officers had summoned him to a separate interrogation. They were friendly, reminding him of his stature on the campus. They said they were willing to forgive almost any transgression should he tell them the truth. He said he would tell them everything and take full responsibility only if they would leave me alone. They consented. Lin Cheng admitted that we had gone into Nanjing together and that we were in love.

The next morning I spoke with him for a moment when we left class. I told him I'd lied in order to protect him. He told me he'd told the truth—told them he loved me—in order to protect me.

"What?" I asked. "You told them you love me?" He had never used the word love in our conversations before. So my anxiety at his confession was tempered by my delight at his revelation of his feelings for me. "How much trouble are we in?" I asked.

"None at all," he assured me. "Truth is the only way. I have their promise that they won't bother you. We have to trust the Party."

That afternoon I was summoned to a meeting with several officers. They waved my confession in my face. The word liar was thrown at me again and again. They demanded I write another confession, or both Lin Cheng and I would be expelled from the PLA and sent home. I panicked. I thought first of saving Lin Cheng's career. The whole thing had been my fault, I told them. I explained how I'd pursued him. I wrote a confession, telling them what I'd written in my first note, how we returned late and climbed over the wall, how we arranged to meet, and what we talked about.

Two days later I was dismissed as class leader for the female cadets. Both of my confessions, I was told, had become part of my permanent record.

Suspending or expelling Lin Cheng would imply that they had made a mistake in admitting him, and they were not prepared to go that far. They decided to settle for a public self-criticism from him that could serve as a deterrent to other cadets.

I managed to meet Lin Cheng in an empty classroom a few days later. We tearfully confessed our love for each other and vowed that we would be husband and wife someday no matter how hard others tried to pull us apart.

The next day the cadets were summoned to the assembly hall to hear the self-criticism of Lin Cheng. All the commanders and junior officers were present. Lin Cheng walked to the middle of the stage. I cringed as I waited to hear my name announced and feel the eyes of everyone in the room on me.

"I am sorry," Lin Cheng began. "Two weeks ago I went to Nanjing for personal reasons and returned late. Please accept my apology." He paused for a moment, looked around the audience, glanced at the officers, smiled weakly, and returned to his seat.

His statement lasted less than ten seconds. The political commissar was uncertain what to do next. A few minutes later he walked to the stage and dismissed us. Lin Cheng had turned his confession into a triumph for himself and for me, and the officers knew it. Yet he had done what had been required—made his public self-criticism. I knew at that moment why I loved him.

Lin Cheng paid for his defiant act. At the end of our senior year, while other class leaders were assigned to choice positions in Beijing, Shanghai, and Guangzhou, he was sent to Taiyuan—the capital of Shanxi Province—to teach English in a military school for submarine officers. It was not a prestigious institution and did not grant degrees. His future no longer seemed promising.

When I was assigned to stay in Nanjing and work at the institute, Lin Cheng and I dreaded the approaching separation. Each time we met, we talked of marriage. But the PLA had its rules—women had to be twenty-four and men twenty-five before they could marry. I was twenty-two at the time, and he was twenty-three. We vowed to marry in two years.

In early December, 1987, we reached the age required by the PLA for marriage. When I told my commanding general of my plan to marry, he was unusually pleased. As a wedding gift to us, he said, he would use his connections to get Lin Cheng transferred to Beijing. He added that he expected to be transferred to the capital himself within a year and that he would keep me as his aide so Lin Cheng and I could finally be united.

The general succeeded in getting Lin Cheng assigned as the foreign-affairs assistant to the president of the NDU. I learned a short time later that the general had been working with others for several years to put promising young officers in influential positions, where they could help promote reform in the PLA. With the prospect of living together in Beijing in the near future, all of our dreams seemed to be coming true.

When Lin Cheng assumed his position at the NDU, one of his first assignments was to take a delegation of American military officers around Beijing. He served as their host, translator, and tour guide. The head of the delegation was so impressed by Lin Cheng's work that he extended an official invitation to him to visit Washington, D.C. His commander approved, and Lin Cheng hastily made preparations for his first journey abroad. He was provided with a generous bonus by the PLA to purchase a new wardrobe for his trip, and his superiors advised him to buy the best clothing available, since they wanted him to impress his American hosts.

We decided to marry before he departed for the United States. In early 1988 General Zhou Erjun, the nephew of the late Premier Zhou Enlai, hosted a reception for us, attended by many top staff officers from the NDU and by representatives of several foreign delegations studying at the school. We had ten uninterrupted days for our honeymoon before Lin Cheng departed for America.

When he returned two weeks later, he phoned me and excitedly told me about America "It's incredible," he said. "It is the most beautiful place I've ever seen." His stories of the United States contrasted dramatically with everything we'd been told about it. He was impressed by the cleanliness of the country—the clean streets and the clear air and water.

"What is the condition of the peasants and of the workers?" I asked him.

He told me there were no peasants and the workers were rich by Chinese standards. I thought he must be exaggerating.

America was a revelation for him, and he said so in his official report. His commanding officer, who had been to America six months earlier and favored closer ties with the United States, read his report and approved it. But a high-ranking political commissar read it and cautioned Lin Cheng about his lack of criticism of the United States. "You didn't see the real America. You only met rich Americans. They have millions of homeless and unemployed, and they conceal them from visitors. Remember that. The real America, the one they hide from us, is ugly."

THE colonel seemed to know almost everything about my husband and me. He held the confessions we'd made, and he was aware of my husband's journey to America, the people he associated with at the NDU, the man who'd hosted our wedding reception, and the names of all those who attended. Any of those people could be suspects for the moment. But I was the key to unlocking the puzzle of a conspiracy, he said.

I didn't want to undergo prolonged questioning about my husband and his associates. I feared that something I might say could cause him trouble and, as in our last year at the institute, jeopardize his career. There was but one way to free him from suspicion.

When the colonel leaned forward to switch on the tape recorder, I asked, "May I write a letter to my husband?"

He sensed that this might be a point on which he could bargain with me. "What is it you wish to tell him?"

"To leave me alone and to never bother me again."

"Why?"

"Because I don't love him anymore."

"Has he done something to make you feel this way?"

"I just want to leave my husband out of this."

"Let's just clear up a few things. Then we can move on. Who sent your husband to the United States?"

"I believe the NDU sent him, Colonel."

"He visited Washington, D.C.?"

"Yes. His hosts lived there."

"Did he make any sight-seeing trips to Virginia?"

"Yes."

"Whom did he visit there? Do you remember any names?"

"Yes. He said he visited the home of George and Martha Washington." The colonel and his aide were about to write down the names. Then they realized I was mocking them.

"He visited San Francisco?"

"Yes."

"Do you know the location of San Jose, California?"

"No."

"Not far from San Francisco. What a coincidence. Didn't Larry Engelmann drive to San Francisco to meet with your husband?"

"No."

"This is important. Are you absolutely sure—*absolutely*—that Larry Engelmann did not meet your husband in San Francisco?"

"Yes, I'm absolutely sure. My husband would have told me."

"And in Beijing, are you sure he never met alone with Larry Engelmann there?"

"Yes, I am sure."

A sudden look of triumph came across the colonel's face. He pulled out a folder. "We have pictures of them together with no one else present. Remember what will happen if you lie to me!"

He lifted a photograph from his folder. It showed my husband and Larry sitting together in what I recognized as the Greenery Restaurant in the Jianguo Hotel in Beijing.

"They were not alone together, Colonel. I took this photograph with Larry's camera. That's why I'm not in it. I was there. If you look carefully, you can see three settings on the table."

That night I reviewed in my mind the questions the colonel had asked. Who was providing him with files and questions? Who was toying with my life, deciding if I should live or die?

The colonel didn't show up during the next five days. On the sixth day he opened a new line of questioning. There was another target now, higher up—my commander at the institute, whom he referred to disdainfully as "the Coffee General."

"Your husband was given his position at the NDU because your commanding officer interceded in his behalf. Isn't that correct?"

"He was helpful."

"Yes," the colonel said. "He's an ambitious man with an interesting past. Let's talk about the general."

He seemed confident that I could be used to undercut the officer he hated more than any other in the PLA.

FIVE 第五章 The General

WHEN the colonel started to question me about the general, it became clear that he imagined a nefarious U.S.-Nanjing-Beijing-Shanghai intelligence conspiracy and that I was in some way central to communication between the various conspirators. He wanted desperately to use me and my relationship with the American to unmask, discredit, and purge a clique of PLA officers who had been working quietly for broad reforms in the military.

The general, a prominent leader of the reformist group, had worked for years for closer ties with the United States and for rapid modernization of politics, economics, and the military. The colonel and his superiors, on the other hand, comprised part of a powerful entrenched conservative clique of PLA officers—many of them elderly—who felt threatened by the ambitious young reformers. When this old guard thought they could link leading reformists with a foreign intelligence agent, they seized their chance. All they required was my cooperation and confession.

The general was a tempting target. Over the years he'd made

powerful friends within the Party and the PLA. But he also had many enemies. He was not unaware of the dangers of endeavoring to change China. He'd warned me to be vigilant. He'd had me swear I'd never betray his trust, and I'd assured him I never would.

"Never sign a confession," he told me several times. "Your signed confession can be your death warrant. Even if it's not, it will remain with you for the rest of your life. And if you are arrested, always remember that your friends will be working for your release, no matter what your interrogators tell you."

So when the colonel asked about my relationship with the general and my knowledge of his activities, I knew what to expect, and I was prepared to protect my friends.

IN THE fall of 1985, three months after I assumed my new position as aide to the executive officer at the Nanjing institute, that elderly officer retired and a new one was assigned. The new executive officer—the man the colonel referred to as the Coffee General—was in his mid-forties, tall, handsome, and very distinguished-looking. A few weeks after his arrival he disclosed his innovative master plan for the institute. He was determined to modernize military intelligence training.

I got along well with him. He soon entrusted me with broader duties and named me his operational manager. I became part of his privileged inner circle of junior officers. Over the course of many months he became increasingly candid with us during private lunches and dinners at his home. He told us he preferred to work with young officers who were still idealists. The older officers, he observed, were often cynical and suspicious of change.

One afternoon I told him that I'd become disillusioned with the army and thought about leaving it because of my unhappy experience as a cadet. Rather than leave the army, he told me, I should work within it. There were still enough good people in the army, he said, to restore it to the status it was meant to achieve.

I wondered what motivated him. I asked him many times about his background, and at first he deflected my questions. But one afternoon, three months after he'd arrived at the institute, he invited me into his office for coffee and told me the story of his life.

His father had joined the Nationalist Army when he was a young man. Over the years he worked his way up and became a two-star general. But he became disillusioned with Chiang Kai-shek, who was more concerned, he found, with remaining in power than improving the lives of the people or expelling the Japanese. In 1948 he split with Chiang and took his army with him to the Communist side. After the Communist victory in 1949 he was honored as a People's Hero. Then he suddenly died, leaving behind a young wife and ten-year-old son.

The general recalled that his mother, with the help of her wealthy and influential family, was able to provide well for him. He followed the path of his father, expecting to rise to a top rank in a modern military force. But his expectations were shattered by the Cultural Revolution, launched in 1966. His mentors were jailed and tortured. Finally he left the PLA and moved to Shanghai, where he formed a secret group to work against the policies of the local leaders of the Cultural Revolution. But the group was betrayed, and the general and his friends were incarcerated. Every day, he said, the names of several men were called and they were taken out and shot. But his name was never called.

In 1978, following the death of Mao and the arrest of the Gang of Four, he was released. His health was broken, but he was vindicated, alive and free. His Party membership was restored, and his opposition to the leaders of the Cultural Revolution was termed heroic. He was reactivated in the PLA. Within a few years he was promoted to general.

When he finished his story, the general told me, "After I was released from prison, I met with my Shanghai group again. All of us are in the PLA once more. We want to make sure that what happened to us and millions of others in China will never happen again. I want you to work with me and my group. But you should be aware that such an undertaking involves risk. The political climate in China changes often. There are beautiful days and stormy days. I was caught in the chaos of the Cultural Revolution and barely survived. If we succeed, you could be a hero. Or you could be denounced and imprisoned. You must be prepared for either."

"I am," I assured him.

"Good," he said. "Then let's get to work."

The general intensified his efforts to improve the training of students in the institute. He worked tirelessly to further the careers of talented young officers who were loyal to him. The opening in Nanjing of the joint educational venture of The Johns Hopkins University and Nanjing University—the Center for Chinese and American Studies—presented an opportunity for officers from our school to study with American teachers. The general had concluded that the English our graduates spoke made them seem like bumpkins in the United States. Their awkward phrasing and pronunciation, along with their discomfort and unfamiliarity with the customs of America, made them stand out when they were supposed to fit in. They didn't know how to drive a car or pump gas, what to order in restaurants off an American-style menu, and they were confused by American banking, checks, and credit cards.

He'd thought about the problem and in the spring of 1988 had come up with his own solution. He wanted to construct a small American city near the institute. He said the KGB had constructed such an installation in the Soviet Union, and it proved to be useful. Officers from around the country could be assigned to our secret installation for final training before being sent to America. The only language spoken in the city would be English.

Although the reform group of officers applauded the scheme, there was outspoken resistance to it from conservatives in the institute and in Beijing. They implied that too much exposure to America could be a dangerous thing, and they wanted to teach no more about Western democracies to our recruits than was necessary. They feared the steady erosion of Marxism and its replacement by liberal Western values.

Late that spring of 1988 the general told me, "I want you to study at the Nanjing University joint venture with The Johns Hopkins University." He said he'd arrange for my admission. I could better learn colloquial English, as well as observe firsthand the teaching methods and styles of the Americans. When I returned from the center, I could incorporate what I'd learned into the curriculum of the institute and use it in putting together the plans for our new American city. He also entertained the idea of bringing one or two American instructors to the institute and of having them lecture to the students about American culture and society. It was important that I make as many friends and contacts as possible at the center, while at the same time making sure I revealed as little as possible about my own background.

THE colonel withdrew a fat folder from his briefcase filled with material on the general. "Did he ask to meet the American?"

"No, he didn't."

"Did the American ask to meet the general?"

"Why would he? He wasn't aware of the general's existence."

"I don't think that's true, Xu Meihong. How many times did the general ask you to bring the American to the institute?"

"Twice, I think."

"You never wondered why?"

"I knew why. The general wanted him to lecture on American life and society."

"And did the American go to the institute?"

"No. He said he was too busy."

"Or perhaps he was awaiting instructions from America?"

"I don't know what you're talking about."

Despite my denials, the colonel went back over the same material day after day to see if my answers were consistent. After questioning me for seven straight days about the general, the colonel suddenly indicated that I might not have been the only officer arrested on December 2. I started to wonder if the general had been arrested that day also. At the same time I wondered if this wasn't an attempt to undermine my confidence by making me believe that my friends and supporters were gone.

"The general and his friends are trying to divide the PLA when they should be trying to unite it. He is a very ambitious man, an individualist. But we know all about him. So if I were you, I would not rely on his help."

"I rely on the truth, Colonel."

Sometimes there was a lapse of several days between sessions. After three weeks the colonel apparently concluded my information on the general was limited, so in mid-January he returned to my relationship with the American.

SIX 第六章 The American

IN EARLY September, 1988, I packed some of my books and belongings in two bags and arranged to be driven to the center in a military car. As I passed through the large glass doors into the lobby, I was unaware that I was not merely moving into another educational institution. I was entering a new world that would change me and my life in ways I'd never dreamed.

It was suggested that each Chinese student select an English name and each American student select a Chinese name. I chose the name Rose, which was a loose interpretation of my Chinese name, Meihong, which means Beautiful Red.

My third-floor room had a private telephone and private bathroom. The facilities was luxurious compared with those provided students in any Chinese university.

I was in my room only a few minutes when the telephone rang. "Welcome," the voice at the other end said. It was vaguely familiar.

"Who is this?" I asked. "How did you know I was here?"

"You don't remember?" he asked. "This is Li Yan."

He had been a top student at the institute, graduating in 1982. I'd heard he had been demobilized in the past year. "I haven't seen you in years. What are you doing?" I asked.

"Can we meet?" he asked. "I can answer your questions then."

"Of course. When? Where?"

He wanted to see me that afternoon. I asked if he'd like to see the center, and he said he'd already been there a number of times. He preferred to meet me somewhere nearby. An hour later I was waiting for him on a street corner when a car pulled up and he jumped out. He was dressed in civilian clothes and wore dark glasses. But there was something I recognized in the way he carried himself, the way he looked at the people around us.

"Are you working for the Ministry of State Security now?"

"Is it that obvious?" he asked, smiling.

"A guess," I said. "Congratulations. Do they pay well?"

He ignored my question and responded, "You've done well for yourself also, *Lieutenant* Xu Meihong. Long time no see. How are things at the institute? How is the general?"

"You know the general?"

"Who doesn't? He's ambitious. He's going places. Are you going with him?"

"No. I'm just going to the center. And I'm going to have tea with you." We both laughed at my feeble attempt at humor.

We walked to a small restaurant and ordered tea. We talked about the institute and about our classmates and friends. Some had risen high in the ranks of the PLA. Some worked abroad under cover as journalists, businessmen, and graduate students.

He told me he was aware of my admission to the center and he'd been awaiting my arrival.

"You must have studied everybody's personnel files at the center," I said.

"Being from where you are, you know how everything works, don't you?" he replied.

As we talked, I realized something in him had changed. There was none of the youthful jocularity that I remembered. I had the feeling also that each of us was curious to know what the other knew without revealing much about ourselves.

"Why did you contact me?" I asked. "Is the MSS monitoring the PLA now?"

"Of course we're not," he said. "It's the Americans. We want to know about the activities of certain Americans, their real reasons for coming here and staying in the center."

"But the center's an educational institution. Why would an agent be sent there?"

"The Americans do these things. If they insert someone into China, even into a place like the center, we have to identify him, watch him, and get rid of him or neutralize him."

"Where do I fit into your agenda? Are you recruiting?"

"Not really," he said. "I'd appreciate your help and understand if you said no. But if you say yes, I'll make it worth your time."

Both of us knew that I could not refuse to cooperate with the MSS if they asked for my help. The only point to be negotiated was how much I must help. "What is it you want me to do?"

"Watch someone—an American."

"Isn't that something the housekeeping staff does for you?"

"I need someone trained for this, like you."

I told him I'd do what I could for him but that I really wanted to devote myself to study. He assured me that my tasks would consume only a minimal amount of time and effort.

When we'd finished our tea, he said he'd like to show me something at his office. It was a nice afternoon. We walked several blocks to the local MSS headquarters. In his office, he laid out some photos. "Take a look at this man," he said.

"Look at his blue eyes!" I said. "Who is he?"

"His name is Engelmann. He is from California. He will be teaching two classes—American history and American culture and society. Help me find out if he is really who he claims to be."

"What exactly do you want to find out?"

"I'm not entirely sure what to look for," he said. "Just watch him for anything unusual. But not a single soul should know what you're doing for me. Agreed?"

"Agreed. But what do I get for my extracurricular activity?" I asked jokingly.

"Dinner? Once a week?" he replied.

"Is that all?"

"We'll see," he said, and smiled.

As I walked back to the center, I worried about what Li Yan had asked me to do. This was an unwelcome intrusion in my life. I decided to do as he requested and not to tell anyone, not even the general. I hoped Li Yan's suspicions would be unfounded and that my work with him would be brief.

THE first week at the center was referred to as shopping week. During that time students attended as many classes as possible, met the professors, listened to their introductory lectures, and then decided which two elective classes to take.

The general asked me to concentrate on American political history and social studies so I could use what I learned to help him with his American city. Keeping both his and Li Yan's requests in mind, I chose two classes taught by Larry Engelmann—American political history and American culture and society. My third class was an intensive English-language course.

Curious about the alleged American agent, I arrived early for his initial class session. He was tall and slender, had curly brown hair and the bluest eyes I'd ever seen. He didn't dress like any professor I'd ever known. He wore blue jeans, a white dress shirt open at the neck, and a sport coat. Before he began, he removed his coat, draped it over a chair, and then sat on the edge of a table in front of the room. He then began talking—not lecturing, as we were accustomed to, but speaking in a low, conversational tone.

"I am going to tell you how I got here," he began. "Mine is an unusual story. Strange in a funny way. Funny strange, we say. Parts of it, though, are funny sad and parts are funny ha-ha."

Was this some arcane American dialect? I wondered. None of us was prepared for this.

After several minutes he noticed our confusion at his language. "If you think I am speaking too fast, please put up your hand," he said. Immediately all but a few hands went into the air. He laughed and said he would speak more slowly. The hands went down.

He explained carefully the various qualifiers for the word funny, and most of us finally grasped what he had been saying. We were amused by the ways in which English could be "twisted," as he put it. Through the remainder of the semester he was constantly pausing to explain English-language structure and idioms to us.

He told us he thought the man most responsible for his presence in Nanjing was Nikita Khrushchev. In 1957, he said, the Soviet Union put up the first earth satellite—Sputnik—and the American Congress was so alarmed by the technological feat that, among other things, it passed a massive student-loan program for students from low-income families. A student loan made it possible for him to attend the University of Minnesota. "God bless Nikita Khrushchev!" he proclaimed. He later earned his graduate degrees—M.A. and Ph.D—at the University of Michigan and then moved to California and started teaching at San Jose State University. "In 1975, because of the collapse of South Vietnam, one hundred and thirty thousand South Vietnamese fled from their country to the United States," he explained. "Several hundred ended up in my university. Many were in my classes. Last year twenty-five percent of my students were Asian-born, mostly Vietnamese. They convinced me to write about Vietnam."

While writing about Vietnam, Engelmann met a *New York Times* correspondent, Fox Butterfield, who had been in Saigon in 1975 and later headed the *Times* office in Beijing. When he visited California, he stayed in Engelmann's home. He told of his experiences in China and encouraged Larry to apply for a teaching job at the center. Larry followed Butterfield's advice and was hired.

"So you see," he said, "without a Communist victory in Vietnam there would have been no Vietnamese students in my class, no visiting correspondent in my home, and no American from California standing before you right now. If you have problems with my class, complain to the Russians, okay? Or blame your own government for helping North Vietnam. It's all their fault." He laughed loudly at his own joke, but the students remained silent.

When he'd completed his introductory lecture, he announced, "I've told you personal things because I think you can learn about America from my experience. I have as much to learn from you as you do from me. I think that's why we're here. Let's make this a memorable experience."

I went to his office to get his approval to enroll in both of his classes. He asked me to sit down. The office was crowded with books, stacks of video and audio tapes, and large boxes of documents. I asked why he'd brought all of the books and papers with him to China and how he could afford the shipping charges.

"It's not as expensive as it looks," he said. "It came by ship, not air. I want to stay here for two years at least, and I want to continue my research. So I brought everything I thought I'd need."

"How many books did you bring?" I asked in amazement.

"I think around two hundred," he said.

"And how many videotapes?"

"Only about fifty. But there are three movies on each tape. So maybe one hundred and fifty movies. There's an auditorium here with a VCR and a big screen, and I can show them to everybody, I hope, with approval. You can all learn a lot about America from our movies and get some good laughs from them. Someone told me I'd need something to keep my spirits up here."

It sounded wonderful to me. I loved American movies too.

I was surprised to see the papers he'd piled along one wall—typed documents marked CLASSIFIED and CIA and DIA. "What are these?" I asked. "Are you allowed to tell me?"

"Oh," he said, laughing, "they're for my next book. These are from Saigon and Washington in April 1975. It's declassified. Field reports from Americans monitoring North and South Vietnamese military units. The black line through the word 'classified' means the stuff is available to researchers."

"They let anyone see these in the United States?"

"If you're doing research."

I believed this was one of the reasons the MSS singled him out. Documents that had been declassified in America would be very interesting to the intelligence services in China. They would at least indicate which kinds of materials have been kept secret, even if the content is no longer important.

"How do I say your name?" he asked, looking at my enrollment form.

"Meihong," I told him. "But you may call me Rose. That's my English name."

"That's nice. Beautiful. I'm learning Chinese, however, so let me use Meihong," he said, mispronouncing my name. "Would that be all right with you?"

"That's fine with me. What should I call you?" I asked. "Don't you have a Chinese name?"

"It's silly. It's La Li. They tried to make it sound like Larry."

"It has no meaning," I told him.

"That's what they tell me. I've also been told in Shanghainese it means 'zipper.' And in other Chinese dialects it means 'diarrhea' or 'bald.' So you'd better just call me Larry."

His openness and candor were disarming. I enjoyed talking with him, and he seemed sincerely interested in everything I had to say.

He'd shipped a computer to the center and had it on his desk. When I asked about it, he showed me how the word-processing functions worked. At that moment Carol Chu, his American colleague and my academic adviser, joined us. Larry suggested the three of us have lunch together outside the center. We walked to a nearby noodle restaurant—Zhou's. After lunch we walked through the campus of Nanjing University, talking and laughing.

Late that night, while reading at my desk, I turned for a moment to look out the window. I noticed a light in a window across the way in another wing of the center complex. It came from Larry's office. I turned out my light so I could see in the dark without being seen. Larry was sitting at his computer, slowly paging through papers and then pausing occasionally to type something. As I watched him, I wondered if he could possibly be anything other than what he said he was—a professor. He seemed completely ingenuous and open.

On my third morning at the center I received a call from my friend at the MSS. I went to his office and described in detail everything I'd learned about Larry. I suggested strongly that he was not the agent the MSS was looking for.

DURING our first class sessions Larry encouraged students to take notes in the margins of their textbooks and to underline critical parts of the narrative. But the center had only purchased four copies of the textbooks for the entire class. We had to check books out of the library, and they were examined by the librarians when they were returned. When we pointed this out to him, he thought about it for a moment and said he'd see that we each got our own copies of the books. We found this hard to believe.

That afternoon he composed a letter to the publisher of the textbooks. He wrote that he'd assigned their books for years in America and then described his work in China and asked the publisher to consider sending free books to his students.

He gave the note to an administrative secretary and asked that it be telexed to the United States. He heard nothing about it for two days. Then his letter was returned to him with a note from the American and the Chinese codirectors stating tersely that it was not the policy of the center to provide textbooks for every student.

The next afternoon he walked to the Jinling Hotel and telexed the message to the publisher himself. One week later a truck arrived at the center and unloaded the books. When the Chinese codirector discovered the gift, he was furious. He branded Larry a troublemaker and from that day on watched for a way to humble him.

The arrival of the books aroused apprehension in the students as well. Surely an obligation accompanied the generous gift. They wanted to know why an American publisher gave away books of such value to students in China they'd never met. Larry tried to explain. "I guess they did it because it was the right thing to do. Sometimes that happens, even in a capitalist society."

The idea of a substantial gift with no strings attached—of a random act of kindness—was something alien to most of the students. A gift implied the cultivation of connections and therefore opened doors. When my friend in the MSS asked me what favors I thought Larry might expect from the students in exchange for the gift, I confessed that I could see none.

The Chinese students at the center were primarily mid-career professionals like myself, ranging in age from their mid-twenties to their mid-forties, who were returning to the classroom to refresh their education and to learn how and what Americans taught. We each belonged to a work unit, where we practiced our profession. That unit maintained a permanent personal file on us that followed us all of our lives. When we completed our year at the center, the Chinese codirector was required to write a report on our activities. It became part of our permanent file.

In the classroom Larry never fully appreciated the pressures under which his students labored. Any politically incorrect remark made casually or humorously might be reported to the Chinese codirector and find its way into our personal file. So when Larry repeatedly asked our opinions on various subjects and then tried to compare them with political policies in China or when he asked us about the importance of some concept—individualism, conformity, privacy, or liberty—in our daily lives, we were reluctant to answer. The most common answer was, "I don't know."

Students enjoyed class most when Larry spent the entire period talking about American writers and philosophers and reading from their works. Outside the classroom, in small groups in the privacy of our rooms, we discussed the questions he'd asked in the classroom—questions that had gone unanswered. And we talked about the books he'd assigned. We were delighted at how Larry made writers like Melville, Hawthorne, Thoreau, Whitman, and Emerson relevant to our experience when he spoke of fanaticism and the burdens of history and witch-hunts and scarlet letters. I am sure he was disappointed at our answers to his questions, and I know he wasn't aware that he was throwing open the windows of our minds. The fact that we could not express our thoughts and feelings did not mean we did not have them. He thought that what he could not see and could not hear wasn't there. But that is a mistake most foreigners make in China.

As the weeks passed, I busied myself in the center with study and also with the social life of the place. In addition to classes, there were parties, dances, movies, and informal discussions every week. I had papers to write and examinations. On the weekends I returned to my institute. What little free time I had I spent in the library poring over books. But every minute of life in the center was enjoyable. I lost myself in it, and I loved it.

ONE afternoon I was taking a walk by myself, and I saw Larry emerge from the front gate and start walking down Beijing Road.

He was very happy when he saw me. "I need to mail these," he said, holding up a fistful of postcards and letters. "How would you like to come with me and translate for me in the post office?"

"You must have many friends in the United States," I said upon seeing the number of items.

"Most of these aren't going to the United States," he said. "They're going to Vietnam." Larry had spent a month in Vietnam before he came to China. He'd gone there to do research for his next book, *Tears Before the Rain.* "Look at this," he said, and showed me one of the envelopes. I recognized the name on it—Colonel Bui Tin, the man who had taken the surrender of South Vietnam in 1975. Tin's address was the Ministry of Defense in Hanoi.

"Is this man your friend?" I asked.

"No. But I interviewed him. I plan to see him again in Hanoi in January. This is a thank-you note and some information on my next visit to Vietnam. He was very helpful and hospitable."

I felt uneasy. I knew that the letters would be copied and placed in the folder my friend at the MSS kept in his safe.

On the way back to the center, Larry waved to a Chinese girl, about fifteen, who sat on a small stool on the sidewalk just across from the old Drum Tower, near the post office. Pieces of automobile tires were stacked around her, and beside her was a small box filled with nails and razor blades. She replaced worn-out shoe soles.

"I'd like to talk to her," Larry said. "Will you translate?"

"Of course," I told him, though I could not imagine what an American professor would have to say to a street shoe-repair girl. I was touched, however, by his concern for this little girl's well-being. I translated as he asked about her school, her hours of work, and her family. He said he wanted to know how people lived—the people most of the tourists never met or talked to or cared about. I asked why. He insisted it was merely curiosity—nothing more.

I accompanied him to the post office again several days later. We sat down in a park across from the Drum Tower to watch people passing by, and he asked me, "How do you like the center?"

"It's luxurious," I said.

He looked at me in astonishment. "You're kidding, aren't you?"

"No, I'm not. Hot water—sometimes—private showers, telephones. That's unusual for students here. Very nice."

"They've cut corners," he said. "It's supposed to be nicer."

"What do you mean?"

"They put fifteen-watt bulbs in our apartments. When I bought new bulbs and tried to change them, the sockets fell out of the ceiling. They were held in with toothpicks. Someone had stolen the screws."

I'd learned to live with dim lightbulbs and couldn't appreciate his concern. "I didn't realize that," I told him.

"The budget for food is way out of line with the quality of the food served. One of the students pointed out how the kitchen manager leaves each day on his bicycle with a large load of food and returns later without it. Do you think he sells it? And all the computer software is pirated. Nobody from the United States—because of cultural sensitivity—tells the Chinese administrators that it's against the law to pirate our software and then sell it."

"Do all Americans complain like this?"

"No. I apologize. I'm not used to this. Everything is so different from what I'd expected. Not just exotic and colorful but also crooked. They say there is little crime here, but petty crime is rampant. Everything that's not tied down is stolen. Everyone with a little power is on the take."

"Larry, things are getting better here. Just try to be positive."

"You're awfully tolerant. Are all Chinese like you?"

"Some things can't be changed very easily. This is China, Larry, and the first thing you have to learn is patience."

He was quiet for several minutes, then conceded, "You're right, Meihong. I'm impatient. I had no idea things were like this. I'm sorry if I offended you. There are a lot of good people here. I like the people working on the street—the shoe-repair girl, the tailors, the fortune-tellers, the noodle makers. They all work hard."

"Nobody here is blind. We see what you see. But we can't change the situation overnight. So we do the best we can. We don't complain. We make adjustments. We do what we must to survive."

"Why don't you help me, then?" he said. "I'll teach you all I know about America, and you teach me about China. Help me see what you think I should see, and help me avoid making mistakes."

"Okay," I said. I realized how easy it was going to be to watch this man, to discover if he really was who he claimed to be, and to provide that information to my friend at the MSS.

And so on the following afternoon, when Larry called my room and asked if I was available for another walk, I agreed to meet him outside the center. It was a beautiful day. We walked to the Jinling Hotel, where we had coffee. He stopped and spoke to a man who had his own noodle stand on the street. The man remembered the Japanese occupation of Nanjing, and Larry listened to him and asked questions for nearly half an hour. People gathered and listened, and the man seemed flattered that a foreigner was interested in his memories. Then Larry spoke to a little girl who stood on the corner with a scale and a measuring device. For three fen she would let you weigh yourself and measure your height.

He began practicing Chinese. He asked me the word for nearly everything as we walked along. He insisted that through repetition he would someday speak fluent Mandarin. I had my doubts. He had no talent for languages, I thought, but I didn't discourage him.

He genuinely enjoyed listening to the people he met, I found, and I enjoyed my walks and conversations with him. "What do you learn when you listen to all these people?" I asked.

"Academics and writers don't have a monopoly on what's happening in the world, you know. They talk about life rather than live it. Sometimes people on the street are better at analyzing what's going on than people in ivory towers or in government offices."

I agreed with him. "If you talk to people like these every day, you'll get a picture of this country that most foreigners miss. The reason some of these people are surprised when you ask them a question is because nobody else is interested in their lives—not the government, not the scholars, not the tourists, not anybody but the police. They are suspicious at first, but if they see you out here on the street often, they may open up to you more and more."

"What about you? If we take walks every day, will you open up to me more and more? Tell me about yourself."

"My life has been like that of anyone else you know here. I studied in a university before I came to the center. And I'm married."

"Are you? Where is your husband, and what does he do?"

I thought it unwise to disclose my military background, so I lied. "He's a businessman in Beijing. We met when we were both university students."

I watched his reaction. He appeared to believe every word I said.

He nearly caught me in a lie one week later, when he came to visit me in my room. On the previous weekend I had returned to my institute and received my commission as first lieutenant. My new officer's uniform was ready for me at that time. I wanted to see myself in it standing before a full-length mirror, so I brought it with me to the center. While I stood looking at myself in the mirror, there was a knock on the door. Without thinking, I opened it a few inches. It was Larry. Through the open door he could see me in the mirror. He was nearly dumbstruck when he saw the uniform. "What's that?" he asked.

"It belongs to a girlfriend," I said. "I'm keeping it for her. She just had it cleaned in Nanjing, and she's picking it up later."

Larry was carrying a pocket camera, and he suddenly said, "Smile!" and snapped a picture.

"I'd like that picture," I told him. "Can you give me the film?"

"There are more exposures on the roll. I'll give you a print when I develop it," he said.

"No," I said, trying not to sound anxious. "It's against military regulations for me to be seen or photographed in this uniform, because I'm not in the army. Please give me the film, Larry."

He told me not to worry and promised he'd give me the film after he'd finished the entire roll. I had to believe him. But by the time the roll was used, he'd forgotten his promise.

I BEGAN meeting with Larry every day. I helped him practice his Chinese, and I translated for him on the street. When the weather was bad, he'd invite me to his apartment, and we'd talk there. Sometimes we'd watch one of his videos. When I asked if I might use his computer to write some of my papers, he said I could use it anytime he wasn't. When I complained that sometimes there was too much noise on the student floor for me to study, he let me read in his apartment while he worked in his office.

Often, when I was reading in his apartment or working on his computer in his office, he'd leave me alone to attend a meeting or to do some work in the library. Thus I gained access to the files in his office as well as his apartment. I read through his papers, letters, and diary, looking for anything that might indicate he was secretly communicating with someone in China or sending reports back to the United States. I found nothing like that. But on his computer I found my name in the letters he'd written to friends in America. "She's right out of a dream," he wrote to a friend. "Or should I say she's right out of a Chinese silk-screen painting, the most lovely creature God has ever seen fit to place in my path."

As I read his words, I felt ashamed, because he had no idea that I was repeating our conversations to the security people. I thought for a long time about him and about what I was doing. He was a complete innocent when it came to comprehending the complexities of the politics of China. I wanted to shield him and prevent him from being hurt. I also felt a stirring in my heart. I knew that any sympathy I felt for him could be dangerous for me. But, like him, I couldn't help it.

I decided not to tell my friend at the MSS that I'd read what Larry wrote privately. I believed that would have been a further violation of Larry's trust, and I decided not to cross that line.

As we spent more and more time together, I found Larry trusted me completely, but I was untrustworthy. I wanted to tell him about the suspicions of the MSS. But I couldn't warn him without revealing my role in watching him. And I couldn't convince the MSS to stop their surveillance. I was not sure what to do.

Late one evening I decided to go to his office to see if there was a way I might warn him that he was being watched. He was writing at his computer. I said hello and asked him how he could work so late. For the first time since I'd known him, I saw weariness in his expression and heard an uncharacteristic sadness in his voice. He said he worked hard to escape from thinking about things that made him unhappy. I asked him if he wasn't happy with China, and he said he wasn't happy with his life. China had nothing to do with it.

He stared out the window and told me he'd been lonely for a long time, since his divorce eleven years earlier. He lived alone and hated it. Yet it seemed to be his fate. He'd come to China, he said, to try to find a new life for himself, but the old emptiness and sadness traveled with him. There was no escaping it.

As he stared out the window at the black starless sky, I wanted to put my hand on his shoulder and tell him that fate changes unexpectedly and unhappiness ends and we can never tell what the future holds for us. But I did not.

Finally he turned, forced himself to smile, and said, "I'm sorry to burden you with this. The last thing I want to do is to share my personal problems with you." He saved his work and then turned his computer off. As we stepped into the hall, he brushed his fingertips against my hair and lightly touched my face and said, "You know, you are so beautiful. You'd probably better stay away from me. I'll make you unhappy, or I'll get in trouble, or I'll make you hate me. I'm good at that."

I didn't respond to his statement. At the stairwell where we parted, I reached out, took his hand, and asked, "Are you going to be all right?"

He seemed to recover from his sadness and told me he would be fine after some sleep. He patted me on the shoulder and wished me good night. I let go of his hand, and he turned and slowly climbed the stairs to his apartment.

In my room, I thought about his words for a long time. I wondered how he'd feel if he knew I read his mail and reported our conversations to the MSS. How could I betray such a trusting soul? I have to stop this, I told myself. I can't do this any longer.

I took out some paper and wrote a brief letter to my husband, saying I missed him and asking him to visit me soon.

I WAS absolutely convinced that Larry had nothing to do with an American intelligence agency. But no matter how adamant I became in my assertions, my friend in the MSS insisted I was naïve.

He pointed out that the first American codirector of the center was a political officer at the American embassy, and the way he said the words "political officer" indicated there was more to the position than simply analyzing the politics of China. When the codirector left the center after two years, the MSS believed he would be replaced. They became convinced Larry was their man. His connections to the American media (journalists were believed generally to double as spies), his correspondence with high-ranking officers in Vietnam, and his possession of declassified CIA documents indicated he was involved in intelligence gathering.

At this stage I concluded that the best way out of the matter was to warn Larry to be careful and not to fall into any political trap set for him. I also needed to remind him not to mention my name in his letters to America, since I sensed that his political innocence might compromise my career and my future.

One afternoon I went to his office and asked him to take a walk with me. "Is anything wrong?" he asked as soon as we stepped outside the center's main gate.

I didn't say anything until we sat on a bench in a nearby park. Then I asked him, "Have you finished your roll of film? The one with me in uniform? You promised to give it to me."

"I just sent it to the local developer. I'll give you the prints when I get them back tomorrow."

"You know, you're going to get me into a lot of trouble with those pictures. You really are a professor, aren't you?"

"First, I don't know how I can get you into any trouble, and second, yes, I am a professor," he asserted with solemnness. "Are my lectures that bad?" He laughed.

"I know you want to learn about China, and I'm trying to help you. But there is an invisible world here. I want you to be aware of it, because if you aren't, you can get into a lot of trouble."

"You've lost me," he said.

"Okay, let me make it very straight. When you write letters to your friends in America, please stop mentioning my name."

"How do you know what I write to my friends in America?"

"All foreigners are under suspicion here. That includes you."

"And how do you fit into all of this? Are you watching me?"

I could not answer his question directly. All I could tell him was that it was routine for agents of the government to read the mail of foreigners. "You have to remember that here in China, you don't have a private life," I cautioned him. "Don't trust anybody, and don't mention my name in your letters, please."

He was quiet for several seconds. "Okay, Meihong. If you say so."

"And that film?"

"I'll get the prints to you tomorrow," he promised.

"I need the negatives too," I told him.

"The negatives too? My God, you are thorough. What are you anyway? A spy?"

"I'm not a spy," I told him. "I'm just a friend who's concerned about your welfare." I was convinced that he believed me and he'd do as I asked. But he didn't. We returned to the center, and he went straight to Carol's room and repeated our conversation. That night he wrote letters to his friends and described our conversation and the paranoia he felt all around him in China. He found my warnings to be half-humorous cloak-and-dagger material.

Every word spoken in Carol's room that afternoon was recorded by the MSS, and his letters were copied and placed in his MSS file.

IN THE next weeks I thought Larry had accepted my warning and changed his behavior. I assumed he would be more cautious and, as a result, the MSS would gradually lose interest in him.

On November 1 the students and faculty took a weeklong field trip to Beijing. I promised Larry and Carol I'd serve as their tour guide. On their first day I took them to the Forbidden City, Tiananmen Square, Mao's Tomb, and the Temple of Heaven. That evening they invited me to dinner. They wanted to thank me by taking me to Justine's, an elegant continental-style restaurant in the Jianguo Hotel, where they were staying. We had a wonderful time.

On his last night in Beijing, Larry invited me to a nightclub. We sat and talked, listened to the music, and watched the dancers. When a slow song played, Larry asked me if I'd like to dance. We walked to the center of the dance floor. He held out his arms in a very formal way, I took his hand, and he pulled me close to him and we danced. The music was very romantic. Larry softly sang the words for me in English, and I felt confused and lost. When the music stopped, I said we should leave, but he asked me for one more dance, and I said yes, and we danced again and then one more time. Each time, it seemed, he held me closer, and each time, I felt myself lost in his embrace. I found I wasn't anxious to leave anymore, but finally he said it was time to go, and he took me to a taxi and paid the driver to return me to the NDU. Before we parted, he kissed me on the forehead and thanked me for the days in Beijing. He said he'd never forget them.

When I returned to Nanjing, most of my time was taken up by studying for examinations. Sometimes, in the evening, I took a short walk to get fresh air. Larry joined me a few blocks from the center, and we walked on a regular route around Nanjing University and back. Sometimes he took my hand and helped guide me through the darkness. But when we approached a streetlight, he continued grasping my hand and I continued to let him. I knew at those moments that we had crossed another line in our friendship. But neither of us dared to give voice to what we were thinking or feeling. Each of us knew, I believe, that it was wonderful and it was wrong, and we didn't care, at least not at the moment.

One night we sat on a bench and looked up at the stars. I asked him if he still felt sad and had moments of gloom. He told me that he'd found a cure for his blues—me. When I asked him if he'd miss me after he left China, he said, "Meihong, I think in a different place, under different circumstances, in a perfect world, I'd fall madly in love with you. I'd love to take you to all the places you want to go, and see the world with you."

That night I stared out the window, my mind filled with dreams. I saw Larry working in his office in front of the computer. I watched until he stood and turned off the light and closed the door and the room went black. He was unaware that I had been watching him. And both of us were unaware that there were others in the dark that night watching us with the confidence of men who already knew how this story would end.

In mid-November I went to visit Li Yan at the MSS and again emphasized that I believed that Larry was not a foreign agent. This time Li Yan agreed with me. "You were right, and we were wrong."

I felt as if a heavy burden had been lifted from my shoulders. At last, I concluded, I am a full-time student. I was unaware that I'd just made one of the biggest mistakes of my life.

"YOU liked this American, didn't you?" the colonel asked me when he resumed my interrogation in mid-January. "In fact, you liked him very much, didn't you?"

"Yes."

"Would you say you *loved* him?"

Almost reflexively, perhaps because I was exhausted, I answered, "Yes, I suppose."

I could tell in a moment by the way he sat forward and glanced at the tape recorder that I'd made a mistake, that I had carelessly agreed with the word he interjected—love. Words were weapons. Now the word was on tape, and there was no taking it back.

There were knowing glances from the colonel to the others, and he smiled broadly. "We knew this a long time ago."

Love alone was not a capital crime, I reminded myself. "That is my only mistake, Colonel," I said. "Is that why I am here? Yes, I loved an American. I am innocent of anything other than that."

"Why didn't you tell us you loved this man from the start?" he asked. "You could have saved all of us so much time."

"I am a married woman. I wanted to keep my life, my career, my marriage, my dignity."

"We know you love your husband, and it's impossible that you'd fall in love with this foreigner. You are a good girl," he said with pretended paternal pride. "We now see things more clearly. He took advantage of your youth and innocence. He seduced you and made you tell him many things you should not have told him."

I shook my head from side to side as the colonel spoke, but he ignored my silent disavowal of his assertions. What he wanted now—what he demanded—was my cooperation in exchange for my future. He proceeded to lay out the tale he wanted me to repeat in my own words. "You knew him for three months. Look what he did to your mind in that short time. Your brain was washed by him, and we want to know how. Did he drug you, perhaps, Meihong, before forcing himself on you? He might even have put something in your tea before . . . *raping* you."

"Colonel, this is only your filthy fantasy."

"Did he buy things for you or promise you anything?"

"You don't understand, Colonel. We are friends. We spent time together. We shared ideas. We danced. We had dinner. That's all. He didn't seduce me. I am the only one guilty of wrongdoing, because I am a married woman, and as an officer, I am not supposed to have any emotional feelings toward a foreigner."

"Meihong, this American forced himself on you. We can finish all of this with a simple document from you. I want you to compose a statement. After you write and sign it, you may leave."

"What do you want me to write?" I asked warily.

"For the sake of the PLA and the Party, for the security of the country, we want this man to leave our country. This man took advantage of your trust, coerced you into revealing your position and rank, and lured you into providing him with information."

"I never told him my rank and position."

"But look at this picture," the colonel said, and pushed a photograph across the table of me in my new uniform.

"You wouldn't believe me if I told you the story of that photo."

"You're right," he said. "I wouldn't believe you. But there is a way to make things right. We have a statement prepared for you that says the American raped you. You want the Chinese authorities to drive him away in order to protect you and all other Chinese women. I want you to copy this statement and then sign it."

Someone had to pay. The colonel could not report that he'd spent all this time and come up with nothing but a little love story. He needed something more scandalous.

I struggled to hold back my tears. I stared at the piece of paper.

"Lieutenant, this is important. For God's sake, this man is just an American."

"But I know him. How can you ask me to destroy an innocent

person? Do you think the American administrators will believe this? I'll look foolish, and so will you."

"The Americans will accept this. This is not your problem."

"You can do anything you want to me, Colonel. But I can't write this. I am not going to help you dispose of him with this lie. From the moment you brought me here, you told me you wanted only the truth. This statement is not the truth."

He pulled the paper back. "Okay, you don't have to write a thing. Just sign your name at the bottom. I'll take care of the rest."

I laughed. I hadn't laughed in weeks. It felt good. I held my arms across my stomach and bent over with laughter from recognition of the absurdity of all this. "I'll never do that. And if you dare to forge my name to the document, I will tell people the truth about it."

"You will tell people the truth? The truth is too big for you. This bastard has destroyed you, and you don't know it. If he did not exist, you would have a good life, a bright future, and a good marriage. Now they have been poisoned. If we reveal that he raped you—repeatedly, like an animal—then you are the victim. Instead of condemnation, you will receive praise for revealing this secret crime." The colonel paused for nearly a minute. "Think about it, Meihong. We have a little more time. Think about it for a few hours." He motioned to his aides to return me to my room.

MY FEMALE guards had prepared a surprise for me. Over the many weeks of my incarceration I had spoken often with Xiao Zhang, the youngest guard. She asked me about my life in the center and at the institute and was genuinely curious about that and my close relationship with a foreigner. She'd never met a foreigner.

I had worn the same clothing for eight weeks. My requests for clean underwear had been denied. One afternoon I asked Xiao Zhang if she could bring me clean underwear. I said I didn't want this favor without repaying her and asked what I could do. She said she knew that I was one of the best dancers among the female officers at the institute. She would bring me underwear, she said, if I could teach her to dance. I agreed.

When I returned to the room after hearing the colonel's persistent pleas for me to charge Larry with rape, I found a small paper bag on my bed. Inside were two new pairs of underwear. When I saw them, I smiled at Xiao Zhang, who beamed back at me.

"Do you want to learn to dance now?" I asked her.

She looked at Li Xia, who nodded approval.

"Just follow me," I told her. "I'll take the man's part." I stood in front of her, put my right arm around her waist, took her right hand in my left, and pulled her gently against me. "Don't be so stiff. This isn't like marching. You're supposed to have fun."

As we practiced, I hummed a song Larry taught me during our walks—"Somewhere Out There." I counted out the steps as we moved in a tight circle around the floor. I remembered dancing to the song with Larry in Beijing. "Close your eyes," I told Xiao Zhang. "Think romantic thoughts, and you can fly away to some other world."

After we'd danced for several minutes, she whispered to me, "We're leaving tomorrow. We're going home."

I felt a sudden chill. "Really?" I said. "How nice."

We circled the room a few more times. Then I stopped humming and released her. "End of lesson number one," I announced. She looked disappointed but didn't object. I lay down on my bed, closed my eyes, and tried to sleep.

WE WERE awakened just before daybreak, when the colonel came to the door and told us to prepare to leave.

"Am I leaving too?" I asked him.

"We are all leaving," he said.

He and I walked to a waiting car. I was guided into the back seat, and the door was locked. We passed quickly through the gate and out onto the main road. Dawn was breaking. Nobody told me where we were heading. I wondered if I was on my way to a military jail or if I was on my way to freedom.

Two hours later the driver stopped in front of a large brick apartment building not far from my military institute. I was led to a small dark room. The only furnishings were two military beds.

"Since this is your new home, you may want to clean it up," the colonel told me before he left.

I poured water into a bucket and scrubbed the floor and walls.

A guard brought me food twice each day. I had no visitors for three days. On the fourth day the colonel and his aides returned. He told me things were not so bad after all. "Everything is clear," he said. "We just need you to write a document telling why you left the Hopkins-Nanjing center. We want you to write that you left because of your fear of the American Larry Engelmann."

"I have a better solution," I said. "Take me to the center and let me stand before the Chinese and American students and faculty and tell them in my own words why I was taken from the center and why I cannot return. Let's give them real Chinese drama!"

"What we need is an official notice of withdrawal signed by you. It is in everyone's best interest."

"Everyone's? Mine? My husband's? Larry Engelmann's?"

"The American is gone for good," the colonel said. "The document is for the record alone. It's a formality."

"What did you do to him?" I asked, my voice shaking.

"He left of his own accord, perhaps because of his guilt. He said he didn't like living in China and asked not to return. The American administrators granted his request. Everything has been taken care of in a satisfactory way. This document will help you get back your position at the institute. It will clear your record."

For the first time I harbored hope that this was going to end less tragically than I had initially expected. The silver bracelet Larry had given me at our last meeting was working its magic for me.

The colonel handed me a writing pad, a sheet of paper, and a pen. I sat on the bed and prepared to write. "I'll dictate it to you," he directed. " 'While I was studying at the Center for Chinese and American Studies, I had an affair with my American professor, and now I regret what happened and feel that I do not want to return to the center again. I am ashamed of what I have done.' "

I stopped writing after the first phrase.

"If you want to stay here in this room the rest of your life," he responded, "then by all means persist in your arrogance. You control your own fate now. If I leave this room without the document, I will nail that door shut and never let you out of here again."

"I have to think about this," I told him. "Come back later."

Surprisingly, he agreed. Two hours later he returned and offered me another option. "We can change the wording. You do not have to say you had an affair with the American."

"Then what is there to write? Our business is finished."

"Say you do not want to return to the center, so you are withdrawing of your own free will. Write this: 'Due to some personal difficulties, I am withdrawing.' " The words could be construed in several ways—not having enough money, not being able to take the pressure of life there, or having personal family problems.

I wrote the statement and signed it. The colonel gave a sigh of relief and, without saying another word, departed.

Three days later six military officers came to the room. One of them was the general. This was the first time I had seen him since he'd summoned me to his home in November. I was true to my word not to betray him, and he knew it.

I could tell by their expressions this was going to be a somber ceremony. One of the senior officers announced, "We have been investigating your case, Xu Meihong, for some time." He said the general would read the decision of the board of inquiry.

I knew why this confrontation had been choreographed this way. The general's enemies wanted to provide me with a final chance to save myself by betraying my commander. As he read my punishment, they expected me to break down and blame him for everything.

The general stepped forward. In a formal, flat voice he read the decision. The PLA had concluded that I had made a serious error in forming a personal relationship with a foreigner. It was suspected that if the relationship had been allowed to continue, I might have been induced to compromise confidential information concerning state security. By my actions I had seriously damaged the image of the PLA and of the People's Republic of China. I had also damaged the image of all good Chinese women.

I was becoming sick to my stomach. Still, I stood at attention.

The PLA headquarters had weighed the charges against my stellar military record prior to September 1988. There would be leniency, therefore, in my sentence. First, I was discharged from the Communist Youth League. Second, I was stripped of my military rank and discharged from the PLA. Third, I was to return to my home village to work as a peasant for the rest of my life. Finally, I was forbidden from contacting any foreigner. If I attempted to do so, "the most severe punishment" awaited me.

As the general read, I turned the silver bracelet back and forth, trying to calm myself. When I touched it, I felt stronger.

The general asked if there was anything I wanted to say.

I remained silent for several seconds. Then I said calmly, "Comrades, I would like to thank all of you. I am innocent of these crimes. But you have made what you consider to be an honest judgment, I know. I accept it like the good soldier I have always been. I will never ever forget my years in the PLA. I will never forget this day, and I promise I will never forget any of you men."

When I'd finished, there was a long moment of silence. My eyes met the general's for a second. I detected relief and gratitude in his look. I had been true to my word. He was the only man in the room who knew I was exactly what I said I was—a good soldier.

That evening, half an hour after I lay down to sleep, the door was flung open and the light switched on. I sat up in bed, my heart racing. I was speechless when I saw the colonel and, standing beside him, my husband. Lin Cheng was wearing his dress uniform, and he looked so dashing and healthy and handsome.

He ran to me and embraced me and kissed me on top of my head. He whispered in my ear, "Smile. Smile for this son of a bitch."

I smiled through my tears. "I didn't know if you would come back for me."

"What are you talking about, you silly girl? You are my wife. I have been here for several days waiting for you. They refused to tell me where you were until tonight. They said you cannot leave until the morning. So I'll be back then."

He embraced me again and then left with the colonel.

When they were gone, I switched off the light and went to bed again. I started to cry. I bit down on my hand so I would make no sound for the guard to hear.

It was over. I had survived. My old life was dead. Tomorrow morning I would start a new life.

Lying there, crying, I asked myself the same question over and over again: Xu Meihong, what have you done?

MY SLEEP that night was fitful, and I was fully awake before dawn. I washed myself at the metal sink. During my eight weeks of interrogation I had not been allowed to shower. On this final morning of incarceration I wanted to appear clean and fresh in order to show my captors that although they had the power to hold me, they had been unable to destroy me.

Around eight o'clock Lin Cheng appeared at the door with the colonel and three armed soldiers. "You look wonderful this morning," he said, and embraced me tightly. Then he removed his military coat and helped me into it. The colonel and the other soldiers were there to escort me back to my room at the institute to pack. Then I was to be driven to my village.

The van let us out just inside the gate of the institute, and we walked the remaining distance. We encountered several soldiers and cadets along the way. They'd been briefed on my case, so none of them dared greet me. I'd become invisible.

The general was waiting inside my building. He asked the others to wait while he accompanied me to my room.

We ascended the stairs without speaking. Once inside, he closed the door behind us. I breathed more easily. I assumed he'd searched the apartment for microphones.

"Did you confess anything?" he asked nervously.

"Didn't you read the transcripts?"

"I'm sure they were edited. I'd prefer to hear what was said from you. Did that son of a bitch downstairs ask about me?"

"Yes," I said. "Many times. He wanted something on you very much. But he knew nothing. He still knows nothing."

"And what did you tell him about me?" the general asked.

"I kept my promise that I'd never betray you. You're safe. I'm the only one in trouble." I went to my dresser and picked out some items of clothing. When I was finished, I turned to him and said, "And how are you, Xu Meihong?"

"What?" he asked.

"Aren't you going to ask about me? I'm the one being punished, remember? What will happen to me now? Are you interested?"

"I'm sorry. You know I am very concerned about you," he said, obviously embarrassed by my statement. He'd begun to regain his composure. "My wife asked me to say good-bye. She wishes you well. She will miss you, she said."

These words warmed me. "I'll miss her too," I said. "Please tell her that for me, will you?"

"You should be aware of what happened while you were being questioned," the general said.

"Tell me. I'm curious even though it will do me no good now."

"Your husband, friends, and I all defended you. But in trying to help you, we came under suspicion. If you had cooperated with them, everyone working to help you would have paid a high price."

"I know. I didn't cooperate."

"They underestimated your determination. They had bigger targets than you, of course. They wanted me—and my friends and associates. They wanted to wipe out a bloc of the reformist wing of the PLA in one big swipe. This was just the beginning, I am sure. It's going to get far worse."

"What am I supposed to do now?" I asked.

"They think you'll become desperate and careless. They suspect once you're in the countryside, you'll be overwhelmed by the hardship around you and you'll eventually crack and make a deal with them. They'll be watching you constantly."

"Why am I still so important to them?" I asked.

"After your arrest someone from Nanjing provided Party General Secretary Zhao Ziyang with an account of accusations against a junior military officer from Nanjing. That was you, Xu Meihong. He took an immediate interest."

"Why?"

"His political reforms aren't working," the general explained. "The real power in Beijing is still with Central Military Commission Chairman Deng Xiaoping and President Yang Shang Kun. Both are from the PLA. Zhao believes the army has been undercutting him. When he was told of your case, he saw an opportunity to taint the army by exposing a group of disloyal officers. The moment Zhao tried to step in, the men who arranged to have you arrested lost their support and their case. General Yang saw the danger in what was happening, and he informed the Nanjing Military Headquarters that he wanted the case disposed of as quickly as possible. So the men who arranged your arrest were caught in their own trap."

"What about you, General?"

"Politics isn't new to me. I've been through this before. You should be thinking about yourself. You caused the conservative old guard to lose face. Yet you are not welcome with the reformists anymore either, because you were almost a weapon in their destruction. They want to distance themselves from you. Remember, there are people waiting for the opportune moment to arrest you again."

"What shall I do?"

"You have to get out of China as soon as possible, but that may be difficult, even impossible. Something will have to happen to divert the attention of those watching you—a national catastrophe, a political upheaval. When it happens, I'd make my move."

"And if I need help?"

"There will be help," he assured me.

We returned down the stairs to the guards and to my husband. A van had been summoned to transport me to my village. I was directed to the rear bank of seats. A guard was seated on each side of me. My husband rode in front with the driver, and the two remaining soldiers sat in the middle seat.

The drive to Danyang took four hours. The longer we rode, the more despairing I became. I knew what shame I was bringing home to my family. I remembered what happened to my aunt Lingdi when she returned to the village. I would be treated like a leper. Knowing my return home escorted by military guards would be hard on my parents, I started to cry. My husband spoke to the colonel and asked that we be let off outside the village. He agreed.

When we arrived, my mother was preparing lunch. I couldn't look into her eyes. Her smile was forced and unconvincing. My father greeted me and then left the room. My mother served lunch a short time later, but I sat silently at the table without eating.

Afterward my husband and I put on our coats and took a walk through the frozen, snow-covered fields.

"I can't live here," I said, "with the realization that I've brought so much humiliation to my family."

"Maybe you should come to Beijing. I'll take care of you."

"I'm not supposed to leave the village. I don't want you to be held responsible for breaking the rules. It would mean the end of your career."

"I have a friend who may be able to help us."

My husband called his friend at the NDU. The friend's father ran a business in the oil fields in western Henan Province and might be able to arrange a job for me there, where no one could trace me. The condition was, however, that nobody, including my parents, know my whereabouts.

It was the eve of the Chinese New Year. That night firecrackers exploded outside every home to drive away evil spirits, and rockets whooshed high into the air and exploded in bright colors.

After my family's New Year's Eve dinner Lin Cheng and I excused ourselves and went to bed. "No matter what happens or what you do, I will always be here to help you," he reassured me. "I didn't marry you just for the good times."

I started to talk about the plans we'd made when we married—to live together in Beijing someday and have a child. My hope of that future was one of the things that kept me alive, I told him.

After a long pause he said, "Meihong, I love you, but we can never have children. Even if you come to Beijing someday and have a baby, he will suffer because of his parents and their reputation. His life and career will be far less than either of us could want for him. That's not fair. And I won't do that to a child. If we stay married, we will live by ourselves without any children."

If we stay married, I thought. If?

When Lin Cheng asked what had happened to me at the center, I couldn't really explain it. I wasn't sure how I had transformed a simple assignment from the MSS and a request from the general into a personal catastrophe. What had attracted me to Larry in the first place? Every time I had made up my mind not to go for a walk with him again or to visit him again and he called, I gave in. I didn't understand my own feelings. How could I hope to explain them to someone else? I was sure my affection and respect for Larry didn't diminish my love for Lin Cheng. I always assumed that someday Larry would return to America and I'd return to my husband and my old life. I never intended to threaten my marriage or my future. But I had done just that.

That night I realized that despite his outspoken support for me upon my release, Lin Cheng's love was different from the love we'd shared in the past. For a long time I lay awake beside my husband and repeated his last sentence silently to myself over and over again. Then I quietly cried myself to sleep.

THE next morning I was visited by my best friend from high school, Zhang Yuhua. She had become a teacher at Qinghua University in Beijing and lived in a dormitory on campus. She'd heard what had happened to me. "Come to Beijing," she suggested, "and live with me. Nobody will find you there. I'll help you."

"Maybe someday," I said, "but not now."

"When?" she asked.

I remembered what the general had advised, and I said, "Shortly after hell breaks loose in Beijing."

"That soon?" she asked, and we both laughed. She held my hand as I walked her outside and said good-bye.

During the weeklong Chinese New Year's festival it is a custom to visit relatives and extend New Year's greetings. So my husband and I walked to the nearby villages to visit my aunts, uncles, and cousins. No one asked about my arrest, but they all knew. I felt comfortable visiting only Lingdi and her husband. She knew what it was like to live as an outcast. She tried to comfort me in the way my mother had comforted her after her return to Lishi from the labor camp.

After New Year's Day we again called Lin Cheng's friend in Beijing. He said that I could go to Henan Province, and I'd be given a job. I wouldn't be reported. I wouldn't be watched.

We decided to go by boat up the Yangtze River as far as Wuhan, then take a train. I didn't tell my parents I was leaving. I wanted to protect them from inquiries by the PLA and the MSS. I'd find a way later to let them know I was safe.

FROM the deck of our ship Wuhan appeared to be a large, crowded, and dreary place. A short distance from the wharf we found a bus to take us to the train station, one of the largest in China. When our train was announced, we became part of a tidal wave of anxious people suddenly rushing to the station platform. The cars were unheated and unventilated. People stood tightly packed together, and it seemed every man in the car smoked furiously. The journey took nearly four hours. Once I put my hands in my coat pockets, it was so crowded, I couldn't get them out. I closed my eyes, and for the first time in my life I fell asleep standing up.

When the train squealed to a stop, the doors were flung open by the attendants. Hundreds of people who had been waiting along the tracks rushed and blocked the open door and then bulldozed their way into the car. For a moment the inrushing mob prevented the exit of those trying to get out. My husband and I locked arms and pushed our way toward the exit, holding tightly to our bags. After several minutes we wedged our way through and jumped to the platform. As we walked away, a bell sounded, and the attendants boarded the train and pulled the doors closed behind them. We heard people inside shouting that they had to get off. But the attendants paid no attention.

The next day we took a bus to the settlement where my new life was to begin. The fifty-mile trip took three hours. In the desolate frozen countryside, peasants in drab clothes walked slowly along the side of the road, carrying children and pulling wagons loaded with sacks of supplies and fodder for the farm animals. Everyone seemed mute or stunned, our groaning bus invisible to them.

I saw a little girl standing outside a large barn a few meters off the road. She was holding a bundle of hay, feeding it little by little to an old brown horse. She petted its nose tenderly. It looked like she was singing to the horse.

I remember, I said to myself. That was me. I did that. I sang to the farm animals too. It wasn't that long ago.

I was now returning to everything I'd once dreamed of escaping. My life had come full circle.

WHEN I was her age, during school vacations I had a job caring for the village's herd of water buffalo. For a ten-year-old child, tending the buffalo was exhausting work. Each day, I cut grass for them and guided them to the river to drink. At night I herded them into a pen. When it rained and when there was thunder and lightning, the animals became restless and jittery and sometimes ran away. But I got along well with them.

They could recognize my scent and the sound of my voice, and they came to trust me. In the morning I'd climb on the back of one of the animals and stay there throughout the day. One of the old females was particularly fond of me. When she saw me approaching, she'd lower her head for me. Then, barefoot, I'd place each of my feet on the smooth part of each of her horns. She'd carefully raise her head, and I'd slide down onto her back.

I daydreamed when I was on her back. My most persistent daydream was of becoming an officer in the PLA. The army meant escape from the drudgery of farm life. In the PLA you could sing in a chorus, be part of an army drama or dance troupe, march in Tiananmen, help the people, fly an airplane, ride in a submarine, see the world, and defend the country. Getting into the PLA was something like getting into heaven for a Christian.

When the sky darkened and I realized rain might soon start

falling, I tried to calm the animals by singing to them, but the only songs I knew were the revolutionary songs I'd learned in school. I sang "The East Is Red" and the "Internationale." It worked. From the moment they heard me begin with *"Red in the east rises the sun, / A man called Mao Zedong was born in China,"* they became calm.

Even though my life on the farm was difficult and I worked long hours when I wasn't in the classroom, I was often reminded of how lucky I was. My mother's childhood had been far more difficult. Her family name was also Xu, a common surname in the village. Her family was poor, but the poverty of the Xus was a relatively new status for them. My mother's grandfather had been among the largest landowners in the village. One evening in the mid-1920s a local warlord and some of his men came through the village. They chose my great-grandfather's place to stay for the night. The warlord had several large trunks carried into the house.

In the morning he departed. But some neighbors believed he had left one trunk behind. Word of this quickly reached a group of bandits who operated in the area. The bandit chief and his men broke into my great-grandfather's home and demanded the trunk. Great-grandfather told them there was no trunk.

So the bandits bound Great-grandfather and his sons and marched them to the village square. They brought a huge cooking pot from one of the homes, filled it with cooking oil, and built a fire under it. Once the oil was boiling, they hoisted Great-grandfather over the pot. The bandit chief demanded that he turn over the trunk. Again and again Great-grandfather said there was no trunk. Finally the bandit chief gave a signal to his men, and they dropped Great-grandfather into the oil. There was an abbreviated scream of terror, a loud crackling, and Great-grandfather was gone.

Great-grandfather's three sons were then lifted into the air and lowered to within a few inches of the boiling oil. And each of them in turn denied that the warlord had left behind any trunk. The bandits finally concluded that the story of the trunk wasn't true. They released the three boys. But before they left, they ransacked Great-grandfather's house, taking everything of value. They killed the farm animals. Finally, they set fire to the house.

That morning Great-grandfather had been one of the wealthiest peasants in Lishi. That afternoon he was dead and his widow and sons were homeless.

My grandfather never forgot what happened, and he found in the Communist Party the justice he had been waiting for. Before the Communists won the civil war, Grandfather became the first member of the Party in our village. Afterward the Party named him head of land redistribution and reform in the village and the surrounding area.

The peasants who owned the largest parcels of land were labeled landlords by the Party, and after their land was confiscated, they were publicly executed. The local warlord and the bandit chief and his men were captured and executed. Grandfather and his brothers were invited to attend the executions.

"The Party was our salvation," my mother was reminded again and again when she was growing up. "They saved us from starvation and warlordism, and they gave us justice and land."

Grandfather worked tirelessly for the Party and justice. He was so fair in redistributing land that the local people came to respect him, and the Party decided to publicize him as the ideal peasant Communist. They brought him to neighboring villages to give speeches on the glories of the Party and what it had done for Lishi. The peasant assemblies loved his speeches and cheered him enthusiastically.

Before long most of his time was spent making speeches rather than working on his land. He traveled to Danyang, Zhenjiang, Nanjing, and other cities to speak, and soon he was the centerpiece of a Party delegation traveling through Jiangsu Province and neighboring provinces. But Grandfather never aspired to be a celebrity. He had received no formal education and could neither read nor write. He spoke Mandarin with a heavy country accent and often mispronounced words. He started to notice people in the audience snickering and laughing at him. After this happened several times, the Party appointed a group of young writers to compose speeches for him. The speechwriters used words and idioms that were incomprehensible to him, and he found himself reciting speeches he couldn't understand. He asked to be sent home but was refused.

After traveling for the Party for several more months, Grandfather began to experience pain in his chest. He fainted on the stage in the middle of a speech in Zhenjiang and was rushed to a hospital. The doctors said he was just tired, but three days later, at an outdoor rally in Nanjing, he collapsed again. Thinking he had only fainted, Party cadres carried him into a nearby building to rest. By the time they found a table and laid him on it, he was dead.

Grandfather's reputation grew to mythic proportions following his death. A short book was written about him, and students in the local schools studied his life and work. In the schoolbooks nothing at all was said about his requests to return to his family to live a simple life far from the propaganda stage.

My grandmother's health declined after her husband's death. Soon she became bedridden. As a result of this double family misfortune, my mother, as the eldest daughter in the family, became the head of her household. Illiterate like her mother and father, she went to work full-time in the fields at age twelve. She became responsible for providing food and shelter for her mother; her younger sister, age two; and two younger brothers, ages seven and five. She got up before dawn each day and worked until dark.

By the time she was fifteen, she'd saved enough money to send her brothers and sister to a village school. When she was nineteen, the Communist Party's Great Leap Forward brought famine to the countryside. In five years nearly thirty million people starved to death. Mother and her cousin Lingdi learned that there were factory jobs in Shenyang, in northeastern China. So the girls took the train to Shenyang. With the money my mother sent home, the family was able to buy enough food on the black market to stay alive, while more than half of the villagers died of starvation.

When Mother returned from Shenyang, she had reached the marrying age. A village boy from another Xu family had just graduated from agricultural school and had become the farm's new veterinarian. When a matchmaker introduced the young veterinarian to my mother in 1962, the two found they liked each other very much. They were married that year on National Day, October 1. Fourteen months later I was born.

I STARTED GRAMMAR SCHOOL when I was seven. The school was in a nearby village, a twenty-minute walk from our house. Several classes met simultaneously in one room. The school day lasted from seven a.m. until four p.m. six days a week, with three weeks of vacation in the winter and three months in the summer. Each fall we had a two-week break to help with the harvest.

Our curriculum stressed political education over academic studies. On the first day in class we were given our own copies of Chairman Mao's *Little Red Book*. We began and ended each day with a recitation from the book.

In the lower grades we studied Chinese literature and history through simple stories and spent several hours each day practicing writing Chinese characters. We also studied math, science, and politics. Every lesson was geared toward making us good Party followers rather than independent analytical thinkers. Obedience and conformity were the Confucian subtext of our education, even though Confucius himself was out of favor with the Party.

Part of each school day was devoted to physical education. Of course, our exercises also had a political component. We learned how to jog long distances in order to confront an enemy, and we worked on strengthening our arms and shoulders so we could throw hand grenades. We played games like Ping-Pong and basketball, the latter a sport that we never realized had originated in America.

During our first school year we were required to fill out applications for membership in the Little Red Guards, a group organized in 1966 to assist the older Red Guards in spearheading the Cultural Revolution. Out of thirty applicants at my school, six were accepted on this first round of applications. I was one of the lucky six. I ran all the way home to tell my mother the good news.

The next afternoon there was a gathering of the Little Red Guards from all classes. After the inductees promised to embrace the principles of the group, the older members of the Red Guards gave each of us a red scarf and showed us how to knot it properly.

Many campaigns took place during my years in primary school. In one campaign the people were instructed to "learn from the PLA." Soldiers came into the countryside and worked among the people. They arrived without fanfare in Lishi. I wasn't aware of their presence until one afternoon. At that time I was frustrated by my difficult experience of writing complex Chinese characters. I was so upset, in fact, that I burst into tears while walking home from school with friends. Suddenly I saw four tall men blocking our path. They were in uniform, and I thought they were the most beautiful men I had ever seen. One bent down beside me and asked, "Why are you crying, Little Red Guard?"

"I can't write my characters. Everyone laughs at my writing."

"Let me help you," he responded. "What is your name?"

"Xu Meihong."

"Well, Xu Meihong, show me your notebook," he said. I showed him my tortured characters.

"That isn't so bad," he assured me. He knelt down beside me and then very slowly in large clean strokes made the characters for me. After doing that, he put the pencil in my hand and guided it over and over again, drawing the characters. I felt I was touched by a god. The other children were envious and awestruck.

The soldiers remained in our village for two weeks. Of course, all the students fell in love with them. Their bright uniforms—a rich green with vermilion piping and epaulets and stars—contrasted starkly with the drab outfits worn by the peasants.

The soldiers labored long hours in the village, helping in the fields and with construction. They camped outside, cooked their own food, and turned down all invitations by villagers to stay in their homes or to eat with them. They would take nothing from us, they said. They had come only to help us. The adults adored these young men as much as the children did.

When they had completed their work in Lishi, they moved on to another village. They cleaned up their camp before departing, leaving behind only affection, goodwill, and a platoon of little dreamers.

WHEN I was in the third grade, our teacher told us that we were going to learn special marching, just like the PLA. She asked each of us to bring a toy gun to school. The next day some of the children showed up with toy guns their parents had purchased for them. Those whose parents were woodworkers had beautiful homemade guns. But most of us were pathetically armed. My weapon was just a rough pointed stick.

When our teacher saw our homemade guns, she frowned for a moment and then changed her request. She said we could carry any homemade weapon—a gun, a sword, or a spear.

We used our ingenuity. We cut tall bamboo shoots, and our fathers fashioned crude spearpoints from wood and tied them to the end of the bamboo, like a traditional Chinese pike. We tried to make the tips and blades as sharp as possible so we could skewer any enemies of the people we might find—landlords, rightists, Americans, or Russians—on the way to school.

Our teachers had begun to tell us frightening stories about the enemies of China. The landlords were the most insidious. Before 1949, we were taught, the landowners were extremely wealthy. They dressed in silk, had many servants and concubines, and overworked and abused the peasants on their lands. We were told life was much better since liberation, but the landlords still lay in wait for their return to power, backed by their allies abroad. If the revolution was overthrown, they would rise up to take back their land and wealth.

Spies were everywhere, we were warned, to win converts to the counterrevolutionary cause. Every stranger was a suspect. Whenever a relative or friend from outside our village came to visit, he was required to report to the head of the village. A permanent file was maintained on every outsider who visited.

In order to provide practical training for what we'd learned in school, our teachers organized scores of field trips for us. We assembled at school to begin our own little version of the Long March. For kids of eight or nine this was a big adventure. As we marched along, shouting patriotic slogans, the teacher would occasionally yell, "Hit the ground!" and we'd all drop to the ground and lie completely still. Then she would shout, "Bombs!" and some of the students would immediately shield their fellow students from bomb fragments by covering their bodies with their own.

After a few minutes she would order us to resume our marching and shouting. We had a wonderful time playing at stealth and combat. Each of us imagined himself a little hero off to save the nation.

Sometimes traitors were found within the village. The Red Guards were merciless, saying they were trying to save the country from its enemies. The rest of us joined in the chorus of denunciation. The children were given little red flags, and we marched behind the accused, berating them, throwing stones at them, demanding they confess. Those identified as enemies of the people were not punished only by public beatings, denunciations, humiliation, and imprisonment. Some were wicked enough to merit execution. I witnessed several public executions when I was a child.

The condemned men and women were marched onto a stage. Wearing a sign listing their crimes, they were rebuked, punched, kicked, slapped, poked, and denounced as hooligans or landlords or capitalist roaders or rightists or spies with relatives in Taiwan, Hong Kong, or the United States. Then they were taken to a field at the edge of the village. Everyone followed, shouting slogans and pausing now and then to listen for confessions or pleas for mercy.

When an execution took place, the family of the criminal was required to pay thirty fen for each bullet used by the National Security Police. Often enough a criminal might move as the bullet was fired, or there would be a misfire. In some cases three or four bullets were required to kill a criminal, and his family had to pay ninety or one hundred twenty fen and was denounced for raising a child who was so troublesome right to the end of his life.

No one asked if the convicted criminal really deserved the fate he suffered. Those who were executed deserved it, we believed, and everyone benefitted by their disposal. The relatives of the condemned dared not show their sadness in public, or they would be accused of complicity or disloyalty.

Later I learned that execution quotas were issued for every province, county, district, and village. The quotas had nothing at all to do with the crime rate. Like everything else in China, they were politically determined. In one case a young man from our village was arrested late one night for attempted rape. He had gotten drunk and sneaked into his girlfriend's house. But he went to the wrong room and tried to embrace her sister. The police were summoned, and the next morning a sign was posted saying he had been executed for "hooliganism." The quota was filled.

Since enemies of the people might be anywhere, our teachers encouraged us to describe in detail our homelife. Our parents or our brothers and sisters might be class enemies. Our primary loyalty, we were told, must be to the Party and the revolution.

My father loved to listen to his radio. Each night at eight he'd listen to a national news broadcast. But late at night, when he thought everyone else was asleep, he'd listen to the BBC and the Voice of America broadcasts in Chinese. Our teachers told us to report anyone who listened to foreign radio broadcasts. I didn't turn my father in, but I expected the Public Security people to come smashing through the door at any moment to arrest him.

MY LAST semester of grammar school began in January 1976. On the morning of January 8 the national news was being broadcast when suddenly there was a long silence. This was followed by slow sad music that played for several minutes. Then the announcer said that Premier Zhou Enlai had died. My heart sank. Chairman Mao was the greatest man in the country, but Zhou Enlai was the most loved. He was like a member of every Chinese family.

At school we were given little white paper flowers to wear. The eyes of all of the teachers were swollen and red from crying.

On Qing Ming Day in April, when we celebrate our ancestors and clean their gravesites, a large crowd gathered at Tiananmen Square to put flowers at the Monument to the People in memory of Zhou. But on the radio it was reported that counterrevolutionaries and hooligans had gathered and were chased away by the police and armed workers. When we heard this story, we were stunned and confused. Why did the hooligans love our late premier? This was the first indication we had that enemies of Chairman Mao and of the Cultural Revolution were numerous, organized, and bold enough to express their dissent openly.

An earthquake struck on July 28 that summer in Tangshan, one hundred miles southeast of Beijing, in Hebei Province.

The night of July 27 had been unusually hot in our village, and

I was unable to sleep. I awakened early—before anyone else was up—and poured water into a large wooden container to bathe in. I climbed in, certain that my privacy would not be interrupted.

I was relaxing in the tub when I felt something like an explosion. This was followed by a severe shaking of the entire house. The water sloshed from side to side in the tub and splashed onto the floor. I tried to stand, but the shaking of the floor made it impossible. When it stopped, I jumped from the tub and ran outside screaming. I stood there petrified, shaking, and totally naked.

Up and down the village paths, people were running, screaming, and crying. I didn't realize I was naked until I noticed neighbors staring at me. I felt more fear than shame and didn't go back into the house, but instead covered myself with my hands. My parents and brother and sister came outside, also crying and hysterical.

My father turned on his radio, but the government news services refused to say anything about the quake, perhaps for fear that it made us vulnerable to an attack from our enemies. The only guidance we received from the government was to sleep outside. (Later we heard initial estimates that 655,000 people had been killed and 779,000 injured in Hebei Province alone.)

In the next months it was as though the villagers of Lishi were one big clan or tribe again. In the central square the people put up a huge plastic tent. Although it protected us from the rain and sun, it did not protect us from the heat. There were no airholes in the tent and no windows. There was only a large opening to go in or out, and that was closed at night to keep out mosquitoes. Inside the tent the temperature rose to well over one hundred degrees.

When classes resumed in September, we were instructed to stay outside the school building, which might collapse in another earthquake. There were no trees nearby, so we studied under the sun. September was particularly hot that year. Our skin burned, and we perspired and soaked our clothing.

I wondered if things could possibly get any worse. Then they did. At four p.m. on September 9, 1976, we heard the news that truly shook our world. A newsman on the radio said, "Our great beloved Chairman Mao Zedong has passed away."

I couldn't move. To me this was an official announcement that God had died. My mother, who had been lying in bed listening to the music and the news, burst into tears. I heard shouts outside as people rushed from their houses, moaning and crying.

With the death of Mao we believed that the sun had died and that the new age would be one of darkness for China. But we were wrong. We soon discovered we had been living in darkness without knowing it, and the new age, which we initially feared, quickly brought us change and light.

I THOUGHT about my childhood years in the village for a long time after seeing the little girl feeding the horse. It was growing dark when we finally arrived at our destination. The bus stopped, and we gathered our luggage and got off. "Where are we?" I asked.

"Near your new home," my husband replied. I saw a cluster of houses and smokestacks in the distance. "That's it," he said, pointing to the buildings. We began walking down the road toward the settlement. We walked slowly, side by side, like two lost and tired souls looking for shelter.

I looked up and saw a shooting star streak across the evening sky. Didn't a shooting star mean good luck? I couldn't remember. I asked my husband, but he said he couldn't remember either.

EIGHT 第八章 Twelve Pandas

WE WERE greeted by a guard inside the headquarters of the Nanyang Oil Company. Lin Cheng gave our names and said we had an appointment with the supervisor. The guard made a phone call, and the supervisor appeared minutes later. He was friendly and said his son in Beijing had told him all about us. He seemed convinced he was helping a friend of his son escape from family difficulties.

We stayed in his home that night. He told me I could live with his family, earning my keep by helping with the cooking and chores. He found me a job selling instant noodles on the street.

My husband remained with me for two nights, then returned to Beijing. I gave him a letter I'd written to my parents and asked him to mail it as soon as he arrived there. I told them I was doing well and was busy with my new job and would not be able to write to them often. I gave no indication that I was not in Beijing.

Selling noodles on the street, I felt completely out of place. None of the people I worked with had even a basic education. Their greatest passion was making a one-fen profit from each bag of noodles. They gawked at me as if I were from another planet.

Each day I got up at five thirty a.m. to clean the rooms in the house where I lived. Then I prepared breakfast. I had a ninety-minute break at lunchtime, when I'd hurry home to make lunch for the family, then clean up. After work I cooked and served dinner and washed the dishes and the clothing for the family. No television, radio, or newspaper was available to me. I was no more than a servant in the household. Letters from Lin Cheng provided my only hope and connection to the outside world.

One month after I began my new job, I received a letter from him with news I dreaded. "I have thought it over," he began, "and I feel I must tell you now that I no longer love you. I want to get a divorce as soon as possible. I know you are facing the most difficult time in your life. But pretending that I still love you would be to mislead you, and I won't do that. We each have our own lives to live now. Please don't be angry with me. In time I think you will understand why this is necessary."

I went to my room, locked the door behind me, and cried the rest of the evening. The next night I sat in a chair next to the window thinking about my life. I saw no reason to continue it. I thought about stepping into the path of one of the oil trucks that passed me on the road each evening when I returned home from work. Crying softly, feeling unloved, unwanted, and doomed, I crossed my arms on the windowsill and rested my head against them. As I did, I felt something cold against my face. I sat up and noticed the small silver bracelet still locked snugly around my wrist. I'd completely forgotten it. I recalled the afternoon Larry had given it to me and promised it would bring me luck. If it weren't for the bracelet, I could almost believe he'd never existed.

THE last time I'd cried with such hopelessness was after I'd heard of the death of Chairman Mao. I was sure I'd never smile again. Then I remembered that I'd been wrong. Mao's death, in fact, opened a door for me to a new life.

Earlier my parents had disagreed about my education. My mother pointed out that we were poor and that if I went to work in the fields, I could add to our income and make life a little better for everyone in the family. My father, on the other hand, had favored further education for me. He had attended a good high school in Danyang and had studied to become a veterinarian. Father prevailed, but there was a compromise. Mother told me that I could attend a good middle school for two years, but to attend high school after that would be useless.

The death of Mao and the arrest of his wife and her associates marked the start of a period of dramatic change for everyone in China. Deng Xiaoping took control of the government. Maoists were removed from positions of power in the Party and replaced by Deng's friends. Deng announced his intention to modernize China. Among the reforms he introduced were fundamental changes in the educational system. Political education was deemphasized in school, and genuine academic achievement became the primary goal.

I completed middle school in the spring of 1978 and earned a high enough score on the high-school examination to qualify to study in Danyang High School, one of the most prestigious high schools in Jiangsu Province. Because I excelled in school and was a class leader at each grade level, my teachers had appealed to my mother to let me continue with my education rather than relegating me to working on the farm. Mother relented and in 1981 gave me permission to pursue my academic dreams. And so, following the completion of my third year, I took the college entrance examination. It was rigorous—eighteen hours of tests in six subjects spread over three days. On the third day, after returning home, I composed a letter to the president of the PLA Institute for International Relations in Nanjing. For the first time since 1965 the institute had announced it would recruit female cadets for admission in the fall of 1981.

Three weeks later I received my scores, which were among the highest in my county. Then I was given special physical examinations for admission to the army. In late July, officers from the institute visited my high school on three occasions to interview me in both English and Chinese. On August 18, 1981, I was informed that I had been selected as one of the twelve girls to be admitted. Later Mother told me that was the happiest day in her life. I was the first individual in her family to attend a university. She felt even her ancestors were proud of my accomplishment.

My parents accompanied me on the train to Nanjing one week later. That evening I had dinner with my parents and new classmates in the campus dining room. The place was large enough to accommodate more than fifteen hundred cadets. The female cadets' quarters were above the offices of the English department. The boys were housed in three barracks, far enough away to see our quarters but too far away to see in through the windows.

A high-ranking officer came to our quarters with his aides to brief us. "This school," he began, "is unique in China. We are part of the PLA's Second Bureau—military intelligence. In order to protect our security, you are never to talk with anyone about this school. Everything you do and see and hear and say here is classified information. If you are ever asked by anyone where you are studying, you will tell them only that you are a student in a military institute. You will not give them the location of this school. Your address will be a post-office-box number only. You will tell no one your telephone number. The penalty for breaching these rules will be most serious."

Not long after this I went into Nanjing one Sunday afternoon with some of the other women. Outside the large Jinling Hotel, a few blocks from Nanjing University, an elderly man noticed our uniforms and stopped us. "I have a nephew studying in the Institute for International Relations," he said. "I am from Henan Province. I've been on the train for twenty hours getting here. I can't find his school on any map. And there are no phone numbers listed for the institute. Can you help me locate him?"

I was the first to speak up. "I am sorry, sir," I said, "but I've never heard of that school before. We can't help you."

We turned and walked quickly away. We dared not help him.

But we were not always as careful as the school wanted us to be. A month later, on National Day (October 1), several of us visited the Dr. Sun Yat-sen Memorial in Nanjing. Some American tourists waved and said hello, and we made the mistake of saying hello back to them. We immediately realized we'd made a mistake, so we hurried away.

When we got back to the institute, a senior officer was waiting for us. Someone had reported our brief exchange to our commanding officer. "Damn it," he said, "didn't you know that those were Americans? Don't you know what a serious breach of security this is?"

Each of us was required to write a lengthy self-criticism. We were questioned together and individually to make sure that this was purely an accidental encounter.

The fall session at the institute commenced officially on September 1. We were designated a special squad in the school's Company 13, which had one hundred and twenty new cadets.

At our barracks, our supervisor called our names one by one, then solemnly told us that we were like no other girls in China. The important role we would play in maintaining the security of our country was emphasized. The sacrifices we could expect to make were listed. He again called us by name and asked us if we were willing to make the required sacrifices. Each of us in turn answered softly, "Yes."

He announced that I had been selected, along with another girl, as a leader of our group. Then he said, "You are not just part of Company Thirteen. You are the Twelve Pandas—twelve national treasures. Live up to it. Work hard."

Before leaving, he said something that we would hear repeated by our officers nearly every week for the next four years. "We will train you, feed you, clothe you, and care for you for a thousand days. But we will only need you for one moment. Be ready!"

The institute's cadets were divided into thirteen companies. Companies 1 through 3 were trained specifically to work with our military attachés. Companies 4 through 6 were trained to work in Japan, Germany, France, Vietnam, and other Asian and European countries, as well as in the Middle East and in Taiwan and Hong Kong. Companies 7 through 9 were trained to work in Russia. Companies 10 through 13 were trained to work in English-speaking countries.

During opening ceremonies we assembled by company on the parade ground and then marched into the auditorium to our assigned seats. An officer appeared on the stage and shouted, "Sit!" Instantly, with a great rustling and clatter, all fifteen hundred cadets and five hundred officers and teachers in the auditorium sat.

For a moment there was complete silence. Then, from a far corner of the room, a company of seniors broke into a rousing martial song. No sooner was the song finished than another company began another song. This was followed by another. It soon became clear to the new cadets that each of the companies competed to see who could sing the loudest.

After fifteen minutes an officer stood and signaled to stop singing. Then someone ordered the female cadets of Company 13 to stand and sing. We stood self-consciously and sang "The Red Flower"—the Red Flower indicating a model soldier. When we finished, the boys hooted, stomped their feet, and applauded. We were embarrassed by this attention, but since our early youth we'd heard the singing PLA soldiers and dreamed of joining their ranks, and now our dreams had come true.

During the first week of orientation the male students were given lectures on how to behave with females on the campus. "We must warn you," they were told, "that it is strictly forbidden that there be contact between you except in the most formal of circumstances. You are not to eat at the same table. There is to be no romance. You are to study and train here. That is all. If secret contacts are discovered, you will be disciplined along with the woman. You could be expelled from the PLA, and there will forever be a black mark on your record." The women were called to our own meeting and also warned. At the time, none of us could imagine allowing a romantic attachment to endanger our military career. We intended to preserve our passion for soldiering alone.

We went through three months of intense military training before regular classes began. The training lasted from sunrise to sunset six days a week. There was a special squad for the student leaders. We were trained to shout slogans and issue marching orders to the other cadets. At first it was interesting. Then it became amusing and, finally, boring and exhausting. We stumbled to our beds at night without even washing. We didn't move until the bugle call the next morning.

We learned kung fu and wrestling. Each of us was issued a pistol—a 9-mm 54 model, copied from a Czechoslovakian weapon. We learned to assemble and disassemble the weapon and then practiced with it on the firing range. We practiced hand-to-hand combat with bayonets. (Usually our assault on the enemy followed the familiar cry "American soldiers, surrender! You are surrounded, and all resistance is futile!") From there we worked our way up the weapons chain, practicing with hand grenades, small artillery pieces, mortars, and, finally, fieldpieces.

We were reminded repeatedly of the PLA's tradition of courage in combat. We were told of fierce struggles—the fight against the Americans at Pork Chop Hill in Korea and the bloody struggle in the mountains along the border with Vietnam. The Nationalists were expelled to Taiwan, and soon we would defeat them there. No one could stand up to the PLA, we learned. We were in training to carry on the glorious tradition.

Near the end of the training we had several emergency drills. These were supposed to serve as a practical test for all we'd learned, as well as a rehearsal for a real international crisis. One morning we were awakened at three a.m. by a burst of bugle blasts. We sprang from our beds, struggled into our uniforms, grabbed our packs, then raced out to the parade ground.

An officer was waiting for us and announced in an unusually serious tone, "Comrades, we have received word that China has been attacked by the United States."

We glanced at each other—this did not sound like a dress rehearsal.

"The Americans have crossed our borders," he continued. "As you know, this means all-out war. American marines have come up the Yangtze River and are at this moment ten miles from here. Our orders are to meet and destroy them within the hour. We will gladly sacrifice ourselves this morning, if necessary, for the security and the survival of our country. Turn right! March!"

We marched through the gate into the darkness. Quickly our pace became a jog. Although we carried full packs, some of the women began to whisper that we had not been issued weapons or ammunition. How were we supposed to fight the marines?

As we neared the river, we saw a ship anchored midstream. The first ranks of men slowed and began to form a skirmish line—still without weapons. Then we could make out the Chinese markings on the ship. Our commanders walked behind us with stopwatches. They announced that this was a drill. There were no marines. There would be no fight. We dropped to the ground, exhausted.

At the completion of our three months of basic training the institute held a dress parade, followed by a formal ceremony. There were no official ranks in the PLA at that time, but we were informed that we were all designated officers. We traded in our training uniforms for officer's uniforms. We, as officers, had four pockets in our tunics, and the enlisted men had two. That was how rank was distinguished in an army without official rank.

Physical conditioning and weapons-utilization training continued during the next four years, but the principal focus of our education shifted to language skills and intelligence gathering. Our most intensive courses concentrated on developing fluency in English. We needed equal facility in colloquial and technical English, because PLA officers stationed in listening posts throughout China monitored American military and diplomatic communications and private telephone conversations. America's Sixth and Seventh fleets were a critical target of our monitors. We were shocked, sometimes, to hear an American naval officer call his wife in the United States, then moments later call his mistress in the Philippines or Hong Kong and use exactly the same romantic idioms.

The conversations we heard not only helped us learn English expressions but also aroused in us a contempt for American moral standards. To us romance and love were still largely textbook concepts. None of the twelve women had even held hands with a man. We expected romance to be as noble and pure as in the novels we read by Jane Austen, Charlotte Brontë, Margaret Mitchell, and even Ernest Hemingway. We'd never imagined language like that overheard in monitoring American servicemen. They were nothing at all like the high-minded PLA officers, we believed. The world would be a better place when America's power and reach abated and her influence retreated to her own shores.

We also studied American politics and international relations, films, and popular culture. We learned to eat with Western utensils and became adept at Western ballroom dancing. These too were skills that could someday open doors to new friendships and information sources, we were told.

Years later, however, when I met Americans at the Center for Chinese and American Studies in Nanjing, I discovered how outdated our training had been. I had difficulty understanding the latest American idioms. I also learned that Americans our age didn't do ballroom dancing anymore. We had been practicing to interact with an America that no longer existed.

About ninety percent of the new cadets were in the Communist Youth League, the organization from which Party members were drawn. League members met weekly in small study groups. Sometimes we were required to write essays about selected subjects or ourselves. The League and Party line was, "There is absolutely nothing that you cannot share with the Party." So each of us wrote down our private thoughts. They were collected and read aloud to the group and then criticized for selfish attitudes or for intimations of bourgeois values or political ignorance. We were also required to keep diaries, and these were collected from time to time and read.

The intent of these sessions was to raise and sharpen our political consciousness. The result, however, was not what the League and the Party expected. We learned what Party and League leaders wanted to hear, and that is what we wrote. We filled our diaries with folksy politically correct fabrications. We learned to tell big, colorful lies about our love and respect for all of our senior officers and fellow cadets even if we found them brutish or ignorant.

We developed a public and a private persona. The public persona never questioned the order of things or officially sanctioned wisdom. The private persona felt doubts and fears and had questions and misgivings. The twelve of us came to trust only each other and to share our real feelings only when we were in our quarters.

By the end of our first year some of the women wondered if they'd made an unwise choice in coming to a PLA school. Our friends in civilian universities enjoyed a far less disciplined life. Already some of our patriotic ardor was starting to dissipate. But we could never indicate that to our commanders and instructors. We hoped for the best and trusted that the larger part of our childhood dreams might in the end be redeemed. And we continued to cultivate our two faces. While the PLA counted twelve girls in our company, we knew there were twenty-four.

AN EYE-OPENING revelation came during graduation ceremonies for the senior cadets in July 1982. Prior to graduation, cadets were given their future assignments. All of us had the expectation that someday we would have important assignments. Now we learned this might not happen. We heard that fifteen graduating cadets had been assigned to Tibet. We had talked about Tibet often. We were told by those whose friends had been sent there that despite government reports to the contrary, the Tibetans did not want us there. The people were unfriendly or openly hostile. No Chinese soldier felt safe when he was alone, particularly at night. Assignment to Tibet was considered tantamount to being sent to hell. It also meant a dead end to a military career. No soldier stationed there had the chance to make the connections or the reputation necessary to rise in the ranks of the PLA.

In 1981, when assignments were made, the commanders of the

institute made a fundamental error. They convinced themselves that because of indoctrination, any recruit would accept any assignment without protest. Very few cadets actually believed that. After all, cadets with parents who were officers in the PLA or high-ranking cadres in the Party had them pull strings to get them into the institute. After graduation they expected to serve either in a metropolitan area of China or in some prestigious post abroad. The unspoken assumption was that hardship assignments would go to cadets who had no connections. Unfortunately, in 1981 the institute's commanders overlooked this important principle.

At the official graduation ceremony the name of each senior was called and his assignment was announced. When the ceremony was over, we marched to the dining room for a lavish banquet. All of the officers were present, sitting at the head table. The young men assigned to Tibet sat together, commiserating.

Beer and wine were served. The graduating seniors consumed large amounts of both. As the evening passed, they became more intoxicated, outspoken, and rowdy. They unbuttoned their tunics, and their faces reddened. Then one of the cadets assigned to Tibet stood on his chair to give a speech.

"During our first year here," he began, pointing to the table of the officers, "you told us we were being trained for important assignments. Well, now we know that you were just full of s___. And you know it too. Everyone in this room knows it."

His words were answered by cheers from the other cadets at his table. The officers glared in disbelief at the young man. He glared right back. "You lied to us every day. And when we're gone to Tibet, you'll still be here to lie to the new cadets."

One by one the senior officers stood and left the room.

"We came here," the cadet said, as they made their exit, "and we gave you our youth. And what did you do with it? You turned it into bulls___."

Every time he finished a sentence, more seniors pounded on the tables and shouted their approval. One after another, those being sent to Tibet stood on their chairs and denounced the commanding officers. They continued until the beer and wine were gone.

Then, like an angry mob, the seniors stormed out of the hall. Within minutes we could hear them tearing up their quarters, smashing windows, throwing furniture into the courtyard. Several young officers escorted the women back to our quarters. They advised us to lock our doors. The seniors were "totally out of control."

The seniors stripped to their underwear and sat outside drinking, singing, and chanting. We huddled around our windows and watched them. Several times they stood and raised their bottles to us and drank a toast before collapsing on the lawn.

The commander of the institute issued an order that night saying that as long as the seniors remained on campus and did their damage, they were not to be approached. They were just letting off steam, he said. But no one would be allowed outside the gate, and extra sentries were posted. Eventually the seniors stumbled to their quarters and went to sleep.

Early the next morning we were awakened by the roar of the engines of several trucks. We dressed and ran outside to the parade ground. All of the senior cadets were gathered outside their barracks. Some of them were embracing. Others were shaking hands, and many were crying. One by one they threw their packs into the trucks and climbed up after them.

When they saw us approaching, they became quiet. We had never spoken personally to each other. One woman shouted, "Good-bye. Take care of yourself. We will never forget you."

The departing cadets waved from the trucks and shouted back, "We will never forget you either! Long live Company Thirteen!"

Someone started to sing the "Internationale," and we all joined in. Then they were gone, and it was quiet again.

Back in our quarters, one girl asked if we weren't sacrificing too much by coming to the institute. "No fun, no romance, no dating," she said. "Study, run, exercise, self-criticism, martial arts. What for? Tibet? Three more years of work and sacrifice for that?"

But we were trapped. We had agreed that in exchange for our education, we would go wherever the PLA sent us. Was the institute really preparing us for important assignments, or was it the graveyard of our dreams?

I RETURNED TO THE INSTITUTE in August to start my second year. We learned that half a dozen of the seniors sent to Tibet had deserted before arriving there. Their punishment was expulsion from the PLA, but the army wanted to keep their protests out of the news. The men were well connected, and the commanders at the institute did not wish to arouse the anger of influential critics. Each of the deserters, we were told, because of the language skills they'd acquired at the institute, had immediately taken good-paying jobs in the cities where they'd expected to be assigned by the PLA. We were shocked at the news, because they had prospered after their dishonorable release from the PLA. We were surprised at how easily they'd slipped from the military harness. There was a kind of heroism in their defiance of PLA authority, we felt, and we couldn't help but feel a bit of admiration for them.

The institute's commanders learned from their mistake. After that the cadets selected for service in Tibet were of peasant background, without influential connections. They prized Party membership, which was given along with the assignment to Tibet. Thus they became grateful and convenient victims for the PLA, and there were no more insurrections following graduation ceremonies.

By our senior year all twelve girls at the institute were both bolder and more melancholy than we'd been in the past. We found boyfriends, defied our commanding officers in small acts of rebellion, and were increasingly aware we would soon be going our separate ways. We also faced the fact that each of us owed the PLA fifteen years of service.

On the day our final banquet was held and we were handed our degrees, we twelve women had our picture taken as a group for the last time. There remains a sacred chamber in my memory for the women of my company. For four years we had practiced on the same parade grounds, studied in the same classrooms, laughed and cried together. We loved each other and showed it daily in our acts. We dreamed and then lost the same dreams, enjoyed the same successes, and suffered the same disappointments.

When we came to Nanjing, we were young and innocent and red, and they told us we were national treasures. And we were.

NIGHT AFTER NIGHT IN Nanyang, alone in my room, I remembered my days at the institute and the eleven women I'd shared those years with. Everything I'd ever dreamed was ashes now—my idealism, my faith, my hope, my career, my husband, and soon my life. I wondered if the other women from the group could understand or sympathize with my plight or if they'd ever know how much I missed them now.

AT THE end of each day I returned from work walking along the side of the road used by the big oil trucks heading for the city of Nanyang. I saw how simple it might be to step in front of a truck and end my life in the blink of an eye. Many times I tried to summon the courage to take that step. I'm still not sure why I could not do it. I wonder, though, if my hesitation wasn't the result of a fragment of hope still hooked on a shard of memory.

Three days after I received Lin Cheng's letter asking for a divorce, a telegram from him arrived. He'd had time to reconsider, he said. He apologized and asked me to forgive him. "I love you and will never leave you. I'll do my utmost to help you and to help us get out of this terrible situation." I realized that, like me, he was still struggling to untangle romantic recollections and hopes from the implacable imperatives we faced.

My problem was already affecting his career. He had been scheduled to escort the president of the NDU—a four-star general—on a visit to the United States and Southeast Asia. But at the last minute he'd been replaced by a junior officer. People looked at him differently since his wife was accused of involvement with an American agent. If I left Lin Cheng, I reasoned, I might repay him for the embarrassment and suffering I'd caused him. He could fulfill most of his dreams. And by accepting the consequences of my actions, I too in time might find peace. But I knew that happiness for me could never be secured in China. The general had advised me to wait for a moment of national chaos and then take advantage of it and leave China. Saving my husband required only that I accept reality. Saving myself meant waiting for a miracle to happen.

In early May I received a short letter from my childhood friend Zhang Yuhua, at Qinghua University in Beijing. "Dear Meihong," she wrote. "Do you remember our talk in Lishi? I must tell you now that hell has broken loose. Come to Beijing."

I felt my heart start pounding. What was she talking about? I hadn't heard a radio or read a newspaper since leaving Nanjing. I hurried back to the mailroom and asked the clerk if she had any newspapers. She rummaged through the papers on her desk and found a week-old copy of the *People's Daily.*

There it was on the first page: Students and workers were in the streets in Beijing calling for an end to corruption and for democracy. Similar disruptions were beginning in other cities.

"Oh, God," I whispered. I was shaking so much I could hardly hold the paper. "Thank you, God. Thank you, thank you."

I contemplated my next move. I reached into my pocket to see if I had my wallet. I did. But I had no money with me. It made no difference, I thought. I didn't want to waste time going home. I'd get by. I knew what I had to do, and I had to do it immediately.

I walked to the road and stood there watching the trucks roll by. After several passed, I spotted a driver I knew. I waved for him to stop. "I need to get to Nanyang," I said. "Can you give me a lift?"

"Sure," he said, and smiled broadly. "I can always use company. Especially that of a pretty girl."

He dropped me off at the train station and wished me luck.

Thousands of people crowded the station. I looked at the schedule and saw when the next train departed for Beijing, then plunged headlong into the sea of people and let myself be pushed along with them onto the long platform outside. Within minutes I was on the Beijing-bound train. Then all I had to do was elude the conductor for the next sixteen hours.

In Beijing, I hopped off the train and walked through the station. Thousands of students were milling around, finding friends and hurrying off. I listened to their excited chatter. Some were going to university campuses and some to Tiananmen Square. I caught a bus to Qinghua University with bus fare a kindly engineer on the train had given me. As I rode through Beijing, I watched the commotion in the streets and felt I was right where I wanted to be—in the middle of it. I glanced down at the tiny silver chain on my wrist and wondered if at last it was working its fabled magic.

The moment Zhang Yuhua saw me standing outside her door in my dusty work clothes, she burst into tears, then pulled me into her room. "Everything is going to be all right again," she assured me. "There's going to be a new future for us."

She tried to tell me everything that had happened in Beijing since mid-April. The universities, including her own, had become centers of protest and insurrection. Huge banners covered the university walls calling for democratic reforms. The numbers of those demanding change multiplied daily. The old order was crumbling by the hour. There was a universal feeling that China had arrived at a turning point. The people were going to stand up and make history again.

Yuhua loaned me clean clothing. That evening I called Lin Cheng at the NDU and told him I was in Beijing. He was surprised and immediately came to see me.

That night we had dinner with a friend and his girlfriend. Afterward I told Lin Cheng I wanted to apply for divorce as quickly as possible. "For your sake, as well as mine. That doesn't mean I don't love you. It means I do love you." When I stopped speaking, it was quiet for a moment. Then both of us started to cry. We embraced for a long time and agreed we had to be strong and help each other.

My first concern after arranging to start divorce proceedings was finding a job so I could earn some money and not burden my husband or Yuhua. Through a military friend, I found one with a large air-cargo business in Beijing that needed hostesses and translators that spring of 1989 for a big international conference. I could live in an employee dormitory in Beijing managed by the company.

Sometimes, during my lunch break, I walked to Tiananmen Square and mixed with the students and workers who were gathered there. I noticed hundreds of foreigners at the square, many of them Americans. I began to wonder about Larry. Had he really left China, or was that merely another lie the colonel had fed me?

I called the Center for Chinese and American Studies in Nanjing and asked for Carol Chu. When she answered the phone, I said, "It's me." She recognized my voice. I told her I was in Beijing. She was cautious and gave only brief answers to my questions. Neither of us used specific names.

"Are you okay?" she asked.

"Yes, I am," I assured her. "Where is our friend? Is he okay?"

"He's in Hong Kong or Thailand," she said. "I'm not sure. He's finishing his book. He's okay too."

"I'm coming to see you at the end of the month."

"Call me when you arrive," she said. Then we hung up.

WHEN my employer's convention concluded at the end of May, my boss thanked me for the work I'd done and asked if I'd stay on. I agreed but told her I'd like a brief break.

I used the money I'd earned to buy a train ticket to Nanjing.

My train was scheduled to leave at ten thirty p.m. Early on the day of my departure I received a phone call from the general, who had been summoned to Beijing for the national emergency. He'd gotten my number from Lin Cheng. He said he would meet me at Kunming Lake early in the evening.

The first thing he asked me was why I'd returned so suddenly. I told him, and confided I thought China might be undergoing a dramatic change.

"There will be no change," he said. "The army is going to wipe out the students." I thought that the army might be called in but only to clear Tiananmen Square. The general told me I was wrong. "If you wish to remain alive, please do not go near the square again. Power is what is most important to the rulers of this country. Don't you know that by now? The demonstrators are threatening their power. So the students will die." He concluded,

"Listen, Xu Meihong, you have caused them trouble once. If they catch you again, here, you are dead."

"Then what shall I do?"

"The student movement is not an important consideration for you. It will be crushed. The most important thing for you is to get out of China."

"I was thinking about ways," I told him. "I know someone who can help me find Larry."

He warned me to prepare for disappointment. "Americans are not like Chinese," he said. "The Chinese are loyal to personal friends. So this Larry Engelmann may not be willing to help you. Don't expect any American to feel an obligation to you."

But I did have faith in Larry. I told the general I believed I could depend on him if I could just find him.

That night I took the train to Nanjing. After I arrived, I called Carol from the post office. She asked to meet me in front of Zhou's restaurant. An hour later I stood in a storefront a few buildings away.

As Carol approached, she looked frightened. She walked by me. I watched the street behind her, trying to see if she'd been followed. When I was sure she was alone, I joined her. We continued walking quickly, looking behind us several times.

I asked what had happened to Larry. "He is doing just fine," she said. "He's in Hong Kong finishing his book. He asks about you every time he writes. I didn't know what happened, so I had nothing to tell him."

"I need your help. Can you give me his address and phone number in Hong Kong?"

"Have you any idea what you did to him?"

"What do you mean?" I asked.

"You signed a statement saying Larry assaulted you at the center. The Chinese codirector described it to the Chinese students at one of their meetings to discredit Larry. The American authorities demanded he resign and leave China."

"Carol, I never signed anything like that."

"People in the center say you hurt him deliberately. Why? He did nothing to hurt you."

"Carol, I played no part in that. I'll explain it all. Just tell me where he is."

"No!" she said with blunt finality. "Absolutely not."

"Carol, who told you these things about me?"

She ignored my question. "You know, Meihong, Larry never believed you signed that statement. Till the day he left, he thought you were forced to write it. He keeps writing letters trying to find you. Are you planning to hurt him again? It will only be worse this time."

She said good-bye. Then she turned and was gone. My one contact with Larry was beyond my reach.

That night I thought, It might take a long time, but if Larry really wants to find me, he will find me.

I left Nanjing the next evening, June 2, and arrived in Beijing on the afternoon of June 3.

BEIJING was warm and humid. I planned to stay in Lin Cheng's quarters until I began my new job, so I found a bus to take me to the NDU, which is outside Beijing. On the way, I saw troops in trucks, bumper to bumper, heading into the city. The soldiers all had weapons at the ready. It reminded me of photographs I'd seen of the PLA going into battle. People along the street watched the soldiers and demanded they turn around and leave the city. Some shook their fists and denounced them. The people in my bus leaned far out the windows and yelled, "Go back! Why are you coming to Beijing? Go home!" But the soldiers stared straight ahead and refused to make eye contact. The trucks, without flags or any military insignia, continued slowly on their way into the city. The soldiers were young—seventeen or eighteen years old, about the age I had been when I came into the army. They looked like provincial forces, thoroughly intimidated by the crowds.

That night Lin Cheng had invited a half-dozen fellow officers to watch television with him in his apartment. While they watched the news, they discussed what they'd heard about troop movements. Some had heard rumors that the soldiers carried tear gas and rubber bullets to clear Tiananmen Square. The consensus was that nobody would be hurt.

None of us could sleep that night. About midnight we turned on the radio to listen to the Voice of America and the BBC. We heard that the troops were clearing Tiananmen Square. We could not tell, beyond that, what was happening.

About six a.m. a friend came to the door and told us, "They killed the students. They killed them all."

We turned on Voice of America again. They were saying that hundreds of students had been killed. There were rumors that fighting had broken out between different units of the army.

We hired a minivan later that morning to take us into the city. Lin Cheng and his friends wanted to see for themselves what had happened. What we saw was unbelievable. Carcasses of cars and military trucks lined the streets all the way into the city. People were standing around watching them burn. I saw no soldiers until we neared the center of the city, where we saw tanks rumbling up and down the boulevards.

Later that day we turned on the TV and heard newsmen announce that the PLA had achieved "another victory" and that Beijing was under their control.

On my way out of the city, I saw enraged crowds of people everywhere denouncing the brutality of the PLA. The soldiers had killed everyone—students, women, children, they said, "from babies to ninety-year-olds"—and had randomly fired into apartment windows. There were also reports that enraged citizens had stopped trucks filled with soldiers and mobbed them. Someone said that an entire company had disappeared in Beijing. "They can't find them." Some said that the soldiers had been killed and cremated in the same way they had killed and burned the students.

People threw food and rocks at the soldiers and almost anything else they could pick up. Some of the country troops threw away their tunics and hid, but they were recognized by their white army shirts and military trousers. They were beaten senseless or killed by mobs.

It seemed China was no longer my country. What had been done secretly to individuals in the past now had been done publicly to masses of people before the eyes of the entire world.

I BEGAN MY NEW JOB TWO weeks after the Tiananmen massacre. I'd worked only for four weeks before agents from the Second Bureau of the PLA found me. They told my manager that I had serious political problems and that I was forbidden to be in contact with foreigners. They warned her that she was responsible if I violated that restriction. She told me the next day she could not keep me much longer and that I'd better make other plans.

Agents from the Second Bureau also warned my husband that his wife did not belong in Beijing. Non-Beijing residents were not allowed to remain there after the Tiananmen massacre. He told them I needed to stay while our divorce was pending. They cautioned him that he was responsible for reporting any wrongdoing he might suspect me of.

That night he told me it would be best if I left the country as soon as possible. "There will never be a normal life for you in China again," he said. "You have to leave."

"But how?" I asked. I was told that the government traced international phone calls and censored all international correspondence. I couldn't afford getting caught contacting Larry. I sought the help of Yuhua. A friend from her university was going to the University of Kansas soon. He agreed to mail a letter to Larry for me once he arrived. I composed a short formal letter. "Dear Professor Engelmann," I wrote. "Do you remember a girl you met in China named Xu Meihong? She remembers you. She thinks of you often. She needs your help. If you would like to help her, please contact me." Then I wrote my phone number at work and Yuhua's address at Qinghua University and requested that my real name not be used on the envelope. I signed my letter, "Yours always, Rose."

My time was running out. I decided to take a gamble and call Larry from my office. I still had his office phone number. I dialed, and as I listened, I felt a wave of panic. A recorded voice came on—I recognized it as his. I said softly, "Professor Engelmann, I need your help. Please call me." Then I hung up without leaving my number. I prayed he might recognize my voice and what? I wasn't sure.

Several days passed. On a Friday morning, August 25, I arrived at work at seven a.m. I heard the phone ringing. Another girl answered it. She said it was for me and that it sounded like an international phone call. I tried to remain calm. I picked up the phone and said in English, "Hello."

"Is this Xu Meihong?" the caller asked. I recognized the voice. I started to cry. Then he said, "Don't cry. I have your letter. I remember you. And I love you."

"Me too," I said.

"We have a lot to talk about," he said.

"Yes," I replied. "I want to explain everything to you."

"You need my help, don't you?"

"You're my last chance. I need to get out of China, Larry. I'm in trouble."

"I can help you, Xu Meihong," he said confidently. They were the sweetest and most assuring words I'd heard in months. "I'll do anything for you," he said. "Anything at all. Just calm down and think about what you want, and we'll get it together."

"You're not angry with me?"

"No. I never doubted you for a moment, Meihong."

"Okay," I said, trying to compose myself.

"Do you want to come to America?" he asked.

"Yes."

"Then let's make it happen. By the way, do you still have the bracelet I gave you?"

"Yes, of course I do."

"Good, because I want it back when you get here," he said, and then laughed.

I knew when I heard his voice that I'd been right about him all along. He called every day during the following week. Together we began to make our plans for me to leave China.

He asked about academic sponsorship, but I was certain they would never let me have a passport to come to America as a student. That would reward someone branded a criminal.

"I have one other idea," he said. "But it is fairly dramatic. What if you were the wife of an American citizen? Would that make it easier?"

"It could. But would you do that for me?" I asked, surprised.

"Would I do that? I love you. Of course I'd do that."

"That might be my best chance."

"We could get divorced after you were settled here, and you could live your own life then."

I waited for a moment to see if he was joking. "Why would I do that?" I asked. "I love you."

"I love you too," he assured me. "I've thought of you every day since I left China. I've thought about dancing with you. I've thought about our walks. I've thought about every word we exchanged. And . . ." He paused. "You've been in my dreams. Every night. We're taking a chance. But I think we don't have much choice. If you'll have me, I'd be happy to be your husband as long as you need me and want me and love me. How does that sound?"

"Larry, you've been in my dreams too. I'll never stop loving you, and I'll never let anyone separate us again. Never."

Our exchange was spontaneous and heartfelt. I think each of us was surprised by the firmness of our determination. There was a pause, then Larry said, "All right. Now that we've settled that much . . ." and then he laughed—a laugh that dispelled my doubts about our ability to accomplish whatever we set out to do.

We set a time line. He would fly to China during the first week in January. I would complete the required paperwork for marrying a foreigner—not an easy task even for someone who had never been in trouble with the government. I had doubts I could do it. But whenever I despaired, Larry encouraged me. We needed to be flexible and creative.

The first thing I had to do was speed through my divorce from Lin Cheng. During the turmoil of the spring our application for divorce had not been acted on. I asked Lin Cheng to use his connections. He pulled strings, and it was finalized in early December. We rode on Lin Cheng's bicycle to the government bureau, where we signed the necessary documents and were given our divorce certificate. That evening I was to return to my village. My boss had asked me to leave the company, because someone in the office had reported to the authorities that I was receiving long-distance calls from the United States. At the train station, Lin Cheng said, "Don't worry, Meihong. I believe in you. You've come a long way from your village. You are capable and deserving."

I kissed him good-bye and turned to get on the train, but he held me and said, "I'm sorry that I didn't make life better for us. I let you go because you deserve a better life in a better place. I don't even have anything valuable to give you when you leave." He handed me the camera he'd purchased on his trip to America and insisted that I bring it with me. "Good-bye. Take care of yourself."

He watched the train leave. I thought it might be the last time I'd ever see him. I gazed at him through my tears until he was out of sight.

IN MY village I began a frantic paper chase. Larry notified me that he'd be arriving in Shanghai on the evening of January 7. He'd arranged to remain in China for one week, which, I assumed, would give us enough time to get married. Then he planned to fly to Hong Kong with our marriage certificate and begin work on getting me into the United States.

But I had no idea how to get married to a foreigner. I sent a friend to Nanjing to meet with the general to get the information. She returned with a contact name and phone number. She also handed me a wedding gift from the general—an envelope containing five thousand yuan. "To buy your way out," my friend said.

I visited the office in Nanjing that issued marriage certificates to Chinese citizens marrying foreigners. I was shown a list of the documents I'd need.

Next I had to decide on a city where we could marry without attracting attention. I was too well known in Danyang and in Nanjing, I feared, and my name might be on a blacklist. I had friends in Zhenjiang, however, and decided my best chance might be there.

The first step in marrying a foreigner was to obtain a certificate of singleness and permission to marry from the neighborhood committee in my village. The committee customarily consists of old women, adept at collecting rumors about all residents. After hearing my request, the two women of my neighborhood committee asked me to return the following afternoon. I knew this meant I had come asking a favor and had not brought gifts.

I took the train to Zhenjiang. Through a friend I was able to buy a carton of Marlboro cigarettes and a carton of Zhonghua cigarettes, a brand smoked only by high officials in China. The next day I visited the two women and gave them the cigarettes. They pushed back my gifts twice—this was the standard ritual—before reluctantly accepting them.

They gave me an application form to fill out. Under the name of the groom I wrote Larry's Chinese name. I wrote it small so that later next to it I could write the name in English. For the work unit I wrote San Jose State University in Chinese. They asked me where it was located in China—they'd not heard of it. I told them it was a new university. "No wonder," they said. "We've heard of Beijing University and Qinghua University but never San Jose State University. We are too old to keep up with these things anymore." All I could do was thank God at that moment for their ignorance. They stamped the document and handed it to me.

The following day I returned to Zhenjiang, where my friend introduced me to two officers who would issue the marriage certificate. What was required, they said, was a certificate of singleness from my future husband, a document, I discovered, that did not seem to exist in America. He was also required to provide a letter of support and sponsorship, a bank statement, and a statement from his employer confirming his employment and salary. Finally, I'd need a medical certificate for each of us, including an AIDS test.

If Larry went to any hospital in China, it would be very difficult to escape the attention of the local MSS. I had a close friend who was a head nurse at the Danyang People's Hospital. She was nervous but was willing to help. We picked up the application forms and went to the head physician, a sixty-year-old man who had very poor eyesight. I told him I was transferring to Zhenjiang from Danyang with my husband and we needed the physical exam reports immediately. The physician said he would see us right away as a favor to my friend. Then I told him my husband was on a business trip, but Zhenjiang needed the papers right away. My friend suggested that we could get the document signed first and then do the exam later. The doctor took the form and started to ask questions about me and Larry regarding our height and weight. "Your husband is 1.84 meters?" he asked. "That's very tall."

"Yes," I said. "He's a basketball player."

"Why do you need an AIDS test? This seems very unusual."

"My husband is in the PLA," I said. "The military has special requirements for their examination."

The doctor looked puzzled. "Oh, so he's a soldier," he said, and seemed for a moment to be convinced of the legitimacy of what I was asking him to do. He checked several boxes on the form.

The final thing I needed him to do was to stamp the pictures attached to the form. "Something is wrong with this photo," he said. "This man is not Chinese."

I had to take a chance, and I blurted out, "You're right, Doctor. He's not Han, like us. He's from a minority group in Xinjiang."

"Oh, I see," he said. "He looks like a Uighur. Is he?"

"Yes, he is," I said. "His ancestors were even part Russian."

"Now I understand," the doctor said.

I could hardly believe the string of lies I'd gotten away with. My future husband, a Uighur PLA officer basketball player! What a combination, I thought. But I was getting used to taking chances with the truth.

I arranged for us to stay at the Jinshan Hotel in Zhenjiang. I told the clerk at the front desk that I was from the Foreign Affairs Office and I wanted to put up an American there. My sister was with me at the time and was stunned by the ease with which I lied. "I can't believe how you lied to them without even blinking."

I told her, "I've been lying ever since the day the government accused me of committing a crime. I'll keep on lying as long as I have to in order to get out of China."

Larry's flight was scheduled to arrive in Shanghai at six p.m. At four p.m. someone knocked on my hotel-room door. I opened it and saw a PLA officer standing there. I nearly fainted. I thought he'd come to arrest me. But instead he said, "I've been sent by a friend to take you to the airport to pick up your friend."

中國的女兒

Above: *November, 11, 1988, at the Center for Chinese and American Studies—the picture Larry took that ended up in Meihong's file.* Below: *Larry and Meihong at the Shanghai train station, on the way to Zhenjiang to get married.*

I had no choice but to trust him.

He parked the car in the airport lot and walked with me to the terminal. All along, in the back of my mind, I had a suspicion that someone high up in the MSS might be orchestrating this and that I was merely being used as bait to get Larry back into China. I had told Larry earlier that when he came out of the terminal, if he saw me and I waved, everything was all right. If I looked away after making eye contact with him, he should immediately turn around and book a return flight.

His flight arrived on time. It was dark and snowing heavily. I stared at faces in the crowd for someone who might be an agent of the MSS, someone who might return my look and betray his true reason for being there. But no one paid me any attention. Then I saw Larry coming through the door. I waved. He rushed to me and embraced me. "Welcome to China again," I said.

Larry kissed me on the forehead and said, "Are you real? Is this really happening?" We held each other tightly for several seconds. Then we walked to the car, and our driver took us to the hotel. We were together again for the first time in thirteen months.

Larry gave me belated birthday and Christmas presents—clothing and shoes. He'd also brought a gold wedding ring for me. But, he reminded me, "I can't slip this on your finger until we are really married." I knew for sure when I saw his face and his smile and heard his voice again that I was doing the right thing and that I loved him. I had been right to trust him to bring me to a new life.

He told me about the campaign against him in the center by the MSS and the Chinese codirector soon after my disappearance. He said he was sustained in those difficult times by faith in me. He knew, deep inside, that I'd never written the document the Chinese insisted they possessed. And when the Americans demanded to see it, the Chinese told them it was classified. In order to defuse the situation, the American administrators provided Larry with his full salary if he agreed to leave the center. They also provided a letter praising his teaching at the center and exonerating him of any wrongdoing. He accepted the arrangement and left Nanjing.

I told him I was sorry. He replied that it wasn't my fault, that if everything turned out all right in the end, then none of those things would matter.

We talked late into the night. I confessed that I'd set up a very romantic image of him in my mind, like a little girl who dreamed about a prince who would come on a white horse and take her away. He told me he was just like that and he'd left his horse and lance at the airport in San Francisco. After we'd laughed, he told me that I was the hero of our story, that I was the one who'd suffered. Perhaps, he suggested, I'd been the one who saved him. Now he was returning the favor. "We were both reckless," he said. "And we were both innocent. If anyone has done anything wrong, it was me. I'm here to make it right now. With your permission."

Before returning to my room, I told Larry to get a good night's sleep because we'd be getting up early in the morning to catch the train to Zhenjiang.

At the Shanghai train station in the morning, we waited in the cavernous lounge for foreign travelers. When Larry had been there a year earlier, there had been thousands of foreigners waiting for trains. Now, in the wake of Tiananmen, there were just the two of us.

All that day, when I was with him, I felt safe for the first time in more than a year. His laughter was so uplifting and his embrace so reassuring. He was convinced that there was a solution for every problem we might confront. All we had to do, he advised me, was to continue to trust each other. I believed that he would allow no one to pull us apart this time. I believed he would die for me, if it came to that. And I would die for him.

We arrived in Zhenjiang and went to our hotel. Larry was given a room on the fourth floor, and I was given one on the first floor. We had dinner and talked long into the night.

I expected to be married the following morning. But suddenly everything became very complicated again. At the marriage registration bureau we were notified that the clerks had discovered my former work unit was the PLA. "Why didn't you tell us?" they snapped. "We have to have a letter from your institute saying your background is cleared."

I panicked. The officials at my institute would never permit me to marry a foreigner, particularly one they believed worked for the CIA. In a desperate gamble I called the general. He said he'd see what he could do. But the person in charge of providing the clearance was his archenemy—the colonel. When I finished talking with him, I thought it was over and I'd been outmaneuvered.

But Larry was unfazed. He said if it didn't work out this time, he'd return during the summer, and we could be married then. My own feeling was that if I failed this time, they'd watch me much more closely. My veil of secrecy would be gone for good.

Then I remembered the name of an old friend of my paternal grandfather. The man was a former mayor of Zhenjiang. He was retired but still had some influence. Grandfather had helped his family decades earlier, and he had never been asked to repay the favor. I went to him and told him I was Mr. Xu's granddaughter and needed help. He agreed to do what he could.

The clerks from the marriage bureau, in the meantime, had called the institute in Nanjing on January 8 to get a report on me and clearance for marriage to a foreigner. They were put through to the office of the colonel. He had left on a vacation with his family to Beijing and would not return for several weeks. His assistants said they could not release information on me without his approval.

Grandfather's friend went to the marriage bureau and told them that he would personally vouch for me. He asked, "What if the PLA does not respond to your inquiry? Will you keep this American friend waiting forever? We must preserve a good image of how the government works here. If Xu Meihong was not eligible to marry the American professor, the PLA would have said so."

The marriage bureau officials accepted this argument, but they decided to wait a little longer. They said if on the afternoon of Saturday, January 13, they had still not heard from the PLA, I could be married on Monday the fifteenth. I told them that was too late—Larry's flight to Hong Kong was on the fourteenth. I wondered if we might get married on the morning of January 14, a Sunday. "This office is closed on Sunday," they said.

I called Grandfather's friend again. Half an hour later he called me back and said, "They will be waiting for you on Sunday at eight a.m. in the marriage bureau."

This was more than luck. It was a miracle.

On Saturday night we went to a large restaurant and enjoyed our wedding banquet. I knew Larry would depart within an hour of our marriage in the morning. I didn't know when I might see him again. So I told him I wanted us to become husband and wife—to have our wedding night before the wedding rather than after.

I went to his room that night. I drew the curtains, locked the door, listened for noises in the hallway. Then I took a chair and tilted it against the door handle. Larry laughed at my transformation of the room into a fortress. I still thought someone would come along to destroy all of our work even at this late moment.

But they didn't.

The next morning we arose at six. It was snowing again. There were no taxis at that hour. The marriage bureau was five miles away, and we had to walk that distance in the snow carrying our luggage.

But we had no choice. Larry kept looking at his watch. We had walked for almost thirty minutes when I saw an old man coming toward us on a large tricycle he used to transport vegetables. I signaled for him to stop and told him I had an emergency and needed a ride. He agreed to take us all the way to the marriage bureau for five yuan. I tried to bargain with him, and Larry said, "My God, what are you arguing about? I want to get married this morning. Give him a hundred yuan, but just get us there on time."

The old man did not look very strong. I got on the back of his tricycle, and Larry put both bags on, then jogged alongside so the man could go faster. We arrived at the marriage bureau at seven fifty-five.

The first thing the two clerks told me was that Larry's certificate of singleness, which I'd given them earlier, said only that Larry had not been married in California in the past twenty-five years. They asked, "What if he was married before that time? What if he was married in another state? We are not sure he is qualified to marry."

I had Larry write in English in large letters, "I am not married," and sign his name. Then we had to go through a question-and-answer session: when we met, how long we'd been in love, how we fell in love. I had to laugh now and then, but this was the standard procedure. They treated us like kids. When they finished, they conferred with each other for several seconds, then smiled and said, "Congratulations. You are now husband and wife."

I handed each of them two cartons of Marlboros that we'd purchased the previous afternoon, and they pushed them back twice before accepting them. They gave us each in return an orange, then handed us our marriage certificates. Everyone was pleased with the morning's proceedings.

Outside again, we kissed and held each other tightly in the cold morning air. "We did it," Larry said. "Now let's get the hell out of here before these guys change their mind."

In the taxi to the train station, Larry suddenly said, "I forgot something," reached into his pocket, and took out the ring. He held my hand gently and then slipped the ring onto my finger. "Congratulations, Mrs. Engelmann," he said. "We're almost home."

Over breakfast at the restaurant across from the station, I said I wished the ceremony could have been a little bit more special, but Larry told me it was the most wonderful morning and the most glorious wedding ceremony he'd ever seen.

On the train, he held me close beside him all the way to Shanghai. I was glowing with optimism now. I couldn't help but think I was almost out of China. Almost home.

At the Shanghai airport, we had cake and ice cream—our wedding cake, Larry called it—at a restaurant in the terminal. It was the most beautiful cake and ice cream I'd ever eaten. I saw some American girls waiting for the plane. They seemed so free, and I envied them. I wanted out of China with my husband so badly now.

Larry paid our bill and then helped me put my coat on. Music was playing in the restaurant, and he asked, "How about a dance after dinner?" Before I could answer, he put an arm around my waist and danced me out the door. He lifted me up when he'd finished, and kissed me. "Don't be unhappy. We'll be together soon."

"I'll try," I promised.

Larry whispered, "See you in California!" I watched as he approached the customs desk. Suddenly all the televisions in the terminal came on and began showing a Donald Duck cartoon. The customs officers nodded to the departing passengers and waved them through so as not to interrupt their viewing of the cartoon. Larry walked into the departure lounge and disappeared from my sight. But somewhere, deep in my heart, for the first time in more than a year I felt happy and safe.

ON MONDAY morning in Hong Kong, Larry faxed copies of the marriage certificate to a friend in the United States, who had envelopes and letters addressed to California Senators Alan Cranston and Pete Wilson asking for their help in getting me out of China. Copies also went to several California Congressmen, including Tom Campbell of Palo Alto, who was interested in U.S.-Chinese relations; to prominent members of Congress; to the Secretary of State and Secretary of Defense; and to the President and the Vice President. Larry told me that he was going to make as much noise and cause as much trouble as he could until I was safely by his side.

On January 15 I returned to my village with my marriage certificate. Larry asked me to give him a few days before going to the Public Security Bureau and requesting a passport.

When I visited the bureau and said what I'd come for, the officer in charge glanced up at me with unconcealed contempt. "Where would you like to go? Perhaps to America? Why don't you go home and stop wasting my time."

"Yes, I'd like to go to America," I told him. "I'd like to join my husband there. I'm the wife of an American citizen."

My words rendered him dumbstruck. I handed him my marriage certificate. He examined it carefully and saw the signatures and chops (stamps) on it and realized it was not a forgery. "What have you done?" he asked. Then he said I'd need a letter from my husband inviting me to America and a letter from my mother and father giving me permission to leave China.

"I am twenty-six years old. Are you telling me I need my parents' permission to join my husband?"

"Even if you were sixty, you would. That's the law."

I returned home and thought about it for a day. I'd told my parents nothing about my divorce and nothing about my remarriage. The less they knew, I believed, the safer they would be. So I composed a letter and signed my parents' names with my left hand to disguise the writing. Larry provided the required documents by express service within days. I then returned with all the documents for the Public Security man. He told me, "This will take at least three months. Don't come back until then."

Larry called every day to check on my progress. I found I had used up all of my connections and influence in Danyang. Then I was notified that a letter had been received from the PLA in Nanjing stating that under no circumstances was I to be allowed to receive a passport or to leave the country.

I received regular visits from the Public Security Bureau and from a military representative from Nanjing. They encouraged me to be a good soldier and annul the marriage and promised there might be some form of rehabilitation available for me if I did. I simply repeated to them that I wished to join my husband in America.

Larry succeeded in getting both California Senators as well as Congressman Campbell to write to the Chinese embassy expressing concern at his inability to get me out of China. They wanted to know why there was a delay. Larry called the State Department and spoke with the young man serving on the China desk, Patrick Freeman, who, Larry discovered, was a graduate of San Jose State University. When Larry told me that, he laughed and said he knew that fate had to be on our side.

In late June I was summoned to the Public Security Bureau and told that the army had decided that my familiarity with intelligence methods and operations meant that allowing me to go abroad would endanger state security. As a result, I was denied a passport and could not apply for one for seven years.

I called Larry and tearfully told him I was willing to end the marriage rather than have him wait seven years. "Damn it," he said. "They are bluffing. This will not take seven years. No way." We planned to meet in Guangzhou in two weeks. His words comforted me, but I knew of no method of getting out of China without the passport.

In July, Larry flew to Hong Kong, did some research for a book he was beginning on the plight of the boat people, and then took the train to Guangzhou. We visited the American consulate to fill out the papers that would be required for my visa.

One afternoon Larry took out a notebook. "Look at this," he said. He'd drawn a map of the northern half of Vietnam, the Gulf of Tonkin, Hainan Island, and the coast of China to Hong Kong. "I've interviewed hundreds of boat people in the camps in Hong Kong. About ninety percent of them are from northern Vietnam." He drew a line with his pencil. "They come this way out of Vietnam, across the South China Sea. They land on the northwest coast of Hainan Island, here," he said, pointing. "Nobody bothers them if they move on. Here's what I want to do. I'll come back to Hong Kong at Christmas. Then I'll fly to Hainan, and we can meet in Haikou, as if we are vacationers. Then we'll go to the coast here, and I'll buy us a place on a boat."

I was amazed by his plan—to make us both boat people.

"Can you do this?"

"Of course I can do this. Chances are we'd be picked up by a ship in the South China Sea. I'll alert the State Department and the consulate in Hong Kong. They'll be waiting for us."

"What if we're caught by the Chinese guards?"

"Great!" he said, and laughed. "What a great news story that will be—American citizen and his Chinese wife try desperately to escape from China as boat people. If we're caught, the news will go around the world. We can't lose, unless the boat sinks. But that won't happen. Are you willing to try?"

I thought about it for a moment and looked into his eyes. He was completely serious. I trusted him. "Yes. I'll come with you."

"If we do it, we'll have a great tale to tell our children. And if we don't make it," he said, placing his hand on my hair, brushing it gently, "we'll still be together. And I want that." He added, "I really think we're going to embarrass them into letting you go."

Before Larry took the train to Hong Kong, we held each other a long time. "I can't keep saying good-bye to you," he said. "The next time I leave China, I am not leaving without you."

Back home, I was visited by the Public Security people. They asked if I'd had a good time in Guangzhou. I told them I had. They asked why, then, I'd cried when Larry and I were talking. I said because we were apart. "Get used to it," they said, and gloated.

In October, Larry's book on the fall of South Vietnam, *Tears Before the Rain,* was published. He began a ten-city book tour to promote the book. In putting together the publicity folder that went to newspapers and radio stations around the country, Larry had the publisher include a page on his marriage to a "former PLA officer, Xu Meihong," in Zhenjiang, China, and the statement that "she remains in China and he is currently working to bring her to America." He appeared on several regional and national radio programs, including National Public Radio in Philadelphia and Washington. Always, after discussing the book, the interviewers had questions about Larry's wife. With the American public still interested in Tiananmen and relations with China, his story of Chinese vindictiveness caught the public eye. Larry even included a note in the acknowledgments of the book: "Finally, thank you, Xu Meihong, who helped me organize and transcribe much of this material during my stay in China. Meihong eventually paid a high price for our friendship. Her dreams and fears and her fate helped me understand some of the bitterness and the behavior of those who won and lost in Vietnam, and why they fought." Larry had written the statement before we'd found each other again in August 1989.

He also continued to send out requests for individuals to write the Chinese embassy. He sent notes to Brent Scowcroft; Henry Kissinger; ex-Presidents Gerald Ford and Jimmy Carter; Winston Lord and his wife, Bette Bao Lord; General William Westmoreland; people within the DIA, the CIA, and the State Department; and people at various think tanks and universities around the country.

In the midst of the book tour, when Larry was in Washington, he received a call from Patrick Freeman at the State Department telling him that someone in the Chinese embassy would like to see him. Larry went to the embassy on Wednesday, October 24.

He was led to a conference room. He smiled when he saw a poorly disguised two-way mirror. He was greeted by Wang Maoheng, the first secretary of the embassy, who was gracious. "Dr. Engelmann," he began, "I sympathize with the plight of you and your wife. I'd like to help you. But I do not understand why she is being detained in China. Do you have any idea?"

"No, sir, I don't. I thought you might be able to tell me."

"All I can tell you is that it has something to do with her former work unit. Do you know what that was?"

"I have some idea. She was in the PLA, I believe."

"Did you ever meet anyone else from her unit?"

"No, I didn't."

"Did she introduce a general to you while you were in Nanjing in 1988?"

"No."

The question-and-answer session lasted for half an hour. Mr. Wang concluded in the end, "I don't know what is going on. So I am not sure how to help you. Perhaps you can help me, and I can provide information that might help."

"I don't know how," Larry said. "My wife is no threat to anyone. She merely wants to be here with me."

The first secretary extended his hand. "Dr. Engelmann, I will do all I can to help you be reunited with your wife. If you come across any information that could help us, please call me here."

Within days David Chang from the U.S. consulate in Shanghai, who had been working hard on my case, reported to Larry that he'd spoken to the Public Security people in Danyang, and they were not straightforward about my case. Chang said he planned to travel to Danyang and confront them face to face. Larry said this was just the kind of pressure we needed, and thanked Chang.

Meanwhile, I flew to Beijing and went to the American embassy. I spoke for a long time with Katherine Dee Robinson. She said she would work on the case and stay on it until there was a better solution than my waiting seven years to get out of the country.

On the morning of December 10 Larry received a call from Patrick Freeman. "Have you heard from your wife?" he asked.

"Not for a couple of days," Larry said. "Why?"

"Something is happening in China," he said. "Don't get your hopes up. All we know is that the Chinese government has indicated that they will resolve her case, but they didn't say how."

Larry feared I'd be rearrested on some trumped-up charge and would disappear forever. He planned to call me on Wednesday morning. There was no way to get in touch with me before then, since I didn't have a phone at home. But I called him on Tuesday evening and told him, "The Public Security people came to my home this morning."

"And?"

"And they've been instructed to give me a passport. I'm to leave the country as soon as possible."

"Oh, God, we've done it," he said. He told me to make the plane reservation to San Francisco as soon as I could and to call him back every day with a progress report.

"It's very strange," I told him. "They told me that the order for issuing my passport came directly from the Party Central Committee in Beijing. Nanjing has been bypassed. I don't know why. I don't know who ordered this, and they don't either."

"Don't worry about that. We can worry about it later. Just buy a plane ticket when you receive your passport, and get out."

One week later I had my passport. When I picked it up at the Public Security Bureau, the officer in charge was furious. He said this was highly unusual. He tried to ask me questions about friends in Beijing, but I wouldn't talk. Then he reminded me ominously, "You may be leaving China, Xu Meihong, but your family is still here. Don't forget that ever. Your family is still here."

I turned and walked out the door.

The next day I flew to Guangzhou and got my immigration visa form from the U.S. consulate there. Then I bought a ticket for a flight from Shanghai to Los Angeles and then on to San Francisco. I was scheduled to arrive December 29 at twelve thirty p.m. I called Larry with the good news.

He was so happy, he could hardly speak. Yet both of us were still cautious. Permission to leave had come from some unknown official—high in the government obviously. And it could just as easily be canceled. I would not be safe till I was in the United States.

"I'll be waiting for you in San Francisco," he said.

There was a pause, and then we both spoke at once. "I love you."

"Don't be late," he said.

"I won't," I promised.

"It looks like our Hainan–Hong Kong cruise will have to be canceled," he said. "That would have been an adventure."

"I think we've had enough adventures for one lifetime, Larry," I said. "No more."

TEN 第十章 Another World

MY FLIGHT landed in Los Angeles on the morning of December 29, 1990. I passed through customs and got my first look at America. It seemed that everyone was smiling and happy. I caught a connecting flight to San Francisco. As soon as we touched down, I took a small mirror from my purse and looked at myself to make sure I was presentable after such a long journey. I applied a little lipstick and powder and ran my fingers through my hair. I was trembling slightly, I noticed, from anticipation. I took several deep breaths and tried to calm myself.

I walked down the long skyway to the terminal. In the distance I saw a crowd of people waiting. I searched for the familiar face of my husband and saw him suddenly emerge from the crowd and approach me, arms outstretched, smiling broadly.

I dropped my bag and reached out for him.

"Welcome home," he said. And then he put his arms around me and lifted me into the air.

That night I returned the silver bracelet to Larry. We decided that neither of us would ever wear it again. Someday we'd give it to our children and tell them where it had been and what magic it had worked.

For several weeks after my arrival I'd awaken in the middle of the night, utterly terrified because of a nightmare that I was still in China, questioned day and night, my life hanging in the balance. On those nights Larry would embrace me and assure me that no one could harm me again. He promised that nothing would ever separate us again. Then I'd fall asleep peacefully in his arms.

And so my old life ended, and my new life began.

THREE years after I left China, I received a letter from Lin Cheng telling me he'd left the PLA and had remarried. I knew that someday this news was sure to arrive. And I was equally certain that I would be as saddened as I was happy for him. I will always love that handsome cadet who won my heart in Nanjing in 1984, when both of us were still so young and red and intoxicated with the dreams of youth.

The general was arrested shortly after I departed from China. For a time, I was told, he was placed under house arrest. Eventually he was cashiered from the PLA. Then he disappeared. I have no idea where he is today.

All of the Twelve Pandas left the PLA. Three of us live abroad today. The others remain in China. I keep the picture of us from our graduation day in my bedroom. And I often look at that picture and remember them, wishing each of them a happy life.

EACH year on September 1, when the new semester begins at the Nanjing Institute for International Relations of the PLA, the new recruits are gathered in a large auditorium and given a lecture detailing the history, heroes, and successes of the institute. Then, as a warning, one of the institute's rare failures is mentioned. I have learned from several former cadets that my story is told to the new students as an example of what might happen when an innocent young soldier fails to heed the lessons of her training and ends up making an imprudent decision, with potentially cataclysmic results. The lights in the room are dimmed, and a picture of me in my cadet's uniform is projected on a large screen. A somber speaker tells the wide-eyed recruits the tragic story of "Xu Meihong, a naïve village girl from Jiangsu Province, who showed great enthusiasm and promise when she arrived here. She worked hard and became a class leader. Much was expected of her. But during an early assignment she allowed herself to be deceived by an American agent. As a result, she betrayed her country. Before she could do serious damage to China's security, however, her deception was discovered. Because of her youth and her prior record of service to the PLA, she was shown mercy following a tearful confession. The damage she might have done was, thanks to her subsequent cooperation, successfully contained. Her life was spared. But she was cashiered from the military and exiled to the countryside for reeducation through hard labor. She died there in the winter of 1990."

Like all of the other stories told to fresh and eager PLA cadets in China, this one is true.

About the Authors

LESLEY STAHL has been a correspondent with *60 Minutes* since 1991, and plans to stay there "forever." She explains, "I feel right now that I will never ever tire of this job, that it will always be challenging and fun and important." The White House correspondent for the *CBS Evening News* during the Carter, Reagan, and Bush administrations, she also hosted *Face the Nation* from 1983 to 1991. Stahl lives in New York City with her husband, screenwriter Aaron Latham, and still calls her mother, Dolly, after every Sunday evening broadcast of *60 Minutes.*

A writer who is also a fireman, **DENNIS SMITH** wields both pen and fire hose with equal skill and dedication. Born in New York City in 1940, he served that city's fire department for eighteen years and was honored for heroism. During that time he was also editor in chief of *Firehouse Magazine* and wrote *Report from Engine Co. 82,* about his adventures with New York's busiest fire station. The book became a best seller and launched Smith on a new career. He has since written eight other books, including three more best sellers.

LISA BELKIN, a reporter for *The New York Times* since 1984, lives ten minutes from Yonkers, New York, whose public-housing struggles she portrays in *Show Me a Hero.* As a first-time homeowner, she was drawn to investigate the story after she saw a small notice for Yonkers's public-housing lottery in her local newspaper. Intrigued, she attended the lottery, began interviewing participants, and was touched by their dream of a safe place to call home—a dream that mirrored her own. Belkin's previous book, *First, Do No Harm,* was an exploration of a hospital's ethics committee.

MEIHONG XU received her B.A. from the Institute for International Relations in Nanjing, China, and her M.B.A. from San Jose State University. Today she works for an Internet service provider in California's Silicon Valley. **LARRY ENGELMANN** teaches history at San Jose State University. His four previous books include *The New York Times* Notable Book *The Goddess and the American Girl.* He is currently at work on a new book—*Toy Soldiers: Stories from the Life of a Child's Military Life.* The authors live in San Jose, California.

Today's Best Nonfiction is issued every two to three months. The typical volume contains four outstanding books in condensed form. Any reader may receive this service by writing The Reader's Digest Association, Inc., Pleasantville, N.Y. 10570 or by calling 800-234-9000.

Visit our Web site at http://www.readersdigest.com

CREDITS

REPORTING LIVE—Pages 6–7, 83 (top): official White House photo. Pages 7 (right), 84 (top, middle), 85 (top): CBS Photo Archive. Pages 9, 40, 66, 95, 124: Corbis/UPI. Pages 82, 83 (bottom), 85 (bottom): courtesy of the author. Page 84 (bottom): courtesy Ronald Reagan Presidential Library.

A SONG FOR MARY—Pages 160, 226, 227: courtesy of the author.

DAUGHTER OF CHINA—Pages 437, 455, 559: courtesy of the authors.

Volume design by Soren Noring.

Author photos—Page 574 (top): Sigrid Estrada. Page 575 (top): John Maggiotto.